Evolution of Cognitive Networks and Self-Adaptive Communication Systems

Thomas D. Lagkas
University of Western Macedonia, Greece & University of Sheffield, UK

Panagiotis Sarigiannidis
University of Western Macedonia, Greece

Malamati Louta
University of Western Macedonia, Greece

Periklis Chatzimisios
Alexander TEI of Thessaloniki, Greece

A volume in the Advances in Wireless Technologies and Telecommunication (AWTT) Book Series

Information Science REFERENCE

An Imprint of IGI Global

Managing Director:	Lindsay Johnston
Editorial Director:	Joel Gamon
Book Production Manager:	Jennifer Yoder
Publishing Systems Analyst:	Adrienne Freeland
Development Editor:	Monica Speca
Assistant Acquisitions Editor:	Kayla Wolfe
Typesetter:	Henry Ulrich
Cover Design:	Jason Mull

Published in the United States of America by
Information Science Reference (an imprint of IGI Global)
701 E. Chocolate Avenue
Hershey PA 17033
Tel: 717-533-8845
Fax: 717-533-8661
E-mail: cust@igi-global.com
Web site: http://www.igi-global.com

Copyright © 2013 by IGI Global. All rights reserved. No part of this publication may be reproduced, stored or distributed in any form or by any means, electronic or mechanical, including photocopying, without written permission from the publisher. Product or company names used in this set are for identification purposes only. Inclusion of the names of the products or companies does not indicate a claim of ownership by IGI Global of the trademark or registered trademark.

Library of Congress Cataloging-in-Publication Data

Evolution of cognitive networks and self-adaptive communication systems / Thomas D. Lagkas, Panagiotis Sarigiannidis, Malamati Louta and Periklis Chatzimisios, editors.
      pages cm
  Summary: "This book overviews innovative technologies combined for the formation of self-aware, self-adaptive, and self-organizing networks, for those interested in clarifying the latest trends toward a unified realization for cognitive networking and communication systems"--Provided by publisher.
  Includes bibliographical references and index.
  ISBN 978-1-4666-4189-1 (hardcover) -- ISBN 978-1-4666-4190-7 (ebook) -- ISBN 978-1-4666-4191-4 (print & perpetual access) 1. Cognitive radio networks. 2. Telecommunication systems. 3. Adaptive signal processing. I. Lagkas, Thomas, 1980- II. Sarigiannidis, Panagiotis, 1979- III. Louta, Malamati, 1975- IV. Chatzimisios, Periklis.
  TK5103.4815.E96 2013
  621.382'15--dc23
                                                2013009731

This book is published in the IGI Global book series Advances in Wireless Technologies and Telecommunication (AWTT) Book Series (ISSN: 2327-3305; eISSN: 2327-3313).

British Cataloguing in Publication Data
A Cataloguing in Publication record for this book is available from the British Library.

All work contributed to this book is new, previously-unpublished material. The views expressed in this book are those of the authors, but not necessarily of the publisher.

Advances in Wireless Technologies and Telecommunication (AWTT) Book Series

Xiaoge Xu
The University of Nottingham Ningbo China

ISSN: 2327-3305
EISSN: 2327-3313

MISSION

The wireless computing industry is constantly evolving, redesigning the ways in which individuals share information. Wireless technology and telecommunication remain one of the most important technologies in business organizations. The utilization of these technologies has enhanced business efficiency by enabling dynamic resources in all aspects of society.

The **Advances in Wireless Technologies and Telecommunication Book Series** aims to provide researchers and academic communities with quality research on the concepts and developments in the wireless technology fields. Developers, engineers, students, research strategists, and IT managers will find this series useful to gain insight into next generation wireless technologies and telecommunication.

COVERAGE

- Cellular Networks
- Digital Communication
- Global Telecommunications
- Grid Communications
- Mobile Technology
- Mobile Web Services
- Network Management
- Virtual Network Operations
- Wireless Broadband
- Wireless Sensor Networks

IGI Global is currently accepting manuscripts for publication within this series. To submit a proposal for a volume in this series, please contact our Acquisition Editors at Acquisitions@igi-global.com or visit: http://www.igi-global.com/publish/.

The Advances in Wireless Technologies and Telecommunication (AWTT) Book Series (ISSN 2327-3305) is published by IGI Global, 701 E. Chocolate Avenue, Hershey, PA 17033-1240, USA, www.igi-global.com. This series is composed of titles available for purchase individually; each title is edited to be contextually exclusive from any other title within the series. For pricing and ordering information please visit http://www.igi-global.com/book-series/advances-wireless-technologies-telecommunication-awtt/73684. Postmaster: Send all address changes to above address. Copyright © 2013 IGI Global. All rights, including translation in other languages reserved by the publisher. No part of this series may be reproduced or used in any form or by any means – graphics, electronic, or mechanical, including photocopying, recording, taping, or information and retrieval systems – without written permission from the publisher, except for non commercial, educational use, including classroom teaching purposes. The views expressed in this series are those of the authors, but not necessarily of IGI Global.

Titles in this Series

www.igi-global.com

701 E. Chocolate Ave., Hershey, PA 17033
Order online at www.igi-global.com or call 717-533-8845 x100
To place a standing order for titles released in this series, contact: cust@igi-global.com
Mon-Fri 8:00 am - 5:00 pm (est) or fax 24 hours a day 717-533-8661

Editorial Advisory Board

Mischa Dohler, *Centre Tecnològic de Telecomunicacions de Catalunya, Spain*
Fabrizio Granelli, *University of Trento, Italy*
Ekram Hossain, *University of Manitoba, Canada*
Ali Imran, *QU Wireless Innovations Center (QUWIC), Qatar*
Jaime Lloret Mauri, *Polytechnic University of Valencia, Spain*
Arturas Medeisis, *Vilnius Gediminas Technical University, Lithuania*
Dusit Niyato, *Nanyang Technological University, Singapore*
R. Venkatesha Prasad, *Delft University of Technology, The Netherlands*
Fernando Jose Velez, *Instituto de Telecomunicacoes, Portugal & Universidade da Beira Interior, Portugal*
Chonggang Wang, *InterDigital Communications, USA*
Honggang Zhang, *Zhejiang University, China*

List of Reviewers

Evgenia Adamopoulou, *Institute of Communication and Computer Systems (ICCS), Greece*
Nancy Alonistioti, *National and Kapodistrian University of Athens, Greece*
Peter Anker, *Ministry of Economic Affairs, Agriculture, and Innovation, The Netherlands & Delft University of Technology, The Netherlands*
Prathima Agrawal, *Auburn University, USA*
Roi Arapoglou, *National and Kapodistrian University of Athens, Greece*
Alireza Babaei, *Auburn University, USA*
Gilberto Berardinelli, *Aalborg University, Denmark*
Athina Bourdena, *University of the Aegean, Greece*
Pascal Bouvry, *University of Luxembourg, Luxembourg*
Andrea F. Cattoni, *Aalborg University, Denmark*
Dimitris E. Charilas, *National Technical University of Athens, Greece*
Konstantinos Chatzikokolakis, *National and Kapodistrian University of Athens, Greece*
Philip Constantinou, *National Technical University of Athens, Greece*
Noel Crespi, *Institut Mines-Télécom, France & Télécom SudParis, France*
Krešimir Dabčević, *University of Genova, Italy*
Rohit Datta, *Technische Universität Dresden, Germany*
Konstantinos Demestichas, *National Technical University of Athens, Greece*

Panagiotis Demestichas, *University of Piraeus, Greece*

Djamel Djenouri, *CERIST, Algeria*

Uddin Shah Muhammad Emad, *Politecnico of Turin, Italy*

Yasir Faheem, *Universit´e Paris-Est Marne-la-Vall´ee, France & Université Paris Nord, France*

Nelson Fonseca, *State University of Campinas, Brazil*

Vasilis Gkamas, *University of Patras, Greece*

Kiam Cheng How, *Nanyang Technological University, Singapore*

Vasiliki Kakali, *Aristotle University of Thessaloniki, Greece*

Alexandros Kaloxylos, *University of Peloponnese, Greece*

George T. Karetsos, *TEI of Larissa, Greece*

George Katsikas, *National and Kapodistrian University of Athens, Greece*

Dzmitry Kliazovich, *University of Luxembourg, Luxembourg*

Yogesh Kondareddy, *Auburn University, USA*

Georgios Kormentzas, *University of the Aegean, Greece*

Yiouli Kritikou, *University of Piraeus, Greece*

Ioannis Loumiotis, *Institute of Communication and Computer Systems (ICCS), Greece*

Maode Ma, *Nanyang Technological University, Singapore*

Prodromos Makris, *University of the Aegean, Greece*

Antonio Manzalini, *Telecom Italia, Italy*

Lucio Marcenaro, *University of Genova, Italy*

George Mastorakis, *Technological Educational Institute of Crete, Greece*

Marja Matinmikko, *VTT, Finland*

Ioanna Mesogiti, *Cosmote Kinites Tilepikoinonies, Greece*

Roberto Minerva, *Telecom Italia, Italy*

Preben Mogensen, *Aalborg University, Denmark*

Evangelos Pallis, *Technological Educational Institute of Crete, Greece*

Athanasios D. Panagopoulos, *National Technical University of Athens, Greece*

George Papadopoulos, *Aristotle University of Thessaloniki, Greece*

Nikolaos Papaoulakis, *Institute of Communication and Computer Systems (ICCS), Greece*

Maria Paradia, *Pedagogical Institute, Greece*

Petar Popovski, *Aalborg University, Denmark*

Marios Poulakis, *National Technical University of Athens, Greece*

Carlo S. Regazzoni, *University of Genova, Italy*

Mubashir Husain Rehmani, *Université Paris Est, France & COMSATS, Pakistan*

Charalabos Skianis, *University of the Aegean, Greece*

Dimitrios N. Skoutas, *University of the Aegean, Greece*

Troels B. Sørensen, *Aalborg University, Denmark*

Panagiotis Spapis, *National and Kapodistrian University of Athens, Greece*

Makis Stamatelatos, *National and Kapodistrian University of Athens, Greece*

Theodora Stamatiadi, *Institute of Communication and Computer Systems (ICCS), Greece*

Dimitrios Stratogiannis, *National Technical University of Athens, Greece*

Efstathios Sykas, *Institute of Communication and Computer Systems (ICCS), Greece*

Fernando M. L. Tavares, *Aalborg University, Denmark*

George Theofilogiannakos, *Aristotle University of Thessaloniki, Greece*

Oscar Tonelli, *Aalborg University, Denmark*

Georgios Tsiropoulos, *National Technical University of Athens, Greece*

Stavroula Vassaki, *National Technical University of Athens, Greece*

Dariusz Wiecek, *National Institute of Telecommunications, Poland*

Table of Contents

Section 1
Physical Layer Issues in Cognitive Networks

Section 2
High Layer Issues in Cognitive Networks

Detailed Table of Contents

Section 1
Physical Layer Issues in Cognitive Networks

This section addresses cognitive networking issues, which are mainly related to the physical layer of the network architecture. It provides a review of cooperative communication technologies and presents state of the art techniques for disseminating data and selecting channels in cognitive radio networks. Resource management is also examined, focusing on the TV White Spaces and the QoS requirements. Moreover, it discusses power control issues in modern mobile networks (such as LTE-Advanced) and explains how regulations affect business aspects related to cognitive radio. Experimental results regarding distributed data dissemination are also presented.

Chapter 1

This chapter discusses the main aspects of cooperative networking starting from the main historical milestones that shaped the idea. It focuses on the main mechanisms and techniques that foster cooperation and continues by studying performance metrics for various possible deployments, such as capacity bounds and outage probabilities. Finally, it examines the aspects related to medium access control design and implementation.

Chapter 2

This chapter provides a comprehensive review of broadcasting and channel selection strategies for wireless cognitive radio networks. Initially, some applications of the data dissemination in wireless cognitive radio networks are discussed and then a detailed classification of broadcasting protocols in the light of the existing literature is provided. Furthermore, data dissemination is briefly discussed in the context of multi-channel environments and cognitive radio networks. A classification of channel selection strategies is also provided.

Athina Bourdena, University of the Aegean, Greece
Prodromos Makris, University of the Aegean, Greece
Dimitrios N. Skoutas, University of the Aegean, Greece
Charalabos Skianis, University of the Aegean, Greece
George Kormentzas, University of the Aegean, Greece
Evangelos Pallis, Technological Educational Institute of Crete, Greece
George Mastorakis, Technological Educational Institute of Crete, Greece

This chapter discusses Joint Radio Resource Management (JRRM) issues in cognitive networks presenting the TV White Spaces (TVWS) spectrum exploitation use case. It initially provides a state-of-the-art work for existing cognitive radio network architectures, while a reference architecture for commons and secondary TVWS trading is proposed. Subsequently, JRRM concepts for heterogeneous Radio Access Technologies' extension over TVWS are presented. Finally, a thorough classification of existing admission control and scheduling techniques is provided.

Stavroula Vassaki, National Technical University of Athens, Greece
Marios I. Poulakis, National Technical University of Athens, Greece
Athanasios D. Panagopoulos, National Technical University of Athens, Greece
Philip Constantinou, National Technical University of Athens, Greece

This chapter focuses on the employment of the effective capacity theory in Cognitive Radio (CR) systems, presenting an extensive survey on QoS-driven resource allocation schemes proposed in the literature. Some useful conclusions are presented and future research directions on this subject are highlighted and discussed.

Konstantinos Chatzikokolakis, National and Kapodistrian University of Athens, Greece
Panagiotis Spapis, National and Kapodistrian University of Athens, Greece
Makis Stamatelatos, National and Kapodistrian University of Athens, Greece
George Katsikas, National and Kapodistrian University of Athens, Greece
Roi Arapoglou, National and Kapodistrian University of Athens, Greece
Alexandros Kaloxylos, University of Peloponnese, Greece
Nancy Alonistioti, National and Kapodistrian University of Athens, Greece

This chapter presents the Spectrum Aggregation scenario as it is proposed to be incorporated in LTE-advanced. Furthermore, the interesting extensions of FP7 SACRA European research project regarding Spectrum Aggregation are described. The business and the functional aspects stemming from the incorporation of this solution in the LTE-Advanced networks are presented in detail. Moreover, a typical power control algorithm is described and enhanced with learning capabilities and policies in order to meet the requirements of the Spectrum Aggregation scenario.

This chapter addresses the impact on the business case for cognitive technologies of the regulatory regime and the choices on the fundamental CR technology that regulators will have to make.

This chapter focuses on the practical aspects related to the real world experimentation with distributed DSA network algorithms over a testbed network. Challenges and solutions are extensively discussed, from the testbed design to the setup of experiments. A practical example of experimentation process with a DSA algorithm is also provided.

Section 2
High Layer Issues in Cognitive Networks

This section addresses issues that are mainly related to cognitive networking layers, which are higher than the physical one. It presents an overview of cutting edge technologies for autonomous software networks and discusses QoS support provision in multiple layers of Cognitive Radio Networks. The suitability of TCP in dynamic access networks in analyzed, while the convergence of optical and wireless networks is also examined. Moreover, the section reviews the latest developments in self-adaptive networks and provides simulation results regarding security issues in Cognitive Networks. Lastly, an application of cognitive techniques for e-learning in broadband networks is presented.

Chapter 8

This chapter addresses the potential impact of technologies like Autonomic, Cognitive, and Software Defined Networking on future networks evolution. It is argued that said technologies, coupled with a wide adoption of virtualization, will bring an impactful disruption at the edge of current networks. The edge will become a business arena with multiple interacting networks and domains operated by diverse players. The chapter elaborates this vision, reports a brief overview of the state of the art of enabling technologies, describes some simulation results of a use-case, and concludes by providing future research directions.

This chapter examines issues that take place on different layers, chiefly the physical, MAC (Medium Access Control), and network layer of Cognitive Radio Networks (CRNs). It also reviews existing proposals to tackle the challenging issue of QoS provisioning in CRNs. In the second part of the chapter, greater QoS provisioning capabilities are provided by two proposed routing protocols for CRNs utilizing a variety of techniques.

Chapter 10

This chapter explains why the typical TCP scheme, which was designed for wired networks, is not suitable for dynamic spectrum access networks. An analytical model is developed to estimate the TCP throughput of dynamic spectrum access networks. The proposed model considers primary and secondary user traffic in estimating the TCP throughput by modeling the spectrum access using continuous-time Markov chains, thus providing more insight on the effect of dynamic spectrum access on TCP performance than the existing models.

Chapter 11

This chapter introduces a novel management system called CONFES, Converged Network Infrastructure Enabling Resource Optimization and Flexible Service Provisioning, aiming at the proactive determination of PON (Passive Optical Network), clients' needs in bandwidth resources, the efficient and reasonable allocation of resources to multiple clients according to such needs, and the corresponding Service Level Agreements. Furthermore, the chapter proposes, studies, and compares physical architecture solutions (both centralized and distributed) that can realize such advanced management systems.

This chapter overviews recent developments of self-awareness, self-management, and self-healing, discussing possible cognitive node structure and candidate cognitive network architecture. It explains the functionality of cognitive algorithms and discusses opportunities for potential optimization. Furthermore, the concept of cognitive information services is introduced. Information signaling techniques are then classified, reviewed in detail, and compared. Finally, the performance of cognitive communication protocols is presented for a choice of examples.

Chapter 13

This chapter focuses on identifying, presenting, and classifying the main potential security attacks and vulnerabilities, as well as proposing appropriate counter-measures and solutions for them. These are supplemented by simulation results and metrics, with the intention of estimating the efficiency of each of the observed attacks and its counter-measure. nSHIELD is used to demonstrate the practicability of the potential implementation of the proposed countermeasures and solutions for the discussed security problems and issues.

Chapter 14

This chapter focuses on an application of cognitive networks, presenting the mechanism by which self-adaptation can be added. More specifically, this chapter discusses e-learning management systems and showcases the methodology by which such a system may be adapted to users' preferences and achieve effective learning. This is achieved by using vocabulary teaching as a specific instance of e-learning. Scenarios and the respective results of this methodology are also presented.

Foreword

Since the formulation of cognitive radio in the late 1990s, there have been a few notable milestones in wireless systems engineering. From my personal perspective one of the most important early milestones was the Dagstuhl[1] workshop in 2004 that accelerated the shift in focus from a cognitive wireless device to cognitive wireless networks. This led to the book *Cooperation in Wireless Networks: Principles and Applications* edited by Frank Fitzek and Marcos Katz, which captured much of the early thinking on this subject. Thomas Lagkas's book on the evolution of cognitive networks and self-adaptive communications systems is another such significant milestone in the development of this critical enabling technology.

Wireless networks have been rapidly expanded in business and home environments making wireless a huge market. Smart phones, digital tablets like Kindle, and other Personal Digital Assistants (PDAs) are spread across the globe. Mobile phones with what once would have been called supercomputer capabilities are almost everywhere and laptops with wireless connections are selling in great numbers. In addition, the Internet of Things is on the rise where every appliance from refrigerator to oven will have a wireless connection for cooperation to use energy more efficiently, to improve the living experience, and much more.

The Evolution of Cognitive Networks and Self-Adaptive Communications Systems brings together important new technical contributions in how to make all of this happen both for growth of the commercial sectors and for the greater good of humankind. The superb chapters provide insights and tools for wireless networks to allow users to stay connected and to be productive anywhere. For example, the chapter by Kritikou develops eLearning as a motivating use case. How's chapter on mesh protocols develops technology for knitting together a robust and supportive environment from devices in the home or workplace.

Driven by the mobility of society, convenience, and ease of use of wireless products, users would like to go beyond the distinction between services offered from wireless and wireline networks. Chapters by Karestos (relay), Rehmani (broadcast channel selection), Manzalini (Self Organizing Networks [SON] and virtual resources), and Demestichas (fiber optics) develop techniques that are helpful in erasing the distinctions between wireless and wireline. As interactive applications such as IP and video telephony, streaming video, and interactive video games have become very popular, they bring tight constraints to the network performance requirements. Vassaki's chapter on Radio Resource Management (RRM) for Quality of Service (Qos), and Chatzikokolakis's chapter on spectrum aggregation show how to enhance the wireless networks to address these and other such challenges. Kondareddy's chapter on TCP in cognitive radio networks addresses an important challenge in wireless-wireline integration.

Wireless communication poses new challenges in wireless network design. Efficient medium access techniques, transmission errors at the wireless medium, variable bit rate adjusting to wireless medium conditions, connection to the most suitable base station as the mobile user moves around, energy saving techniques due to limited battery power of mobile devices, best path selection in multi-hop mesh networks and admission control of new stations are some of the critical issues that should be addressed in efficient Network Design. These new and challenging problems of mobile and wireless network design, combined with the tight constraints and QoS required by interactive applications offer fruitful new areas of research. Kliazovich's chapter on signaling for the cognitive media access control layer, and Bourdena's chapter on TV white space markets offer important new insights in addressing such challenges.

Policy questions loom large. For example, such convenience at home, work, and play may be both a benefit and a curse without attention to security and privacy, so Dabčević's chapter on security stands out as a particularly important contribution. Regulatory policy can be an impediment or an enabler as Anker's chapter addresses. Finally, careful attention to experimentation as developed in Tonelli's chapter is the foundation of progress.

In short, this book will be a valuable reference to researchers and developers in the fields of wireless network design. In addition, it should help new entrants in this field with its contributions in the most important topics in the field. The book presents the wireless network community with the current research trends for efficient MAC design and QoS in wireless networks to inspire future research in these important areas. The variety of topics and the depth and breadth of treatment should make it a valuable reference to active researchers as well.

Joseph Mitola
Allied Communications, USA

Joseph Mitola III, *recognized globally as the father of software radio and cognitive radio, Dr. Mitola is founder and Chief Technology Officer of Mitola's STATISfaction, where his research interests focus on trustable, teachable cognitive systems including multifunction trustable agile radio frequency (RF) systems, and mathematically secure computing and communications. STATISfaction's publications have included the first commercial software radio architecture (May 1995 issue of the IEEE Communications Magazine) and the first cognitive radio architecture (Wiley, 2006). STATISfaction focuses on user satisfaction; intellectual property includes analytical models of classes of user, use context, and wireless infrastructure capabilities and limitations as well as high fidelity multi-media digital vignettes for advanced wearable information prosthetics. Previously, Dr. Mitola was Vice President for the Research Enterprise of Stevens Institute of Technology where he led faculty teams in pursuit and execution of a wide range of technologies. He also has served as Chief Scientist of the U.S. Department of Defense (DoD) Federally Funded Research and Development Center for The MITRE Corporation; Joint Special Assistant to the Director of the US Defense Advanced Research Projects Agency (DARPA) and to the Deputy Director of the US National Security Agency (NSA) for trustable cognitive systems; DARPA Program Manager; Technical Advisor to the Executive Office of the President of the United States; and Technical Director of Modeling and Simulation for DoD. He has held positions of technical leadership with E-Systems, Harris Corporation, Advanced Decision Systems, and ITT Corporation. Dr. Mitola began his career as an engineering student assistant with DoD in 1967. His graduate textbooks include Software Radio Architecture (Wiley 2000) and Cognitive Radio Architecture (Wiley, 2006). Dr. Mitola received the B.S. degree in electrical engineering from Northeastern University, Boston, MA, in 1971, the M.S.E. degree from The Johns Hopkins University, Baltimore, MD, in 1974, and the Licentiate (1999) and doctorate degrees in teleinformatics from KTH, The Royal Institute of Technology, Stockholm, Sweden, in 1999 and 2000, respectively.*

ENDNOTES

[1]   IBFI Schloss Dagstuhl, 66687 Wadern, Germany.

Preface

"Cognitive Networking" is a term of a broad meaning that refers to "smart" communicating entities that are capable of identifying current networking conditions and adapting to them. The combined objective is the optimization of the overall network behavior via the exploitation of the current network resources. Since the communication conditions may change radically based on excessively dynamic factors, networking devices are now expected to be self-aware, in order to efficiently adapt to this varying environment.

Research on cognitive networks was focused until lately on radio and spectrum related aspects. However, these can now be considered just a part of the subject area. The current trends reveal major activity in other relevant fields towards the integration of different techniques for the realization of completely self-aware and self-adaptive communication systems. For instance, learning automata, self-organizing ad hoc networks, dynamic resource allocation, node cooperation, natural systems, and automated network access selection can be taken into account when researching cognitive networking solutions.

The implications of cognitive networks can be proven critical for the evolution of future communication systems. Optimizing the coexistence terms of the wireless devices is expected to lead to significantly improved reliability, robustness, performance, cost management, and resource utilization. Hence, it is now evident that extensively studying the specific area is a necessity.

The overall objective of this publication is to provide the reader with advanced material related to the modern and multivariable area of cognitive networking. The book is intended to provide a complete overview of the cutting edge technologies that are combined for the formation of self-aware, self-adaptive, and self-organizing networks.

Our mission through this publication is to inform the research community and the related industry of the state-of-the-art solutions on cognitive networks, bring the involved technologies together, and clarify the latest trends towards a unified, cross-layer architecture for the realization of cognitive networking.

The book can be used as a library reference, useful in computer science, informatics, electronic-electrical engineering, and telecommunications engineering departments. It could also serve as a course supplement for computer networks and data telecommunications units.

In total, this publication is aimed at students, instructors, researchers, and professionals. It could be considered as a modern guide for students and instructors to cognitive, wireless, adaptive, and next generation networks. Researches will find it to be a valuable source of information on the related area, on which source they could rely to develop novel methods and techniques. Lastly, the book may assist professionals in acquiring cutting edge knowledge on their field and motivate them towards the implementation of self-managing networking solutions.

The book is composed of fourteen chapters that are divided in two sections: "Physical Layer Issues in Cognitive Networks" and "High Layer Issues in Cognitive Networks." Section 1 includes seven chapters that address cognitive networking issues that are mainly related to the physical layer of the network architecture. This section provides a review of cooperative communication technologies and presents state-of-the-art techniques for disseminating data and selecting channels in cognitive radio networks. Resource management is also examined, focusing on the TV White Spaces and the QoS requirements. Moreover, it discusses power control issues in modern mobile networks (such as LTE-Advanced) and explains how regulations affect business aspects related to cognitive radio. Experimental results regarding distributed data dissemination are also presented.

Chapter 1 discusses the main aspects of cooperative networking starting from the main historical milestones that shaped the idea. It focuses on the main mechanisms and techniques that foster cooperation and continues by studying performance metrics for various possible deployments, such as capacity bounds and outage probabilities. Finally, it examines the aspects related to medium access control design and implementation.

Chapter 2 provides a comprehensive review of broadcasting and channel selection strategies for wireless cognitive radio networks. Initially, some applications of the data dissemination in wireless cognitive radio networks are discussed, and then a detailed classification of broadcasting protocols in the light of the existing literature is provided. Furthermore, data dissemination is briefly discussed in the context of multi-channel environments and cognitive radio networks. A classification of channel selection strategies is also provided.

Chapter 3 discusses Joint Radio Resource Management (JRRM) issues in cognitive networks by presenting the TV White Spaces (TVWS) spectrum exploitation use case. It initially provides a state-of-the-art work for existing cognitive radio network architectures, while a reference architecture for commons and secondary TVWS trading is proposed. Subsequently, JRRM concepts for heterogeneous Radio Access Technologies' extension over TVWS are presented. Finally, a thorough classification of existing admission control and scheduling techniques is provided.

Chapter 4 focuses on the employment of the effective capacity theory in Cognitive Radio (CR) systems, presenting an extensive survey on QoS-driven resource allocation schemes proposed in the literature. Some useful conclusions are presented, and future research directions on this subject are highlighted and discussed.

Chapter 5 presents the Spectrum Aggregation scenario as it is proposed to be incorporated in LTE-advanced. Furthermore, the interesting extensions of FP7 SACRA European research project regarding Spectrum Aggregation are described. The business and the functional aspects stemming from the incorporation of this solution in the LTE-Advanced networks are presented in detail. Moreover, a typical power control algorithm is described and enhanced with learning capabilities and policies in order to meet the requirements of the Spectrum Aggregation scenario.

Chapter 6 addresses the impact on the business case for cognitive technologies of the regulatory regime and the choices on the fundamental CR technology that regulators will have to make. It concludes that despite the fact that cognitive radio holds an interesting promise for improved utilisation of the radio spectrum, there is a considerable degree of uncertainty regarding the potential application of cognitive radio. In addressing these uncertainties, the perspective of the entrepreneur is considered centre point. It is ultimately up to the entrepreneur to find viable product-market combinations for the exploitation of cognitive radio.

Chapter 7 focuses on the practical aspects related to the real world experimentation with distributed DSA network algorithms over a testbed network. Challenges and solutions are extensively discussed, from the testbed design to the setup of experiments. A practical example of experimentation process with a DSA algorithm is also provided.

Section 2 addresses issues that are related to cognitive networking layers that are higher than the physical one. It presents an overview of cutting edge technologies for autonomous software networks and discusses QoS support provision in multiple layers of Cognitive Radio Networks. The suitability of TCP in dynamic access networks in analyzed, while the convergence of optical and wireless networks is also examined. Moreover, the section reviews the latest developments in self-adaptive networks and provides simulation results regarding security issues in Cognitive Networks. Lastly, an application of cognitive techniques for e-learning in broadband networks is presented.

Chapter 8 addresses the potential impact of technologies like Autonomic, Cognitive, and Software Defined Networking on future network evolution. It is argued that said technologies, coupled with a wide adoption of virtualization, will bring an impactful disruption at the edge of current networks. The edge will become a business arena with multiple interacting networks and domains operated by diverse players. The chapter elaborates this vision, reports a brief overview of the state-of-the-art of enabling technologies, describes some simulation results of a use-case, and concludes by providing future research directions.

Chapter 9 examines issues that take place on different layers, chiefly the physical, MAC (Medium Access Control), and network layer of Cognitive Radio Networks (CRNs). It also reviews existing proposals to tackle the challenging issue of QoS provisioning in CRNs. In the second part of the chapter, it is studied how greater QoS provisioning capabilities are provided by two proposed routing protocols for CRNs utilizing a variety of techniques.

Chapter 10 explains why the typical TCP scheme, which was designed for wired networks, is not suitable for dynamic spectrum access networks. An analytical model was developed to estimate the TCP throughput of Dynamic spectrum access networks. The proposed model considers primary and secondary user traffic in estimating the TCP throughput by modeling the spectrum access using continuous-time Markov chains, thus providing more insight on effect of dynamic spectrum access on TCP performance than the existing models.

Chapter 11 introduces a novel management system called CONFES, Converged Network Infrastructure Enabling Resource Optimization and Flexible Service Provisioning, aiming at the proactive determination of PON (Passive Optical Network), clients' needs in bandwidth resources, and the efficient and reasonable allocation of resources to multiple clients according to such needs and the corresponding Service Level Agreements. Furthermore, the chapter proposes, studies, and compares physical architecture solutions (both centralized and distributed) that can realize such advanced management systems.

Chapter 12 overviews recent developments of self-awareness, self-management, and self-healing, discussing possible cognitive node structure and candidate cognitive network architecture. It explains the functionality of cognitive algorithms and discusses opportunities for potential optimization. Furthermore, the concept of cognitive information services is introduced. Information signaling techniques are then classified, reviewed in detail, and compared among them. Finally, the performance of cognitive communication protocols is presented for a choice of examples.

Chapter 13 focuses on identifying, presenting, and classifying the main potential security attacks and vulnerabilities, as well as proposing appropriate countermeasures and solutions for them. These are supplemented by simulation results and metrics, with the intention of estimating the efficiency of each of the observed attacks and its counter-measure. nSHIELD is used to demonstrate the practicability of the potential implementation of the proposed countermeasures and solutions for the discussed security problems and issues.

Chapter 14 focuses on an application of cognitive networks, presenting the mechanism by which self-adaptation can be added. More specifically, this chapter discusses on e-learning management systems and showcases the methodology by which such a system may be adapted to users' preferences and achieve effective learning. This is achieved by using vocabulary teaching as a specific instance of e-learning. Scenarios and the respective results of this methodology are also presented.

Conclusively, this book includes both lower layer and higher layer approaches, all targeting improving network behavior and user experience via enhancing device intelligence. It is certainly a fact that until this moment there was a strong distinction between lower layer approaches that aim at efficient utilization of the radio spectrum and higher layer approaches that try to ensure effective network performance depending on the current conditions. This publication is an effort towards the integration of the different techniques under a common cognitive networking architecture.

Thomas D. Lagkas
University of Western Macedonia, Greece & University of Sheffield, UK

Panagiotis Sarigiannidis
University of Western Macedonia, Greece

Malamati Louta
University of Western Macedonia, Greece

Periklis Chatzimisios
Alexander TEI of Thessaloniki, Greece

Acknowledgment

The editors would like to thank all people involved in the editing process. Without their efforts the completion of this project would not have been possible. Special thanks are sent to all chapter reviewers for their dedicated and consistent work. The editors are of course thankful to all chapter authors for contributing their qualitative work. Finally, special thanks to our families for their steady encouragement and understanding throughout this project.

Section 1
Physical Layer Issues in Cognitive Networks

Chapter 1
Lending a Hand:
Enhancing the Performance of Wireless Communication Networks Through Cooperation

George T. Karetsos
TEI of Larissa, Greece

ABSTRACT

Cooperative networking is considered one of the main enablers for achieving enhanced data rates in wireless communications. This is due to the fact that through cooperation the adverse effects of fading can be alleviated significantly. Thus, more reliable communication systems deployments can be devised, and performance enhancements can be achieved. In this chapter, the authors discuss the main aspects of cooperative networking starting from the main historical milestones that shaped the idea. Then they focus on the main mechanisms and techniques that foster cooperation and continue by studying performance metrics for various possible deployments, such as capacity bounds and outage probabilities. Finally, the authors take a more practical viewpoint and discuss aspects related to medium access control design and implementation that can serve as a stepping stone for the widespread deployment of cooperative networking.

INTRODUCTION

Cooperative networking is a means of enhancing a communication node's performance through assistance from another node in a network. In such a set up the number of the required nodes is at least three. Although cooperation is possible in fixed networks also, it is in wireless communications where its deployment leads to important performance enhancements. For example, in a wireless network cooperation enhances reliability, due to the fact that if a cooperating node exists, a signal

DOI: 10.4018/978-1-4666-4189-1.ch001

Copyright © 2013, IGI Global. Copying or distributing in print or electronic forms without written permission of IGI Global is prohibited.

will reach the destination node from two different paths. The first path is normally the direct signal from the transmitter while the second path is the relayed signal from the cooperating node. The existence of two paths enhances the decoding probability at the receiver either because one of the paths carries an adequately strong signal or the combination of the two signal instances leads to an easily decodable composite version. This situation, i.e. the availability of two or more copies of the transmitter's signals at the receiver, is called diversity and is considered one the most important methods to enhance the performance of wireless communication networks.

Cooperative diversity is the main enabler for achieving enhanced performance in modern wireless networks and results when a set of nodes assist each other for transmitting their data more efficiently. In such a scheme a source node transmits its data to one or many cooperative relay nodes that process and forward them to the destination node. Then the receiver combines the signals received from the relays with the signal received directly from the source and a performance gain is manifested in both BER and capacity achievements. Cooperation diversity has been studied extensively by the research community and can be performed via the employment of single or multiple relays. Numerous publications and research initiatives have been performed, particularly during the last decade, that treat the subject from various viewpoints. The most representative approaches will be reviewed in this chapter.

The cooperation performance is further enhanced with the employment of techniques such as space-time coding which introduces a temporal diversity dimension apart from the already existing spatial one. The benefits of cooperative diversity and in particular its capacity enhancements are capitalized by the end users via the employment of proper networking protocols that deploy the spatial diversity created from the relay nodes. In particular specially designed MAC protocols exploit the existence of one or multiple relays so

that the forwarded traffic can be treated much more flexibly and in a way that maximizes the system's overall performance. Another important consequence from cooperation is energy savings which may result, for example, from the need to transmit in shorter distances when cooperation is enabled.

In this chapter we provide a thorough review of the latest developments in cooperative networking. We start by providing background information regarding the main milestones in the evolutionary path towards cooperative communications. The details on how cooperation diversity is achieved in fading channels are presented together with the methods via which the receivers combine receptions from different paths so as to extract a strong and easily decodable signal. Then we present the protocols that have been devised so far for achieving cooperation diversity. Subsequently we deal with aspects related to distributed space time coding as it is applied in cooperative networking deployments and then we study capacity related issues. In the sequel cooperative multiple access schemes and their incorporation in legacy wireless networks are presented. Finally power allocation aspects are discussed since they are important for the assessment of the interference in a cooperative communication environment and we close the chapter by providing future research directions and conclusions.

BACKGROUND

The history of cooperative communications started with the work of Edward C. Van Der Meulen who introduced the relay communication channel and analyzed their information theoretic aspects (Van Der Meulen, 1971). It has been also studied by Sato who also provided insights regarding the achievable capacity (Sato, 1976). Then Cover and Gamal provided an extensive study and closed form expressions regarding the achievable capacity of the relay channel with various options regarding the presence of noise and feedback information availability (Cover and Gamal, 1979). The proposed channel model is made of a source node, a relay node and a destination node as shown in Figure 1. In this model the channel consists of a broadcast and a multiple access part since the source's transmission is received by both the relay and the destination and the destination receives from both the relay and the source.

In (Cover and Gamal, 1979) the authors show that the discrete memory-less Additive White Gaussian Noise (AWGN) relay channel achieves better capacity than that of the simple source-destination channel. Three different random coding schemes are proposed and the lower bounds on the channel capacity are derived.

Modern cooperative communications employ basic concepts from the relay channel model but they have a significant difference. While the conventional model was studied for AWGN channels in order to enhance their capacity, modern deployments aim at counter-fighting the adverse effects of fading through diversity. This scheme has been proposed by Sendonaris et. al. in 1998, almost twenty years after the studies for the relay channel took place (Sendonaris, Erkip and Aazhang, 1998). The authors assumed a cellular networking deployment where each user in a cell has a partner which retransmits any information that receives from him together of course with his own data. Since the mobile terminals employ omni-directional antennas there is no cost associated with this operation for the source and a new form of diversity is achieved that is called user cooperation diversity. From then on, research on cooperative communications proliferated and numerous related algorithms, protocols and architectures have been devised and studied.

Cooperative communications and networking is now considered one of the main focal points of research in wireless communications. The main aspects and outcomes of this research field will be presented in detail in the following sections of this chapter.

COOPERATIVE DIVERSITY AND COMBINING METHODS

Diversity may be achieved in space, time, frequency or in combinations of them but however spatial diversity is the scheme that provides the most significant performance improvements in wireless networking. It has been realized already in many practical deployments with the introduc-

Figure 1. The three terminal relay channel model

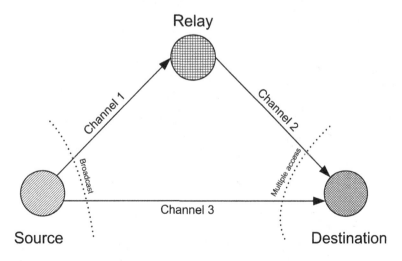

tion of multiple input multiple output (MIMO) communication systems.

Cooperative diversity in wireless networks results when a set of nodes assist each other for transmitting their data more efficiently. The formulated system consists of a source node that transmits its data to a number of cooperative relay nodes which, after some processing, forward them to the destination node. The receiving node makes a combination of the signals received from the relays with the signal received directly from the source as depicted in Figure 2. In this way a set up similar to MIMO systems is realized that can achieve similar transmission rates when the signal propagation conditions allow. In particular when the correlation among the transmission paths is low, spatial diversity gains are obtained (Laneman, Tse and Wornell, 2004). Cooperation diversity is enabled by the broadcast nature of wireless transmissions which allows the signals to reach many receivers. With cooperation diversity transmission reliability and radio coverage are enhanced.

MIMO deployments can offer significant improvements in reliability and throughput in wireless communication systems but however a full rank set up is usually possible only at the base stations due to sizing related constraints at the terminals (Telatar, 1999). Based on the principles of cooperative communications we can realize a MIMO like deployment for the uplink that can serve as an equivalent peer to the corresponding base station.

Diversity combining techniques are employed at the destination nodes so that the intended signals are efficiently reconstructed. They are based on the fact that if the received signals are independent, the combination of more signals leads to smaller error variance. In the case of one user, this means that receiving multiple copies of the same signal from different paths maximizes the probability of receiving at least one signal that has reasonable power and can be decoded successfully. This situation is most possible in urban environments where several uncorrelated multipath components could arrive at the receiver.

Several diversity methods have been proposed and studied for application in different cooperative communications set-ups. In the following we present the most representative techniques together with respective studies that highlight their expected performance. We have to note here that

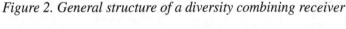

Figure 2. General structure of a diversity combining receiver

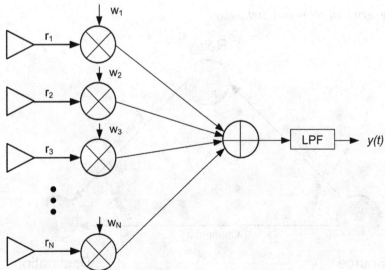

the combining techniques may be applied before or after detection has taken place. There exist small differences between the two approaches but however the way each technique works remains the same so we do not discriminate between the two approaches and in fact we focus and describe the pre-combining schemes.

Maximal Ratio Combining (MRC)

MRC is the optimum combining technique for coherent reception when we have independent fading at each receive path in the presence of AWGN but without considering co-channel interference. It works well in dual-hop configurations and has been analyzed for various systems and channel models. It requires that the channels' attenuation and phase shift are known at the receiver. The signals from both the relay and the source are weighted according to their individual signal to noise power ratios so as to give maximum SNR. Then it is checked and ensured that the signals have the same phase before being summed. MRC outputs a signal with an acceptable SNR even if none of the input signals is decodable. On the other hand, MRC has the highest complexity of all combining techniques since it requires the knowledge of the fading amplitude on each receiving path.

We will review now the way that MRC works when slow flat fading is considered for the channel gains of each receiving path. This means that the channel gain $h_i(t)$ remains constant over a symbol's period. Furthermore the channel gain and the additive white Gaussian noise $n_i(t)$ of each receiving path are assumed independent and identically distributed (i.i.d.) statistical processes. If $s(t) = A(t)\cos(2pf_c t + \vartheta(t))$ is the transmitted signal from the source and $|h_i(t)|$, $\phi_i(t)$ are the magnitude and phase shift imposed by the channel respectively then the received signal at each diversity branch of the combining receiver will be:

$$r_i(t) = \left|h_i(t)\right| A(t)\cos(2\pi f_c t + \vartheta(t) + \phi_i(t)) + n_i(t)$$

with $i=1,2,...,N$. The received signals $r_i(t)$ are then weighted, co-phased and added together. The weights at each branch are $w_i(t) = a_i(t)\cos(2\pi f_c t + \phi_i(t))$ and the amplitude $a_i(t)$ is selected to be proportional to the corresponding signal's amplitude. In this way the strongest signals are amplified while the weak ones are further attenuated. In particular it holds that if $a_i(t) = \left|h_i(t)\right|$ the instantaneous SNR at the output of the receiver is maximized. This rule, however, is not valid when the set of noise components at the diversity branches are not identically distributed.

In (Shin and Song, 2008) the authors derive the exact performance of MRC in dual-hop systems and Nakagami-m fading channels. Dual-hop systems correspond in fact to the same configuration as the three terminal relay channel model depicted in Figure 1. In the presented configuration the source and the relay have a single transmission antenna whereas the destination employs multiple receive antennas (corresponding in essence to the number of the receive paths). The relay performs an amplify and forward operation on the signals received from the source. Unfortunately the noise at the relay is also forwarded to the destination. It is shown that the cooperative diversity benefit is limited by the characteristics of the links (represented by the respective Nakagami parameters) between the source and the relay and between the relay and the destination.

Co-Channel Interference (CCI) is another factor that affects the performance of diversity combining and should be taken into account. This problem has been studied extensively in (Shah and Haimovich, 2000). The authors considered Rayleigh and Ricean fading for the desired signals and Rayleigh fading for the CCI sources. It is shown that fading of the interference sources has significant impact on the performance of the diversity combining scheme. When CCI is the major factor affecting the desired signals then the technique employed is called Optimum Combining (OC) and will be reviewed in the next paragraphs.

Optimum Combining (OC)

It reduces the power of the interfering signals at the combining receiver by exploiting the correlation present among them. Indeed, if we consider a diversity combining receiver as in Figure 2 an interfering signal will be present in all of its antenna elements. This fact is exploited by OC to maximize the resulting signal to interference plus noise ratio (SINR) at the output. The analysis that highlights the operation of the optimum combiner for equal power interferers is done in (Winters, 1984). It is shown that OC achieves significant improvements over MRC in the presence of CCI as the number of the involved antennas at the receiver increases. In particular the improvement is marginal when the number of antennas is much greater than the number of interferers whereas it is considerably large when the interferers surpass the number of the antennas employed at the receiver. Closed form expressions regarding the upper bounds on the achievable BER for BPSK, QAM and differential detection of DPSK for any number of antennas and interferers are provided in (Winters and Salz, 1998). These results are extended in (Chiani, Win, Zanella, Mallik, and Winters, 2003) for the general case of M-ary phase shift keying and by taking into account the existence of thermal noise.

Soft-Bit Maximal Ratio Combining

A problem that may arise in cooperative diversity networking is the fact that when Adaptive Modulation and Coding (AMC) is being employed the signals from the different links may reach the receiver with a different constellation size of the employed modulation scheme. This due to the possible variability of the channel quality characteristics among the different paths, direct and indirect, that the signal may follow to reach the

destination. Thus in order to get full advantage of both AMC and diversity combining there is a need for a technique that will overcome the possible differences in the constellation size of the modulated signals arriving at the receiver. Such a mechanism, called Soft Bit Maximal Ratio Combiner (SBMRC) is proposed in (Bin Sediq and Yanikomeroglu, 2009). Symbols belonging to different constellations are mapped onto soft bits which are then decoded using the Log Likelihood Ratio (LLR) technique. Soft bits contain not only values but reliability information that will help the detector to perform correct decoding. One important advantage of this technique is that its complexity grows linearly with the number of soft bits employed whereas the employment of the Maximum Likelihood Detector (MLD) grows exponentially. In particular if C is the number of bits per symbol the SBMRC technique will decide on the value of the bit $\hat{s}_l$, $l \in \left\{0, 1, \ldots, C-1\right\}$ according to the following rule

$$\begin{cases} \hat{s} = 1 \ \ if \ \ \overline{s}_l \succ 0, \\ \hat{s} = -1 \ \ otherwise \end{cases}$$

where $\overline{s}_l$ is the sum of the soft bits received at the combining receiver from the different paths (direct and indirect). Finally it is proved that the performance of SBMRC regarding BER is slightly inferior to that of the MLD making it the detector of choice when complexity is the critical factor.

Selection Combining (SC)

This approach can also appear in various versions depending on the system under study and on the chosen channel model. In its simplest form only the best signal is selected and decoded at the receiver. In the Generalized Selection Combining (GSC) method N out of M signals are selected and combined at the receiver (Ikki and Ahmed,

2009a). GSC can be considered as a combination of MRC and SC. Only the knowledge of the signal powers suffices for the selection and there is no need for weight balancing or phase shifting. Thus both coherent and non-coherent modulation techniques can be employed. As with MRC the best performance is achieved when the receive diversity branches experience independent and identical fading. The probability of achieving a high SNR at the output increases proportionally with the number of available receive branches.

Selection diversity combing has been studied extensively by the research community. Emphasis has been put on modeling and taking into account the fact that the fading statistics over the different receive branches are in fact correlated due to the insufficient space among the employed antennas. In particular there exists a big number of studies on the dual branch diversity combiner with correlated inputs for different fading models (Simon and Alouini, 1999; Tellambura, Annamalai and Bhargava, 2003; Karagiannidis, 2003). In (Simon and Alouini, 1999) closed form expressions for the error probability and for the outage probability are derived in a dual diversity combining communication system for various coherent and non-coherent modulation schemes over correlated Rayleigh fading channels. It is shown that the correlation degree, expressed via a suitable correlation co-efficient, affects proportionally the performance of the receiver. Correlated Nakagami-m fading is tackled in (Tellambura, Annamalai and Bhargava, 2003) and (Karagiannidis, 2003). In particular in (Tellambura, Annamalai and Bhargava, 2003) closed-form expressions are presented that can be used for the evaluation of average error performance of dual-branch SC for coherent, differentially coherent, and noncoherent communications systems. Finally, the analysis done in (Karagiannidis, 2003) is more practical since it is based on the Signal to Interference Ratio (SIR). Outage and error probability closed-form expressions are provided that are then employed for the system's performance assessment for both

coherent and non-coherent modulations. Again it is shown that the degree of correlation among the two receive branches has negative impact on the achievable performance.

The employment of three or more SC branches is making the problem of performance assessment even harsher. However since it holds that, the larger the number of branches the larger the performance advantage, there is a need to quantify this advantage and to assess its trade off with the induced implementation complexity. Such results have been presented in (Karagiannidis, Zogas and Kotsopoulos, 2003; Chen and Tellambura, 2005; Zhang and Lu, 2002).

The practical alternative of SC, that presents comparatively reduced complexity, is the so-called switched diversity (SWC). Its operation is very simple. The receiver system relies on a particular antenna as long as the signal's quality remains above a certain threshold that ensures reliable communication. If the signal's quality falls below this threshold, the remaining branches are examined for discovering a suitable one (Simon and Alouini, 2005). There exist two main variations of SWC. The first one is called switch and stay combining (SSC) and the second one Switch and Examine Combining (SEC). A thorough analysis of the former for various M-ary modulations and for Rayleigh, Rice and Nakagami-m fading channel models can be found in (Young-Chai, Alouini and Simon, 2000). From the comparison between MRC and SSC regarding the outage probability a 2dB difference in the diversity gain is observed in favour of MRC. As far as the probability of error is concerned MRC presents again a slightly better performance against SSC and SC for both binary and M-ary modulations. SEC is an improvement of SSC in the sense that it switches between the available branches until a suitable one is found whereas SSC will transmit in the next slot irrespectively of the channel's condition in relation to the pre-set threshold. It has been proved that SEC outperforms SSC for a diversity combining scheme with more than two branches (Yang and Alouini, 2003).

SC can be effectively applied in a dual hope cooperative environment with single or multiple relays. A simple method to select the best path between a source and a destination when multiple relays are employed in between is presented in (Bletsas, Khisti, Reed and Lippman, 2006). Instantaneous channel measurements are employed and localization information between the source and the destination is avoided with the simple assumption that the source and the relays transmit at orthogonal time-slots. The wireless channel conditions between both the source and the relays as well as between the relays and the destination are taken into account and the final decision regarding path selection is done via specific policies that ensure end-to-end link quality.

As we mentioned already, when GSC is employed, the signals from more than one relays are combined together with the direct link. This approach is more complex but however its usage compensates for significant performance improvements and has been studied also extensively. Closed-form expressions regarding the probability of error, the outage probability and the achievable capacity for amplify and forward relays and Rayleigh fading environment are provided in (Ikki and Ahmed, 2009a). Further results regarding the first two performance metrics are provided in (Chu, 2012). The provided outcomes are considered more generic since Nakagami-m fading is assumed for the channel models. The performance of GSC can be further enhanced if an error detection technique is employed at the destination (Choi, Hong, Kim and Kim, 2009). Despite the added complexity of error detection the fact that the receiver may not need to combine transmissions from several paths when the first arrival is decoded successfully make this approach attractive.

Equal Gain Combining (EGC)

With this technique each incoming signal is equally weighted before combining. In this way the estimation of each path's fading characteristics is not required. However co-phasing is still required to cope with the possibility that one signal may cancel another one before being combined. These facts make the practical implementation of EGC to be much easier when compared for example with MRC but it requires balanced diversity systems where all diversity paths have identical noise power (Ikki and Ahmed, 2009b). EGC has been also studied extensively by the research community. Exact closed form expressions regarding the outage probability in Rayleigh fading channels in the presence of co-channel interference are provided in (Yi, Blostein and Julian, 2003). The results are obtained are obtained for both equal and distinct interference powers by varying either the number of antennas or the number of interferers or both. Besides the expected outcome that the outage probability increases proportionally with the number of interferers and inversely proportionally with the number of antennas an important observation is that interference should be considered to affect incoherently the desired signals. This result leads to more accurate predictions regarding the outage probability. In (Abu-Dayya and Beaulieu, 1992) the outage probabilities for equal gain, selection and switched diversity combining in generalized Nakagami fading are derived with a focus on the L-branch equal gain combiner. In addition the effects of diversity on frequency reuse and spectrum efficiency in cellular mobile systems are presented. These are important factors that should be taken into account in practical deployments. Finally an alternative and simpler approach in obtaining closed form expressions for BER performance and outage probabilities is presented in (Zogas, Karagiannidis and Kotsopoulos, 2005).

Various possibilities exist regarding the usage of EGC in a cooperative communications environment. In (Ikki and Ahmed, 2009b) and (Ikki and Ahmed, 2007) the outage probabilities of differential EGC for various numbers of amplify and forward relays are derived as well as the BER performance for binary DPSK modulation in Nakagami-m fading environments. In addition in (Ikki and Ahmed, 2007) the impact of the relay location on the performance is also highlighted. It is shown that the obtained performance of differential ECG is comparable to that of MRC, an outcome that makes this technique attractive due to its lower implementation complexity. A general approach for analyzing the performance of dual-hop cooperative diversity networks with amplify-and-forward variable-gain relays is presented in (da Costa and Aissa, 2009). Both Equal-Gain Combining (EGC) and Maximal-Ratio Combining (MRC) techniques are considered at the destination. Closed-form approximations for the outage probability and average symbol error rate (SER) are given which can be employed to assess the system's performance with relatively low computational efforts especially as the number of relays increases.

In Figure 3, we present numerical results that reveal the BER performance of MRC, EGC and SC in relation to E_b / N_0 in a Rayleigh fading environment. The results are obtained for a set-up as in Figure 1 that employs one relay node while the receiver antennas at the destination are varying from 1 to 4. In particular it shown that MRC (dashed lines with squares) performs better than EGC (solid lines with circles) which again performs better than SC (dotted-dashed lines with stars). The performance of the direct transmission (DT) between the source and the destination (i.e. without the employment of the relay node) is also depicted.

Until now, we have focused in two-hop cooperative networking scenarios. However due to the broadcast nature of wireless communications the signals sent by a relay terminal may be received,

apart from the destination, by other relay terminals as well. In this way a multihop diversity network is established which can further enhance the communication performance as introduced in (Boyer, Falconer and Yanikomeroglu, 2004). It is shown, for various relaying schemes, that the multihop diversity channels outperform the singlehop ones given that the intermediate relays are properly selected. In the next section we study the particular protocols that allow for the efficient exploitation of cooperative diversity and combining for either singlehop or multihop configurations.

COOPERATIVE NETWORKING PROTOCOLS

Cooperative networking protocols are the rules via which the spatial diversity created from the relay nodes is exploited in a way that maximizes the system's overall performance. In other words, they define how the received data is processed at the relay node before it is sent to the destination. We report on the various possible implementations of these protocols and we provide the corresponding performance insights that will help in the selection of the best possible combination for a considered deployment (Laneman, Tse, and Wornell, 2004). Finally, a part of this section will be devoted on the impact of relay selection on the performance of the aforementioned protocols. There exist three main forwarding strategies that the relay node may follow for that purpose (Zimmermann, Herhold, and Fettweis, 2003).

Amplify-and-Forward (AF) Transmission

It is the simplest method and it has been introduced in (Laneman, Wornell and Tse, 2004). It is also known as opportunistic relaying. The relay amplifies and re-transmits the received signals from the source. Of course at the same time noise is amplified. However since the destination receives

Figure 3. BER performance of MRC, EGC, and SC in a Rayleigh fading environment of a three terminal cooperative system with variable receive branches and comparison with a Direct Transmission (DT) only set-up

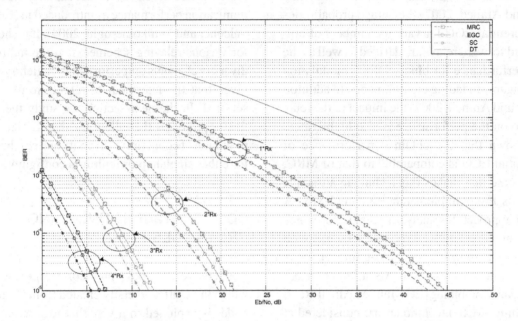

Figure 4. System model for amplify-and-forward cooperation

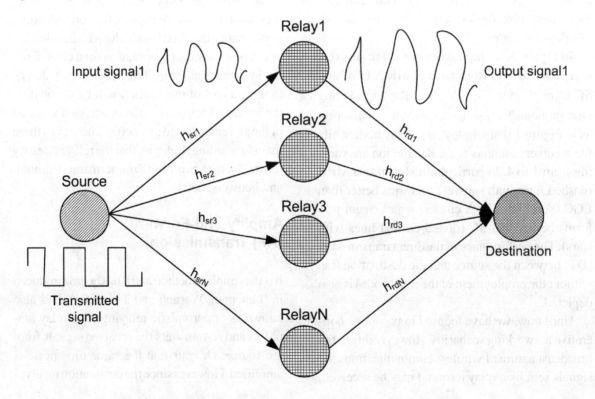

two, most possibly independently faded versions of the same signal, diversity is achieved and the communication performance can be enhanced. The system model of the amplify-and-forward cooperation method is shown in Figure 4. For optimal decoding the receiving station should know the respective channels' co-efficients, a fact that makes the implementation of the AF method not so trivial.

It has been shown that AF can achieve full diversity gain at high SNR regimes (Zhao, Adve and Lim, 2007). In the same work the authors present also two optimal power allocation schemes for all the participating relay nodes that maximize throughput and minimize outage probability and symbol error rate. The possibility to select only one of the relays, this that achieves the higher SNR at the receiver, is also examined. It is proved that the relay selection approach not only maintains the diversity order but it also achieves higher throughput and lower outage probability since the information is only repeated once. Furthermore it has been shown that when MRC is employed at the destination in an AF cooperation environment the full diversity order of $M+1$, where M is the number of relays can be achieved (Anghel and Kaveh, 2004).

Relay selection in amplify-and-forward cooperation could also form the basis for enhancing the lifetime of the formulated networking infrastructure. In (Wan-Jen, Hong and Kuo, 2008) it is proved that this can be achieved even with only local channel state information availability at the relays and residual energy information at the users. Four different selection strategies are examined i.e. minimum transmission power (MTP) strategy, maximum residual energy (MRE) strategy, maximal energy-efficiency index (MEI) strategy, and minimum outage probability (MOP). MEI and MOP are shown to achieve the best performance regarding network lifetime prolongation with reduced complexity.

Energy usage at the relays is a very important aspect in cooperative networking and should be carefully taken into account. Since the cooperating nodes are offering part of their energy so that the communication QoS enjoyed by the source node is enhanced, it is obvious that when multiple relays are involved, a degree of fairness regarding energy consumption should be ensured among them. This problem is studied thoroughly in (Michalopoulos and Karagiannidis, 2008). In particular the relay that will be utilized in the next transmission is selected based on the instantaneous and average channel conditions which are weighted so that the average selection time and power consumption are controlled accordingly. The channels are assumed independent and follow slowly varying Rayleigh fading. Performance results regarding outage probability and average symbol error probability reveal that this scheme is very efficient in achieving fairness especially in high SNRs or when the number of relays is small.

The cross layer performance of amplify-and-forward cooperative wireless networks is analyzed in (Issariyakul and Krishnamurthy, 2009). In particular, using a suitably devised Markov model the following aspects are treated a) amplify-and-forward cooperative diversity at the physical layer, b) flow control and error recovery at the data link layer, and c) traffic generation at the application layer. Several performance metrics are introduced and studied focusing mostly on packet delivery and packet delay probability in relation to the SNR levels and number of cooperating nodes. Finally two power allocation algorithms are presented that affect the upper bound of the packet transmission probability.

Decode-and-Forward (DF) Transmission

In this approach the relay fully decodes and re-encodes the received signal before forwarding it to the destination (Laneman, Tse and Wornell, 2004). It is obvious that the complexity of this scheme is higher than that of AF and CSI between the source and the relay is required for optimum decoding.

Achieving full diversity order is the target in this scheme also and detection and combining play the most important role in this framework. To this end, several techniques have been proposed in the literature. The usage of the maximum likelihood detector is studied in (Chen and Laneman, 2006). In particular a general framework for ML detection of both coherent and non-coherent un-coded modulation schemes that rely on cooperative diversity is presented. Furthermore in the high SNR regime, non-coherent DF achieves full diversity order. Thus ML detection is considered as the optimal scheme that can be employed in DF diversity receivers. A major obstacle, however, in studying ML detection in DF deployments is that their performance analysis is very complicated (Sendonaris, Erkip and Aazhang, 2003). Recently though, a solution to this problem has been presented in (Ju and Kim, 2009) by defining the ML detection rule through the usage of the max-log approximation. In this way it was possible to derive closed-form expressions regarding

BER performance for both M-PAM and M-QAM modulations.

Due to the difficulties that exist in the analysis of ML detection a modified MRC scheme is proposed, called λ-MRC, via which the performance analysis can be accomplished much easier and closed formed expressions for the outage and error probability can be derived (Sendonaris, Erkip and Aazhang, 2003). Apart from λ-MRC, other sub-optimal detection schemes include Cooperative-MRC (C-MRC) and link adaptive regeneration (LAR). C-MRC is introduced in (Tairan, Cano and Giannakis, 2005) and it achieves full diversity for DF cooperation protocols and coherent modulations by exploiting the instantaneous bit error probability of each fading channel between the source and the destination. C-MRC's performance is very close to that of ML detection with the advantage of less complex realization. With LAR the decoded bits at the relays are scaled in power before being forwarded to the destination (Tairan, Giannakis and Renqiu, 2008). Scaling is based on the actual conditions, determined by

Figure 5. System model for decode-and-forward cooperation

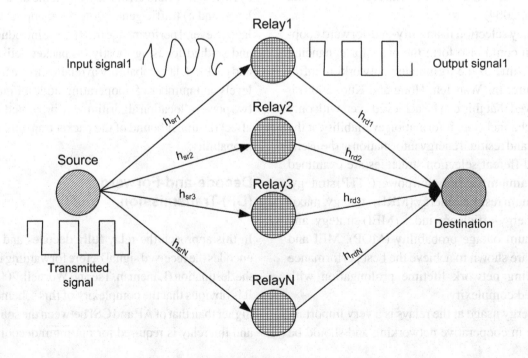

the SNR, on the links between the source and the employed relay and between the employed relay and the destination. Furthermore channel state availability information at the relay regarding the link between the relay and the destination is assumed. Based on these conditions MRC is properly formulated and applied at the destination. This technique also achieves close to optimal diversity gains and in addition it copes efficiently with quantization and feedback errors. Furthermore it leads to energy savings at both the relays and the destination nodes. The general system model of the decode-and-forward cooperation method is shown in Figure 5.

Relay selection can lead to significant performance enhancements in this scheme also. In particular it has been shown in (Yi and Kim, 2008) that the combination of C-MRC with relay selection can achieve the full diversity order. Furthermore, in the same study, LAR is also examined and for two relays the achievable diversity is upper bounded by 3 and lower bounded by 3-ξ where ξ is an arbitrarily small number. Despite the fact that LAR does not achieve the full diversity order

it presents the advantage of lower implementation complexity, in particular for fast fading channels, when compared with C-MRC.

Coded Cooperation (CC) Transmission

In coded cooperation, after the user's data are augmented with cyclic redundancy check, they are partitioned into two segments each one containing N1 and N2 bits respectively. The different portions of each user's code word are transmitted via two independent fading paths (Hunter and Nosratinia, 2006). In this way incremental redundancy is produced. In more detail, if we consider a three-user cooperating scheme as in Figure 6, after user 1 has transmitted his own N1 bits in the second part of the frame he will either transmit his partner's N2 bits if he was able to decode them successfully or his own N2 bits if he cannot decode what he has received from his partner. In this way the transmitted frame consists always of N=N1+N2 bits and the level of cooperation is defined as

Figure 6. System model for coded cooperation transmission

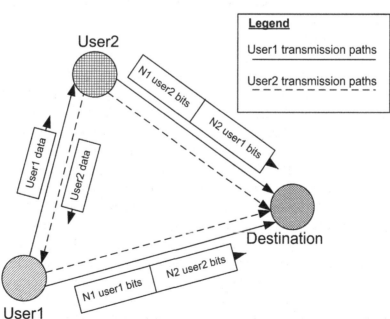

N2/N i.e the larger the number of the forwarded partner's bits the bigger the level of cooperation.

Coded cooperation can achieve important gains when compared to the non-cooperative approach. The respective closed-form expressions as well as numerical results are presented in (Hunter and Nosratinia, 2006). The analysis is taking place for both fast and slow Rayleigh fading channels and for deriving the numerical results Rate-Compatible Punctured Convolutional (RCPC) codes are being employed. Coded cooperation is also tackled in (Lei, Fuja, Kliewer and Costello, 2007) where the cooperating partners transmit an algebraic superposition of the local and relayed information.

Compress and Forward (CF) Transmission

With this strategy the relay produces a quantized and compressed version from the signal that is received from the source that is then forwarded towards the destination node. The destination decodes the source's message by combining the relay's output with his output that was derived from the manipulation of the directly received signal from the source. The statistical dependence of the outputs is exploited using Wyner-Ziv source coding (Wyner and Ziv, 1976). CF technique was already introduced in (Cover and Gamal, 1979) and has again received attention with the introduction of the cooperative networking concept in late 90's. In (Kramer, Gastpar and Gupta, 2005) the work of Cover and Gamal in (Cover and Gamal, 1979) is extended for various cooperative networking configurations that employ either DF or CF strategy or a mixture of them. For the CF strategy the upper bound on the achievable rate with employment of multiple relays is derived. The possibility that different relays are employing different forwarding schemes, i.e. some of them are using decode-and-forward while the rest employ compress-and-forward, is also studied and the upper bounds on the possible rates are obtained.

Furthermore it is shown that the decode-and-forward strategy with phase fading achieves the ergodic capacity if the phase information is only locally available to the receivers and if the relays are near the source. On the contrary compress-and-forward performs better when it is applied to relays that are close to the destination. These are important trade-off aspects that should be considered during practical deployments of the aforementioned schemes.

Recently it was also shown that the performance of CF can be improved if a distributed Karhunen-Loève transform is applied before Wyner-Ziv coding (Simoens, Muñoz Medina, Vidal and del Coso 2010). The achievable rates of the proposed scheme are derived for various coding strategies. Then it is illustrated via simulations that the proposed CF outperforms DF and the achievable rates approach the channel's capacity given that full Channel State Information (CSI) is available. These results show that CF is a possible alternative of AF and DF in some cases but one needs to take also into account the associated complexity before selecting it for implementation.

The last three strategies, i.e. DF, CC, and CF, require more computational resources but lead to a more reliable communication result when compared with the *amplify-and-forward* strategy. Hybrid schemes are also possible and have been proposed and studied by the research community. In (Bao and Li, 2007) a combination of AF and DF is introduced that is called Decode-Amplify and Forward (DAF). For the AF part the scheme exploits the channel's reliability information and not the actual transmissions, via the computation of the LLRs from the received signals for each bit. It is known that both the re-transmitted signal and the channel LLR scale linearly to the received signal at the relay and they are linearly proportional to each other. The idea behind DAF is that the relaying node first decodes the received data via the employed error correction code and instead of making a decision regarding the value of each bit it amplifies the respective LLRs and sends them to the destination. The destination is then trying to recover the original information by jointly decoding the received packets from the source and from the relay. It is shown that this approach outperforms simple AF and simple DF but cannot beat the performance of CC. For this, a combination of DAF with CC is also proposed and studied and it is proved that it achieves the best performance when compared with the other schemes (Bao and Li, 2007). On the other hand it is obvious that DAF presents higher implementation complexity in relation to AF only but this difference can be compensated from the achievable performance gains. In the next section we review efficient coding schemes that are specially designed to cope with the peculiarities of a cooperative communications environment.

COOPERATIVE DISTRIBUTED SPACE-TIME CODING

In cooperative communications, a virtual antenna array is formed with a number of distributed antennas belonging to the same number of users each one of them having their own information to transmit. However the achieved spatial diversity leads to decreased bandwidth efficiency since each relay requires each own sub-channel to transmit (Laneman and Wornell, 2003). The most efficient solution in order to overcome this problem is the development and inclusion of distributed space-time codes that allow all the relays to transmit on the same sub-channel. With this approach the employed space-time codes are generated cooperatively by the participating nodes. It has been shown that with this approach full spatial diversity can be achieved at the cost of enhanced computational complexity at the receivers. In this section we provide a short review of space-time codes and then we highlight the latest results regarding their application in cooperative communication deployments.

With Space Time Coding (STC) temporal correlation is introduced in the signals that are transmitted from different antennas. Since the signals are transmitted from different antennas spatial correlation already exists. For example, in its simpler form, the same information is transmitted by the employment of multiple antennas but a delay of one symbol period is introduced between the different transmissions and thus temporal diversity is introduced. Despite the technically introduced delay there is no increase in bandwidth consumption since at the end two symbols are transmitted during each time slot. The same holds for the transmission power which is not increased with the introduction of temporal diversity. Space time code usage in wireless communications were introduced and studied in (Tarokh, Seshadri and Calderbank, 1998) and (Alamouti, 1998). The initial research efforts on the subject have focused on narrowband flat-fading channels. The application on broadband channels is more challenging. In (Tarokh, Seshadri and Calderbank, 1998) the authors have focused in channel coding design that can perform better than the simplistic error correcting coding approach of repeating the same information via the different transmission paths. Repetition coding is in fact a specific case of space-time coding. Coded modulation M-PSK and M-QAM schemes are provided which show excellent performance and decoding complexity similar to the codes used in Gaussian channels.

In (Laneman and Wornell, 2003) the application and performance analysis of space time codes in a cooperative diversity communication environment is presented. It is shown that full spatial diversity can be achieved which is actually determined by the number of the cooperating relays and not just by the number of the relays that are able to decode and forward. This is because with space time codes it is possible for all the relays to transmit on the same channel. Furthermore it is corroborated that the achievable spectral efficiency of space time codes is higher than that of repetition based coding. Similar results regarding the diversity order that can be achieved in a cooperative wireless networking environment are derived in (Yindi and Hassibi, 2006) but for Linear Dispersion (LD) space time codes.

A more practical study regarding the application of space time codes in a cooperative environment is given (Scutari and Barbarossa, 2005). In particular, the assumption that the relays are error free is removed and the impact of intermediate decoding errors at the relays is examined. Indeed due to the fact that the source and the relays are not collocated, their packets will most probably arrive at the destination at different times. Also the statistical properties of the channels between the source and the relay and between the relay and the destination generally differ. With distributed STC these aspects may lead to error generation that should handled effectively. In (Scutari and Barbarossa, 2005) the authors are dealing with such a situation and they provide the design of an optimum ML detector for such a case given that the vector of the error probabilities at the relays is known at the destination. If the error probabilities are unknown the decision criteria are also provided which however correspond to suboptimal ML detection. The derived results indicate that the BER performance of the suboptimal scheme is close to that of the optimal one when the SNR at the relay is sufficiently high something that makes the former scheme a tempting implementation candidate with reduced complexity.

Since timing and frequency offsets are common in a cooperative networking environment, careful choices regarding the way the participating elements are implemented and operate may alleviate them. In (Wang, Yin and Xia, 2010) both timing and frequency offsets are tackled via a special transceiver design that employs distributed linear convolutive space-time codes and a Minimum Mean Square Error (MMSE) or MMSE Decision Feedback Equalizer (MMSE-DFE) detector with fast Kalman equalizations at the receiver. Performance results of the proposed approach show that significant diversity gains can

be achieved when channel frequency offsets are present and taken into account. Finally in (Guo and Xia, 2008) OFDM together with special code design is being employed for fighting timing errors which leads to full diversity gains. It is obvious that the resolution of these problems will unveil the full potentials of cooperative communications and pave the way towards efficient implementation deployments. It has already been shown that the application of distributed space time coding leads to important capacity improvements in well established wireless networking standards such as Wimax and IEEE 802.11n (Liu, Tao, Narayanan, Korakis and Panwar, 2007; Skordoulis, Ni, Chen, Stephens, Liu, and Jamalipour, 2008). The impact of cooperation on the achievable capacity with or without STC employment is treated in the following section.

COOPERATIVE CAPACITY

Studies on the achievable capacity when a node intervenes, as a facilitator, in the transmission path between a communicating pair have started already in the seventies with the introduction of the relay channel (Cover and Gamal, 1979). This is of course natural since capacity is a practical performance metric that defines the rate of information that can be transferred by the system and the type of services that can be supported. The authors treat the noise degraded discrete memoryless relay channel. In particular, the following situations are studied:

- Degraded relay channel and its achievable capacity;
- Reversely degraded relay channel and its achievable capacity;
- Arbitrary relay channel with feedback and its achievable capacity.

For each case, the upper bounds on the capacity are derived. Subsequently the Gaussian degraded relay channel is introduced and a closed-form expression on the achievable capacity is derived. The general relay channel with feedback is also studied. Finally, the achievable rate of the general relay channel is obtained. In the coming years research on the subject did not progress significantly and only a few theoretical studies appeared in the literature (Zhang, 1988).

Capacity related studies flourished with the introduction of cooperative communications in fading channels due to the important performance enhancements achieved with this approach. One of the most critical parameters in determining capacity in a cooperative environment is of course the SNR levels at the destination. On the other hand, the SNR levels affect energy consumption and the induced interference on neighbouring links. In the following, we will present the main factors that determine and affect the achievable capacity in various cooperative networking deployments.

In (Kramer, Gastpar and Gupta, 2005) the authors deal with the capacity of DF and CF schemes for various decoding strategies and cooperative networking configurations. In particular the achievable rates for relay channels, Multiaccess Relay Channels (MARCs), and Broadcast Relay Channels (BRCs) are derived for the decode-and forward scheme for various decoding strategies. If we consider a network with four relay nodes MARC corresponds to a scenario where two nodes use a single relay to forward their independent data to a destination. On the other hand, BRC corresponds to a scenario where one node uses a relay to forward the same message to two destination

nodes. These scenarios are illustrated in Figure 7. In addition for the CF scheme the upper bound on the achievable rate for multiple relays is derived.

The problem of maximizing the minimum capacity of all sources via relay assignment in a cooperative network with multiple sources, multiple relays and one destination is studied in (Pham, Nguyen and Tuan, 2012). Since we have multiple sources, relay assignment means that each source's signal is forwarded by only one relay. For that purpose CSI is employed by the destination which informs the relays via a control channel about which source should be forwarded by which relay. The fact that a successful transmission may occur at just one step i.e. via the direct path between the source and the destination and without the need for any relay intervention is also exploited. If we consider K sources and L relays the optimization problem can be written as follows:

$$\max_{\{u_{kl}\}} \min_{k \in \{1,2,\dots K\}} C_k$$

$$s.t. \sum_{l=1}^{L+1} u_{kl} = 1, \forall k$$

where and $C_k = \max\{C_k^{(direct)}, C_{kl_k}^{(AF)}\}$ and $u_{kl} = 1$ if the k_{th} source is assisted by the l_{th} relay and 0 otherwise. Such a problem is non-linear and non-convex and thus finding a solution is a very challenging task. However it can be faced by reformulating it as a mixed-integer linear programming (MILP) which can be solved by

Figure 7. Multi-access and broadcast relay channels

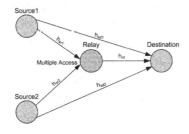 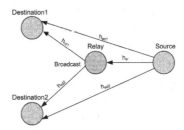

Figure 8. A Multi-source and multi-relay cooperative network deployment

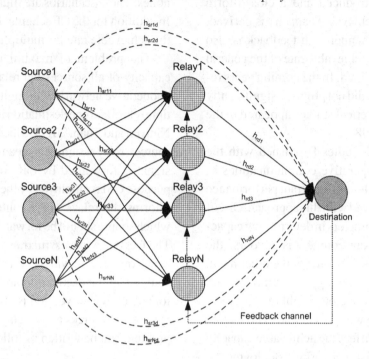

branch-and-bound algorithms. Furthermore a greedy algorithm is developed that is based on the principles of an integer programming class of algorithms named lexicographic bottleneck assignment (Burkard and Rendl, 1991). Simulation results show that the complexity of the greedy algorithm is low and the required computation time increases slowly as the number of the involved sources increases. Furthermore it obtains a close to optimal solution and thus it can be the method of choice for studying configurations such as the one depicted in Figure 8.

Cooperative diversity presents distinct advantages for usage in ad-hoc wireless networks also. In (Host-Madsen, 2004) the author derives the upper and lower bounds for the information-theoretic capacity of four-node *ad hoc* networks with two transmitters and two receivers. In the considered deployment both the cooperation among the transmitters as well as among the receivers is possible. However the existence of multiple signal sources introduces interference into the system which should be taken into account

in the analysis. The system model of the scheme studied is depicted in Figure 9, where T1 and T2 indicate the transmitters and R1 and R2 the receivers. Through an extensive study that covers both system sides it is shown however that there is no multiplexing gain from either the transmitter or the receiver cooperation but there is an additive gain in the high SNR regime. In particular it is shown that transmitter cooperation provides additional gain when the induced interference is weak but there is no gain at all in the event of strong interference. However even in the case of weak interference transmitter cooperation is essential for acquiring the additional again. At the receiver's side on the other hand, cooperation enhances the system's capacity in the presence of both weak and strong interference.

Capacity outage is of particular importance and a more challenging problem when we have to deal with a system with mobile nodes. Indeed cooperating systems with mobile nodes are more close to what is being implemented in reality and thus of more importance for studying them. The

Figure 9. System model for a four-node ad-hoc cooperative network

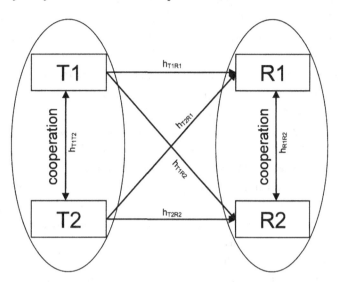

critical aspect that affects performance in such a deployment is the time-varying nature of the channel gains. In (Zlatanov, Hadzi-Velkov, Karagiannidis, and Schober, 2011) this aspect is recognized and studied. In particular the authors focus on deriving closed-form expressions for the average capacity outage rate and for the average capacity outage duration for variable-gain amplify-and-forward, decode-and-forward, and selection decode-and-forward relaying protocols. These performance metrics are more representative for assessing the operational conditions of the system under study given the fact that the channel capacities in neighboring coding blocks are correlated in time. Furthermore, the obtained results can serve as design guidelines for protocol fine-tuning not only in cooperative wireless communication systems. For example, the dimensioning of the retransmission interval of ARQ systems or the scheduling of the slot duration in multiuser systems can be accomplished. Finally the knowledge of the average capacity outage duration can lead to energy savings at the receivers since they may be switched off when decoding is not possible.

It is well known that Adaptive Modulation and Coding (AMC) is one of the most important methods to exploit efficiently the time-varying nature of the wireless channel (Alouini and Goldsmith, 2000). This concept can be exploited in cooperative communications environment also so that the channel conditions are exploited in the best possible way for achieving maximum spectral efficiency. Throughput analysis for direct transmission, multihop and coded cooperation for a three node cooperative network that employs adaptive modulation is performed in (Lin, Erkip and Ghosh, 2005). For each link in the network independent flat Rayleigh fading is assumed that does not change during a packets transmission period. Thus for the direct and multihop transmissions a quasi-static channel is assumed while for the coded cooperation scheme block fading is considered. Furthermore three possible modulations, BPSK, QPSK, and 16-QAM, are employed for the adaptive modulation. Throughput formulas for each scheme are presented and the corresponding numerical results reveal that coded cooperation with adaptive modulation leads to much higher throughput than multihop or direct transmission with adaptive modulation.

Multihop and direct transmission throughputs are almost similar with multihop being better at low to average SNR levels while direct transmission performs better at high SNRs.

The combination of adaptive modulation with or without cooperation is studied in (Strinati, Yang, and Belfiore, 2007). In order to reduce the signaling cost of cooperation the authors propose that a system with one source, one destination and N relays can switch to non-cooperation mode when the quality conditions of the direct link between the source and the destination permit. In this way the signaling overhead required for cooperation is minimized and the system's performance is improved. In particular it is shown that the achieved throughput with the hybrid scheme is higher for both AMC combined cooperative and non cooperative deployments. Furthermore, the cooperation probing delay and the average power consumption are reduced.

COOPERATIVE MULTIPLE ACCESS AND POWER ALLOCATION

In this section we provide MAC protocol designs for cooperative wireless networks that aim in maximizing the throughput of the participating nodes. Furthermore, we examine power allocation aspects which in a multi-user deployment play a very important role on the sum rate that can be achieved by the participating nodes.

Several cooperative MAC protocol designs have been proposed in the literature. In (Liu,

Tao, Narayanan, Korakis and Panwar, 2007) the authors present a MAC scheme that allows low data rate nodes in a WLAN to take help from high rate nodes that are used as relays so as to improve their own data rates. In particular a suitable table is maintained at each low data rate state station that stores essential information that facilitates the selection of a helping node. This information includes the MAC address of the helping station, the transmission rates possible between the source and the helper and between the helper and the destination, number of sequential transmission failures between them and the time when the last packet was heard from the helping node. The table is updated by passively listening to all ongoing transmissions and a helping node is inserted and kept in the table if the transmission delay via it is less than the direct transmission delay between the source and the destination. This condition is expressed by the following equation:

$$\frac{1}{R_{sh}} + \frac{1}{R_{hd}} > \frac{1}{R_{sd}}$$

where R_{sh}, R_{hd} and R_{sd} are the achievable rates between the source-helper, helper-destination and source-destination pairs respectively. The proposed approach is backwards compatible with the IEEE 802.11 family of protocols. In particular the RTS/CTS mechanism is extended with the inclusion of the HTS (Helper ready To Send) that is used by the helper station to acknowledge

Figure 10. Connection establishment and data transfer in a cooperative WLAN deployment

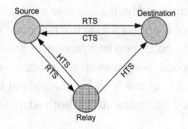
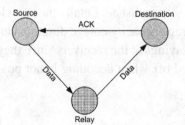

its participation and has the same format as CTS. Such a set-up is presented in Figure 10.

Analytical and simulation results are presented that reveal the achieved throughput improvements from the proposed design. It is known that the size of the MAC Service Data Unit (MSDU) affects the throughput considerably in legacy deployments with the larger size to lead into larger throughput due to the fact that the average packet overhead decreases. This fact is also present in the cooperative WLAN deployment but the throughputs achieved are much larger than those of the legacy systems. In addition, the impact of mobility on the achievable throughput is assessed and the energy expenses of the helper nodes are calculated. It shown, that in a densely deployed environment with multiple cells the presented approach induces almost 35% less interference when compared with legacy 802.11 systems. This is possible since with the employment of helping stations we can reduce the interference caused from the usage of adjacent channels by increasing the distance between the involved APs. Furthermore, power efficiency is achieved since the same amount of traffic is transmitted in less time.

Another very similar approach is presented in (Zhu and Cao, 2006). A relay-enabled distributed coordination function (rDCF) protocol is presented and its performance is assessed. The proposed scheme exploits the multirate capability of 802.11 by helping the participating nodes (source, relay, and destination) to agree on which data rate to use and if it is worth to forward the data via the relay. This is achieved by exploiting the channel conditions of each AP with its neighbours. In particular, the AP collects the channel conditions and if they are favourable it assumes the role of the relay and starts to advertise this capability periodically. Now, when a station wants to transmit, it initiates a handshake procedure in order to decide if the advertised relay will be employed and to agree on which rate to use according to the channel conditions. For the handshake procedure rDCF employs two new packets called relay RTS and relay CTS. Through analysis and simulation it is shown that rDCF achieves better fairness than the Receiver-Based Auto Rate (RBAR) protocol that is considered a better alternative to Auto Rate Fallback (ARF) scheme (Holland, Vaidya and Bahl, 2001; Kamerman and Monteban, 1997).

Another technique called CODE that exploits the existence of multiple relays is presented in (Tan, Wan, Zhu and Andrian, 2007). It is built on top of RBAR but achieves much better performance than RBAR and even than rDCF. One major enhancement compared to rDCF is that CODE cares for bidirectional traffic for which network coding is employed (Katti, Rahul, Hu, Katabi, Medard and Crowcroft, 2008; Fragouli, Le Boudec and Widmer, 2006). However networking coding achieves its full potential for symmetric traffic flows such as those produced by peer-to-peer applications and thus this option should be carefully implemented in a cooperative networking deployment. Simulation results, regarding the impact of mobility and multipath fading on throughput and delay, show that CODE achieves significantly much better performance than RBAR.

In (Grauballe, Jensen, Paramanathan, Fitzek, and Madsen, 2009) the authors provide a cooperative MAC design that results in low access channel delays. A comparative review of the various cooperative MAC designs is provided emphasizing on practical and implementation aspects of their characteristics. In particular the authors are using a suitable testbed to implement a cooperative MAC to be employed for aggregating and forwarding the traffic of a cluster of mobile devices via a suitably elected cluster head node towards a base station. Performance comparisons carried out among plain CSMA/CA, packet aggregation and cooperative MAC reveal that the latter achieves significant packet access delay reduction and a slight increase on the achievable saturated throughput as the number of mobile devices involved in the cluster becomes higher.

Finally if one wants to further fine tune the operation of the MAC protocol in a cooperative networking deployment power allocation should be taken into account so that the most suitable coding and decoding strategies are employed (Kaya and Ulukus, 2007). In particular this approach requires full channel state information at the transmitters and the receiver. The transmitters can then adapt their coding strategy based on the channel state by adjusting their transmit powers (Hanly and Tse, 1998). Furthermore a balance must be achieved between the power used for the transmission of one's own data and the power used for relaying. An optimization problem on the sum rate subject to average transmit power constraints is formulated and solved. It is shown both analytically and via simulations that controlling the transmit powers i.e. deriving optimal power allocation policies, in a cooperative wireless networking environment leads to significant enhancements on the average achievable rates.

FUTURE RESEARCH DIRECTIONS

Cooperative networking has a long way to go as far as the related research aspects are considered and many applications will benefit from the achieved performance enhancements that it offers. In the following we highlight briefly some of the most important future research items in this domain. First of all resource allocation and management will continue to be the focal point of most research initiatives since it affects the involved building blocks of the deployed infrastructures in a horizontal way. Another item, somehow related to the previous one, is energy allocation in particular among the participating relays. This aspect lies within the more general framework of green communications which is now an inseparable feature of almost all major communication research projects. On the other hand, as we move towards practical implementations of cooperative networks, protocol design

aspects e.g. related to routing, need to be studied more intensively. Finally coding techniques will continue to be in the mainstream of research efforts due to the significant throughput enhancements that they offer which however need to be carefully considered due to their significant computational requirements.

CONCLUSION

In this chapter, the main aspects and recent advances on cooperative networking are reviewed and discussed. Comparative studies are provided where possible that can serve as design guidelines in the deployment of cooperative networks since they are now moving towards their implementation phase. The most important diversity combining methods are presented and their performance is assessed for various fading channel models with or without considering co-channel interference. Then we study the main protocols being employed for the efficient forwarding of data in cooperative networking deployments. Insights on the achievable BER and outage probability are provided and the impact of relay selection on these metrics is also highlighted. The principles of space-time coding as applied in cooperative communications are presented and performance aspects are discussed. Subsequently the impact of cooperation on the achievable capacity is studied and we report the latest results on the subject for various deployments. Finally, issues related to MAC protocol design in cooperative networks are treated together with applications to legacy systems. These practical examples illustrate that the concept of cooperative communications, if carefully adopted, is an effective way to enhance the performance of wireless networks. We conclude by highlighting the research items that are envisaged to play a crucial role in the domain of cooperative networking in the near future.

REFERENCES

Abu-Dayya, A. A., & Beaulieu, N. C. (1992). Outage probabilities of diversity cellular systems with cochannel interference in Nakagami fading. *IEEE Transactions on Vehicular Technology*, *41*(4), 343–355. doi:10.1109/25.182583.

Alamouti, S. M. (1998). A simple transmit diversity technique for wireless communications. *IEEE Journal on Selected Areas in Communications*, *16*(8), 1451–1458. doi:10.1109/49.730453.

Alouini, M.-S., & Goldsmith, A. J. (2000). Adaptive modulation over Nakagami fading channels. *Wireless Personal Communications*, *13*, 119–143. doi:10.1023/A:1008979107539.

Anghel, P. A., & Kaveh, M. (2004). Exact symbol error probability of a cooperative network in a Rayleigh-fading environment. *IEEE Transactions on Wireless Communications*, *3*(5), 1416–1421. doi:10.1109/TWC.2004.833431.

Bao, X., & Li, J. (2007). Efficient message relaying for wireless user cooperation: Decode-amplify-forward (DAF) and hybrid DAF and coded-cooperation. *IEEE Transactions on Wireless Communications*, *6*(11), 3975–3984. doi:10.1109/TWC.2007.06117.

Bin Sediq, A., & Yanikomeroglu, H. (2009). Performance analysis of soft-bit maximal ratio combining in cooperative relay networks. *IEEE Transactions on Wireless Communications*, *8*(10), 4934–4939. doi:10.1109/TWC.2009.081187.

Bletsas, A., Khisti, A., Reed, D. P., & Lippman, A. (2006). A simple cooperative diversity method based on network path selection. *IEEE Journal on Selected Areas in Communications*, *24*(3), 659–672. doi:10.1109/JSAC.2005.862417.

Boyer, J., Falconer, D. D., & Yanikomeroglu, H. (2004). Multihop diversity in wireless relaying channels. *IEEE Transactions on Communications*, *52*(10), 1820–1830. doi:10.1109/TCOMM.2004.836447.

Burkard, R. E., & Rendl, F. (1991). Lexicographic bottleneck problems. *Operations Research Letters*, *10*(5), 303–308. doi:10.1016/0167-6377(91)90018-K.

Chen, D., & Laneman, J. N. (2006). Modulation and demodulation for cooperative diversity in wireless systems. *IEEE Transactions on Wireless Communications*, *5*(7), 1785–1794. doi:10.1109/TWC.2006.1673090.

Chen, Y. X., & Tellambura, C. (2005). Performance analysis of three-branch selection combining over arbitrarily correlated Rayleigh fading channels. *IEEE Transactions on Wireless Communications*, *4*(3), 861–865. doi:10.1109/TWC.2005.847109.

Chiani, M., Win, M. Z., Zanella, A., Mallik, R. K., & Winters, J. H. (2003). Bounds and approximations for optimum combining of signals in the presence of multiple cochannel interferers and thermal noise. *IEEE Transactions on Communications*, *51*(2), 296–307. doi:10.1109/TCOMM.2003.809265.

Choi, W., Hong, J.-P., Kim, D. I., & Kim, B.-H. (2009). An error detection aided GSC/MRC switching scheme in AF based cooperative communications. In *Proceedings of the IEEE 69th Vehicular Technology Conference (VTC Spring 2009)*, (pp. 1-5). IEEE.

Chu, S.-I. (2012). Performance of amplify-and-forward cooperative diversity networks with generalized selection combining over Nakagami-m fading channels. *IEEE Communications Letters*, *16*(5), 634–637. doi:10.1109/LCOMM.2012.031212.112443.

Cover, T. M., & Gamal, A. A. E. (1979). Capacity theorems for the relay channel. *IEEE Transactions on Information Theory*, *25*(5), 572–584. doi:10.1109/TIT.1979.1056084.

da Costa, D. B., & Aissa, S. (2009). Performance of cooperative diversity networks: Analysis of amplify-and-forward relaying under equal-gain and maximal-ratio combining. In *Proceedings of the IEEE International Conference on Communications, (ICC 2009)*, (pp. 1-5). Dresden, Germany: IEEE.

Fragouli, C., Le Boudec, J. Y., & Widmer, J. (2006). Network coding: An instant primer. *ACM Computer Communication Review*, *36*(1), 63–68. doi:10.1145/1111322.1111337.

Grauballe, A., Jensen, M. G., Paramanathan, A., Fitzek, F. H. P., & Madsen, T. K. (2009). Implementation and performance analysis of cooperative medium access control protocol for CSMA/CA based technologies. In *Proceedings of the European Wireless Conference (EW 2009)*, (pp. 107-112). EW.

Guo, X., & Xia, X.-G. (2008). A distributed space-time coding in asynchronous wireless relay networks. *IEEE Transactions on Wireless Communications*, *7*(5), 1812–1816. doi:10.1109/TWC.2008.070042.

Hanly, S., & Tse, D. N. C. (1998). Multiaccess fading channels–Part I: Polymatroid structure, optimal resource allocation and throughput capacities. *IEEE Transactions on Information Theory*, *44*(7), 2796–2815. doi:10.1109/18.737513.

Holland, G., Vaidya, N., & Bahl, P. (2001). A rate-adaptive MAC protocol for multihop wireless networks. In *Proceedings of the ACM Mobicom Conference*, (pp. 236-251). Rome, Italy: ACM Press.

Host-Madsen, A. (2004). Capacity bounds for cooperative diversity. *IEEE Transactions on Information Theory*, *52*(4), 1522–1544. doi:10.1109/TIT.2006.871576.

Hunter, T. E., & Nosratinia, A. (2006). Diversity through coded cooperation. *IEEE Transactions on Wireless Communications*, *5*(2), 283–289. doi:10.1109/TWC.2006.1611050.

Ikki, S., & Ahmed, M. H. (2007). Performance analysis of cooperative diversity using equal gain combining (EGC) technique over Rayleigh fading channels. In *Proceedings of the IEEE International Conference on Communications (ICC 2007)*, (pp. 5336-5341). Glasgow, UK: IEEE.

Ikki, S. S., & Ahmed, M. H. (2009a). Performance analysis of generalized selection combining for amplify-and-forward cooperative-diversity networks. In *Proceedings of the IEEE International Conference on Communications (ICC '09)*, (pp. 1-6). Dresden, Germany: IEEE.

Ikki, S. S., & Ahmed, M. H. (2009b). Performance of cooperative diversity using equal gain combining (EGC) over Nakagami-m fading channels. *IEEE Transactions on Wireless Communications*, *8*(2), 557–562. doi:10.1109/TWC.2009.070966.

Issariyakul, T., & Krishnamurthy, V. (2009). Amplify-and-forward cooperative diversity wireless networks: Model, analysis, and monotonicity properties. *IEEE/ACM Transactions on Networking*, *17*(1), 225–238. doi:10.1109/TNET.2008.925090.

Ju, M., & Kim, I.-M. (2009). ML performance analysis of the decode-and-forward protocol in cooperative diversity networks. *IEEE Transactions on Wireless Communications*, *8*(7), 3855–3867. doi:10.1109/TWC.2009.081470.

Kamerman, A., & Monteban, L. (1997). WLAN-II: A high-performance wireless LAN for the unlicensed band. *Bell Labs Technical Journal*, *2*(3), 118–133. doi:10.1002/bltj.2069.

Karagiannidis, G. K. (2003). Performance analysis of SIR-based dual selection diversity over correlated Nakagami-m fading channels. *IEEE Transactions on Vehicular Technology*, *52*(5), 1207–1216. doi:10.1109/TVT.2003.816612.

Karagiannidis, G. K., Zogas, D. A., & Kotsopoulos, S. A. (2003). Performance analysis of triple selection diversity over exponentially correlated Nakagami-m fading channels. *IEEE Transactions on Communications*, *51*(8), 1245–1248. doi:10.1109/TCOMM.2003.815070.

Katti, S., Rahul, H., Hu, W., Katabi, D., Medard, M., & Crowcroft, J. (2008). XORs in the air: Practical wireless network coding. *IEEE/ACM Transactions on Networking*, *16*(3), 497–510. doi:10.1109/TNET.2008.923722.

Kaya, O., & Ulukus, S. (2007). Power control for fading cooperative multiple access channels. *IEEE Transactions on Wireless Communications*, *6*(8), 2915–2923. doi:10.1109/TWC.2007.05858.

Kramer, G., Gastpar, M., & Gupta, P. (2005). Cooperative strategies and capacity theorems for relay networks. *IEEE Transactions on Information Theory*, *51*(9), 3037–3063. doi:10.1109/TIT.2005.853304.

Laneman, J. N., Tse, D. N. C., & Wornell, G. W. (2004). Cooperative diversity in wireless networks: Efficient protocols and outage behavior. *IEEE Transactions on Information Theory*, *50*(12), 3062–3080. doi:10.1109/TIT.2004.838089.

Laneman, J. N., & Wornell, G. W. (2003). Distributed space-time-coded protocols for exploiting cooperative diversity in wireless networks. *IEEE Transactions on Information Theory*, *49*(10), 2415–2425. doi:10.1109/TIT.2003.817829.

Laneman, J. N., Wornell, G. W., & Tse, D. N. C. (2001). An efficient protocol for realizing cooperative diversity in wireless networks. In *Proceedings of the IEEE International Symposium on Information Theory (ISIT 2001)*, (p. 294). Washington, DC: IEEE.

Lei, X., Fuja, T., Kliewer, J., & Costello, D. (2007). A network coding approach to cooperative diversity. *IEEE Transactions on Information Theory*, *53*(10), 3714–3722. doi:10.1109/TIT.2007.904990.

Lin, Z., Erkip, E., & Ghosh, M. (2005). Adaptive modulation for coded cooperative systems. In *Proceedings of the International Workshop on Signal Processing Advances for Wireless Communications (SPAWC 2005)*. New York: SPAWC.

Liu, P., Tao, Z., Narayanan, S., Korakis, T., & Panwar, S. S. (2007). CoopMAC: A cooperative MAC for wireless LANs. *IEEE Journal on Selected Areas in Communications*, *25*(2), 340–354. doi:10.1109/JSAC.2007.070210.

Michalopoulos, D. S., & Karagiannidis, G. K. (2008). PHY-layer fairness in amplify and forward cooperative diversity systems. *IEEE Transactions on Wireless Communications*, *7*(3), 1073–1082. doi:10.1109/TWC.2008.060825.

Pham, T. T., Nguyen, H. H., & Tuan, H. D. (2012). Relay assignment for max-min capacity in cooperative wireless networks. *IEEE Transactions on Vehicular Technology*, *61*(5), 2387–2394. doi:10.1109/TVT.2012.2192508.

Sato, H. (1976). *Information transmission through a channel with relay*. Tech Report B76-7. Honolulu, HI: University of Hawaii.

Scutari, G., & Barbarossa, S. (2005). Distributed space-time coding for regenerative relay networks. *IEEE Transactions on Wireless Communications*, *4*(5), 2387–2399. doi:10.1109/TWC.2005.853883.

Sendonaris, A., Erkip, E., & Aazhang, B. (1998). Increasing uplink capacity via user cooperation diversity. In *Proceedings 1998 IEEE International Symposium on Information Theory*. IEEE.

Sendonaris, A., Erkip, E., & Aazhang, B. (2003). User cooperation diversity: Part II: Implementation aspects and performance analysis. *IEEE Transactions on Communications*, *51*(11), 1939–1948. doi:10.1109/TCOMM.2003.819238.

Shah, A., & Haimovich, A. M. (2000). Performance analysis of maximal ratio combining and comparison with optimum combining for mobile radio communications with cochannel interference. *IEEE Transactions on Vehicular Technology*, *49*(4), 1454–1463. doi:10.1109/25.875282.

Shin, H., & Song, J. B. (2008). MRC analysis of cooperative diversity with fixed-gain relays in Nakagami-m fading channels. *IEEE Transactions on Wireless Communications*, *7*(6), 2069–2074. doi:10.1109/TWC.2008.070812.

Simoens, S., Muñoz Medina, O., Vidal, J., & del Coso, A. (2010). Compress-and-forward cooperative MIMO relaying with full channel state information. *IEEE Transactions on Signal Processing*, *58*(2), 781–791. doi:10.1109/TSP.2009.2030622.

Simon, M. K., & Alouini, M.-S. (1999). A unified performance analysis of digital communication with dual selective combining diversity over correlated Rayleigh and Nakagami-m fading channels. *IEEE Transactions on Communications*, *47*(1), 33–44. doi:10.1109/26.747811.

Simon, M. K., & Alouini, M.-S. (2005). *Digital communications over fading channels* (2nd ed.). New York: Wiley-IEEE Press.

Skordoulis, D., Ni, Q., Chen, H.-H., Stephens, A. P., Liu, C., & Jamalipour, A. (2008). IEEE 802.11n MAC frame aggregation mechanisms for next-generation high-throughput WLANs. *IEEE Transactions on Wireless Communications*, *15*(1), 40–47. doi:10.1109/MWC.2008.4454703.

Strinati, E., Yang, S., & Belfiore, J.-C. (2007). Adaptive modulation and coding for hybrid cooperative networks. In *Proceedings of the IEEE International Conference on Communications (ICC '07)*, (pp. 4191–4195). Glasgow, UK: IEEE.

Tairan, W., Cano, A., & Giannakis, G. B. (2005). Efficient demodulation in cooperative schemes using decode-and-forward relays. In *Proceedings of the Conference Record of the Thirty-Ninth Asilomar Conference on Signals, Systems and Computers*, (pp. 1051- 1055). Asilomar.

Tairan, W., Giannakis, G. B., & Renqiu, W. (2008). Smart regenerative relays for link-adaptive cooperative communications. *IEEE Transactions on Communications*, *56*(11), 1950–1960. doi:10.1109/TCOMM.2008.060688.

Tan, K., Wan, Z., Zhu, H., & Andrian, J. (2007). CODE: Cooperative medium access for multirate wireless ad hoc network. In *Proceedings of the 4th Annual IEEE Communications Society Conference on Sensor, Mesh and Ad Hoc Communications and Networks (SECON '07)*, (pp. 1-10). IEEE.

Tarokh, V., Seshadri, N., & Calderbank, A. R. (1998). Space-time codes for high data rate wireless communication: Performance criterion and code construction. *IEEE Transactions on Information Theory*, *44*(2), 744–764. doi:10.1109/18.661517.

Telatar, E. (1999). Capacity of multi-antenna Gaussian channels. *European Transactions on Telecommunications*, *10*(6), 585–595. doi:10.1002/ett.4460100604.

Tellambura, C., Annamalai, A., & Bhargava, V. K. (2003). Closed-form and infinite series solutions for the MGF of a dual-diversity selection combiner output in bivariate Nakagami fading. *IEEE Transactions on Communications*, *51*(4), 539–542. doi:10.1109/TCOMM.2003.810870.

Van Der Meulen, E. C. (1971). Three-terminal communication channels. *Advances in Applied Probability*, *3*, 120–154. doi:10.2307/1426331.

Wan-Jen, H., Hong, Y.-W. P., & Kuo, C.-C. J. (2008). Lifetime maximization for amplify-and-forward cooperative networks. *IEEE Transactions on Wireless Communications*, *7*(5), 1800–1805. doi:10.1109/TWC.2008.061075.

Wang, H.-M., Yin, Q., & Xia, X.-G. (2010). Fast Kalman equalization for time-frequency asynchronous cooperative relay networks with distributed space-time codes. *IEEE Transactions on Vehicular Technology*, *59*(9), 4651–4658. doi:10.1109/TVT.2010.2076352.

Winters, J. H. (1984). Optimum combining in digital mobile radio with cochannel interference. *IEEE Journal on Selected Areas in Communications*, *2*(4), 528–539. doi:10.1109/JSAC.1984.1146095.

Winters, J. H., & Salz, J. (1998). Upper bounds on the bit-error rate of optimum combining in wireless systems. *IEEE Transactions on Communications*, *46*(12), 1619–1624. doi:10.1109/26.737400.

Wyner, A. D., & Ziv, J. (1976). The rate-distortion function for source coding with side information at the receiver. *IEEE Transactions on Information Theory*, *22*(1), 1–11. doi:10.1109/TIT.1976.1055508.

Yang, H.-C., & Alouini, M.-S. (2003). Performance analysis of multibranch switched diversity systems. *IEEE Transactions on Communications*, *51*(5), 782–794. doi:10.1109/TCOMM.2003.811408.

Yi, S., Blostein, S. D., & Julian, C. (2003). Exact outage probability for equal gain combining with cochannel interference in Rayleigh fading. *IEEE Transactions on Wireless Communications*, *2*(5), 865–870. doi:10.1109/TWC.2003.816796.

Yi, Z., & Kim, I.-M. (2008). Diversity order analysis of the decode-and-forward cooperative networks with relay selection. *IEEE Transactions on Wireless Communications*, *7*(5), 1792–1799. doi:10.1109/TWC.2008.061041.

Yindi, J., & Hassibi, B. (2006). Distributed space-time coding in wireless relay networks. *IEEE Transactions on Wireless Communications*, *5*(12), 3524–3536. doi:10.1109/TWC.2006.256975.

Young-Chai, K., Alouini, M.-S., & Simon, M. K. (2000). Analysis and optimization of switched diversity systems. *IEEE Transactions on Vehicular Technology*, *49*(5), 1813–1831. doi:10.1109/25.892586.

Zhang, Q. T., & Lu, H. G. (2002). A general analytical approach to multi-branch selection combining over various spatially correlated fading channels. *IEEE Transactions on Communications*, *50*(7), 1066–1073. doi:10.1109/TCOMM.2002.800804.

Zhang, Z. (1988). Partial converse for a relay channel. *IEEE Transactions on Information Theory*, *34*(5), 1106–1110. doi:10.1109/18.21243.

Zhao, Y., Adve, R., & Lim, T. J. (2007). Improving amplify-and-forward relay networks: Optimal power allocation versus selection. *IEEE Transactions on Wireless Communications*, *6*(8), 3114–3123.

Zhu, H., & Cao, G. (2006). rDCF: A relay-enabled medium access control protocol for wireless ad hoc networks. *IEEE Transactions on Mobile Computing*, *5*(9), 1201–1214. doi:10.1109/TMC.2006.137.

Zimmermann, E., Herhold, P., & Fettweis, G. (2003). On the performance of cooperative diversity protocols in practical wireless systems. In *Proceedings of the IEEE 58th Vehicular Technology Conference (VTC 2003-Fall)*, (pp. 2212-2216). Orlando, FL: IEEE.

Zlatanov, N., Hadzi-Velkov, Z., Karagiannidis, G. K., & Schober, R. (2011). Cooperative diversity with mobile nodes: Capacity outage rate and duration. *IEEE Transactions on Information Theory*, *57*(10), 6555–6568. doi:10.1109/TIT.2011.2165794.

Zogas, D. A., Karagiannidis, G. K., & Kotso-poulos, S. A. (2005). Equal gain combining over Nakagami-*n* (Rice) and Nakagami-*q* (Hoyt) generalzied fading channels. *IEEE Transactions on Wireless Communications*, *4*(2), 374–379. doi:10.1109/TWC.2004.842953.

ADDITIONAL READING

Akay, E., & Ayanoglu, E. (2006). Achieving full frequency and space diversity in wireless systems via BICM, OFDM, STBC, and viterbi decoding. *IEEE Transactions on Communications*, *54*(12), 2164–2172. doi:10.1109/TCOMM.2006.885089.

Bai, Z., Yuan, D., & Kwak, K. (2008). Performance evaluation of STBC based cooperative systems over slow Rayleigh fading channel. *Computer Communications*, *31*(17), 4206–4211. doi:10.1016/j.comcom.2008.09.010.

Baidas, M. W., & MacKenzie, A. B. (2012). An auction mechanism for power allocation in multi-source multi-relay cooperative wireless networks. *IEEE Transactions on Wireless Communications*, *11*(9), 3250–3260. doi:10.1109/TWC.2012.071612.111722.

Campolo, C., Iera, A., Militano, L., & Molinaro, A. (2012). Scenario-adaptive and gain-aware content sharing policies for cooperative wireless environments. *Computer Communications*, *35*(10), 1259–1271. doi:10.1016/j.comcom.2012.03.017.

Chen, D., Ji, H., & Leung, V. C. M. (2012). Distributed best-relay selection for improving TCP performance over cognitive radio networks: A cross-layer design approach. *IEEE Journal on Selected Areas in Communications*, *30*(2), 315–322. doi:10.1109/JSAC.2012.120210.

Chen, Y., & Fang, X. (2012). Energy-efficient dynamic resource allocation with opportunistic network coding in OFDMA relay networks. *Computer Networks*, *56*(15), 3446–3455. doi:10.1016/j.comnet.2012.07.002.

D'Arienzo, M., Oliviero, F., & Romano, S. P. (2012). Can cooperation improve energy efficiency in ad hoc wireless networks? *Computer Communications*, *35*(14), 1707–1714. doi:10.1016/j.comcom.2012.05.004.

Ding, Z., & Leung, K. K. (2011). On the combination of cooperative diversity and network coding for wireless uplink transmissions. *IEEE Transactions on Vehicular Technology*, *60*(4), 1590–1601. doi:10.1109/TVT.2011.2112787.

Herhold, P., Zimmermann, E., & Fettweis, G. (2005). Cooperative multi-hop transmission in wireless networks. *Computer Networks*, *49*(3), 299–324. doi:10.1016/j.comnet.2005.05.009.

Kadloor, S., & Adve, R. (2010). Relay selection and power allocation in cooperative cellular networks. *IEEE Transactions on Wireless Communications*, *9*(5), 1676–1685. doi:10.1109/TWC.2010.05.090307.

Kim, S.-Y., & Lee, J.-W. (2012). To cooperate or not to cooperate: System throughput and fairness perspective. *IEEE Journal on Selected Areas in Communications*, *30*(9), 1649–1657. doi:10.1109/JSAC.2012.121008.

Lee, J., Mo, J., Trung, T. M., Walrand, J., & So, H.-S. W. (2010). Design and analysis of a cooperative multichannel MAC protocol for heterogeneous networks. *IEEE Transactions on Vehicular Technology*, *59*(7), 3536–3548. doi:10.1109/TVT.2010.2051691.

Li, Y., Zhang, W., & Xia, X.-G. (2009). Distributive high-rate space–frequency codes achieving full cooperative and multipath diversities for asynchronous cooperative communications. *IEEE Transactions on Vehicular Technology*, *58*(1), 207–217. doi:10.1109/TVT.2008.923678.

Li, Z., Xia, X.-G., & Li, B. (2009). Achieving full diversity and fast ML decoding via simple analog network coding for asynchronous two-way relay networks. *IEEE Transactions on Communications*, *57*(12), 3672–3681. doi:10.1109/TCOMM.2009.12.090005.

Liu, J., Shroff, N. B., & Sherali, H. D. (2012). Optimal power allocation in multi-relay MIMO cooperative networks: Theory and algorithms. *IEEE Journal on Selected Areas in Communications*, *30*(2), 331–340. doi:10.1109/JSAC.2012.120212.

Luo, T., Motani, M., & Srinivasan, V. (2009). Cooperative asynchronous multichannel MAC: Design, analysis, and implementation. *IEEE Transactions on Mobile Computing*, *8*(3), 338–352. doi:10.1109/TMC.2008.109.

Peng, M., Yang, C., Zhao, Z., Wang, W., & Chen, H.-H. (2012). Cooperative network coding in relay-based IMT-advanced systems. *IEEE Communications Magazine*, *50*(4), 76–84. doi:10.1109/MCOM.2012.6178837.

ShahbazPanahi, S., & Dong, M. (2012). Achievable rate region under joint distributed beamforming and power allocation for two-way relay networks. *IEEE Transactions on Wireless Communications*, *11*(11), 4026–4037. doi:10.1109/TWC.2012.092112.112072.

Shiguo, W., & Hong, J. (2012). Distributed power allocation scheme for multi-relay shared-bandwidth (MRSB) wireless cooperative communication. *IEEE Communications Letters*, *16*(8), 1263–1265. doi:10.1109/LCOMM.2012.060812.121088.

Singh, S. R., & Motani, M. (2012). Cooperative multi-channel access for 802.11 mesh networks. *IEEE Journal on Selected Areas in Communications*, *30*(9), 1684–1693. doi:10.1109/JSAC.2012.121012.

Sun, L., Zhang, T., Lu, L., & Niu, H. (2010). On the combination of cooperative diversity and multiuser diversity in multi-source multi-relay wireless networks. *IEEE Signal Processing Letters*, *17*(6), 535–538. doi:10.1109/LSP.2010.2046350.

Yu, Y., Hu, R. Q., Bontu, C. S., & Cai, Z. (2011). Mobile association and load balancing in a cooperative relay cellular network. *IEEE Communications Magazine*, *49*(5), 83–89. doi:10.1109/MCOM.2011.5762802.

Zhang, G., Yang, K., & Chen, H.-H. (2012). Resource allocation for wireless cooperative networks: A unified cooperative bargaining game theoretic framework. *IEEE Wireless Communications*, *19*(2), 38–43. doi:10.1109/MWC.2012.6189411.

Zhang, S., Xia, X.-G., & Wang, J. (2012). Cooperative performance and diversity gain of wireless relay networks. *IEEE Journal on Selected Areas in Communications*, *30*(9), 1623–1632. doi:10.1109/JSAC.2012.121005.

Zou, Y., Zhu, J., Zheng, B., & Yao, Y.-D. (2010). An adaptive cooperation diversity scheme with best-relay selection in cognitive radio networks. *IEEE Transactions on Signal Processing*, *58*(10), 5438–5445. doi:10.1109/TSP.2010.2053708.

Chapter 2
Data Dissemination and Channel Selection in Cognitive Radio Networks

Mubashir Husain Rehmani
Université Paris Est, France & COMSATS Institute of Information Technology, Pakistan

Yasir Faheem
Université Paris Nord, France & COMSATS Institute of Information Technology, Pakistan

ABSTRACT

In this chapter, the authors provide a comprehensive review of broadcasting and channel selection strategies for wireless cognitive radio networks. In the beginning, some applications of the data dissemination in wireless cognitive radio networks are discussed to highlight their importance and utility. Next, the authors provide a detailed classification of broadcasting protocols in light of the existing literature, and the pros and cons of each classified category are discussed. Afterwards, the data dissemination is briefly discussed in the context of multi-channel environments and the related issues are highlighted. Then, the authors discuss the challenges of data dissemination in cognitive radio networks, followed by the classification of channel selection strategies along with their advantages and disadvantages for various classes of applications. In the last part, the authors conclude this chapter with open research issues that need to be addressed to provide efficient channel selection and data dissemination strategies in cognitive radio networks.

INTRODUCTION

Data dissemination is a classical and a fundamental function in any kind of network. Data Dissemination corresponds to the spreading of information through broadcasting. Its main objective is to reach the maximum number of neighbors with every sent packet i.e., no explicit routing is used and no end-to-end path is maintained. Data Dissemination has been studied in different wireless networks such as Wireless Sensor Networks (WSNs), Vehicular Ad-Hoc Networks (VANETs), Wireless Mesh Networks (WMNs), and Mobile Ad-Hoc Networks (MANETs).

DOI: 10.4018/978-1-4666-4189-1.ch002

Copyright © 2013, IGI Global. Copying or distributing in print or electronic forms without written permission of IGI Global is prohibited.

In wireless networks, the characteristics and problems intrinsic to the wireless links bring several challenges in data dissemination (broadcasting) in the shape of message losses, collisions, and broadcast storm problem, just to name a few. If broadcasting is done blindly through flooding, serious redundancy, contention, and collision could exist (Ni, 1999). First, many broadcasts are considered to be redundant as geographical location may be covered by the transmission ranges of only a small subset of hosts because the radio propagation is omni-directional. Second, after a node broadcasts a message, if many of its neighbors decide to rebroadcast, these transmissions may severely contend with each other. Third, the timing of rebroadcast of the neighboring nodes may cause collisions. All these three problems associated with flooding collectively referred to as broadcast storm problem. One method to reduce the broadcast storm problem is to inhibit some wireless nodes from rebroadcasting which results in less contention and collision. It has been proved that if a simple counter-based scheme is used instead of simple flooding, it can eliminate many redundant rebroadcasts (Ni, 1999). One such method is probabilistic broadcasting, where wireless nodes rebroadcast with certain probability.

In cognitive radio networks, broadcasting is expected to be done more frequently due to the higher spatio-temporal availability of channels. The situation is more complex than multi-channel wireless networks, where the availability of multiple channels is static. Static means the number of channel do not change. On the contrary, channels are dynamic in cognitive radio networks due to the primary radio activity. Therefore, the broadcast storm problem is also present in cognitive radio networks. In cognitive radio networks, an important step in having efficient data dissemination is to know how to select best channels. In fact, channel selection plays a vital role in robust data dissemination.

The goal of this chapter is to provide a comprehensive review of broadcasting and channel selection strategies, for both wireless and cogni-tive radio networks. The methodology we adopt in this chapter is to first discuss background in which we discuss some applications of data dissemination in wireless networks. We then provide the classification of broadcasting protocols. Data dissemination in multi-channel environments is then discussed. Challenges of data dissemination in cognitive radio networks are discussed, followed by the classification of channel selection strategies. We discuss SURF channel selection study as a case study. We then discuss future research directions. Finally, we conclude this chapter.

BACKGROUND

In vehicular ad-hoc networks, an interesting application is to disseminate emergency messages to the specific area while guaranteeing all relevant vehicles receive the emergency message, such that people can change their routes to destination in time. In this way, people can avoid getting into a traffic jam. In this context, an analysis of emergency message dissemination in vehicular networks is done in (Rostamzadeh, 2011). In (Lee, 2010), a fast and reliable emergency message dissemination mechanism was proposed to disseminate emergency message in VANETs. In addition, the authors discussed how to solve the broadcast storm problem, achieving low dissemination delay, and providing a high reliability in freeway scenario.

Data dissemination in wireless sensor networks has been widely studied in the literature. In WSNs, data dissemination is generally performed from sensor nodes to a static sink. This data could be an emergency message such as a fire alarm, and it must be transmitted rapidly and reliably towards the sink. Note that in emergency situations the sink could be mobile, e.g., a fire fighter roaming in the area or an Unattended Aerial Vehicle (UAV). For instance, the authors in (Erman, 2010) proposed data dissemination protocol for emergency message transmission in mobile multi-sink WSNs. In (Vecchio, 2010), the authors proposed density-based proactive data dissemination protocol, Deep, for wireless sensor networks with uncontrolled sink mobility. Similarly, a proactive data dissemination approach, called Supple, for data gathering in self-organized Wireless Sensor Networks is proposed in (Viana, 2010). Supple effectively distributes and stores monitored data in WSNs such that it can be later sent to or retrieved by a sink.

Epidemic dissemination has huge potential, enabling, for instance, a wide range of mobile ad-hoc communication and social networking applications, supported entirely through opportunistic contacts in the physical world. For instance, the authors in (Zyba, 2011) improved the understanding of data dissemination in opportunistic mobile ad hoc networks. In fact, their work is a first step in studying the impact of social behaviour of users on information dissemination. Another application where epidemic dissemination could be used is WSNs. Directed diffusion (Intanagonwiwat, 2003) is one such example, where interest propagation is done through flooding. At the following, we discuss the classification of broadcasting protocols.

CLASSIFICATION OF BROADCASTING PROTCOLS

Broadcasting protocols in wireless networks can be classified into two major categories: (1) stateful broadcasting protocols, and (2) stateless

broadcasting protocols. Stateful broadcasting algorithms require the nodes the knowledge of network topology in their local neighborhood and this is commonly achieved by proactive exchange of hello messages between neighbors. On the opposite, stateless broadcasting protocols do not require any knowledge of the neighborhood. Stateless broadcasting protocols were shown to perform well in specific scenarios but very poorly in others, e.g. for varying node density and traffic loads. A very detailed discussion on the taxonomy of broadcasting protocols for wireless mobile ad-hoc networks can be found in (Heissenbuttel, 2006). Figure 1 shows the classification of broadcasting protocols, as briefly described in the following:

- **Stateful Broadcasting Protocols:** Stateful broadcasting protocols can be classified according to the way the neighbor is designated.
  - **Neighbor Designated:** In neighbor designated broadcasting protocols (Liang, 2006), a node that transmits a packet specifies which one of its one-hop neighbors should broadcast the packet.
  - **Self Pruning:** In self pruning broadcasting protocols (Ya-Feng, 2004), a node receiving a packet will decide itself whether or not to transmit the packet.

Figure 1. Broadcasting protocols and their classification

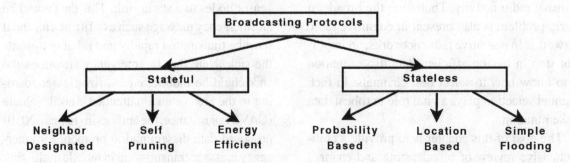

- ◦ **Energy Efficient:** Energy efficient broadcasting protocols (Wieselthier, 2000) are those protocols that consider the energy consumption during broadcasting.
- **Stateless Broadcasting Protocols:** Stateless broadcasting protocols can be classified as follows:
  - ◦ **Probability Based:** In probability-based broadcasting protocols (Ni, 1999), (Tseng, 2001), (Haas, 2002), each node broadcasts with a certain probability p and drops the packet with a probability of 1 − p.
  - ◦ **Simple Flooding:** Simple flooding is the broadcasting scheme in which each node broadcast a packet with probability 1.
  - ◦ **Location Based:** Location-based broadcasting protocols (Ni, 1999) are those protocols in which a node rebroadcasts a packet on the distance between itself and the node from which that packet is received.

Note that all the aforementioned broadcasting schemes cannot be directly applied to cognitive radio networks. Primarily, due to the challenges specific to cognitive radio networks, as classified in section IV.

DATA DISSEMINATION IN MULTI-CHANNEL ENVIRONMENT

In this section, our goal is to briefly discuss some data dissemination protocols for multi-channel environment.

In (Simon, 2005), the authors proposed two protocols, McSynch and McTorrent, for data dissemination in multi-channel wireless sensor networks. McTorrent achieves end-to-end data dissemination in less time than the single channel protocols, while McSynch can substantially reduce the time required for a cluster-wide synchronization. In (Starobinski, 2010), the authors analyzed the performance limits of data dissemination with multi-channel, single radio sensors under random packet loss. The authors showed that, for an arbitrary topology, the problem of minimizing the expected delay of data dissemination can be treated as a stochastic shortest path problem. Broadcasting on multiple access channels by deterministic distributed protocols are studied by authors in (Anantharamu, 2010). The authors compared the packet latency of deterministic protocols and backoff-type randomized protocols.

Broadcasting protocols for multi-channel wireless networks in the presence of adversary attacks are proposed in (Asterjadhi, 2011). The authors used network coding for data dissemination in order to reduce the impact of suck adversary attacks on dissemination performance and derived the optimum number of channels that nodes have to access in order to minimize the reception delay. A power saving data dissemination architecture for mobile clients' units in multi-channel environment is proposed in (Al-Mogren, 2008). The authors proposed a concurrency control technique suitable for the multi-channel dissemination-based architectural model. A data scheduling algorithm over multiple channels in mobile computing environment is proposed in (Feng, 2010). The authors formulated the average expected delay of multiple channels considering data items' access frequencies, variable length, and different bandwidth of each channel.

In cognitive radio networks, very less work has been done on data dissemination. For instance, in (Sun, 2011), the authors investigated the distribution and limits of information dissemination latency and speed in cognitive radio networks. In fact, data dissemination in CRNs has not been discussed widely. For this reason, we first highlight the challenges of data dissemination in cognitive radio networks.

CHALLENGES OF DATA DISSEMINATION IN COGNITIVE RADIO NETWORKS

Robust data dissemination is a challenge in cognitive radio networks due to its intrinsic properties such as:

- **Availability of Multiple-Channels:** CR nodes have more than one channel in the available channel set. Compared to traditional wireless networks, where a single channel is used for communication such as WiFi, cognitive radio networks can communicate over multiple channels. Available channel set is the set of channels eligible by CR nodes for any communication.
- **Diversity in the Number of Available Channels:** CR nodes have diverse set of available channels in the available channel set. Diversity means that CR nodes in the network can access different channels.
- **Primary Radio Activity:** Channels are occupied by the PR nodes and are only available to CR nodes for transmission when they are idle. In fact, the spatiotemporal utilization of spectrum by PR nodes (i.e. primary radio nodes' activity) adds another challenge to data dissemination. As a consequence, the number of available channels to CR nodes changes with time and location leading to the diversity in the number of available channel set. Because of PR's activity, the usability of the channels by CR nodes becomes uncertain.

Moreover, without any centralized entity, as in the case of multi-hop ad hoc cognitive radio network, data dissemination is even more challenging because CR nodes have to rely on locally inferred information for their channel selection decision. If a channel selection is done in an intelligent way, higher data dissemination reachability can be achieved. Furthermore, the consideration of PR activity during channel selection can enhance the effectiveness of data dissemination reachability and can reduce the harmful interference to PR nodes by CR transmissions.

Considering the previously described observations, hereafter we describe the key characteristics required by a channel selection strategy for improving data dissemination robustness in infrastructureless multi-hop cognitive radio ad-hoc networks:

1. **CR Neighbor Reception:** A good channel selection strategy is the one that increases the probability of higher message delivery to the CR neighbors in multi-hop context.
2. **Primary Radio Constraints:** The channel selection strategy should ensure that the transmission on the selected channel does not create harmful interference to primary radio nodes.
3. **Autonomous Decision by CR Nodes:** In decentralized infrastructureless multihop cognitive radio networks, CR nodes are required to take autonomous decisions. It means that the channel selection strategy should work well without any centralized authority and channel selection decision should be based on locally inferred information.
4. **Sender/Receiver Tuning:** The channel selection strategy should guarantee that the CR transmitter and receiver select the same channel with high probability.

In the following section, we provide a classification of channel selection strategies in cognitive radio networks.

CLASSIFICATION OF CHANNEL SELECTION STRATEGIES IN CRNS

Recently, a lot of channel selection strategies have been proposed for cognitive radio networks (Yang, 2008; Cordeiro, 2006; Hoyhtya, 2010;

Zhao, 2007; Niyato, 2008; Rahual, 2008; Hou, 2010; Rao, 2010; Nguyen, 2010; Anggraeni, 2008; Acharya, 2006). These channel selection strategies are designed to achieve different performance goals like optimization of throughput and delay. Besides achieving these goals, each channel selection strategy has a nature, according to its reaction with the appearance of PR nodes on the CR communicating channel. Therefore, channel selection strategies can be classified into three categories by nature: (1) proactive (predictive), (2) threshold based, and (3) reactive. From the algorithmic perspective, channel selection strategies can be classified into centralized and distributed. The classification of channel selection strategies in cognitive radio networks is shown in Figure 2. Table I compares different channel selection strategies for cognitive radio networks and their features. In the following, we discuss each classification in detail.

Goals of Channel Selection Strategies

Channel selection strategies have been used to achieve different goals, e.g., load balancing, throughput maximization, channel switching delay minimization etc. Authors in (Yang, 2008) proposed a channel selection strategy to satisfy the traffic demands of Access Points. *Throughput maximization* is another goal and several channel selection strategies were proposed for throughput maximization (Acharya, 2006; Xiao, 2009; Nguyen, 2010; Zhao, 2007; Zhao, 2008). In (Nguyen, 2010), the authors determined the transmission schedule of the CR nodes in order to improve the network throughput. In (Acharya, 2006), the authors improved the throughput of the CR users in the TV broadcast network. In fact, the authors proposed a predictive channel selection scheme to maximize spectrum utilization and minimize disruptions to PR nodes. They considered a single-hop network in which CR nodes coordinate with the TV receiver to collect information regarding PR activity. Two opportunistic channel selection

schemes, CSS-MCRA and CSS-MHRA, are proposed in (Xiao, 2009). In CSS-MCRA, the goal was to maximize the throughput while minimize the collision rate. In CSS-MHRA, the goal was to maximize the throughput while minimizing the handoff rate. CSS-MCRA and CSS-MHRA both considered single user and are predictive in nature.

Load balancing is another important goal of channel selection strategies (Wang, 2010, 2011). In (Wang, 2010), the authors proposed a channel and power allocation scheme for CR networks. The objective was to maximize the sum data rate of all CRs. They considered the availability of a centralized authority, which monitors the PR activity and assign channels to CR nodes. Sensing-based and probability-based spectrum decision schemes are proposed in (Wang, 2011) to distribute the load of CR nodes to multiple channels. The authors derived the optimal number of candidate channels for sensing-based scheme and the optimal channel selection probability for probability-based spectrum decision scheme. The objective of both schemes was to minimize the overall system time of the CR users.

The authors in (Feng, 2009) proposed a predictive channel selection scheme to minimize the *channel switching delay* of a single CR node. Other channel selection strategies focus on optimizing the expected waiting time (Hus, 2007), (Ma, 2009), remaining idle time (Yoon, 2010), (Song, 2010), reducing *system overhead and improving CR QoS* (Zhu, 2007). A predictive channel selection strategy, Voluntary Spectrum Handoff (VSH) (Yoon, 2010), is proposed to reduce the *communication disruption* duration due to handoffs and to select the channel that has maximum remaining idle time. However, VSH requires the presence of Spectrum Server (SS), a centralized entity, to monitor the activities of PR and CR nodes. In (Hou, 2010), the authors proposed a channel selection scheme to maximize the *total channel utilization*. In their paper, the authors consider source-destination pairs in single-hop context. Channel selection strategies can also be used in conjunction with routing protocols for

Figure 2. Classification of channel selection strategies for cognitive radio networks

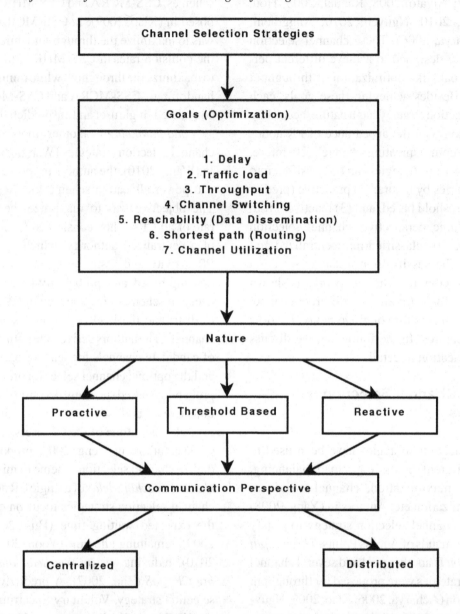

reliable path selection (Khalife, 2008) and good route selection for delay sensitive applications (Shiang, 2008).

Nature of Channel Selection Strategies

Every channel selection strategy reacts differently according to its working nature upon the appearance of PR nodes on the CR communicating

channel. Here, we classify his reactive decision making behavior of the channel selection strategies into proactive (predictive), threshold based, and reactive, as presented in Table 1.

- **Proactive Channel Selection Strategies:** In proactive channel selection strategies (Hoyhtya, 2010; Vartianen, 2010; Yang, 2008; Hoyhtya, 2008; Clancy, 2006; Acharya, 2006; Feng, 2009), the activity of

Table 1. Channel selection strategies and their features

Strategy	Goal	Nature	Hop/User
VSH (Yoon, 2010)	Remaining idle time	Predictive	Centralized
(Acharya, 2006)	Maximize channel utilization, throughput maximization and minimize disruptions to PRs	Predictive	Single-hop
SWIFT (Rahul, 2008)	Combine multiple non-contiguous unoccupied bands to create a high-throughput wideband link	work on unlicensed band	N/A
CBH, LH (Rao, 2010)	Maximize channel utilization & decrease message overhead	Reactive	Multi-hop
WAIT (Anggraeni, 2008)	Maximize throughput	Reactive	Single-hop
CSS-MCRA (Xiao, 2009)	Minimize collision rate and Throughput Maximization	Predictive	Single user
CSS-MHRA (Xiao, 2009)	Minimize handoff rate and Throughput Maximization	Predictive	Single user
(Nguyen, 2010)	Throughput maximization	Threshold based	Centralized
PS-OSA (Zhao, 2008)	Throughput maximization	N/A	CR pairs
(Wang, 2010)	Load balancing	Reactive	Centralized
(Wang, 2010)	Load balancing	Predictive/Reactive	Single-hop
(Feng, 2009)	Reduce channel switching delay	Predictive	Single user
SCA-MAC (Hsu, 2007)	Expected waiting time	Predictive	N/A
POSH (Ma, 2009)	Expected waiting time	Predictive	N/A
FLEX (Yang, 2008)	Traffic demands of Access Points	N/A	Single-hop
IEEE 802.22 (Cordeiro, 2006)	International wireless standard based on CR technology to use TV spectrum without causing harmful interference to TV devices	N/A	Centralized
(Song, 2010)	Remaining idle time	Proactive	CR pairs
(Zhu, 2007)	Reduce system overhead and improve CR QoS	N/A	N/A
(Hou, 2010)	Maximize total channel utilization	Reactive	CR pairs
MPP (Khalife, 2007)	Reliable path selection	N/A	Multi-hop
(Shiang, 2008)	Route selection for delay sensitive applications	Reactive	Distributed
(Zhao, 2005)	Route selection for delay sensitive applications	Reactive	Distributed
(Hoyhtya, 2010)	Find longest idle time channel	Predictive	N/A
(Vartiainen, 2010)	Optimize delay in finding the channel	Proactive	N/A
PRO-I, PRO-II (Yang, 2008)	Minimize disruptions to PRs, throughput Maximization	Proactive	Single pair
(Hoyhtya, 2008)	Reduce delay & channel switching, maximize Throughput	Predictive	N/A
PDSA (Clancy, 2006)	To determine expected channel idle time	Predictive	N/A
(Liu, 2006)	Outage requirement of PR user CR	Reactive	Centralized
RMC-MAC (Fourati, 2011)	Reduce forced termination probability and increase bandwidth utilization	Reactive	Single-hop
DFHC (Hu, 2007)	Better QoS and maximize throughput	Reactive	Centralized
SB (Kondareddy, 2008)	Data Reachability	N/A	Distributed
SURF	Data Reachability, minimize disruptions to PRs	Predictive	Distributed

PR nodes is predicted and the CR nodes move to the channel according to the prediction. In (Hoyhtya, 2008), the authors proposed a predictive channel selection strategy to reduce delay and channel switching, while maximizing the throughput. The same authors further extend their work in (Hoyhtya, 2010) and classified the PR traffic and applied different prediction rules. These prediction rules were then used in the predictive channel selection scheme to find the channels with the longest idle times for CR use. In (Clancy, 2006), the authors explored two approaches of Predictive Dynamic Spectrum Access (PDSA). The first approach uses cyclostationary detection on the primary users' channel access pattern to determine expected channel idle times. The second approach briefly examines the use of Hidden Markov Models (HMMs) for use in PDSA. Their basic goal was to predict when the channels will be idle, based on observations of the primary radio nodes channel usage. They determined the expected channel idle times for CR usage. Two proactive channel selection strategies, PRO-I and PRO-II are proposed in (Yang, 2008). The goals of these schemes were to minimize disruptions of PR nodes and throughput maximization of CR nodes. The authors used a single pair of CR nodes and they ignored the impact of other CR nodes contending for the channel. The authors in (Vartianen, 2010) proposed a proactive channel selection scheme. Through their scheme, the authors tried to optimize the delay in finding the channels using the history. Their scheme is based on two steps: the database step and the signal detection step. In the database step, the database collects information about the channels. The CR node, when required a channel for transmission, sends a query to the database. The database then provides the most probable unoccupied channels, which are the best candidates for searching the channels. These channels are then submitted to the CR node. CR node then selects the channels according to the priority which is based on the signal detection history.

- **Threshold-Based Channel Selection Strategies:** The threshold based schemes are those channel selection schemes in which the PR node is active all the time i.e., occupy the channel 100% and no idle channel is available to CR nodes. In these schemes, CR nodes are allowed to share the channel as long as the interference caused by the CR nodes to the PR nodes is below a certain threshold. Threshold-based schemes are also known as schemes that uses grey spaces. For instance, (Nguyen, 2010) is a threshold based channel selection scheme, in which the authors determined the transmission schedule for the CR nodes to maximize their throughput.

- **Reactive Channel Selection Strategies:** In reactive channel selection strategies (Liu, 2006; Fourati, 2011; Mishra, 2006; Sahai, 2004; Sahai, 2004), channel switching occurs after the PR node appears. In fact, in reactive channel selection schemes, CR nodes monitor local spectrum through individual or collaborative sensing. A lot of work has been done on individual or collaborative sensing, which can be found here (Mishra, 2006; Sahai, 2004; Ganesan, 2005; Ghasemi, 2005; Cabric, 2004). After detecting a change in the spectrum, e.g., channel is occupied by PR node, CR nodes stop the transmission, return back the channel to the PR node and search for other channel to resume the transmission. In (Wang, 2010), the co-authors of (Wang, 2008) provided the modeling and analysis of reactive spectrum handoff scheme in more detail. In (Liu, 2006), the authors proposed a sensing-based opportunistic channel access scheme. They considered a Primary TV broadcast network. They also considered a single PR node and a single CR node and a base station is required for keeping the primary channel's statistics. A reactive multi-channel mac protocol, RMC-MAC, for opportunistic spectrum access is proposed in (Fourati, 2011). Their objective was to increase the bandwidth utilization and to reduce the forced termination probability. However, they considered a single-hop CR network. Dynamic Frequency Hopping Communities (DFHC) (Hu, 2007) is also a reactive approach, which is designed for IEEE 802.22 networks and requires the presence of base station.

In (Wang, 2008), the authors compared the proactive (predictive) and reactive spectrum handoff schemes. The authors mentioned that the advantage of reactive spectrum handoff scheme resides in the accuracy of the selected target channel, but incurs the cost of sensing time. On the contrary, the proactive spectrum handoff scheme avoids the sensing time, but the pre-determined channel may not be available.

Channel Selection Strategies from the Communication Perspective

From the communication perspective, channel selection strategies can be classified into centralized and distributed. In (Salami, 2011), a comparison between centralized and distributed approaches for spectrum management is provided.

- **Centralized Channel Selection Strategies:** In centralized channel selection strategies, a centralized entity is present, which helps CR nodes in their channel selection decision (Pereirasamy, 2005; Buddhikot, 2005; Kulkarni, 2006). The authors in (Leaves, 2004) investigat-

ed different steps for the development of centralized algorithms for different radio networks. They discussed the current interests of regulators, technical requirements, and the possible schemes for dynamic spectrum allocation. In (Yang, 2008), the authors proposed an efficient spectrum allocation architecture that adapts to dynamic traffic demands but they considered a single-hop scenario of Access Points (APs) in Wi-Fi networks. An approach that uses non-continuous unoccupied band to create a high throughput link is discussed in (Rahul, 2008). In (Nguyen, 2010), the authors proposed a threshold-based channel sharing scheme between CR nodes. Their algorithm is designed for source-destination pairs and is specially designed for single-hop communication. In their paper, the authors assumed that all the PRs are active all the time and no idle channel is available to CR nodes for their communication. A centralized channel allocation scheme for IEEE 802.22 standard is proposed in (Zhu, 2006). The proposed channel allocation scheme allocates the channel based upon three rules: (1) maximum throughput rule, (2) utility fairness rule, and (3) time fairness rule. The authors in (Niyato, 2009) proposed an opportunistic channel selection scheme for IEEE 802.11-based wireless mesh networks. In this channel selection scheme, an Access Point (AP) is required to connect the nodes to the Internet via mesh router.

- **Distributed Channel Selection Strategies:** In distributed channel selection strategies, there is no centralized entity that helps CR nodes in their channel selection decision. CR nodes need to take channel selection decision on their locally available information. Very few works has been done on distributed channel selection strategies in the context of cognitive radio networks (Kondraeddy, 2008; Zhao, 2005; Shiang, 2008). In (Zhao, 2005; Shiang, 2008), the authors proposed a dynamic resource management scheme for multi-hop cognitive radio networks, in which routes are maintained for delay sensitive applications, such a multimedia streaming. The authors studied the amount of information exchange required in the multi-hop network. Based on the available information exchange, the authors proposed a multi-agent learning approach which allows the various nodes to optimize their transmission strategies autonomously, in a distributed manner, in multi-hop cognitive radio networks. In addition, the channel selection scheme proposed in (Zhao, 2005; Shiang, 2008) is designed to work with routing protocols, and thus cannot be used for broadcasting. Selective broadcasting (SB) (Kondareddy, 2008) is a distributed channel selection strategy. In SB, each cognitive node selects a minimum set of channels (ECS) covering all of its geographic neighbors to disseminate messages in multi-hop cognitive radio networks. There are however, several challenges in the practicality of SB. Indeed, from the communication perspective, simultaneous transmission over a ECS requires more than one transceiver, which means having bigger and more complex devices, as it is done for military applications (Younis, 2009). On the contrary, using a single transceiver to transmit over minimum set of channels requires determining the correct channel to overhearing a transmission, increases delay, and brings frequent channel switching. Secondly, from the perspective of overhearing, either neighbor nodes need to simultaneously overhear over multiple channels or synchronization is required among neighbors, which incurs scheduling overhead.

SURF CHANNEL SELECTION STUDY: A CASE STUDY

SURF is a packet-based channel selection scheme for data dissemination and not a routing algorithm. SURF classifies available channels on the basis of primary radio unoccupancy and the number of CR neighbors using the channels. More precisely with SURF, every CR node autonomously classifies available channels based on the observed PR-unoccupancy over these channels. This classification is then refined by identifying the number of CRs over each channel. The best channel for transmission is the channel that has the lowest PR activity and a highest number of CR neighbors. Indeed, choosing a channel with few CRs increases the probability of having a disconnected network. Practically, every CR after classifying available channels, switches dynamically to the best one and broadcasts the stored message. Moreover, SURF tries to learn with previous wrong channel state estimation. This learning process allows better tuning the future estimations and helps CR nodes to recover from their bad channel selection decisions.

Additionally, CRs with no messages to transmit implement the SURF strategy in order to tune to the best channel for data reception. Clearly, using the same strategy implemented by the sender increases the chance that receivers in close geographic areas select the same used-to-send channel for overhearing. This is also due to the fact that, intuitively, it is likely that CRs in the sender's vicinity have the same PR unoccupancy. Hence, channels available to a CR sender are also available, with high probability, to its neighbors. In this way, SURF increases the probability of creating a connected topology. Once a packet is received, every CR receiver undergoes again the same procedure to choose the appropriate channel for conveying the message to its neighbors.

We compare SURF with random strategy (RD), highest degree strategy (HD) and selective broadcasting, proposed in with multiple transmissions (SB). We suggested RD strategy, which is the simplest one and no information is required. In RD, channels are randomly selected to be used by CR nodes for transmission and/or overhearing, without any consideration to the ongoing PR and CR activity over these channels. HD approach only considers CR activities and is inspired by SB approach. In HD, CR nodes select the highest CR degree channel for transmission and overhearing, without any consideration of PR activity. The highest degree channel covers, consequently, the highest number of neighbors in the available list of channels. In SB, each CR node calculates a minimum set of channels, Essential Channel Set (ECS), for transmission that covers all its geographic neighbors, without considering the PR unoccupancy. In SB, a CR node transmits on multiple channels in round-robin fashion present in the ECS list, until all neighbors are covered. Note that in nothing is mentioned about how nodes overhear over the channels. Therefore, we consider nodes select for overhearing the highest degree channel from their ECS list only. If more than one option is available, a random choice for transmission/overhearing is performed among those channels with the same degree.

In this chapter, we include few results. We encourage the readers to read the paper (Rehmani, 2011) for detailed analysis.

We characterize the probable interference caused by CR transmissions to PR nodes for SURF, RD, HD, and SB. Figure 3 compares the harmful interference ratio for the four strategies i.e. RD, HD, SB and SURF, for Ch=5 and Ch=10. It can be clearly seen in the figure that SURF, as expected, causes less harmful interference to PR nodes, compared to RD, HD, and SB. This is primarily because, when using SURF, CR nodes select those channels that have very high probability of being in OFF state, reducing thus PR interference. Note that in SURF, if all channels are occupied, the CR transmission will not take place. In addition, when the number of channels is low, i.e. Ch=5, the value of HIR is higher

than Ch=10. This is due to the fact that a lower number of channels also reduce the chances for CR nodes finding PR-unoccupied channels for their transmission. As a result, SURF protects PR nodes, by reducing the amount of collisions with primary radios.

We have chosen two parameters to evaluate robust data dissemination: (1) average delivery ratio, and (2) ratio of accumulative receivers.

Average Delivery Ratio: In order to better observe the impact on delivery ratio of such dynamic neighborhood, we first consider a scenario where PR activity equals to 0. Figure 4 shows the average delivery ratio per node ID for Ch=5 and Ch=10 when PR activity equals to 0. The results attest the obtained low delivery ratios are mainly due to the creation of different topologies resulted from the multi-channel availability and distributed channel selection by CRs. More specifically, even when no PR competition exists, the maximum average delivery ratio is lower than 35%. It is worth mentioning that the diversity in terms of available channels and PR activities, and the consequent lower neighborhood density after CRs local channel selection result in the creation of different topologies (i.e., dynamic neighborhood) at each transmission/overhearing of CR nodes. These issues make hard the achievement of a higher delivery ratio than SURF, as it can be observed in Figure 4.

We now consider PR activity in our analysis. Figure 5 compares the average delivery ratio of RD, HD, SB and SURF, for Ch=5 and Ch=10. SURF increases considerably the delivery ratio compared to the other solutions. In particular, for Ch=5, SURF guarantees a maximum delivery ratio of approximately 40% compared to almost 0% in the case of RD, HD, and SB. And when Ch=10, SURF allows some nodes to reach a maximum delivery ratio of 50%, while in RD, it is almost 0% and 2% in HD and SB. In fact, RD, HD, and SB, do not guarantee that the selected channel is unoccupied for transmission thus causing a severe decrease in the delivery ratio. While

Figure 3. PR harmful interference ratio for RD, HD, SB, and SURF, when Ch=5 and Ch=10

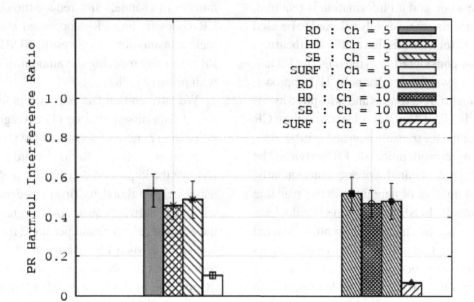

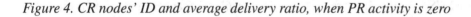

Figure 4. CR nodes' ID and average delivery ratio, when PR activity is zero

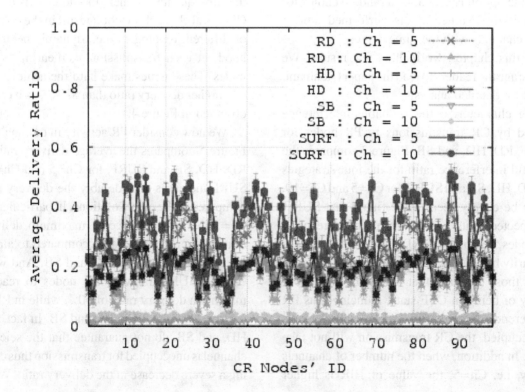

Figure 5. CR nodes' ID and average delivery ratio

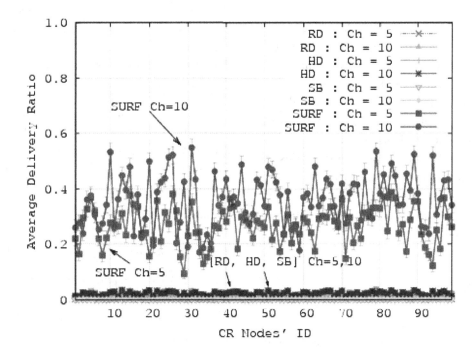

in SURF, the average delivery ratio is higher because CR nodes select the channel that has higher P_OFF (t) and higher CR neighbors. Nevertheless, it is worth noting that SURF is the approach less impacted by the PR activities: By intelligently taking profit of channels availabilities, SURF is able to ensure a stable delivery ratio even when CRs transmission is competing with the PR ones.

FUTURE RESEARCH DIRECTIONS

SURF channel selection strategy can be further enhanced by considering the primary radio nodes activity pattern. As we have pointed out in this thesis that the intermittent primary radio activity case is the case where clever solutions need to operate. In this regard, we can incorporate other history-based metrics (that try to better infer the quality of channels) combined with the current Pw of SURF. One example could be: How often the channel is free? Here, SURF may keep history of channel ON/OFF states. SURF will consider an "observation time window". The observation time window is defined as the duration of time during which the channel ON/OFF states are observed. In this manner, SURF will compute the ratio of being free over the time window (the size of the time window could be varied to evaluate the impact of ON/OFF states). In addition, we can also consider How long channels stay in OFF state? Here, SURF may compute the duration of OFF state over the total time of window size, in the considered time window. This metric depends on how SURF keeps the history of channel states. This could be done on per time slot basis or combining two or more time slots. Finally, in SURF, we can consider What was the ratio of success (reception or transmission) over the times the channel was in OFF state? This metric will give the quality of the channel in terms of contention. By using this metric, SURF may avoid those channels that are quality wise poor.

CONCLUSION

In this chapter, we gave an introduction on data dissemination in these types of networks. We then discussed the related works and the challenges associated with data dissemination in cognitive radio networks. Additionally, we highlighted that channel selection plays a vital role in efficient and robust data dissemination. We provided an in-depth study of channel selection strategies in cognitive radio networks. Furthermore, classification of channel selection strategies according to their goals, nature, and communication perspective has been provided.

REFERENCES

Acharya, P. A. K., Singh, S., & Zheng, H. (2006). Reliable open spectrum communications through proactive spectrum access. In *Proceedings of TAPAS*. TAPAS.

Al-Mogren, A. (2008). Energy adaptive approach in a multi-channel dissemination-based network. In Proceedings of New Technologies, Mobility and Security, NTMS '08, (pp. 1 –6). NTMS.

Anantharamu, L., Chlebus, B., Kowalski, D., & Rokicki, M. (2010). Deterministic broadcast on multiple access channels. In *Proceedings IEEE INFOCOM*. IEEE.

Anggraeni, P., Mahmood, N., Berthod, J., Chaussonniere, N., My, L., & Yomo, H. (2008). Dynamic channel selection for cognitive radios with heterogenous primary bands. *Wireless Personal Communications, 45*, 369–384. doi:10.1007/s11277-008-9464-7.

Asterjadhi, A., Kumar, R., La Porta, T., & Zorzi, M. (2011). Broadcasting in multi channel wireless networks in the presence of adversaries. In *Proceedings of the 8th Annual IEEE Communications Society Conference on Sensor, Mesh and Ad Hoc Communications and Networks (SECON)*, (pp. 377 –385). IEEE.

Buddhikot, M., & Ryan, K. (2005). Spectrum management in coordinated dynamic spectrum access based cellular networks. In *Proceedings of the First IEEE International Symposium on New Frontiers in Dynamic Spectrum Access Networks, DySPAN'05*, (pp. 299 –307). IEEE.

Cabric, D., Mishra, S. M., & Brodersen, R. W. (2004). Implementation issues in spectrum sensing for cognitive radios. In *Proceedings of Asilomar Conference on Signals, Systems and Computers*. Asilomar.

Clancy, T. C., & Walker, B. D. (2006). Predictive dynamic spectrum access. In *Proceedings of SDR Forum Technical Conference*. Orlando, FL: SDR.

Cordeiro, C., Challapali, K., Birru, D., & Shanka, S. N. (2006). IEEE 802.22: An introduction to the first wireless standard based on cognitive radios. *The Journal of Communication, 1*(1), 38–47.

Erman, A. T., & Havinga, P. (2010). Data dissemination of emergency messages in mobile multi-sink wireless sensor networks. In *Proceedings of the 9th IFIP Annual Mediterranean Ad Hoc Networking Workshop (Med-Hoc-Net)*, (pp. 1 –8). IFIP.

Feng, Q. Xue, Guangxi, S., & Yanchun, L. (2009). Smart channel switching in cognitive radio networks. In *Proceedings of CISP, 2009*. CISP.

Feng, W. Liang, & Zhu. (2010). A greedy strategy of data dissemination over multi-channel in mobile computing environments. In *Proceedings of the 3rd International Conference on Advanced Computer Theory and Engineering (ICACTE)*, (vol. 5, pp. V5–322 –V5–326). ICACTE.

Fourati, S., Hamouda, S., & Tabbane, S. (2011). Rmc-mac: A reactive multi-channel mac protocol for opportunistic spectrum access. In *Proceedings of the 4th IFIP International Conference on New Technologies, Mobility and Security (NTMS)*, (pp. 1 –5). IFIP.

Ganesan, G., & Li, Y. G. (2005). Cooperative spectrum sensing in cognitive radio networks. In *Proceedings of IEEE DySPAN*. DySPAN.

Ghasemi, A., & Sousa, E. S. (2005). Collaborative spectrum sensing for opportunistic access in fading environments. In *Proceedings of IEEE DySPAN*. DySPAN.

Haas, Z., Halpern, J., & Li, L. (2002). Gossip-based ad hoc routing. In *Proceedings of the Twenty-First Annual Joint Conference of the IEEE Computer and Communications Societies INFOCOM*, (vol. 3, pp. 1707 – 1716). IEEE.

Heissenbuttel, M., Braun, T., Walchli, M., & Bernoulli, T. (2006). Optimized stateless broadcasting in wireless multi-hop networks. In *Proceedings of the 25th IEEE International Conference on Computer Communications INFOCOM*. IEEE.

Hou, F., & Huang, J. (2010). Dynamic channel selection in cognitive radio network with channel heterogeneity. In *Proceedings of IEEE Globecom*. IEEE.

Hoyhtya, M., Pollin, S., & Mammela, A. (2008). Performance improvement with predictive channel selection for cognitive radios. In *Proceedings of the First International Workshop on Cognitive Radio and Advanced Spectrum Management, CogART 2008*. CogART.

Hoyhtya, M., Pollin, S., & Mammela, A. (2010). Classification-based predictive channel selection for cognitive radios. In *Proceedings of IEEE ICC*. IEEE.

Hsu, A. C.-C., Wei, D. S.-L., & Kua, C.-C. J. (2007). A cognitive mac protocol using statistical channel allocation for wireless ad-hoc networks. In *Proceedings of WCNC*. WCNC.

Hu, W., Willkomm, D., Abusubaih, M., Gross, J., Vlantis, G., Gerla, M., & Wolisz, A. (2007). Cognitive radios for dynamic spectrum access - Dynamic frequency hopping communities for efficient IEEE 802.22 operation. *IEEE Communications Magazine*, *45*(5), 80–87. doi:10.1109/MCOM.2007.358853.

Intanagonwiwat, C., Govindan, R., Estrin, D., Heidemann, J., & Silva, F. (2003). Directed diffusion for wireless sensor networking. *IEEE/ACM Transactions on Networking*, *11*(1), 2–16. doi:10.1109/TNET.2002.808417.

Khalife, H., Ahuja, S., Malouch, N., & Krunz, M. (2008). Probabilistic path selection in opportunistic cognitive radio networks. In *Proceedings of the IEEE Globecom Conference*. IEEE.

Kondareddy, Y. R., & Agrawal, P. (2008). Selective broadcasting in multi-hop cognitive radio networks. In *Proceedings of the IEEE Sarnoff Symposium*. IEEE.

Kulkarni, R., & Zekavat, S. A. (2006). Traffic-aware inter-vendor dynamic spectrum allocation: Performance in multi-vendor environments. In *Proceedings of the 2006 International Conference on Wireless Communications and Mobile Computing*. ACM Press.

Leaves, P., Moessner, K., Tafazolli, R., Grandblaise, D., Bourse, D., Tonjes, R., & Breveglieri, M. (2004). Dynamic spectrum allocation in composite reconfigurable wireless networks. *IEEE Communications Magazine*, *42*(5), 72–81. doi:10.1109/MCOM.2004.1299346.

Lee, J.-F., Wang, C.-S., & Chuang, M.-C. (2010). Fast and reliable emergency message dissemination mechanism in vehicular ad hoc networks. In *Proceedings of the IEEE Wireless Communications and Networking Conference (WCNC)*. IEEE.

Liang, O., Sekercioglu, Y. A., & Mani, N. (2006). A survey of multipoint relay based broadcast schemes in wireless ad hoc networks. *IEEE Communications Surveys Tutorials*, *8*(4), 30–46. doi:10.1109/COMST.2006.283820.

Liu, X. (2006). Sensing-based opportunistic channel access. *Mobile Networks and Applications*, *11*, 577–591. doi:10.1007/s11036-006-7323-x.

Ma, R.-T., Hsu, Y.-P., & Feng, K.-T. (2009). A pomdp-based spectrum handoff protocol for partially observable cognitive radio networks. In *Proceedings of WCNC*. WCNC.

Mishra, A. S. S., & Brodersen, R. (2006). Cooperative sensing among cognitive radios. In *Proceedings of IEEE ICC*. IEEE.

Nguyen, G. D., & Kompella, S. (2010). Channel sharing in cognitive radio networks. In *Proceedings of MILCOM*. MILCOM.

Ni, S.-Y., Tsend, Y.-C., Chen, Y.-S., & Sheu, J.-P. (1999). The broadcast storm problem in a mobile ad hoc network. In *Proceedings of the 5th Annual ACM/IEEE International Conference on Mobile Computing and Networking (MOBICOM '99)*. ACM/IEEE.

Niyato, D., & Hossain, E. (2008). Competitive spectrum sharing in cognitive radio networks: A dynamic game approach. *IEEE Transactions on Wireless Communications*, *7*(7), 2651–2660. doi:10.1109/TWC.2008.070073.

Niyato, D., & Hossain, E. (2009). Cognitive radio for next-generation wireless networks: An approach to opportunistic channel selection in IEEE 802.11-based wireless mesh. *IEEE Wireless Communications*, *16*(1), 46–54. doi:10.1109/MWC.2009.4804368.

Pereirasamy, M., Luo, J., Dillinger, M., & Hartmann, C. (2005). Dynamic inter-operator spectrum sharing for umts fdd with displaced cellular networks. In *Proceedings of the IEEE Wireless Communications and Networking Conference*, (vol. 3, pp. 1720 – 1725). IEEE.

Rahul, H., Kushman, N., Katabi, D., Sodini, C., & Edalat, F. (2008). Learning to share: Narrowband-friendly wideband wireless networks. *ACM SIGCOMM*, *38*(4), 147–158. doi:10.1145/1402946.1402976.

Rao, V. S., Prasad, R. V., Yadati, C., & Niemegeers, I. (2010). Distributed heuristics for allocating spectrum in cr ad hoc networks. In *Proceedings of IEEE Globecom*. IEEE.

Rehmani, M. H., Viana, A. C., Khalife, H., & Fdida, S. (2011). Improving data dissemination in multi-hop cognitive radio ad-hoc networks. In *Proceedings of the 3rd International ICST Conference on Ad Hoc Networks (ADHOCNETS 2011)*. Paris, France: ADHOCNETS.

Rostamzadeh, K., & Gopalakrishnan, S. (2011). Analysis of emergency message dissemination in vehicular networks. In *Proceedings of the IEEE Wireless Communications and Networking Conference (WCNC)*, (pp. 575 –580). IEEE.

Sahai, N. H. A., & Tandra, R. (2004). Some fundamental limits on cognitive radios. In *Proceedings of the 42 Allerton Conference on Communication, Control and Computing*. Allerton.

Sahai, R. T. A., & Hoven, N. (2006). Opportunistic spectrum use for sensor networks: The need for local cooperation. In *Proceedings of IPSN*. IPSN.

Salami, G., Attar, A., Holland, R. T., Oliver, & Aghvami, H. (2011). A comparison between the centralized and distributed approaches for spectrum management. *IEEE Communications Surveys and Tutorials, 13*(2), 274–290.

Shiang, H. P., & Schaar, M. V. D. (2008). Delay-sensitive resource management in multi-hop cognitive radio networks. In *Proceedings of IEEE DySpan*. IEEE.

Simon, R., Huang, L., Farrugia, E., & Setia, S. (2005). Using multiple communication channels for efficient data dissemination in wireless sensor networks. In *Proceedings of the IEEE International Conference on Mobile Adhoc and Sensor Systems Conference*. IEEE.

Song, Y., & Xie, J. (2010). Common hopping based proactive spectrum handoff in cognitive radio ad hoc networks. In *Proceedings of GlobeCom*. IEEE. doi:10.1109/GLOCOM.2010.5683840.

Starobinski, D., & Xiao, W. (2010). Asymptotically optimal data dissemination in multichannel wireless sensor networks: Single radios suffice. *IEEE/ACM Transactions on Networking*, *18*(3), 695–707. doi:10.1109/TNET.2009.2032230.

Sun, L., & Wang, W. (2011). On distribution and limits of information dissemination latency and speed in mobile cognitive radio networks. In *Proceedings IEEE INFOCOM*. IEEE.

Tseng, Y.-C., Ni, S.-Y., & Shih, E.-Y. (2001). Adaptive approaches to relieving broadcast storms in a wireless multihop mobile ad hoc network. In *Proceedings of the 21st International Conference on Distributed Computing Systems*. IEEE.

Vartiainen, J., Hoyhtya, M., Lehtomaki, J., & Braysy, T. (2010). Priority channel selection based on detection history database. In *Proceedings of CROWNCOM*. CROWNCOM.

Vecchio, M., Viana, A. C., Ziviani, A., & Friedman, R. (2010). Deep: Density-based proactive data dissemination protocol for wireless sensor networks with uncontrolled sink mobility. *Computer Communications*, *33*(8), 929–939. doi:10.1016/j.comcom.2010.01.003.

Viana, A. C., Herault, T., Largilliers, T., Peyronnet, S., & Zaidi, F. (2010). Supple: A flexible probabilistic data dissemination protocol for wireless sensor networks. In *Proceedings of the 13th ACM International Conference on Modeling, Analysis, and Simulation of Wireless and Mobile Systems*. ACM Press.

Wang, C.-W., Wang, L.-C., & Adachi, F. (2010). Modeling and analysis for reactive-decision spectrum handoff in cognitive radio networks. In *Proceedings of the IEEE Global Telecommunications Conference (GLOBECOM 2010)*. IEEE.

Wang, H., Ren, J., & Li, T. (2010). Resource allocation with load balancing for cogntive radio networks. In *Proceedings of IEEE GlobeCom*. IEEE.

Wang, L.-C., & Wang, C.-W. (2008). Spectrum handoff for cognitive radio networks: Reactive-sensing or proactive-sensins? In *Proceedings of the IEEE International Performance, Computing and Communications Conference (IPCCC 2008)*. IEEE.

Wang, L.-C., Wang, C.-W., & Adachi, F. (2011). Load-balancing spectrum decision for cognitive radio networks. *IEEE Journal on Selected Areas in Communications*, *29*(4), 757–769. doi:10.1109/JSAC.2011.110408.

Wieselthier, J., Nguyen, G., & Ephremides, A. (2000). On the construction of energy-efficient broadcast and multicast trees in wireless networks. In *Proceedings of the Nineteenth Annual Joint Conference of the IEEE Computer and Communications Societies INFOCOM*, (vol. 2, pp. 585–594). IEEE.

Xiao, Q., Li, Y., Zhao, M., Zhou, S., & Wang, J. (2009). Opportunistic channel selection approach under collision probability constraint in cognitive radio systems. *Computer Communications*, *32*(18), 1914–1922. doi:10.1016/j.comcom.2009.06.015.

Ya-Feng, W., Yin-long, X., Guo-Liang, C., & Kun, W. (2004). On the construction of virtual multicast backbone for wireless ad hoc networks. In *Proceedings of the IEEE International Conference on Mobile Ad-hoc and Sensor Systems*, (pp. 294 – 303). IEEE.

Yang, L., Cao, L., & Zheng, H. (2008). Proactive channel access in dynamic spectrum networks. *Elsevier Physical Communications Journal*, *1*, 103–111. doi:10.1016/j.phycom.2008.05.001.

Yang, L., Cao, L., Zheng, H., & Belding, E. (2008). Traffic-aware dynamic spectrum access. In *Proceedings of the Fourth International Wireless Internet Conference (WICON 2008)*. WICON.

Yoon, S.-U., & Ekici, E. (2010). Voluntary spectrum handoff: A novel approach to spectrum management in CRNS. *Proceedings of, ICC*, ICC.

Younis, O., Kant, L., Chang, K., & Young, K. (2009). Cognitive manet design for mission-critical networks. *IEEE Communications Magazine*, 64–71. doi:10.1109/MCOM.2009.5273810.

Zhao, J., Zheng, H., & Yang, G. H. (2005). Distributed coordination in dynamic spectrum allocation networks. In *Proceedings of the First IEEE International Symposium on New Frontiers in Dynamic Spectrum Access Networks (DySPAN)*, (pp. 259–268). IEEE.

Zhao, Q., Geirhofer, S., Tong, L., & Sadler, B. M. (2008). Opportunistic spectrum access via periodic channel sensing. *IEEE Transactions on Signal Processing*, *56*(2), 785–796. doi:10.1109/TSP.2007.907867.

Zhao, Q., Tong, L., Swami, A., & Chen, Y. (2007). Decentralized cognitive mac for opportunistic spectrum access in ad hoc networks: A pomdp framewrok. *IEEE Journal on Selected Areas in Communications*, *25*(3), 589–600. doi:10.1109/JSAC.2007.070409.

Zhu, J., & Li, S. (2006). Channel allocation mechanisms for cognitive radio networks via repeated multi-bid auction. In *Proceedings of ICWMMN 2006*. ICWMMN.

Zhu, P., Li, J., & Wang, X. (2007). A new channel parameter for cognitive radio. In *Proceedings of CrownCom, 2007*. CrownCom. doi:10.1109/CROWNCOM.2007.4549845.

Zyba, G., Voelker, G., Ioannidis, S., & Diot, C. (2011). Dissemination in opportunistic mobile ad-hoc networks: The power of the crowd. In *Proceedings IEEE INFOCOM* (pp. 1179–1187). IEEE. doi:10.1109/INFCOM.2011.5934896.

ADDITIONAL READING

Clancy, T. C., & Walker, B. D. (2006). Predictive dynamic spectrum access. In *Proceedings of SDR Forum Technical Conference*. Orlando, FL: SDR.

Cordeiro, C., Challapali, K., Birru, D., & Shanka, S. N. (2006). IEEE 802.22: An introduction to the first wireless standard based on cognitive radios. *The Journal of Communication*, *1*(1), 38–47.

Hoyhtya, M., Pollin, S., & Mammela, A. (2008). Performance improvement with predictive channel selection for cognitive radios. In *Proceedings of the First International Workshop on Cognitive Radio and Advanced Spectrum Management, CogART 2008*. CogART.

Nguyen, G. D., & Kompella, S. (2010). Channel sharing in cognitive radio networks. In *Proceedings of MILCOM, 2010*. MILCOM.

Niyato, D., & Hossain, E. (2008). Competitive spectrum sharing in cognitive radio networks: A dynamic game approach. *IEEE Transactions on Wireless Communications*, *7*(7), 2651–2660. doi:10.1109/TWC.2008.070073.

Wang, L.-C., Wang, C.-W., & Adachi, F. (2011). Load-balancing spectrum decision for cognitive radio networks. *IEEE Journal on Selected Areas in Communications*, *29*(4), 757–769. doi:10.1109/JSAC.2011.110408.

KEY TERMS AND DEFINITIONS

Channel Selection: Channel selection means the selection of spectrum band or frequency for communication.

Cognitive Radio Networks: Cognitive radio networks are composed of cognitive radio devices in which cognitive radio changes its transmission parameters based on interaction with the environment in which it operates.

Data Dissemination: Data dissemination is commonly defined as the spreading of information to multiple destinations through broadcasting. The main objective is to reach the maximum number of neighbors with every sent packet.

Dynamic Spectrum Access Networks: Dynamic spectrum access networks define a set of protocols for sharing spectrum among different networks. Dynamic spectrum access networks are also called as cognitive radio networks.

Chapter 3
Joint Radio Resource Management in Cognitive Networks:
TV White Spaces Exploitation Paradigm

Athina Bourdena
University of the Aegean, Greece

Charalabos Skianis
University of the Aegean, Greece

Prodromos Makris
University of the Aegean, Greece

George Kormentzas
University of the Aegean, Greece

Dimitrios N. Skoutas
University of the Aegean, Greece

Evangelos Pallis
Technological Educational Institute of Crete, Greece

George Mastorakis
Technological Educational Institute of Crete, Greece

ABSTRACT

In this chapter, Joint Radio Resource Management (JRRM) issues in cognitive networks are discussed presenting the TV White Spaces (TVWS) spectrum exploitation use case. TVWS are portions of UHF spectrum, which will be released and interleaved according to the geographical region due to the gradual switch-off of analogue TV and the adoption of digital TV. With the availability of TVWS and their temporary lease, traditional network planning and RRM design rationale points need to be enhanced. This chapter provides state-of-the-art work for existing cognitive radio network architectures, while a reference architecture for commons and secondary TVWS trading is proposed. Subsequently, JRRM concepts for heterogeneous Radio Access Technologies' extension over TVWS aiming to continuously guarantee the QoS, the network key performance indicators, and at the same time targeting the overall highest system capacity, are presented. Finally, a thorough classification of existing admission control and scheduling techniques are provided, outlining the need for including continuously more cognitive and context-aware features in JRRM algorithms being applicable in advanced Heterogeneous Networking (HetNet) environments.

DOI: 10.4018/978-1-4666-4189-1.ch003

Copyright © 2013, IGI Global. Copying or distributing in print or electronic forms without written permission of IGI Global is prohibited.

1. INTRODUCTION

Emerging types of wireless network services and applications, rich in multimedia content with increased requirements for network resources and guaranteed end-to-end QoS provisioning, raise the needs for higher frequency availability and create new challenges in radio-spectrum (i.e. the fundamental resource in wireless telecommunication networks) management and administration. While the utilization of advanced digital signal processing techniques enable for efficient radio-spectrum exploitation, even under the traditional "command-and-control" spectrum administration/management policy, there is a worldwide recognition that such methods have reached their limit and are no longer optimal. In fact, radio-spectrum utilization studies have resulted that most of the licensed spectrum is under-utilized (McHenry et al., 2004), and considerable parts of it would be available when both space and time dimensions are taken into account. An example of under-utilized radio-spectrum, is the so-called "television white spaces" (TVWS) that comprise of VHF/UHF frequencies, either released/freed by the digital switchover process ("Spectrum/Digital Dividend"), or being totally unexploited, mainly at local level, due to frequency planning issues and/or network design principles ("Interleaved Spectrum") (Australian Communication & Media Authority, 2007). TVWS include tenths of MHz at local/regional level (OFCOM, 2008), enable for low cost and low power systems design, provide superior propagation conditions for building penetration, while at the same time their sufficiently short wavelength facilitate the construction of resonant antennas, at a size and shape that is acceptable for many handheld devices. Therefore, TVWS are well suited for wireless network applications and services, provided by sophisticated telecommunication systems. However, the current "command-and-control" administration/management policy allows only for primary (i.e. licensed) systems to exploit TVWS for the provision of primary services, such as terrestrial digital video broadcasting (DVB-T), handheld digital video broadcasting (DVB-H), interactive (iTV), Programme Making and Special Events (PMSE), while prohibiting any other secondary transmission. Hence, the problem of spectrum scarcity, as perceived today, is due to inefficient radio-spectrum management/administration, rather than the wireless resources shortage. The envisioned frameworks and schemes that are proposed in this book chapter include policies (Unlicensed Operation in the TV broadcast bands, 2009) in which secondary (i.e. unlicensed) systems are allowed to opportunistically utilize the underused primary TV channels. TVWS spectrum exploitation paradigm will be used as a vehicle in order to address joint radio resource management (JRRM) issues in cognitive radio networks, too.

Cognitive Radio (CR) techniques provide the ability in a network to share the available radio spectrum, under an opportunistic basis. Cognitive radio networks adapt their transmitter parameters, based on real-time interaction with their spectral environment, by exploiting portions of frequency bands that are unused at a specific time or a geographical location. The choice of radio spectrum selection has to be performed, under an efficient process without causing interference with other licensed systems operating in the same frequency band. A cognitive radio network can be set to transmit and receive on a variety of different frequencies, exploiting alternative access technologies supported by its hardware design. Through this ability, the most optimum radio spectrum band and the most appropriate operating parameters can be selected and reconfigured.

Towards making full use of cognitive radio networks benefits and improving spectrum efficiency, cognition, intelligent decision-making and the reconfiguration abilities are adopted based on a cognition cycle. More specifically, cognition ability includes acquisition of multi-domain environment cognition information, efficient cognition information transmission and usage. Intelligent decision making ability includes the ability of making decision adaptively, according to the dynamic changing environment and the ability of improving the end-to-end efficiency. Reconfiguration ability includes the reconfiguration of cognitive radio networks, according to previous intelligent decisions for an end-to-end efficiency purpose. Finally, cognition cycle is also exploited, in order to observe the network, perceive current network conditions and make an optimum decision.

The main learning objectives of this book chapter are the following: a) investigate JRRM issues to optimize spectrum utilization, minimize interference, guarantee fairness in TVWS access and minimize spectrum fragmentations, b) propose an abstract cognitive radio architectural framework for TVWS exploitation paradigm, c) provide means for design and implementation of enabling technologies based on cognitive radio to support mobile applications over TVWS for various spectrum sharing models, d) introduce techniques that integrate QoS/QoE aspects in dynamic spectrum management, and e) introduce context-aware and autonomous networking functionalities for JRRM algorithms in cognitive networks. The purpose of the chapter is to present ways that a traditional but always up-to-date research topic such as JRRM can be applicable in efficient TVWS spectrum exploitation. The rationale of the technical content included, is to give to intended audience an overall view of TVWS paradigm and to present specific means that general cognitive and context-awareness concepts can be integrated in related state-of-the-art frameworks towards envisioning the real evolution of cognitive networks and self-adaptive communication systems.

The remainder of the book chapter is structured as follows. In section 2, a comprehensive classification of state-of-the-art cognitive radio architectures is provided accompanied by an exhaustive categorization of existing RRM optimization algorithms, which can be used in the TVWS exploitation paradigm. Section 3 proposes a novel CR framework for TVWS exploitation based on real-time secondary spectrum market (RTSSM)

policy undertaken in the context of FP7-ICT-COGEU project (COGEU, 2012), while various TVWS allocation policies are analyzed. In section 4, the concept of Joint Radio Resource Management (JRRM) for heterogeneous Radio Access Technologies' (RATs) extension over TVWS is introduced by focusing on JRRM both from the spectrum broker and Local Resource Manager (LRM) perspectives. In sections 5 and 6, the two most important LRM functionalities are extensively analyzed. More specifically, context-aware joint admission control and scheduling techniques are presented in sections 5 and 6 correspondingly. Future research trends and directions are given in section 7 providing insightful considerations about the future of cognitive networks and self-adaptive communication systems from the perspective of efficient TVWS exploitation paradigm. The chapter ends up with some concluding remarks, while extensive related bibliography list is provided for additional reading, too.

2. BACKGROUND

2.1. State of the Art of Existing Cognitive Radio Network Architectures

Cognitive radio concept (Mitola & Maguire, 1999) is researched and developed in response to the current wireless networks' needs for increased spectrum availability, as well as to efficiently exploit the available radio resources (McHenry et al., 2004). Deployment of CR networks may satisfy/fulfil the increasing users' demand for bandwidth-hungry QoS-sensitive mobile services, by allowing dynamic access to the available spectrum portions, along with on-demand utilization of the radio resources. In this respect, CR technologies allow for the establishment of frequency-agile devices, utilizing sensing mechanisms, in order to detect TVWS channels and adapt their transmission characteristics, so that primary users are not interfered by secondary ones. To achieve these, CR networks are exploiting network architectures that can be characterized either as infrastructure-based or ad-hoc, single-hop or multi-hop and centralized or distributed ones (Hossain et al., 2009). As shown in Figure 1, distributed network architectures can be implemented in both infrastructure-based and ad-hoc cognitive radio networks. Nevertheless, a centralized dynamic spectrum access can be obtained only in an infrastructure-based network, thus a central controller is required to orchestrate the spectrum access of secondary users. In the case of a multi-hop infrastructure-based network, one of the relay stations can assume the responsibility of controlling dynamic spectrum access.

More specifically, if the network topology frequently differentiates/changes, CR architectures can be characterised as infrastructure or ad-hoc, while the communication along the nodes characterizes the architecture as single or multi-hop. For instance, in a single-hop, infrastructure-based CR architecture, communication among secondary users is assured, via a central controller, which is responsible for the secondary spectrum access coordination. On the other hand, in a multi-hop, infrastructure-based CR architecture, a number of base stations are utilized (i.e. relay nodes), enabling secondary users to exchange data, even though they are not in the same transmission range of each other. Furthermore, if a central controller takes the decision, regarding the spectrum allocation process, then the network architecture is a centralized one. The central controller is responsible to collect information, regarding spectrum usage of the primary users, as well as information about the transmission requirements of the secondary ones. Based on this information, an optimal allocation solution that maximizes spectrum utilization can be performed. The decisions of the central controller are communicated/broadcasted to all secondary users that are connected in the network. Alternatively, in case of distributed decision process for dynamic radio-resource exploitation, a secondary user can autonomously decide on spectrum access. Since each secondary user has to collect information, regarding the radio environment and make its decision locally, the CR transceiver of each secondary user requires greater computational resources than those required in centralized architectures. The communication overhead in this case would be smaller, but since each user has only local information, the optimal solution for spectrum access may not be achievable by all unlicensed users.

Figure 1. Categories of CR network architectures

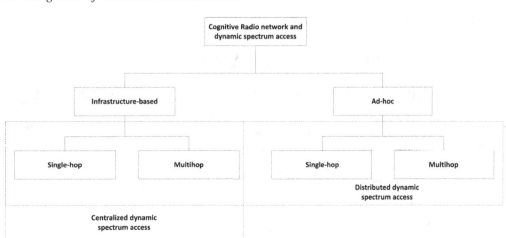

2.2. Radio Resource Management Approaches

In all cases, and no matter which architecture is utilized, vital part of CR networks is the Radio Resource Management (RRM) entity (Bourdena et al., in press, 2011, 2012), which is considered as an optimized solution for optimally allocating network resources. While this optimization can be generally focused on optimizing either a single objective or a set of objectives, the nature of the wireless communications most of the times requires the multi-objective one. More specifically, the optimization goal in CR paradigm, is focused on formulating networking problems, as optimization ones considering resource allocation. Usually, multi-objective optimization can be performed, following either the decision making theory concept or the game theory concept. Whereas the former tries to find an optimal solution through classical mathematical rationalization, the latter considers the optimization problem, as a game theory process (Niyato & Hossain, 2007, 2008).

The decision making approach is based on formulating, (by maximizing or minimizing an objective function), as well as on setting equality and inequality constraints that the optimal solution is required to respect (Hossain et al., 2009). As it is illustrated in Figure 2, three groups of solutions arise for this type of optimization approach:

1. Closed form solution, which can be exploited in cases that at least one solution can be expressed as a closed-form expression and it has an analytic solution. An equation is considered to be a closed-form solution if it solves a given problem in terms of functions and mathematical operations from a given generally accepted set. For example, an infinite sum would generally not be considered closed-form.

2. The next group of decision-making approach is the integer/combinatorial programming that involves parameters with integer values or with combinatorial nature, thus means that a finite number of possible solutions exist. These problems are referred as multi-objective ones and they can be solved by searching for the optimal solutions among the entire set of possible solutions. The goal of the integer/combinatorial programming is shortening the search space to a smaller one. Such an example is backtracking algorithm (Skiena, 2008) that is discussed below in the next paragraphs. In CR networks, integer/combinatorial optimization problem formulations can be used to perform efficient resource allocation methods, which meet the desired objectives when the values of some or all of the decision constraints have

Figure 2. Categories of optimization algorithms

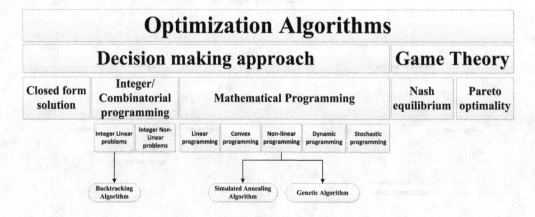

to be integers, such as modulation, channel allocation, and coding rate.

3. Furthermore, the last group of the decision making approaches is the mathematical programming that is used for most real-world optimization problems and can be divided into five major subfields, i.e. linear, convex, non-linear, dynamic and stochastic programming.

   a. Linear programming is used to determine a way to achieve the best solution in a given mathematical model for some list of requirements, represented as linear relationships, subject to linear equality and linear inequality constraints.

   b. The convex programming is based on convergence of the considered values towards the highest local value by exploiting the equality of the local and global optimum.

   c. The optimization process, involving non-linear objective functions and constraints, is called non-linear programming, where the key difference with the linear one is the inequality between the local optimum and the global optimum. One of the greatest challenges in non-linear programming is that several problems perform local optima. These situations are similar to the multiple peaks. It is difficult for an algorithm that tries to move from point to point only by climbing uphill, since the peak it achieves might not be the highest. Algorithms that propose to overcome this difficulty are termed as "global optimization" algorithms. Popular solutions for solving a non-linear programming problem are genetic algorithms and simulated annealing (Skiena, 2008) that are presented below in this section.

   d. Also, the dynamic programming approach solves a high complexity problem by combining the solutions of a series of low complexity sub-problems. Dynamic programming relies on the principle of optimality, which states that in an optimal sequence of decisions or choices, each subsequence must be optimal, too.

   e. The last subfield of mathematical programming is the stochastic programming, which is an optimization process that includes probabilistic elements in the problem formulation and refers to the minimization/maximization of a function in the presence of randomness in the optimization process.

On the other hand, for game theory approach, two groups of optimization solutions arise as it is illustrated in Figure 2:

1. Nash equilibrium, which is a solution concept of a non-cooperative game, involving two or more players. Each player is assumed to know the equilibrium strategies of the other players, and no player, has anything to gain by changing only his own strategy unilaterally (Osborne & Rubinstein, 1994). If each player has chosen a strategy and no player can benefit by changing his/her strategy while the other players keep theirs unchanged, then the current set of strategy choices and the corresponding payoffs constitute a Nash equilibrium.

2. Pareto optimality, where no one can be made better off without making at least one individual worse off. Given an initial allocation of goods among a set of individuals, a change to a different allocation that makes at least one individual better off without making any other individual worse off is called a Pareto improvement. An allocation is defined as

"Pareto efficient" or "Pareto optimal" when no further Pareto improvements can be made. Pareto efficiency is a minimal notion of efficiency and does not necessarily result in a socially desirable distribution of resources: it makes no statement about equality, or the overall well-being of a society (Barr, 2004; Sen, 1993).

At the remainder of this section, we emphasize on three specific algorithms namely backtracking, simulated annealing and genetic ones, as these seem to have the best applicability in the TVWS exploitation paradigm.

Based on the above, backtracking is a general algorithm for finding all possible solutions to some computational problem, that incrementally builds candidates to the solutions, and abandons each partial candidate ("backtracks") as soon as it determines that the partial candidate cannot possibly be completed to a valid solution. Backtracking can be applied only for problems, which admit the concept of a "partial candidate solution" and a relatively quick test of whether it can possibly be completed to a valid solution. Backtracking is often much faster than brute force enumeration of all complete candidates, since it can eliminate a large number of candidates with a single test. Backtracking is an important tool for solving constraint satisfaction problems, such as spectrum allocation in CR networks. Backtracking depends on user-given "black box procedures" that define the problem to be solved, the nature of the partial candidates, and how they are extended into complete candidates. In case of frequency allocation problem in CR, the algorithm generates all possible solutions based on the available network resources and secondary systems requests by repeatedly choosing an optimum spectrum allocation solution. It is therefore a meta-heuristic rather than a specific algorithm, although, unlike many other meta-heuristics, it is guaranteed to find

all solutions to a finite problem, avoiding both repetitions and missing solutions in a bounded timeframe.

On the other hand, Simulated Annealing (SA) is a heuristic computational technique derived from statistical mechanics for finding near globally-minimum-cost solutions to large optimization problems, which can be applied in a network resource allocation process. SA algorithm gives an initial solution in the solution set with objective value, searching its neighborhood for a solution of lower value, and repeating until no further improvement is possible. The final solution obtained is optimal within its neighborhood, or locally optimal. Neighbors of a solution are usually obtained by performing small transformations to it, called moves. The two main issues in local search are the design of effective neighborhood functions and the design of search strategies that are able to escape from poor local optima. In case of TVWS allocation, the SA algorithm tries to avoid local optima, thus creating and evaluating solutions, as a matter of spectrum utilization and spectrum fragmentation values/measurements.

Finally, Genetic Algorithms (GA) are search algorithms that operate via the process of natural evolution and selection. The algorithms are initiated with a sample set of potential solutions, which then evolve towards a set of more optimal solutions. Within the sample set, solutions that are poor tend to die out, while better solutions propagate their advantageous attributes, thus introducing more solutions into the set that feature greater potential. A random mutation process allows to guarantee that a set of potential allocation solution, in case of TVWS allocation problem, will not remain stagnant and it can be efficiently filled up with numerous copies of the same solution. Moreover, GA perform better than traditional optimization algorithms because they are capable to avoid local optima, by taking advantage of an entire set of solutions spread throughout the solution space.

3. TV WHITE SPACES ALLOCATION POLICIES

Although conceptually quite simple, the introduction of CR networks in TVWS represents a disruption to the current "command and control" paradigm of TV/UHF spectrum management, and therefore the exploitation of the pre-mentioned architectural/technological CR solutions is highly intertwined with the regulation models that would eventually be adopted. More specifically, command and control spectrum management regime is employed by the most regulators. This approach adopts that the regulators are the centralized authorities for radio spectrum allocation and usage decisions. The allocation decisions are often static in temporal and spatial dimensions, meaning that they are valid for extended periods of time (i.e. usually decades) and for large geographical regions (i.e. country wide). The usage of radio spectrum is often set to be exclusive, where each band is dedicated to a single network provider, maintaining interference free communication. Command and control spectrum management regime dates back when the technologies employed required interference-free mediums for achieving acceptable quality. Thus, it is often argued that the exclusive nature of the command and control approach is an artifact of outdated technologies. Among the envisaged regulation models are the "Real-time Secondary Spectrum Market" (or licensed policy) and the "Spectrum of Commons" (or unlicensed policy), as depicted in Figure 3.

The "Real-time Secondary Spectrum Market" (RTSSM) (or licensed policy) may be the most appropriate solution, especially for applications that require sporadic access to spectrum and for which QoS guarantees are important. RTSSM regime adopts spectrum trading, which allows primary users (license holders) to sell/lease spectrum usage rights and secondary players to buy them (license vendees), thereby establishing a secondary market for spectrum leasing and spectrum auction. The license holder runs an admission control algorithm, which allows secondary users to access spectrum only when QoS of both primary and secondary users is adequate. The trading of secondary use may also occur through intermediaries, such as a spectrum broker, exploiting radio resource management algorithms (RRM) for determining the frequency, at which a secondary user should operate along with the economics of such transactions. TVWS availability is provided by a geo-location spectrum database to spectrum broker for specific geographical locations. Secondary users, on the other hand, dynamically request access when-and-only-when spectrum is needed and are charged based on spectrum utilization basis, as a matter of types of services, access characteristics and QoS level

Figure 3. TVWS allocation policies

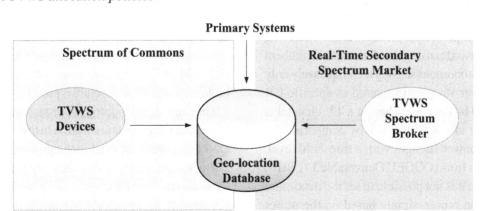

requests. The access types could consist of a long-term lease, a scheduled lease and a short-term lease or spot markets. Each type requires different discovery mechanisms and applies with different levels of service agreements.

On the other hand, "Spectrum of Commons" (or unlicensed policy), represents the case where coexistence with incumbent primary transmissions (e.g. DVB-T) is assured via the control of interference levels rather than by fixed spectrum assignment. In a "spectrum of commons" usage model there is no spectrum manager to preside over the resource allocation, similarly to the wireless ISM bands, where users have to fulfill the technical rules ensuring good coexistence, but do not need to negotiate with existing players. However, despite the fact that unlicensed spectrum promotes efficiency through sharing, QoS cannot be guaranteed, which is a serious problem especially for QoS-sensitive applications. Sensing techniques for reliable detection of TVWS and coexistence mechanisms for interference avoidance are the main technical challenge. Defining spectrum policies and etiquette rules to promote fairness and avoid the "tragedy of the commons" (Australian Communication & Media Authority, 2007) are also key challenges.

Spectrum sensing is a key functionality of cognitive radio systems that may incorporate power control mechanisms, able to dynamically adjust transmission power for an efficient exploitation of spectrum opportunities in TVWS. Therefore, the objective of sensing is to get reliable context information, in order to flexibly set the maximum transmission power per channel at the operating location to avoid causing interference to incumbent devices. Autonomous sensing techniques rely only on the power strength measured in specific CR locations. The decision whether a TV channel is occupied or idle is performed, by comparing the measured power strength with a threshold level. The analysis from (COGEU Deliverable 3.1, 2010) showed that it is not possible to set the maximum transmission power, simply based on the power

strength detected by the CR device. Therefore, a CR network may adopt a hybrid approach, where local sensing information is combined with geo-location database information to compute the TVWS spectrum pool.

There are several advantages for the use of geo-location information to support the detection of incumbent systems. The most important is that the database stores the required information to compute the TVWS spectrum pool available in a specific location. Information, such as DVB protected areas; specifications of DVB transmitters, advance propagation models, protection rules, can be used to compute the maximum transmission power. With a database, part of the complexity associated with sensing and maximum power computation is transferred to the core network, decreasing complexity and power demand of TVWS devices. The database has the ability to be dynamically updated and continuously adjust interference protection parameters in line with the evolution of incumbent standards, e.g. DVB-T2. In addition, TVWS spectral utilization efficiency is better than using sensing alone detection. This is primarily due to the ability of geo-location enabled TVWS devices to accurately determine protected service contours.

3.1. Proposed CR Framework for TVWS Exploitation Based on RTSSM Policy

The proposed approach considers a centralized topology with a Geo-location Spectrum database dealing directly with TVWS Devices (Spectrum of Commons policy) or with Spectrum Broker (RTSSM policy). An overview of the spectrum broker reference architecture is presented in Figure 4. The centralized topology approach was adopted as the most appropriate solution in this case, since QoS guarantee is crucial in the proposed system. Furthermore, such a centralized topology enables for radio spectrum trading, establishing a secondary market for spectrum leasing and spectrum

Figure 4. Reference architecture for commons and secondary TVWS trading

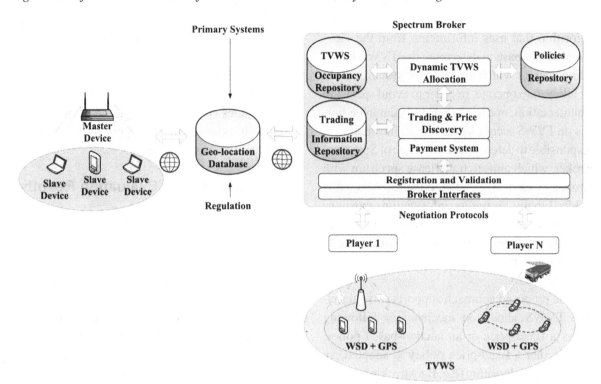

auction. Spectrum broker entity in this network topology controls the amount of bandwidth and power assigned to each secondary user, in order to keep the desired QoS and interference below the regulatory limits. In this reference model, the centralized broker is an intermediary between the Geo-location database (TVWS information supplier) and players that negotiate spectrum on behalf of spectrum users. The reference architecture supports both Spectrum of Commons and RTSSM.

More specifically, this approach supports a broker-based CR network architecture for the efficient exploitation of TVWS under the RTSSM regime and comprises of two core subsystems: a) a Spectrum Broker responsible for coordinating TVWS access and administrating the economics of radio-spectrum exploitation, and b) a number of Secondary Systems (i.e. mobile network operators and wireless network providers), competing/requesting for TVWS utilization. In particular, this network architecture consists of secondary systems that provide different services classes depending on the type of service, voice data, etc.

According to this architecture, Spectrum Broker consists of several sub-entities, such as a Payment System, a Dynamic TVWS Allocation Mechanism (RRM module), Trading and Price Discovery mechanism (Trading module), Registration and Validation mechanism and a number of repositories. More specifically, the TVWS occupancy repository obtains information from the national database, namely the Geo-location spectrum database, which includes data regarding the available TVWS in specific locations and the maximum allowable transmission power of secondary systems per channel, in order to avoid causing interference to primary systems. The TVWS occupancy repository creates a spectrum-portfolio, including all the above-mentioned information that is advertised to bidders. Moreover, the RRM module matches the secondary systems' requirements with available resources and thus allocates the TVWS based on QoS requirements. The TVWS allocation mechanism implements an algorithm that uses information from the Geolocation database to determine the TVWS bands and power, at which a secondary system should be allowed to operate, in order to avoid spectrum fragmentation, optimize QoS and guarantee fairness in TVWS access. Moreover, trading module is responsible to determine the revenue of Spectrum Broker, which aims to trade/lease spectrum with temporary exclusive rights to the most valuable bidder. Finally, the trading information repository hosts information about the TVWS selling/leasing procedure, as well as the spectrum-unit price to be exploited during the trading phase, creating a price-portfolio.

The proposed approach supports two alternative TVWS allocation mechanisms following either a fixed-price or an auction-based policy. In case that a fixed-price policy is adopted, an optimization algorithm (e.g. Backtracking, Simulated Annealing, Genetic Algorithm) obtains the best-matching/optimal solution by minimizing an objective function, as a matter of spectrum fragmentation and/or Secondary Systems' prioritization (e.g. in case that some secondary technologies must be served before others). Alternatively, in the auction-based policy, the spectrum broker collects bids from the secondary systems, and subsequently determines the allocation solution along with the price for each spectrum portion from a price portfolio in order to maximize the spectrum broker profit. The auction process is then being repeated as soon as spectrum portions are available.

On the other hand, the proposed approach considers two types of TVWS Devices (TVWSD or WSD), exploiting Spectrum of Commons policy. Master devices contact Geo-location spectrum database (see Figure 4) in order to obtain a set of available frequencies in their geographical location and Slave devices obtain the relevant information from master ones. The main information that needs to be communicated by master devices to

the geo-location database is expected to be location, location accuracy, expected area of operation (optional), coverage area, and device type. Moreover, technical information that is required to be transferred to the master devices originate from the Geo-location database and include available frequencies (minimum requirement), maximum transmit power and the appropriate national/regional database to consult.

3.2. Performance Evaluation Results

Towards verifying the validity of the proposed RRM algorithms and the capacity of the proposed CR network architecture for efficient TVWS exploitation and QoS provisioning within the RTSSM policy, a decision making process was implemented, by exploiting Simulated Annealing, Genetic Algorithms, Backtracking and Pruning algorithms. A number of several experimental tests was designed and conducted, under controlled-conditions (i.e. simulations) evaluating the performance of the above algorithms, as a matter of spectrum fragmentation and simulation time. The experimental test-bed consists of a TVWS Occupancy Repository, which keeps records about UHF/TV frequencies that can be utilized by LTE secondary systems. Information in this repository was built around actual/real spectrum data gathered within the framework of the ICT-FP7 "COGEU" project (COGEU, 2012), concerning TVWS availability between 626MHz (Ch.40) and 752MHz (Ch.60) around Munich in Germany. It should be noted that in the simulation tests that were conducted, fixed-price mode was selected, based on a single spectrum-unit price that was applied for every TVWS trading process.

In this context, the simulation scenario includes seven LTE secondary systems with different radio characteristics that were simultaneously competing for the available TVWS (see Figure 5) during 4 different time periods. LTE systems operate under Time-Division-Duplexing (TDD) mode, while a different QoS level was adopted for each

Figure 5. Time periods of simulation scenario

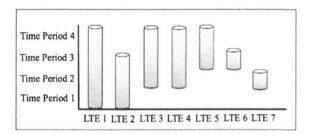

system, based on specific services requirements. This QoS level was respected, by the optimization algorithms for the fixed-price mode, during radio spectrum allocation process. Additionally, for each new simulation period (namely as Time Period in the experimental tests) secondary systems with different QoS expectation were entering the test-bed, under a fixed schedule, requesting access to the available (at the given Time Period) TVWS. The technical specifications of such LTE secondary systems are presented in Table 1.

From Table 1, it comes that there are two major types of services defined with guaranteed bit rate (GBR) and non-guaranteed bit rate (Non-GBR). GBR services are real-time applications, such as conversational voice and video, while Non-GBR services include P2P and Web applications. For a GBR service, a minimum amount of bandwidth is reserved by the proposed system and the network resources provision is guaranteed, by taking into account specific QoS requirements. GBR services should not experience packet losses or high latency in case of network congestion. On the other hand, Non-GBR services are provided under a best effort scheme and a maximum bit rate is not guaranteed on a per-service basis. Based on the above-mentioned simulation scenario, four time periods were defined as depicted in Figure 5.

Figure 6 depicts the performance evaluation results obtained in every time period for each RRM implementation. From the upper plot, it can be verified that all algorithms provide an acceptable fragmentation score, taking into account that: a)

the value "0" represents an "un-fragmented" spectrum, while when moving towards "1" spectrum becomes more-and-more fragmented, i.e. there exist many blocks of unexploited frequencies. The lower plot represents a qualitative comparison among Backtracking (with and without Pruning technique), Simulated Annealing and Genetic Algorithm, as a matter of the duration of the simulation before obtaining the optimum solution. From this plot, it can be observed that Simulated Annealing performs slightly better in comparison to the other algorithms, obtaining faster the best-matching solution in a shorter simulation time.

3.3. Applicability of the Proposed Solutions

Towards proving the applicability of the proposed solutions, a TVWS occupancy repository was implemented, acting as a geo-location database that holds information about secondary networks operating over TVWS around Munich area in Germany (COGEU Deliverable 3.1, 2010). The main objective is to keep the track of the allocated radio spectrum, provide data to the TVWS allocation mechanism for the provision of QoS to

Table 1. Technical specifications of each secondary system

Secondary System	Services Provided	Bandwidth (MHz)	Priority/ QoS Level
LTE 1	TCP-based services (GBR)	20	Medium
LTE 2	P2P (Non-GBR)	5	Low – Best Effort
LTE 3	Internet (Non-GBR)	20	Low – Best Effort
LTE 4	Video (GBR)	20	High
LTE 5	Video (GBR)	10	High
LTE 6	P2P (Non-GBR)	5	Low – Best Effort
LTE 7	Video (GBR)	5	Medium

Figure 6. Simulation results

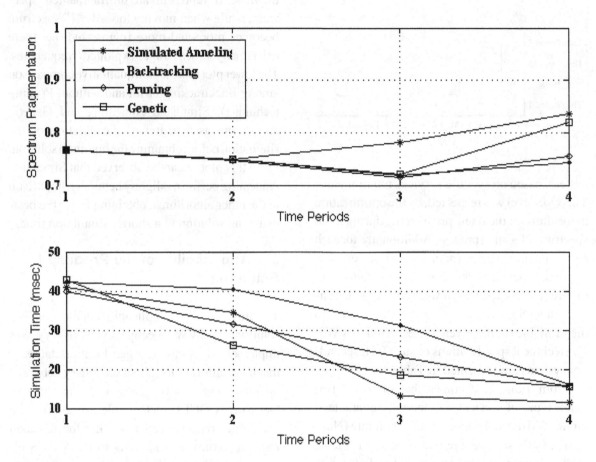

the secondary players in the relevant frequency bands and advertise the TVWS portfolio available for trading. The technical characteristics of the deployed secondary networks, operating in TVWS are stored in the repository. Such information entities are needed, in order to evaluate current and future requests from spectrum buyers (i.e. players). The repository is divided in three time periods, two during the day, and one for the night. During the day period, specific sites are on the market, and existing Mobile Network Operators can lease TVWS to operate extra LTE-downlink carriers. An auction-based approach is used for the day period. During the night period, spectrum demand is lower than spectrum supply; therefore the available TVWS are leased with a fix\benchmark price, for instance, to a wireless network operator that implements smart metering applications. The TVWS occupancy repository

is the unit that contains information on active TVWS networks and their operational parameters. The repository carries all information required to compute mutual interference between TVWS systems. This repository also hosts the methods to manage the database and generate events or reacts on external events relevant for the management of TVWS systems.

4. JOINT RADIO RESOURCE MANAGEMENT FOR HETEROGENEOUS RADIO ACCESS TECHNOLOGIES' EXTENSION OVER TVWS

The system operation is based on three layers/entities, as depicted in Figure 7, each one denoting a significant process for the resource allocation. The

Figure 7. Layers of system operation

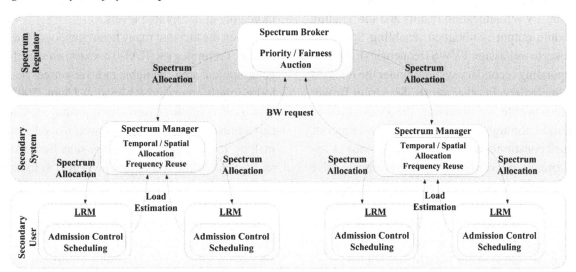

layers of the system consist of the Local Resource Manager (LRM), the Spectrum Manager (SM), and the Spectrum Broker (SB).

The LRM is responsible for the disposal/assignment of spectral resources within the area of each secondary system. More specifically, LRM calculates the required bandwidth needed for each class, taking into account the radio link operation and the traffic load. Depending on the requests sent by secondary users through the LRMs, the spectrum manager of each secondary system assigns to them the TVWS resources. Moreover, each spectrum manager sends information to the Spectrum Broker based on the requested bandwidth of each secondary system, the load handled, and the priority of classes. It also sends a negotiation request, in case that a secondary system requests for more bandwidth than the initial needs for bandwidth. The Spectrum Broker is responsible for conducting the spectrum allocation process, either utilizing a fixed-price or an auction-based approach, based on negotiations and requests for required bandwidth.

The Spectrum Broker of the proposed CR network architecture initially advertises data regarding spectrum portions that are available to be leased to secondary systems, as well as

relevant maximum allowable transmission power thresholds. This information originated from the Geo-location database, is hosted within the TVWS Occupancy Repository. Thus, the Spectrum Broker firstly advertises the spectrum-portfolio and the price-portfolio to the secondary systems, in order to be informed for the transmission characteristics and the call price of the TVWS spectrum. After this stage, bidders (i.e. secondary systems) send/define their needs/bids for the spectrum of interest, as well as the offered price, in case of auctions. Spectrum Broker collects all interests/bids and the dynamic TVWS allocation module analyzes and processes them as a matter of secondary systems technical requirements and the locally available TVWS channel characteristics (cf. Figure 4). For each spectrum portion/fragment, Spectrum Broker creates and maintains a list with interest/bids per time period, namely as auction-portfolio, in order to choose the most valuable bidder for each specific time slot, in case of auction process, or to assign TVWS to secondary systems that cause the least spectrum fragmentation, in case of fixed-price. The auction portfolio is also analyzed/elaborated by Trading Module, taking into account a spectrum-unit price or call price (e.g. cost per MHz) that is based on spectrum-auction policies.

Finally, an optimized solution combining the dynamic TVWS allocation results and the Trading Module output is obtained, enabling Spectrum Broker to sell/assign TVWS frequencies to the corresponding secondary systems under the RTSSM regime/policy. In other words, Spectrum Broker is responsible for obtaining the best-matching solution, through an optimization-based process, which constitutes a NP-hard problem, thus an approximation algorithm is required in order to solve either the fixed-price or the auction-based process.

Even though optimized TVWS spectrum allocation policies have to be adopted from a business logic point of view, dynamic joint radio resource management (JRRM) techniques need also to be implemented at the Local Resource Manager (LRM) level. As shown in Figure 7, each secondary system, via its Spectrum Manager module, allocates the required spectrum to its LRM entities and the latter serve all the mobile end users being in a specific geographical area. More specifically, secondary systems can be considered LTE, WiMAX, WiFi, HSPA, GSM systems etc, while at the secondary user level (cf. Figure 7), each LRM is deployed in one of the heterogeneous radio access technologies' (RATs) base stations. For example, in Figure 7, the first spectrum manager entity depicted at the left hand side, could reside in an LTE system, which serves many geographical areas by its corresponding e-NodeBs. In each e-NodeB, a LRM entity is deployed mainly dealing with interference management, admission control and scheduling issues. The second spectrum manager entity depicted at the right hand side could represent a WiMAX system following the same rationale with the pre-mentioned LTE system. LRM entities, apart from implementing admission control and scheduling algorithms, send feedback to their inter-related spectrum managers, too. This context information being delivered enables the LRM entities to provide optimal QoS/QoE services to the mobile end users and the whole proposed CR network

architecture to keep the network key performance indicators at acceptable levels.

Given the fact that many heterogeneous Radio Access Technologies (RATs) coexist in a specific geographical area, available radio resources need to be jointly managed (Falowo & Chan, 2008). When radio resources are jointly managed, joint call admission control algorithms are needed for making radio access technology selection decisions. Scheduling techniques need also to follow context-aware mobile and wireless networking (CAMoWiN) principles (Makris et al., in press). In the following two sections (i.e. sections 5 and 6), a thorough overview of the state-of-the-art admission control and scheduling algorithms and techniques are presented. These JRRM techniques are complementary to the ones being adopted at the spectrum broker and spectrum manager layers and have already been discussed in the previous sections. The main differential feature of the JRRM techniques being implemented at the LRM level, is that the decision making procedures should be extensively dynamic since decision loops take place even every 1 ms (e.g. LTE-A scheduler). As discussed in section 3, other CR-related phases are also included and interconnected with RRM modules and these are network monitoring, context acquisition, TVWS carrier's assessment, trading and price discovery modules etc. These phases can be carried out in larger time intervals (e.g. every one hour/day) as they are more business logic oriented and thus decision making procedures are made within a timeframe of several hours, days or even months (e.g. spectrum allocation policies, accounting strategies, policies for personalization services, etc). Even though self-organized networking (SON) principles are gaining ground via 3GPP LTE-A latest standardization activities (3GPP, 2011), there are a lot of things to be done by the research community until all RRM-related processes of the proposed CR network architecture become cognitive.

In the following two sections of this book chapter, we discuss on the two main components of the

Local Resource Manager, namely the Admission Control and the Packet Scheduling procedures. Through a brief survey of the related literature, we identify the main features that each of these components should have, as well as potential building blocks for their implementation.

5. CONTEXT AWARE JOINT ADMISSION CONTROL AND RESOURCE PARTITIONING TECHNIQUES

According to the descriptions having been made in the previous section regarding the LRM functionalities (Figure 7) and specifically the joint call admission control (JCAC)-related operations (Figure 8), we will further present a classification of JCAC techniques being applicable in heterogeneous wireless access networks emphasizing in emerging cognitive and context-aware enhancements recently proposed in the international literature. Based on the efficient TVWS exploitation paradigm presented in this book chapter, when radio resources are allocated to LRM entities, JCAC schemes are needed in order radio resources

to be jointly managed. JCAC is a major category of JRRM and is responsible for deciding whether an incoming call/service can be accepted or not and which of the available radio access networks (RANs) is/are most suitable to accommodate the incoming call/service. The decision strategy for the admission of new connections consists of guaranteeing that the sum of the minimum rate requirements of all accepted connections does not surpass specific thresholds. This strategy guarantees that the resources available to the scheduler (cf. section 6) are sufficient to provide the QoS requirements for all accepted connections. The major factors that need joint management from a JCAC perspective are: a) multiple heterogeneous RATs (cf. section 4), b) multiple user groups with diversified priorities and needs, and c) multiple service groups with diversified QoS requirements. Furthermore, the major network key performance indicators that have to be taken into account and are the objectives of JCAC in cognitive networking are (Falowo & Chan, 2008): a) guarantee QoS/QoE requirements (data rate, delay, jitter, PER, BER) of accepted calls/services, b) minimize call blocking and dropping probabilities, c) maximize operators' revenues, d) maximize radio resource

Figure 8. The main components of the local resource manager

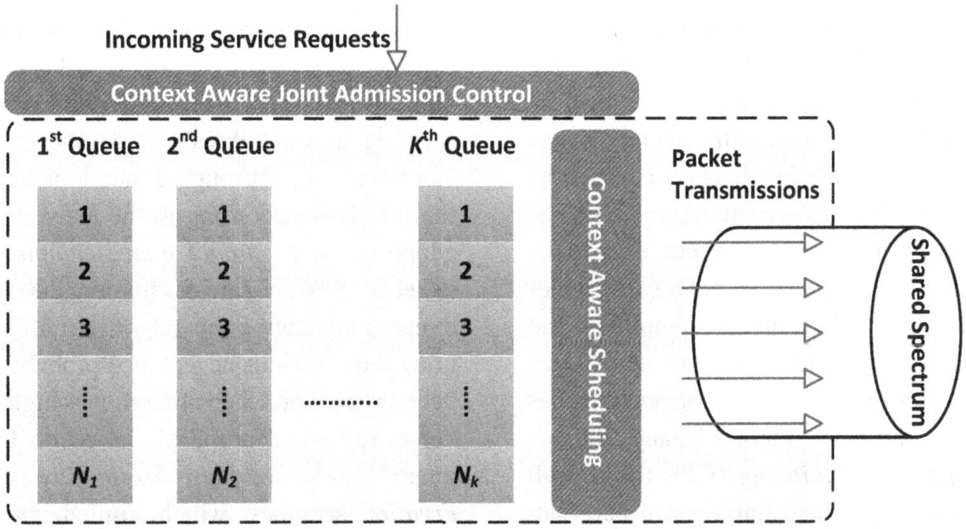

utilization, e) maximize user satisfaction by granting additional resources beyond those required in the initial AC process, f) minimize the number of handoffs from one RAT to another, and g) uniform distribution and balancing of the total network load. From the above, it can be easily inferred that there are trade-offs when trying to satisfy some of the pre-referred objectives. As already mentioned in section 2.2, multi-objective decision making rationale can be applied in such kind of problems. In this section, we further elaborate on various partitioning techniques ending up by describing a roadmap for future JCAC implementations being applicable in next generation networking environments (e.g. 3GPP heterogeneous networks (HetNets), mobile cloud, etc). Partitioning refers to various algorithmic techniques that can be applied to a pool of resources trying to fulfill multiple and diversified objectives. In the following, complete sharing, complete partitioning, hybrid/virtual partitioning and advanced related context-aware approaches are described.

5.1. Complete Sharing and Complete Partitioning

Complete Sharing (CS) is the most trivial technique and considers one unique pool of resources, which is common for all combinations of user groups, service groups, and available RATs. A new call is admitted into the system, if there are adequate resources from the unique common pool, otherwise it is rejected. That is, when the total network resources get to their limits, a new call will be blocked while a handoff call will be dropped. CS is a First-Come-First-Served (FCFS) non-prioritization scheme and thus adopts the simplest resource allocation policy. Its major advantages are implementation simplicity and high radio resource utilization. However, CS does not provide any QoS differentiation and thus has poor QoS performance (Fang & Zhang, 2002).

In *Complete Partitioning* (CP), the overall resources are partitioned into several parts ac-

cording to a combination of RAN, user group and service type and a new call request is rejected, if the resource mapped to the corresponding combination is used up (Chen et al., 2006). In other words, by the term "partitioning", we mean that a fixed capacity is allocated to each combination and thus no resources from one partition can be allocated to more than one combination. The size of each partition is defined according to a priori knowledge that the system already acquires taken from extensive past statistical measurements. From this kind of measurements, various mobility and load traffic patterns are derived and thus a good calculation of the size of each fixed partition can be done. Whenever a radical change in JCAC-related key performance indicators is observed, a network administrator can manually calibrate various parameters assuring the system's proper operation. The main advantage of CP is that it has good QoS performance and ensures the fairness of different priority calls, but due to the fixed partition policy, the radio resource utilization can be severely decreased. Another main drawback is that there is no elasticity/dynamicity in the size of the partitions and no intelligence is included in the JCAC process.

Towards providing more intelligence in both CS and CP schemes, many algorithmic proposals have been made in the literature during the last decade. *Guard channel* is one of the earliest techniques and it proposes to reserve some extra capacity for prioritized calls (e.g. handoff calls, high-priority user/service groups, etc) by implementing a static threshold. Higher utilization can be achieved through dynamic adaptation of the threshold according to the network state by adopting the *fractional guard channel* scheme (Li et al, 2004; Niyato & Hossain, 2005). As the dynamic adaptation depends on the radio resource utilization, various acceptance probabilities can become smaller, when utilization is high and vice versa. Enhanced proposals based on fractional guard channel are *multi-threshold resource reservation* schemes, which implement multiple dynamic thresholds in order to assign different priorities to multiple combinations of service calls (Ogbonmwan & Li, 2006; Makris & Skianis, 2008). *Thinning* algorithms (Fang, 2003) follow the same rationale by supporting multiple types of services and calculating the admission probability based on the priority and the current traffic situation. Finally, in *queuing priority* schemes, when utilization reaches 100%, high-priority calls are queued and are served when some radio resources become available. In this case, the queuing delay has to be inter-related with other types of delay imposed by scheduling process (cf. section 6). The main drawback of queuing priority scheme is that is needs a lot of buffers to deal with real-time multimedia traffic. It also needs a sophisticated scheduling mechanism in order to meet the QoS requirements of delay-sensitive calls (Falowo & Chan, 2008).

5.2. Hybrid and Virtual Partitioning

The problem with CS and CP schemes is that they are not flexible enough in order to cope with all emerging JCAC challenges (e.g. multi-homing, innovative mobile services/business models, etc). Nowadays, users' demands are not only restricted in enjoying different types of services from various heterogeneous RATs but they continuously and increasingly demand for more flexibility and elasticity in order their QoE to be enhanced. Innovative business models are also pushing towards this direction as an individual user may have more than one profile according to the mobile device he/she uses, his/her location, etc. As a result, the number of the corresponding combinations referred in section 5.1 has become very large and conventional partitioning schemes cannot handle the incurred algorithmic complexity.

Hybrid/virtual partitioning is a JCAC scheme, which manages to combine the advantages of CS and CP and strikes a balance between unrestricted sharing in CS and unrestricted isolation in CP. More specifically, hybrid/virtual partitioning

scheme behaves like unrestricted sharing when the overall traffic is light and like complete isolation when the overall traffic is heavy. Hence, the best characteristics of CS and CP under different loadings are combined (Yao et al., 2004). The general structure of a partition in hybrid/virtual partitioning is explicitly explained in (Skoutas et al., in press). More specifically, each partition has two main parts namely the "commonly shared" and the "reserved" area. Each partition is allowed to accept "external" service calls (i.e. calls which were initially aimed to be served by other partitions). However, this has to be performed in a controlled manner in order to prevent the flooding of the partitions with external calls. While an "external" service call can be placed only at the commonly shared area, a "native" service call (i.e. a call which is mapped to be served by the specific partition) can be placed in any of the defined areas. By considering a dynamically changing reservation factor, the "commonly shared" area of the partition can be obtained by subtracting the "reserved" area capacity from the total capacity of the partition. As a result, as the reservation factor increases, the "commonly shared" area decreases thus accepting fewer "external" service calls and vice versa. It has to be noted that an accompanied preemption scheme is needed in order the robustness of the overall hybrid/virtual partitioning scheme to be supported. Hence, the main drawback is that the preemption scheme may lead to lower utilization.

Towards confronting this drawback, many supplementary algorithmic proposals have been made. *Spillover-partitioning* algorithms are proposed in (Yilmaz et al., 2010), where utilization is improved by sharing certain partitions among different service calls. *QoS degradation* (Niyato & Hossain, 2005; Chou & Shin, 2004; Wan et al., 2005) is also a well-known technique and is used in situations of network congestion. For example, when the network becomes congested, the amount of bandwidth allocated to some of the ongoing calls (also called degradable calls) is revoked to accommodate more incoming calls so that call dropping/blocking probabilities can be maintained at the target level without affecting resource utilization maximization targets. In case of light traffic load, some revenue maximization algorithms have been proposed such as (Chen et al., 2006). In order to increase the resources utilization, some calls (also called upgradable) can be allocated with more resources. A typical example is Web browsing or file downloading. In this scenario, the mobile user can enjoy better QoS (by first giving his consent for being excessively charged) and at the same time the operator can increase its revenues.

5.3. Advanced Context-Aware Approaches

As previously described, hybrid/virtual partitioning family of JCAC techniques seems be able to adequately and simultaneously satisfy most of the JCAC-related objectives in cognitive networking (Falowo & Chan, 2008). However, research community envisions even more challenges regarding the future-networking continuum, which need to be addressed. For example, JCAC-related architectural innovations proposed by various IEEE standards like P1900.4 (IEEE P1900.4, 2008) and 802.21 (IEEE Standard 802.21, 2009) stress the need for dealing with distributed radio resource usage optimization issues from an overall system perspective. Radio resource management in LTE-Advanced networks including related emerging challenges in HetNets (Lopez-Perez et al., 2011), machine-to-machine communications (M2M) (Zheng et al., 2012), device-to-device communications (D2D) (Yu et al., 2011) and cooperative communications (Elkourdi & Simeone, 2011) are also fields of research that are continuously gaining ground. Finally, novel JCAC principles have to be stressed for mobile cloud computing environments as the idea of integrating cloud computing into heterogeneous mobile and wireless networking is promising, too (Makris et al., 2012; Hoang et al., 2012).

Regarding the afore-mentioned JCAC-related architectural innovations, the main objective is to define an appropriate system architecture and protocols, which will facilitate the optimization of radio resource usage by exploiting context information exchanged between network and mobile terminals, regardless of their support for multiple simultaneous links and dynamic spectrum access. The "Distributed Radio Resource Usage Optimization" use case introduced in (IEEE P1900.4, 2008), contains many cognitive and context-aware JCAC-related building blocks, while reconfiguration and self-management features play a critical role, too.

Regarding LTE-Advanced innovations, the main breakthrough lies in the fact that the case of mobile terminals (MTs) being directly (i.e. via one hop) connected to base stations (BSs) of heterogeneous RATs in order to acquire access to services is not a panacea. In fact, many wireless/wired nodes can be relays of information, while small base stations (e.g. femtocells) can operate as relays, too (Elkourdi & Simeone, 2011). Moreover, the concepts of M2M and D2D communications introduce the idea of MTs communicating directly with each other over M2M/D2D links, while remaining control under BSs. Due to this potential, location-aware and geo-referenced services can be developed and thus novel JCAC design has to be adopted.

In mobile cloud computing/networking, the main novelty feature, which has to be stressed is that a JCAC framework has to simultaneously take into account both: a) wireless/radio access resources pool and b) computing resources pool for data processing/storage aiming at flexible virtualized infrastructure sharing solutions. That is, there is no sense in allocating only networking resources to MTs, because there may not be corresponding sufficient computing resources to support the ongoing calls/services. Finally, joint design and optimization of access and backhaul is needed and hence JCAC modules have to be accordingly enhanced.

6. CONTEXT AWARE SCHEDULING TECHNIQUES

Following the centralized spectrum sharing model described at section 4, the spectrum distribution to the secondary systems is based on a dynamic negotiation procedure, which involves the Local Resource Manager, the Spectrum Manager and the Spectrum Broker. Thus, the spectrum available to the end users of a secondary system is periodically adapted to their requirements in a cognitive manner by utilizing either a fixed-price or an auction-based approach. As discussed at the previous section, within each secondary system a CAC scheme should be employed in order to maintain the traffic load within a manageable range, while a packet scheduling mechanism is responsible for the efficient sharing of the available capacity among the ongoing traffic flows.

This centralized dynamic spectrum approach can only be used with infrastructure based wireless networks, where a central controller is able to coordinate the spectrum access of the secondary users. Consequently, the most likely candidates for the exploitation of TVWS under this scheme are Mobile Broadband Wireless Networks (MBWN) such as LTE and Mobile WiMAX which, despite their diverse origin, are slowly converging towards the same design goals. Regarding the packet transmission process, MBWNs have adopted similar features, such as Fast Scheduling, Hybrid ARQ (HARQ) and Adaptive Modulation and Coding (AMC) and as a result, it is feasible to identify a theoretical scheduling framework with wide applicability (Skoutas & Rouskas, 2010).

The main trade-off when designing a context aware scheduling mechanism is between the speed and accuracy of decision making. In general, the scheduler's computational complexity and the optimality of the scheduling decisions are both reduced when decreasing the amount of the information that is required for each scheduling decision. While low computation complexity is essential for supporting the fast scheduling feature of mobile broadband and wireless networks (MBWNs), it is expected that future context aware scheduling schemes will be required to process increasingly more data. In order to circumvent this problem we have to define heuristic scheduling disciplines which will help us to avoid, to the extent possible, the use of computationally expensive, exhaustive search algorithms (Skoutas & Rouskas, 2009).

Another important trade-off that should be considered when designing a wireless scheduler is the one between the efficient utilization of the available bandwidth and the fair sharing of resources among the users. In wireless networks it is always more efficient, in terms of system's throughput, to share the bandwidth only among users with good channel conditions. However, this policy can be proven to be highly unfair for users that experience low SINR (Signal to Interference plus Noise Ratio) for extended time periods. Therefore, the scheduler should be able to maximize the utilization of the bandwidth and at the same time to maintain fairness among all users by utilizing compensation mechanisms (Capozzi et al., in press).

Furthermore, the scheduler should be capable of providing different QoS levels to the current and future applications and services. This feature is very important as we move towards all-IP network architectures, which, inherently, are not well suited for QoS demanding services. The QoS is usually expressed as a set of minimum or maximum allowable values for specific metrics such as end-to-end latency, jitter, Bit Error Rate (BER) and minimum guaranteed bit rate. With the advent of cognitive networks, more network metrics are made available, enabling thus the scheduling mechanism to provide personalized services and take into account constraints such as energy consumption. In the following, we will briefly discuss the evolution of packet scheduling from a simple fair capacity sharing problem in the first network deployments to a multi-parameter optimization problem in current context aware wireless networks.

6.1. Fundamental Scheduling Disciplines

The first scheduling schemes were designed for low QoS demanding services, which were transmitted over wireline networks. Therefore, the goal they had to accomplish was the equal sharing of the available capacity among the end users. The Round Robin (RR) approach, which aims to assign the shared channel for equal amount of time to each traffic flow is a typical example of this category of schedulers. RR can be combined with a Resource Preemption (RP) mechanism in order to achieve QoS differentiation between low priority and high priority traffic flows (Capozzi et al., in press).

Generalized Processor Sharing (Parekh & Gallager, 1993) is a more advanced scheduling discipline, which aims to provide differentiated allocation of the available capacity among the ongoing traffic flows. According to the GPS discipline, each traffic flow receives at each scheduling period a fraction of the total capacity, which is proportional to a positive real number (weight) assigned to the flow. While GPS is more efficient that RR and RP, it cannot be applied to real networks as it assumes that the transmitted packet traffic is infinitely divisible. The Weighted Round Robin (WRR) scheduler (Fattah & Leung, 2002) is a simple and realistic approximation of the GPS scheduling discipline. According to WRR, the number of transmitted packets from each non-empty queue is proportional to the respective weight of the queue. However, the use of WRR can be problematic when the size of the data packets is variable. A better approximation of GPS for packet transmission is Packet by Packet GPS (PGPS), also known as Weighted Fair Queuing (WFQ) (Fattah & Leung, 2002), which emulates the GPS operation. Specifically, PGPS emulates a hypothetical GPS server and on each packet arrival, a virtual service time is calculated according to the GPS discipline. Then, the packets from different flows are sequenced and arranged for transmission in increasing order of their virtual departure times. The Earliest Due Date (EDD) scheduler (Capozzi et al, in press) is a scheme able to provide QoS differentiation based on packet delay. EDD associates each incoming packet with a deadline and then it serves the packets following an increasing order of their respective deadlines. Shortest Time to Extinction (STE) (Panwar et al., 1988) is a scheduling discipline similar to EDD, which discards the packets that exceed their deadlines instead of keeping them in the queue.

The abovementioned scheduling schemes are able to provide a basic form of QoS differentiation together with a worst-case delay guarantee in the case of leaky bucket constrained sources. However, as they are designed for wireline networks, they are not aware of the variations of the wireless channel capacity and therefore they cannot be directly applied to wireless networks.

6.2. Wireless Channel Aware Scheduling Schemes

Moving in the era of wireless networks, the scheduler designers tried to transfer the wireline scheduling disciplines in the wireless environment. Thus, for example, the GPS discipline was evolved towards this direction, producing a class of Wireless Fair Queuing (WiFQ) schemes such as Channel condition Independent Fair Queuing algorithm (CIF-Q), Idealized Wireless Fair Queuing algorithm (IWFQ) and Server Based Fairness Approach (SBFA) (Fattah & Leung, 2002). The main idea behind all these schemes is the same; a GPS based scheduler is emulated in an error free environment and used as a reference model for the actual rate allocation. A compensation mechanism ensures that flows, which are lagging in comparison to their error-free service model will be compensated in the subsequent scheduling periods.

Credit Based (CB) schemes (Kam et al., 2001) are also developed for the sharing of a wireless channel and their scheduling discipline of resembles, in a sense, to that of Wireless Fair Queuing. The CB schemes assign to each ongoing traffic flow a guaranteed transmission rate, which, as in WFQ, is a fraction of the available capacity. The service priority of the flows is then defined based on a priority variable, which is called the credit. The credit of each flow is calculated as the difference between the amount of data that should have been transmitted (i.e. error free service model), and the actual amount of data that has been transmitted so far from the specific flow. All the schemes that are following rate-based disciplines, such as CB and WFQ, are able to provide data rate guarantees to the ongoing connections as long as a perfect power control is assumed.

Following a similar evolutionary path as GPS, the earliest due date (EDD) scheduling discipline has been introduced to the wireless environment through the Feasible-EDD (FEDD) scheme (Shakkottai & Srikant, 2002). As a variant of EDD, FEDD transmits at each scheduling period the packets with the lowest deadlines; however, in contrast to EDD, it does not consider all the ongoing traffic streams but only those with good channel conditions. A Proactive variant of EDD (PEDD) (The et al., 2003) takes into account expected future changes in the state of the wireless channel and adjusts accordingly the packet's deadline. A main disadvantage of both FEDD and PEDD is that they assume ideal knowledge of the channel conditions. Thus, Realistic PEDD (R-PEDD) and R-PEDD+ (Kong & Teh, 2004) pointed out the need for separate probing mechanisms for the acquisition of the required channel information.

The scheduling schemes of this category are adapted to the wireless environment and are able to provide QoS differentiation. Nevertheless, they are still missing important features and they cannot be directly applied to the current and future mobile wireless broadband networks.

6.3. Context Aware Scheduling Schemes

Since the advent of MBWNs, applications and services were classified into QoS classes according to the delay sensitivity of the corresponding traffic, and hence it has become apparent that future packet schedulers should be able to support delay based QoS differentiation. Another fundamental feature of MBWNs is fast scheduling, which dictates that the scheduling decisions should be performed in a fast and accurate manner. Moreover, a scheduler should be aware of the Channel State Information (CSI) in order to able to select at each transmission interval the proper modulation scheme that offers the required Bit Error Rate (BER). Hence, a modulation scheme with reduced constellation can be used over noisy channels while a higher constellation modulation scheme can be used when the channel conditions are good, providing thus increased data rates. The conclusion that emerges from the above is that the early wireless scheduling schemes discussed previously, are not suitable for the current and future MBWNs. Rate based algorithms such as WiFQ cannot be used in MBWNs because they are not able to provide delay based QoS differentiation while others which can provide such kind of QoS differentiation (i.e. FEDD, PEDD and R-PEDD) are too complex and their use can be problematic.

A scheduling algorithm with Dynamic Priority Assignment (DPA), proposed in (Skoutas & Rouskas, 2009) is one of the first approaches that aimed to combine all the required characteristics of a MBWN scheduler and at the same time to provide a deterministic delay bound to each connection. DPA is aware: a) of the available shared capacity, b) the number of queued packets at each queue, c) the state of the wireless path and d) the available transmission power. DPA utilizes the processing gain of CDMA networks instead of AMC in order to achieve the required BER. Dynamic Hybrid Scheduler (DHS) (Skoutas & Rouskas, 2010) is a more generalized scheduling approach that

.

utilizes AMC and extends the DPA discipline so that it can be applied to the most of the currently evolving broadband wireless technologies.

More recent approaches (Piro et al., 2011; Esmailpour & Nasser, 2011) exploit the concept of combining scheduling disciplines in a two level scheduling process which offers a more accurate and effective handling of the shared capacity. Thus, the desired QoS can be preserved together with a better utilization of the available resources. Furthermore, one could additionally consider multi-cell scheduling aiming to achieve efficient resource allocation and inter-cell interference mitigation in multi-cell environments. At (Pateromichelakis et al., in press), the evolution of interference management techniques is studied and their common features and differences are discussed. Scheduling in relay assisted MBWNs is also a topic that becomes to draw the attention of the scientific community. Future scheduling schemes should be aware of the characteristics of the upcoming relay enhanced cellular networks. Centralized schemes (Salem et al., 2010) as well as fully distributed scheduling algorithms (Suzhi & Zhang, 2012) have been recently presented in the related literature aiming to reduce outage probability and preserve user fairness, which is crucial in such environments. Finally, one should also consider the need for more energy-efficient wireless communications. At (Feng-Seng et al., 2012), a scheme that reduces the energy consumption at the mobile terminal by scheduling its transmissions into fewer time slots is proposed while at (Wang et al., 2012) a number of techniques that can be employed in future green mobile networks are presented.

7. FUTURE RESEARCH DIRECTIONS

This section discusses emerging research trends providing insightful considerations about the future of cognitive networks and self-adaptive communication systems from the perspective of

efficient TVWS exploitation paradigm. Several related ongoing projects co-funded by the EU Commission pave the way for new research innovations in the future. Apart from COGEU project's concepts (COGEU, 2012), which are presented in this book chapter, QUASAR (QUASAR, 2012), QoSMOS (QoSMOS, 2012) and SACRA (SACRA, 2012) projects provide future roadmaps regarding JRRM challenges for TVWS exploitation paradigm. More specifically, COGEU project proposes: a) JRRM techniques to optimize spectrum utilization, minimize interference, guarantee fairness in TVWS access and integrate QoS aspects in dynamic spectrum management, b) ways that reliable data delivery can be realized by routing and transport protocols across regions of different spectrum availability, and c) protocols that will allow system players to efficiently negotiate spectrum information parameters with a centralized spectrum broker. QUASAR provides specific and reasoned proposals to go beyond the current regulatory frameworks defined in specifications of various federated organizations such as FCC (Federal Communications Commission) in USA and CEPT-SE (Conference of Postal and Telecommunications Administrations Spectrum Engineering) in Europe, while many national regulators from the globe such as ACMA (Australia), KCC (Korea), Ofcom (UK), iDEA (Singapore) can exploit the project's recent research outcomes, too. Regarding JRRM concepts, QUASAR proposes: a) a cognitive management architecture to implement decision-making processes as well as to support mobility and QoS provisioning at the radio access/link level and b) a cognitive spectrum management framework accompanied by corresponding RRM algorithms to optimize spectrum utilization. QoSMOS project main focus is to make use of technology and service neutral spectrum opportunistically. It proposes an overall TVWS exploitation framework applicable to both centralized and distributed CR architectures including: a) a cognitive manager for resource management (CM-RM) to manage the problem of efficiently enforcing QoS for coexisting heterogeneous wireless networks with intermittently available spectrum resources and b) a cognitive manager for spectrum management (CM-SM). SACRA project mainly focuses on physical-layer studies by designing hardware components to support the CR approach viewing the TVWS exploitation problem from an energy-efficient perspective, too. It proposes a cognitive RRM inner and outer loop architecture, which enables collection of key information from bands sensed by the SACRA sensing system to make decisions on data partitioning across spectrum bands and on resource allocation to secondary users within TVWS bands. JRRM rationale is also adopted to determine the amount of resources to allocate to each link via optimization algorithms enhanced by prediction and learning techniques.

In addition to the above-mentioned short-term future research directions, there are some longer-term future research insights incurred by the evolution of cognitive networks and TVWS exploitation paradigm. In (Wu, et al., 2012), a Cognitive Radio Cloud Networking (CRCN) model is proposed that is able to support CR access in TVWS. Making use of the flexible and vast computing capacity of the cloud, the proposed cloud infrastructure has virtually unlimited resources to collect, analyze, process, and coordinate the massive and dynamic CR communications activities. Moreover, a primitive CRCN prototype is presented, which integrates functions of cooperative spectrum sensing (CSS), dynamic spectrum access (DSA), mobility management and QoS provisioning on a unified cloud platform. Conclusively, scalable cloud-based CSS and JRRM schemes remain crucial to justify the feasibility of the envisioned CRCN concept in the support of large-scale public access.

Extensive research efforts are also expected to take place in the field of worldwide trends in regulation of secondary access to TVWS using CR techniques, as indicated in (Nekovee M. et al., 2012). Some of these regulatory trends are: a) elaboration on consensus points regarding CEPT

SE43 and FCC rules, b) geo-location databases versus cooperative spectrum sensing trade-off investigations, c) alternative options for secondary licensing, d) aggregate interference management in TVWS, and e) generalize TVWS exploitation paradigm to other potential candidates such as military and radar bands. In any case, all these regulation mentality shift needs to be jointly addressed by regulators, industry and academia.

Promising applicability area candidates for TVWS exploitation can also be machine-to-machine (M2M) and rural broadband communications as the state-of-the-art experience has indicated that white spaces are better suited to deploying new network infrastructures and not peer-to-peer communications (Webb W., 2012). In (Yan Z., 2012), the use of CR technology in M2M communications from different point of views, including technical, applications, industry support, and standardization perspectives is motivated. Cognitive M2M system coexistence in TVWS is a new research challenge, which needs careful design to ensure fair and efficient sharing among heterogeneous users, while JRRM concepts have to be effectively mapped to new network system design prerequisites.

8. CONCLUSION

Nowadays, cognitive radio is being intensively researched for proper access to the TV White Spaces, which become available on a geographical basis after the gradual switch-off of analogue TV and adoption of digital TV. Due to the excellent propagation conditions of the released UHF/VHF band, efficient TVWS exploitation paradigm is seen as an opportunity for new services and business. In the context of FP7 ICT COGEU project (COGEU, 2012), the general idea is to move away from the binary choice of optimizing current spectrum (not always possible) or buy new spectrum with exclusive rights (too costly) by including a third option, which is the secondary use of TVWS (e.g. new spectrum commons, real-time secondary spectrum market and auction-based market). In this book chapter, a centralized CR topology is proposed with a spectrum broker trading with various secondary systems. Various spectrum sharing models and TVWS allocation policies are also investigated. Apart from our proposed architectural innovations, we further focused on emerging JRRM challenges. Indeed, with the availability of TVWS and their temporary lease, the traditional concepts of network planning and RRM have to be significantly enhanced. More specifically, as TVWS extend the pool of available radio resources for every heterogeneous RAT, it is necessary to manage them on the general context of JRRM (i.e. new TVWS carriers and legacy carriers from each heterogeneous RAT). We emphasized on context-aware JCAC and joint scheduling techniques by providing a comprehensive classification of past, state-of-the-art and emerging algorithmic proposals having been made in the international literature. Means of advanced context-aware and cognitive approaches are also introduced regarding the applicability of novel JRRM design and development in emerging research fields, such as LTE-Advanced systems, cooperative communications and mobile cloud computing/networking environments. Hence, by reading this book chapter, researchers from both academia and industry can effectively identify technical challenges regarding their ongoing/future work on JRRM issues in a broad range of cognitive and context-aware mobile and wireless networking area.

ACKNOWLEDGMENT

The work presented in this chapter has been undertaken in the context of the project COGEU (Cognitive Radio Systems for Efficient Sharing of TV White Spaces in European Context). COGEU is a Specific Targeted Research Project (STREP) supported by the European 7th Framework Programme, Contract number ICT-248560, Project duration 1st January 2010 to 31st December 2012 (36 months). The authors would like to acknowledge the contributions of their colleagues from the COGEU consortium.

REFERENCES

Australian Communication and Media Authority (ACMA). (2007). *The economics of spectrum management: A review*. ACMA.

Barr, N. (2004). *Economics of the welfare state. New York*. USA: Oxford University Press.

Bourdena, A., Pallis, E., Kormentzas, G., & Mastorakis, G. (2012). A centralised broker-based CR network architecture for TVWS exploitation under the RTSSM policy. In *Proceedings of the 2nd IEEE Workshop on Convergence among Heterogeneous Wireless Systems in Future Internet (CONWIRE 2012)*. IEEE.

Bourdena, A., Pallis, E., Kormentzas, G., & Mastorakis, G. (2013). A prototype cognitive radio architecture for TVWS exploitation under the real time secondary spectrum market policy. *Physical Communication*.

Bourdena, A., Pallis, E., Kormentzas, G., Skianis, C., & Mastorakis, G. (2011). Real-time TVWS trading based on a centralised CR network architecture. In *Proceedings of the IEEE Globecom2011*. IEEE.

Capozzi, F., Piro, G., Grieco, L., Boggia, G., & Camarda, P. (2013). *Downlink packet scheduling in LTE cellular networks: Key design issues and a survey*. IEEE Communications Surveys & Tutorials.

Chen, I. R., Yilmaz, O., & Yen, I. L. (2006). Admission control algorithms for revenue optimization with QoS guarantees in mobile wireless networks. *Springer Wireless Personal Communications*, *38*(3), 357–376. doi:10.1007/s11277-006-9037-6.

Chou, C. T., & Shin, K. G. (2004). Analysis of adaptive bandwidth allocation in wireless networks with multilevel degradable quality of service. *IEEE Transactions on Mobile Computing*, *3*(1), 5–17. doi:10.1109/TMC.2004.1261813.

Elkourdi, T., & Simeone, O. (2011). Femtocell as a relay: An outage analysis. *IEEE Transactions on Wireless Communications*, *10*(12), 4204–4213. doi:10.1109/TWC.2011.100611.102046.

Esmailpour, A., & Nasser, N. (2011). Dynamic QoS-based bandwidth allocation framework for broadband wireless networks. *IEEE Transactions on Vehicular Technology*, *60*(6), 2690–2700. doi:10.1109/TVT.2011.2158674.

FP7-ICT-248303 QUASAR Project. (n.d.). Retrieved from http://www.quasarspectrum.eu/

FP7-ICT-248454 QoSMOS Project. (n.d.). Retrieved from http://www.ict-qosmos.eu/

FP7-ICT-248560 COGEU Deliverable 3.1. (2010). *Use-cases analysis and TVWS systems requirements*. Retrieved December 2012 from http://www.ict-cogeu.eu/deliverables.html

FP7-ICT-248560 COGEU Project. (2012). *Cognitive radio systems for efficient sharing of TV white spaces in European context*. Retrieved from http://www.ict-cogeu.eu

FP7-ICT-249060 SACRA Project. (n.d.). Retrieved from http://www.ict-sacra.eu/

Falowo, O. E., & Chan, H. A. (2008). Joint call admission control algorithms: Requirements, approaches and design considerations. *Elsevier Computer Communications*, *31*(6), 1200–1217. doi:10.1016/j.comcom.2007.10.044.

Fang, Y. (2003). Thinning algorithms for call admission control in wireless networks. *IEEE Transactions on Computers*, *52*(5), 685–687. doi:10.1109/TC.2003.1197135.

Fang, Y., & Zhang, Y. (2002). Call admission control schemes and performance analysis in wireless mobile networks. *IEEE Transactions on Vehicular Technology*, *51*(2), 371–382. doi:10.1109/25.994812.

Fattah, H., & Leung, C. (2002). An overview of scheduling algorithms in wireless multimedia networks. *IEEE Wireless Communications*, *9*(5), 76–83. doi:10.1109/MWC.2002.1043857.

Feng-Seng, C., Kwang-Cheng, C., & Fettweis, G. (2012). Green resource allocation to minimize receiving energy in OFDMA cellular systems. *IEEE Communications Letters*, *16*(3), 372–374. doi:10.1109/LCOMM.2012.010512.2339.

3. GPP. (2011). *Technical specification group radio access network, evolved universal terrestrial radio access network (E-UTRAN), self-configuring and self-optimizing network (SON) use cases and solutions, TR 36.902, V9.3.1, release 9.*

Hoang, D. T., Niyato, D., & Wang, P. (2012). Optimal admission control policy for mobile cloud computing hotspot with cloudlet. In *Proceedings of the IEEE Wireless Communications and Networking Conference (WCNC)*. Paris, France: IEEE.

Hossain, E., Niyato, D., & Han, Z. (2009). *Dynamic spectrum access and management in cognitive radio networks*. Cambridge, UK: Cambridge University Press. doi:10.1017/CBO9780511609909.

IEEE P1900.4/D1.5. (2008). *Draft standard for architectural building blocks enabling network-device distributed decision making for optimized radio resource usage in heterogeneous wireless access networks*. IEEE.

IEEE Standard 802.21. (2009). *IEEE standard for local and metropolitan area networks-part 21: Media independent handover services*. IEEE.

Kam, A. C., Minn, T., & Siu, K. Y. (2001). Supporting rate guarantee and fair access for bursty data traffic in W-CDMA. *IEEE Journal on Selected Areas in Communications*, 19(11), 2121–2130. doi:10.1109/49.963799.

Kong, P. Y., & the, K. H. (2004). Performance of proactive earliest due date packet scheduling in wireless networks. *IEEE Transactions on Vehicular Technology*, 53(4), 1224–1234. doi:10.1109/TVT.2004.830942.

Li, B., Li, L., Li, B., Sivalingam, K. M., & Cao, X.-R. (2004). Call admission control for voice/data integrated cellular networks: performance analysis and comparative study. *IEEE Journal on Selected Areas in Communications*, 22(4), 706–718. doi:10.1109/JSAC.2004.825987.

Lopez-Perez, D., Guvenc, I., De La Roche, G., Kountouris, M., Quek, T. Q. S., & Zhang, J. (2011). Enhanced intercell interference coordination challenges in heterogeneous networks. *IEEE Wireless Communications Magazine*, 18(3), 22–30. doi:10.1109/MWC.2011.5876497.

Makris, P., & Skianis, C. (2008). Multi-scenario based call admission control for coexisting heterogeneous wireless technologies. In *Proceedings of IEEE GLOBECOM*. New Orleans, LA: IEEE.

Makris, P., Skoutas, D. N., & Skianis, C. (2012). On networking and computing environments' integration: A novel mobile cloud resources provisioning approach. In *Proceedings of the IEEE International Conference on Telecommunications and Multimedia (TEMU)*. IEEE.

Makris, P., Skoutas, D. N., & Skianis, C. (2013). *A survey on context-aware mobile and wireless networking: On networking and computing environments integration*. IEEE Communications Surveys & Tutorials. doi:10.1109/SURV.2012.040912.00180.

McHenry, M. A., McCloskey, D., & Lane-Roberts, G. (2004). *New York City spectrum occupancy measurements*. Shared Spectrum Company.

Mitola, J., III, & Maguire, G. Q. (1999). Cognitive radio: Making software defined radio more personal. In *Proceedings of the IEEE International Conference of Personal Communications*. IEEE.

Nekovee, M., Irnich, T., & Karlsson, J. (2012). Worldwide trends in regulation of secondary access to white spaces using cognitive radio. *IEEE Wireless Communications*, 19(4), 32–40. doi:10.1109/MWC.2012.6272421.

Niyato, D., & Hossain, E. (2005). Call admission control for QoS provisioning in 4G wireless networks: Issues and approaches. *IEEE Network Magazine*, 19(5), 5–11. doi:10.1109/MNET.2005.1509946.

Niyato, D., & Hossain, E. (2007). A game-theoretic approach to competitive spectrum sharing in cognitive radio networks. In *Proceedings of the Wireless Communications and Networking Conference, WCNC 2007*. Hong Kong: WCNC.

Niyato, D., & Hossain, E. (2008). Spectrum trading in cognitive radio networks: A market-equilibrium-based approach. *Wireless Communications*, 15(6).

OFCOM. (2008). *Digital dividend review: Geographic interleaved awards 470 - 550 MHz and 630 - 790 MHz consultation on detailed award design*. OFCOM.

Ogbonmwan, S. E., & Li, W. (2006). Multi-threshold bandwidth reservation scheme of an integrated voice/data wireless network. *Elsevier Journal on Computer Communications*, 29(9), 1504–1515. doi:10.1016/j.comcom.2005.09.007.

Osborne, M. J., & Rubinstein, A. (1994). *A course in game theory*. Cambridge, MA: MIT.

Panwar, S. S., Towsley, D., & Wolf, J. K. (1988). Optimal scheduling policies for a class of queues with customer deadlines to the beginning of service. *Journal of the ACM, 35*(4), 832–844. doi:10.1145/48014.48019.

Parekh, A. K., & Gallager, R. G. (1993). A generalized processor sharing approach to flow control in integrated services networks: The single-node case. *IEEE/ACM Transactions on Networking, 1*(3), 344–357. doi:10.1109/90.234856.

Pateromichelakis, E., Shariat, M., Quddus, A., & Tafazolli, R. (2013). *On the evolution of multicell scheduling in 3GPP*. IEEE Communications Surveys & Tutorials.

Piro, G., Grieco, L. A., Boggia, G., Fortuna, R., & Camarda, P. (2011). Two-level downlink scheduling for real-time multimedia services in LTE networks. *IEEE Transactions on Multimedia, 13*(5), 1052–1065. doi:10.1109/TMM.2011.2152381.

Salem, M., Adinoyi, A., Rahman, M., Yanikomeroglu, H., Falconer, D., & Young-Doo, K. et al. (2010). An overview of radio resource management in relay-enhanced OFDMA-based networks. *IEEE Communications Surveys & Tutorials, 12*(3), 422–438. doi:10.1109/SURV.2010.032210.00071.

Sen, A. (1993). Markets and freedom: Achievements and limitations of the market mechanism in promoting individual freedoms. *Oxford Economic Papers, 45*(4), 519–541.

Shakkottai, S., & Srikant, R. (2002). Scheduling real-time traffic with deadlines over a wireless channel. *Springer Wireless Networks, 8*(1), 13–26. doi:10.1023/A:1012763307361.

Skiena, S. S. (2008). *The algorithm design manual* (2nd ed.). Berlin: Springer. doi:10.1007/978-1-84800-070-4.

Skoutas, D. N., Makris, P., & Skianis, C. (2013). *Optimized admission control scheme for coexisting femtocell, wireless and wireline networks*. Springer Telecommunication Systems Journal.

Skoutas, D. N., & Rouskas, A. N. (2009). A scheduling algorithm with dynamic priority assignment for WCDMA systems. *IEEE Transactions on Mobile Computing, 8*(1), 126–138. doi:10.1109/TMC.2008.106.

Skoutas, D. N., & Rouskas, A. N. (2010). Scheduling with QoS provisioning in mobile broadband wireless systems. In *Proceedings of the European Wireless Conference (EW)*, (pp. 422-428). EW.

Suzhi, B., & Zhang, Y. J. A. (2012). Outage-optimal TDMA based scheduling in relay-assisted MIMO cellular networks. *IEEE Transactions on Wireless Communications, 11*(4), 1488–1499. doi:10.1109/TWC.2012.021512.111150.

The, K. H., Kong, P. Y., & Jiang, S. (2003). Proactive earliest due date scheduling in wireless packet networks. In *Proceedings of the International Conference on Communication Technology*, (pp. 816–820). ACM.

Wang, X., Vasilakos, A. V., Chen, M., Liu, Y., & Kwon, T. T. (2012). A survey of green mobile networks: Opportunities and challenges. *Springer Mobile Networks and Applications, 17*(1), 4–20. doi:10.1007/s11036-011-0316-4.

Wang, X. G., Min, G., Mellor, J. E., Al-Begain, K., & Guan, L. (2005). An adaptive QoS framework for integrated cellular and WLAN networks. *Elsevier Journal on Computer Networks, 47*(2), 167–183. doi:10.1016/j.comnet.2004.07.003.

Webb, W. (2012). On using white space spectrum. *IEEE Communications Magazine, 50*(8), 145–151. doi:10.1109/MCOM.2012.6257541.

Wu, S. H., Chao, H. L., Ko, C. H., Mo, S. R., Jiang, C. T., & Li, T. L. et al. (2012). A cloud model and concept prototype for cognitive radio networks. *IEEE Wireless Communications, 19*(4), 49–58. doi:10.1109/MWC.2012.6272423.

Yan, Z., Rong, Y., Nekovee, M., Yi, L., Shengli, X., & Gjessing, S. (2012). Cognitive machine-to-machine communications: visions and potentials for the smart grid. *IEEE Network, 26*(3), 6–13. doi:10.1109/MNET.2012.6201210.

Yao, J., Mark, J. W., Wong, T. C., Chew, Y. H., Lye, K. M., & Chua, K.-C. (2004). Virtual partitioning resource allocation for multiclass traffic in cellular systems with QoS constraints. *IEEE Transactions on Vehicular Technology, 53*(3), 847–864. doi:10.1109/TVT.2004.825746.

Yilmaz, O., Chen, I. R., Kulczycki, G., & Frakes, W. B. (2010). Performance analysis of spillover-partitioning call admission control in mobile wireless networks. *Springer Wireless Personal Communications, 53*(1), 111–131. doi:10.1007/s11277-009-9673-8.

Yu, C. H., Doppler, K., Ribeiro, C. B., & Tirkkonen, O. (2011). Resource sharing optimization for device-to-device communication underlaying cellular networks. *IEEE Transactions on Wireless Communications, 10*(8), 2752–2763. doi:10.1109/TWC.2011.060811.102120.

Zheng, K., Hu, F., Wang, W., Xiang, W., & Dohler, M. (2012). Radio resource allocation in LTE-advanced cellular networks with M2M communications. *IEEE Communications Magazine, 50*(7), 184–192. doi:10.1109/MCOM.2012.6231296.

ADDITIONAL READING

Akyldiz, I. F., Lee, W., Vuran, M. C., & Mohanthy, S. (2008). A survey on spectrum management in cognitive radio networks. *IEEE Communications Magazine, 46*(4), 40–48. doi:10.1109/MCOM.2008.4481339.

Anagnostopoulos, C., Tsounis, A., & Hadjiefthymiades, S. (2007). Context awareness in mobile computing environments: A survey. *Wireless Personal Communications, 42*(3), 445–464. doi:10.1007/s11277-006-9187-6.

Bellavista, P., Corradi, A., & Giannelli, C. (2011). A unifying perspective on context-aware evaluation and management of heterogeneous wireless connectivity. *IEEE Communications Surveys & Tutorials, 13*(3), 337–357. doi:10.1109/SURV.2011.060710.00060.

Bourdena, A., Mastorakis, G., Pallis, E., Mavromoustakis, C. X., Kormentzas, G., & Karditsis, E. (2012). A radio resource management framework for opportunistic TVWS access. In *Proceedings of the 1st ACM Workshop on High Performance Mobile Opportunistic Systems, HP-MOSys 2012*. Paphos, Cyprus: ACM.

Bourdena, A., Pallis, E., Kormentzas, G., & Mastorakis, G. (2012). A radio resource management framework for TVWS exploitation under an auction-based approach. In *Proceedings of the 8th International Conference on Network and Service Management, CNSM 2012*. CNSM.

Bourdena, A., Pallis, E., Kormentzas, G., Skianis, C., & Mastorakis, G. (2012). QoS provisioning and policy management in a broker-based CR network architecture. In *Proceedings of the IEEE Globecom2012*. IEEE.

Coutaz, J., Crowley, J. L., Dobson, S., & Garlan, D. (2005). Context is key. *ACM Communications Magazine, 48*(3), 49–53. doi:10.1145/1047671.1047703.

Deaton, J. D., Ahmad, S. A., Shukla, U., Irwin, R. E., DaSilva, L. A., & MacKenzie, A. B. (2012). Evaluation of dynamic channel and power assignment for cognitive networks. *Wireless Personal Communications, 62*(2), 277–290. doi:10.1007/s11277-010-0053-1.

Demestichas, P. (2010). Introducing cognitive systems in the wireless B3G world: Motivations and basic engineering challenges. *Elsevier Telematics and Informatics*, *27*(3), 256–268. doi:10.1016/j.tele.2009.08.002.

Feng, Z., Zhang, O., Tian, F., Tan, L., & Zhang, P. (2012). Novel research on cognitive pilot channel in cognitive wireless network. *Wireless Personal Communications*, *62*(2), 455–478. doi:10.1007/s11277-010-0064-y.

Fitch, M., Nekovee, M., Kawade, S., Briggs, K., & MacKenzie, R. (2011). Wireless service provision in tv white space with cognitive radio technology: A telecom operator's perspective and experience. *IEEE Communications Magazine*, *49*(3), 64–73. doi:10.1109/MCOM.2011.5723802.

Galani, A., Tsagkaris, K., & Demestichas, P. (2010). Information flow for optimized management of spectrum and radio resources in cognitive B3G wireless networks. *Springer Network and Systems Management*, *18*(2), 125–149. doi:10.1007/s10922-009-9150-4.

Galani, A., Tsagkaris, K., Koutsouris, N., & Demestichas, P. (2010). Design and assessment of functional architecture for optimized spectrum and radio resource management in heterogeneous wireless networks. *Wiley International Journal of Network Management*, *20*(4), 219–241.

IEEE P1900.4/D1.5. (2008). *Draft standard for architectural building blocks enabling network-device distributed decision making for optimized radio resource usage in heterogeneous wireless access networks*. IEEE.

Linehan, E., Tsang, S. L., & Clarke, S. (2008). *Supporting context-awareness: A taxonomic review*. TCD-CS-2008-37.

Ma, M., & Tsang, D. H. K. (2009). Joint design of spectrum sharing and routing with channel heterogeneity in cognitive radio networks. *Elsevier Physical Communication*, *2*(1-2), 127–137. doi:10.1016/j.phycom.2009.02.007.

Moltchanov, B., Mannweiler, C., & Simoes, J. (2010). *Context-awareness enabling new business models in smart spaces*. Berlin: Springer Verlag. doi:10.1007/978-3-642-14891-0_2.

Raychaudhuri, D., Jing, X., Seskar, I., Le, K., & Evans, J. B. (2008). Cognitive radio technology: From distributed spectrum coordination to adaptive network collaboration. *Elsevier Pervasive and Mobile Computing*, *4*(3), 278–302. doi:10.1016/j.pmcj.2008.01.004.

Saatsakis, A., & Demestichas, P. (2010). Context matching for realizing cognitive wireless networks segments. *Wireless Personal Communications*, *55*(3), 407–440. doi:10.1007/s11277-009-9807-z.

Wang, B., & Liu, K. J. R. (2011). Advances in cognitive radio networks: A survey. *IEEE Journal of Selected Topics in Signal Processing*, *5*(1), 5–23. doi:10.1109/JSTSP.2010.2093210.

Wu, Y., & Tsang, D. H. K. (2011). Joint bandwidth and power allocations for cognitive radio networks with imperfect spectrum sensing. *Wireless Personal Communications*, *57*(1), 19–31. doi:10.1007/s11277-010-0004-x.

Zhang, R., Liang, Y., & Cui, S. (2010). Dynamic resource allocation in cognitive radio networks - A convex optimization perspective. *IEEE Signal Processing Magazine*, *27*(3), 102–114. doi:10.1109/MSP.2010.936022.

KEY TERMS AND DEFINITIONS

Context Awareness (CA): CA refers, in general, to the ability of computing systems to acquire and reason about the context information and adapt the corresponding applications accordingly.

Dynamic Spectrum Management (DSM): DSM also referred to as dynamic spectrum access (DSA), is a set of techniques based on theoretical concepts in network information theory and game theory that is being researched to improve the performance of a wireless communication network and efficiently exploit radio spectrum resources.

Fragmentation Factor: Fragmentation factor defines the optimal spectrum usage over time in order to avoid that TVWS will be divided into discrete fragments.

Joint Call Admission Control (JCAC) Algorithms: JCAC algorithms are one subset of JRRM algorithms, which decide whether an incoming call can be accepted or not in a wireless access network. They also decide which of the available radio access networks is most suitable to accommodate the incoming call.

Joint Radio Resource Management (JRRM): RRM is the system level control of co-channel interference and other radio transmission characteristics in wireless communication systems. RRM involves strategies and algorithms for controlling parameters, such as transmission power, data rates, handover criteria, modulation scheme and error coding scheme. Joint Radio Resource Management (JRRM) algorithms define ways of achieving an efficient usage of a joint pool of resources belonging to several radio access networks.

Real Time Secondary Spectrum Markets (RTSSM): RTSSM policy used in cognitive radio systems adopts spectrum trading, which allows primary users to sell/lease spectrum usage rights and secondary players to buy them, thereby establishing a secondary market for spectrum leasing and spectrum auction.

TV White Spaces (TVWS): TVWS are the unexploited portions of radio spectrum in the TV bands, such as the guard bands between broadcasting channels and channels freed up, by the transition from analogue to digital terrestrial television.

Chapter 4
Resource Allocation Strategies in Cognitive Radio Networks Under QoS Constraints

Stavroula Vassaki
National Technical University of Athens, Greece

Athanasios D. Panagopoulos
National Technical University of Athens, Greece

Marios I. Poulakis
National Technical University of Athens, Greece

Philip Constantinou
National Technical University of Athens, Greece

ABSTRACT

The rapid growth of spectral resources' demands, as well as the increasing Quality of Service (QoS) requirements of wireless users have led to the necessity for new resource allocation schemes which will take into account the differentiated QoS needs of each wireless user. Towards this direction, the researchers have introduced the concept of effective capacity, which is defined as the maximum rate that the channel can support in order to guarantee a specified QoS requirement. This concept has been considered as a "bridge" among the physical layer characteristics and the upper-layer metrics of QoS. During the last years, it has been widely employed for resource allocation problems in various wireless networks leading to efficient mechanisms. This chapter focuses on the employment of the effective capacity theory in Cognitive Radio (CR) systems, presenting an extensive survey on QoS-driven resource allocation schemes proposed in the literature. Some useful conclusions are presented and future research directions on this subject are highlighted and discussed.

1. INTRODUCTION

The emerging services of modern wireless networks raise an increasing demand for spectral bandwidth resulting in the congestion of this scarce resource. At the same time, the limited spectrum is used inefficiently most of the times leading to low utilization. To overcome these problems, the concept of CR technology has been introduced. The research community defines CR as a radio platform that can rapidly reconfigure its operating parameters through a process of cognition, based

DOI: 10.4018/978-1-4666-4189-1.ch004

Copyright © 2013, IGI Global. Copying or distributing in print or electronic forms without written permission of IGI Global is prohibited.

on changing requirements and conditions. It is considered that in a CR system, the licensed wireless spectrum can be opportunistically accessed by unlicensed users (Secondary Users, SUs) in an intelligent and flexible way, without causing harmful interference to the licensed users (Primary Users, PUs). The spectrum sharing techniques can be divided in the spectrum interweave, spectrum underlay and spectrum overlay (Goldsmith, Jafar, Maric & Srinisava, 2009) approaches. In the first approach, the SUs are allowed to transmit their data only in the absence of PUs' transmission, whereas in the spectrum underlay approach, the SUs are allowed to transmit at the same time with the PUs guaranteeing specific interference constraints. Finally, in the spectrum overlay approach the SUs are allowed to transmit simultaneously with the PUs but they are obligated to help the PUs and relay their messages so as to offset the caused interference. Each of these approaches is characterized by its own challenges and benefits.

Furthermore, the fact that CRs can sense the environment and adapt their operating characteristics correspondingly, leads to their potential use in many applications and scenarios. One of the possible approaches for exploiting CR networking is the case of the Opportunistic Networks (ONs) (Stavroulaki et al, 2011) which constitute dynamically created networks and operate as extensions of the existing telecommunication systems. Given the dynamic environment of ONs, cognitive mechanisms should be proposed so as to allocate efficiently the network resources. Various resource management algorithms can be found in (Georgakopoulos et al, 2012; Karvounas et al, 2012) for a more detailed analysis based on the specific networks.

At the same time, apart from the number of the wireless users and the consumed spectral resources, the QoS requirements of the various services increase dramatically. Moreover, different services (such as video, VoIP, multimedia etc.) demand different QoS constraints leading the wireless users to tolerate different levels of delay

for each service. Especially for real time applications, it is important to take into consideration the impact of the QoS provisioning metric in the system's performance analysis. Therefore, there is an obvious need for new resource allocation schemes that will also take into account the quality requirements of the users. The combination of these schemes with the concept of CR will lead to much more efficient use of spectrum guaranteeing also the QoS satisfaction of each user. Typically, in a CR system, the SUs are either not allowed to transmit at all when a PU is present or they have to bound their transmit power so as not to harm the PU's communication, depending on the spectrum sharing approach. This constitutes an additional barrier for the SUs in order to satisfy their QoS requirements, compared with the PUs whose transmission is mainly limited due to the propagation phenomena and intra-system interference constraints. Thus, the QoS provisioning is more challenging in CR systems and particularly for the SUs, since they also have to take into account the activity of the PU and the imposed interference constraints. Consequently, cognitive users have to allocate their resources properly in order to be able to achieve specific QoS requirements.

The objective of this chapter is to present a survey on resource allocation techniques for the SUs considering that they have to meet specific quality constraints. Firstly, a suitable tool that can integrate the performance rate of a wireless link and the key metric of delay QoS requirements known as the effective capacity of the wireless link is described. As it is analyzed in this section, this function refers to the maximum constant arrival rate that the channel can support in order to guarantee a certain QoS requirement. After having presented the concept of the effective capacity, some research works regarding the use of this concept for resource allocation problems in various wireless networks (ad hoc, relay networks, etc) are briefly described. More specifically, a variety of power allocation schemes which optimize the user's throughput for specific

QoS constraints as well as their characteristics is presented. Significant remarks are analyzed and interesting conclusions for the resource allocation mechanisms are drawn.

Furthermore, an extended survey of the recent research work in the area of SU's resource allocation with QoS constraints is presented. This section of the chapter is separated in two subsections: the first part refers to schemes that consider the underlay spectrum sharing approach whereas in the second part, resource allocation mechanisms for a hybrid (underlay/interweave) spectrum sharing approach are discussed. The reason why these approaches have drawn the interest of the majority of the researchers is that in these cases the achievement of SUs' QoS is more challenging as their transmission is limited by various interference constraints. Particularly, at first, the basic model of a CR system is presented as well as the general form of the power allocation problem given specific QoS restrictions. Subsequently, an extended presentation of the power allocation schemes for underlay spectrum sharing CRs proposed in the literature is discussed. The impact of various interference and power constraints to the optimal power allocation policy and the corresponding effective capacity is investigated. Moreover, the influence of different degrees of channel state information (CSI) knowledge to the optimal effective capacity is discussed. At last, the power allocation problem for a hybrid spectrum sharing approach taking into account both the cases of perfect and imperfect CSI, is analyzed.

Afterwards, a discussion on open issues and future research subjects in this area follows. The chapter finishes with a brief conclusion highlighting the most important remarks regarding SUs' resource allocation for specific QoS constraints. The goal of this chapter is to present a unified survey which will indicate how the SUs have to allocate their power in order to guarantee a specific communication quality for different system architectures and for different interference assumptions.

2. EFFECTIVE CAPACITY

Before presenting various efficient resource allocation mechanisms which will guarantee the quality requirements of wireless users, the effective capacity theory, which is employed in the mechanisms, is analytically described. The concept of effective capacity was first introduced by Wu and Negi (Wu & Negi, 2003) in order to be able to characterize effectively the statistical delay QoS provisioning for data transmission in time-varying wireless channels. As it was proven a hard delay bound could not be guaranteed in mobile wireless networks due to the impact of time-varying fading over wireless channels. For this reason, this concept has been established as an alternative solution by guaranteeing a specific delay bound with small violation probability, providing in this way, statistical QoS guarantees. In this section, at first, a brief introduction of the theory of statistical QoS guarantees is presented and afterwards a formal definition and analysis for the concept of effective capacity is provided.

2.1. Theory of Statistical QoS Guarantees

The theory of statistical QoS guarantees has been thoroughly studied in the early 90s, under the concept of the effective bandwidth theory focused on wired Asynchronous Transfer Mode networks (ATM). Based on large deviation theory, in (Chang, 1994), it has been proven that considering a dynamic queuing system with stationary, ergodic arrival and service processes and under the condition that the average arrival rate is smaller than the average service rate, the queue length process $Q(t)$ will converge in distribution to a random variable $Q(\infty)$ for which the following equality will hold:

$$-\lim_{x \to \infty} \frac{\log\left(\Pr\left\{Q(\infty) > x\right\}\right)}{x} = \theta \qquad (1)$$

In different words, this means that the probability, the queue size Q exceeds a given threshold x, can be given by the following expression:

$$\Pr\{Q > x\} \approx \begin{cases} \varepsilon e^{-\theta x} & \text{, for small values of x} \\ e^{-\theta x} & \text{, for large values of x} \end{cases} \quad (2)$$

where, ε is defined as the probability that the buffer is non empty. Therefore, it can be observed that the probability that the queue length exceeds a specific threshold x decays exponentially as this threshold increases. It should be noted that the parameter θ is defined as the QoS exponent and represents the decaying speed of the QoS violation probability. As it can be seen, this parameter plays a very important role to the provisioning of the QoS requirements. More specifically, smaller values of θ denote slower decaying rate, meaning that the system can guarantee only looser QoS constraints. On the contrary, larger values of θ correspond to faster decaying rate leading to more stringent QoS requirements.

Similarly, it has been proven that in case where delay-bound is the metric of interest, the delay-bound violation probability can be expressed as:

$$\Pr\{Delay > D_{\max}\} \approx \varepsilon \cdot e^{-\theta \delta D_{\max}} \quad (3)$$

where, D_{max} denotes the delay threshold and the parameter δ can be jointly determined by both the arrival and service processes (Chang, 2000).

2.2. Definition of Effective Capacity

Effective capacity has been introduced as the dual concept of the effective bandwidth (El-walid & Mitra, 1993; Chang, 1994), which represents the minimum service rate that is required by a specific arrival process in order to guarantee a QoS requirement determined by the parameter θ. Correspondingly, effective capacity has been defined in (Wu & Negi, 2003) as

the maximum arrival rate that the time-varying channel can support so as to guarantee a specific delay-bound violation probability controlled by the QoS exponent θ. Particularly, considering a discrete-time, stationary and ergodic stochastic service process $\{R[i], i = 1, 2, ...\}$, the time-accumulated service process $S(t) = \sum_{i=1}^{t} R[i]$ and given that the asymptotic log-moment generation function:

$$\Lambda_C(\theta) = \lim_{t \to \infty} \frac{1}{t} \log\left(\mathbf{E}\left\{e^{\theta S(t)}\right\}\right) \quad (4)$$

exists, and it is a convex function, differentiable for all real values of θ, the effective capacity function can be given by:

$$E_C(\theta) = -\frac{\Lambda_C(-\theta)}{\theta} = -\lim_{t \to \infty} \frac{1}{\theta t} \log\left(\mathbf{E}\left\{e^{-\theta S(t)}\right\}\right). \quad (5)$$

where, $\mathbf{E}\{\cdot\}$ corresponds to the expected value function.

Specifically, for uncorrelated, block-fading channels in which the service process $R[i]$ is also uncorrelated, the effective capacity can be simplified to the following expression:

$$E_C(\theta) = -\frac{1}{\theta} \log\left(\mathbf{E}\left\{e^{-\theta R[i]}\right\}\right). \quad (6)$$

In the literature, usually, the function $R[i]$ represents the Shannon capacity and it is given from the following expression:

$$R[i] = T_f B \log_2(1 + SINR) \quad (7)$$

where, T_f denotes the duration of the data link-layer frames, B is the system's total spectral bandwidth and $SINR$ refers to the link's signal to interference and noise ratio. In this case, the channel is considered invariant within a frame's duration T_f whereas it varies from one frame to another. Thus, the unit for the effective capacity is "bits per frame". Here, it should be noted that, in the literature, the reader can often find the concept of the normalized effective capacity which is defined as the effective capacity divided by the factor $T_f B$ and has the unit of "bits/sec/Hz".

In order to demonstrate more analytically the properties of the concepts defined above and highlight the relationship between effective bandwidth and effective capacity function, Figure 1 presents these two functions versus the QoS parameter θ. As it can be seen from this Figure, the effective capacity function is a decreasing function of the QoS exponent θ whereas the opposite is true for the effective bandwidth function. This can be explained considering that as the QoS constraint becomes stricter (θ increases), the channel can guarantee the quality requirements by supporting only lower traffic arrival rates. Thus, when θ tends to infinity, the effective capacity function converges to the minimum service rate. On the other hand, when the system can tolerate long delays (small values of QoS exponent θ), the maximum arrival rate that the channel can

support is equal to the average service rate. Trying to explain this behavior in terms of capacity, it can be said that for $\theta \to 0$, the effective capacity converges to the ergodic capacity whereas for $\theta \to \infty$, it converges to the delay-limited capacity. Correspondingly, regarding the behavior of the effective bandwidth function, it can be explained considering that as the QoS requirements become more stringent, the channel has to support higher service rates in order to ensure the quality guarantees. On the other hand, lower service rate is needed when there are looser QoS constraints (small values of θ) as it can also be seen in Figure 1.

Except from the illustration of the properties of the two above functions, Figure 1 can help the readers to understand how the delay-bound violation probability can be computed for specific arrival and service processes. In order to find this probability, at first, the intersection point of the effective capacity with the effective bandwidth function should be found. At this point, as it can be seen in Figure 1, the QoS exponent is equal to θ^* and the corresponding rate is equal to δ. Thus, using (3), the violation probability for any predetermined delay threshold is given by the following equation:

Figure 1. Effective capacity and effective bandwidth functions versus QoS exponent θ

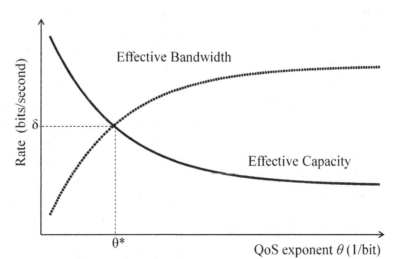

$$\Pr\left\{Delay > D_{\max}\right\} \approx e^{-\theta^{*}\delta D_{\max}} \tag{8}$$

Concluding this sub-section, it is noted that the concept of effective capacity constitutes a powerful tool for the design of efficient mechanisms providing QoS guarantees. Moreover, it should be highlighted that this concept can be employed as a bridge in the cross-layer design among the physical layer and the upper data-link layer as it achieves to relate the wireless channel service rate to the network QoS performance through a single simple parameter, the QoS exponent θ. This final remark explains the reason why during the last years, the researchers have employed the effective capacity approach in order to study various resource allocation problems integrating the concept of QoS provisioning.

3. RESOURCE ALLOCATION IN WIRELESS NETWORKS UNDER QOS CONSTRAINTS

The analysis of effective capacity theory has shown that this concept constitutes an extremely useful tool which has helped the researchers to investigate the impact of various physical layer characteristics on upper-layer performance metrics as well as to develop efficient resource allocation schemes. Thus, over the last years, a plethora of resource allocation mechanisms has been proposed taking into account the QoS requirements of the wireless users through the use of effective capacity theory. This section mainly focuses on the existing QoS-driven power allocation schemes for various technologies and architectures of wireless networks.

One of the first research works on this subject is found in (Tang & Zhang, 2007a), where the authors propose a power allocation mechanism for wireless networks that maximizes the system throughput for specific delay QoS requirements. In order to be able to integrate in their approach the system's quality requirements with the infor-

mation theoretic approach of Shannon capacity, they employ the concept of effective capacity. Specifically, at first, they consider uncorrelated fading channels and they find the optimal power allocation that maximizes the effective capacity given a mean power constraint. The optimization problem can be expressed as follows:

$$\max_{P(\theta,\gamma)}\left\{-\frac{1}{\theta}\log\left(\mathbf{E}\left\{e^{-\theta R(P(\theta,\gamma))}\right\}\right)\right\}$$
$$\text{s.t}\quad \mathbf{E}\left\{P(\theta,\gamma)\right\} = \text{constant} \tag{9}$$

where $R(P(\theta,\gamma))$ represents the Shannon capacity and $P(\theta,\gamma)$ represents the power allocation that depends both on the signal-to-noise ratio (SNR) of the link denoted as γ and the QoS exponent θ.

In Figure 2, the optimal power allocation resulting from the solution of the above maximization problem is depicted. As it can be seen, there is a significant tradeoff between the achieved throughput and the provided QoS guarantees. More particularly, it can be observed that when there are looser QoS requirements and the system can tolerate a long delay (small values of θ), the optimal power allocation policy converges to the well-known water-filling scheme (Li & Goldsmith, 2001). As it is proven in (Goldsmith, 2005), this scheme optimizes the ergodic capacity function and it allocates more power when the channel experiences good channel conditions and less power when the channel is getting worse. On the other hand, when there are strict delay constraints (larger values of θ), the optimal power allocation is similar to the total channel inversion mechanism (Goldsmith, 1997). In this mechanism, more power is allocated when the channel conditions are bad and less power is assigned in good channel conditions so as to achieve constant SNR and thus constant Shannon capacity. Regarding the intermediate values of the QoS exponent θ, the power allocation policy varies between the water-filling and the total channel inversion schemes as it is shown in Figure 2.

Figure 2. Optimal power allocation under QoS constraints

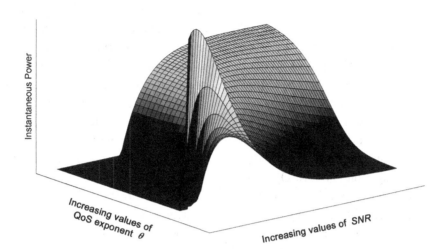

In the same paper, (Tang & Zhang, 2007a), the authors study the optimal power allocation scheme considering more practical scenarios with adaptive modulation techniques for both uncorrelated and correlated fading channels. As it is proven, the behavior of the power allocation policy for different values of QoS parameter θ remains the same in these schemes. However, a basic remark observed from these scenarios is that the channel correlation influences significantly the power mechanism. More specifically, considering Markov model fading channels, the authors have proven that as the channel correlation increases, the power control mechanism converges faster to the total channel inversion technique for large values of θ.

In (Tang & Zhang, 2007b), the same authors take into account the advances in physical layer infrastructure and propose a power allocation mechanism for multichannel communications, referring either to diversity or multiplexing systems, over wireless links. Similarly to (Tang & Zhang, 2007a), their goal is to find the power allocation that maximizes the system's throughput for specific QoS constraints. However, their analysis for multichannel communications shows that there are significant differences comparing the proposed

scheme with the single-channel case referred in (Tang & Zhang, 2007a). More specifically, as it is proven, for looser QoS constraints, the optimal power allocation mechanism converges also to the water-filling algorithm achieving the ergodic capacity. However, in case the QoS exponent takes large values (strict quality constraints), the optimal power allocation policy leads to a constant rate scheme which approaches the ergodic capacity as the number of sub-channels increases. Thus, it can be seen that the multichannel scheme offers a significant advantage for large values of the QoS exponent θ as it can combine both high values of throughput and strict QoS guarantees at the same time, contrary to the single channel case.

Another QoS-driven mechanism for multichannel communications can also be found in (Zhang, Tang, Chen, Ci & Guizani, 2006; Tang & Zhang, 2007c), where the authors present a cross-layer model so as to study the influence of physical layer infrastructure characteristics on data-link layer performance employing the concept of effective capacity. More specifically, in their approach, they integrate multiple-input multiple-output (MIMO) diversity techniques with adaptive modulation and coding techniques (AMC) and they analyze how the infrastructure of the physical layer affects the effective capacity of the mobile wireless network. Using this approach, they study various statistical QoS metrics which are critical for real-time services such as the delay bound probability, buffer overflow probability etc. A basic remark from their numerical investigation is that the use of MIMO techniques compared to single-input single-output (SISO) techniques increase significantly the effective capacity of the system. Regarding the comparison of MIMO with multiple-input single-output (MISO) techniques, an interesting remark is that for looser QoS constraints the effective capacity of the MISO systems may be higher from the effective capacity of some MIMO systems depending on the exploitation of the CSI. However, for stricter QoS requirements, MIMO systems lead always to better effective capacity values. Moreover, in this work, the authors compare the constant power control allocation with the well-known water-filling algorithm showing that the power control scheme that maximizes the effective capacity is not the same with the scheme that optimizes the ergodic capacity but it depends mainly on the values of the QoS exponent θ.

The same authors, in another study (Tang & Zhang, 2008), analyze the downlink case of a mobile wireless network and they propose a resource allocation mechanism in order to guarantee specific QoS characteristics to the mobile users. In this work, they employ the effective capacity theory as a "bridge" so as to study the influence of various physical layer techniques, such as adaptive power control and CSI feedback delay, on the upper-protocol layers characteristics. Particularly, they present a dynamic resource management scheme that allocates power and timeslots to heterogeneous mobile users depending on their characteristics (fading channel state, QoS requirements, etc) so as to guarantee certain bounded delays for each user. In their algorithm, they study how the adaptive power control scheme influences the provision of QoS guarantees applying three different power allocation schemes: the water-filling scheme, a constant power allocation

algorithm and the optimal power allocation scheme proposed in (Tang & Zhang, 2007a). As it can be seen from their numerical analysis, the third scheme outperforms significantly the other two mechanisms in terms of QoS guarantees. Their proposed joint power and timeslot assignment scheme guarantees the QoS requirements of each user while on the same time it minimizes the total energy of the system, leading to either reduce the transmission power or increase the admission region of the users.

An interesting approach for a similar resource allocation problem in cooperative relay networks can be found in (Ren & Letaief, 2009). In this work, the authors study the case of a relay wireless network and propose a timeslot allocation mechanism so as to optimize the system's throughput for specific QoS constraints. At first, they consider block fading channels and they find the optimal timeslot's length that should be allocated to each relay for detecting and forwarding the source's signal in order to maximize the system's effective capacity. As it is proven in their work, when there are looser QoS constraints, the optimal allocation boils down to choosing only the relay with the best average condition whereas for strict QoS requirements, more relays have to cooperate in order to optimize the effective capacity. The proposed optimal timeslot allocation mechanism is compared with two other timeslot allocation mechanisms: an opportunistic allocation scheme in which only the relay with the best average channel condition is chosen and an equal allocation scheme where all the relays are allocated the same timeslot's length. It is shown that the proposed scheme outperforms both these schemes in terms of effective capacity for any given value of the QoS exponent θ. Another interesting observation is that, given a specific effective capacity goal, there is a tradeoff between the transmission power and the number of relays. Moreover, the authors study the more practical scenario of correlated fading channels and they show that the channel correlation influences negatively the effective capacity.

Except the use of effective capacity for resource allocation problems in terrestrial networks, this concept has also been introduced in satellite communication systems in (Vassaki, Panagopoulos & Constantinou, 2012). In this paper, the authors study the QoS–driven power allocation problem for the downlink of a land mobile satellite system. Specifically, closed form expressions for the optimal power allocation and the corresponding effective capacity are obtained. Moreover, the impact of significant satellite link's characteristics, such as the propagation conditions and the elevation angle of the satellite, on the power allocation and the effective capacity are investigated. As it is proven, the increase of elevation angle influences positively the effective capacity values whereas the shadowing has negative influence meaning that heavy shadowing conditions lead to much lower values of effective capacity.

Finally, since game theory has provided a powerful tool for the analysis of various resource allocation problems in wireless networks during the last decade (Wang, Wu & Liu, 2010; Charilas & Panagopoulos, 2010), the researchers have started to employ the concept of effective capacity in game-theoretic approaches in order to develop distributed allocation mechanisms. More specifically, some recent results towards the direction of game-theoretic delay-constrained resource management can be found in (Du & Zhang, 2009; Qiao, Gursoy & Velipasar, 2010), where the authors study a non cooperative power control game between mobile users who want to maximize their effective capacity. In particular, they consider that each mobile user has complete knowledge of CSI and is a selfish, rational player with specific quality constraints who tries to optimize its effective capacity subject to average power constraints. In their works, they focus on the two-user case and they prove that the power control game has always a unique Nash equilibrium. Moreover, they compare the performance of the specific game and the water-filling game proposed in (Lai & El Gamal, 2008). As it is shown, for stringent quality requirements, the QoS-driven game leads to better effective capacity than the water-filling game whereas for small values of the QoS-exponent, the two games lead to the same results. However, an interesting remark is that the introduction of the QoS restrictions has led to an equilibrium in which both users can transmit simultaneously opposite to the simple water-filling game where at most one user can transmit data in every fading state. Finally, a similar approach is presented in (Mao, Xu, Fu &Huang, 2012), where the authors study the QoS-driven power allocation problem of users in a high-speed mobile environment employing also concepts from non-cooperative game theory.

4. POWER CONTROL IN COGNITIVE RADIOS UNDER QOS CONSTRAINTS

The basic priority in the CR systems is to ensure the unaffected communication of PUs. However, cognitive SUs should also transmit at high rates and limit the delay experienced by the data in the buffers in order to satisfy their own QoS requirements. All these have to be achieved given the fact that the wireless channel conditions vary randomly over time due to mobility and changing environment. Furthermore, the provisioning of QoS guarantees is more challenging in a CR system, since the SUs have also to take into account the activity of the PU and the imposed interference constraints. These considerations are critical for the successful deployment of CR systems and emerge the necessity of efficient radio resource management schemes.

This section makes an extended presentation of the research works proposed in the literature which are focusing on the area of SUs' resource allocation with QoS constraints. The first part presents different power allocation schemes for the underlay spectrum sharing approach; while the second part refers to similar mechanisms which consider a hybrid (interweave/underlay) spectrum sharing approach. More specifically, the first part starts with the description of the basic CR system model that is commonly used in resource management problems. Afterwards, the general power allocation problem under specific QoS constraints is presented and an extended survey of various resource management schemes is discussed considering different power and interference constraints, the use of AMC, as well as different degrees of CSI (perfect/imperfect) knowledge. Furthermore, an extension of the basic model to multi-user systems is presented. Finally, in the second part, the power allocation problem for the hybrid approach taking into account both the cases of perfect and imperfect CSI, is studied.

4.1. Power Allocation Schemes for the Underlay Spectrum Sharing Approach

4.1.1. System Model and Problem Formulation

The most common system model that is employed for the investigation of the underlay spectrum sharing approach is presented in Figure 3. In the

specific case, a secondary transmitter attempts to communicate with a secondary receiver in the presence of a PU. Thus, it is considered a pair of secondary transmitter (SU-Tx) and receiver (SU-Rx) that coexists with a pair of primary transmitter (PU-Tx) and receiver (PU-Rx). Assuming discrete-time block-fading channels for the secondary and primary links, the received signals at the primary and the secondary receiver, at a specific time n, are correspondingly:

$$y_p[n] = \sqrt{h_p[n]}x_p[n] + \sqrt{h_{sp}[n]}x_s[n] + z_p[n] \quad (10)$$

$$y_s[n] = \sqrt{h_s[n]}x_s[n] + \sqrt{h_{ps}[n]}x_p[n] + z_s[n] \quad (11)$$

where, x_p and x_s represent the transmitted signals from the primary and the secondary transmitter respectively, and z_p, z_s represent the Additive White Gaussian Noise (AWGN) for the primary and the secondary link. Moreover, h_s, h_{sp}, h_p, h_{ps} denote the channel power gains between the secondary/

Figure 3. Basic CR system model: SU coexists with PU

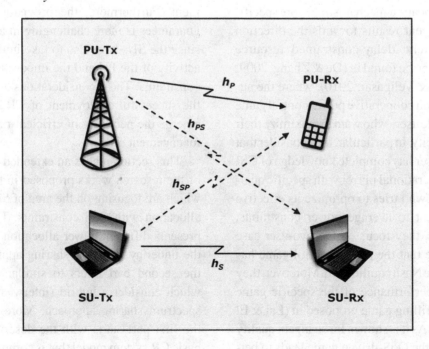

primary transmitter and the secondary/primary receiver, according to Figure 3.

As it has been already noted, since different services have different QoS requirements, the wireless users are expected to tolerate different delay levels for each service. Hence, it is crucial to take into account the impact of the QoS provisioning metric in the formulation of an efficient radio resource management problem. For that reason, the concept of effective capacity is used as an appropriate tool as it can be seen in the previous section. In the case of CRs and specifically in the underlay spectrum sharing approach, the SUs are allowed to transmit simultaneously with the PUs. However, their transmission power is limited by strict interference constraints so as to protect the communication of PUs. These constraints that are imposed to ensure the reliable communication of the PUs, at the same time, degrade the QoS of the SUs who may not be allowed to transmit at the optimal power level. This constitutes a significant problem in providing QoS guarantees for the communication of SUs and it has started to draw attention of the research community. As it can be seen in the rest of this section, recent research works deal with the problem of resource allocation for cognitive radio systems under QoS requirements proposing efficient power control algorithms.

The general form of the SUs' power allocation problem, in an underlay spectrum sharing approach, considering that the SUs have specific QoS requirements, can be expressed as the following maximization problem of the SUs' effective capacity:

$$\max_{P_s}\left\{-\frac{1}{\theta}\ln\left(\mathbf{E}\left[e^{-\theta R(P_s)}\right]\right)\right\}$$

s.t. *Power* and *Interference Constraints*

$$(12)$$

where, P_s denotes the transmission power of the SU-Tx, $R(P_s)$ denotes the channel capacity of the

SU link and θ represents the corresponding QoS exponent. The *Power Constraints* refer to power restrictions that depend on the device capabilities and they can be expressed in terms of maximum peak or maximum average transmission power limit at SU-Tx. On the other hand, the *Interference Constraints* refer to the maximum acceptable interference in order to ensure the unperturbed communication of the PU and they can be expressed in terms of maximum peak or maximum average interference power limit at the PU-Rx. In the literature, some other constraints (e.g. outage probability constraints of PU) have also been proposed but most of them can be reduced to the fundamental interference-power constraints. In the rest of this subsection, a survey of the proposed power allocation mechanisms is presented.

4.1.2. Perfect Knowledge of CSI

This subsection focuses on the research works that have as a basic assumption that the SU has complete CSI knowledge of all the links. Thus, since it is aware of all the instantaneous channel gains, it is considered that the SU can adapt its power depending on these values.

More specifically, in (Ma, Zhang, Yuan & Chen, 2009), the authors propose a cross-layer scheme and study the optimal power allocation problem given that the SUs have specific communication quality requirements. They consider the case of one SU coexisting with a PU sharing the spectrum, using the underlay approach, in a way that its transmission parameters are limited by an average interference-power constraint. The authors propose a maximization problem of the SUs' effective capacity subject to certain average and peak transmission power constraints as well as to an average interference power restriction. The channels are assumed to experience Nakagami-*m* fading. The optimization problem is decomposed into two sub-problems in order to reduce the overall computational complexity and a recursive algorithm under the power constraints is developed to find the optimal solution. Furthermore, in this work, the authors investigate the solution of the dual problem. Particularly, they present the SU's power control policy that minimizes the average interference power at the PU guaranteeing at the same time a specified delay QoS for the SU expressed in terms of effective capacity constraints. Thus, the limits of the average interference power for specific SU's QoS requirements are derived. Some basic remarks obtained from the numerical analysis are that the effective capacity is a monotonically decreasing function of QoS exponent θ and that the power control policy for more relaxed interference constraints performs better in terms of the effective capacity. Moreover, it is proven that the average interference power increases with the increase of effective capacity threshold due to the fact that higher power is needed from the SU to enhance its effective capacity, resulting in generating more interference on the PU. In a similar manner, it is shown that the average interference power increases as the SUs' QoS requirement becomes more stringent.

Another delay-constrained power and rate allocation scheme for the SU link considering an underlay spectrum sharing approach and Nakagami-m block fading environment, has also been presented in (Musavian & Aïssa, 2010). In this paper, it is assumed that a SU is allowed to access the spectrum occupied by a PU subject to interference limitations imposed by the PU. Particularly, the authors consider an average interference power constraint at the PU receiver so as to guarantee the communication quality of the primary link, forcing the transmission power of the SU to adhere to this interference limitation. The optimal power and rate adaptation policy that maximizes the effective capacity of the SUs' channel is derived, and closed-form expressions for the effective capacity as well as for the optimal power allocation are provided. Furthermore, the authors present closed-form expressions for the expenditure power of the SU transmitter in order to achieve the optimal effective capacity. In order

to be able to compare their scheme in terms of effective capacity, two widely employed power allocation policies are considered: the optimal power and rate allocation that maximizes the corresponding channel capacity, and the channel inversion policy which leads to constant link's rate. Thus, the effective capacity of the channel under these power allocation techniques is also investigated. As it can be seen from the numerical analysis, the proposed power allocation policy outperforms the other two power allocation algorithms in terms of effective capacity. Moreover, an interesting observation is that the normalized effective capacity of the SUs' link increases as the Nakagami parameter m of the SU-Tx – SU-Rx (h_s) channel increases but with no significant gain. It should be noted here that the Nakagami parameter m denotes the ratio of the Line of Sight (LoS) signal power to that of the multi-path component and thus it models the severity of fading for the corresponding channel. The analysis also reveals that the normalized effective capacity decreases significantly when the fading parameter of the SU-Tx - PU-Rx link increases. This remark leads to the conclusion that the interference link (h_{sp}) has a much greater impact on the optimal power allocation and the corresponding effective capacity than the secondary link (h_s). Another basic remark, which has also has been discussed in (Tang & Zhang, 2007a), is that the effective capacity decreases for increasing values of the QoS exponent, meaning that as the quality requirements are getting stricter, the channel can support only lower throughput values. In Figure 4, the behavior of effective capacity versus the delay QoS exponent for various interference-limit values at PU-Rx is shown. As it can be seen, regarding the behavior of the normalized effective capacity for different values of interference-limit, the increase of the interference limit leads to higher values of effective capacity. This observation can be justified considering that given a looser interference constraint, the SU is allowed to transmit at higher power levels and thus increase its effective capacity.

Figure 4. Effective capacity vs. delay QoS exponent θ, for various interference limits at PU-Rx

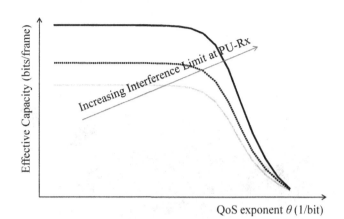

In (Vassaki, Poulakis, Panagopoulos & Constantinou, 2011), a spectrum underlay cognitive radio system operating in Rayleigh block fading environment is considered. In particular, the authors study the QoS-driven optimal power allocation policy that maximizes the normalized effective capacity of the secondary link considering an average interference power restriction so as to guarantee the communication quality of the primary link. The authors take into consideration a peak transmit power constraint that expresses the maximum power capability of the SU-Tx device's power amplifier. Contrary to the research works referred above, in this paper, the interfering power from the primary transmitter to the secondary receiver is taken into account for the derivation of the SU's optimal power allocation in order to study a more realistic scenario. The authors derive expressions of the optimal power allocation and the corresponding effective capacity. For comparison reasons, the effective capacity of a constant power allocation scheme is also studied. As it can be seen in the numerical analysis, the proposed optimal power allocation scheme leads to better values of effective capacity compared to the constant power allocation algorithm. Moreover, an interesting remark, regarding the optimal power allocation for different values of interfering power from the primary transmitter and for varying normalized exponent, is that when the system has looser QoS requirements, the SU assigns more power when the interference caused from the PU takes lower values and less power (or zero) when the experienced interference is significant as it is depicted in Figure 5. On the other hand, when the system has strict QoS requirements, the SU transmits at higher power levels when the PU causes significant interference to the secondary link so as to eliminate its impact to the quality of the secondary link. Thus, it is shown that the impact of the primary transmitter-secondary receiver link is very important for the optimal power allocation policy.

Another factor that impacts the performance of delay-constrained resource allocation schemes and, recently, the researchers started to take into account, is the use of adaptive modulation techniques. The authors in (Musavian, Aissa & Lambotharan, 2011) propose a variable-rate variable-power M-level Quadrature Amplitude Modulation (MQAM) scheme employed under delay QoS constraints in underlay spectrum sharing CR systems. In this approach, it is considered that certain service outage constraints for the PUs should be satisfied, independently of the existence of the SUs in the network. Thus, the transmission parameters of the secondary transmitter should be limited such that the PU experiences a minimum

Figure 5. SU's optimal power allocation vs. the QoS exponent θ and for various values of interference caused from the PU

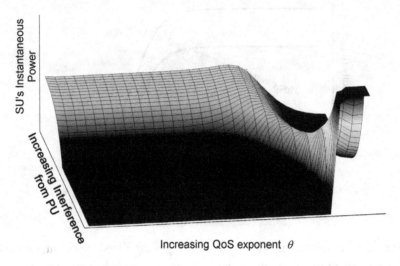

rate for a specific percentage of time. The PU can choose its transmit power without taking into consideration the existence of the SU in the network, following a constant transmission power scheme or an optimal transmission power scheme that maximizes its channel's capacity. The authors translate the outage probability constraints on either average or peak interference power constraints for Rayleigh or Nakagami-m fading channels correspondingly, studying both PU's transmission power strategies. Given these interference power constraints, the maximum throughput of the SU's channel under delay QoS constraint is obtained in terms of effective capacity. Specifically, the authors solve the optimization problem considering that the SU can employ adaptive MQAM with continuous or discrete constellations and they determine the optimal power and rate allocation strategies that maximize the effective capacity for these modulation schemes (continuous/discrete) both for the average and the peak interference constraints. In addition, closed-form expressions for the optimal effective capacity and the corresponding power allocation are obtained. A first remark from the numerical results is that the effective capacity of the SU is more sensitive

to the fading severity of the interference link between the secondary transmitter and the primary receiver, compared with that between the secondary transmitter and receiver of the SU. Moreover, the interference-power constraint obtained when the PU employs constant power techniques is much tighter than the corresponding constraint of the PU's optimal power allocation policy. Additionally, it can be seen that the effective capacity under average interference constraints is considerably higher than that under peak interference power constraints due to the fact that in the first case, the SU is more flexible to allocate its power compared to the case of strict peak power constraints. Another interesting observation from the numerical investigation is that the effective capacity achieved with the use of discrete MQAM is smaller than that achieved with the use of continuous MQAM. However, the loss in terms of effective capacity in this case is small compared to the loss between the optimal case, where there is no restriction on the modulation, and the continuous MQAM case. Finally, as it is shown in the numerical analysis, the effective capacity decreases significantly when the minimum rate required by the PU increases or as the outage probability decreases. This can be explained considering that both these changes in PU's characteristics eventually lead to stricter interference constraints.

4.1.3. Imperfect Knowledge of CSI

All the previous works have assumed perfect knowledge of CSI in the formulation of the resource allocation problem. However, in wireless communications, where channel conditions fluctuate over time, the estimation of these channel variations is an extremely difficult task. Furthermore, in case of CR systems where the operating parameters need to be reconfigured based on changing requirements and conditions, the estimation and knowledge of the channel conditions constitute a crucial part of their efficient operation. In general, if the channel conditions are not known a priori, the wireless systems employ training sequences to perform channel estimation. However, in practice, perfect CSI is not possible due to the channel estimation errors and delays. It should be noted that, in case of imperfect CSI, the exact value of the corresponding channel coefficient (h) can be expressed as the sum of the channel estimation $\hat{h}$ and the channel estimation error $\tilde{h}$, as follows:

$$h = \hat{h} + \tilde{h} \tag{13}$$

The channel estimation can be performed using a minimum mean-square error (MMSE) estimator. The error is commonly considered that it follows a known distribution (e.g. zero-mean Gaussian) with a known variance to both the transmitter and the receiver, which captures the quality of the channel estimation and it is treated as another source of Gaussian noise.

Therefore, the investigation of the imperfect CSI and its effects on resource allocation schemes remains an interesting problem. In (Musavian & Aissa, 2009; Rezki & Alouini, 2012), the authors

consider a CR system where the SU is provided with incomplete information of the link between its transmitter and the PU's receiver and they discuss the resource allocation problem for different interference constrains. Moreover, it is described how the optimal power allocation and the corresponding ergodic capacity are affected by the channel estimation errors reaching the conclusion that they both decrease as the channel estimation error variance increases. However, in both of these works, the SUs are not considered to have specific QoS requirements. The impact of channel uncertainty on QoS-driven resource management schemes has very recently started to draw the attention of the researchers and the results are still limited. More specifically, in (Xie & Guo, 2011), the authors take into account the influence of imperfect CSI in a QoS-driven resource allocation problem. In this work, the authors analyze the effective capacity gains of opportunistic underlay spectrum-sharing with imperfect CSI. They consider that a SU may access the spectrum allocated to a PU as long as the caused average interference power remains below predefined power limits. Moreover, it is assumed that the SU has partial knowledge of the CSI of the link between the SU transmitter and PU receiver, whereas complete knowledge of CSI for the rest of the links is considered. Thus, the channel power gain can be estimated imperfectly having channel estimation error with a known variance. The optimal power allocation strategy is derived in order to achieve the maximum effective capacity under the average interference power constraints and the assumption of imperfect channel information. Furthermore, the expressions of the corresponding effective capacity and the average expenditure-power required to achieve the optimal effective capacity are obtained, associated with the channel estimation error variance. A significant conclusion from the presented results is that the optimal effective capacity as well as the expenditure power required achieving these values of effective capacity increase as channel estimation error variance decreases.

4.1.4. Multi-User Case

Finally, the case of a multi-user system is studied in (Kiskani, Khalaj & Vakilinia, 2010), where the authors consider a CR model in which some SUs coexist with a network of PUs using underlay spectrum sharing in Nakagami-*m* fading environments. In this approach, the concept of effective capacity is considered so as to guarantee a desired delay QoS for every SU. The authors propose an optimal adaptive modulation scheme in order to support the desired QoS and to maximize the sum of SU's effective capacities. More specifically, a network of secondary transmitters has been considered, which are competing to send their data to some secondary receivers in the presence of a network of primary transceivers. Each of the secondary transmitters is using MQAM adaptive modulation. Regarding the fading status of each link, the secondary transmitter decides the power level and which modulation type to use so that the delay QoS requirement is fulfilled. In order to determine the optimal adaptive modulation scheme at each time slot, the authors maximize the network utility function that is considered as the sum of effective capacities of all of the secondary users under the individual average constraints of maximum transmit power for each SU and the average interference power constraints which are common for all the SUs for each individual PU. The continuous adaptive modulation case is firstly studied and the optimal constellation size is found for such modulations. Moreover, the suboptimal discrete modulation is derived from the optimal modulation, since the continuous modulation size is not practically possible. After finding the constellation size, the authors obtain the optimal rate using the optimal power allocation that is found as a solution to the optimization problem, to guarantee a specific bit error rate. Finally, they analytically show that the proposed scheme is optimal and derive a feasible suboptimal adaptive modulation scheme for the SUs.

4.2. Power Allocation Schemes for Hybrid Spectrum Sharing Approach

In contrast with the underlay approach, where it is considered that the PUs communicate with each other continuously, this subsection studies the case where the PUs are not active all the time. In this case the SUs have first to detect the activity periods of the PUs (e.g. using the well-suited energy-based detection methods) in order to adapt their power. This approach can be considered as a hybrid (underlay/interweave) approach, because the SU can communicate with or without the absence of PU's activity, either constrained to transmit at low power levels in order not to disturb PU communication or not constrained under specific acceptable interference limits. The system model is the same to that of the previous section in which a secondary transmitter attempts to send information to a secondary receiver coexisting with a PU. However, in this case, it is considered that SU performs channel sensing before transmitting data, and then depending on the PU's activity, the secondary transmitter selects its transmission power and rate. In the rest of this subsection, the QoS-driven power allocation schemes, which have been proposed in the literature for this hybrid spectrum sharing approach, are presented.

In (Akin & Gursoy, 2010), the performance of CR systems, for the hybrid spectrum sharing approach, is studied considering that the SUs operate under statistical QoS constraints. The effective capacity of CR channels is analyzed in order to identify the performance levels and to determine the impact of channel sensing parameters to the achieved throughput in the presence of QoS constraints. More specifically, in this CR model, SUs initially perform channel sensing, and then the secondary transmitter selects its transmission power and rate depending on the channel sensing results. Since the transmission strategies of the PUs are not known, energy-based detection methods that are well-suited for the detection of the activities of PUs are used. Thus, the channel sensing can be formulated as a hypothesis testing problem between the noise and the PU's signal plus noise. The optimal Neyman-Pearson detector for the hypothesis testing problem is used for a given detection threshold and the probabilities of false alarm and detection are established. Furthermore, the authors propose a state transition model defining the transition probabilities for the two following cases: perfect CSI at the SU receiver only and perfect CSI at both the SU receiver and transmitter. For the first case, the SU transmits at two fixed rates not knowing the channel conditions, depending on the sensed PU activity and the normalized effective capacity for this case is computed. Regarding the second case, the SU transmitter adapts its rate and power with respect to the channel conditions and depending on the sensed PU activity. The normalized effective capacity and the optimal power adaptation policies are computed under specified average power constraints for the cases of busy and idle channel. Simulation results are provided for three different transmission schemes: fixed-power/fixed-rate, fixed-power/variable-rate, and variable-power/variable-rate. As it is shown in this work, the effective capacity increases as the values of false alarm probability are decreasing. At the same time, as the detection threshold increases or the duration of channel sensing increases, the probabilities of false alarm and detection decrease. Thus, the increase of detection threshold leads also to higher values of effective capacity as the SU incorrectly assumes that the channel is idle and transmits at higher power levels. On the contrary, the increase of the channel sensing duration results in decreasing the effective capacity due to the fact that there is less time available for the SU to transmit its data. Moreover, it is remarked that diminishing detection probabilities have a different effect in fixed-rate and variable-rate schemes. Variable-rate schemes outperform fixed-rate transmission methods if the detection probabilities are sufficiently high whereas otherwise, fixed-power/fixed-rate transmission should be preferred. Furthermore, comparing the variable-rate/variable-power scheme with the variable-rate/fixed power allocation, it is shown that the first scheme always outperforms the second one. Finally, a significant observation is that both the effective capacity and transmission rates get smaller with increasing QoS exponent θ and the gains through adapting rate and power diminish as θ increases.

The same authors, in (Akin & Gursoy, 2011) analyze the effective capacity of cognitive radio channels for the hybrid spectrum sharing approach in the presence of QoS constraints, transmission power limitations and channel uncertainty. In this paper, SUs initially perform channel sensing to detect the activities of the PUs, and then, depending on the channel sensing results, the secondary transmitter selects the pilot symbol as well as the data transmission power policy. The pilot symbol is employed for the estimation of the channel coefficients using different Minimum Mean-Square-Error (MMSE) estimation methods (mismatched MMSE, linear MMSE and MMSE). However, in channel sensing and channel estimation phase, erroneous decisions can be made, and thus channel uncertainty is not completely eliminated. The authors assume that the secondary transmitter and the secondary receiver are unaware of the channel conditions, thus the transmitter is considered to send the data at fixed average power and rate levels depending on whether the channel is sensed as idle or not. In the data transmission phase, depending on the capabilities of the SU transmitters and the energy resources that they are equipped with, there exist maximum constraints on the average transmit powers and also an extra average power constraint to limit the interference to the PUs' receiver. Moreover, statistical boundaries on the buffer lengths are imposed to take into account the SU's QoS constraints. A state-transition model is proposed by taking into account the reliability of the transmissions, the channel sensing decisions, their correctness and the evolution of PU's activity which is modeled as a two-state Markov process. Since it is generally difficult to characterize the channel capacity in the presence of channel uncertainty; the authors present the achievable rate expressions as lower bounds to the instantaneous channel capacities, considering the channel estimation results and the interference caused by the PUs. Moreover, the maximum throughput under statistical QoS constraints is identified by deriving the normalized effective capacity of the cognitive radio channel for the considered state transition model. In the numerical investigation, various results for the power and rate policies and the impact of several parameters such as detection and false probabilities, average power constraints and training power value, on the system's performance are presented. More specifically, it is shown that the effective capacity value increases, as the interference limit at PU receiver increases. Moreover, it is shown that the optimal transmission rate of the SU is larger when the channel is detected as idle compared to the case where the channel is busy. Comparing the effective capacity values obtained using mismatched MMSE and linear MMSE techniques, it is noticed that linear MMSE provides a slightly better performance for lower interference limits and for higher detection probabilities, a remark that highlights the significant relationship between channel sensing and channel estimation.

5. FUTURE RESEARCH DIRECTIONS

As it can be concluded from the previous sections, the integration of communication quality requirements in resource allocation schemes has attracted the interest of many researchers during the last years. However, the effective capacity concept in order to develop efficient resource management mechanisms for CRs has been employed only recently for specific cases of CRs. Thus, there are many open issues that the researchers should deal with so as to investigate and develop new resource allocation schemes which will improve even more the performance of the CR systems. Towards this direction, this section highlights

and discusses some of the issues that should be addressed in the future.

At first, a subject that should be investigated in more details is the resource allocation problem for specific QoS constraints in a multiuser CR system. As it can be seen through the chapter, there is limited work in which the case of multiuser network is considered. However, the concept of CRs implies the coexistence of many pairs of PUs and SUs. Thus, the analysis of a resource management problem in which the performance of the system will be optimized given that each SU has its own QoS requirements constitutes a crucial task that should be addressed in the future.

Towards the same direction, an interesting subject for future research is the development of distributed efficient QoS-driven allocation mechanisms. Given that CRs should be flexible enough so as to reconfigure their operating parameters based on the changing environment, the existence of a centralized entity seems rather impractical. Thus, centralized resource allocation schemes should be replaced by new mechanisms which will take into consideration the inherent distributed nature of CR networks. In order to accomplish this, game-theoretic techniques could be used. More specifically, principles from cooperative and non cooperative game theory could be employed so as to model the resource allocation problem as a game in which SUs represent selfish players who want to maximize their effective capacity subject to specific interference constraints. However, in case of game-theoretic approaches, other issues arise and should be carefully studied such as the overall complexity of the schemes as well as the existence, uniqueness and the optimality of the equilibrium. Thus, other distributed allocation schemes could also be studied inspired by mechanism design theory (auction mechanisms, etc.) or classic optimization theory.

Another subject that should be addressed is the analytical calculation of effective capacity in CR systems under composite fading channels that incorporate large and small scale effects. The impact of correlation should also be taken into account in order to develop advanced interference mitigation mechanisms and efficient resource allocation schemes.

Finally, it would be interesting to investigate how the existing QoS-driven resource allocation schemes influence the communication quality of the PUs in terms of its effective capacity. Furthermore, the use and the impact of the other interference constraints apart from the traditional interference power constraint on the derivation of optimal power allocation and the corresponding effective capacity should be investigated. Concluding, it must be noted that there are still a lot of open research issues lying on this area that should be addressed in order to derive efficient mechanisms for realistic CRs networks.

6. CONCLUSION

This chapter dealt with the problem of resource allocation in CR networks given that the wireless users have to satisfy specified communication quality requirements. At first, the theory that relates the wireless channel rate to the system QoS performance, known as effective capacity theory, was presented. Afterwards, a brief survey of the resource management techniques proposed in the literature was given. In particular, this section has focused on QoS-driven power allocation schemes for various wireless networks. Apart from the impact of QoS requirements, the influence of various physical layer infrastructure parameters on the optimal power allocation and the corresponding effective capacity were investigated. Moreover, the observation that the optimal power allocation for users with strict quality requirements boils down to the total channel inversion algorithm whereas for users with looser quality constraints, it is similar to the water-filling mechanism and other interesting remarks from the literature were discussed. In the next section, the incorporation of effective capacity in CR systems was studied. More specifically, the basic model of a CR sys-

tem and the general form of the power allocation problem were presented. Furthermore, an extended presentation of the existing resource allocation techniques that optimize the effective capacity of the SUs was followed. The proposed optimal SU's power allocation policies for both the cases of underlay and hybrid spectrum sharing approaches were investigated. Basic remarks for the impact of interference constraints on the allocation policy, as well as the influence of different degrees of CSI knowledge and the use of AMC on the optimal effective capacity, were presented. Finally, some open issues that should be addressed in the future in order to develop even more efficient resource allocation mechanisms for realistic CR systems, have been discussed.

ACKNOWLEDGMENT

This research has been co-financed by the European Union (European Social Fund – ESF) and Greek national funds through the Operational Program "Education and Lifelong Learning" of the National Strategic Reference Framework (NSRF) – Research Funding Program: Heracleitus II: Investing in knowledge society through the European Social Fund.

REFERENCES

Akin, S., & Gursoy, M. C. (2010). Effective capacity analysis of cognitive radio channels for quality of service provisioning. *IEEE Transactions on Wireless Communications*, *9*(11), 3354–3364. doi:10.1109/TWC.2010.092410.090751.

Akin, S., & Gursoy, M. C. (2011). Performance analysis of cognitive radio systems under QoS constraints and channel uncertainty. *IEEE Transactions on Wireless Communications*, *10*(9), 2883–2895. doi:10.1109/TWC.2011.062911.100743.

Chang, C. S. (1994). Stability, queue length, and delay of deterministic and stochastic queuing networks. *IEEE Transactions on Automatic Control, 39*(5), 913–931. doi:10.1109/9.284868.

Chang, C. S. (2000). *Performance guarantees in communication networks*. Berlin, Germany: Springer-Verlag. doi:10.1007/978-1-4471-0459-9.

Charilas, D. E., & Panagopoulos, A. D. (2010). A survey on game theory applications in wireless networks. *Computer Networks, 54*(18), 3421–3430. doi:10.1016/j.comnet.2010.06.020.

Du, Q., & Zhang, X. (2009). *QoS-driven power-allocation game over fading multiple-access channels*. Paper presented at IEEE Global Telecommunications Conference (GLOBECOM). New York, NY.

Elwalid, A. I., & Mitra, D. (1993). Effective bandwidth of general Markovian traffic sources and admission control of high speed networks. *IEEE/ACM Transactions on Networking, 1*(3), 329–343. doi:10.1109/90.234855.

Georgakopoulos, A., Karvounas, D., Stavroulaki, V., Tsagkaris, K., Tosic, M., Boskovic, D., & Demestichas, P. (2012). Scheme for expanding the capacity of wireless access infrastructures through the exploitation of opportunistic networks. *Mobile Networks and Applications, 17*(4), 463–478. doi:10.1007/s11036-012-0379-x.

Goldsmith, A., Jafar, S. A., Maric, I., & Srinivasa, S. (2009). Breaking spectrum gridlock with cognitive radios: An information theoretic perspective. *Proceedings of the IEEE, 97*(5), 894–914. doi:10.1109/JPROC.2009.2015717.

Goldsmith, A. J. (2005). *Wireless communications*. Cambridge, UK: Cambridge University Press. doi:10.1017/CBO9780511841224.

Goldsmith, A. J., & Varaiya, P. (1997). Capacity of fading channels with channel side information. *IEEE Transactions on Information Theory, 43*(6), 1986–1992. doi:10.1109/18.641562.

Karvounas, D., Georgakopoulos, A., Stavroulaki, V., Koutsouris, N., Tsagkaris, K., & Demestichas, P. (2012). Resource allocation to femtocells for coordinated capacity expansion of wireless access infrastructures. *EURASIP Journal on Wireless Communications and Networking*, (1): 310. doi:10.1186/1687-1499-2012-310.

Kesidis, G., Walrand, J., & Chang, C. S. (1993). Effective bandwidths for multiclass Markov fluids and other ATM sources. *IEEE/ACM Transactions on Networking, 1*(4), 424–428. doi:10.1109/90.251894.

Kiskani, M. K., Khalaj, B. H., & Vakilinia, S. (2010). Delay QoS provisioning in cognitive radio systems using adaptive modulation. In *Proceedings of the 6th ACM Workshop on QoS and Security for Wireless and Mobile Networks (Q2SWinet)*. ACM.

Lai, L., & El Gamal, H. (2008). The water-filling game in fading multiple-access channels. *IEEE Transactions on Information Theory, 54*(5), 2110–2122. doi:10.1109/TIT.2008.920340.

Li, L., & Goldsmith, A. J. (2001). Capacity and optimal resource allocation for fading broadcast channels: Ergodic capacity. *IEEE Transactions on Information Theory, 47*(3), 1083–1102. doi:10.1109/18.915665.

Ma, Y., Zhang, H., Yuan, D., & Chen, H. H. (2009). Adaptive power allocation with quality-of-service guarantee in cognitive radio networks. *Computer Communications, 32*(18), 1975–1982. doi:10.1016/j.comcom.2009.06.012.

Mao, L., Xu, S., Fu, T., & Huang, Q. (2012). *Game theory based power allocation algorithm in high-speed mobile environment*. Paper presented at Vehicular Technology Conference Fall (VTC 2012-Fall). Québec City, Canada.

Musavian, L., & Aissa, S. (2009). Fundamental capacity limits of cognitive radio in fading environments with imperfect channel information. *IEEE Transactions on Communications, 57*(11), 3472–3480. doi:10.1109/TCOMM.2009.11.070410.

Musavian, L., & Aissa, S. (2010). Effective capacity of delay-constrained cognitive radio in Nakagami fading channels. *IEEE Transactions on Wireless Communications, 9*(3), 1054–1062. doi:10.1109/TWC.2010.03.081253.

Musavian, L., Aissa, S., & Lambotharan, S. (2011). Adaptive modulation in spectrum-sharing channels under delay quality-of-service constraints. *IEEE Transactions on Vehicular Technology, 60*(3), 901–911. doi:10.1109/TVT.2010.2097282.

Qiao, D., Gursoy, M. C., & Velipasalar, S. (2010). A noncooperative power control game in multi-access fading channels with quality of service (QoS) constraints. *Physical Communication, 3*(2), 97–104. doi:10.1016/j.phycom.2010.03.003.

Ren, S., & Letaief, K. B. (2009). Maximizing the effective capacity for wireless cooperative relay networks with QoS guarantees. *IEEE Transactions on Communications, 57*(7), 2148–2159. doi:10.1109/TCOMM.2009.07.070585.

Rezki, Z., & Alouini, M. (2012). Ergodic capacity of cognitive radio under imperfect channel-state information. *IEEE Transactions on Vehicular Technology, 61*(5), 2108–2119. doi:10.1109/TVT.2012.2195042.

Stavroulaki, V., Tsagkaris, K., Logothetis, M., Georgakopoulos, A., Demestichas, P., Gebert, J., & Filo, M. (2011). Opportunistic networks: An approach for exploiting cognitive radio networking technologies in the future Internet. *IEEE Vehicular Technology Magazine, 6*(3), 52–59. doi:10.1109/MVT.2011.941892.

Tang, J., & Zhang, X. (2007a). Quality-of-service driven power and rate adaptation over wireless links. *IEEE Transactions on Wireless Communications, 6*(8), 3058–3068. doi:10.1109/TWC.2007.051075.

Tang, J., & Zhang, X. (2007b). Quality-of-service driven power and rate adaptation for multichannel communications over wireless links. *IEEE Transactions on Wireless Communications, 6*(12), 4349–4360. doi:10.1109/TWC.2007.06031.

Tang, J., & Zhang, X. (2007c). Cross-layer modeling for quality of service guarantees over wireless links. *IEEE Transactions on Wireless Communications, 6*(12), 4504–4512. doi:10.1109/TWC.2007.06087.

Tang, J., & Zhang, X. (2008). Cross-layer-model based adaptive resource allocation for statistical QoS guarantees in mobile wireless networks. *IEEE Transactions on Wireless Communications, 7*(6), 2318–2328. doi:10.1109/TWC.2008.060293.

Vassaki, S., Panagopoulos, A. D., & Constantinou, P. (2012). Effective capacity and optimal power allocation for mobile satellite systems and services. *IEEE Communications Letters, 16*(1), 60–63. doi:10.1109/LCOMM.2011.110711.111881.

Vassaki, S., Poulakis, M., & Panagopoulos, A. D., & Constantinou, P. (2011). *Optimal power allocation under QoS constraints in cognitive radio systems.* Paper presented at the IEEE 8th International Symposium on Wireless Communication Systems (ISWCS '11). Aachen, Germany.

Wang, B., Wu, Y., & Liu, K., J., R. (2010). Game theory for cognitive radio networks: An overview. *Computer Networks, 54*(14), 2537–2561. doi:10.1016/j.comnet.2010.04.004.

Wu, D., & Negi, R. (2003). Effective capacity: a wireless link model for support of quality of service. *IEEE Transactions on Wireless Communications, 2*(4), 630–643.

Xie, X., & Guo, W. (2011). *Fundamental effective capacity limits of cognitive radio in fading environments with imperfect channel information.* Paper presented at International Conference on Computational Problem-Solving (ICCP '11). Aachen, Germany.

Zhang, X., Tang, J., Chen, H. H., Ci, S., & Guizani, M. (2006). Cross-layer-based modeling for quality of service guarantees in mobile wireless networks. *IEEE Communications Magazine, 44*(1), 100–106. doi:10.1109/MCOM.2006.1580939.

ADDITIONAL READING

Abdrabou, A., & Zhuang, W. (2011). *Statistical QoS evaluation for cognitive radio networks*. Paper presented at Global Telecommunications Conference (GLOBECOM 2011). Houston, TX.

Akyildiz, I. F., Lee, W.-Y., & Chowdhury, K. R. (2009). CRAHNs: Cognitive radio ad hoc networks. *Ad Hoc Networks*, 7(5), 810–836. doi:10.1016/j.adhoc.2009.01.001.

Akyildiz, I. F., Lee, W.-Y., Vuran, M. C., & Mohanty, S. (2008). A survey on spectrum management in cognitive radio networks. *IEEE Communications Magazine*, 46(4), 40–48. doi:10.1109/MCOM.2008.4481339.

Asghari, V., & Aissa, S. (2011). End-to-end performance of cooperative relaying in spectrum-sharing systems with quality of service requirements. *IEEE Transactions on Vehicular Technology*, 60(6), 2656–2668. doi:10.1109/TVT.2011.2136391.

Asghari, V., & Aissa, S. (2011). Resource management in spectrum-sharing cognitive radio broadcast channels: Adaptive time and power allocation. *IEEE Transactions on Communications*, 59(5), 1446–1457. doi:10.1109/TCOMM.2011.022811.090623.

Chen, D., Ji, H., & Leung, V. C. M. (2011). *Cross-layer QoS provisioning for cooperative transmissions over cognitive radio relay networks with imperfect spectrum sensing*. Paper presented at Global Telecommunications Conference (GLOBECOM 2011). Houston, TX.

Chen, Y., Yu, G., Zhang, Z., Chen, H.-H., & Qiu, P. (2008). On cognitive radio networks with opportunistic power control strategies in fading channels. *IEEE Transactions on Wireless Communications*, 7(7), 2752–2761. doi:10.1109/TWC.2008.070145.

Du, Q., Huang, Y., Ren, P., & Zhang, C. (2011). *Statistical delay control and QoS-driven power allocation over two-hop wireless relay links*. Paper presented at Global Telecommunications Conference (GLOBECOM 2011). Houston, TX.

Gong, X., Vorobyov, S. A., & Tellambura, C. (2011). Optimal bandwidth and power allocation for sum ergodic capacity under fading channels in cognitive radio networks. *IEEE Transactions on Signal Processing*, 59(4), 1814–1826. doi:10.1109/TSP.2010.2101069.

Han, Z., & Liu, K. J. (2008). *Resource allocation for wireless networks: Basics, techniques, and applications*. New York: Cambridge University Press. doi:10.1017/CBO9780511619748.

Harsini, J. S., & Lahouti, F. (2012). Effective capacity optimization for multiuser diversity systems with adaptive transmission. *Transactions on Emerging Telecommunications Technologies*, 23(6), 567–584. doi:10.1002/ett.2511.

Haykin, S. (2005). Cognitive radio: Brain-empowered wireless communications. *IEEE Journal on Selected Areas in Communications*, 23(2), 201–220. doi:10.1109/JSAC.2004.839380.

Hossain, E., & Bhargava, V. K. (2007). *Cognitive wireless communication networks*. Berlin: Springer. doi:10.1007/978-0-387-68832-9.

Hossain, E., Niyato, D., & Han, Z. (2009). *Dynamic spectrum access in cognitive radio networks*. New York: Cambridge University Press. doi:10.1017/CBO9780511609909.

Kang, X., Liang, Y.-C., Nallanathan, A., Garg, H. K., & Zhang, R. (2009). Optimal power allocation for fading channels in cognitive radio networks: Ergodic capacity and outage capacity. *IEEE Transactions on Wireless Communications*, 8(2), 940–950. doi:10.1109/TWC.2009.071448.

Kang, X., Zhang, R., Liang, Y.-C., & Garg, H. K. (2011). Optimal power allocation strategies for fading cognitive radio channels with primary user outage constraint. *IEEE Journal on Selected Areas in Communications, 29*(2), 374–383. doi:10.1109/JSAC.2011.110210.

Le, L. B., & Hossain, E. (2008). Resource allocation for spectrum underlay in cognitive radio networks. *IEEE Transactions on Wireless Communications, 7*(12), 5306–5315. doi:10.1109/T-WC.2008.070890.

Lien, S. Y., Lin, Y.-Y., & Chen, K.-C. (2011). Cognitive and game-theoretical radio resource management for autonomous femtocells with QoS guarantees. *IEEE Transactions on Wireless Communications, 10*(7), 2196–2206. doi:10.1109/TWC.2011.060711.100737.

Musavian, L., & Aissa, S. (2009). Capacity and power allocation for spectrum-sharing communications in fading channels. *IEEE Transactions on Wireless Communications, 8*(1), 148–156. doi:10.1109/T-WC.2009.070265.

Musavian, L., Aissa, S., & Lambotharan, S. (2010). Effective capacity for interference and delay constrained cognitive radio relay channels. *IEEE Transactions on Wireless Communications, 9*(5), 1698–1707. doi:10.1109/TCOMM.2010.05.090600.

Nadkar, T., Thumar, V., Tej, G. P. S., Merchant, S. N., & Desai, U. B. (2012). Distributed power allocation for secondary users in a cognitive radio scenario. *IEEE Transactions on Wireless Communications, 11*(4), 1576–1586. doi:10.1109/TWC.2012.020712.111502.

Qiao, D., Gursoy, M. C., & Velipasalar, S. (2012). Encrgy efficiency in multiaccess fading channels under QoS constraints. *EURASIP Journal on Wireless Communications and Networking,* (126): 1–16.

Qiao, D., Gursoy, M. C., & Velipasalar, S. (2012). Transmission strategies in multiple access fading channels with statistical QoS constraints. *IEEE Transactions on Information Theory, 58*(3), 1578–1593. doi:10.1109/TIT.2011.2175900.

Soret, B., Aguayo-Torres, M. C., & Entrambasaguas, J. T. (2010). Capacity with explicit delay guarantees for generic sources over correlated rayleigh channel. *IEEE Transactions on Wireless Communications, 9*(6), 1901–1911. doi:10.1109/TWC.2010.06.081599.

Wang, Y., Ren, P., Du, Q., & Su, Z. (2012). *Resource allocation and access strategy selection for QoS provisioning in cognitive networks.* Paper presented at IEEE International Conference on Communication (ICC 2012). Ottawa, Canada.

Wang, Y., Ren, P., Du, Q., & Zhang, C. (2012). Optimal resource allocation for spectrum sensing based cognitive radio networks with statistical QoS guarantees. *Mobile Networks and Applications, 17*(6), 711–720. doi:10.1007/s11036-012-0388-9.

Wang, Y., Ren, P., Li, F., & Su, Z. (2012). Cross-layer based power allocation over cognitive wireless relay link with statistical delay QoS guarantees. *Concurrency and Computation, 24*(11), 1239–1251. doi:10.1002/cpe.1895.

Wu, D., & Negi, R. (2006). Effective capacity-based quality of service measures for wireless networks. *ACM Mobile Networks and Applications, 11*(1), 91–99. doi:10.1007/s11036-005-4463-3.

Xie, R., Yu, F. R., & Ji, H. (2012). Dynamic resource allocation for heterogeneous services in cognitive radio networks with imperfect channel sensing. *IEEE Transactions on Vehicular Technology, 61*(2), 770–780. doi:10.1109/TVT.2011.2181966.

Xie, X., & Guo, W. (2012). Effective capacity analysis of spectrum sharing system based on multi-user diversity. *Journal of Computer Information Systems*, 8(7), 2941–2948.

Yang, Y., & Aissa, S. (2011). *On the capacity of multiple cognitive links through common relay under spectrum-sharing constraints*. Paper presented at IEEE International Conference on Communications (ICC 2011). Kyoto, Japan.

Zhang, C., Wang, X., Guan, X., & Chen, H.-H. (2009). *Quality-of-service in cognitive radio networks with collaborative sensing*. Paper presented at Global Telecommunications Conference (GLOBECOM 2009). Hawaii, HI.

Zhang, R., Liang, Y.-C., & Cui, S. (2010). Dynamic resource allocation in cognitive radio networks. *IEEE Signal Processing Magazine*, 27(3), 102–114. doi:10.1109/MSP.2010.936022.

Chapter 5
Spectrum Aggregation in Cognitive Radio Access Networks from Power Control Perspective

Konstantinos Chatzikokolakis
National and Kapodistrian University of Athens, Greece

George Katsikas
National and Kapodistrian University of Athens, Greece

Panagiotis Spapis
National and Kapodistrian University of Athens, Greece

Roi Arapoglou
National and Kapodistrian University of Athens, Greece

Makis Stamatelatos
National and Kapodistrian University of Athens, Greece

Alexandros Kaloxylos
University of Peloponnese, Greece

Nancy Alonistioti
National and Kapodistrian University of Athens, Greece

ABSTRACT

Spectrum scarcity has motivated researchers and standardization bodies to work towards flexible spectrum usage. One of the solutions, Spectrum Aggregation, as proposed by 3GPP, is a way to increase wireless capacity through providing additional bandwidth to users. This chapter presents the Spectrum Aggregation scenario as it is proposed to be incorporated in LTE-Advanced. Furthermore, the interesting extensions of FP7 SACRA European research project regarding Spectrum Aggregation are described. The business and the functional aspects stemming from the incorporation of this solution in the LTE-Advanced networks are presented in detail. From the functionalities that are the cornerstone of the Spectrum Aggregation, namely spectrum sensing, admission control, and power control, the latter one is studied, which is not thoroughly investigated yet, and the authors present its key features. Moreover, a typical power control algorithm is described and enhanced with learning capabilities and policies in order to meet the requirements of the Spectrum Aggregation scenario; the simulation results highlight the need for power control schemes in Spectrum Aggregation cases.

DOI: 10.4018/978-1-4666-4189-1.ch005

Copyright © 2013, IGI Global. Copying or distributing in print or electronic forms without written permission of IGI Global is prohibited.

INTRODUCTION

The vast proliferation of wireless devices and services for mobile communications, WiFi and TV broadcast serves as a characteristic example of how much the society depends on radio spectrum which is becoming increasingly scarce. Towards this direction, Federal Communications Commission (FCC) (Federal Communications Commission, 2012) has been investigating the exploitation of innovative radio design techniques to optimally manage the radio resource frequencies. In addition, FCC has recommended over the past years that spectral efficiency could be significantly improved by deploying wireless devices which can coexist with the incumbent licensed (primary) users. Thus, motivated by the increasing needs for efficient spectrum usage, 3GPP has defined three functionalities that increase the provided capacity to the users, namely, Spectrum Aggregation (or Carrier Aggregation), enhanced use of multi-antenna techniques (MIMO), and support for Relay Nodes (RN). These functionalities have been introduced in the Long Term Evolution Advanced (LTE-advanced) so as 3G devices would exploit unused component carriers, in order to increase bitrate and to achieve efficient heterogeneous network planning. The Spectrum Aggregation increases the users' capacity by providing to them more spectrum carriers (licensed or unlicensed) through novel spectrum sensing and spectrum allocation techniques that comprise admission control, power control and user partitioning algorithms. Enhanced use of multi-antenna techniques is used to increase the overall bitrate through transmission of at least two different data streams on at least two different antennas—using the same resources in both frequency and time, separated only through the use of different reference signals—to be received by two or more antennas. RNs are small-sized base stations operating at low power levels; they are used for providing enhanced coverage and capacity at cell edges, or connection to remote areas

without fiber infrastructure. RN is expected to be connected to the Evolved Node B (eNodeBs) via a radio interface, whilst the radio resources are shared among the User Equipments (UEs) which are served directly by either the Donor eNodeB or the RN. Two types of RNs have been identified, based on whether they use the same frequency as the Donor eNodeB or not. In the former type, RN could suffer from self-interference issues which could be surpassed with a time sharing scheme between transmitting and receiving, or by placing the transmitter and the receiver at different locations. The RNs enable the efficient network planning by providing enhanced coverage and capacity at cell edges; RNs can also be used to connect to remote areas without fiber connection. Out of the three functionalities Spectrum Aggregation has received the most attention as the most straightforward way to increase the capacity offered to the users is to increase the available bandwidth.

The Spectrum Aggregation scenario considers as prerequisite a set of functionalities for efficient usage of the available resources. A typical cognitive radio network comprises of nodes that attempt to transmit opportunistically in unused frequency bands that are not licensed to operate at; spectrum sensing realizes the identification of the potential spectrum holes that a CR user could exploit. The admission control mechanism aims at identifying whether a CR user can be served using the available network resources, without causing interference to existing incumbent ones. However, unlicensed users also compete with each other for resource allocation, thus a power control mechanism that will address the interference mitigation among opportunistic users is also required. The spectrum sensing and the admission control functionalities are topics well investigated in the literature, whereas the opportunistic usage of resources has recently started attracting the interest of the research community, especially in such scenarios.

This chapter aims at presenting initially the concept of Spectrum Aggregation, as it is defined by 3GPP and endorsed by European research projects and standardization bodies. The introduction of Spectrum Aggregation concept is then followed by the analysis of the enhancements and views designed in the context of the EU funded project called SACRA (FP7 EU SACRA, 2010); these views and enhancements discuss apart from the functionality of evolved mechanisms, the business aspects and the mapping of these mechanisms in the LTE-advanced network. After the description of Spectrum Aggregation and its advancements we focus on the involved mechanisms that are required for the realization of this concept as well as the constraints imposed. Taking into account that the coordination for resource usage, and more specifically the power control among the users, is a topic that needs to be further investigated, we briefly present and categorize a set of solutions available in the literature. Also, we choose a typical power control mechanism, the Cooperative Power Control that is applicable in a variety of environments (i.e., sensors, WiFi, LTE-advanced) and describe it thoroughly. Furthermore, following the analysis of the power control algorithm, we apply a set of enhancements in the mechanism in order to highlight its expendability; the enhancements concern the incorporation of learning capabilities and policies for guaranteeing important telecom aspects (e.g., QoS, fairness among opportunistic users etc). Finally, the chapter concludes with some very interesting findings regarding the use of power control schemes and their necessity in Spectrum Aggregation use cases.

SPECTRUM AGGREGATION SCENARIO

As mentioned in the introduction the growing need for radio resources has made essential the elaboration of innovative concepts such as the Spectrum Aggregation, the Cognitive Relays and the design and realization of enhanced hardware parts such as the multi-antennas to improve spectral efficiency. Out of these three techniques Spectrum Aggregation has attracted most of the attention of researchers, standardization bodies and companies. In this section we present the Spectrum Aggregation scenario the advancements and the functionalities this concept comprises in order to utilize discrete spectrum bands and increase the capacity provided to the users. Also, we describe the business benefits for the operators and the users stemming from a Spectrum Aggregation scenario in the context of a European research project, namely FP7 SACRA. Additionally we show the way various mechanisms (that are related to the Spectrum Aggregation scenario) are placed into SACRA's functional architecture.

Spectrum Aggregation: Current Trends and State of the Art Approach

Spectral efficiency is generally defined as "the information rate that can be transmitted over a given bandwidth in a specific communication system." Ofcom, an independent regulator for the UK communications industries, considers the fragmentation of spectrum as a result of the adoption of more spectrally efficient technologies, of old techniques not using frequencies efficiently, of allocations not being used and also for historical reasons of allocating spectrum (QinetiQ, 2006). In such demanding context where the services' needs for spectrum is increasing, Spectrum Aggregation has been introduced by 3GPP as an enabler for overall spectrum efficiency, as it will increase the capacity in wireless and mobile communications by providing additional bandwidth.

As presented in QinetiQ's report (QinetiQ, 2006) "the concept of Spectrum Aggregation is to exploit spectrum fragments simultaneously to create wider bandwidths for communications systems". As mentioned by Wang & Huang (2010), "the discrete spectrum bands can sustain information flow transmission service as the same as the continuous spectrum bands"; in this way, cognitive radio enables support of highly demanding—in terms of bandwidth—services through sensing and utilizing discrete (idle) spectrum bands.

Figure 1 illustrates the Spectrum Aggregation Scenario as in 3GPP. In this 3GPP scenario, the aggregated spectrum component can have a bandwidth of 1.4, 3, 5, 10, 15, or 20 MHz. Thus, up to five (5) component carriers (i.e., the individual component carriers can be of different bandwidths) can be aggregated leading thus to maximum bandwidth of 100 MHz. The number of aggregated carriers can be different in DownLink (DL) and Uplink (UL).

Two ways for Spectrum Aggregation have been incorporated in the LTE-A (Figure 1):

- Intra-band
  - Contiguous allocation featuring use of contiguous component carriers within the same operating frequency band (as defined for LTE – user A with component carriers A1 and A2). Different frequency allocation scenarios may limit applicability of intra-band contiguous Spectrum Aggregation.

  - Non-contiguous allocation; in this scenario the component carriers belong to the same operating frequency band but are separated by a frequency gap (user A with component carrier A4).
- Inter-band non-contiguous allocation; in this case the component carriers belong to different operating frequency bands (user B with component carriers A3 and B1).

The coverage of the serving cells may differ – both due to component carrier frequencies but also from power planning – useful for heterogeneous network planning. Different component carriers can be planned to provide different coverage, i.e. different cell size. In the case of inter-band Carrier Aggregation, the component carriers will experience different path loss, which is proportional to frequency.

The introduction of Spectrum Aggregation concept has attracted the attention of research activities, standardization bodies and companies since it was standardized for Long Term Evolution Advanced (LTE-A) based on the 3rd generation

Figure 1. Intra and inter-band spectrum aggregation

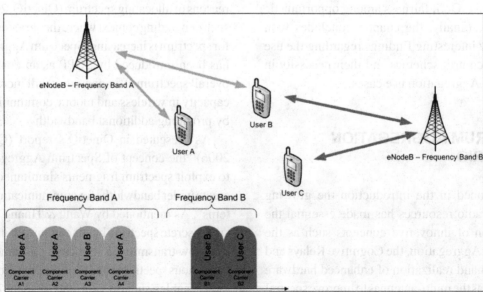

telecommunication (3G) systems. QinetiQ is a research organization aiming at exploiting the advantages of Spectrum Aggregation technique to sustain broadband services, and study the causes of spectrum fragmentation, the utilization principles and the realization methods. Furthermore, FCC is working on the production of a framework that will set the rules operators should follow in order to allocate temporarily spectrum for opportunistic usage. Additionally, many researchers have shown great interest over the past years in Spectrum Aggregation cases. Robinson, Shukla, Burns & Atefi (2005) have introduced a spectrum trading scheme that enables spectrum owners to exchange component carriers of their own bands and aggregate the resources for increasing the provided capacity and satisfy thus, the user demands. Chen, Zhang and Jia (2005) propose a discontiguous spectrum access and aggregation scheme that allows the aggregation of discrete spectrum bands and a spectrum assignment algorithm in cognitive ad-hoc networks, namely Aggregation-Aware Spectrum Assignment (AASA), that takes Spectrum Aggregation into consideration. Ratasuk, Tolli & Ghosh (2010) provide an overview of Carrier Aggregation concept and focus on the technical issues of the concept regarding the implementation, control signaling design and coexistence analysis.

Besides the standardization bodies and the research organizations, several European Union research projects have been working on the concept of Spectrum Aggregation and the way the available spectrum could be further exploited in a more efficient and sophisticated manner (FP7 EU COGEU, 2010; FP7 EU QoSMOS 2010; FP7 EU SENDORA, 2008; FP7 EU SACRA, 2010). SENDORA project has developed innovative techniques based on sensor networks that will support the coexistence of licensed and unlicensed wireless users in a same area, while QoSMOS project aims at Quality of Service provision and mobility driven cognitive radio systems design. COGEU project is a composite of technical, business, and regulatory/policy domains, with the objective of taking advantage of the TV digital switch-over (or analog switch-off) by developing cognitive radio systems that leverage the favorable propagation characteristics of the TVWS through the introduction and promotion of real-time secondary spectrum trading and the creation of new spectrum commons regime. SACRA project aims at designing and demonstrating advanced techniques for mobile communications, focusing on dynamic management of dual band license (i.e., Digital Dividend – 790 to 862 MHz – and LTE – 2.6 GHz – bands) and usage of TV White Space (470 to 790 MHz) when required by the needs of the users. SACRA's project objective is the study and demonstration of spectrum and energy efficient communications through multi-band cognitive radio. The project aims at providing an integrated hardware and software platform to support cognitive operation. SACRA project helps filling the gap in the Cognitive Radio area by providing the SACRA multi-band cognitive radio technology and addressing the need for new regulation policies regarding the use of the radio spectrum. In this section we present SACRA's views and extensions regarding Spectrum Aggregation. The innovative features brought by SACRA are the combination of advanced hardware design with new cognitive radio algorithms for spectrum sensing and radio resource management to support flexible communications on several bands, allowing an optimized use of the radio frequency spectrum in the considered bands. Furthermore, the key characteristic that discriminates SACRA from other EU projects is the integration of those features into the aforementioned demonstrator platform that will realize the identified mechanisms and functionalities of the Spectrum Aggregation concept.

Spectrum Aggregation: The SACRA Approach

SACRA project offers a complete view of the business, and spectrum utilization benefits stemming from the Spectrum Aggregation concept.

More specifically, in the considered approach, SACRA extends the concept of Spectrum Aggregation as defined in the release 10 of 3GPP LTE-Advanced standard, by considering a system able to manage the aggregation of licensed spectrum in the 2.6 GHz and in the digital dividend bands, and, available spectrum in the TV white spaces (TVWS) band. Operating in the TVWS will improve the throughput experienced by the users of a given cell, in particular at the border of the cell, provided that the network has the capability to protect the incumbent users from a noticeable degradation of their QoS. The network operator, using both licensed and non-licensed spectrum, could monitor the use of the TVWS thanks to the access to databases containing the information about the licensed and unlicensed users in any channel of the TVWS band, accordingly to the current trends in regulation (ECC Report 159, 2011; FCC 10-174, 2010). The aforementioned databases should be based on existing national databases, which could suffer from not being up-to-date, and which could provide more information than expected. The UEs should also be able to enrich the information provided by the geo-location database with the result of sensing operations performed to get up-to-date informa-

tion on the channels of interest, and also needed to protect the communications of the Programme Making and Special Events (PMSE) equipments, which do not register. Even though that querying a database will not give a precise estimation of the spectrum holes but will just provide information on probable spectrum holes, it is crucial to have access to such information because sensing tasks for the whole band would be time and energy consuming (Ofcom 2012).

Furthermore, in the SACRA Spectrum Aggregation case, compared to the current status of the LTE-A standard, the spectrum to operate (i.e., licensed or unlicensed) is selected dynamically in relation to the user needs (Figure 2). The resource managers of the eNodeB make this dynamic selection and perform the Spectrum Aggregation using certain knowledge on the characteristics (capacity, range, etc.) of the channels of interest: the licensed and the available channels for an opportunistic use in the TVWS band.

Motivation, opportunities, and benefits for the involved business players can be captured by a business architecture model as presented in the sequel. For clarity, we need to differentiate between a business player (an organization, a company, etc.) and the various business roles, which reflect

Figure 2. SACRA spectrum aggregation (adopted by FP7 EU SACRA, 2010)

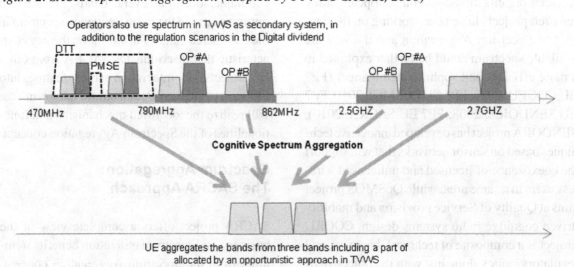

specific value propositions and can be assigned to different players according to different scenarios.

Business and Regulatory Considerations

The need for additional spectrum to support rapidly growing mobile traffic growth is recognized. The TV white space band and digital dividend has been identified as potential bands for wireless broadband services which will allow supporting this traffic growth. Deploying a new spectrum band (e.g. TVWS) allows Network Operator (NO) to avoid significant costs. NO can initially upgrade existing base stations with a supplemental component carrier rather than using the more expensive option of building additional base stations. Once the additional capacity from the spectrum upgrades is used up, the NO can deploy new base stations which are more effective in terms of expenses. In a competitive market these lower costs will result in lower end user prices for mobile broadband and mobile multimedia services.

As reported in (Gigaom, 2012) European Commission wants license holders to share spectrum and hand over spectrum usage to address radiowave logjam due to explosion of Wi-Fi, 4G, smart grids and the Internet of Things. Wireless spectrum is running out, and those who own it must play nicely with others who want it. At least, that's according to the European Commission, which is hoping to avoid a spectrum crunch. As indicated in European Union press release (EU 2012) advances in technology make efficient spectrum sharing possible. Many new wireless technologies are designed to share bands in which no license is required (license-exempt bands), while others make additional spectrum resources available by, for example, providing wireless broadband services in between TV frequencies (the 'white spaces'). To maximize the benefits of spectrum sharing, regulatory barriers need to be removed and incentives to be provided. This requires new

regulatory approaches to give different users the right to use a given frequency band on a shared basis.

In the regulatory field, the CEPT SE43 working group has defined the technical and operational requirements for wireless systems operating in the TVWS (ECC Report 159, 2011). In this context, cognitive radio devices may be granted access to TVWS spectrum, provided that they are not causing harmful interference to the incumbent users; this is achieved by using cognitive spectrum access techniques. The report refers to different kinds of devices, including, for example, personal/portable devices, home/office devices and private and public access points. In the specific case of personal and portable devices they should be small enough to be carried, in the manner of mobile phones, personal media players, or laptops according to the report. The ECC report 159 (ECC Report 159, 2011) also provides the transmission parameters that should be used to protect the licensed services in the TVWS (including TV broadcasting and PMSE systems). Moreover, FCC has published a memorandum (FCC 10-174, 2010) that allows "Super Wi-Fi" technologies operating in the TVWS. The "Super Wi-Fi" devices must include geo-location capabilities and a database access, but the implementation of sensing techniques is not required anymore.

Therefore, the Spectrum Aggregation, as extended by SACRA, addresses the regulatory aspects and raises new business aspects, including enhanced bandwidth demands, new services and new types of user terminals - mainly smart phones and tablets, leading to corresponding motivation opportunities and value propositions for the roles in this scenario. A business architecture which has been elaborated based on the scenario implications and the regulatory trends is presented in Figure 3 which illustrates the main business and the revenue flows corresponding to value proposed among roles, based on their motivation around the considered business scenario.

Provision of better QoS, enhanced service provision and efficient infrastructure operation and management form key interests for the Network Service provider. The Platform HW Developer is motivated to design and develop the needed hardware for operation in aggregated bands and opportunistic access to TVWS in order to join the business case; hardware design costs are a critical point for a new market sector which could be formed by the availability and provision of aggregating devices. This is also affected by the fact that the number of spectrum fragments participating in Spectrum Aggregation tends to increase (Analysis of Mason, 2012). The Platform Software Developer is interested in developing software modules for operation in aggregated spectrum bands as well as to support the aggregating tasks and the access of TVWS spectrum portions. The Spectrum Legislator has to consider methods for retaining power for Spectrum Aggregation taking into account that this would have

an impact to licensees; policies and rules should be issued accordingly and compliance costs can be claimed. Spectrum Owner has to determine regulated/unregulated spectrum based on regulation rules thus addressing directives which have been made available by CEPT, for example.

As mentioned, Figure 3 implies a set of interactions among the players, value propositions, and revenue flows. More specifically, the End User pays the Network Service Provider and Application Service Provider as well as Platform HW Developer for device acquisition; respective software is provided as "built-in" the UE as developed by the Platform SW Developer. The Network Service Provider pays the Spectrum Owner for spectrum licenses, Platform HW Developer and Platform SW Developer for hardware and software acquisition, and Application Service Provider (revenue sharing) for application service provision; the Network Service Provider also pays the Spectrum Legislation for Spectrum compli-

Figure 3. Business architecture model

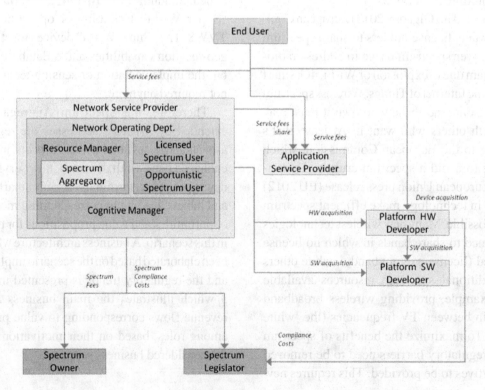

ance. Regarding the infrastructure management, the Network Service Provider compensates the Network Operating Department for infrastructure management, and the Spectrum Aggregator and the Cognitive Manager for opportunistic access to TVWS bands. The link between the Network Operating Department and the Spectrum Legislator implies interaction for Spectrum Aggregation compliance. Regarding the Spectrum Owner, he holds and manages the (primary) spectrum access rights and manages the knowledge concerning opportunistic spectrum usage and aggregated bands. Finally, the Spectrum Legislator is being paid by the Platform HW Developer for the product's compliance to the legislator rules.

Spectrum Aggregation Extended Functionalities in SACRA Context

In the SACRA methodology the aforementioned benefits arising from the business model are being captured by two cases of Spectrum Aggregation, namely intra-cell Spectrum Aggregation and inter-cell Spectrum Aggregation. It should be noted that this type of discrimination is based on the serving eNodeBs and is different from the intra-band/inter-band categorization which is based on the type of radio resources used (i.e. whether the component carriers are from the same band or not). Figure 4 (a) illustrates the intra-cell case. In such case each eNodeB is capable of providing services using the licensed band and improving its capacity with additional resources available (for secondary use) in the TVWS. Thus, UEs are served from a single eNodeB (having component carriers for LTE and TVWS). Figure 4 (b) highlights the inter-cell case where carriers across two cells, either co-located (with several sectors) or distant, are considered to serve one single UE. In both cases, a multi-operator environment is assumed.

For both intra and inter-cell cases, a set of Radio Resource Management mechanisms that will lead to the optimum allocation of the available radio resources in conjunction to a spectrum

sensing mechanism is required. Each UE must be capable to select the most suitable sensing algorithm and perform the sensing process, decide whether it should transmit in unlicensed band or not and tune its transmitting parameters to reduce mutual interference with other UEs. Additionally, a mechanism that makes the decision of partitioning the opportunistic users to the available component carriers is required. So, in the considered cases, initially, the UE, with the sensing configuration mechanism identifies which is the most suitable sensing algorithm for the considered environment. The decision is made locally in the UE, using local information and information stemming from the base station as well. Then, when the user tries to access a specific service, the local sensing algorithm senses the environment in order to detect primary signals in the considered area, and the (local) spectrum access control algorithm decides whether a user shall be permitted to operate in TVWS. The cooperative power control algorithm (located in the terminals) undertakes the coordination of the transmission power of each device (i.e. UE) participating in the scheme. It must be clarified that among the users that are associated to the same base station, the operation of a cooperative power control scheme is not required. However, such scheme is necessary for coordination among users associated to neighboring cells; the base station at this case operates for information fusion among the UEs in the area under consideration. In such scenario, the base station, using a user partitioning algorithm, decides the optimal aggregation of the available spectrum so as to fulfill users' demands.

In case a primary user appears in the environment, he will be detected by the local sensing algorithm of each user's equipment. Such information is being communicated to the spectrum access control algorithm (operating in the UE) which decides whether the user will be allowed to transmit in the TVWS taking into account the primary outage probability, in order to ensure

Figure 4. (a) Intra-cell spectrum aggregation, (b) inter-cell spectrum aggregation

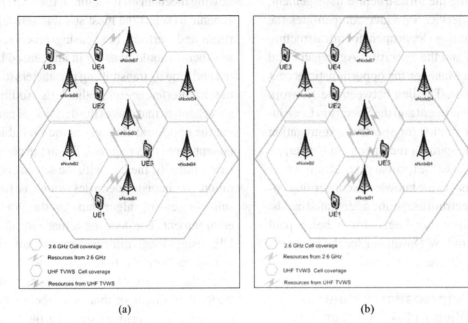

(a)   (b)

that the interference which the primary users will perceive is not going to exceed a maximum allowed threshold. The base station, again, decides the optimal aggregation of the available spectrum, so as to fulfill users' demands.

The afore-described scenario is a typical storyline, materializing the concept of Spectrum Aggregation and identifying the required functionalities for its incorporation in LTE advanced networks. Trying to go a step beyond, in SACRA they have linked the user perceived QoS with the inability of the sensing algorithm to detect correctly the presence of primary users in the area. Thus, in case QoS degradation is identified the sensing configuration system takes into account this information and modifies the sensing parameters (i.e. sensing frequency etc.), or even selects another algorithm for the sensing procedure, in order for the UEs to proceed in more accurate sensing.

For addressing both intra and inter-cell Spectrum Aggregation, the UEs and the eNodeBs should be enhanced with mechanisms for more sophisticated sensing, and accessing the wireless medium. These mechanisms, as mentioned afore,

include: *sensing for detecting primary signals in the served area, radio resource management for checking the operation of UE(s) in TVWS bands, spectrum aggregation decision mechanism, interference mitigation mechanism* in cases of present primary users and *transmission power coordination among users associated to neighboring cells*. Such functionalities should be placed in the LTE-advanced network elements in order to highlight the applicability of the enhanced Spectrum Aggregation scenario.

Figure 5 presents the SACRA reference architecture consisting of a set of functional blocks, necessary for materializing the concept of Spectrum Aggregation. The Cognitive Radio Resource Management, the Cognitive Engine and the Joint Radio Resource Management are responsible for tuning the transmitting and receiving parameters (e.g., power control, coding) and providing flexible spectrum allocation among the opportunistic users based on the sensed environment. The Information Management undertakes the message exchange scheme required for the coordination of the network entities (i.e. UEs and

Figure 5. Reference functional architecture

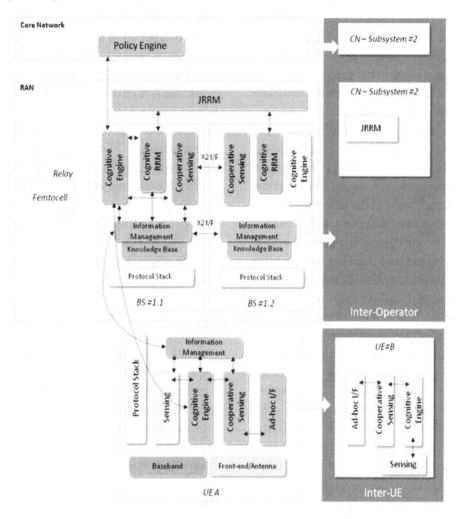

eNodeBs from various operators). The Cooperative Sensing evaluates all area measurement and information regarding the spectrum, interference, primary user and neighbor sensing/detection and selects the neighbour's UEs with the aid of sensing rules. Finally, the Policy Engine manages all the high level rules, by deriving or/and disseminating policies (including global policies).

As spectrum aggregation scenarios involve management of component carriers from various frequency bands, efficient and flexible mechanisms that will enable the UE to switch among bands when needed (i.e. when a primary user is present) are required. These mechanisms will facilitate the UE to exploit the available resources in an optimal way so as to fulfill his demands for bandwidth. In the following section we present these techniques that are necessary for the realization of the Spectrum Aggregation concept.

Spectrum Sensing and Radio Resource Management Functionalities in Spectrum Aggregation

The Spectrum Aggregation concept implies that a set of novel radio resource management techniques are required to optimize the way opportunistic users transmit in unlicensed bands, given the presence of primary users. These techniques comprise a set of mechanisms so that the opportunistic users will be capable to dynamically select a sensing algorithm to detect the presence of primary users and adapt their transmitting and receiving parameters accordingly.

Firstly, spectrum sensing mechanisms are necessary as it is required from opportunistic users to perform real-time wideband monitoring of the licensed spectrum they intend to use. Three methods are widely used in the literature; the energy detector, the feature detector and the matched filtering and coherent detection. Energy Detector is easy to implement and does not require prior knowledge about primary signals, but suffers from high false alarm probability and is unreliable in low SNR regimes. Moreover, this method cannot determine whether the sensed signals are coming from primary users, or other signal sources. Feature Detector overcomes the problems of energy detector, is more robust against noise uncertainty and is capable to distinguish primary system's signals from other types of transmissions but specific features (e.g. cyclostationary features) is required to be associated with primary signals. Matched filtering and coherent detection is even more robust than feature detector to noise uncertainty, but is a very complex method that requires prior information regarding the primary signals. Besides the advantages and the disadvantages of each method, there is also one additional obstacle that these techniques cannot overcome. Factors such as noise uncertainty, multipath effect and shadowing effects, reduce significantly the detection performance of a single user. Therefore, cooperative sensing has been considered as a potential solution that will improve the detection accuracy due to the spatial and multi-user diversity. Cooperative spectrum sensing could follow a centralized approach where a secondary base plays the role of the central controller that aggregates information received from the users and based on decision making process determines which channels could

be accessed from opportunistic users and informs them accordingly. On the other hand, this process could be applied in a distributed manner; in that case a message exchange scheme among users is required. All the aforementioned approaches are sensitive to the environment and very careful selection of their parameters is needed. Furthermore, none of those approaches outperforms the rest in all circumstances. Therefore, in a Cognitive Radio device (where more than one sensing mechanisms are available) a sensing selection and configuration mechanism is required. This mechanism is considered part of the Radio Resource Management and interacts with the sensing algorithms and the admission control as shown in Figure 6. Sensing algorithm selection and configuration is responsible for the dynamic selection and adaptation of the most suitable mechanism available that will perform the sensing procedure.

Each of the opportunistic users, based on the sensed environment, decides whether he should transmit in the unlicensed band or not. As the number of opportunistic users increases the problem of accessing the unlicensed spectrum becomes more complex and necessitates the usage of access control mechanisms that will maximize the number of opportunistic users allowed to transmit. This decision could be based on the maximum interference that the user will cause to the primary users present in the area, as well as the corresponding decisions of other opportunistic users present in the area. Therefore, various approaches are available in the literature and can be classified based on the network architecture (i.e. centralized or distributed), the collaborative behavior of the UEs (i.e. cooperative or non-cooperative), the spectrum management principle (i.e. spectrum overlay or spectrum underlay) and the spectrum bands the secondary users are using (i.e., open spectrum sharing or licensed spectrum sharing) (Wang & Liu, 2011).

As described above, spectrum sensing and admission control are two well investigated areas. Power control on the contrary, has not

Figure 6. Spectrum sensing and radio resource management interactions

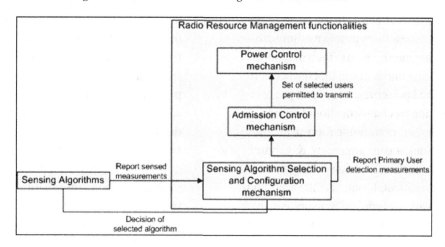

received similar attention over the past years. Such a mechanism is required as its functionality is twofold; on the one hand energy spent by the UE if it transmitted always at the maximum allowed level is conserved and on the other hand interference among the users is mitigated. The latter functionality could be further split into two categories; interference mitigation among primary-secondary users and interference mitigation only among secondary users. The first category is well investigated and many approaches based game-theoretic solutions or function optimization techniques are available in the literature. On the other hand, the latter category is an open research area and the available possible solutions of this problem are presented in the following section.

Power Control in Spectrum Aggregation

As mentioned in the previous section, the Spectrum Aggregation scenario is strongly related to three functions that act as enablers for its incorporation in LTE advanced environments, namely, the spectrum sensing, the admission control and the power control. The two first ones have been thoroughly studied, whereas the latter has recently started attracting the interest of the research community especially in cases of mitigating mutual interference among opportunistic users. In the past, power control schemes have been applied mainly in sensor networks, in order to extend the sensors' battery life. More recent researches have been focusing on other networks as well, such as WiFi and cellular ones. In this section, we briefly present some solutions available in the literature for the three identified application areas (i.e., WSN, WLANs, and cellular networks). Also, we choose a typical power control mechanism, applicable in all three cases and present it in details. The objective of this mechanism is twofold; the energy gains on the one hand, the minimization of the interference on the other. The motivation behind such selection is related to the mechanism's adaptability to various wireless environments and its extendibility, thus enabling the incorporation of policies, learning capabilities etc.

Power Control Schemes State of the Art Analysis

Power control techniques have been applied in wireless networks in three application areas, namely wireless sensor networks (WSNs), wireless local area networks (WLANs) and cellular networks. Each application area has its specific purposes that should be served, thus the objectives (i.e., power consumption in WSNs, interference mitigation in WLANs and cellular networks etc) in each category are different. In every case, the wireless devices access the wireless medium arbitrarily thus causing interference to their neighbors.

In WSNs, taking into account that the network nodes have limited power resources and processing capabilities, the mechanisms should minimize the computation and communication overheads (Akyildiz, Su, Sankarasubramaniam, & Cayirci, 2002. Sensor networks have been widely used to monitor the environmental context of the users and may comprise various types of sensors capable to measure temperature, pressure, presence or absence of certain objects, characteristics of an object (e.g.., current speed, direction and size, etc). Furthermore, interference mitigation is not the main objective in WSNs and this is the main reason why it is addressed as a generic power control issue. Solutions available in the literature could be considered mainly as power control mechanisms and divided into two categories, namely Sleep/Wakeup Protocols and MAC Protocols with Low Duty-Cycle ones:

- Sleep/Wakeup schemes, (i.e., on-demand, scheduled rendezvous, or asynchronous schemes) (Yue, Sun, & Jin, 2010; Jin, Yue, & Sun, 2012) implemented as independent protocols on top of the MAC protocol (i.e. at the network or the application layer). Independent sleep/wakeup protocols can be further subdivided into three main categories: on-demand, scheduled rendezvous, and asynchronous schemes. The former ones are based on the idea that nodes should wake up only when other nodes need to communicate with them. Typical problem for this category is the identification of the conditions under which a node needs to communicate with other nodes and therefore the triggering of the mechanism that will inform these nodes to wake up. The scheduling rendezvous approaches have been introduced to overcome this

problem. Based on these solutions the nodes follow a coordinated wake up procedure with their neighbors and remain active for a short time slot in order to exchange information with the neighbors. Such approaches though, cause extra energy consumption as nodes needs to communicate do not always follow a typical periodicity. In such cases asynchronous sleep/wakeup approaches could be applied when sophisticated mechanisms enable the nodes to wake up only when they have to receive information from the neighbors (Rezaei, & Mobininejad, 2012).

- MAC protocols for wireless sensor networks focusing on the implementation of a low duty-cycle scheme for power management (Alavi. Walsh, & Hayes, 2009; Ye, Heidemann, & Estrin, 2002; Hu, & Tang, 2011; Tang, Sun, Gurewitz, & Johnson, 2011). MAC protocols for wireless sensor networks focusing on the implementation of a low duty-cycle scheme for power management (Alavi. Walsh, & Hayes, 2009; Ye, Heidemann, & Estrin, 2002; Hu, & Tang, 2011; Tang, Sun, Gurewitz, & Johnson, 2011). These solutions can be categorized into contention-based, TDMA-based, hybrid, and cross layer MAC protocols according to the used channel access policy. Contention-based MAC protocols are based on the idea that a node will compete for the wireless channel when it needs to send data; such approach requires no coordination among the nodes accessing the channel. TDMA-based MAC Protocols offer an inherent collision-free scheme by assigning unique time slot for every node to send or receive data and solve the hidden terminal problem. The hybrid MAC protocols use the random access channel for the control packets and the data packets are transmitted in the scheduled access channel thus achieving higher energy gains and better scalability and flexibility. Finally, the cross layer MAC protocols optimize the communication in terms of transmitting only the necessary information, omitting the transmission of corrupted or useless packets (Rezaei, & Mobininejad, 2012).

In 802.11 WiFi networks (i.e., WLANs), the power control among the Access Points is related to the interference mitigation. The interference mitigation concerns APs operating in the same, or adjacent channels, due to the overlap among them. Given the vast proliferation of the 802.11 technology, the interference mitigation is a very attractive research area. In the literature many approaches exist for the interference mitigation in WiFi networks; the available solutions could be grouped in:

- Protocol based solutions focusing into the available links and the corresponding links' quality. Such solutions might be synchronous or asynchronous given the nature of the approach (Spapis, et. al, 2011; Kowalik, Bykowski, Keegan, & Davis, 2008; Ramachandran, Kokku, Zhang, & Gruteser, 2010; Wei, Song, & Song, 2008; ElBatt, Krishnamurthy, Connors, & Dao, 2000).
- Fairness schemes focusing on starvation free solutions, setting higher transmission power to APs that are heavily loaded (Mhatre, Papagiannaki, Baccelli, 2007).
- Transmission power management schemes that take into account mobility patterns for setting the transmission power levels (Merentitis, Triantafyllopoulou, 2010). Such schemes usually exploit clusters in order to reduce the transmission power (however this might lead to formation of many clusters and increase in the overall interference of the network even if each cluster's interference levels decrease – local minimum).

The available solutions use centralized and decentralized approaches, materialized using several mechanisms (i.e., game theoretic approaches, utility based solutions etc). The aspects that should be taken into consideration are related mainly to the nature of the mechanism (i.e., ad-hoc, centralized, cooperative etc). Such aspects affect the system in terms of the communication overhead and the processing cost to be added to the network; in cases where power limitations exist, should be taken also into consideration.

In LTE networks, FDM offers interference-free communication within a cell; however interference issues may arise among neighboring cells, as they use the same frequency band and the same resources. Such cases have been widely studied and the interference management problem has been solved through Inter Cell Interference Coordination (ICIC) techniques (Pauli, & Seidel, 2011; Fodor Koutsimanis, Racz, Reider, Simonsson, & Muller, 2009) that are applied to the cells of an operator. An issue that should be taken into consideration is that the existing interference coordination schemes in LTE (Autonomous Component Carrier Selection [ACCS], Garcia, Pedersen, & Mogensen, 2009) and (enhanced) inter-cell interference coordination, eICIC) lack robustness and flexibility when applied in scenarios of ultra-dense and dynamic-infrastructure environments. Furthermore, the introduction of the Spectrum Aggregation scenarios gives the flexibility to LTE operators to exploit resources from different bands (i.e. unlicensed use of TVWS); thus increasing the sources of interference and making the introduction of interference coordination schemes imperative. The opportunistic spectrum access should be carefully considered, as the unlicensed use of TVWS will be common for all the operators, leading thus not only to interference to primary users but also to undesirable side effects (i.e. unexpected interference, QoS degradation) to other opportunistic users assigned to other network operators. In (Mihovska, Meucci, Prasad, Velez, & Cabral, 2009) a combination of centralized and decentralized Radio Resource Management techniques is investigated for achieving higher performance and capacity gains. Based on the proposed framework, operators will be able to share spectrum via a time division strategy. The challenges of the proposed approach in the context of IMT-A systems is given and as it is presented, power control techniques should be developed to realize higher capacity gains. In (Lien, Tseng, Chen, & Su, 2010) an autonomous interference mitigation technique for femto-networks is presented and the necessity to develop novel power control techniques that will be able to cope with the ultra dense LTE environments in the future is described. The proposed RRM scheme allows femto-network to perform channel sensing periodically and estimate the radio resource usage of the Macro-network. Furthermore, an optimization approach regarding the sensing period and the resource allocation is proposed. Results presented show improved efficiency regarding the resource utilization as compared with that of a randomized scheme. In (Chatzikokolakis, Arapoglou, Merentitis & Alonistioti, 2012) the authors propose a mechanism for cooperative power control among TVWS opportunistic users; in such scheme the opportunistic users coordinate their transmission power levels in order to have the best tradeoff between the links' capacity and the interference they experience to their neighbors for all users.

Cooperative Power Control Algorithm

In this section, we choose a typical power control mechanism from the previous literature proposals based on an objective function optimization. Such approach is a generic one and has been initially proposed by Huang, Berry and Honig (2005, 2006) for its application in WSNs. The selection of such algorithm is based on the applicability of such solution on various environments The solution provided there has been adapted in Merentitis & Triantaffylopoulou (2010) in order to be applied

in networks with high uncertainty rates (i.e., loss of messages, increased mobility, etc.). In (Spapis et. al, 2011), another modified version of the initial algorithm for its deployment in 802.11 WiFi networks is proposed; such solution also incorporates learning capabilities in order to enable the network nodes (i.e., WiFi APs) to adapt the way they interpret their environment (ex., by adapting what is considered "low" packet error rate, "high" channel utilization, "high" mobility, etc.). In (Chatzikokolakis, Arapoglou, Merentitis & Alonistioti, 2012) the initial algorithm is being adapted in order to be applied in LTE advanced environments, for opportunistic spectrum access of TVWS. In the latter solution, the incorporation of policies is also being proposed in order to have fair resource usage. The presented case is a subcase of the inter-cell SA as it is described in the corresponding subsection; the power control is required for transmission power adjustments among the opportunistic users. Thus, the reader can observe that the solution can be enhanced with learning and policies. This section also provides the mapping of the enhanced Cooperative Power Control to the SACRA Functional Architecture and contains the messages exchange for the solution's incorporation in LTE advanced environments. Finally, the section concludes with the performance results of the Cooperative Power Control that also provides an analysis of the available results.

Algorithm Description

In (Huang, Berry & Honig, 2005) and (Huang, Berry & Honig, 2006) the authors proposed an algorithm for interference compensation using transmission power adjustments. The algorithm is being applied in WSNs and aims at maximizing a network utility, consisting of the weighted sum of the Shannon capacity and the SINR. This formula prevents users from always setting their power to the maximum valid power level. The considered mechanism identifies links among the users belonging in the scheme, as depicted in

Figure 7; every user is modeled by a set of links, the ones that cause interference to their neighbors and the ones that their neighbors cause interference to them.

Initially, a set of L pair nodes-users is considered operating at the same frequency band, where K channels are available. The SINR of the i-th pair (i ϵ {1, 2,.., L}) in k-th channel (k ϵ {1, 2, ..., K}) is calculated by the equation:

$$\gamma_i(p_i^k) = \frac{p_i^k \cdot h_{ii}}{n_o + \sum_{j \neq i} p_j^k \cdot h_{ji}} \qquad (1)$$

where,

- p_i^k is the power of i-th transmitter on channel k
- h_{ii} is the link gain between i-th receiver and i-th transmitter
- n_0 is the ambient noise level (equals 10^{-2})
- p_j^k is the power for all other users on channel k, assuming that j {1,2,...,L} and j≠i
- h_{ji} is the link gain between i-th receiver and j-th transmitter

A flat faded channel without shadowing effects is considered. Since the channel is static, the only identified attenuation is the path loss h (channel attenuation or channel gain). Given that indoor urban environments are considered, the channel gain is:

$$h_{ji} = d_{ji}^{-3} \qquad (2)$$

where,

- d is the distance between the j-th transmitter and the i-th receiver.

The notion of interference price has been adopted from the literature (Huang, Berry, & Honig, 2005). This metric expresses the marginal reduction of utility due to the marginal increase in interference user i will sustain if the other users increase their transmission power. Interference prices are disseminated through the eNodeBs to all the UEs and act as a counter motive for setting the transmission power at maximum allowed level. The equation below computes the interference price for user i:

Figure 7. Representation of link gain among UEs in the network

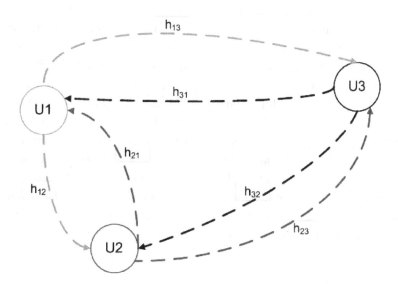

$$\pi_i^k = \frac{\partial u_i(\gamma_i(p_i^k))}{\partial(\sum_{j \neq i} p_j^k \cdot h_{ji})} \qquad (3)$$

where,

- $u_i(\gamma_i(p_i^k)) = \theta_i \log(\gamma_i(p_i^k))$ is a logarithmic utility function
- θ_i is a user dependent parameter

As mentioned afore, cognitive users select their transmission power value, by taking into consideration their own utility and the degradation in utility of the other users. They compute the appropriate power value to transmit by maximizing the formula given below:

$$\max_i \left\{ (u_i(\gamma_i(p_i^k)) - \alpha \cdot p_i^k \sum_{j \neq i} \pi_j^k \cdot h_{ji} \right\} \qquad (4)$$

The first part of the equation is closely related to the Shannon capacity of the channel, while the second part expresses the utility loss to other users if user i increases its power level. It should be noted that factor α (alpha) is included as a weight in order to prevent underestimation of interference that user i will cause to the others. Underestimation is caused due to uncertainties in message exchange (i.e. message loss), large delays in the message exchange between users, and users' mobility. In (Huang, Berry & Honig, 2005, 2006) solutions, α is set in a static manner as 25%. In (Merentitis & Triantaffylopoulou, 2010) a fuzzy reasoner is introduced in order to identify, in a more dynamic way, uncertainties in the network based on the network's status; the inputs (number of users, mobility, update interval) of the fuzzy reasoner capture the volatile nature of the ad-hoc network, whereas the output of the fuzzy reasoner is the Interference Weight. The

a factor is defined as 1/β Interference Weight + 1 (β has the maximum value of the Interference Weight). The Fuzzy reasoner used in this case is of type "Mamdani", because this type of reasoner is intuitive, well suited for human input, flexible and widely accepted.

The algorithm consists of three steps. The first is the initialization, where each user sets its power value to a valid value (usually a minimum one) and calculates its interference price. The second step is the power update, where each user computes the appropriate power value in order to maximize Equation 4. The third step is the interference price update, where each user computes its interference price based on the updated power value from the second step. Finally, it announces its interference price to the other users. The second and the third step take place asynchronously for all users until a final steady state is reached. As a steady state we define a state where no further enhancement in utility of any UE pair can be achieved without negatively affecting the total network utility.

As obvious from Equation 4, there are no limitations and lower bounds for an appropriate minimum power value a user chooses to transmit, apart from the hardware and regulatory ones (i.e., safety limitations, wireless cards higher and lower transmission power levels etc). Each user only attempts to balance the trade-off between utility optimization and interference mitigation. Furthermore, recalculating appropriate power values for L users is a multi-dimensional problem. In order to find the optimal power values, a search space of L-dimensions needs to be investigated. A simplified scheme would be to assign higher power values to underprivileged cognitive users, (for example the maximum allowed). However, this would lead to increased interference to other users and sharp degradation to the utility of the network. As a consequence, a trade-off between enhanced power value assignment and increased interference exists.

High Level Policies for the Cooperative Power Control Algorithm

Even though that the cooperative power control enables the network elements to operate collaboratively and to aim to maximize the overall network utility, it is not guaranteed that the operators objectives will be met and enforced. Thus, in (Chatzikokolakis, Arapoglou, Merentitis & Alonistioti, 2012) the authors have introduced a method to incorporate policies in the Cooperative Power Control (CPC) so as to strengthen its capabilities. The aim of such policies is to enrich the capabilities of Cognitive Radio Systems with other equivalently important aspects for the Cognitive Users, in addition to interference management. More specifically, the policies considered are:

- **Fairness:** Cooperative Power Control algorithm guarantees interference mitigation and network performance optimization. This behavior might lead to undesired side effects (i.e. a portion of cognitive users will be obliged to transmit in low power values). Network operator could decide to enforce a fairness policy in order to allow these users to transmit in higher power levels for a specific time period (Chatzikokolakis, Arapoglou, Merentitis, & Alonistioti, 2012).
- **Convergence Time:** Rapidly reallocated spectrum resources and battery consumption of the cognitive users suggest an urgent need for algorithms that converge quickly to a steady state. Although algorithm described in (Merentitis, Triantafyllopoulou, 2010) is proven to converge, there is no conclusion about the number of steps that are needed. A higher level in the Radio Resource Management infrastructure could decide to enforce a policy for faster convergence.
- **QoS:** From the perspective of network operators a lower bound on performance for cognitive users is often required. SINR is a primary factor of the actual QoS the cognitive user is experiencing. This factor expresses the influence of undesired signals at the receiver and indicates whether a transmission was successful. For this purpose network operators could enforce a threshold value for SINR.

In the following analysis, we present firstly the policy architectural principles that have set the basis for the development of the aforementioned policies. This analysis is then followed by a subsection for each policy that presents the characteristics, the assumptions and the constraints imposed in each case.

General Policy Architectural Principles

In the proposed scheme we follow the policy architecture introduced by (Pavloska, Denkovski, Atanasovski, & Gavrikovska, 2010) which consists of two main components, Policy Enforcing Point (PEP) and Policy Decision Point (PDP, also referred to as Policy Engine - PE), as depicted in Figure 8. The PEP is an entity equipped with RF transceiver and sensors; such entity is responsible for determining the state of the radio environment in which it operates and collecting information about spectrum usage, available channels and networks.

On the other hand, the role of PDP is to perform reasoning (i.e. decision making) process. It comprises of two entities, a Policy Database (DB) and a Policy Reasoner (PR). PDP receives policy requests from several PEPs and sends policy replies (positive or negative). The DB contains active policies of the system, originated from operators, regulators and cognitive users. Policy Reasoner performs reasoning for each PEP request. It checks the rules forming a policy and evaluates through a conflict resolution mechanism, whether the policies are contradictive. Finally, PDP allows or disallows the policy request.

Figure 8. Policy architecture

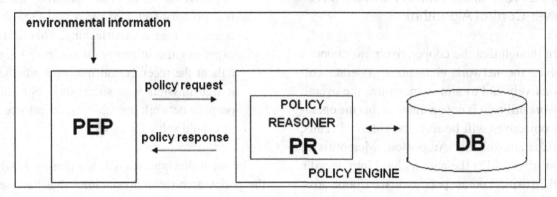

Consequently, when a cognitive radio wants to transmit, PEP sends policy requests to PDP. After receiving a reply from PDP, it controls the transmission of the radio according to PDP policies, contained in a positive reply. In case of a negative reply, PEP searches for a new channel and sends requests. PEP also sends requests in case channel conditions are getting worse. In addition, PEPs are present in every cognitive radio node, whereas PDP is not mandatory for each node in a cognitive radio network.

Mapping of Enhanced Cooperative Power Control to the SACRA Functional Architecture

Given the wide range of applicability of the Cooperative Power Control we have mapped its functionalities in the SACRA functional architecture. The CPC includes the core algorithm, which is based on the utility optimization and the cooperation among the UEs, regarding the information exchange, the conformance to policies (simple and more sophisticated ones) and the adaptation to the environment feedback (i.e. learning capabilities). Such functionalities are distributed among the functional blocks of the SACRA reference architecture (Figure 5).

Figure 9 captures the message sequence exchange among the functional blocks of the SACRA

functional architecture (presented afore in Figure 5) that are involved during the execution of the Cooperative Power Control mechanism. The core CPC functionalities, which concern the TxPower adjustment of the terminals, are located in the UEs' cognitive engine regarding the objective function and the interference prices calculation as well as the termination condition identification. Regarding the information fusion, among terminals from neighboring cells the information management blocks from both the UEs and the RAN system are being used. The policy engine block of the Core Network is invoked by the RAN system in case policies are being incorporated. Such engine sets the rules and policies that govern the overall system's behaviour.

Performance Analysis of the Cooperative Power Control Mechanism

The benefits stemming from the introduction of a power control scheme move towards several directions. On the one hand, the cooperative power control mechanism enables the network to proceed in power adjustments that maximize the network's utilization in an efficient manner (setting the transmission power in the most appropriate level for having acceptable data rates and not causing interference to the neighbors). On the other hand, the mechanism enables the network operator to

Figure 9. Message sequence chart for the cooperative power control mechanism

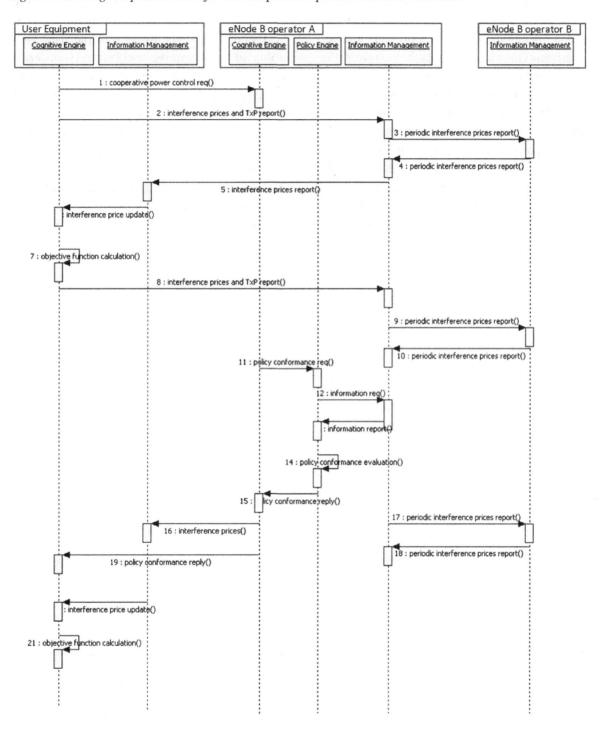

induce policies and adaptation mechanisms in the network elements so as to optimize the network's operation. This section presents a set of experiments in order to quantify the gains from the incorporation of such mechanism in the network.

The cases under investigation examine topologies with small number of cognitive users; in the first case 5 opportunistic users are considered in the respective area. These users attempt to identify an optimal transmission power based on the mechanism described afore. Then, algorithm's robustness against a gradually increasing number of users is evaluated. In the following three cases it

is assumed that 1, 2 and 5 additional opportunistic users have been added to the network respectively.

Figure 10 (a)-(d) illustrates the mean network utility of the cognitive users over 10 different topologies. The network utility is given from the Equation 4. The equation gives a tradeoff between the positive impact of the increase in the transmission power (capacity) and the negative impact (interference to the neighboring users). Maximizing the network utility underlines the benefit to the network by jointly increasing the users' Shannon capacity and decreasing the caused interference. In every topology we consider users

Figure 10. Network utility of cooperative power control vs. MAXP approach for (a) 5 users, (b) 6 users, (c) 7 users, (d) 10 users

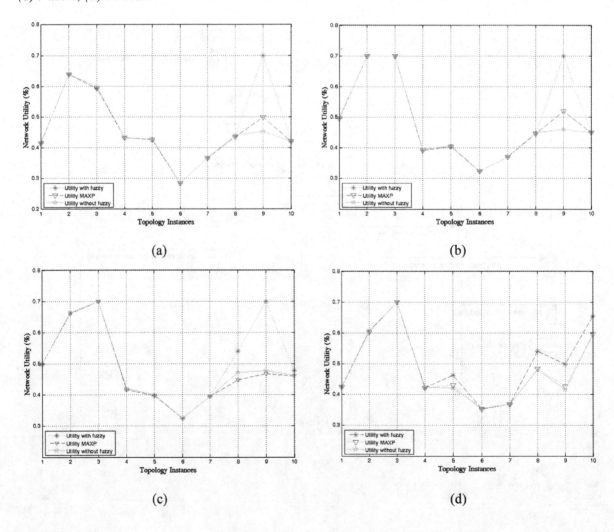

(a)

(b)

(c)

(d)

with specific mobility patterns (i.e. the location of each user in every experiment test is randomly changed compared to the previous one with maximum derivation equal to 1%). Figure 10 (a) to (d) present the transmission power for 5, 6, 7, and 10 cognitive users participating in the cooperative power control scheme, respectively. In every case the cooperative power control outperforms the utility with maximum transmission power set in the users. Furthermore, the experiments show that the identification of uncertainties also increases the network's utility, given the fact that the users do not underestimate the negative impact they have to their neighbors. Finally, the experimental procedure highlights that as the number of cognitive users participate in the scheme gradually increases the energy utility gains we have are also increased; thus implying better utilization of the resources (i.e. transmission power) and scalable performance of the algorithm.

Figure 11 (a) presents the network utility of the cooperative power control for different number of users. The users in all cases have the same mobility partners and the corresponding topologies are the same, however the number of users participating in the power control scheme differs.

The figure shows that network utility is not related to the number of users but is strongly related to the topology of the network. This is a reasonable outcome of the algorithm, which shows that if users assigned to different operators are in short distance, network utility will be decreased due to interference issues that cannot be avoided. Figure 11(b) shows the mean transmission power of the cooperative power control for different number of users. As afore, the figure shows that the selected transmission power of the users is not related to the number of users but strongly related to the topology of the network as well; such outcome shows that if users assigned to different operators are in short distance, cognitive users will choose to transmit in lower power levels to reduce interference issues that cannot be avoided.

Learning Enhancement for the Cooperative Power Control Algorithm

In the previous sections the generic Cooperative Power Control mechanism's principles and the corresponding enhancement with policies have been described. Such solution implies that all

Figure 11. (a) Network utility of the cooperative power control for 5, 6, 7, and 10 users, (b) mean power of the cooperative power control for 5, 6, 7, and 10 users

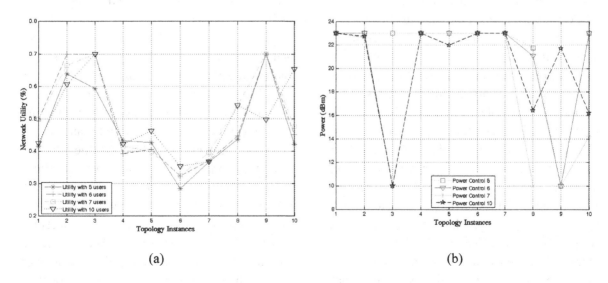

(a)   (b)

the UEs participating in the Cooperative Power Control scheme will have the same static situation perception, despite that each UE may have different preferences or special characteristics (e.g., regarding mobility, QoS etc). Factor α of Equation 4, (initially statically defined – 25% and later computed using fuzzy reasoners) aims at capturing uncertainties in the network; these uncertainties are related to how correctly each terminal has received and compiled information regarding the interference price which should have been available by the user's neighbors given the asynchronous nature of the communication. This information impacts the way a UE adjusts its transmission power. However, both in Huang, Berry, & Honig (2005) and Merentitis & Triantaffylopoulou (2010), all network elements that participate in the scheme have the same definition of α which also implies a static perception of the environment. More specifically, all network elements given the fact that they have the same reasoning scheme (i.e., fuzzy reasoner) interpret their environment in the same way. This might be problematic, because the same environment stimuli might need to be interpreted differently by two terminals.

A fuzzy logic controller consists of three parts, namely the fuzzifier, the inference engine and the defuzzifier. The fuzzifier undertakes the task to transform the input values (crisp values) to a degree with which these inputs belong to a specific state (low, medium, high, etc.), using specific input membership functions; the overlapping areas in the input membership functions denote the uncertainty among two states. Then the inference part of a fuzzy logic controller correlates the inputs and the outputs using simple "IF...THEN..." rules. Each rule results to a specific degree of certainty for each output; these degrees are then aggregated. The rule building procedure is based on experts' knowledge, so as to capture the network and services limitation as well as the operator's policies. The output of the decision-making procedure comes from the last phase of the process, the defuzzification procedure; such

a procedure captures the degree with which the decision maker belongs to a specific state and provides one crisp output value to be used by the controller – i.e. the output metric is x ($0 < x < 1$). The nature of a fuzzy logic controller implies that there are two methods for adapting its operation. The first approach is to adapt the fuzzy logic controller input and output membership functions and the latter is to adapt the correlations among the inputs and the outputs. The former has been applied by (Magdalinos et al, 2011) using a supervised learning method (via clustering) for the reshaping of the input membership functions of fuzzy reasoners. The second approach is to use reinforcement learning techniques (evaluation of each decision) for changing the links between the inputs and the outputs (Razavi et al, 2010).

Regarding the CPC in (Spapis et al, 2011) the authors propose to use of an approach similar to the first one. More specifically, they propose the use of clustering schemes for the extraction of the input membership functions according to the clustering of the decisions. The adaptation mechanism, modified to operate in LTE advanced environments, is based on the scheme/information exchange of Figure 12. As depicted, the UEs gather information and proceed to the first step of processing and provide this information to the learning points (i.e. the eNodeBs). Then, the eNodeBs process the available data and provide their feedback to the UEs.

The learning algorithm consists of three parts, namely, the monitoring/labeling, the classification and the adaptation of the fuzzy reasoner. Each UE of the cooperative power control scheme – monitors its environment and evaluates the uncertainties; then it proceeds to the transmission power adjustment. Every time that the UEs collaboratively proceed in transmission power adjustment (i.e. periodically, after a complete cycle), their interference prices are being classified as low, medium and high according to the effect they have to the neighboring UEs. In other words, each UE might have low, medium or high interference effect to the neighboring UEs. Such classification

Figure 12. Overview of the learning scheme

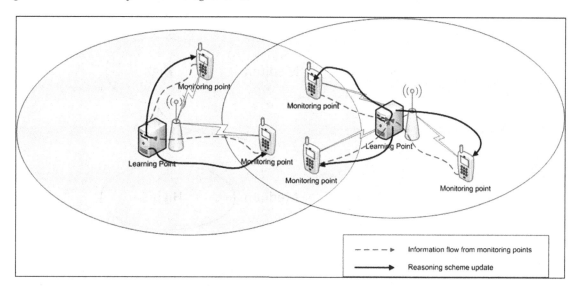

might be performed using simple static bounds/ thresholds, or more sophisticated data mining methods such as kNN (k-Nearest Neighbors). In case the kNN is being used the system has to be fed with a set of vectors that their validity is certain. Then, the rest of the inputs are being classified according to their proximity to the initially imported input set. The classified values are being provided to the learning points as illustrated in Figure 12. Once the learning points have gathered enough data they proceed in identification of the correlations of the input data by using data mining techniques.

We consider the input vector Z_i (i.e., UE pairs, update interval, mobility level) of each user, which is being evaluated against a predefined fuzzy inference system and results to an α value which is used in conjunction to the interference prices, for the calculation of the optimum transmission power. The interference prices are gathered and classified locally as low, medium and high using kNN classification. This procedure results to a set (S) of labeled decisions which have been categorized into three categories (i.e. low/medium/high).

The labeled data may contain misclassified data, due to the fact that we are not certain about the classification using kNN. In order to tackle the aforementioned problem, we proceed in data clustering so as to identify the similarities among the measurements. Thus, clustering is performed to each of the sets (low, medium and high) into three sets low, medium and high so as to identify the measurements that significantly deviate from the rest of the inputs and are misclassified. Once the sets are divided the three clusters with overlapping areas have been created. These overlapping areas are the uncertainty areas, given the fact that include input vectors from two types of interference effect, low and medium between the low and medium clusters and medium and high on the medium and high clusters respectively – as shown in Figure 13.

For each couple of clusters i, j, the cluster centers C_i, C_j define a line ε that interconnects the two points. This line can be described by the following set of equations:

$$p_m = x_m + u \cdot (y_m - x_m), \; m = 1...d \qquad (5)$$

Line ε intersects with spheres S_i and S_j in four points which can be retrieved by substituting the p_m values into the following hypersphere equations:

$$D_i \rightarrow \sum_{m=1}^{d} (p_m - x_m)^2 = R_i^2 \qquad (6)$$

Figure 13. Classification and clustering algorithms

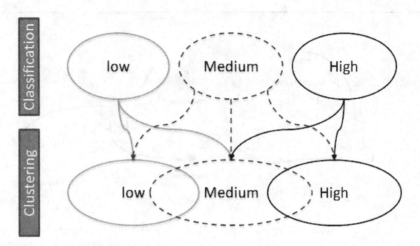

$$D_j \rightarrow \sum_{m=1}^{d} (p_m - y_m)^2 = R_j^2 \qquad (7)$$

A simple way of identifying the bounds would be to extract the intersection points which belong to different hyperspheres and exhibit minimum distance from each other. Then, as shown in Figure 14, the identified bounds are mapped to the input membership functions of the fuzzy reasoner; this results to the modification of the environment perception of each network element.

Mapping of the Learning Enhancement for the Cooperative Power Control Algorithm to the SACRA Functional Architecture

The learning functionalities are located in the terminals' cognitive engine and information management and the RAN's information management and cognitive engine (as illustrated in Figure 15). More specifically, the monitoring part of the algorithm is placed in the UE's cognitive engine and the labeling part is placed in the information management block. The information manage-

Figure 14. Clustering and bounds extraction mechanisms

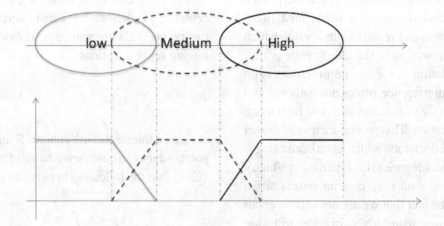

Figure 15. Message sequence chart for the learning process of the cooperative power control mechanism

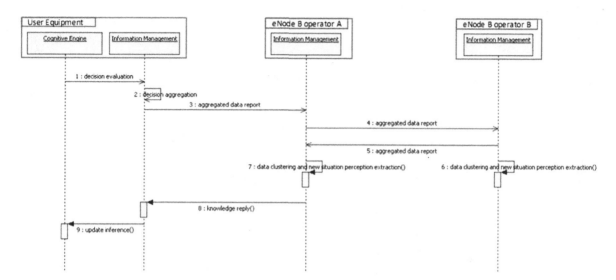

ment of the RAN is invoked for the information gathering from the UEs and for the corresponding harmonization. The cognitive engine undertakes to extract the new environment modeling (i.e. new input membership functions) which is being disseminated to the terminals.

Performance Analysis of the Learning Enhanced Cooperative Power Control Mechanism

As thoroughly described in the previous section, the purpose of the enhancement of the Cooperative Power Control mechanism with learning capabilities is related to the evolution of the situation perception of each UE based on the effect each of his decisions has to the neighboring UEs. Each Cooperative Power Control cycle might have positive (i.e., decrease in the interference price) or negative effect (i.e., increase in the interference price) on other UEs.

The overall evaluation procedure is based on 1000 input vectors randomly generated in order to model the mobility pattern of each UE, which also affects the UEs that participate in the Cooperative Power Control scheme as well. This dataset reflects network topologies with a relatively small number of secondary UEs.

The aforementioned situation perception is related to the inputs mapping of the fuzzy reasoner and the interpretation of the environment stimuli. The output of the fuzzy reasoner is the interference weight (alpha factor). Figure 16 (a) shows the 8th polynomial degree function before and after the learning for the interference weight. As shown in the figure, the fuzzy reasoner has become more sensitive to the environment after the learning procedure given the fact that the interference weight variation after the learning procedure is 0.0458 instead of 0.0091 before the procedure.

The results shown in Figure 16 (b) indicate that the learning enhanced algorithm achieved equal or improved overall network utility in the same topologies and with the same mobility patterns as without learning. This is being achieved because the UEs have better situation perception, thus concluding in more appropriate transmission power levels.

FUTURE RESEARCH DIRECTIONS

As mentioned afore in this chapter, RNs and enhanced antennas with MIMO technologies are the two directions that 3GPP has identified as promising paradigms besides Spectrum Aggrega-

Figure 16. (a) 8th polynomial degree of the interference weight before and after the learning procedure, (b) overall network utility with and without the learning

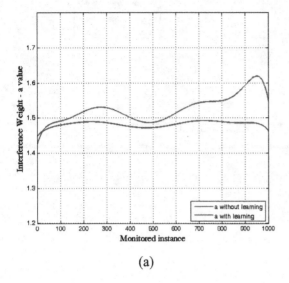

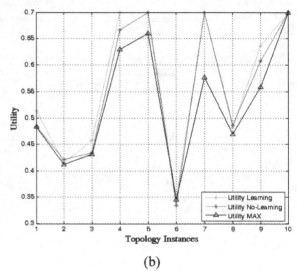

(a)   (b)

tion. The target of the introduction of such new promising technologies is the increased spectral efficiency, optimized resource allocation and efficient heterogeneous planning. In this section we briefly describe the current status of the exploitation of those directions, the requirements for their operation and the trends that is expected to set the basis for the advancements of those two functionalities in the future.

Certain requirements for the deployment and exploitation of RNs should be met. Careful study of the benefits coming from the usage of such nodes compared to the cost of deploying them is an open issue that is expected to be addressed in the future. Furthermore, RNs impose certain additional constraints, which should not be disregarded. For example, exploiting RNs, results in an additional hop in the communication which could lead to QoS degradation to the user.

Current works on RNs elaborate the exploitation of this functionality for provision of QoS to users in high-speed vehicles. As these vehicles are electromagnetically well insulated, in particular for the recently opened multi-gigabit carrier frequency bands, the onboard capacity was not sufficient. Mobile Relays (i.e. RNs attached to a vehicle and

connected remotely to the network infrastructure) could be a potential solution to mitigate the vehicular penetration loss, so that the onboard capacity could be met. Conclusively, we could say that it is expected that this functionality will be a key trend for communications beyond 2020 and will evolve based on the future application scenarios, as more companies and standardization bodies will follow the instructions from the 3GPP LTE-Advanced for the beyond 3rd generation (3G) mobile devices.

MIMO technology is currently used in many wireless telecommunication systems (e.g. IEEE802.11.n, WiMax, and LTE) and has enabled considerable system performance improvement. Deployed MIMO requires the use of multiple antennas in both the infrastructure and the UE side. This means, that MIMO has more than one tracks to explore/research for further evolution and corresponding system performance improvement. At the same time, it is expected that a system exploiting all the different aspects of MIMO technologies will be either complex, or difficult to deploy, or maintain, or expensive to develop. From a general viewpoint, today's vendors deliver MIMO products with four antennas for base stations whilst eight antennas have been announced. At the UE part, size and space limitations have been overcome utilizing co-existing methods; however, bigger UEs such as tablet PCs are becoming more and more popular thus getting an increasing market share and offering less limitations regarding to space.

Currently, LTE standardization activities around MIMO are not intensely differentiated comparing to other wireless systems: effort focused on efficient schemes for downlink single user MIMO; multi-user schemes have been left to manufacturers. However, as mentioned in Telecom Insights (2012) "MIMO development and usage is not going to be finished by standardization". Quite a few future trends have been reported and the most indicative are presented in the following paragraphs.

Given the current trend of digital dividend, the exploitation of cognitive radio as enabler for the utilization of TVWS spectrum bands for wireless and mobile data communications, it is more than expected that MIMO technologies will be exploited in MM-wave bands. Green communications stands for concept gaining increasing attention thus imposing additional constraints; MIMO offers an excellent case for addressing those energy efficiency constraints and requirements and maintain a desired level of spectral efficiency. Moreover, MIMO and RF SIM card comparing with expected advances in nanotechnology and increase in frequency bands is foreseen to make the MIMO application in this context efficient and promising.

MIMO is expected to be deployed in additional propagation environment. The emerging scenarios for dense home/office, motorway, train-scenarios, may get benefit by appropriate deployment of MIMO technologies (e.g. optimized deployment of multiple antennas etc). Alike, the explosion of deployment of Wireless Sensor Network (WSN) and their inherent strict constraints for energy optimization may demand corresponding extension of MIMO technologies towards using different antenna types and approaches of their deployment location to serve WSN data flows.

Last but not least, MIMO and Internet of Things (i.e. M2M communications) imposing additional requirements due to expected data traffic explosion in scenarios that were previously providing voice communications only.

Another aspect that has recently been proposed in the literature and the standardization bodies is the introduction of the Distributed Node-Bs or Cloud Radio Access Network (C-RAN). The C-RAN is a new paradigm in base stations that aims at reducing the cell sites and at the same time increasing the base stations deployed in the area under discussion. This will be performed by decomposing the functionalities of the BS to Base Unit (BU) and the Remote Radio Head (RRH) that obtains the digital (optical) signals (Li, J., Chen, D., Wang Y., & Wu J.). The idea is to have centralized functionalities related to the BU operation which will be connected to the RRH using fiber creating cloud-like radio access network topology. In 3GPP, Coordinated Multi-Point (CoMP) transmission has been accepted; such approach focuses on traditional eNodeB structure where one site and another are connected through backhaul and the number of the eNodeBs participating in the scheme is rather small (i.e., 3 and 9 in the intra-site and inter-site CoMP respectively). Such approaches could also be used in conjunction to another new trend, the virtualization of the resources in order to enable efficient management and sharing. Such approaches could enable the operators to interoperate for increasing their profits. Furthermore, this introduces a new market and the operators become service providers as well; the services could be enhanced towards other directions as well, such as the applications servers sharing for application delivery close to the application user (Andersen, P., (2012).).

CONCLUSION

This book chapter aims at capturing the business and power control aspects of a novel concept; that of Spectrum Aggregation. Such concept, introduced by 3GPP, increases the capacity in wireless and mobile communications through exploiting the unused spectrum in order to provide additional bandwidth when needed; the proposed approach by 3GPP exploits the intra-band and the inter-band derivatives based on the component carriers that are being used every time. Several EU research projects and initiatives are building on the 3GPP directions in order to materialize the benefits from such proposal.

In SACRA FP7 EU project, the Spectrum Aggregation concept has been implemented by using the 2.6GHz, the digital dividend and the TVWS bands. This approach is very beneficiary for the operators and the users, as shown by the presented SACRA business scenario. The detailed description of an enhanced Spectrum Aggregation scenario enables the identification of the main functionalities for the incorporation of such concept in the LTE-Advanced; in order to be materialized in LTE-Advanced networks we have to implement as well three radio resource management mechanisms, namely the sensing configuration mechanism, the admission control, and the power control. The two former mechanisms are well investigated in the literature; the power control is a relative new concept, especially in terms of solutions regarding opportunistic spectrum access cases.

In order to capture the main tracks of way forward for power control, we have provided a short description and grouping of mechanisms available in the literature. Furthermore, aiming at identifying the benefits from the incorporation of a power control mechanism we have chosen one, the Cooperative Power Control, and we described it thoroughly. Its extensions regarding the mechanism's adaptability (learning capabilities) and the incorporation of policies are presented as well. The described mechanism has been linked to the SACRA functional architecture for proving its applicability on the LTE-advanced. Finally,

we have provided some very interesting results regarding the energy gains from the incorporation of the Cooperative Power Control to the Spectrum Aggregation concept.

ACKNOWLEDGMENT

The research leading to these results has received funding from the European Community's Seventh Framework Programme (FP7/2007-2013) under grant agreement SACRA n° 249060.

REFERENCES

Akyildiz, I., Won-Yeol, L., Vuran, M., & Mohanty, S. (2006). NeXt generation/dynamic. *Computer and Telecommunications Networking*, *50*(13), 2127–2159. doi:10.1016/j.comnet.2006.05.001.

Akyildiz, I. F., Su, W., Sankarasubramaniam, Y., & Cayirci, E. (2002). Wireless sensor networks: A survey. *Computer Networks*, *38*(4), 393–422. doi:10.1016/S1389-1286(01)00302-4.

Alavi, S. M. M., Walsh, M., & Hayes, M. (2009). Robust distributed active power control technique for IEEE 802.15.4 wireless sensor networks — A quantitative feedback theory approach. *Journal in Control Engineering Practice*, *17*(7), 805–814. doi:10.1016/j.conengprac.2009.02.001.

Analysis of Mason. (2012). Retrieved February 12, 2012 from http://www.analysysmason.com/consulting/services/strategy-consulting/spectrummanagement/Digital-dividend/Our-digital-dividend-experience/Digital-dividend-study-forDutch-Ministry-of-Economic-Affairs/

Andersen, P. (2012). *Application delivery networking in the cloud*. Retrieved October 13, 2012, from http://cloudtimes.org/2012/08/27/application-delivery-networking-in-the-cloud/

Bennis, M., & Niyato, D. (2010). A q-learning based approach to interference avoidance in self-organized femtocell networks. In *Proceedings of GLOBECOM Workshops (GC Wkshps)* (pp. 706-710). doi: 10.1109/GLOCOMW.2010.5700414

Bloem, M., Alpcan, T., & Başar, T. (2007). A stackelberg game for power control and channel allocation in cognitive radio networks. In *Proceedings of the 2nd International Conference on Performance Evaluation Methodologies and Tools*. ICST. ISBN: 978-963-9799-00-4

Cao, L., & Zheng, H. (2005). Distributed spectrum allocation via local bargaining. In *Proceedings of the IEEE Sensor and Ad Hoc Communications and Networks (SECON '05)*, (pp. 475–486). IEEE.

Cave, M. (2002). *Review of radio resource management*. Retrieved May 24, 2012, from http://icttoolkit.infodev.org/en/Document.2245.pdf

Chatzikokolakis, K., Arapoglou, R., Merentitis, A., & Alonistioti, N. (2012). Fair power control in cooperative systems based on evolutionary techniques. In *Proceedings of the International Conference on Mobile Ubiquitous Computing, Systems, Services and Technologies, UBICOMM 2012*. ACM.

Chen, D., Zhang, Q., & Jia, W. (2008). Aggregation aware spectrum assignment in cognitive ad-hoc networks. In *Proceedings of the Third International Conference on Cognitive Radio Oriented Wireless Networks and Communications (CrownCom 2008)*, (pp. 1-6). CrownCom.

Cognitive Radio Tutorial. (2012). Retrieved June 11, 2012, from http://www.radio-electronics.com/info/rf-technology-design/cognitive-radio-cr/technology-tutorial.php

Dirani, M., & Altman, Z. (2010). A cooperative reinforcement learning approach for inter-cell interference coordination in OFDMA cellular networks. In *Proceedings of the 8th International Symposium on Modeling and Optimization in Mobile, Ad Hoc and Wireless Networks (WiOpt)*, (pp. 170-176). WiOpt.

ECC REPORT 159. (2011). *Technical and operational requirements for the possible operation of cognitive radio systems in 'white space' of the frequency band 470-790 MHz*. Retrieved on July 27, 2012 from http://www.erodocdb.dk/Docs/doc98/official/pdf/ECCREP159.PDF

ElBatt, T. A., Krishnamurthy, S. V., Connors, D., & Dao, S. (2000). Power management for throughput enhancement in wireless ad-hoc networks. In *Proceedings of the IEEE Communications, 2000*, (pp. 1506-1513). IEEE. doi: 10.1109/ICC.2000.853748

EU. (n.d.). *Press release on maximising radio spectrum efficiency by sharing it*. Retrieved on October 15, 2012 from http://europa.eu/rapid/press-release_MEMO-12-636_en.htm

FP7 EU COGEU. (2010). *COGnitive radio systems for efficient sharing of TV white spaces in EUropean context*. Retrieved June 10, 2012, from http://www.ict-cogeu.eu/index.htm

FP7 EU FEDERICA. (2008). *Federated e-infrastructure dedicated to European researchers innovating in computing network architectures*. Retrieved June 10, 2012, from www.fp7-federica.eu

FP7 EU GEYSERS. (2010). *Generalized architecture for dynamic infrastructure services*. Retrieved June 10, 2012, from www.geysers.eu/

FP7 EU NOVI. (2010). *Networking innovation over virtualized infrastructures*. Retrieved June 10, 2012, from www.fp7-novi.eu

FP7 EU QoSMOS. (2010). *Quality of service and mobility driven cognitive radio systems*. Retrieved June 10, 2012, from http://www.ict-qosmos.eu/home.html

FP7 EU SACRA. (2010). *Spectrum and energy efficiency through multi-band cognivite radio*. Retrieved June 10, 2012, from http://www.ict-sacra.eu/

FP7 EU SENDORA. (2008). *Sensor network for dynamic and cognitive radio access*. Retrieved June 10, 2012, from http://www.sendora.eu/

FP7 EU UniverSelf. (2010). Retrieved June 10, 2012, from http://www.univerself-project.eu/

FCC 10-174. (2010). *Second memorandum opinion and order*. Retrieved July 27, 2012 from http://www.ic.gc.ca/eic/site/smt-gst.nsf/vwapj/SMSE-012-11-adaptrum-annexj.pdf/$FILE/SMSE-012-11-adaptrum-annexj.pdf

FCC Spectrum Policy Task Force. (2002). *Report of the spectrum efficiency working group*. Retrieved July 15, 2012 from http://www.fcc.gov/sptf/reports.html

Federal Communications Commission. (2012). Retrieved from http://www.fcc.gov/

Fodor, G., Koutsimanis, C., Racz, A., Reider, N., Simonsson, A., & Muller, W. (2009). Intercell interference coordination in OFDMA networks and in the 3GPP long term evolution system. *The Journal of Communication, 4*(7), 445–453.

Frisanco, T., Tafertshofer, P., Lurin, P., & Ang, R. (2008). Infrastructure sharing and shared operations for mobile network operators: From a deployment and operations view. In *Proceedings of Network Operations and Management Symposium (NOMS 2008)*, (pp. 129-136). NOMS. doi: 10.1109/NOMS.2008.4575126

Garcia, L. G. U., Pedersen, K. I., & Mogensen, P. E. (2009). Autonomous component carrier selection: Interference management in local area environments for LTE-advanced. *IEEE Communications Magazine, 47*(9), 110–116. doi:10.1109/MCOM.2009.5277463.

Gigaom. (2012). *Article on spectrum sharing among operators*. Retrieved October 13, 2012 from http://gigaom.com/europe/europe-wants-operators-to-share-their-spectrum/

Hu, Q., & Tang, Z. (2011). ATPM: An energy efficient MAC protocol with adaptive transmit power scheme for wireless sensor networks. *Journal of Multimedia, 6*(2), 122–128. doi:10.4304/jmm.6.2.122-128.

Huang, J., Berry, R. A., & Honig, M. L. (2005). Spectrum sharing with distributed interference compensation. In *Proceedings of the 1st IEEE International Symposium on New Frontiers in Dynamic Spectrum Access Networks 2005 (DySPAN '05)*, (pp. 88-93). IEEE. doi: 10.1109/DYSPAN.2005.1542621

Huang, J., Berry, R. A., & Honig, M. L. (2006). Distributed interference compensation for wireless networks. *IEEE Journal on Selected Areas in Communications, 24*(5), 88–93.

Insights, T. (2012). *Report on current and future prospects for MIMO – A bird's eye view*. Retrieved September 10, 2012, from http://trends-in-telecoms.blogspot.gr/2012/07/current-and-future-prospects-for-mimo.html

Jin, S., Yue, W., & Sun, Q. (2012). Performance analysis of the sleep/wakeup protocol in a wireless sensor network. [ICIC]. *International Journal of Innovative Computing, Information, & Control, 8*(5), 3833–3844.

Kowalik, K., Bykowski, M., Keegan, B., & Davis, M. (2008). An evaluation of a conservative transmit power control mechanism on an indoor 802.11 wireless mesh testbed. In *Proceedings of the International Conference on Wireless Information Networks and Systems (WINSYS'08)*, (pp. 5-14). ISBN: 978-989-8111-61-6

Li, J., Chen, D., Wang, Y., & Wu, J. (2013). Performance evaluation of cloud-RAN system with carrier frequency offset. In *Proceedings of the IEEE Global Communications Conference, Exhibition & Industry Forum*. IEEE.

Lien, S. Y., Tseng, C. C., Chen, K. C., & Su, C. W. (2010). Cognitive radio resource management for QoS guarantees in autonomous femtocell networks. In *Proceedings of the IEEE International Conference on Communications (ICC)*, (pp. 1-6). IEEE. doi: 10.1109/ICC.2010.5502784

Ma, L., Han, X., & Shen, C. C. (2005). Dynamic open spectrum sharing MAC protocol for wireless ad hoc networks. In *Proceedings of the 1st IEEE International Symposium on New Frontiers in Dynamic Spectrum Access Networks 2005 (DySPAN '05)*, (pp. 203-213). IEEE.

Magdalinos, P., Kousaridas, A., Spapis, P., Katsikas, G., & Alonistioti, N. (2011). Enhancing a fuzzy logic inference engine through machine learning for a self- managed network. *ACM Springer Mobile Networks and Applications*, *16*(4), 475–489. doi:10.1007/s11036-011-0327-1.

Meddour, D. E., Rasheed, T., & Gourhant, Y. (2011). On the role of infrastructure sharing for mobile network operators in emerging markets. *International Journal of Computer and Telecommunications Networking*, *55*(7), 1576–1591.

Merentitis, A., Kaloxylos, A., Stamatelatos, M., & Alonistioti, N. (2010). Optimal periodic radio sensing and low energy reasoning for cognitive devices. In *Proceedings of the 15th IEEE Mediterranean Electrotechnical Conference (MELECON 2010)*, (pp. 470-475). IEEE. doi: 10.1109/MELCON.2010.5476231

Merentitis, A., Patouni, E., Alonistioti, N., & Doubrava, M. (2008). To reconfigure or not to reconfigure: Cognitive mechanisms for mobile devices decision making. In *Proceedings of the Vehicular Technology Conference (VTC 2008)*, (pp. 1-5). IEEE. doi: 10.1109/VETECF.2008.267

Merentitis, A., & Triantafyllopoulou, D. (2010). Transmission power regulation in cooperative cognitive radio systems under uncertainties. In *Proceedings of the IEEE International Symposium on Wireless Pervasive Computing (ISWPC)*, (pp. 134-139). IEEE. doi: 10.1109/ISWPC.2010.5483742

Mhatre, V. P., Papagiannaki, K., & Baccelli, F. (2007). Interference mitigation through power control in high density 802.11 WLANs. In *Proceedings of INFOCOM 2007 26th IEEE International Conference on Computer Communications* (pp. 535-543). IEEE. doi: 10.1109/INFCOM.2007.69

Mihovska, A., Meucci, F., Prasad, N. R., Velez, F. J., & Cabral, O. (2009). Multi-operator resource sharing scenario in the context of IMT-advanced systems. In *Proceedings of the Second International Workshop on Cognitive Radio and Advanced Spectrum Management (CogART 2009)*, (pp. 12-16). CogART. doi: 10.1109/COGART.2009.5167225

Mitola, J. III. (1995). The software radio architecture. *IEEE Communications Magazine*, *33*(5), 26–38. doi:10.1109/35.393001.

Mitola, J., III. (2000). *Cognitive radio: An integrated agent architecture for software defined radio*. (PhD Dissertation). Royal Institute of Technology, Stockholm, Sweden.

Mitola, J. III, & Maguire, G. Q. (1999). Cognitive radio: Making software radios more personal. *IEEE Personal Communications*, *6*(4), 13–18. doi:10.1109/98.788210.

Nash, J. F. (1950). Equilibrium points in n-person games. *Proceedings of the National Academy of Sciences of the United States of America*, *36*(1), 48–49. doi:10.1073/pnas.36.1.48 PMID:16588946.

Nolte, K., Kaloxylos, A., Tsagkaris, K., Rosowski, T., Stamatelatos, M., & Galani, A. et al. (2010). The E3 architecture: Enabling future cellular networks with cognitive and self-x capabilities. *International Journal of Network Management.*

Ofcom Consultation on White Space Device Requirements. (2012). Retrieved November 23, 2012 from http://stakeholders.ofcom.org.uk/consultations/whitespaces/?utm_source=updates&utm_medium=email&utm_campaign=whitespaces

Pauli, V., & Seidel, E. (2011). *Inter-cell interference coordination for LTE-A.* Retrieved May 28, 2012 from http://www.nomor.de/uploads/1d/19/1d196a493af5511cc92466089924cc5c/2011-09-WhitePaper-LTE-A-HetNet-ICIC.pdf

Pavloska, V., Denkovski, D., Atanasovksi, V., & Gavrikovska, L. (2010). A policy reasoning architecture for cognitive radio networks. In *Proceedings of the 8th International Conference in Communications (COMM),* (pp. 531-534). ACM. doi: 10.1109/ICCOMM.2010.5509059

Peng, C., Zheng, H., & Zhao, B. Y. (2006). Utilization and fairness in spectrum assignment for opportunistic spectrum access. *Journal in Mobile Network Applications, 11*(4), 555–576. doi:10.1007/s11036-006-7322-y.

QinetiQ, Ltd. (2006). *A study of the provision of aggregation of frequency to provide wider bandwidth services.* Final report for Office of Communications(Ofcom). Ofcom.

Ramachandran, K., Kokku, R., Zhang, H., & Gruteser, M. (2010). Symphony: Synchronous two-phase rate and power control in 802.11 WLANs. *IEEE/ACM Transactions on Networking, 18*(4), 1289–1302. doi:10.1109/TNET.2010.2040036.

Ratasuk, R., Tolli, D., & Ghosh, A. (2010). Carrier aggregation in LTE-advanced. In *Proceedings of the Seventy-First IEEE Vehicular Technology Conference (VTC 2010 Spring),* (pp. 1-5). IEEE.

Razavi, R., Klein, S., & Claussen, H. (2010). A fuzzy reinforcement learning approach for self-optimization of coverage in LTE networks. *Bell Labs Technical Journal, 15*(3), 153–175. doi:10.1002/bltj.20463.

Rezaei, Z., & Mobininejad, S. (2012). Energy saving in wireless sensor networks. *International Journal of Computer Science & Engineering Survey, 3*(1), 20–27. doi:10.5121/ijcses.2012.3103.

Robinson, D. L., Shukla, A. K., Burns, J., & Atefi, A. (2005). Resource trading for spectrum aggregation and management. In *Proceedings of the First IEEE International Symposium on New Frontiers in Dynamic Spectrum Access Networks (DySPAN'05),* (pp. 666-671). IEEE.

Shannon, P. C. E. (1949). Communication in the presence of noise. *Proceedings of the Institute of Radio Engineers, 37,* 10–21.

Spapis, P., Katsikas, G., Stamatelatos, M., Chatzikokolakis, K., Arapoglou, R., & Alonistioti, N. (2011). Learning enhanced environment perception for cooperative power control. In *Proceedings of the International Conference on Mobile Ubiquitous Computing, Systems, Services and Technologies, UBICOMM 2011.* UBICOMM. ISBN: 978-1-61208-171-7

Sun, Q., Zeng, X., Chen, N., Ke, Z., & Rasool, R. (2008). A non-cooperative power control algorithm for wireless ad hoc and sensor networks. In *Proceedings of the Second International Conference on Genetic and Evolutionary Computing (WGEC '08),* (pp. 181-184). WGEC. doi: 10.1109/WGEC.2008.95

Tang, L., Sun, Y., Gurewitz, O., & Johnson, D. (2011). PW-MAC: An energy-efficient predictive-wakeup MAC protocol for wireless sensor networks. In *Proceedings of the IEEE Infocom* (pp. 1305-1313). IEEE. doi: 10.1109/INFCOM.2011.5934913

Wang, B., & Liu, K. J. R. (2011). Advances in cognitive radio networks: A survey. *IEEE Journal of Selected Topics in Signal Processing, 5*(1), 5–23. doi:10.1109/JSTSP.2010.2093210.

Wang, F., Krunz, M., & Cui, S. (2008). Price-based spectrum management in cognitive radio networks. *IEEE Journal of Selected Topics in Signal Processing, 2*(1), 74–87. doi:10.1109/JSTSP.2007.914877.

Wang, W., & Huang, A. (2010). Spectrum aggregation: Overview and challenges. *Network Protocols and Algorithms, 2*(1), 184–196. doi:10.5296/npa.v2i1.329.

Wannstrom, J. (2012). *LTE-advanced*. Retrieved May 10, 2012, from http://www.3gpp.org/IMG/pdf/lte_advanced_v2.pdf

Wei, Y., Song, M., & Song, J. (2008). An AODV-improved routing based on power control in WiFi mesh networks. In *Proceedings of Electrical and Computer Engineering, 2008* (pp. 001349–001352). CCECE.

Wyglinski, A. M., Nekovee, M., & Hou, Y. T. (2009). *Cognitive radio communications and networks: Principles and practice*. London: Elsevier.

Yang, C. G., Li, J. D., & Tian, Z. (2010). Optimal power control for cognitive radio networks under coupled interference constraints: A cooperative game-theoretic perspective. *IEEE Transactions on Vehicular Technology, 59*(4), 1696–1706. doi:10.1109/TVT.2009.2039502.

Ye, W., Heidemann, J., & Estrin, D. (2002). An energy-efficient MAC protocol for wireless sensor networks. In *Proceedings of the IEEE Infocom,* (pp. 1567-1576). IEEE. doi: 10.1109/INFCOM.2002.1019408

Yick, J., Mukherjee, B., & Ghosal, D. (2008). Wireless sensor network survey. *The International Journal of Computer and Telecommunications Networking, 52*(12), 2292–2330.

Yue, W., Sun, Q., & Jin, S. (2010). Performance analysis of sensor nodes in a WSN with sleep/wakeup protocol. In *Proceedings of the Ninth International Symposium on Operations Research and Its Applications (ISORA'10),* (pp. 370–377). ISORA.

Zhao, J., Zheng, H., & Yang, G. H. (2005). Distributed coordination in dynamic spectrum allocation networks. In *Proceedings of the 1st IEEE International Symposium on New Frontiers in Dynamic Spectrum Access Networks (DySPAN '05),* (pp. 259-268). IEEE.

Zhao, Qing, & Sadler, B.M. (2007). A survey of dynamic spectrum access. *IEEE Signal Processing Magazine, 24*(3), 79–89. doi:10.1109/MSP.2007.361604.

Zhao, Q., & Sadler, B. M. (2007). A survey of dynamic spectrum access. *IEEE Signal Processing Magazine, 24*(3), 79–89. doi:10.1109/MSP.2007.361604.

ADDITIONAL READING

Akter, L., & Natarajan, B. (2010). Modeling fairness in resource allocation for secondary users in a competitive cognitive radio network. In *Proceedings of the Wireless Telecommunications Symposium (WTS 2010),* (pp. 1-6). WTS.

Fette, B. (2006). Cognitive radio technology. In *Communications Policy and Spectrum Management* (pp. 29–71). London: Elsevier.

Georgoulas, S., Moessner, K., Mansour, A., Pissarides, M., & Spapis, P. (2012). A fuzzy reinforcement learning approach for pre-congestion notification based admission control. In Sandre, R. et al. (Eds.), *Dependable Networks and Services (LNCS) (Vol. 7279,* pp. 26–37). Springer Link Press. doi:10.1007/978-3-642-30633-4_4.

Guibene, W., Hayar, A., & Turki, M. (2010). Distribution discontinuities detection using algebraic technique for spectrum sensing in cognitive radio. In *Proceedings of the Fifth International Conference on Cognitive Radio Oriented Wireless Networks & Communications (CROWNCOM 2010),* (pp. 1-5). CrownCom.

Irmer, R., Droste, H., Marsch, P., Grieger, M., Fettweis, G., & Brueck, S. et al. (2011). Coordinated multipoint: Concepts, performance, and field trial Results. *IEEE Communications Magazine, 49*(2), 102–111. doi:10.1109/MCOM.2011.5706317.

Jia, J., Zhang, Q., & Shen, X. (2008). HC-MAC: A hardware-constrained cognitive MAC for efficient spectrum management. *IEEE Journal on Selected Areas in Communications, 26*(1), 106–117. doi:10.1109/JSAC.2008.080110.

Karakayli, M. K., Foschini, G. J., & Valenzuela, R. A. (2006). Network coordination for spectrally efficient communications in cellular systems. *IEEE Wireless Communications Magazine, 13*(4), 56–61. doi:10.1109/MWC.2006.1678166.

Kawadia, V., & Kumar, P. R. (2005). Principles and protocols for power control in wireless ad hoc networks. *IEEE Journal on Selected Areas in Communications, 23*(1), 76–88. doi:10.1109/JSAC.2004.837354.

Liang, Y. C., Chen, K. C., Li, G. Y., & Mahonen, P. (2011). Cognitive radio networking and communications: An overview. *IEEE Transactions on Vehicular Technology,* 99.

Lotfinezhad, M., Liang, B., & Sousa, E. S. (2010). Optimal control of constrained cognitive radio networks with dynamic population size. In *Proceedings of the IEEE Infocom,* (pp. 1-9). IEEE.

Magdalinos, P., Kousaridas, A., Spapis, P., Katsikas, G., & Alonistioti, N. (2011). Feedback-based learning for self-managed network elements. In *Proceedings of the 12th IEEE International Symposium on Integrated Network Management.* IEEE.

Malla, A., El-Kadi, M., & Todorova, P. (2001). A fair resource allocation protocol for multimedia wireless networks. In *Proceedings of the International Conference on Parallel Processing,* (pp. 437- 443). IEEE.

Müller, A., & Frank, P. (2010). Cooperative interference prediction for enhanced link adaptation in the 3GPP LTE uplink. In *Proceedings of the Seventy-First IEEE Vehicular Technology Conference (VTC 2010 Spring),* (pp. 1-5). IEEE.

Raju, A., Delaere, S., Lindmark, S., Stamatelatos, M., & Ballon, P. (2011). *Sustainability of business ecosystems for next generation cognitive networks.* Paper presented at the Wireless Innovation Forum European Conference on Communications Technologies and Software Defined Radio. Brussels, Belgium.

Raju, A., Lindmark, S., Delaere, S., Gonçalves, V., Stamatelatos, M., & Ballon, P. (2011). Multi-actor analysis for self-organizing energy efficient business ecosystems. In *Proceedings of the Tenth Conference of Telecommunication, Media and Internet Techno-Economics (CTTE 2011),* (pp. 1-9). CTTE.

Qu, Q., Milstein, L.B., & Vaman, D.R. (2007). Distributed spectrum and power control in cognitive radio based wireless ad hoc networks. In *Proceedings of the IEEE Sarnoff Symposium,* (pp. 1-6). IEEE.

Report, B. C. (2012). *Application delivery networks: The new imperative for IT visibility, acceleration and security.* Retrieved October 15, 2012, from http://www.bluecoat.com/sites/default/files/documents/files/Application_Delivery_Networks-_The_New_Imperative_for_IT_Visibility,_Acceleration_and_Security.d.pdf

Zayen, B., Guibène, W., & Hayar, A. (2010). Performance comparison for low complexity blind sensing techniques in cognitive radio systems. In *Proceedings of the Second International Workshop on Cognitive Information Processing (CIP 2010),* (pp. 328-332). ACM.

KEY TERMS AND DEFINITIONS

Cognitive Radio Resource Management: Mechanisms controlling the communication schemes between mobile terminals and radio networks.

Cognitive Radio: A transceiver which automatically detects available channels in wireless spectrum.

Evolved Node B: The element in E-UTRA of LTE that is the evolution of the element Node B in UTRA of UMTS. It is the hardware part responsible for direct communication with the mobile handsets (UEs) in the mobile phone network. It is also known as E-UTRAN Node B and abbreviated as eNodeB or eNB.

Policy Based Management: A way to allocate network resources, primarily network bandwidth, QoS, and security (firewalls), according to defined business rules.

Power Control: The intelligent selection of transmit power in a communication system to achieve good performance within the system.

Q-Learning: A reinforcement learning technique that works by learning an action-value function.

Spectrum Aggregation: Technique for multiple spectrum bands to be utilized by the same user in order to satisfy the large bandwidth demand.

Spectrum Sensing: The process required so that a UE will perceive signals coming from other sources in the environment.

Chapter 6
The Impact of Regulations on the Business Case for Cognitive Radio

Peter Anker
Ministry of Economic Affairs, The Netherlands & Delft University of Technology, The Netherlands

ABSTRACT

Cognitive Radio holds an interesting promise for improved utilisation of the radio spectrum. However, there is a considerable degree of uncertainty regarding the potential application of cognitive radio. One of the reasons for this uncertainty is the need for changes in the regulatory regime to allow for more dynamic forms of spectrum access. In addressing the necessary changes in regulations, the regulator should be well aware of the perspective of the entrepreneur. Eventually, it is the entrepreneur who invests in CR technology and thereby realises the goal of improved utilisation of the radio spectrum. This chapter addresses the impact on the business case for cognitive technologies of the regulatory regime and the choices on the fundamental CR technology that regulators will have to make.

INTRODUCTION

Cognitive Radio (CR) and Cognitive Networks (CN) are promising innovative technologies that can be used to improve spectrum utilisation. Especially the ability of cognitive technology to provide access to spectrum that is already assigned to other user(s) or usage, but partly unused when considered on a time or geographical basis holds an interesting promise. This CR capability is considered as highly valuable for the introduction of new radio communication services, as essentially all (usable) radio spectrum has been allocated and assigned. However, there still is a large degree of

DOI: 10.4018/978-1-4666-4189-1.ch006

Copyright © 2013, IGI Global. Copying or distributing in print or electronic forms without written permission of IGI Global is prohibited.

uncertainty associated with CR that will have to be mitigated before successful, large scale deployment may be expected and the potential economic and social value can be realised.

One of the reasons for this uncertainty is that the current regulatory model is not compatible with this new technology. In the current model, radio spectrum is divided into fixed and non-overlapping blocks, which are exclusively assigned to different users, services or wireless technologies. Regulatory provisions are needed to align the regulatory model with the new capabilities of cognitive technology to realise the goal of more efficient and flexible utilisation of the radio spectrum.

In addressing the necessary changes in regulations, governments should be well aware of the perspective of the entrepreneur. Ultimately it is through the actions of the entrepreneurs, individually and collectively, that the realisation of improved utilisation of the radio spectrum can become a reality.

In a somewhat simplistic view of the world, governments, as custodians of the radio spectrum, allocate and assign rights to the use of the radio spectrum with an aim of efficient use of the radio spectrum, while firms develop products and services that use radio waves with an aim to maximize profit. Hence, governments and firms have different roles and different objectives. Nonetheless, in the realisation of their objectives they are highly interdependent. If as a result of profit maximisation considerations firms decide not to use the radio spectrum as intended or decide not to use the radio spectrum efficiently, the government fails in realising its governance objectives related to the radio spectrum.

In general firms will only decide to invest in new products and/or services if they can expect a future return. These investment decisions are driven by three major considerations: (1) the prospective demand and willingness to pay for new products and/or services; (2) the magnitude of the investments required; and (3) the degree of risk or uncertainty involved.

The profile of the business case, in terms of depth of investment and the recovery period required, will influence the ability to obtain the necessary (external) funding. As such the business case is especially challenging for communication services provisioning that requires an associated infrastructure roll-out. In these cases the right to exploit the radio spectrum over a significant period of time and on an exclusive basis will contribute to the willingness of entrepreneurs to invest, as it lowers the degree of uncertainty.

The dilemma that governments are now facing is that, since the liberalisation, prevailing policy suggest a technology neutral assignment of radio spectrum to improve dynamic efficiency, while enabling the deployment of a specific technology, i.e. cognitive radio technology, is of public interest to achieve more efficient utilisation of the radio spectrum. It appears that in this light regulations to allow deployment of a specific type of CR technology in parts of the radio spectrum that would otherwise be underutilised or not used at all is justified (Lemstra, Anker et al., 2011).

The subsequent challenge governments will be facing is the choice among some of the more fundamental features of CR, such as sensing and/ or the use of database and the band in which the CR is allowed to operate. Their choices will need to be well informed as their choices play a pivotal role in the business models of the entrepreneurs. The way governments allocate the use of radio spectrum to particular radio communication services on the (inter)national level and assign the rights to use the radio spectrum on the national level is determining the viability of the business case for particular radio communication products and services. In this respect there is the issue of 'the chicken and the egg': certain types of radio spectrum rights assignment facilitate certain types of usage, while certain types of perceived usage will require a particular type of assignment. In other words, entrepreneurs are reluctant to invest in new products and/or services based on CR technology because of the degree of regulatory uncertainty and regulators are not in a position to provide this certainty because it is uncertain if their choices will support a viable business case.

This chapter explains the relationship between the fundamental choices regulators will have to make and possible business cases for the introduction of CR technology. The chapter starts with an introduction on the regulatory environment and the relationship between the regulatory regime and possible business cases. It will address the regulatory environment, the changes that will have to be made to allow CR and CN technology and more dynamic forms of spectrum access, the activities that are currently carried out on both an international level and national level to allow for cognitive radio and dynamic spectrum access and the relationship between the regulatory regime and possible business cases. It is followed by a description of the basic technological solutions that are possible for CR and CN and the relationship between the CR capabilities and possible business cases.

This exploration is used to assess the impact of a chosen regulatory environment and associated CR technology on possible business cases. This approach will be illustrated by an assessment of the best known business case for the deployment of CR technology, the BuC for white spot access in the TV bands.

BACKGROUND ON THE CURRENT PARADIGM OF SPECTRUM REGULATIONS

Radio waves are used to deliver a broad range of services and applications, for instance, mobile telephony, radio and television broadcasting, maritime radio, research into the (birth of) the universe, and even for heating food in a microwave oven. However, it is not possible for users to use this resource without limitations. The use of radio waves at a particular frequency by one user will influence the use of the same, or nearby

frequencies, by other users at the same time. Radio receivers will have difficulties to distinguish the intended signal from all other signals it receives. This phenomenon is called interference. Hence, co-ordination is needed in the use of radio waves between the various users to manage the problems associated with interference. As the propagation of radio waves is not hindered by national borders, this coordination will need to be performed on an international level.

Particularly for users, it is also often important that services and the equipment needed for them are standardized. This means that these services operate with similar equipment in different countries on the same frequencies. More efficient use can be made of the spectrum, as a result of this harmonisation of allocations, and the equipment can also be used over much wider geographical areas, increasing the size of the market for such equipment and reducing production costs. In the case of a number of applications, international harmonisation of use is even necessary owing to the nature of the application.

Historical developments have led to a situation in which governments have taken the role of 'supreme coordinator' in the use of the radio spectrum. Spectrum management has become based on the avoidance of interference and technically efficient use of spectrum. This section gives a short overview of the international and national regulatory framework for spectrum regulations. The section focuses thereby on the framework for Europe.

ITU

Spectrum is globally governed by the International Telecommunications Union (ITU). The Radiocommunication Sector of the ITU (ITU-R) develops and adopts the Radio Regulations, a binding international treaty, with a voluminous set of rules, recommendations and procedures for the regulation of radiocommunications. The Radio Regulations are based on avoidance of radio interference through the division of spectrum in bands which are allocated to one or more services out of some 40 different radio services. These radio services include services such as fixed, mobile, satellite, amateur, radio navigation and radio astronomy. Most bands are shared among primary and secondary services. Primary services have priority in case of conflicts resulting in harmful interference. Harmful interference is defined as *Interference* which endangers the functioning of a *radionavigation service* or of other *safety services* or seriously degrades, obstructs, or repeatedly interrupts a *radiocommunication service* operating in accordance with Radio Regulations (ITU, 2008: article 1.169)

A wide range of regulatory, operational, and technical provisions ensure that radio services are compatible with one another and harmful interference among services of different countries is avoided. The Radio Regulations are regularly updated in response to changes in needs and to new demands at World Radiocommunication Conferences (WRC), which are held every three to four years (ITU, 2004).

The Radio Regulations are an international treaty between countries. This means that it only concerns the relations between countries. Individual countries can adopt some or all of the allocated services of each band and they are allowed to deviate from the Radio Regulations as long as no harmful interference is caused to the services in other countries.

CEPT/ECC

The Electronic Communications Committee (ECC) of the European Conference of Postal and Telecommunications Administrations (CEPT) brings together 48 countries to develop common policies and regulations in electronic communications and related applications for Europe. Its primary objective is to harmonize efficient use of the radio spectrum, satellite orbits and numbering

resources across Europe. It takes an active role at the international level, preparing common European proposals to represent European interests in the ITU and other international organisations. The ECC work is carried out in partnership with all stakeholders including the European Commission and ETSI.

There are four different regulatory deliveries developed by the ECC:

- *ECC Decisions* are regulatory texts providing measures on significant harmonisation matters, which CEPT member administrations are strongly urged to follow. ECC Decisions are not obligatory legislative documents, as any other CEPT deliverable; however, they are normally implemented by many CEPT administrations.
- *ECC Recommendations* are measures which national administrations are encouraged to apply. They are principally intended as harmonisation measures for those matters where ECC Decisions are not yet relevant, or as guidance to CEPT member administrations.
- *ECC Reports* are the result of studies by the ECC normally in support of a harmonisation measure.
- *CEPT Reports* are the final results of studies developed in order to support responses to European Commission (EC) mandates. In many cases the results in the report form the basis for future EC Decisions on harmonized technical conditions of use (see the following section on the European Union).

CEPT deliverables are non-binding, as noted above, and this gives the national administrators a large degree of flexibility when it comes to adapting these to country specific conditions, legacy usages and circumstances.

European Union

Throughout the 1990s the European Commission gradually increased its involvement in spectrum issues, as the RF spectrum use started to affect the 'internal market'. The first intervention was related to the creation of a single European (internal) market for equipment. On the 9th of March 1999 the European Commission published the R&TTE Directive 1999/5/EC (EC, 1999). This Directive covers most products which use the radio frequency spectrum, including unlicensed devices. All equipment that is placed on the market must comply with a set of essential requirements, covering the protection of health and safety, electromagnetic emission and immunity of the equipment and effective use of the radio spectrum so as to avoid harmful interference.

Equipment manufactured in accordance with a "Harmonised Standard" may be placed on the market within the whole European Union (see also the following section on ETSI). However, certain restrictions may apply to the use of radio equipment if the frequencies are not harmonised in the European Union. If a Harmonised Standard is used, the manufacturer has to perform some specific radio tests and can make its own declaration of conformity (self declaration) which states that the product satisfies the essential requirements. There is no need for an external body to perform the testing. When a Harmonised Standard is not available or not appropriate, a manufacturer needs to demonstrate more extensively how the requirements of the Directive are being met through testing, to be documented in a 'technical construction file'. This file has to be reviewed and approved by a notified body.

Another intervention of the European Union in radio spectrum management came with the introduction of the new regulatory framework. This framework was aimed at further liberalisation, harmonisation and simplification of the regulations in the telecommunications sector. The Framework Directive (2002/21/EC), *on a common regulatory framework for electronic communications networks and services*, states that the allocation and assignment of radio frequencies by national regulatory authorities are to be based on objective, transparent, non-discriminatory and proportionate criteria (EC, 2002c). The related Authorisation Directive (2002/20/EC) specifies the circumstances under which the granting of an individual license is being allowed (EC, 2002b). The Directive states that granting of an individual license is only allowed to ensure efficient use of radio frequencies. The Directive also limits the conditions that may be attached to the rights of use for radio frequencies. The licensing and the formulation of the conditions under which the radio frequencies may be used are left to the Member States.

Under this new regime harmonisation of spectrum is still left to CEPT. However, the associated Radio Spectrum Decision by the European Commission (2002/676/EC) created the possibility to impose technical harmonisation measures upon the Member States (EC, 2002a). This Decision created a legal framework for 'the harmonised availability and efficient use of radio spectrum in the European Union for the establishment and functioning of the internal market in Community policy areas, such as electronic communications, broadcasting and transport'. In the implementation of the Decision the European Commission is assisted by the newly formed Radio Spectrum Committee (RSC). The RSC is composed of experts from the Member States.

The European Commission can issue mandates to CEPT to advice on technical harmonisation measures. The RSC approves the CEPT Report and associated technical implementation measures prepared by the Commission. The implementation of these measures is mandatory for the EU Member States.

Next to the RSC, the Radio Spectrum Policy Group (RSPG) was set up to facilitate consultation and to develop and support radio spectrum policy. The Radio Spectrum Policy Group (RSPG) is a group of high-level representatives of the Member States which advises the European Commission on radio spectrum policy at a strategic level.

The revision of the regulatory framework in 2009 introduces two governing principles that will have implications on the future regulation. Firstly, general authorisation should be the general rule when authorizing access to spectrum. Individual licensing can still be used but such deviations from the general principle must be justified. Secondly, the principles of technology and service neutrality should be the general rule for both general and individual authorisation of access to spectrum. Deviations from this principle will still be allowed but must be justified. As the allocation of spectrum to specific technologies or services is an exception to the principles of technology and service neutrality and reduces the freedom to choose the service provided or technology used, any proposal for such allocation should be transparent and subject to public consultation (EC, 2009).

ETSI

The European Telecommunications Standards Institute (ETSI) is an independent, non-profit organisation, whose mission is to produce globally applicable standards for Information & Communications Technologies including fixed, mobile, radio, broadcast, Internet and several other areas. ETSI plays a major role in developing a wide range of standards and other technical documentation as Europe's contribution to world-wide ICT standardisation. This activity is supplemented by other activities such as interoperability testing services. ETSI's prime objective is to support global harmonisation by providing a forum in which all the key players can contribute actively.

ETSI is recognised as an official European standards organisation by the European Commission and works under mandates from the Commission to prepare Harmonised Standards for the R&TTE Directive. Membership is open to all interested parties. Harmonised Standards are standards adopted by European standards Organisations, prepared in accordance with the General Guidelines agreed between the Commission and the European standards organisations (ETSI, CEN and CENELEC), and in response to a mandate issued by the Commission after consultation with the Member States. The reference of a Harmonised Standard must be published in the Official Journal (OJEU) under the R&TTE Directive in order to give a presumption of conformity to the essential requirements of the R&TTE Directive.

ETSI is an officially recognized partner of the ECC, which is reflected in a Memorandum of Understanding (MoU). The cooperation between ETSI and the ECC plays an important role to ensure the objective of harmonized and efficient use of the radio spectrum across Europe.

National Spectrum Management Authority

Based on the international allocations and regulatory provisions the national spectrum regulator grants access to spectrum for users. An EU Member State has the right to set conditions on the use of spectrum under the Framework Directive. These conditions can include appropriate limits that aim to avoid harmful interference to other radio services. These conditions can be harmonised on a European wide basis either through a European Commission Spectrum Decision (which is mandatory for EU Member states to implement) or by an ECC Decision or Recommendation. Alternatively, if no mandatory harmonised guidance is available a regulatory deliverable can be developed on a national basis.

Usually a license gives an exclusive right to operate in a specific frequency range, in a specific location or geographic area and under specific technical conditions (e.g., power level, antenna height, antenna location etc.) and other conditions such as service obligations and (network) build-out requirements. The compliance of spectrum users with the license obligations is monitored and enforced.

If the demand for spectrum within a particular band is considered to be significantly less than the supply licenses are usually granted on a first come first served basis. When spectrum demand exceeds the supply, the spectrum regulator has to use another mechanism to award the licenses. Increasingly, regulators have turned to comparative hearings or "beauty contests" and more recently to spectrum auctions (Anker, 2010b).

Concluding Remarks

The current spectrum management model operates on both a national and international level as depicted in Figure 1.

In the current paradigm all decisions are made by the spectrum regulator. Therefore, this traditional spectrum management model is commonly referred to as Command & Control. This Command and Control model has its limitations. The two most eminent are: all (usable) spectrum is allocated but some of the portions of the spectrum are hardly used, and the method to allocate and assign spectrum is slow in responding to changes in market and technology.

In the past, the inefficiencies in spectrum utilisation introduced by this bureaucratic command and control spectrum management model were tolerable. As demand grew, advancing technology ensured that new frequency bands were available, and there was no need to deal with economically inefficiently used spectrum. More recently, de-

Figure 1. The international and national regulatory framework for spectrum regulations in Europe

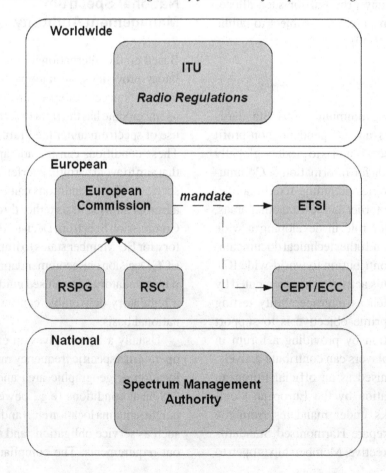

mand has grown very rapidly and technology has delivered new services and devices to serve that demand. However, the opening up of even higher frequency bands is not going in the same pace and not all frequencies are alike. More bandwidth (capacity) is available in the higher frequency range, but higher frequencies have a shorter range, ceteris paribus. E.g. for mobile communications the ideal frequency range is roughly 1-3 GHz. Below this frequency range there is not enough data throughput capacity available and above this range the coverage area of the base stations becomes too small.

This means that Spectrum Management Authorities more or less ran out of useable spectrum to assign for new services and technologies. Hence, services based on new technologies can only be introduced at the expense of existing services. Consequently, Spectrum Management Authorities all over the world are in the process of modernising their spectrum policies, and are seeking alternative spectrum management models which allow a much more efficient and flexible utilisation of the spectrum (Nekovee, 2006; Anker, 2010b).

THE NEW REGULATORY PARADIGM OF DYNAMIC SPECTRUM ACCESS

Solutions have to address the lack of available (accessible) spectrum in the current static model. In the current spectrum management model, radio spectrum is divided into fixed and non-overlapping blocks, separated by so-called guard bands, and exclusively assigned to different services and wireless technologies, while a lot of spectrum usage is only local and limited in time. In an economic sense, there appears to be a paradox whereby the rights to the radio spectrum are fully assigned, but a lot of radio spectrum remains unused in practice when considered on a time or geographical basis. Under the current command and control model it is very difficult to make this unused spectrum available.

There are two basic alternative regimes considered, a regime based on exclusive property rights and a regime based on a commons for spectrum with strict general rules on the use of spectrum without the need for individual licenses (Faulhaber and Farber, 2003; Anker, 2010b). In these discussions, cognitive radio has been closely linked to the commons. Advocates of the commons see CR technology as an enabler to realise a radio spectrum commons (Faulhaber, 2005). However, technologies such as cognitive radio do not favour one regime over another. Cognitive radio can be used in both spectrum management regimes, as it can also be used to facilitate an efficient market-based regime based on property rights (Anker, 2010b). Cognitive radio, as a technology, is an enabling tool to realise this goal of increased flexibility in access to spectrum.

The key feature of such a cognitive radio is its ability to recognize unused parts of spectrum that are assigned to conventional users and adapt its communication strategy to use these parts while minimizing the interference that it causes to the conventional users. An important consequence is that cognitive radio can be an enabling technology to facilitate a paradigm shift for spectrum management from a regime based on static spectrum assignments to a regime based on more dynamic forms of spectrum access (Olafsson, Glover et al., 2007; Anker, 2010b).

ADAPTING THE REGULATORY FRAMEWORK FOR DYNAMIC SPECTRUM ACCESS

The first question is if there is any international regulation in place that prohibits dynamic spectrum access through the use of cognitive radio. The short answer to that question is: No. Administrations that wish to implement cognitive radio have two different alternatives to do so (Anker, 2010a).

Firstly, cognitive radio can be used under any service defined in the Radio Regulations, i.e., if the cognitive radio is used to deliver mobile communications, the cognitive radio can be treated in the same way as an ordinary mobile radio, and will be allowed to operate under the provisions for the mobile service. This means that the cognitive radio can use bands that are allocated to the mobile service as far as the (international) regulations on interference and sharing conditions are met.

A second option is to implement cognitive radio on a so-called non-interference basis (ITU, 2008: article 4.4). This means that the cognitive radio shall not cause harmful interference to, and shall not claim protection from, harmful interference caused by a station operating in accordance with the provisions of the Radio Regulations. These provisions only apply for cross-border communications (and interference), since the Radio Regulations are an international treaty between countries. Individual countries are allowed to deviate from the Radio Regulations as long as no harmful interference is caused to the services in other countries.

However, to realise the full potential of cognitive radio, the radio will need to have dynamic access to a wide range of spectrum bands, which might currently be designated for different radio services. Introduction of dynamic spectrum access is only possible if these exclusively designated frequency bands are opened up for other services and technologies. Hence, there is a need to enhance the regulatory framework to allow for more flexibility in the use of radio spectrum.

Next to the need for more flexibility in the designation of frequency band to radio services, there are different regulatory adaptations that can be made to improve the possibilities for dynamic spectrum access. Both regimes that are considered to improve the efficiency and flexibility (open access and property rights) need to be linked to the new technological capabilities of cognitive radio's and dynamic spectrum access.

Within both regimes there are different possibilities to exploit dynamic spectrum access. In both regimes dynamic spectrum access can be used to pool spectrum between a number of users or user groups or it can be used to dynamically access white spots. Spectrum pooling is the situation in which a common "*pool of spectrum*" is shared among multiple users (Lehr and Jesuale, 2008). Access to the pool may be restricted to a closed group of users or the pool may be open to all under certain use restrictions. All users have the same rights to access the spectrum. Therefore, this kind of sharing is also referred to as horizontal sharing.

This is in contrast to the other case in which white spot users are only allowed access to the spectrum as long as the primary users are not using it. The white spot users are on a secondary level of usage of the spectrum. Therefore this type of sharing is also referred to as vertical sharing. This secondary usage may also be restricted to a closed user group or open to all.

This leads to four different scenarios for the implementation of dynamic spectrum access. The different scenarios are summarized in Table 1.

The role of the spectrum regulator will differ with the regulatory regime under which dynamic spectrum access is realised. In the following two subsections, the role of the spectrum regulator in implementing dynamic spectrum access is further explored for the different scenarios.

Table 1. Four different regulatory scenarios for dynamic spectrum access

	Horizontal sharing (spectrum pooling)	Vertical sharing (white spot access)
Property rights regime (Closed user groups)	Spectrum owners dynamically share spectrum.	Owners of the spectrum grant specific Cognitive Radio's access to their white spots.
Open access regime (Commons)	All users dynamically share spectrum on an equal footing.	Cognitive Radio's dynamically access white spots from incumbent users.

Dynamic Spectrum Access in an Open Access Regime

In an open access regime, any user can obtain access to spectrum under certain specified conditions. These conditions will have to be clearly defined to limit the interference level. In the vertical sharing regime, a commons is created by giving devices access to the unused parts of the spectrum of licensed users. This type of sharing is also referred to as Opportunistic Spectrum Access. In this case, the rules for spectrum access will have to guarantee that the interference to the primary user(s) of the band is kept below an acceptable level. The spectrum regulator will need to provide the necessary information to detect and protect incumbent users.

The definition of an appropriate level is not an easy task. If the level is too restrictive the potential gains of Opportunistic Spectrum Access are marginal, while a level that is too permissive may affect the Quality of Service of the primary user. The regulator will have to cooperate with industry to set a realistic level, which is based on the state of the art of technology. The level will have to be re-assessed if the primary user changes its technology. In the case of a true commons in which a frequency band is dynamically shared among all users, there is less need for involvement by the spectrum regulator. The main task of the regulator is in that case to designate a band for such purposes.

The regulator can also support OSA by providing information on the use of the band that will be dynamically shared between primary users and OSA devices.

Dynamic Spectrum Access in a Property Rights Regime

A property rights regime is based on the introduction of property rights. These property rights go a step further than the licenses of today. They are used to create a market for spectrum in which these rights can be sold, leased and rented. The spectrum regulator will have to define these rights, with as few restrictions as possible. A number of countries have already introduced the possibility of secondary trading. However, in most cases there is an approval mechanism involving the authorities before trading may take place. This kind of barrier induces a delay before a trade can take place and thus makes real-time trading impossible. Hence, this barrier will have to be removed to exploit the full potential of dynamic spectrum access. Trading based on a much shorter time basis may make the market for spectrum more fluid. A central entity (a spectrum broker) could be used to facilitate this spot market.

A spectrum market can only function if information about the actual ownership of the spectrum property rights is readily available to facilitate trading. The regulator is ideally positioned to perform the task to keep a record of the ownership of these rights. Inclusion of monitoring information about actual usage of spectrum can further facilitate trading by giving more insights in the possibilities for trading and secondary usage.

Enforcement and Dispute Resolution

To successfully introduce dynamic spectrum access, there must be some assurance for the incumbent users of the spectrum that their usage will not be subject to (harmful) interference. This means that there is a need for a dispute resolution mechanism. To ease the settlement of disputes, it may be necessary to introduce a unique identifier for all cognitive radios that is send alongside with the message with all radio transmissions. This will require that regulators are actively involved in the development and/or standardisation of CR technology (Atia, Sahai et al., 2008).

A related point is that regulators will have to be very active in enforcement, especially in the start up phase of the use of CR technology. This will provide the necessary confidence to existing users of the band that all efforts are taken to prevent cognitive radios from inducing harmful interference and at the same time it will provide useful information to the industry to further develop their product (Anker, 2010a).

Conclusion

The role of the regulator and the necessary conditions in the various regulatory regimes is outlined in Table 2.

CURRENT REGULATORY ACTIVITIES FOR DYNAMIC SPECTRUM ACCESS

Spectrum regulators all over the world are active to provide more flexibility in the use of spectrum and other activities to allow for more dynamic forms of access to spectrum.

Activities Within the ITU

At the World Radio Conference 2007 (WRC-07) it was decided to put Software Defined Radio and Cognitive Radio on the agenda for the World Radio Conference of 2012 under agenda item 1.19. Study Group 1 (Spectrum management) of the

Table 2. Necessary conditions for dynamic spectrum access in various regulatory regimes

Regulatory regime	Necessary conditions
Open access	• Strict protection rules needed to keep the interference to the primary users at an acceptable level • Rules to promote fair sharing of spectrum resources among OSA devices • Availability of information on primary use to detect and protect incumbent users
Property rights	• Well defined exclusive licenses granted to primary users or brokers • As few usage restrictions as possible • No barriers to instant trading • Electronic information about ownership and actual usage should be available

ITU-R was responsible for the studies needed in preparation of this agenda item of the WRC-12. As part of these studies, the following definition was developed (ITU-R, 2009):

Cognitive Radio System. A radio system employing technology that allows the system to obtain knowledge of its operational and geographical environment, established policies and its internal state; to dynamically and autonomously adjust its operational parameters and protocols according to its obtained knowledge in order to achieve predefined objectives; and to learn from the results obtained.

This definition is illustrated in Figure 2.

WRC-12 came to the conclusion that Software Defined Radio (SDR) and Cognitive Radio Systems (CRS) are related technologies which can be used in any radio service within the Radio Regulations. There is no need to incorporate the definitions of SDR and CRS in the Radio Regulations. However, WRC-12 reiterated that any radio system implementing CRS technology needs to operate in accordance with the provisions of the Radio Regulations.

In other words, administrations that wish to implement cognitive radio already can do so. Cognitive Radio Systems can be used under any of the in the Radio Regulations defined services. However, it was also noted that there remain questions around the deployment and use of Cognitive Radio Systems. A common concern was expressed within the ITU-R about how the protection of existing services from potential interference from the services implementing CRS technology, especially from the dynamic spectrum access capability of CRS, could be realised. ITU-R and the WRC-12 came to the conclusion that there is need for further studies within ITU-R on the implementation of CRS technologies within a radiocommunication service and on sharing among different radiocommunication services with regard to the capabilities of CRS, in particular dynamic access to frequency

Figure 2. The definition of a cognitive radio system

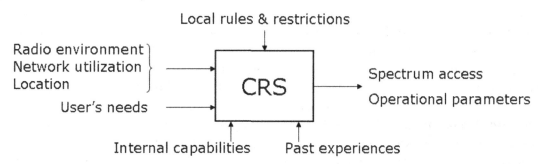

bands. ITU-R came to the conclusion that there is a need for further studies on CRS during the discussions on the future work programme of the ITU-R at the Radiocommunications Assembly. This need for further studies is expressed in ITU-R Resolution 58. The RA was held in January 2012, in the week prior to the WRC-12. The WRC-12 confirmed the need for further studies in WRC-12 Recommendation 76.

ITU-R Study Group 5 (Terrestrial services) already started work on the possibilities for the introduction of cognitive radio in the mobile service and the operational implications of this introduction. ITU-R Report M.2225 provides a general description of cognitive radio systems and describes a set of deployment scenarios for the introduction of cognitive radio systems in the land mobile service (excluding International Mobile Telecommunications [IMT]). ITU-R Report M.2242 describes how introduction of CRS in the IMT systems may be used for more dynamic and flexible radio resource management and optimisation. It is now up to the other study groups to study possibilities for the introduction of cognitive radio technology for the radio services under their purview.

Activities Within the European Union

Within the European Union, there are a number of activities to introduce more flexibility in the use of spectrum and to introduce secondary trading. Both issues were included in the amendment of the regulatory framework for electronic communications networks and services of 2009 (EC, 2009).

The European Parliament and Council adopted on 14 March 2012 the first Radio Spectrum Policy Programme (RSPP). The RSPP outlines at a strategic level how the use of spectrum can contribute to the most important political objectives of the European Union from 2011 to 2015. The programme sets general regulatory principles and policy objectives to be applied for spectrum in all sectors of the internal market, defines actions and common principles to enhance efficiency and flexibility, preserve and promote competition, support wireless broadband communications as well as other EU policies. The guiding principles for spectrum management are spectrum efficiency and flexibility, technology and service neutrality and competition. In addition, collective use of spectrum and spectrum trading would be promoted. In article 4, which deals with sharing, is an explicit reference made to cognitive radio (EU, 2012):

Member States, in cooperation with the Commission, shall, where appropriate, foster the collective use of spectrum as well as shared use of spectrum.

Member States shall also foster the development of current and new technologies, for example, in cognitive radio, including those using "white spaces."

The European Commission started an initiative to promote shared use of spectrum resources. The initiative started with the commissioning of a study "Perspectives on the value of shared spectrum access" (Forge, Horvitz, et al., 2012). The aim of the study was to contribute to a better understanding of the socio-economic value of shared spectrum access, including its impact on competition, innovation, and investment. It is intended to support the European Commission's plans to publish a Communication on these issues. In its recommendations it sees cognitive technology as a way forward to increase the possibilities for sharing. It promotes Authorized Shared Access (ASA) or Licensed Shared Access (LSA) as steps on the way to more shared spectrum (Forge, Horvitz, et al., 2012). ASA and LSA are comparable concepts to share spectrum between licensed incumbents and licensed secondary users.

The RSPG (Radio Spectrum Policy Group) developed a Report and an Opinion on Cognitive Technology (RSPG, 2010, 2011a). The Report provides an overview of the various aspects related to CR technology and to identify challenging regulatory issues which require further attention. The use of cognitive radio technologies is seen as an enabler providing more efficient spectrum sharing and providing more dynamic access to spectrum. The report also highlighted that the use of so-called "white spaces" in the UHF band might be one of the first applications of CR.

The Opinion is a follow up of the report and should be considered as a generic initiative to approach the issue of the implementation of CR technologies on a European level. The main conclusion of this Opinion is that there is no need to adapt the current regulatory framework for the introduction of Cognitive Radio. The introduction of CR could be left to Member States as long as border coordination issues are addressed for each band concerned. The necessary coordination activities related to the implementation of CR technologies can be left to CEPT and standardisation bodies, such as ETSI.

The RSPG sees usage of a database as the most feasible and flexible way forward to provide reliable real time information updates on spectrum usage. The following important issues will have to be addressed by the regulators to implement a database:

- Indicating how the database should be certified or accredited;
- Providing information on actual spectrum usage;
- Providing information to database managers on algorithms to calculate white spaces.

The development of the database technology itself can be left to the standardisation bodies. RSPG recommends standardization of the technology on a European level, i.e. by ETSI. This process could be supported by the regulators by giving ETSI relevant information on the data elements needed to describe actual spectrum usage, expected behaviour of the equipment and the radio characteristics of the radio devices.

RSPG further recommends to create a platform to allow researchers, academia, manufacturers, operators, service providers and regulators to coordinate research activities. This platform could build upon already existing platforms with comparable purposes, notably COST-TERRA.

The RSPG acknowledged LSA in a recent report on collective use of spectrum. The concept involves granting a LSA user the right to utilize under-used spectrum without interfering with the incumbent user. It is argued that LSA allows licensees to maintain a certain level of quality of service (RSPG, 2011b).

Activities Within the ECC

The European Commission mandated the European Communications Committee in 2007 to perform a study on the introduction of Cognitive Radio in the television bands. CEPT responded with CEPT Report 24. This report indicates that the feasibility of the introduction of Cognitive Radio systems has not yet been conclusively demonstrated. Since the CR technology is at a very early stage, the CEPT recommends looking further into the requirements within the European environment for CR devices to be deployed in white space spectrum in order to facilitate the further development of CR technology. The initial CEPT view was that any new white space applications should be used on a non-protected non-interfering basis (ECC, 2008). At its meeting in March 2009, the ECC has decided to task WG SE to investigate and define technical requirements for white spaces operation in the UHF broadcasting band (470-790 MHz). In ECC Report 159 "Technical and Operational requirements for the possible operation of cognitive radio systems in the "White Spaces" of the frequency band 470-790 MHz" CEPT thoroughly addressed the way forward for secondary use of TV White Spaces in Europe, assessing both geolocation databases and spectrum sensing, based on some preset goals. In particular, CEPT concluded that the technologies under consideration should:

- Protect Broadcast service;
- Protect Programme Making and Special Events (PMSE);
- Protect Radio Astronomy in the 608-614 MHz frequency band;
- Protect Aeronautical radio navigation in the 645-790 MHz frequency band.

The report concludes that spectrum sensing could succeed in protecting radio astronomy, but it falls short on the first two conditions and further research is needed on the last condition. A suitable technology to exploit white spaces needs to be able to avoid interference to any other (primary) operation, especially the incumbent broadcast service. As spectrum sensing in its current stage of development fails to do so, alternative technologies may need to be considered (ECC, 2011).

Activities Within the United States

The Federal Communication Commission (FCC) already proposed to permit unlicensed opportunis-

tic access to white spaces in the TV bands in 2004 (FCC, 2004). In response to this notice the IEEE has created the IEEE 802.22 Wireless Regional Area Network (WRAN) working group with an aim to develop a standard based on opportunistic spectrum access for the television bands to provide fixed wireless broadband access in rural and remote areas.

The FCC issued a First Report and Order and Further Notice of Proposed Rule Making in October 2006 in which the FCC takes a number of important first steps towards the allowance of new low power devices in the broadcast television spectrum on frequencies that are not being used for authorized services and asks questions and set forth certain proposals with regard to the provisions necessary to implement complete and final rules (FCC, 2006). In its Second Report and Order of 2008 the FCC permitted both fixed and portable unlicensed devices to operate in the TV band at locations where that spectrum is not being used by licensed services. All devices are required to consult a database to obtain a list of the permitted channels in their geographic location before they are allowed to transmit. The only exceptions to that rule are portable devices that work in a client mode under control of another fixed or portable device with access to the database. In addition, all devices must also have a capability to sense TV broadcast and low power auxiliary service station signals. Other requirements include the transmission of identifying information to ease enforcement in case of interference and the requirement for all devices to be certified by the FCC laboratory (FCC, 2008).

In its Second Memorandum Opinion and Order of 2010 the FCC removed the requirement that white spot devices that incorporate geo-location and database access must also include sensing technology to detect the signals of TV stations and low-power auxiliary service stations (FCC, 2010).

Subsequently the FCC issued a call for proposal for geolocation database providers. After evaluating the response received from the interested parties, it conditionally designated nine entities as TV band database administrators in January 2011. Until mid 2012, the FCC granted preliminary approval to two entities to actually exploit a database, SpectrumBridge Inc. and Telcordia Technologies.

The Rules were further refined in a Third Memorandum Opinion and Order. In particular the following changes were made: (1) increasing the maximum height above average terrain (HAAT) for sites where fixed devices may operate; (2) modifying the adjacent channel emission limits to specify fixed rather than relative levels; and (3) slightly increasing the maximum permissible power spectral density (PSD) for each category of TV bands device. These changes will result in decreased operating costs for fixed TV band devices and allow them to provide greater coverage, thus increasing the availability of wireless broadband services in rural and underserved areas without increasing the risk of interference to incumbent services (FCC, 2012).

Activities Within the UK

Ofcom was the first regulator in Europe which considered secondary access to white spaces in the television bands. In a statement of December 2007, Ofcom proposes to allow licence exempt use of these white spaces for cognitive devices (Ofcom, 2007). This use will need to protect licensed users of this spectrum, including digital terrestrial television (DTT) and PMSE, against harmful interference. After consulting the market Ofcom concluded that the licensed users could be protected by both sensing and geolocation. However, the implementation of detection-only devices is likely many years away. The most important mechanism in the short to medium term will be geolocation (Ofcom, 2009).

Ofcom decided to consult the stakeholders to further develop the concepts and algorithms necessary for geolocation. As a result of that consultation, Ofcom will now investigate arrange-

ments, in co-operation with industry partners, with a view to specify the requirements to be met by geolocation databases and their providers that wish to be accredited by Ofcom (2011).

Activities Within Other Countries

Another European country that is quite active on the field of cognitive radio is Finland. In 2009 a statement was published which states that cognitive radios are allowed to use white space in the 470-790 MHz band provided that they do not cause harmful interference to other systems in the band. A white space test bed has been set up to develop and validate technical solutions, accelerate commercial utilisation of white spaces, and to contribute to the regulatory work on cognitive radios (Paavola and Ekman, 2011).

The Singapore regulator, iDA, has commenced trials in March 2011, named Cognitive Radio Venues ("CRAVE"), in order to develop the regulatory framework for the use of TV white spaces. As a follow up on these trials the Singapore White Spaces Pilot Group was set up in April 2012. The group is to undertake commercial pilot deployments to explore how white space technology could supplement the existing wireless infrastructures and develop innovative consumer and business applications (iDa, 2012). Other countries in the Asia Pacific region, including Korea and Japan, have set up trials to investigate possibilities for secondary access to TV white spaces (Nekovee, 2012).

Industry Canada released in august 2011 a consultation document on a Policy and Technical Framework for the Use of white space devices in the television broadcasting bands below 698 MHz (Industry Canada, 2012). Industry Canada has not yet proposed detailed regulations for these white space devices. However, Industry Canada focuses on the use of geolocation databases to protect incumbent users of the band and recommends that a Canadian database should be developed (Nekovee, 2012).

THE IMPACT OF THE REGULATIONS ON THE BUSINESS CASE

The way in which the regulatory regime allows access to spectrum will greatly influence the business opportunities. This section gives an overview of the impact of the regulatory regime on the business opportunities.

White Spot Access

In the white spot access regimes, the CR devices will always have to respect the needs of the primary user. White spot access is only possible as long as there is no need for the spectrum by the primary user and no interference is created to the primary user.

This sets limitations to the business case for unlicensed white spot access with an unrestricted number of devices. There will never be a guarantee that a CR device can have access to a white spot and there is always the possibility that a CR device has to cease its operation because a primary user wants access to the spectrum. This makes this regulatory regime less suitable for time critical CR applications.

Restriction of access to white spots to a specific user group provides the possibility for active coordination between the incumbent user and the secondary (cognitive) user about the likelihood of interference, and on guarantees about access to spectrum. Restricted access may also increase the level of trust for the incumbent user and may make them more willing to share their white spots with a known and trusted CR user.

Spectrum Pooling

In case spectrum is pooled between a number of users or user groups, CR technology is used to dynamically share the spectrum resources. Pooling of spectrum in a closed user group between spectrum owners is only a viable option if the various owners are not in direct competition with each other. This is for instance the case if spectrum is used for company internal purposes, such as fixed links or private mobile radio. It is also possible to pool spectrum between various owners which have a completely different service, e.g. between a terrestrial service and a satellite service. Coordination between various owners will be easier if there already is a relationship whereby spectrum is shared at present. This will increase the level of trust and will make it easier to come to an agreement.

CR technology can also be used to pool spectrum between unlicensed applications. Knowledge of the radio environment is in this case used to realise a fair distribution of access to spectrum between the devices.

Conclusion

The regulatory regime has a huge impact on the business case for Cognitive Radio. Each regulatory regime will facilitate a different kind of CR applications and/or service offerings. A mixture of these regimes will be necessary to unlock the full potential of CR technology in increased spectrum efficiency. The impact on the business case of the regulatory regime under which the CR application will operate is summarised in Table 3.

Especially the use of CR technology in a closed user group can help to bring this technology further for two reasons. First, restricting access to a controlled group may increase the level of trust between the users who share the spectrum. Second, restricted (licensed) access can provide certainty about access to spectrum over a longer period of time needed to recover the investments to be made in CR technology.

THE IMPACT OF COGNITIVE RADIO CAPABILITIES ON THE BUSINESS CASE

The fundamental difference between a cognitive radio and a conventional radio is that a cognitive radio uses information of the radio environment

Table 3. Impact of the regulatory regime for spectrum access on the business case for CR applications

	Horizontal sharing (Spectrum pooling)	Vertical sharing (white spot access)
Open acces (commons)	Fair distribution of spectrum access	No guarantees for spectrum access, i.e. less suitable for time critical applications.
Closed user group (licensed)	■ Increased level of trust ■ More certainty about access to spectrum	
	CR user groups not in direct competition with each other.	Possibility for active coordination. More guarantees for spectrum access.

to select and deploy the most appropriate communications profile, such as frequency band, access technique and modulation method. There are various techniques possible to obtain information about the radio environment.

The regulator will have to make fundamental choices about the radio environment in which the CR will operate and on the way in which the cognitive radio collects information of the radio environment. Each of them will have different implications for potential CR applications and the magnitude of the required investments.

The Radio Environment

CR technology is proposed to improve utilisation by using spectrum that is allocated but actually not used at a given time and location. The question is whether there is enough capacity in these unused spots that can be made available to support the underlying business case for CR technology and if the business case is solid enough to recoup the necessary investments in this new technology.

The ease of making unused spectrum available for cognitive use depends on the characteristics

of the incumbent user. It is easier to find a white spot if conventional user(s) and usage is relatively static than when conventional users are mobile and/or their usage fluctuates.

Moreover, the fact that large parts of the spectrum are not utilised does not imply that an attractive business case for the remaining unused parts exists. The fact that in rural areas GSM spectrum is underutilised does not necessarily mean that there is a viable business case for these unused GSM frequency channels, at least not for mobile communications. The business case for the exploitation of these white spots will have to be distinctively different from the business case of the conventional user.

Sensing

In its basic form a cognitive radio senses the radio environment to acquire information on the local usage. The CR device relies thereby on its own judgment of the local use of the spectrum to transmit over sections of the spectrum that are considered free. No matter how good the sensing technology is, a system that only relies on its own judgment to obtain information about spectrum usage might come in a situation where it inadvertently is not able to detect usage of a radio channel. This means that with a cognitive radio based on sensing alone, there is always the possibility of interference to the conventional users of the band. To limit this risk, restrictions on the output power of the CR devices will have to be set. As a consequence, the CR can only be used for applications which use low power in relation to the incumbent usage.

Sensing can be used without the need for coordination with the "outside world". Hence, sensing can be used for standalone applications, whereby there is no need for investments in the roll-out of associated infrastructure.

The probability of finding a white spot that can be utilised depends on the activities of the incumbent user(s), the range of frequencies which is sensed and the number of active white spot devices. Sensing will have to take place over a sufficiently large frequency range to support the capacity needed by the CR application. Sensing becomes more challenging, and more expensive, when a wider range of frequencies and/or a wider range of conventional user applications are to be taken into account. At the current state of technology and field experience on sensing, a case-by-case approach will be required which takes into consideration the existing spectrum usage. Hence, for new CR regulations to be meaningfully applied, i.e. before making available a band for white spot devices, an assessment should be made of the amount of white spots that can be made available against the capacity needed for the introduction of the application that uses these white spots.

Sensing can be made more reliable by co-operation between the sensing devices (Mishra, Sahai et al., 2006). Cooperation can improve the probability of detection and reduces the detection time and thus increase the overall agility of the system. Drawbacks are the need for a common signalling channel between the devices and the additional overhead needed to exchange sensing information over this channel.

Especially the need for a signalling channel makes this coordinated approach complex. The cognitive devices become part of a network. This makes this coordinated approach especially feasible in applications where the CR device is already part of a (local) network, e.g. in-house networks. Coordination is a less attractive option for stand-alone CR applications.

Database

A second option is to get information about the local use of the spectrum from a database. Such a database should contain the relevant information on the frequencies that can be used at a certain location as well as the applicable restrictions. The database will have to be kept up-to-date, which

makes this option especially suitable in cases where spectrum usage of the conventional user(s) does not change frequently, e.g., in a broadcasting band or a band for fixed satellite communications.

The restrictions for the CR application imposed by the use of a database are twofold. First of all, the CR device needs to be aware of its geographical location. This information can be programmed in the device during the installation of the CR device for fixed applications. Mobile CR devices will need a means to acquire that information, for instance by incorporating radio navigation in the terminal. However, the use of radio navigation will be difficult for indoor applications.

Secondly, the CR device will need to have access to this database on a regular basis. Access to the database is easier to arrange if the CR device is already part of a network than for stand-alone CR applications. The rate at which the CR devices have to obtain updated information on the local radio environment depends on the rate at which the information on the incumbent user may change and on the degree of mobility of the CR device.

Cognitive Pilot Channel

Coordination between CR devices can be realised through a so-called Cognitive Pilot Channel (CPC). A CPC is a dedicated carrier providing information about the availability of spectrum and possibly usage restrictions to the CR devices in a certain area. The CPC can be used to (1) give general –local– information on the availability of white spots in relation to the service to be protected, or (2) to coordinate the use of the spectrum resources by the CR devices competing for spectrum access or (3) a combination of both (Bourse, Agusti et al., 2007; ETSI, 2009).

The first option requires that the CPC broadcasts information on channels that are available and possibly the associated use restrictions, unless these restrictions are already known beforehand by the CR device. The second option is more complex because there is also a need for the network to know which channels are actually used by the CR devices and therefore there is a need for a feedback channel.

Implementation of a CPC will require a radio-infrastructure to support the CPC. The CPC can be provided by a dedicated, autonomous network, but this will require substantial investments. The necessary investments can be lowered if the CPC uses a logical channel within an existing network, e.g. within a mobile network. Standardisation activities in this field are on-going (ETSI, 2009).

Because a CPC can provide real-time information, a CPC is highly suitable in cases where spectrum usage of the user(s) with which the band has to be shared is more dynamic. In this case, the network will need to have up-to-date information of the spectrum usage of all user(s) at all times.

Conclusion

The means a CR uses to acquire information on the radio environment has a significant impact on the business case for CR applications. An outline of the main conclusions of the impact of the CR technology on the CR application, and thereby on restrictions for a viable business case, are given in Table 4.

An apparent difference between sensing on the one hand and a database or Cognitive Pilot Channel on the other hand, is that the latter two will require investments in infrastructure. This means that sensing can be used for stand-alone applications, whilst the other options are better suited for the delivery of services with an associated infrastructure roll-out, i.e. sensing can be used in a business case based on the sales of equipment whereas the database and CPC are better suited for a service provider driven business case based on the sales of a service. In that case there will be a direct relationship between the service provider and the customer. This relationship is necessary to recoup the investments in infrastructure.

Of course, it is always possible to use a combination of techniques. Especially a combination of database access and sensing seems promising. The database can be used to protect existing services with which the band is shared and sensing can be used to assess whether the opportunity is really available or already in use by another CR device.

Another possibility is the use of a local CPC (or so-called beacon) to reduce some of the drawbacks of sensing, especially the complexity and associated costs of sensing devices. A relatively complex master device can be used to process the

Table 4. The impact of the CR technology on the CR application

	Implication to potential CR applications	Remarks
Sensing	Low power in relation to the primary user. Sensing over a relatively small band sets limits to the data transfer capacity available. Wide band sensing increases the capacity available, but is more complex and expensive. Can be used for stand-alone applications.	There remains a potential for interference to the conventional user.
Database	Can be used for applications which need a higher power. CR device needs to be aware of its location. Application needs a connection to the database on a regular basis.	Only useful in bands with relatively static conventional users. Costs of database service will have to be recovered.
Cognitive Pilot Channel	Can be used for applications which need a higher power. CR device is part of a network.	Can also be used for more dynamic conventional use. Large scale deployment more expensive than a database

sensing results of a range of locally connected devices. The master device decides based on this information on what channel the connected devices may operate and sends this information to these devices over a local beacon. This solution can only be used if these devices form a local network. The relatively expensive master device acts as an intelligent central node for the relatively cheap connected devices.

POSSIBLE BUSINESS OPPORTUNITIES FOR COGNITIVE RADIO

The previous two sections show that both the regulatory regime and the fundamental choices that will have to be made on the use of CR technology will create certain business opportunities and at the same time will pose limitations on other business opportunities for CR and dynamic access to spectrum. There needs to be a fit between the regulatory regime, the fundamental choices on technology and a perceived business opportunity.

Opportunistic spectrum access based on sensing will always have a likelihood of interference and there are no guarantees that an OSA-device can find an opportunity to communicate. This will depend on the amount of OSA-devices and their communication needs in relation to the amount of capacity available. This sets limitations to the use and on the types of applications that can be supported. Since there is no need to build infrastructure there is a match with a device oriented open access regime of a commons. OSA based on sensing is expected to be restricted to low-end applications involving low power devices.

Opportunistic spectrum access can be used to share bands between licensed users and unlicensed short-range devices in bands that were difficult in the classic scenario. A good example of this is the use of the 5 GHz band. RLANs use sensing to detect and avoid incumbent radar systems.

OSA is also of interest to military users but for a completely different reason. A true OSA-device acts solitary without the need for coordination with the outside world. This makes it possible to communicate without making the whereabouts and communication needs of the military radios known to others. This will make their communications less vulnerable.

Since sensing is in its present form is not reliable enough, regulators around the world have turned their focus from sensing towards a geo-location database. This will require investments in a database and related infrastructure that need to be recouped. Entrepreneurs will only invest in this infrastructure if there is long-term assurance for access to spectrum and willingness to pay from customers. This shifts the orientation from a device centric approach to a service centric approach. Such a business case is better supported by a regulatory regime based on property rights.

A possibility to ease the problem of the (un) reliability of sensing is to focus sensing in a band that is not too-wide in a completely unlicensed environment to create a true commons for short range devices. The regulator should pinpoint a band for dynamic spectrum access in cooperation with industry. To reach economies of scale this band could be designated on a regional level, for example on a European level.

A very promising application for a true commons whereby unlicensed devices pool their spectrum is in-house networking. An in-house network is an ad-hoc network by its very nature. No two in-house networks are exactly alike and devices are turned on and off during the day, new devices are brought in, devices leave the house and the neighbouring houses have the same ad-hoc way of working. The number of wireless devices in a household is rising while the users want to have new equipment that is "plug and play". A new device that is put into service should be able to find its own possibilities to communicate within the in-house network. OSA can be used to realise this goal. A new OSA device senses its environment and coordinates its use within the local in-house network. A possible band to start is e.g. the 60 GHz band.

A second example of ad-hoc networking is the radio network between vehicles as part of Intelligent Transportation Systems (ITS). Restricting access to the pool for certain applications with a polite cognitive protocol, may alleviate the tragedy of the commons. In that case, the number of devices outnumbers the available spectrum in such amount that the spectrum is of no use to all. However, even if a polite cognitive protocol is used and the band is restricted to a certain type of applications, the amount of spectrum that is made available must be enough to cater for the intended business case.

Another possibility is to use sensing in a more controlled environment between licensed users. This will give more control over the environment, because the users are known. This type of sharing could be used to broaden the amount of accessible spectrum for temporarily users who need a guaranteed Quality of Service. This makes this type of sharing a perfect fit for e.g. Electronic News Gathering and other Programme Making and Special Events services. Electronic News Gathering only requires spectrum for short periods of time and for a restricted local area but it requires guaranteed access during the operation.

Another service that needs guaranteed access to spectrum but only in a very local area and for a short period of time is public safety. Public safety organisations have their own network for day-to-day operations. However during an emergency situation they have a huge demand for communications on the spot (Pawelczak, Prasad, et al., 2005). A public safety organisation might make an agreement to alleviate their urgent local needs with other frequency users. In the agreement sharing arrangements are covered but the actual spectrum usage can be based on the local conditions and spectrum sensing of the local use of the primary user.

A good opportunity to start this form of sharing is in bands of the military. The military already have a longstanding practice of sharing with both the ENG community and public safety organisations. This may raise the level of trust to a level that is high enough to start an experiment.

In a true property rights regime dynamic access to spectrum is obtained through buying, leasing or renting access rights from the owners of the spectrum. This regime provides the possibility for active coordination between the incumbent user and the cognitive user about the likelihood of interference, and on guarantees about access to spectrum. If the barriers to instant trading are removed, the opportunity to buy and sell rights to access spectrum can be based on the actual demand for spectrum. This creates the opportunity to use DSA systems for higher valued services, such as mobile telephony, and for a spot market to be introduced. A spot market is a perfect means to acquire or sell rights to spectrum access based on the actual demand at any given moment in time.

This property rights regime can be used among operators to pool the spectrum in such a way that the rights to spectrum access are based on the actual demand for spectrum by their respective users. One of the suggested implementation scenarios is that mobile operators use a part of their spectrum to provide the basic services to their respective customers and pool the rest of their spectrum to facilitate temporarily high demands for spectrum. However, cooperation between mobile operators that are in direct competition to each other is not likely to happen (Bourse, Agusti et al., 2007).

This kind of sharing spectrum might be a more viable option for implementation in border areas to ease the problem of border coordination. Nowadays the use of spectrum in border areas is based on an equal split of the use of spectrum between neighbouring countries through the definition of preferential rights. However, there is no relationship with the actual demand for spectrum at either side of the border. A prerequisite is that the spectrum market is introduced at both sides of the border or in a region, e.g., the European Union.

Pooling spectrum between different services that are not in direct competition to each other might be a more promising approach. A property rights regime can help to make licensed spectrum that is not fully used available to others users. In this case access to spectrum is based on an negotiable acceptable level of interference, instead of the worst case scenarios based on harmful interference that are used by regulators to introduce a new service in an already used band. This may open bands for alternative use which might otherwise be kept closed. The incumbent licensee may now have an incentive to open its spectrum for other, secondary, users. The incumbent licensee is in full control because it can earn money with unused spectrum, whilst the access to its spectrum of the secondary user is on the incumbents own conditions.

Licensed owners of spectrum can also grant access to parts of their spectrum that they do not need in a certain geographic area and/or for a certain period of time to secondary devices. These devices can get access to this spectrum after an explicit request for permission to the owner of the spectrum. The owner will need a mechanism to facilitate requests from secondary devices for permission to use spectrum. Cellular operators can use their existing infrastructure to handle these requests. E.g. a mobile operator can set aside a mobile channel for this purpose. The owner of the spectrum and the secondary user can negotiate their own terms under which the secondary user may have access to spectrum. This provides possibilities for active coordination between the incumbent and the secondary user about the acceptable level of interference and guarantees to access spectrum.

A spectrum market can only function if information about the actual ownership of the spectrum property rights is readily available to facilitate trading. The regulator is ideally positioned to perform the task to keep a record of the ownership of these rights. Inclusion of monitoring information about actual usage of spectrum can further facilitate trading by giving more insights in the possibilities for secondary usage.

A second incentive might be to introduce easements in spectrum property rights. In other words, if a spectrum owner is in possession of spectrum that (s)he actually does not use, everybody is entitled to use this spectrum in an opportunistic way as long as the transmissions of the rightful owner are not subject to interference from this opportunistic spectrum access. This is an incentive which might prevent market players from hoarding spectrum (Anker, 2010a).

A special case of licensed spectrum pooling is pooling whereby a single operator who is the exclusive owner of the spectrum uses cognitive radio technology to perform a flexible redistribution of resources among different radio access technologies within its own licensed frequency bands to maximize the overall traffic by an optimum use of spatial and temporal variations of the demand. This could be used by mobile operators to realise a flexible spectrum allocation to the various radio access technologies in use or to have an optimal distribution of spectrum between the different hierarchical layers of the network. E.g. to realise an optimal allocation of spectrum to femto cells that takes account of the actual user demand without affecting the macro network. A prime requisite for such a scenario is that the license from the operator is flexible enough and technology neutral.

ANALYSIS OF THE BUSINESS CASE FOR WHITE SPOT ACCESS IN THE UHF TELEVISION BANDS

The first application for CR that was put forward was the use of white spots in the TV broadcasting bands. The US Federal Communication Commission (FCC) made these white spots available for unlicensed broadband Internet. Its intended use is above all to provide more affordable broadband deployment in rural areas (FCC, 2010).

CR technology is used to share the TV-band with the legitimate primary users, TV broadcasting stations and low power auxiliary service stations (notably wireless microphones). It is understandable that the FCC removed sensing from the original requirements and took other measures to guarantee access to spectrum for wireless microphones and to prevent wireless microphones from getting interference from CR devices. Sensing is at the current state of technology not sufficiently reliable. This puts restrictions on the use of white spots by CR devices. To prevent interference to the primary user, the output power of the CR device should be low relative to the primary users. These primary users are not only TV broadcasting stations but also low power wireless microphones. Restriction of the output power of CR devices to a level that is low compared to the wireless microphones would be detrimental for the business case of rural broadband access.

The first question one has to ask on the business case for rural broadband access is: Why is there no service provided at the moment? The main reason is that the costs to provide the service are too high in relation to the willingness to pay for the provided service. Under the FCC white spot ruling, rural broadband access is made more feasible due to the fact that a lower frequency range is made available, which extends the coverage area of a base station, compared to the existing alternatives to provide the service. However, the business case is only viable if the cost reduction is bigger than the additional costs associated with the new cognitive technology.

Existing mobile networks operate at frequencies that are just above the television band. This means that the gains of using a lower frequency are limited. Therefore the business case for deployment of a wide area network in rural areas based on white spot access remains questionable. It is much more likely that white spot access will be used to provide localised access to the Internet at specific nodes. This is a business case that is comparable to Wi-Fi hot spot access, although over larger distances.

The next question is whether the capacity that can be supported by white spot access is high enough to support the demand of the users. In areas where the required demand for capacity is bigger, the coverage area of the base station may have to be made smaller. This conflicts with the reason to make these lower frequencies available. This means that the business case will be restricted to areas with a population density below a certain limit. This limit will be lower if the demand per customer is higher. It remains to be seen whether the assigned band will have enough white spot capacity available for the intended application – broadband Internet access – to support a successful business case.

Studies performed of European use of the UHF broadcasting bands for cognitive radio showed that the amount of white space is limited in Europe, because of the tight digital broadcast planning. Moreover, the TV band is already heavily used "opportunistically" for Program Making and Special Event services, especially wireless microphones. Furthermore, the upper part of the band has to be made available as a harmonized subband for mobile use (ECC, 2008). Hence, the amount of available spectrum for white space devices is less than in the United States (ECC, 2008; Beek and Riihijarvi, 2011). This amount may be even further reduced in Europe through the decision of the World Radio Conference 2012 to extend the possibility of the use of the TV band for mobile services to the 694 - 790 MHz band.

To conclude, the white spot access regulations appear to be a technological fit instead of a business case fit driven by the regulator to reach a social goal. Whether the BuC is viable remains questionable. This would also explain why the intended service providers are relatively absent in the standardisation activities and other discussions around white spot access in the UHF band. Moreover, the business model for commercial operation of the database is not very clear.

An alternative is to use CR technology to 'automate' the already existing opportunistic access to the band for wireless microphones. But the use of CR technology will make the wireless microphone more expensive, so is there enough to be gained to make this a viable business case? There are indications that this might be the case. The current way of working with a manual scan of available spectrum is time consuming and is performed before the microphone is used. If a CR device automatically performs a scan of available spectrum the costs associated with a manual scan fall away. In a number of scenarios the time to do an extensive manual search is not available, e.g. when the wireless microphones are used to provide a live report of an unannounced news event. In these cases, automatic scanning will give a better sharing of the white spots among the wireless microphones with a lower probability of interference between these microphones.

Another much cited option lately, is the use of white spots for machine-to-machine communications. If this white spot access is based on a database, the M2M communications is restricted to fixed applications In order to allow for mobility, there is need to include sensing, which restricts the communications to a rather low power. Since there are no guarantees to spectrum access, M2M communications is restricted to applications which tolerate a rather high latency, such as meter reading. The unresolved issue is if there is enough capacity in this white spots available to support the business case.

A POSSIBLE WAY FORWARD

Although there are possibilities to use cognitive radio under the current radio spectrum management regime, there is still no compelling business case. For the promise of CR to be unlocked, the regulator and industry should closely cooperate to reduce the uncertainties that now cloud the market for CR applications. As the custodian of spectrum aiming for more efficient use of spectrum, the regulator is in a good position to take the first step. Regulation is about giving certainty. Not only by restricting spectrum use, but also by enabling and facilitating innovative use (Baldwin and Cave, 1999; Anker, 2010a).

A possible way forward is to review potential product-market combinations where CR functionality provides a 'value add' and determine whether these cases are attractive enough to be taken up by the industry as first applications of CR. The regulator can provide a platform to facilitate the coordination needed to find the 'sweet spot' and provide the necessary specific regulations to enable this 'sweet spot'.

The RSPG (Radio Spectrum Policy Group) already recommended to create a platform to allow researchers, academia, manufacturers, operators, service providers and regulators to coordinate research activities. This platform could build upon already existing platforms with comparable purposes, notably COST-TERRA (RSPG, 2011a). As COST-TERRA is focused on research activities, it will be necessary to extend the membership to include the user communities and service providers to have a successful and well informed discussion on the deployment of CR technology.

To facilitate coordination by the actors a Community of Practice (CoP) related to CR has been established in the Netherlands (CRplatform.NL). This CoP aims to identify the uncertainties surrounding potential deployment areas of CR and through discussion among stakeholders to find ways and means of addressing and reducing these uncertainties; thereby facilitating the successful deployment of CR-based products and services. This initiative evolved from the regular interaction between representatives of the Ministry of Economic Affairs and the industry.

In addressing uncertainties and finding ways towards resolution, the CoP organizes workshops to explore potential application areas of CR, the so-called Use Cases. The following application areas have been the topic of a Use Case Workshop: Container Terminals in the Rotterdam harbour; Special Events capture by broadcasting organisations; Public safety communications by the police force; High intensity communications at airports; and CR facilitating Domotica. Each Workshop brought together potential users, potential suppliers, policy makers and regulators, as well as academic researchers.

The Use Cases as discussed suggest that CR functionality adds most value in situations that are typically niche applications or are a small segment of the overall market for wireless technologies. One of the reasons for that is the fact that CR technology is basically a technology to (more efficiently) share spectrum. As CR provides additional functionality compared to current radio technology this will come at increased costs, at least initially. Situations of high intensity demand are expected to provide the highest willingness-to-pay by the end-users.

Each Use Case discussed so far addressed a specific market segment, or even a market niche. Hence, potential market volumes are (relatively) low to moderate, which impacts the viability of the CR business case. Nonetheless, the Use Cases also show similarities, in particular if CR-based solutions are considered as variants of a more generic CR-platform solution. Especially the combined business case of the communication needs of the public safety services in case of an emergency and the registration of this emergency and other news gathering seems to be logical and promising. This became apparent during the Use Case Workshop on Special Events, as during (ad-hoc) events the needs of public safety and broadcasting converge at the same place and time. The type of communication needs show a strong parallel. Hence, pursuing solutions for one group of actors (broadcasters) should best be done cognisant of the needs of the other group of actors (public safety).

This example shows that finding a sweet spot for CR might be easier if the solutions for one group are similar to the solutions for the other group,

at least on the platform level. This increases the addressable market and hence the viability of the business case. The unresolved issue is the capacity issue. How much capacity is available for CR use and is there enough capacity available to support the (combined) business case?

The Use Cases further show that a viable business case for CR will require economies of scale. This extends the need for coordination to the European Union level, if not at the global level. Such coordination may still be left to be organized by the industry actors. However, the use case experience suggests that lacking a very compelling business case the likelihood that industry actors will take the lead is expected to be low. The discussions within the CoP confirmed the role of the regulator to facilitate this search for a sweet spot.

CONCLUSION

Cognitive radio holds an interesting promise for improved utilisation of the radio spectrum. However, there is a considerable degree of uncertainty regarding the potential application of cognitive radio. In addressing these uncertainties the perspective of the entrepreneur is considered centre point. It is ultimately up to the entrepreneur to find viable product-market combinations for the exploitation of cognitive radio.

The initial target of CR-based services, provisioning of Internet access in rural areas in television white spaces seems to be desirable from a policy perspective but seems not to be a an easy business case.

Successful introduction of CR will require a fit between an initial business opportunity, the characteristics of the cognitive radio and the regulatory regime under which the cognitive radio will operate. What is needed is a more congruent approach towards the implementation of cognitive radio. Regulators, industry actors, service providers and user groups are well advised to share their insights to arrive at outcomes that are considered optimal under circumstances of uncertainty. This coordination is necessary to find and enable a "sweet spot" for CR deployment. A sweet spot is enabled if the regulatory environment and the characteristics of the CR technology are aligned in such a way that the intended business opportunity can be realised. Exploring Use Cases can be a good instrument to bring all interested parties together and in an explorative modus find viable product-market combinations. The regulator is in a perfect position to initiate and facilitate such a platform.

In this explorations, one of the first questions one have to ask is: what are the gains from the use of CR technology, and are these gains high enough to cover the increased cost of the use of CR technology compared to the alternatives? Once, there is an initial business case in sight, the question is whether enough unused spectrum can be made available through the use of CR technology.

The type of CR technology to be used and the appropriate regulatory regime to support it depend on the specifics of the intended business case and the specifics of the users with which the bands will be shared. When such a combination is found, the regulator should set up the specific regulations to facilitate the CR deployment and thereby make a step towards a more efficient utilisation of the radio spectrum.

ACKNOWLEDGMENT

The author acknowledges COST Action ICC0905 (COST TERRA) for the useful and inspiring discussions that took place at the meetings.

REFERENCES

Anker, P. (2010a). Cognitive radio, the market and the regulator. In *Proceedings of the IEEE Symposium on New Frontiers in Dynamic Spectrum Access Networks*. IEEE.

Anker, P. (2010b). Does cognitive radio need policy innovation? *Competition and Regulation in Network Industries, 11*(1), 2–26.

Atia, G., Sahai, A., et al. (2008). spectrum enforcement and liability assignment in cognitive radio systems. In *Proceedings of the 3rd IEEE Symposium on New Frontiers in Dynamic Spectrum Access Networks*. IEEE.

Baldwin, R., & Cave, M. (1999). *Understanding regulation: Theory, strategy, and practice.* Oxford, UK: Oxford University Press.

Beek, J. V. D., & Riihijarvi, J. (2011). UHF white space in Europe – A quantitative study into the potential of the 470–790MHz band. In *Proceedings of the IEEE International Symposium on Dynamic Spectrum Access Networks (DySPAN)*. Aachen, Germany: IEEE.

Bourse, D., Agusti, R., et al. (2007). *The E2R II flexible spectrum management (FSM) framework and cognitive pilot channel (CPC) concept – Technical and business analysis and recommendations.* E2R II White Paper.

EC. (1999). Directive 1999/5/EC of the European parliament and of the council of 9 March 1999 on radio equipment and telecommunications terminal equipment and the mutual recognition of their conformity. *Official Journal, L 091*, 0010 - 0028.

EC. (2002a). *Decision no 676/2002/EC of the European parliament and of the council of 7 March 2002 on a regulatory framework for radio spectrum policy in the European community (radio spectrum decision)*. Brussels, Belgium: EC.

EC. (2002b). Directive 2002/20/EC of the European parliament and of the council of 7 March 2002 on the authorisation of electronic communications networks and services (authorisation directive). *Official Journal, L 108*, 0021 - 0032.

EC. (2002c). Directive 2002/21/EC of the European parliament and of the council of 7 March 2002 on a common regulatory framework for electronic communications networks and services (framework directive). *Official Journal. L 108*, 0033 - 0050.

EC. (2009). Directive 2009/140/EC of the European parliament and of the council of 25 November 2009 amending directives 2002/21/EC on a common regulatory framework for electronic communications networks and services, 2002/19/EC on access to, and interconnection of, electronic communications networks and associated facilities, and 2002/20/EC on the authorisation of electronic communications networks and services. *Official Journal, L 337*, 0037 - 0069.

ECC. (2008). *CEPT report 24: A preliminary assessment of the feasibility of fitting new/future applications/services into non-harmonised spectrum of the digital dividend (namely the so-called white spaces between allotments)*. Electronic Communications Committee (ECC) within the European Conference of Postal and Telecommunications Administrations (CEPT).

ECC. (2011). ECC report 159 technical and operational requirements for the possible operation of cognitive radio systems in the 'white spaces' of the frequency: *Vol. 470-790. MHz*. Cardiff: ECC.

ETSI. (2009). *ETSI TR 102 683 V1.1.1: Reconfigurable radio systems (RRS), cognitive pilot channel (CPC)*. ETSI.

EU. (2012). Decision no 243/2012/EU of the European parliament and of the council of 14 March 2012 establishing a multiannual radio spectrum policy programme. *Official Journal, L. 81*, 7-17.

Faulhaber, G. R. (2005). *The question of spectrum: Technology, management, and regime change*. AEI-Brookings Joint Center for Regulatory Studies.

Faulhaber, G. R., & Farber, D. J. (2003). Spectrum management: Property rights, markets and the commons. In Craven, F., & Wildeman, S. (Eds.), *Rethinking Rights and Regulations: Institutional Response to New Communications Technologies*. MIT Press.

FCC. (2004). FCC 04-113 notice of proposed rulemaking: In the matter of unlicensed operation in the TV broadcast bands (ET docket no. 04-186) and additional spectrum for unlicensed devices below 900 MHz and in the 3 GHz band (ET docket no. 02-380). Washington, DC: Federal Communications Commission.

FCC. (2006). FCC 06-156 first report and order and further notice of proposed rule making in the matter of unlicensed operation in the TV broadcast bands (ET docket No. 04-186) and additional spectrum for unlicensed devices below 900 MHz and in the 3 GHz band (ET docket No. 02-380). Washington, DC: Federal Communications Commission.

FCC. (2008). *FCC 08-260 second report and order and memorandum opinion and order in the matter of unlicensed operation in the TV broadcast bands*. Washington, DC: Federal Communications Commission.

FCC. (2010). FCC 10-174 second memorandum opinion and order in the matter of unlicensed operation in the TV broadcast bands (ET docket No. 04-186) and additional spectrum for unlicensed devices below 900 MHz and in the 3 GHz band (ET docket No. 02-380). Washington, DC: Federal Communications Commission.

FCC. (2012). FCC 12-36 third memorandum opinion and order in the matter of unlicensed operation in the TV broadcast bands (ET docket No. 04-186) and additional spectrum for unlicensed devices below 900 MHz and in the 3 GHz band (ET docket No. 02-380). Washington, DC: Federal Communications Commission.

Forge, S., Horvitz, R., et al. (2012). *Perspectives on the value of shared spectrum access.* Princes Risborough: SCF Associates Ltd. IDA. (2012). *Commercial trial for white space applications.* Retrieved from http://www.ida.gov.sg/Policies%20and%20Regulation/20100730141139.aspx

Industry Canada. (2012). *Consultation on policy and technical framework for the use of non-broadcasting applications in the television broadcasting bands below 698 MHz.* Industry Canada. ITU-R. (2009). *Report ITU-R SM.2152 definitions of software defined radio (SDR) and cognitive radio system (CRS).* Geneva: ITU.

ITU. (2004). *Radio spectrum management for a converging world.* Paper presented at the Workshop on Radio Spectrum Management for a Converging World. Geneva, Switzerland.

ITU. (2008). Radio regulations: *Vol. 1. Articles.* Geneva: International Telecomunication Union.

Lehr, W., & Jesuale, N. (2008). Spectrum pooling for next generation public safety radio systems. In *Proceedings of the 3rd IEEE Symposium on New Frontiers in Dynamic Spectrum Access Networks, 2008.* IEEE.

Lemstra, W., & Anker, P. et al. (2011). Cognitive radio: Enabling technology in need of coordination. *Competition and Regulation in Network Industries, 12*(3), 210–235.

Mishra, S., Sahai, A., et al. (2006). Cooperative sensing among cognitive radios. In *Proceedings of the IEEE International Conference on Communications, 2006.* IEEE.

Nekovee, M. (2006). Dynamic spectrum access - Concepts and future architectures. *BT Technology Journal, 24*(2), 111–116. doi:10.1007/s10550-006-0047-4.

Nekovee, M. (2012). *QUASAR deliverable D 1.4: Final report on regulatory feasibility assessment.* Retrieved from http://www.quasarspectrum.eu/

Ofcom. (2007). *Digital dividend review - A statement on our approach to awarding the digital dividend.* OFCOM.

Ofcom. (2009). *Digital dividend: Cognitive access - Statement on licence-exempting cognitive devices using interleaved spectrum.* OFCOM.

Ofcom. (2011). *Implementing geolocation - Summary of consultation responses and next steps.* OFCOM.

Olafsson, S., & Glover, B. et al. (2007). Future management of spectrum. *BT Technology Journal, 25*(2), 52–63. doi:10.1007/s10550-007-0028-2.

Paavola, J., & Ekman, R. (2011). *WISE – White space test environment for broadcast frequencies.* Retrieved from http://wise.turkuamk.fi

Pawelczak, P., Prasad, R. V., et al. (2005). Cognitive radio emergency networks–Requirements and design. In *Proceedings of the First IEEE International Symposium on New Frontiers in Dynamic Spectrum Access Networks.* IEEE.

RSPG. (2010). *RSPG10-306 radio spectrum policy group report on cognitive technologies.* Brussels: RSPG.

RSPG. (2011a). *RSPG10-348 final RSPG opinion on cognitive technologies.* Brussels: RSPG.

RSPG. (2011b). *RSPG11-392 report on collective use of spectrum (CUS) and other spectrum sharing approaches.* Brussels: RSPG.

ADDITIONAL READING

Barrie, M., & Delaere, S. et al. (2012). Aligning technology, business and regulatory scenarios for cognitive radio. *Telecommunications Policy, 36*(7), 546–559. doi:10.1016/j.telpol.2012.03.001.

Cave, M., & Doyle, C. et al. (2007). *Essentials of modern spectrum management*. Cambridge, UK: Cambridge University Press. doi:10.1017/CBO9780511536724.

Chapin, J. M., & Lehr, W. H. (2007). Cognitive radios for dynamic spectrum access-the path to market success for dynamic spectrum access technology. *IEEE Communications Magazine*, *45*(5), 96–103. doi:10.1109/MCOM.2007.358855.

Nekovee, M. (Ed.). (2012). QUASAR deliverable D 1.4: Final report on regulatory feasibility assessment. Retrieved from http://www.quasarspectrum.eu/

KEY TERMS AND DEFINITIONS

Community of Practice: A group of people with a common interest, who share knowledge, insights and experiences.

Dynamic Spectrum Access: A new spectrum sharing paradigm that allows users to dynamically access empty spectrum holes in a band that is also used by others.

Open Access: Regime whereby any user can obtain access to spectrum under certain specified conditions.

Property Right Regime: Regime whereby access to spectrum is only possible for owners of a tradable property right.

Spectrum Pooling: A situation in which a common "*pool of spectrum*" is shared among multiple users. Access to the pool may be restricted to a closed group of users or the pool may be open to all under certain use restrictions.

Spectrum Regulations: National and international rules to govern the use of the radio spectrum.

White Spot Access: A situation in which white spots are available for use by secondary users as long as this usage doesn't interfere with the usage of the primary user.

White Spot: Frequencies assigned to a primary user, but, at a particular time and specific geographical location, not being used by the primary user.

Chapter 7
Real–World Experimentation of Distributed DSA Network Algorithms

Oscar Tonelli
Aalborg University, Denmark

Andrea F. Cattoni
Aalborg University, Denmark

Gilberto Berardinelli
Aalborg University, Denmark

Petar Popovski
Aalborg University, Denmark

Fernando M. L. Tavares
Aalborg University, Denmark

Troels B. Sørensen
Aalborg University, Denmark

Preben Mogensen
Aalborg University, Denmark

ABSTRACT

The problem of spectrum scarcity in uncoordinated and/or heterogeneous wireless networks is the key aspect driving the research in the field of flexible management of frequency resources. In particular, distributed Dynamic Spectrum Access (DSA) algorithms enable an efficient sharing of the available spectrum by nodes in a network without centralized coordination. While proof-of-concept and statistical validation of such algorithms is typically achieved by using system level simulations, experimental activities are valuable contributions for the investigation of particular aspects such as a dynamic propagation environment, human presence impact, and terminals mobility. This chapter focuses on the practical aspects related to the real world-experimentation with distributed DSA network algorithms over a testbed network. Challenges and solutions are extensively discussed, from the testbed design to the setup of experiments. A practical example of experimentation process with a DSA algorithm is also provided.

INTRODUCTION

The scarcity of frequency spectrum resources and their increasing fragmentation are among the main issues hindering the achievement of very large data rates in future wireless communication networks. In this context the improvement of network capacity by exploiting large continuous spectrum chunks is becoming increasingly challenging. The traditional rigid and exclusive assignation of frequency bands to licensed users may represent an obstacle to the efficient utili-

DOI: 10.4018/978-1-4666-4189-1.ch007

Copyright © 2013, IGI Global. Copying or distributing in print or electronic forms without written permission of IGI Global is prohibited.

zation of the spectrum. Discussions were raised for example, concerning the under-utilization of UHF frequency channels and about the limited adaptability of standard frequency reuse schemes to the operations in dynamic scenarios. Dynamic Spectrum Access (DSA) techniques have drawn considerable attention, by both industry and academia, providing increased opportunities for the sharing and reusing of spectrum resources among multiple and heterogeneous wireless networks. The concept of DSA may be discussed within the broader research paradigm of Cognitive Radio (CR)(Haykin, 2005). Cognitive radios are devices able to "learn" from the surrounding environment and reconfigure their transmission parameters in order to optimize their communication capabilities.

A large variety of CR/DSA solutions has been presented in literature, covering a wide set of application areas. CR concepts for military or public safety purposes for example, focus on the setup of a communication network in challenging transmission conditions and/or deployment scenarios. The exploitation of TV white spaces instead, aims at enabling opportunistic spectrum access to secondary users. DSA concepts can also be applied to commercial mobile networks. Future generation wireless standards such as Long Term Evolution – Advanced (LTE-A) (3GPP, 2008) are expected to cope with the dramatic increase of demand in data services. Very high data rate in local-area (LA) is foreseen as a challenging requirement in relation to the limited and very costly resources in current licensed bands. In a potential operative scenario, operators may share frequency resources in order to enable the usage of a large transmission bandwidth. Moreover, the setup of a network in indoor home/office environments is expected to be characterized by dense and uncoordinated deployment of access points (APs)(Chandrasekhar, Andrews, & Gatherer, 2008). A planned reuse of frequencies under these circumstances is likely to be uneffective and thus the network may experience unbearable inter-cell interference. The exploitation of DSA and CR techniques in such scenarios can provide significant advantages. By dynamically adapting the allocated resources by the APs, the generated interference is reduced and an increased spectrum utilization can be achieved. In addition, if considering the applicability of these concetps over wide network deployments, distributed algorithmic solutions typically provide a larger scalability in respect to pure centralized approaches.

Current research activities with CR/DSA algorithms for resource management at network level mainly rely on the extensive usage of Monte Carlo simulations for validation purposes. The benefits of simulation-based studies are evident in terms of reduced implementation effort and statistical coverage of scenario parameters. In simulators it is however challenging to accurately model the propagation environment; simplified deployment scenarios and standard channel models are therefore commonly utilized (e.g., WINNER model(Hentilä, Kyösti, Käske, Narandzic, & Alatossava, 2012)). Despite the predominance of simulation-based works in literature, there is an increasing interest for more tangible evidence of the effectiveness of CR concepts. Experimental activities in realistic deployment environments, including terminals mobility and human presence, can provide the missing proofs for a complete validation of the proposed solutions. The setup of experiments for distributed network algorithms requires the realization of a testbed and the definition of adequate experimental procedures. In literature a considerable amount of work has been proposed in the field of platforms and development tools for CR testbeds. The early interest by the research community for the opportunistic usage of the spectrum, and military applications, resulted in the early development of testbed platforms primarily focusing on specific physical (PHY) layer features such as spectrum sensing, waveform adaptation and reconfigurable transceivers. The related experimental experiences mainly consider a limited number of nodes in the network testbeds and focus on point-to-point communication aspects.

In this chapter we discuss the practical aspects related to the implementation and execution of experiments with CR and DSA concepts. In particular, we focus on the specific needs of DSA algorithms for distributed resource management. This contribution aims at providing an insight on the issues related to the setup of a testbed network, and at individuating the elements enabling the agile management of repeatable experimental activities. The review of the current state-of-the-art of existing testbeds for CR development provides a starting point for the discussion. The impact of the testbed platform characteristics in the implementation and execution of novel cross-layer system architectures is then analyzed in the chapter. The design aspects of the considered algorithms as well as practical issues such as testbed management and hardware impairments calibration are also widely discussed. A description of the experimental works with a distributed DSA algorithm carried on at Aalborg University is also included in the chapter.

BACKGROUND

The CR paradigm has born in tight connection with the concept of Software Defined Radio (SDR) (Mitola & Maguire, 1999). Most of CR realizations are indeed based on SDR, with the aim of exploiting the flexibility of the software (for the definition of the communication protocol stack) with versatile hardware solutions. A unique architecture for CR products is not yet defined; the configuration of an SDR node may indeed vary according to the specific application. Product-oriented devices typically feature fully integrated hardware solutions, often relying on Field-Programmable-Gate-Arrays (FPGAs) and Digital Signal Processors (DSPs). Prototypes for research purposes instead, typically employ programmable hardware along with host PCs or

other General Purpose Processor (GPP) -based hosts (Chowdhury & Melodia, 2010).

In an ideal SDR system, the hardware platform provides support for digital/analog conversion and up/down-sampling of incoming/outgoing signals. All the baseband signal processing tasks are instead left to the host. In practice, several limitations due to connection bus latencies, limited buffer sizes and high sample rates, may require to move critical signal processing functionalities to the FPGA (Polson, 2004). In the recent years a large number of platform solutions for CR systems prototyping have been proposed; the trade-offs between hardware complexity, signal processing capabilities and implementation flexibility, are at the base of this great variety. The software/hardware characteristics of the platforms are a fundamental aspect to consider for the design of an experimental network testbed. In this section, an overview on the existing research-oriented CR platforms as well as on the most relevant hardware solutions is provided. The state-of-art on experimental activities with SDR testbeds for CR is also presented.

Hardware Solutions and Software Platforms for SDR

Programmable and reconfigurable radio hardware equipment is the basic component of a CR node. In this context, several solutions are currently available as commercial products or experimental prototypes. By far, the most popular SDR device for research applications is the Ettus Research Universal Software Radio Peripheral (USRP) (Ettus Research, 2012), available in different models. The most common configuration of the USRP consists of a motherboard hosting a Xilinx Spartan 3 FPGA and a Gigabit Ethernet (GbE) interface to the host computer. Other configurations, support embedded system implementation or different connection interfaces such Universal Serial Bus (USB). All USRP models operate with a set of daughterboards providing RF front-end across a wide range of operational frequency bands. The large diffusion of the USRP hardware among the research community is mostly to be found in the compact and cost-effective solution provided; the USRPs moreover, utilize the open-source Universal Hardware Drivers (UHD) (Ettus Research, 2012) which ensures compatibility with most of host PC software environments. Another example of commercial device for SDR design is the Small Form Factor (SFF) SDR development platform from Lyrtech (Lyrtech RD Incorporated, 2012) which aims at providing a powerful solutios for the integrated implementation of high-end military, public safety and commercial applications.

A non-commercial setup, but widely known in literature especially for its powerful signal processing capabilities, is the Berkeley Emulation Engine 2 (BEE2) (Chang, Wawrzynek, & Brodersen, 2005). The BEE2 consists in a computational module featuring 5 FPGA cores plus RF front-end. BEE2 supports up to 500 giga-operations per second and implements optical connections for high speed data transfer. The SDR development over the BEE2 relies on FPGA and DSP programming with Matlab Simulink and Xilinx System Generator environments. The Microsoft Research Software Radio (SORA) (Tan, et al., 2009) is another powerful platform for SDR. SORA provides support for baseband processing over multi-core GPPs while it relies on other hardware solutions for the RF front-end. SORA also features a software development kit enabling the system design over the hardware. A strong focus on real-time processing performance is at the base of the development of OpenAirInterface (OAI) from Eurecom, France (Kaltenberger, Ghaffar, Knopp, Anouar, & Bonnet, 2010). OAI relies on various customized hardware solutions, also enabling Multi User-MIMO communication and the execution of an almost-LTE compliant softmodem. One of the main characteristics of OAI is that in order to fully exploit the processing resources available on the host computer, the realized communication system runs as a kernel

module in Linux OS. According to the recent literature one of the most significant platforms for SDR implementation and realization of testbeds is the Wireless open-Access Research Platform (WARP) (Khattab, Camp, Hunter, Murphy, Sabharwarl, & Knightly, 2008) from Rice University Houston. WARP enables multilayer design from Very-High-speed integrated circuit hardware Description Language (VHDL) to Matlab modeling; the WARP hardware features a motherboard with an FPGA core and supports up to 4 daughterboards with RF front-ends. In comparison to the USRPs the WARP is generally a more costly solution; on the other hand it offers greater signal processing capabilities. WARP is one of the few experimental prototypes that managed to go beyond the use in the institution of origin and become a reference tool in the field of CR/DSA experimental research.

Most of the previously mentioned SDR platforms aim at the improvement of low-level signal processing features, in particular related to data-rate transfer problems between hardware components, computation capabilities and end-to-end latency. Other typologies of platforms focus instead increased system design flexibility and runtime reconfigurability. In these cases the adopted approach is to carry out the majority of the signal processing in software, thus following closer the ideal SDR concept.

One of the first platforms realized, featuring a more software-oriented development framework, is the Open Source SCA Implementation::Embedded (OSSIE)(Gonzalez, et al., 2009) mostly used at Virginia Tech. The SCA (Software Communications Architecture) has been originally developed under the Joint Tactical Radio Systems program of the US Department of Defense, aiming at providing support for secure signal-processing applications on heterogeneous and distributed hardware. The SCA defines a set of interfaces for the deployment and management of waveforms and system components. Additional interfaces enable the exploitation of multiple physical devices such as GPPs and DSP, thus allowing the platform usage with both commercial SDR hardware and embedded solutions.

The most popular software platform for SDR is GNU Radio (GNU Radio, 2012), an open-source software framework which is characterized by a component-based architecture and large library of SDR building blocks. GNU Radio's popularity is due to its intuitive design abstraction which enables the realization of a communication system as a flow graph of processing components. The contribution of the GNU Radio software to the CR research is evident in the several system prototypes presented in literature and conferences (Pawelczak, Nolan, Doyle, Ser Wah Oh, & Cabric, 2011). A similar platform, also providing a component-based architecture, is Iris (Sutton, et al., 2010), developed at Trinity College Dublin. On top of GNU Radio capabilities, Iris adds support for runtime re-configuration and system design based on eXtensible Markup Language (XML). Iris introduces support for higher layers in the network stack and features a number of engines enabling the execution of asynchronous tasks in the system.

Experimentation Activities with Testbeds for CR and DSA

While considerable amount of work has already been published in relation to the development of both CR algorithms and experimental platforms, the literature on practical experiments for CRs performance analysis has not reached a mature stage yet. In(Pawelczak, Nolan, Doyle, Ser Wah Oh, & Cabric, 2011) a comprehensive summary of major demonstrational and experimental activities with testbeds is provided. In this paper, the authors analyze the contribution of testbed-based research to CR development, identifying that currently available works are still suffering of limited network focus, small testbed scale and lack of out-of-the-lab test experiences.

Due to the interest of the regulatory agencies in novel solutions for increasing the utilization of the available spectrum resources, research activities in the field of opportunistic spectrum access have received primary attention. A great part of the CR experimental work available in literature, focuses therefore on topics such as white spaces utilization, spectrum sensing techniques and primary user protection. An example of experimental activities carried on in this area is provided in (Sutton, Nolan, & Doyle, 2008) where the proposed cyclostationary signatures for transmission identification are implemented over an experimental setup based on the Iris platform and USRP hardware. Another experience, involving two independently developed testbed for experimentation purposes with spectrum white spaces, is presented in (Nolan, Sutton, Doyle, Rondeau, Le, & Bostian, 2007). In (Tkachenko, Cabric, & Brodersen, 2007) a detector of cyclostationary features is implemented over the BEE2 platform: the impact of system design parameters such as FFT size is investigated while the performance of the detection algorithm is experimentally evaluated with respect to parameters such as sampling offsets sensitivity, sensing time, detection probability and robustness to out-of-band interference. An experimental experience with a CR system featuring a Genetic Algorithm (GA) is presented in (Sokolowski, Petrova, de Baynast, & Mähönen, 2008). The GA attempts to optimize parameters such as transmission power, modulation order and frequency channel, thus enabling interference avoidance and opportunistic spectrum access: a testbed composed by two nodes featuring USRP hardware and GNU Radio software has been realized; the experimentation focuses on convergence speed of the algorithm in respect to a target bit error rate (BER).

Another research area with a solid background of experimental activities is the one of WiFi-oriented applications. The great availability of commercial hardware solutions, open-source drivers and well-established system architectures eases indeed the realization of testbeds for such research purposes. DSA concepts are also of major interest, with particular focus on distributed resource management and heterogeneous networks coexistence. In (Sengupta, Hong, Chandramouli, & Subbalakshmi, 2011) for example, a modified version of the IEEE 802.11 MAC layer is proposed for enabling DSA across the 16 WiFi channels. A testbed relying on open-source drivers and commercial WiFi hardware has been implemented, featuring two nodes for the experiments execution. The performed experiments focus on the evaluation of the synchronization performance of the cognitive nodes in presence of coordinated switching of transmission channels. In(Bajaj, Wooseong, Oh, & Gerla, 2011) another DSA approach for WiFi networks is proposed. Energy detection features and channel workload calculation algorithms are implemented with the aim of improving the network utilization of the available WiFi channels. The experimental validation relies on a testbed composed by three nodes using the Microsoft SORA platform.

Other notable experimental activities have been carried out in the areas of cooperative networking and mobile ad-hoc networks. Though not always strictly related to CR and DSA, the experimental literature in these areas is still relevant given the frequent choice of relying on SDR equipment, and the contributions in the analysis of propagation environment aspects and network deployment scenarios. An example of experimental trials in this context can be found in (Bradford & Laneman, 2009), where a testbed consisting of 3 USRP nodes is implemented for the evaluation of a cooperative communication technique, and in(Korakis, Knox, Erkip, & Panwar, 2009), where an architecture for cooperative PHY/MAC layer schemes is implemented on SDR testbeds featuring both GNU Radio/USRP and WARP platforms.

The previously mentioned experimental trials mostly rely on testbeds networks with a very limited number of nodes (2-3 in most of the cases). Experiments with distributed DSA concepts require however, a much larger number of devices in order to fully characterize a realistic operative scenario. In this sense, a significant experimental activity with 80+ devices is presented in (Meshkova, et al., 2011). In this experience the testbed nodes (composed by WARP, USRPs and other devices) are used as measurement terminals for the characterization of the signal propagation and pathloss estimation in an indoor office environment. Despite the absence of specific CR/DSA features in the described setup, the experiments highlighted critical aspects for the management of experimental runs with large testbed networks. In particular, the execution of repetitive time-controlled experiments, hardware calibration and centralized data collection, are issues of primary concern in the development of a testbed infrastructure. An important aspect related to the setup and management of experiments with testbeds is the actual deployment of the nodes. It may be indeed quite challenging to remotely control an experiment with large number of nodes over a wide building deployment. An important contribution addressing this problem is given by the experiences with the Cognitive Radio Network Testbed (CORNET) at Virginia Tech (USA) (Newman, Hasan, DePoy, Bose, & Reed, 2010). In CORNET a testbed with 48 SDR nodes, mainly consisting of USRP devices, is deployed across building facilities in a fashion resembling the typical WiFi access points arrangement. Such setup is made possible by exploiting the hardware GbE interfaces and long cabling, up to 100 meters. Decoupling the RF front-end from the processing hosts allows to regroup the core of the testbed nodes in a single room thus considerably easing the control of the running devices.

SYSTEM ARCHITECTURE DESIGN

The advent of CR pushes in the direction of overcoming the traditional stacked architecture in order to fully exploit the new possibilities provided by flexible and reconfigurable communication systems. In an ideal CR device every communication parameter, from the RF front-end to the application layer, may be instantaneously adapted to the channel conditions. In respect to this, particular design methodologies such as Cross-Layer (CL) can be applied to develop adaptive and optimized smart systems (Cattoni, Sørensen, & Mogensen, 2012). The CL approach is particularly suited for DSA since a DSA algorithm should be able to interface itself with the entire protocol stack in order to properly make a decision on the spectrum allocation. As presented by Akyildiz *et al.* in (Akyildiz, Lee, Vuran, & Mohanty, 2008), CL and network-wise entities can be involved in the process of dynamically assigning the proper channel set to a CR device. A similar approach, that can involve network entities for cooperation in the cognitive processes is also proposed in (Reddy & Bullmaster, 2008).

In later years, it has been preponderant the usage in the CR world of a particular CL design methodology, consisting in the insertion of a parallel entity that takes care of the stack-wise adaptation, namely the Cognitive Engine (CE). A good overview of the usage of Cross-layering in CR is presented in(Arslan & Yarkan, 2007), where the authors define a general CL architecture, including a CE and multiple interfaces for layer-to-layer direct communication. Furthermore, they present a state of the art of the optimization techniques that can be used within the proposed framework.

Besides the algorithmic design, the usage of CL entities has a significant impact also on the development of software platforms for CR experimental activities. In fact, such tools should allow researchers to investigate architectures with information flows that are more challenging than the traditional layer-to-layer, top-down, and bottom-up ones. Parallel processing and information flow loops, have been indeed carefully evaluated from a theoretical point of view, but only practical testing could confirm their capabilities in meeting the CR objectives. In particular, in (Cattoni, Sørensen, & Mogensen, 2012) an implementation-oriented analysis is performed in order to provide insights

to designers and developers about the possibilities and issues of such evolved architectures. Many of the platform tools previously mentioned in the chapter, do not provide agile support for the implementation of complex architectures and advanced CL features. Other tools, like GNU Radio and Iris, offer some possibilities, but they still have limitations when compared to the full-blown potential of truly CL CEs. In the following, a more detailed overview of the platforms will be presented, in order to provide the reader with a clear picture of the offered possibilities available.

The GNU Radio framework defines a stable and intuitive development framework particularly suited for the realization of signal processing applications relying on linear graphs of components. In GNU Radio the data exchange between blocks always occurs through buffers; the number of supported data types is limited. When creating a new processing block, the rates between input and output data elements, must be precisely specified in advance. The design rules of GNU Radio are essential to the development of an open-source platform with a large community of contributors and restrictions over the data-exchange ensure straightforward compatibility of the implemented components.

The Iris platform supports all the basic functionalities of GNU Radio, but on top of these it also enables runtime reconfiguration of system components and multiple threads of execution. The Iris framework allows the definition of a communication system architecture, directly from eXtensible Markup Language (XML) files. Moreover, additional elements named controllers can be used for managing events and parameters related to non-contiguous components, thus enabling cross-layer functionalities and runtime system reconfigurability typical of cognitive radio applications. A general overview of the Iris software architecture is provided in Figure 1. The Iris architecture is well suited for the design of CR/DSA systems; however, some aspects are still cumbersome. For instance, a strict distinction

Figure 1. Key aspects of the Iris architecture (adapted from Sutton, et al., 2010)

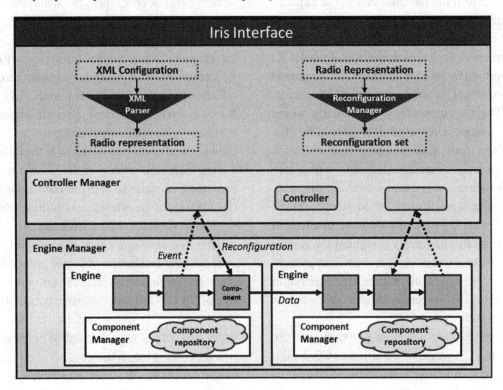

between processing components and controllers is enforced by the framework: the functionalities of these two elements as well as the data types handled are very different, and should be identified in advance by the designer. Such framework restrictions are intended to ensure a deterministic behavior of the system during runtime execution. On the other hand however, they may also hinder the development of novel communication architectures where a clear categorization of system elements may not be possible.

PHYSICAL LAYER ASPECTS: ROBUST BASEBAND DESIGN AND HARDWARE CALIBRATION

When approaching the realization of a testbed it is important to be aware of the limitations that the employed devices may pose to the experimentation process. In particular, the design of the PHY layer is sensitive to the characteristics of the available hardware solution. Specific measures must then be taken, in order to properly support the investigation of the features of interest.

In this chapter we are interested in distributed DSA algorithms which aim at improving the link quality between APs and User Equipments (UEs) by dynamically optimizing the frequency reuse and minimizing the inter-cell interference. The algorithm decision-making process typically assumes the possibility of acquiring information about the interference coupling between the AP and the neighboring nodes. The PHY layer design should then provide solutions for the identification of the interfering devices and the reliable measurement of their associated signal power; in this context measurements on reference signals (e.g., Reference Signal Received Power, RSRP, using the 3rd Generation Partnership Project - 3GPP terminology) can be exploited. Moreover, the algorithms assume the APs to be able of dynamically adjusting the transmission bandwidth across the whole available spectrum. Note that this is a significant difference compared to experimentation activities based, for instance, on WiFi technology, where the design flexibility is limited by the standardized physical layer, which impedes the direct user access to the significant parameters/procedures (e.g., dynamic channel selection is not possible). The aforementioned considerations justify then the adoption of a customized physical layer design for distributed DSA experimentation.

Orthogonal Frequency Division Multiplexing (OFDM) modulation is considered particularly suited for DSA applications since the IFFT/FFT-based transceiver allows to easily exploiting the frequency granularity of the system bandwidth. The reference signal associated with a node can be then generated in the frequency domain as in an OFDM transmitter, and then converted to time through IFFT. In order to distinguish the signals sent by different nodes, they can be designed as predefined pilot sequences that are univocally associated to the node identifiers, and multiplexed in frequency.

The design of the frequency multiplexed pilot patterns has necessarily to deal with the non-idealities of the testbed hardware; the limited precision of the local oscillators mounted on cost-effective commercial hardware boards (e.g., USRP) leads indeed to frequency offset and phase noise phenomena. For instance, the nominal accuracy of the 100 MHz Voltage Controlled Oscillator (**VCO**) mounted on the USRP2 boards is of 10 ppm, which leads to an expected maximum frequency offset of around +/-50 kHz at a 5 GHz carrier, while the phase noise is estimated to be of around -65 dBc/Hz at 10 kHz offset. The frequency offset can significantly affect the accuracy of the RSRP measurements since the received pilots may shift from their nominal frequency position. Moreover, each received pilot may leak its energy to the adjacent frequency bins, thus generating inter-pilot interference. Of course, the problem can be solved by locking both transmit and receive boards to a

high precision external reference clock, but this solution would require additional equipment and is not scalable to a large number of nodes.

The frequency spacing between different pilot patterns should then be designed according to the experienced power leakage. For example, a practical test has been carried out where an USRP board transmitting a single pilot at 0 dBm in a predefined frequency position is connected via cable and 50 dB attenuators to a receiver USRP board, which measures the power in the neighboring frequency bins and average it over a number of 1000 received time vectors. A pilot spacing of 180 kHz proves to be sufficient for obtaining a power leakage below the noise level, thus avoiding inter-pilot interference.

It is worth to notice that, in case each node is transmitting an unique pilot tone, the reliability of the RSRP measurements may be affected by the instantaneous fading in that frequency bin. The number of pilots of each transmit node has then to be set with the aim of capturing the frequency selectivity of the channel and average it out. This requirement, together with the frequency spacing one, may pose a severe limit on the testbed scalability for a given available bandwidth. Moreover, the phase noise may cause a further instantaneous random shift of the frequency position of the pilots at the receiver. It is then advisable to integrate the receive power within a limited set of bins centered on the nominal frequency position in order to capture the overall pilot energy. From practical experiments with USRP boards, a power integration over a region of around 60 kHz allows to achieve the same measurement accuracy which is obtainable with both transmit and receive boards connected to a common external reference clock with 1 ppm precision.

While the described physical layer design allows coping with motherboard inaccuracies, the usage of daughterboards affected by unequal transmit/receive power levels can still impact the experimentation outcome. The Ettus XCVR2450 daughterboards (used with USRP) have shown variations in the transmit/received power up to 10 dB, variable from device to device at the same frequency and with the same reference signal. A statistical validation of the DSA concepts over a testbed networks requires a common reference for aligning transmit power and measurements of each node at each experiment. A calibration procedure needs then to be carried out for both transmit and receive chains. Note that the hardware calibration, which has fundamental importance for the statistical validation of network algorithms, is instead typically disregarded by testbeds focusing on point-to-point applications.

The transmit chain can be calibrated by connecting by cable the board to a spectrum analyzer, recording the transmit power level and computing a correction coefficient for aligning the effective power to a reference level. The receiver chain can be instead connected to a high precision signal generator, which outputs a reference signal at a predefined power. Correction coefficients are then computed for aligning the measured power. Furthermore, different boards can also experience different noise floors. For instance, the Analog-to-Digital Converter (ADC) in the USRP N200 board has 3 dB of analog front-end gain with respect to previous versions of the USRP boards, thus reducing the noise level. We suggest to establish a common noise floor for the whole set of boards in the testbed regardless of their effective measured noise. Such common noise floor has reasonably to be set as the highest noise value measured among the testbed boards, despite of a reduction in the dynamic range.

MANAGEMENT OF EXPERIMENTS

The execution of experiment trials requires careful planning and the development of specific practical methodologies. As a starting point, the desired outcome of the experiments must be identified and specified under the form of measurable key performance indicators (KPIs).

DSA, as any other communication technology, has as a primary goal the improvement of communication performance between terminals of a network. Such performance can be intuitively described by referring to fundamental communication parameters such as signal-to-interference and Noise Ratio (SINR), maximum transfer data rate or bit-error-rate (BER). Distributed DSA algorithms embedding cognitive capabilities may also be characterized by additional parameters depending on their specific features: for example, the detection probability of spectrum opportunities and rendezvous signals as well as the estimation precision of node locations are possible KPIs of interest for typical cognitive applications. Moreover, the number of iterations (or the time) required for an algorithm to converge, is also a critical aspect to be investigated during the experiments.

EXPERIMENT DESIGN

In the previous section we highlighted the importance, for distributed DSA algorithms, of signal power measurements in respect to neighboring nodes. Given the aforementioned difficulties in modeling the real propagation environment, in Monte Carlo simulations such information is typically derived from the path loss between the network nodes, whose position is randomly generated at each iteration. In a testbed, the reverse process occurs and measurements of RSRPs can then be exploited for creating the inter-node pathloss maps, which provide useful information for the analysis of the testbed deployment and the algorithm's performance. A reliable estimation of pathloss between nodes in a testbed is however statistically challenging to achieve; RSRP values measured within a single experiment run are indeed strictly depending on the specific multipath propagation. The pathloss can be estimated in principle by averaging out the multipath over a large set of uncorrelated measurements, obtained without significantly varying the mutual inter-node distance. The variability of the experienced multipath fading is one of the elements providing additional richness in the experiments with respect to pathloss – based simulations for the algorithm's performance evaluation.

The most intuitive approach for obtaining a large set of multipath realizations would be mechanical: i.e. moving the transmit/receive antenna position at each experiment of few wavelengths (thus not varying significantly the mutual internode distance) in order to undergo uncorrelated fading. However, the mechanical approach requires either continuous human interaction or expensive remotely controlled mechanical features. An easier solution for obtaining uncorrelated multipath realizations consists in running the experiment at different carrier frequencies within a band where the pathloss conditions are not expected to be significantly altered. Obviously, the minimum frequency difference between the carriers has to be set larger than the coherence bandwidth of the channel (e.g., typically 20 MHz in a local area environment). As a consequence, this approach can be constrained by the effective available band, given the used RF front-end.

Besides static propagation environment characteristics, the performance of the network running the DSA algorithm may also vary considerably according to other scenario features such as human presence or mobility of the terminals. Moreover, the allocation of spectrum resources in the network is a dynamic process which may be affected (and thus providing variable results) by events such as variable traffic request in time or nodes (de)/activation order. A large variety of scenario configurations should be therefore considered for ensuring a good statistical coverage of the experiments.

The previous consideration highlights the need of tools enabling the execution and management of a large number of experiment runs. Repeatable experiments should have a well-defined program schedule specifying events such as system reconfigurations or nodes de-/activation. Such operations require time synchronization in order to be enforced across the whole testbed network. A critical aspect enabling the automatic control of complex experiment runs is then the definition of a common time reference.

Another aspect related to the experiments execution is the centralized control of testbed operations. The setup and configuration of the testbed is a very time-consuming activity. It is therefore important to reduce the complexity of these tasks by centralizing the procedures for testbed configuration, experiment execution and acquisition of the results. Related to the problem of centralized testbed control, are also the issues of error-handling and recovery from failure. A runtime error on a node may compromise the execution of an entire experiment run. Proper measures must then be taken to minimize this risk. While system implementation bugs can be mostly avoided with proper software testing methodologies, hardware failures are more difficult to predict; it would therefore be desirable to develop automatic procedures for controlled rebooting of devices, reset of parameters configuration and recovery of the experimental run from the failure point.

EXPERIMENTAL INSIGHT

The usage of a testbed platform for the proof of concept of CR/DSA algorithms is justified when it provides additional insights relative to the simulation studies. As briefly discussed earlier in the chapter, simulation-based studies provide only a limited support for the validation of distributed cognitive features. This is due to the several assumptions typically made in modeling the propagation environment and the complexity of the scenario dynamics. The usage of a network testbed can enable investigation of those aspects that are difficult to implement in simulators, such as:

- **More Realistic and Dynamic Propagation Environment:** In a simulation the impact of, for example, furniture is typically not considered. Especially in the office environment, the presence of large metallic surfaces such as cabinets, shelves and similar furnishings, can lead to propagation effects not easily captured by the commonly considered propagation models. Moreover the dynamics of an office environment during working hours is considerably different from a home scenario (including effects of human presence) thus having a different impact over the behavior of a cognitive/dynamic algorithm.

- **Impact of Realistic Deployment of Nodes and Terminals in Complex Building Scenarios:** A real deployment of nodes, APs in particular, is usually not random in space but follows precise guidelines in order for example to gurantee best signal coverage. Testbed setups can be used to investigate specific deployment situations which may be critical for the algorithm execution.

- **PHY-Layer:** Impact of synchronization/equalization issues on various emerging PHY-layer techniques, for example implementing mechanisms for interference cancellation.

- **Exploiting Long Term Statistics:** Gathering large amount of data in realistic environment conditions can provide a valuable data set for the evaluation of the algorithms performance. Especially when considering cognitive applications, the effectiveness of the learning process can be examined under realistic conditions.

We believe that a joint usage of simulations and experimental studies should therefore be pursued. Moreover, experimental measurements can be directly used as input to feed a simulator with real-world data.

THE ASGARD PLATFORM

The Application-oriented Software on General-purpose-processors for Advanced Radio Development (ASGARD) (ASGARD, 2012) software platform has been developed at Aalborg University, Denmark, by following the specific design requirements of both centralized and distributed CR/DSA algorithms, identified in the previous sections of this chapter. ASGARD has been originally conceived for maximum design flexibility for the implementation of reconfigurable communication systems architectures along with the integrated support of experimental activities. Similarly to GNU Radio and Iris, ASGARD is a component-based development framework. The platform is available for Linux Operating System (OS) and entirely written in C++.

The main novelty of ASGARD with respect to other platforms is the minimization of the architectural restrictions that the SDR development framework imposes in terms of communication system design and data exchange between system components. Such concept aims at easing the implementation of novel communication protocols and thus enabling the fast-prototyping of cognitive cross-layer architectures.

Software Platform Architecture

The architecture of ASGARD is object-oriented and extremely modular. The design process of a communication system consists in the definition of its basic computational tasks as elementary processing blocks, and their assembly into structured protocol routines. ASGARD provides several building elements for the management of key design aspects such as definition of the data processing, system execution-flow control and management of memory objects. A reference scheme of the ASGARD architecture is provided in Figure 2. The basic building elements in ASGARD are the following:

Figure 2. Asgard software architecture

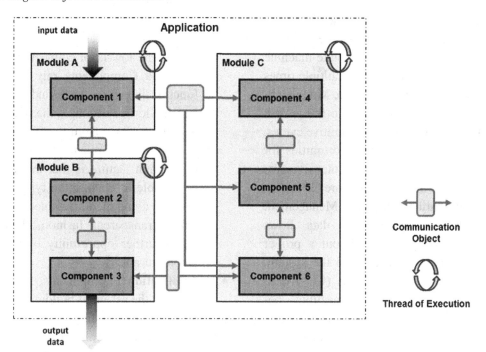

- **Components:** Components are responsible for a specific processing job over the data given in input. In ASGARD, no restrictions apply to the data types and rates that Components can handle, therefore various communication-related routines can be specified. Generic PHY-layer processing (e.g., encoder, modulator) as well as data sources and sinks, or interfaces with the host OS, are examples of tasks that can be implemented in a Component container. An ASGARD Component can also easily support the implementation of state-machines, and is therefore particularly suited for hosting decision-making units and advanced reasoning features for CR. Components can in principle manage a great amount of different (I/O) connections, thus enabling multiple, parallel, data flows. Lastly, Components may be used for managing system events and reconfigurations of other Components, thus easing the realization of control units in the system.

The mutual control between components enabled by ASGARD allows to fully pursue both flat and/or cross-layered system architectures.

- **Modules:** Components are static architectural elements, and do not specify how processing tasks should be executed in time. This aspect is handled in ASGARD by Modules, software containers which allow loading groups of Components onto independent threads of execution. The management of multiple threads is a critical issue within an SDR application: performance optimization problems in respect to the execution over the General Purpose Processor (GPP) should be indeed carefully evaluated along with the need of asynchronous protocol routines in a communication system. The abstraction offered by the ASGARD Modules allows to deal with the problem of threads of execution in a practical, object-oriented design fashion. The Components loaded into a

Module are iteratively processed at every cycle. The designer is given the possibility of specifying different component execution patterns; for instance, a state-machine component can be executed multiple times per cycle. The flexibility of the Module abstraction provides an intuitive framework for the implementation of cognitive cycles. Moreover, it also offers opportunities for the optimization of the most intensive processing tasks over multiple-core GPPs.

- **Communication Objects:** Management of multiple, asynchronous data flows would not be possible without a proper support for data exchange in the system. The Communication Objects (COs) used in ASGARD provide connections between two or more components and enable thread-safe data transfer between asynchronous modules. Different typologies of data can be embedded in a CO (e.g., buffers, containers for shared variables, events, TCP sockets, etc.). In Figure 3 a scheme of the functionalities provided by the COs is shown. A practical example of particular usage of the COs is the implementation of a system register storing organized information about the sta-

tus of a cognitive network. Such register, embedded into a CO, can easily be shared among multiple decision-making components. The low-level connections between COs and Components rely on call-back function interfaces (Alexandrescu, 2001), which allow to decouple the function calls at software level from the function definition itself. The practical consequence of this design feature is that in ASGARD it is possible to change the typology of the system components connections in an almost-transparent fashion, thus achieving a further opportunity of architecture reconfigurability.

- **Application:** Components, Modules and COs are the essential building components of ASGARD; a higher abstraction container named Application, is responsible for their specific use. Within an Asgard Application are specified the processing Components in the system, their mutual connections, their allocation over multiple Modules and the types of COs to be used. An Application is also responsible for loading system configuration parameters from XML files, and for managing external input (e.g. from the users) to the system.

Figure 3. Communication objects usage in ASGARD

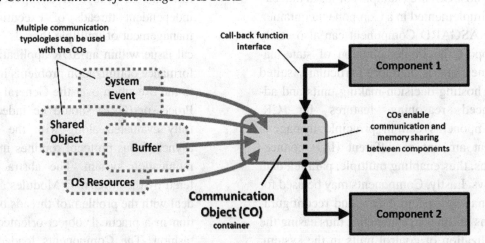

The variety of design options provided by the ASGARD software elements aims at easing the research process with novel CR/DSA solutions. The obtained framework flexibility enables cross-layer design, multiple data-flows and data rates in the system, and it also supports full run-time reconfigurability of parameters and system architecture. Removing architectural constraints however, may severely impact the stability of a poorly designed system. Data flows and runtime behavior may be difficult to monitor in a complex architecture, and even more challenging when analyzing network-wide processes across the entire testbed. In such context it is extremely important to utilize structured software testing procedures in conjunction with ASGARD-based system design. Procedures such as Test-Driven-Development (Beck, 2002) should be applied throughout the entire development process.

Support to Experimental Activities

We previously mentioned how the statistical validation of distributed network algorithms over a testbed network can hardly be achieved with prolonged static experimental sessions only. Proper "stress" performance tests or investigation of specific operational scenarios, require the testbed setup to dynamically manage node reconfigurations and node activation sequences. A precise goal in the development of ASGARD is to integrate the support for centralized testbed management and time-controlled operations within the fundamental platform capabilities, thus avoiding the need of additional tools.

In ASGARD, specific components for intra-testbed communication and control procedures have been implemented: a testbed manager application for example, has been realized to remotely operate the activation and the configuration of the nodes. The testbed manager exploits a backhaul network connection across the testbed and features a customized protocol of commands for controlling the nodes. Moreover, the backhaul

connectivity can be exploited for the centralized acquisition of testbed parameters and logging of operations. The definition of an experiment with ASGARD consists in the creation of an Application which specifies what system configuration will be executed in each testbed node and which parameters will be modified during execution time. It is possible to manage multiple system architectures and eventually modify the role of a node (access point, user device, relay, etc.) during an experimental session.

In order to enable common time reference and synchronization among testbed elements, ASGARD widely exploits the Network Time Protocol (NTP) (typically supported by the host OS) within its software components. A testbed node acting as a NTP server and connected to the backhaul network can then provide synchronization to all other ASGARD nodes, in the orders of tens of milliseconds. Experiment Applications can rely on NTP-based synchronization for enabling automatic experiment procedures and further time-dependent operations.

EXAMPLE OF PRACTICAL EXPERIMENTATION

In this section, we finally provide the description of an experimentation process aiming at the proof-of-concept of a distributed DSA algorithm. The design and realization of a network testbed is described as well as the setup of experiments for the performance evaluation of the DSA-enabled network.

ACCS Algorithm Description

The ACCS algorithm is a distributed DSA technique originally conceived for managing the spectrum resources in a network of LTE-A femtocells(Garcia, Pedersen, & Mogensen, 2009). In a context of uncoordinated indoor home/office deployment scenario, the unplanned reuse of frequencies of the APs may generate unbearable inter-cell interference levels. ACCS aims at boosting the overall network capacity by coordinating the spectrum occupation in a distributed fashion.

ACCS assumes that the transmission frequency band can be divided in a number of Component Carriers (CCs) which are shared among the APs, named evolved Node Bs (eNBs) following the 3GPP terminology. The algorithm's decision making process runs locally on each eNB, but relies on shared information about CCs usage and inter-cell interference coupling. Such information is conveyed over a common control channel. The decision making and the control data exchange are performed periodically on a time-frame basis. ACCS framing is supposed to be rather slow compared to baseline Radio Resource Management (RRM) techniques (e.g., time/frequency domain packet scheduling).

In ACCS, each eNB selects at least a Base Component Carrier (BCC), which is intended to be the main communication carrier between the eNB and the UEs. Its selection procedure is performed is such a way that overlapping allocations of BCCs by different cells are preferably avoided, or their occurrences minimized. The purpose is to guarantee a sufficient link quality between the eNB and its affiliated UEs. The BCC selection occurs at the eNB startup. It exploits local pathloss estimations with respect to other eNBs already active in the network, and the control data information regarding CCs allocation. The pathloss estimations can be derived from RSRP measurements of reference signals sent by neighboring eNBs. Note that the BCC is always allocated regardless of the presence of active UEs in the network.

The Supplementary Component Carriers (SCCs) are additional channel resources that the eNB can allocate in order to satisfy the traffic request from the UEs. The SCCs allocation procedure aims at obtaining a fair allocation of resources among the cells, limiting greedy behaviors in the network. While the BCC selection is based on inter-eNB measurements, the SCCs activation is

performed by evaluating a background interference matrix (BIM) which is built from a set of RSRP measurements reported by the affiliated UEs. The BIMs are exchanged by the eNBs over the control channel, and contain information about inter-cell interference coupling, in the form of estimations of Carrier to Interference (**C/I**) power ratio, i.e. the ratio between the useful and the interference power which would occur in case two nodes share the same CC.

A certain SCC is allocated only if it does not harm above a predefined threshold the signal quality of another cell which is using the same CC. Different thresholds are defined for BCC and SCCs, respectively: being the main communication link, the BCC has typically more demanding SINR requirements. SCCs can be de-allocated in case of decreasing traffic demand or unsatisfactory channel quality experienced in the cell. Further information about the ACCS can be found in (3GPP, Nokia Siemens Networks, 2009 and 2010).

Testbed Design

The testbed realized for ACCS enables the full algorithm execution, over a number of nodes in a network. The testbed uses Ettus USRP N200 hardware and host computers running the ASGARD software. The RF front-end consists in the Ettus XCVR2450 daughterboards, able to operate in the 2.4 and 5 GHz bands. The interface between the ASGARD system applications and the hardware is provided by the UHD.

One of the main design assumptions of our testbed is that the entire ACCS control plane (i.e. information exchange among the eNBs and measurements report by the UEs) runs over a backhaul network, Ethernet or WiFi. This allows simplifying the physical layer design which can be the main bottleneck of an agile experimentation; in our testbed it is used for basic operations such as transmission of reference signals and RSRP measurements. As mentioned before, we opted indeed for a basic physical layer where eNBs are continuously transmitting pilot symbols over orthogonal frequency patterns, which can be easily discriminated by the receiving UEs. The CC allocation is simply obtained by transmitting pilots only over the assigned portion of bandwidth.

eNB and UE systems have been entirely designed with ASGARD building components. Their main functionalities are:

- **eNB:** In the testbed setup the eNB is responsible for the ACCS algorithm execution; a scheme of the implemented eNB architecture is provided in Figure 4. The ACCS cognitive engine dynamically selects BCC and SCC and triggers the reconfiguration of the used CCs. The generated ACCS control data is sent for broadcast over the control channel. RSRP measurements computation is performed in the Sensing module. The Network Register module is responsible for the organized storage and periodic update of information related to the network status, e.g. CCs usage by active cells, SINR on the CCs, and UE activity information. Such data can then be exploited by the ACCS cognitive engine, as well as other DSA-type solutions. As mentioned above, the PHY takes care of generating pilots and performing RSRP measurements. The baseband signal is streamed to/from the hardware by using an UHD interface. A number of ASGARD Modules have been employed to cope with the different time-processing requirements of the ACCS cognitive engine, the sensing procedures and the data transfer between the hardware and the UHD-based transceiver.

- **UE:** Its implementation is minimal and features only the PHY and the Communication Client for reporting the measurements to the eNB over the backhaul network. The purpose of the UE is to periodically provide the affiliated eNB with sensing information about the signal power from the serving eNB, as well as from the interferers.

A general overview of the ACCS testbed architecture is given in Figure 5. The backhaul testbed infrastructure connects all the nodes and, besides enabling inter-node communication, also provides means for experiment control and testbed data collection. The control channel is emulated by a centralized unit that routes the control data among the nodes. The feedback channel connecting the UEs to the affiliated eNBs is also emulated and enables the reporting of the downlink (DL) RSRP measurements. The UE logical affiliation to an eNB is completely transparent to the Feedback Channel Emulator, thus enabling runtime reconfigurations of the UE cell subscription. The overall synchronization of the control plan in the backhaul network is obtained by relying on NTP (one of the testbed nodes also acts as a time server). All the testbed control units including channel emulators and testbed manager have been implemented with ASGARD components and can run on any computer connected to the testbed network (see Table 1).

ACCS Experimentation

In this example, the setup of three experimental trials with the ACCS testbed is considered. The experiments focus on the impact, over the network performance, of variable CCs system configurations, UE spatial positioning in the cell, and human presence. Experiments have been carried out inside the office premises of Aalborg University. The office environment is characterized by several rooms on the same building floor, arranged in a double stripe fashion with a corridor in the middle (see Figure 6).

In order to obtain comparable results, an identical spatial deployment of the nodes is considered for the three experiments. The experimental setup features 6 testbed nodes: a configuration with 3

Figure 4. eNB architecture in the ACCS testbed. In the rectangles are shown the implemented ASGARD components.

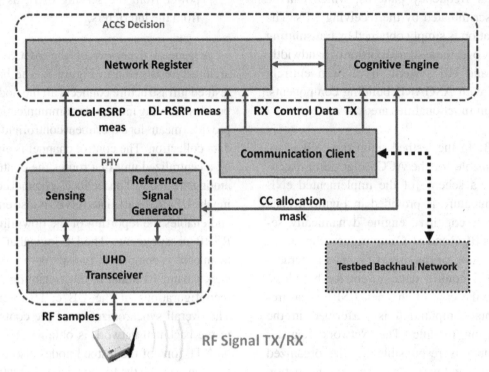

Figure 5. ACCS testbed architecture

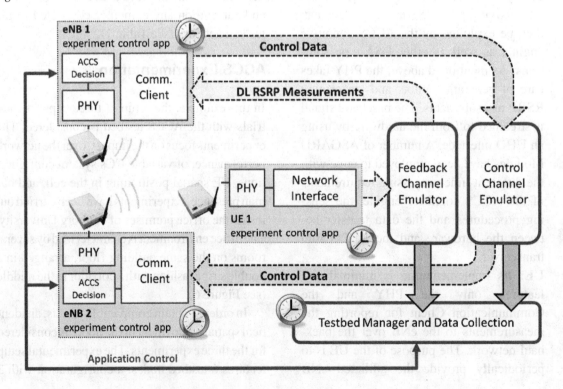

Table 1. Summary of the ACCS testbed features.

Hardware Setup	Host PCs + Ettus USRP N200
Radio Front-End	XCVR2450 operating in 2.4 and 5 GHz bands
Software Platform	Asgard
Implemented Architectures	eNB/UE
DSA features	Distributed execution of ACCS at the eNBs
Inter-cell communication	Control channel over the backhaul
Network synchronization	provided by NTP protocol
Measurements collection	centralized via backhaul
Additional features	Full runtime reconfigurability of the devices, centralized management of the experiments

cells is obtained by considering 1 eNB and 1 UE per cell. The cells are placed in 3 separate rooms generating a well-defined interference scenario. Cell 1 is separated by the corridor, while cells 2 and 3 are placed in contiguous rooms. Two specific configurations for cell 3 have been foreseen: in position a) the eNB 2 is placed very close to the UE 3, thus expecting to generate strong interference; position b) aims at reducing this effect. Despite the limited number of nodes, such deployment of the nodes provides diversified interference coupling combinations which are challenging for the ACCS performance evaluation.

All experiments share a number of common system configuration parameters that are briefly summarized in Table 2.

A sample rate of 12.5 MS/s is used, which leads to a band-pass of 12.5 MHz. The size of the I/FFT is set to 1024 bins, offering a large granularity for the spectrum division in CCs and the frequency allocation of the reference pilots of different eNBs across the same CC. A minimum spacing of 180 kHz between adjacent pilots is set in order to avoid power leakage due to frequency offset. A distinction is made between the radio bandwidth and the emulated bandwidth. The radio

bandwidth is the effective over-the-air band-pass where the reference pilots are mapped, while the emulated bandwidth is the abstraction reference value for the computation of the KPIs.

During the experiments the BCC and SCCs selection procedures, previously described, are executed. The algorithm iteration period (ACCS frame) is 400 ms while the UE measurements reporting period is 200 ms. The considered traffic model is full-buffer: once the UE connects to the cell, the eNB attempts to allocate the maximum number of SCCs.

An interesting aspect addressed during the experiments is the evaluation of target BCC and SCC C/I thresholds, upon which the allocation of SCCs depends. The values selected for the thresholds greatly impact the ACCS capabilities of frequency reuse and thus the overall network capacity. Restrictive thresholds for example, may excessively prevent the allocation of shared resources between cells. Low C/I requirements generate instead larger spectrum allocations which increase the probability of coupled cells to interfere each other. In this work, the values of 10 dB

Figure 6. Testbed network deployment across office rooms. Two positions a) and b) are considered in the experiments for the UE 3

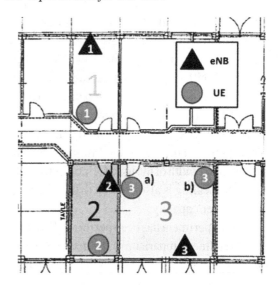

Table 2. Overview of the ACCS experiments configuration parameters.

Experiments	1	2	3
Environment characteristics	Static	Static	Dynamic
Deployment setup	a)	b)	a)
CCs configuration	2/3/4	4	4
System Carrier Frequency	Variable from 4.91 to 5.81 GHz	Variable from 4.91 to 5.81 GHz	5.41 GHz
Tx power per CC	0 dBm		
Transceiver I/FFT size	1024 points		
Channel configuration	2/3/4 CCs over 12.5 MHz		
Total Emulated Bandwidth	12 MHz		
Antenna configuration	SISO		
ACCS frame	400 ms		
UE Traffic model	Full buffer		
Target C/I for BCC	10 dB		
Target C/I for SCC	4 dB		

and 4 dB have been selected as thresholds on the basis of an empirical observation of the network during the experimentation.

The ACCS algorithm is executed on the testbed in real-time, thus generating time data traces of the eNBs control data and UEs RSRP measurements. These experimental results have been processed in order to extract network-wide statistics about downlink SINR experienced in the cells, and the corresponding estimated capacity which is obtained through Shannon mapping (Shannon, 1948). The SINR is first measured on the narrowband pilots, and then scaled to the effective emulated bandwidth of the used CC configuration. Bandwidth scaling is also applied to the Shannon mapping over capacity.

A first experiment has been performed in order to get a baseline comparison of the network maximum capacity when ACCS is enabled, in respect

to a frequency reuse 1 scheme (i.e., all the eNBs are transmitting over the whole bandwidth, thus are fully interfering each other). The experiments has been executed in static propagation environment conditions. The impact of a variable number (2, 3, and 4) of CCs has also been analyzed. A single run of the experiment consists in the steps reported below:

- eNBs are activated sequentially and a single BCC is selected per cell.
- UEs are activated sequentially within an interval of a few ACCS frames: the maximum number of SCCs allowed by the algorithm is allocated in the cell as soon as the UE connects, and before the following UE is activated.

In order to ensure a good statistical coverage, multiple runs of the experiments have been executed. In particular, the problem of variable multipath fading contributions is addressed by repeating the experiment over 10 different carrier frequencies ranging from 4.91 to 5.81 GHz. Moreover, changing the activation delays of eNBs and UEs (thus also their activation order) at each experiment contributes in obtaining a larger set of results. Considering also all possible CCs configurations, the total amount of experiment runs is 1080. The obtained results in terms of channel capacity in the cells are reported in Figure 7a. The cumulative distribution functions (CDFs) show a clear benefit of ACCS in respect to Reuse 1, and a decreasing marginal gain at the increase of the CCs cardinality.

A second experiment focused on the impact of the relative position between eNB and UE within a single cell. Assuming a similar configuration of parameters as in the first experiment, the network performance is evaluated in respect to the variable position of the UE node in cell 2 (i.e. positions *a* and *b* in Figure 6). The obtained capacity results have shown that the variable interference coupling between cells 2 and 3, given

Figure 7. a) Experiment 1: cells' capacity CDFs, b) experiment 3: snapshot of C/I variations in time measured by cell 1 in respect to cell 2 and cell 3. Values experienced in static scenario and in simulation environment are also included as terms of comparison.

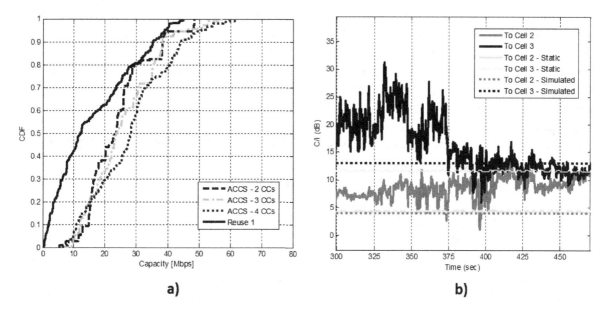

a)   b)

by the different amount of interference experienced by the UE2, has network-wide implications, greatly impacting the capacity of other surrounding cells (cell 1 in this case). The fairness principles adopted in ACCS prevent the greedy allocation of resources by one cell in respect to a highly coupled neighbor, thus leading to an overall reduction of the amount of interference in the network.

In a static environment, the variations of received signal power due to the fading are negligible. In simulation studies, whenever the fast-fading contribution is not considered, the environment is assumed to be static. The validation process of an algorithm, occurring with such simulation assumptions, often focuses on the spatial analysis (e.g. short simulation duration, large amount of network deployment configurations), rather than on the long-term behavior of the network. In such context, the usage of static decision-making thresholds appears as an effective solution to the DSA problem. In a dynamic propagation environment,

accounting for the effects of human presence and terminal mobility, the assumption of stationary signal power measurements (and related values, such as the C/I) in relation to a specific spatial deployment, no longer holds. The algorithm performance in terms of spectrum resources allocation can be therefore affected. A third experimental trial with ACCS aimed then at providing a first insight into such issues.

The experiment focused on the variations of the C/I values registered at the UEs during long experimental sessions. The testbed network is deployed according to the same configuration of the previous cases, considering trials of 1 hour execution time. Experiments are performed during working hours thus allowing human presence in the scenario. A single carrier frequency is used.

A relevant time snapshot of the C/I measurements (related to cell 1 in respect to cell 2 and cell 3) during the experiment, is reported in Figure 7b. In the Figure, are also included the C/I values measured in static scenario conditions, and the values generated in a simulated context (no fast fading, inter-node pathloss relations equal to the real-world case are assumed). More general results from the same set of experiments are summarized in Table 3. In this case, the mean C/I values $\overline{X}$ and the standard deviation σ are listed considering different simulation and experimental scenarios. Two different data time-averaging configurations have been analyzed.

The provided results show that the testbed execution in a static environment reasonably meets the expectations from the simulation-based analysis. In a dynamic environment instead, the human activity strongly affects the C/I measurements, producing fluctuations up to 25 dB. The C/I oscillations, well across the two BCC and SCC thresholds (fixed at 10 and 4 dB), are complex to track for the ACCS algorithm, which tends to performs frequent re-configurations of the allocated spectrum resources. In such context, the experimental results suggest that an algorithm optimization in respect to static decision-thresholds may be uneffective. A dynamic management of the thresholds is instead desirable: cognitive processes considering learning capabilities may provide, for example, an interesting solution in this direction.

The simple experimental activities previously described, highlight how the algorithm implementation over a testbed network, can provide valuable insight about challenging aspects of the execution in a realistic environment. Further improvements of the ACCS testbed setup are however needed, in order to provide a more complete analysis of the algorithm performance.

FUTURE RESEARCH DIRECTIONS

The aim of the experimentation activities is to reduce the gap between the assumptions made in a simulation environment, and the behavior of a device in a realistic utilization context. In order to achieve this ambitious goal, a gradual process can be pursued. As a start, testbed implementations providing signal power measurements can improve the understanding of specific propagation scenarios. More advanced testbed realizations, with greater hardware and software capabilities, will then enable the investigation of more challenging aspects, such as: distributed network synchronization, protocols timing and real-time computation constraints. The ultimate goal in the development

Table 3. Comparison between simulation and experimental results of cell 1 C/I in respect to cell 2 and cell. All values in the table are in dB.

(dB)	Simulation		Exp. Static Scenario		Exp. Dynamic Scenario	
	$\overline{X}$	σ	$\overline{X}$	σ	$\overline{X}$	σ
$(C/I)_{1/2}$ 0.5 sec avg. window	4	0	4.254	0.146	10.48	4.075
$(C/I)_{1/2}$ 5 mins avg. window	4	0	4.26	0.059	10.21	3.869
$(C/I)_{1/3}$ 0.5 sec avg. window	13	0	11.6	0.133	18.03	3.905
$(C/I)_{1/3}$ 5 mins avg. window	13	0	11.6	0.037	17.69	3.588

of a testbed is enabling the execution of the entire protocol stack of a communication system, thus achieving a full interaction between the testbed devices and the user. Such a tool will then enable a complete experimental analysis of cognitive network concepts, in a context of realistic usage.

In this chapter we highlighted the inherent complexity of implementing and exploiting a network testbed for experimentation purposes. In particular, we summarize here some of the most critical aspects still hindering the applicability of testbeds for a wide range of CR/DSA studies, and thus requiring further developments:

- Hardware limitations in terms of oscillators phase noise, data transfer from/to the host computer and latency of the processing components chain.
- Software platforms compatibility with a wide range of hardware devices and RF front-ends
- Computational burden of the signal processing tasks in the software platform
- Hardware support for multiple antennas configurations
- Remote and centralized control of movable nodes, for repeatable experimental sessions.
- Distributed testbed synchronization at microsecond level
- Deployment of the testbed out of controlled areas (e.g. within residential premises).

From the research perspective, the exploitation of network a testbed has a large number of use cases. In particular, the experimental approach can provide unique insights in the study of the interactions of a large number of autonomous/cognitive devices. The evaluation of the actual performance of network solutions relying on multiple antennas configurations is also of major interest. Specific research areas relate then to:

- Real-time execution of fast communication protocols (e.g., in the order of microseconds)
- Distributed over-the-air network synchronization
- Design of over-the-air inter-cells communication (common control channel).
- Realistic performance assessment of advanced PHY layer techniques (e.g. multiple antennas transceiver algorithms, interference cancellation)
- Combination of heterogeneous techniques (DSA, interference cancellation, network coding)
- Algorithms adaptability to different operative scenarios (deployment in office, residential or large public areas)
- Characterization of the performance losses due to communication delays and hardware limitations (e.g., power leakage in adjacent channels)

CONCLUSION

Research in the field of Cognitive Radio has reached to a maturity stage in which practical demonstrations of theoretical concepts are becoming increasingly important. Commercial solutions and research platforms have been developed, enabling the realization of communication prototypes featuring cognitive features. In literature, several examples of platforms and demonstrators have been proposed. Network testbeds have been realized mainly relying on SDR hardware.

DSA is one of the most important applications for CR. The flexibility of DSA-enabled systems in relation to the problems of spectrum scarcity and fragmentation represents a major opportunity for introducing CR concepts in the market of wireless communications. Despite several demonstration activities successfully presented in international conferences and scientific publications, extensive experimental campaigns with CR/DSA solutions are still widely disregarded. Experiments with large network testbeds should be performed in order to provide additional contributions to simulation-based studies. The development of proper tools and methodologies for this purpose is the fundamental step enabling effective experimentation activities.

When approaching the realization of a testbed it is fundamental to clearly identify the design and execution characteristics of the algorithms of interest, in order to proceed to the choice of the most suited execution platform. In this chapter, we focused on the aspects related to the implementation and experimentation with distributed network algorithms for DSA. In the proposed discussion, we have highlighted the fundamental impact of the testbed platform architecture for the design of cross-layer communication systems and for the management of the experimental sessions. The majority of existing platform solutions for CR has been primarily designed for the optimization of PHY layer and signal processing features. The software ASGARD has been instead specifically conceived for the needs of distributed DSA algorithms and provides integrated support for the centralized control of the testbed.

The execution of experiments with distributed network algorithms aims at the analysis of relevant network KPIs such as SINR at the user and maximum capacity achievable in the network. In order to achieve a statistically significant coverage of the network behavior in different deployment scenarios, it is important to execute a large number of experiments varying sensitive configuration parameters. Proper management of environment contributions such as multipath fading should also be included in the picture when planning the experiment execution. In order to provide a practical example of the entire design process and setup of experiments for a distributed DSA algorithm, the activities carried out at Aalborg University in relation to the ACCS algorithm have been described in the chapter.

REFERENCES

Akyildiz, I. F., Lee, W.-Y., Vuran, M. C., & Mohanty, S. (2008, April). A Survey on Spectrum Management in Cognitive Radio Networks. *IEEE Communications Magazine*, 40–48. doi:10.1109/MCOM.2008.4481339.

Alexandrescu, A. (2001). *Modern C++ Design*. Addison Wesley.

Arslan, H., & Yarkan, S. (2007). Cross-Layer Adaptation and Optimization for Cognitive Radio. I H. Arslan, Cognitive Radio, Software Defined Radio, and Adaptive Wireless Systems (s. 421-452). Springer.

ASGARD. (2012). Retrieved from ASGARD: Cognitive Radio Experimentation Platform: http://asgard.lab.es.aau.dk

Bajaj, J., Wooseong, K., Oh, S. Y., & Gerla, M. (2011). Cognitive Radio Implementation in ISM Bands with Microsoft SORA., (s. 531-535).

Beck, K. (2002). *Test Driven Development: By Example*. Addison-Wesley Professional.

Bradford, G. J., & Laneman, J. (2009). An experimental framework for the evaluation of cooperative diversity. *43rd Annual Conference on Information Sciences and Systems*, (s. 641-645).

Cattoni, A. F., Sørensen, T. B., & Mogensen, P. E. (2012). Architecture Design Approaches and Issues in Cross Layer Systems. I H. F. Rashvand, & Y. S. Kavian, Using Cross-Layer Techniques for Communication Systems (s. 29-52). IGI Global.

Chandrasekhar, V., Andrews, J., & Gatherer, A. (2008). Femtocell Networks: a survey. *IEEE Communications Magazine*, 46(9), 59–67. doi:10.1109/MCOM.2008.4623708.

Chang, C., Wawrzynek, J., & Brodersen, R. W. (2005). BEE2: a high-end reconfigurable computing system. *IEEE Design & Test of Computers*, 22(2), 114–125. doi:10.1109/MDT.2005.30.

Chowdhury, K. R., & Melodia, T. (2010). Platforms and testbeds for experimental evaluation of cognitive ad hoc networks. *IEEE Communications Magazine, 48*(9), 96–104. doi:10.1109/MCOM.2010.5560593.

Ettus Research. (2012). Retrieved from Ettus Research: http://www.ettus.com

Garcia, L. G., Kovács, I. Z., Pedersen, K. I., Costa, G. W., & Mogensen, P. E. (2012). Autonomous Component Carrier Selection for 4G Femtocells - A Fresh Look at an Old Problem. *IEEE Journal on Selected Areas in Communications, 30*(3), 525–537. doi:10.1109/JSAC.2012.120403.

Garcia, L. G., Pedersen, K. I., & Mogensen, P. E. (2009). Autonomous component carrier selection: interference management in local area environments for LTE-advanced. *IEEE Communications Magazine, 47*(9), 110–116. doi:10.1109/MCOM.2009.5277463.

GNU Radio. (2012). Retrieved from GNU Radio: http://www.gnuradio.org

Gonzalez, C., Dietrich, C. B., Sayed, S., Volos, H. I., Gaeddert, J. D., & Robert, P. M. et al. (2009). Open-source SCA-based core framework and rapid development tools enable software-defined radio education and research. *IEEE Communications Magazine, 47*(10), 48–55. doi:10.1109/MCOM.2009.5273808.

3 GPP. (2008). *TR 36.913, Requirements for further advancements for E-UTRA (LTE-Advanced).* Technical Report.

Haykin, S. (2005). Cognitive radio: brain-empowered wireless communications. *IEEE Journal on Selected Areas in Communications, 23*(2), 201–220. doi:10.1109/JSAC.2004.839380.

Hentilä, L., Kyösti, P., Käske, M., Narandzic, M., & Alatossava, M. (2012, July 16). *MATLAB Implementation of the WINNER Phase II Channel Model.* Retrieved from WINNER+: http://projects.celtic-initiative.org/winner+/phase_2_model.html

Kaltenberger, F., Ghaffar, R., Knopp, R., Anouar, H., & Bonnet, C. (2010, April). Design and implementation of a single-frequency mesh network using OpenAirInterface. *EURASIP Journal on Wireless Communications and Networking.* doi:10.1155/2010/719523.

Khattab, A., Camp, J., Hunter, C., Murphy, P., Sabharwarl, A., & Knightly, E. (2008). WARP - A Flexible Platform for Clean-Slate Wireless Medium Access Protocol Design. *ACM SIGMOBILE Mobile Computing and Communications Review, 12*(1), 56–58. doi:10.1145/1374512.1374532.

Korakis, T., Knox, M., Erkip, E., & Panwar, S. (2009). Cooperative Network Implementation Using Open-Source Platforms. *IEEE Communications Magazine, 47*(2), 134–141. doi:10.1109/MCOM.2009.4785391.

Lyrtech, R. D. Incorporated. (2012). *Small form factor SDR development platforms.* Retrieved July 2012, from Lyrtech RD: http://lyrtechrd.com/en/products/view/+small-form-factor-sdr-development-platforms

Meshkova, E., Ansari, J., Denkovski, D., Riihijärvi, J., Nasreddine, J., Pavlovski, M., et al. (2011). Experimental Spectrum Sensor Testbed for Constructing Indoor Radio Environmental Maps. *International Symposium on Dynamic Spectrum Access Networks (DySPAN).* IEEE.

Mitola, J., & Maguire, G. (1999). Cognitive radio: making software radios more personal. *IEEE Personal Communications, 6*(4), 13–18. doi:10.1109/98.788210.

Newman, T. R., Hasan, S. M., DePoy, D., Bose, T., & Reed, J. H. (2010). Designing and Deploying a Building-Wide Cognitive Radio Network Testbed. *IEEE Communications Magazine*, *48*(9), 106–112. doi:10.1109/MCOM.2010.5560594.

Nolan, K. E., Sutton, P. D., Doyle, L. E., Rondeau, T. W., Le, B., & Bostian, C. W. (2007). Dynamic Spectrum Access and Coexistence Experiences Involving Two Independently Developed Cognitive Radio Testbeds. *2nd IEEE International Symposium on New Frontiers in Dynamic Spectrum Access Networks*, (s. 270-275).

Pawelczak, P., Nolan, K., & Doyle, L., Ser Wah Oh, & Cabric, D. (2011). Cognitive Radio: Ten years of experimentation and development. *IEEE Communications Magazine*, *49*(3), 90–100. doi:10.1109/MCOM.2011.5723805.

Polson, J. (2004). Cognitive Radio Applications in Software Defined Radio. *Software Defined Radio Technical Conference*. Phoenix.

Reddy, Y. B., & Bullmaster, C. (2008). Cross-Layer Design in Wireless Cognitive Networks. *International Conference on Parallel and Distributed Computing, Applications and technologies* (s. 462-467). IEEE Computer Society.

Sengupta, S., Hong, K., Chandramouli, R., & Subbalakshmi, K. P. (2011). SpiderRadio: A Cognitive Radio Network with Commodity Hardware and Open Source Software. *IEEE Communications Magazine*, *49*(3), 101–109. doi:10.1109/MCOM.2011.5723806.

Shannon, C. E. (1948). A mathematical theory of communication. *The Bell System Technical Journal*, *27*, 379–423.

Sokolowski, C., Petrova, M., de Baynast, A., & Mähönen, P. (2008). Cognitive Radio Testbed: Exploiting Limited Feedback in Tomorrow's Wireless Communication Networks. *IEEE International Conference on Communications Workshops*, (s. 493-498).

Sutton, P., Lotze, J., Lahlou, H., Fahmy, S., Nolan, K. E., & Rondeau, T. W. et al. (2010, September). Iris: An Architecture for Cognitive Radio Networking Testbeds. *IEEE Communications Magazine*, 114–122. doi:10.1109/MCOM.2010.5560595.

Sutton, P. D., Nolan, K. E., & Doyle, L. E. (2008). Cyclostationary Signatures in Practical Cognitive Radio Applications. *IEEE Journal on Selected Areas in Communications*, *26*(1), 13–24. doi:10.1109/JSAC.2008.080103.

Tan, K., Zhang, J., Fang, J., Liu, H., Ye, Y., & Wang, S. et al. (2009). *Sora: High Performance Software Radio using General Purpose Multi-core Processors*. Boston: USENIX NSDI.

Tkachenko, A., Cabric, D., & Brodersen, R. W. (2007). Cyclostationary Feature Detector Experiments using Reconfigurable BEE2. *International Conference on Dynamic Spectrum Access Networks*.

ADDITIONAL READING

Arslan, M. Y., Yoon, J., Sundaresan, K., Krishnamurthy, S. V., & Banerjee, S. (2011). FERMI: A FEmtocell Resource Management System for Interference Mitigation in OFDMA Networks. *International Conference on Mobile Computing and Networking (Mobicom)*, (s. 25-36).

Baldo, N., & Zorzi, M. (2008, April). Fuzzy Logic for Cross-Layer Optimization in Cognitive Radio networks. *IEEE Communications Magazine*, 64–71. doi:10.1109/MCOM.2008.4481342.

DaSilva, L. A., MacKenzie, A. B., da Silva, C. R., & Thomas, R. W. (2008). Requirements of an Open Platform for Cognitive Networks Experiments. *3rd Symposium on New Frontiers in Dynamic Spectrum Access Networks. DySPAN 2008* (s. 1-8). IEEE.

Fernández-Prades, C., Arribas, J., Closas, P., Avilés, C., & Esteve, L. (2011). GNSS-SDR: an open source tool for researchers and developers. *ION GNSS Conference*. Portland.

Garcia, L. G., Costa, G. W., Cattoni, A. F., Pedersen, K. I., & Mogensens, P. E. (2010). Self-Organizing Coalitions for Conflict Evaluation and Resolution in Femtocells. *Global Telecommunications Conference (GLOBECOM)* (pp. 1-6). IEEE.

Pawelczak, P., Hoeksema, F., Prasad, R. V., & Hekmat, R. (2010). Dynamic Spectrum Access: An Emergency Network Case Study. IEEE DySPAN (s. 601-606). Singapore: IEEE Press.

Petrova, M., & Mahonen, P. (2007). Cognitive Resource Manager. I F. H. Fitzek, & M. D. Katz (Red.), Cognitive Wireless Networks (s. 397-422). Springer.

Wyglinski, A. M., Nekovee, M., & Hou, T. (2010). *Cognitive Radio Communications and Networks: Principles and Practice*. Academic Press.

Zhao, Y., Mao, S., Neel, J. O., & Reed, J. H. (April 2009). Performance Evaluation of Cognitive Radios: Metrics, Utility Functions, and Methodology. *Proceedings of the IEEE*, 642-659.

KEY TERMS AND DEFINITIONS

Background Interference Matrix: Data structure potentially exchanged by nodes in a network, containing information on all the potential interfering cells and corresponding conditional Carrier to Interference (C/I) values. The BIM can be generated from RSRP measurements performed by users in the cell.

Conditional Carrier to Interference (C/I) Ratio: The C/I, expressed in decibel, describes the Reference Signal Received Power (RSRP) difference between the serving cell and the surrounding cells. The C/I is a measure of mutual interference coupling between cells in the case they would use the same component carrier simultaneously.

Cross-Layer Design: The process of involving multiple layers in the optimization of the system. Such improvements can be general, or focused on a specific application or type of traffic, allowing the system to be polarized on use-cases of interest, like for example video streaming.

Distributed Dynamic Spectrum Access: A solution for the management of spectrum resources in the network, considering an independent decision making process over each of the enabled nodes. Information can be shared among network peers but no centralized decision is enforced.

Software Defined Radio: Radio capable device where the processing tasks related to the generation, transmission and reception of data are implemented by means of software on a personal computer or embedded system.

Software Framework: Basic set of software tools, constraints and methodologies enabling the realization of a complex software application. In the case of a SDR development platform, the software framework typically defines the means for data transfer, management of threads of execution and interaction between processing components.

Thread of Execution: Sequence of programming instructions which are managed independently by an operating system. Exploiting threads enables the parallel execution of multiple processing tasks within the software implementation of the communication system architecture.

USRP: Universal Software Radio Peripheral, radio device produced by Ettus. Available in multiple hardware configurations and compatible with a wide range of radio-frequency front-ends, it is one of the most popular solutions for software defined radio implementations.

Section 2
High Layer Issues in Cognitive Networks

Chapter 8
Software Networks at the Edge

Antonio Manzalini
Telecom Italia, Italy

Roberto Minerva
Telecom Italia, Italy

Noel Crespi
Institut Mines-Télécom, France & Télécom SudParis, France

Uddin Shah Muhammad Emad
Politecnico of Turin, Italy

ABSTRACT

The chapter addresses the potential impact of technologies like Autonomic, Cognitive, and Software Defined Networking on future networks evolution. It is argued that said technologies, coupled with a wide adoption of virtualization, will bring an impactful disruption at the edge of current networks: in less than a decade developing distributed clouds of cheap edge nodes powerful enough to run virtualized network functions and services on standard hardware will be possible. This will improve network flexibility and programmability, creating the conditions for the development of new Telco-ICT ecosystems. The edge will become a business arena with multiple interacting networks and domains operated by diverse players. We are already witnessing this transformation, looking at the shift of value towards the users' terminals. The chapter elaborates this vision, reports a brief overview of the state of the art of enabling technologies, describes some simulation results of a use-case, and concludes by providing future research directions.

INTRODUCTION

Socio-economic drivers and technology progresses (with their down-spiraling costs) are steering the evolution of current networks towards becoming a programmable environment of resources, dynamically interconnected by links that are created and destroyed to serve multiple applications.

Technology trends are progressing at an impressive rate: processing is continuing to follow Moore's curve and it is doubling in capability roughly every 18 months; storage capacity on a given chip is doubling every 12 months, driving increases in connectivity demand for access to the network; and optical bandwidth is doubling every 9 months by increasing the capacity of a single

DOI: 10.4018/978-1-4666-4189-1.ch008

Copyright © 2013, IGI Global. Copying or distributing in print or electronic forms without written permission of IGI Global is prohibited.

wave length and by putting multiple wavelengths of light on a single fiber.

These tendencies will impact dramatically the evolution of network architectures: future networks are likely to become less hierarchical and based on optical core infrastructures (with a limited number and types of large nodes) interconnecting different local areas (via optical and/or radio connectivity), populated, at the edge (in a range of few meters around Users) with a sheer number of heterogeneous nodes. The edge, where already we are witnessing already today the migration of "intelligence" will become the business area where a new galaxy of ecosystems will be created.

The performance of processing and storage technologies are making impressive progress, but software will be the true challenge. In fact, future networks will rely more and more on software, which will accelerate the pace of innovation (as it is doing continuously in the computing and storage domains). Already today, advances in resource virtualization are allowing the deployment, on the same physical infrastructure, of diverse coexisting and isolated virtual networks of resources, thereby best fitting, dynamically, a variety of service demands (just like having different OSs - Window, Linux - on the same laptop). This has multiple advantages: for example, the crash, or the misuse, of a virtual resource is confined in a virtual network (e.g., by applying fault recovery policies enforced by self-healing capabilities) and it has no impact on other virtual networks; it is possible to put in place, in each virtual network, specific logics and policies (e.g. to optimize the usage of allocated resources according to SLA); the use of physical resources is optimized, etc.

Software Defined Networking (SDN) (McKeown, 2009) can be seen as a further step in this direction. In particular, in SDN architecture network control and data planes are decoupled, so that network infrastructure is abstracted from business applications. SDN should not be confused with network virtualization, even if the two trajectories

could intersect with interesting possibilities. Network virtualization is the second most-important trend allowing the set-up of virtual networks by connecting virtual IT and networking resources. This is expected to bring about programmability and flexibility: for example it will be possible to build multiple overlay networks (on the same physical infrastructure) offering multiple services.

On the other hand, this evolution is also bringing an increase in design and management complexity. Future networks will start exhibiting the characteristics of complex systems consisting of many diverse and autonomous, but interrelated software and hardware components. As known, complex systems cannot be easily described by rules and their characteristics are not reducible to one level of description: they exhibit properties (e.g. self-organization) that emerge from the local interactions of their parts and which cannot be predicted from the properties of the single parts.

Traditional management and control approaches will no longer be applicable. Networks should be able to self-adapt and self-configure themselves (with limited human intervention). These capabilities can be achieved by introducing cognition as a transformative software technology. As from the prior-art there are already technologies and solutions empowering cognitive networks with the ability to learn and to reason, which involve observations of network states, planning, decisions and actions while taking into account optimization goals. These kind of actions are intended to improve a network's state with respect to these design goals and learning is a product of their accumulated knowledge about past actions and their results. Given these characteristics, we may even argue that the behavior of a cognitive network environment can be view as a sort of self-organization pursuing network-wide constrained optimization (CO). In fact, said behavior can be viewed as the result of a dynamic game, which is influenced by the local actions and the degree of coupling that may exist between the actions of different players (i.e., nodes) The coupling may have the effect of amplifying local perturbations as in Hebb's postulate of learning, which accounts for self-amplification in self-organizing systems.

On the other hand, this means that in future networks there will run the risk of having transition to instability as the complexity increases. As in self-organizing critical systems, unexpected propagation of long-range interactions based on local effects can bring about a state of network criticality at which any further, even low-impact event may trigger an abrupt, critical phase transition. Since networks are strategic assets, it is of paramount importance to mitigate these risks, whose primary effects might not only jeopardize the performance, but even create the meltdown of a portion of the network.

BACKGROUND

It is argued that in less than a decade the three main technology drivers, i.e., decoupling hardware from software (SDN), virtualization and introduction of cognitive and autonomic capabilities, will profoundly transform today networks. This section will provide an overview of the background of said technology drivers.

Software Defined Networking

In Software Defined Networking (SDN), network control and data planes are decoupled, so that network infrastructure is abstracted from business applications (McKeown, 2009). This is expected to bring programmability and flexibility by providing network services that will include routing, multicast, security, access control, bandwidth management, traffic engineering, quality of service, processor and storage optimization, energy usage, and all forms of policy management, all custom tailored to meet business objectives. To give a typical example, SDN moves "intelligence" from the network nodes to a (decoupled) controller or hierarchy of controllers in which

switching paths can be centrally calculated and then downloaded to the distributed switching architecture, which simply forwards the packets. This is called OpenFlow, a first step toward full SDN, i.e. a messaging protocol between the controller and the individual switches making up the forwarding plane. In other words, OpenFlow is an open interface for remotely controlling the forwarding tables in network switches, routers, and access points. Researchers can build networks with new high-level properties on top of this low-level primitive. OpenFlow enables more secure default-off networks, wireless networks with smooth handoffs, scalable data center networks, host mobility, more energy-efficient networks and new wide-area networks.

The IETF's Forwarding and Control Element Separation (Forces) working group is also working on the transition to SDN.

This network transformation towards SDN is simultaneously evaluating open-source initiatives aimed at providing "network connectivity as a service".

For example, OpenStack is an open source cloud project developing two technologies: OpenStack Compute and OpenStack Object Storage (Openstack, 2012). OpenStack Compute is the internal fabric of the cloud, creating and managing large groups of virtual private servers. OpenStack Object Storage is a software for creating redundant, scalable object storage using clusters of commodity servers to store terabytes or even petabytes of data. Interestingly, Quantum is a project of OpenStack aimed at providing "network connectivity as a service" between interface devices managed by other OpenStack services. In other words, Quantum is an application-level abstraction of networking; it requires additional software (in the form of a plug-in) and it can talk to SDN via an API.

In this direction, the idea of developing an Open Source Network Operating System for Carriers' Class nodes is even more disruptive, but technically feasible in less than five years (Figure 1). In

Figure 1. Network operating system

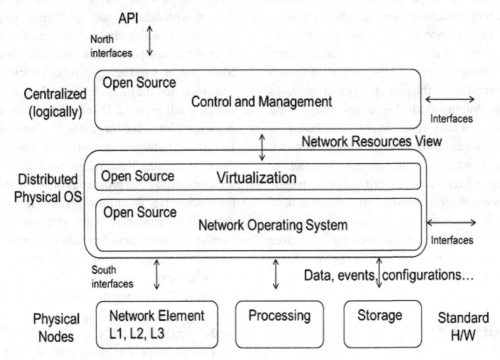

fact, we should not forget the rise of large-scale cooperative efforts under the form of open source s/w and h/w development and production, which might create soon a further ripple in the Telco-ICT Vendor markets.

Virtualization technology, introduced by IBM in 1973, became very popular with systems like the hypervisor Xen and VMware (Anderson et al., 2005). These systems have been widely used to enhance isolation, mobility, dynamic reconfiguration and fault tolerance of IT systems. Virtualization of physical resources will also have a significant impact on network evolution. In the IT context, virtualization is already well known and widely deployed in Data Centers for enabling the execution of multiple isolated instances of a software entity on top of a single physical server. IT Virtualization has several advantages, for example it increases resource utilization and improves state encapsulation.

These principles have not been fully extended to networks. Of course, network virtualization already exists in virtual private networks (VPNs) which generally use the multi-protocol label switching (MPLS) technology, operating on the link level layer. Another form of virtualization is to segment the physical local area networks into virtual local area networks (VLANs). An overlay network is yet another form of network virtualization which is typically implemented in the application layer, though various implementations at lower layers of the network stack are also being used. Extension of IT virtualization principles to network equipment (such as routers and switches) (Wang et al., 2008) could determine several advantages as well, i.e. optimizing the use of physical resources and allowing a deeper integration of IT and network resources. Moreover, as proposed in the Network Function Virtualization (NFV, 2012) initiative, implementing network processing functions fully in software (possible today) will allow running them on standard hardware. Operations normally carried out in Data Centers, such as migration and cloning of virtual resource and functions (e.g. for server consolidation, load balancing, etc.) could be also actuated in the network.

Network Virtualization could bring the ability to co-locate multiple instances of network functions on the same hardware – each running in one (or more) different Virtual Machine (VM).

Figure 2 show an example of network virtualization. This is giving the Network Operators not only the ability to dynamically instantiate, activate and re-allocate resources and functions, but even programming them according to need and policies. It should be noted that virtualization is complementary to SDN but not dependent on it: the two concepts should not be confused even if they can be combined in ways that can create potentially greater value.

Network virtualization is a diversifying attribute of future networks; it provides multiple advantages while posing many challenges to be overcome. The ability to control and move these virtual nodes creates the need for an intelligent architecture that can adapt to changing demands and conditions by autonomically tuning performance, isolation, migration, and sliver resizing. Among other concerns, it is important to find

innovative solutions for developing cross-domain virtual control planes, high performance virtual forwarding planes, and to make forwarding planes re-programmable: with these capabilities, it will be possible to conceive of self-organizing forwarding paths that adapt dynamically to incoming traffic and application requests.

This evolution will require new management approaches, capable of operating, in an integrated fashion, both real and virtual network resources. One means to implement this operational intelligence could be to decouple data processing-forwarding from sets of controllers (interacting with each other and properly orchestrated), embedding certain levels of automaticity (to ease human operation and mitigate mistakes).

Cognition, Autonomics, and Self-Organization

The term cognitive communications is very broad and it encompasses more than the standard areas of cognitive radio and cognitive networks, including other areas such as cognitive environments and cognitive acoustics.

Figure 2. Example of node virtualization

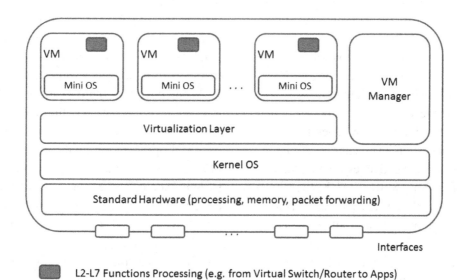

L2-L7 Functions Processing (e.g. from Virtual Switch/Router to Apps)

VM = Virtual Machine

Cognitive radio has been viewed initially as an approach for improving the utilization of a valuable resource, such as the radio electromagnetic spectrum. Specifically, built on a software-defined radio, has been defined as an intelligent wireless communication system that is aware of its environment and uses learning techniques and other methodologies to adapt to its statistical variations.

In general, cognitive network can be distinguished from a network of cognitive radios as it aims at network-wide optimization: said goals are normally achieved involving all network elements and functions from the physical to the application layer across the data path. As mentioned, we may even argue that emergent behavior of a cognitive network environment can be viewed as a self-organization directed in way to pursue network-wide constrained optimization (CO).

This chapter explores also this perspective of exploiting cognitive and autonomic capabilities in software networks in order to achieve network-wide constrained optimizations, seen as expression of self-organization. CO problems are often mathematically modeled using objective functions, functions of decision variables or parameters that produce a scalar value that must be either minimized or maximized: the challenge is to find the values of those parameters that either minimize or maximize, i.e., optimize, the objective function value subject to some constraints on the decision variables. Example of objective functions are sum of utility functions by Users (e.g. QoE/QoS, functions of rate, reliability, delay, jitter, power level, response time, etc.), and network-wide cost functions by Operators (e.g., functions of congestion level, energy efficiency, network lifetime, collective estimation errors, etc.). In this direction, (Kelly, 1997; Kelly, 1998)) are providing the interesting example of TCP as a network-wide optimization problem solved by maximizing a utility function where the variables are the source rates constrained by link's capacities and where the objective function captures the design goals. Utility functions can also provide a pragmatic basis for self-optimization in autonomic

computing systems (Dong, 2004), (Walsh, 2004) for a dynamic, heterogeneous environment.

Autonomic solutions take their inspiration from the biological characteristics of the human Autonomic Nervous System. This part of the nervous system, which acts and reacts to stimuli independent of the individual's conscious input, regulates the behavior of internal organs (e.g., of the heart to control blood flow and heartbeat, of the stomach and intestines to control digestive movement and secretions). It sends commands to the organ and receives feedback, via sensory fibers, on the condition of internal organs, information that helps it to maintain "homeostasis". In this way the Autonomic Nervous System implements a control loop, through which it can react, according to "predefined policies", to the changes of the internal organs and of the environmental conditions (e.g., external temperature), hiding the complexity of the control to the conscious part of the Nervous System.

State of the art on Cognitive Communications is very rich, falling fall into broad areas: from spectrum sensing, to spectrum access, from spectrum management and power control, to cognitive radio physical layers, from learning applied to cognitive communications, etc. Significant efforts in progressing the prior-art on cognitive communications are made by Worldwide Universities Network Cognitive Communications Consortium (WUN CogCom, www.wun-cogcom.org) which has members from over 90 organizations worldwide.

While cognitive radio (Thomas, 2005), (Mitola, 2001), is concerned to the ability to tune the parameters of physical and link layers for achieving local optimization goals, a broader concept of cognitive networks (Thomas, 2006) considers system-wide optimization goals and cross-layer design (Winter, 2006; Bourse, 2003). This sections will provide a brief overview of the prior-art on cognitive networking, addressing those aspects which are felt by the Authors nearer to the context of the vision proposed by the Chapter.

The E2R project leverages on the benefits of Next Generation Network (NGN) and exploits a wide range of network technologies, such as cellular, fixed or WLAN (Bourse, 2005). The goal of E2R is an all-IP network fully integrated with reconfigurable equipment. However, the assumption of simultaneous re-configurability support at all the layers for all the involved actors/devices represents a drawback, limiting its incremental deployment.

OneFIT project has applied the cognitive techniques (Kephart & Chess, 2003; Winter, 2006; Bourse, 2003; Bourse 2005; Demestichas, 2006)) for the management of the opportunistic networks and for coordinating the infrastructure. This innovation will lead to robustness and dependability. The approach capitalizes on the self-management features and also on the learning capabilities that must be intrinsic to cognitive systems. Cognitive management system hosts and implements capabilities for: (i) context acquisition and reasoning, profile management, and policy-awareness; (ii) the cooperation with other cognitive management systems, through the exchange of profiles, policies and context information; (iii) building and sharing knowledge, which, in principle, refers to the situations (contexts) typically encountered, the policies applied, the optimization decisions taken, and the resulting efficiency achieved; (iv) decision-making through cross-layer optimization functionality that takes into account the context of an operation, the profiles, the policies (potentially, of various business level stakeholders), and the acquired knowledge and experience.

(Fitzek & Katz, 2006; Fitzek & Katz, 2007) advocated the vision of breaking up cellular communications by introducing cooperative strategies among wireless devices through cognitive wireless networking. Interestingly they provide details about the potentialities of cooperative and cognitive aspects for future wireless communication networks, including social and bio-inspired behaviors for wireless networks, peer-to-peer, cooperative networks, and spectrum sensing and management.

(Haykin, 2005) argued the potential for cognitive radio to make a significant difference to wireless communications is immense, hence, the reference to it as a "disruptive, but unobtrusive technology." In the final analysis, however, the key issue that will shape the evolution of cognitive radio in the course of time, be that for civilian or military applications, is trust, which is two-fold: trust by the users of cognitive radio; trust by all other users who might be interfered with.

(Haykin, 2012) elaborated on Cognitive Dynamic Systems, which builds on ideas in statistical signal processing, stochastic control, and information theory, and weaves those well-developed ideas into new ones drawn from neuroscience, statistical learning theory, and game principled tools for the design and development of a new generation of wireless dynamic systems exemplified by cognitive radio and cognitive radar with efficiency, effectiveness, and robustness as the hallmarks of performance.

The m@ANGEL platform (Demestichas, 20006) introduces a special approach for solving mobility problems in heterogeneous network environments with the support of cognition. The cognitive process is considered to be implemented in the access part of the network, between base stations and mobile users. The structure of the access network consists of two planes: the infrastructure plane, which includes reconfigurable elements (such as hardware transceivers, base stations, and the network core) and the management plane, composed of m@ANGEL entities. Each m@ANGEL entity is responsible for monitoring, resource brokerage, goals management, and reconfigurable element control functionalities. A certain degree of cooperation is considered between m@ANGEL elements. However, this cooperation is usually performed within the scope of network elements located in neighboring cells and it is not propagated to the network core, somehow limiting the scope of a unified solution.

Differently from the above approaches, (Sutton, 2006) presented a general framework for implementing the cognitive functionality. This work focuses on node architecture capable of enabling reconfigurable properties, implying logical separation between network nodes and the cognitive engine running in the network. While the cognitive engine performs learning, orientation, planning, and decision-making functions, observation and action are left to the reconfigurable node. Node reconfiguration can be requested by the cognitive engine, the core of the reconfigurable node architecture. This approach relies on techniques to make the cognitive node capable of modifying or adjusting its protocol stack as a function of the dynamics of the network environment.

CogNet (Raychaudhuri, 2006) has proposed new cognitive network architecture designed to maintain the layered abstraction of TCP/IP protocol stacks. In CogNet, each protocol layer is extended with so-called Intralayer Cognition Modules, which are software agents performing intra-layer monitoring, control, and coordination functions. Modules are interconnected through the Cognitive Bus, a part of the Cognitive Plane, to coordinate the cognition modules, and are implemented in parallel to the protocol stack. A unique property of the proposed architecture is that the cognitive functions implemented in intra-layer cognitive elements are distributed between different protocol layers. Such a design simplifies the cognitive processes running in the network and reduces signaling overhead. However, the performance of the proposed architecture seems to be highly dependent on Cognitive Plane operation, which is responsible for the translation of end-to-end goals into objectives and configuration parameters at each layer. Consequently, a lack of proper coordination or effective intra-layer cognitive agents' monitoring could lead to unpredictable performance results. The cognitive network model proposed by Thomas at el. (Thomas, 2006) is composed of three horizontal layers. The top level is responsible for specification and translation of user/application requirements into goals understandable by cognitive processes. Several cognitive processes can run in the immediate plane, with implementation potentially distributed among several network nodes. The cognitive process involves learning, knowledge, and decision

making, and operates when information about the network is limited. The bottom layer of the model corresponds to the Software Adaptable Network (SAN), consisting of modifiable network elements and sensors. The communication between modifiable elements and the cognitive plane is performed using the software-adaptable network API. Such an architectural solution brings modularity and flexibility into the design of modifiable elements.

(Gelenbe et al., 1999) proposed the idea of cognitive packet networks, which basically moves routing and flow control capabilities from network nodes into packets. Such packets, called cognitive packets, "route themselves" and learn to avoid congestion and to avoid being destroyed. Each cognitive packet contains a cognitive map and a piece of code that is executed every time the packet arrives at the network node (or router). Routing decisions are taken relying on the cognitive map, as well as based on mailbox messages left by other packets or by the network node. The idea of cognitive packets bears similarities to the concept of active networking (Bush & Kulkarni, 2001), related to custom code execution. However, a unique feature of cognitive packets is their ability to change their behavior based on the state of the network.

Another approach to overcoming the limitations of traditional IP networks was presented by (Lake, 2005). Their Software Programmable Intelligent Network (SPIN) merges concepts from IP, PSTN, cellular, and ad hoc networks to overcome the fundamental limitations of IP networks (such as in-band signaling and the impact of long, nested feedback loops on network performance). SPIN architecture consists of three planes interconnected by layer-2 transport infrastructure characterized by three planes. The forwarding plane is responsible for switching and monitoring and it can provide connectionless packet forwarding, connection oriented packet forwarding, tag switching, and label switching; the Control/management plane manages forwarding plane devices targeting data, forwarding optimization based on the received measurements; and the Cognitive plane which resides on top of the control/management and forwarding planes, providing intelligence for and administration of the entire system. It operates multiple functions dedicated to performing single tasks, including schemas for optimal routing and load balancing, as well as managing responses to legacy control protocols.

Finally, Self-NET (Self-NET, 2007) aims at defining a paradigm for Future Internet self-management based on cognitive behavior with a high degree of autonomy, utilizing a novel feedback-control cycle.

Autonomic Systems

IBM (Kephart & Chess, 2003) as part of its autonomic computing initiative, derived a management architecture able to cope with the increasing complexity of IT systems from the metaphor of the Autonomic Nervous System. This architecture is based on the so-called MAPE-K (Monitor Analyze Plan Execute – Knowledge) implemented in autonomic managers (in charge of controlling any resource). Essentially, sensors, probes, etc. feed information to a Monitor function; the system then proceeds to Analyze the information, forms a Plan, and then Executes it. This plan is then fed back to the effectors which exploit the plan of action. Continually increasing the store of knowledge is a fundamental aspect for the correct functioning of this cycle: it consists of the data shared among the MAPE-K functions of an autonomic component, such as symptoms and policies.

A system that implements a MAPE-K cycle is capable of sensing environmental changes and sending commands to adapt the behavior to the environment; in this way it is possible to achieve self-* autonomic capabilities (e.g. self-CHOP: configuration, healing, optimization, protection).

In this proposal, there is a separation between the supervisor, which implement the MAPE-K cycle, and the system under supervision. This model can be recursively applied so as to create a cascade of supervisors/system under supervision, in a hierarchical manner.

The original MAPE-K model is not suitable to exploit fully autonomic behavior, since components are structured in strict hierarchies. However, in nature, such manager-managed relationships are much less relevant to those established in a peer-wise way. Moreover, individuals are able to react independently, i.e., "autonomously", to most of the external events they perceive, and are able to cooperate by activating peer-to-peer relationships amongst themselves.

Therefore, this approach must overcome the distinction between supervisors/supervised systems by embedding an autonomic control loop in each of the system components. This loop monitors each component's internal behavior and adapts it to internal events and to the changes in its external environment. The components themselves thus become "self-aware" by integrating self-CHOP features into their behavior. In this way, the strict distinction between managed and managing components is removed, since all the components can implement self-management logic by cooperating through interactions with other components in the system.

The embedding of autonomic control loops in the components also enables grassroots approaches. In this case, the control loops are extremely simple, e.g., based on the monitoring and adjustment of just a few local variables, and oriented to handle the simple exchange of information with the environment through local interactions. It is the local interactions of larger numbers of components, embedding much simpler control-loops, that enable the emergence of global system properties.

In particular, the control loops can introduce self-awareness, oriented to achieve self-CHOP features internally to each element, and self-organization, oriented to create, maintain and tune cooperation inside ensembles of elements, and to rule the emergence of properties.

Specifically, unpredictable events may cause a system to drift away from the desired objective, it is thus important that a system can configure its parameters, at run time, to enable the optimal response to any changes. An autonomic system is, by definition, capable of deciding on the fly which elements to update, remove or aggregate in the new configuration. This requires knowledge about the local and global states and configuration of the single components, of the system as a whole, as well as a valid model of the external environment.

Self-awareness of a single element could be defined as a component's awareness of being a single entity of a global autonomic system, at any point in time. This implies that the component knows certain internal/external data, transforms them into knowledge (e.g., with reasoning) and uses that knowledge to control its own behavior according to its plans. The process undergone to maintain homeostasis is an example of self-awareness.

In contrast, the self-organization of ensembles of components derives its inspiration from biological processes where patterns at the global level

of a system emerge from numerous interactions among the elements in the system: the rules specifying interactions among the components and the reaction to them are executed by using only information local to the components.

Self-awareness and self-organization can be achieved by means of two complementary types of control loops implemented by computing elements (Figure 3):

- An Internal/Local Control Loop to tune the behavior according to the planned and unplanned internal events, e.g., to improve the performance of internal functions or for detection of and recovery from internal faults; it introduces self-awareness features in the elements by encompassing reflection, self-control, planning and reasoning;
- An External/Global Control Loop to react to environmental changes and adapt the internal behavior, coordinating it with

Figure 3. Self-awareness and self-organization through autonomic control loops

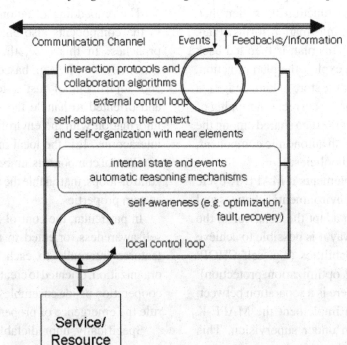

those of other elements according to information exchanged with them; it enables self-organization features for achieving the emergence of global properties/behavior through simple cooperative interactions (inspired by biological, social metaphors), and self-adaptation of the internal behavior to environmental changes.

A variety of architectural frameworks based on "self-regulating" autonomic components have been proposed (White et al., 2004; Liu & Parashar, 2004; XU et al., 2007) based on the common underlying idea of coupling service components with software components called "autonomic managers" in charge of regulating the functional and non-functional activities of components.

In Autonomia framework (Dong at al., 2003) the autonomic behavior of a system and its individual applications is handled by so-called mobile agents. Each mobile agent is responsible for monitoring a particular behavior of the system and for reacting to any changes accordingly.

A slightly different approach is provided by the AutoMate framework (Agarwal et al., 2006). Similar to Autonomia, autonomic behavior in the AutoMate framework is handled by the agents and is implemented in the form of first-order logic rules. Agents continuously process these rules and policies among themselves and perform the desired actions.

In (Jennings et al., 2007), FOCALE architecture is based on mapping business-level system constraints down to low-level process constraints in an approach called the policy continuum (Van der Meer, 2006). This policy-based approach for specifying autonomic system behavior allows network administrators to specify business-level policies for network management (using natural language), for example, defining different Internet connection bandwidth rates for different users, SLA, QoS policies etc.

The Autonomic Communication Element (ACE) model is described in (Manzalini, 2009).

ACEs can autonomously enter, execute in, and leave the ACE execution environment. In general, the behavior of autonomic elements is typically provided in relation to the high-level policies that define an element's original behavior (Parashar & Hariri, (2005). Within the ACE model, such policies (called plans) are specified through a number of states, along with the transitions that lead the ACE execution process from one state to another. Plans distinguish between the ACE's "regular" behavior, which is its behavior when no events undermine the ordinary execution occur, and the "special cases" that can occur during the plan execution process and which could affect the regular ACE execution process. If such occurrences are foreseen, the ACE behavior can be enhanced with rule modification specifying the circumstances under which the original behavior can be relinquished, along with the new behavioral directions to follow.

A very similar endeavor also characterizes several research efforts in the area of Multi-Agent Systems (Biegel & Cahill, 2004). Multi-agents represent (de facto) the types of autonomic components which are capable of self-regulating their activities in accordance with some specific individual goal(s) and, by cooperating and coordinating with each other, according to some global application goal. However, it is worth emphasizing that that Multi-Agents System does not imply an autonomic behavior per-se. At the level of internal structure, Belief Desire Intention (BDI) agent systems, as implemented in agent programming systems like Jadex, JACK or Jason or in the context of the Cortex project (Klein, 2008), propose the use of intelligent agents to deal with autonomic and context-aware components. At the core of this model there is a rule-based engine acting on the basis of an internal component state that is explicitly represented by means of facts and rules (Li et al., 2009, AFI (2012). At the level of multi-agent systems and their interactions, agents are generally expected to discover each other via specific agent-discovery services, and are supposed to be able to interact.

It should be mentioned that RTD activities on autonomic networking and self-managing networks have reached a maturity level, and so have started to move towards standardizing the architectural principles of the Self-Managing Future Internet. This is being accomplished in the Industry Specification Group (ISG) on Autonomic network engineering for the self-managing Future Internet (AFI), under the auspices of the European Telecommunications Standards Institute (ETSI). Specifically, the AFI architectural reference model is a set of fundamental design and operational principles, describing the functions, processes, and interfaces involved, and so it provides the Decision-making Elements (DEs) responsible for the autonomic management and control of network resources (Chiang et al., 2006).

Common to most of the proposed approaches (both those based on autonomic components and multi-agent systems) is the existence of a traditional middleware substrate to implement discovery and interactions among components or agents. On the other hand, none of the above approaches addresses the problem of globally re-thinking networks as complex environments with emerging properties.

FLEXIBLE AND PROGRAMMABLE NETWORKS

Internet has almost lost its initial end-to-end paradigm, which was simply forwarding packets across the network. In current IP networks, functions and services are processed in intermediate nodes which are not placed at the end-points. Current "ossification" of IP is creating limitations for Operators in the development and deployment of new network functionality, services, management policies and other elements which are essential to cope with the increasing complexity and dynamicity of future networks.

Launching a new network service today is complex and expensive, inhibiting the roll out of new revenue earnings. A process of simplification and automation needs to be initiated to speed up the rollout of new revenue earning services. Entities using network services and functionalities should be able to select and combine from a range of alternatives with varying performances and costs.

Future networks should also allow reducing operational (OPEX) and capital expenditures (CAPEX): OPEX could be reduced by easing human operators (i.e. limiting human mistakes, improving processes, etc) by automating management and configuration of equipment and network functionality; CAPEX savings could be achieved by reducing equipment costs and postponing network investments, through an optimized use of physical resources.

Emerging technologies and solutions as SDN and network function virtualization could contribute meeting above requirements. On the other hand, as mentioned, an increasing level of network complexity will make design and management highly challenging: traditional management and control approaches will no longer be applicable. This will involve introducing adaptive control and learning techniques (e.g. autonomic controls loops and cognitive features) and other methods empowering networks with ability to learn and to reason, which in turn involves observations of network states, planning, decisions and actions while taking into account optimization goals.

In summary, the direction is looking for highly flexible and programmable network architectures capable of meeting the challenging requirements of future Telco-ICT markets. There has been considerable interest and a large number of RTD initiatives in defining such network architectures.

Today, one of the main challenges is how exploiting the many different technical solutions that have proposed in recent years, and especially how accomplishing that in accordance with the dynamic requirements of Users, Operators and the market in general. The ideal solution(s) would allow innovative technical solutions, rewarded directly by the market (an essential encouragement for further investments). Ideally, future network infrastructure should be based on modular building blocks which can be view also as constrained optimization problem solvers: in this way it will be possible creating, programming, instantiating or migrating dynamically different types of functionalities and services as well as alternatives of the same. In other words this would also mean increasing the level of network self-organization by pursuing network-wide multi objective optimizations, by means of interacting CO solvers or controllers (Figure 4).

Network Decomposition and Orchestration

It is argued that future edge networks will be so pervasive and composed by a sheer number of resources that they will like large scale systems. As known, there are strict analogies between large scale systems and statistical mechanics. In this section we'll elaborate how statistical mechanics and bio-inspired principles can help us in understanding the basic laws governing future edge networks.

Statistical mechanics provides a framework for relating the microscopic properties of individual atoms or molecules to the macroscopic bulk properties of materials that can be observed in everyday life, therefore explaining thermodynamics as a

Figure 4. Self-organization achieved though interacting solvers of constrained optimization problems

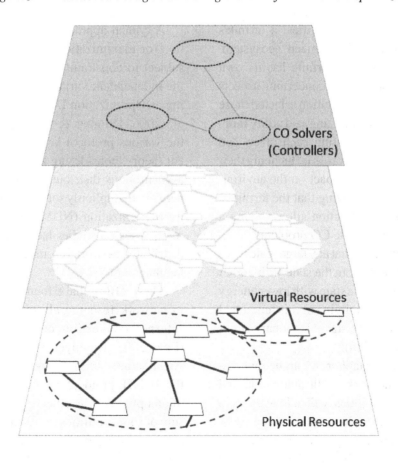

result of description of statistics and mechanics at the microscopic level. In other words provides a molecular-level interpretation of macroscopic thermodynamic quantities such as work, heat, free energy, and entropy. For example, the behavior of a gas (state equation) can be described at the microscopic level in terms of the position and velocity of each molecule, which appear as random processes. Local random behavior of the molecules causes the gas as a whole to solve a large scale constrained optimization problem.

Similarly the behavior of electrons in an electrical network can be described in terms of random walks. This simple description at the microscopic level leads to rather sophisticated behavior at the macroscopic level: pattern of potentials in a network of resistors is minimizing heat dissipation for a given level of current. Again this is like to say that the local random behavior of the electrons causes the network as a whole to solve a large scale constrained optimization problem.

Moving to small living entities, a termites colony can be seen self-organized ecosystem. We can imagine that each termite has its own utility functions (for example concerning aspects related its survivability): evolution selected those behaviors capable of maximizing said utility functions. Termites are interacting each other, and with the environment, thus cross influencing their behaviors and having an impact on the environment. Again this is like saying that the termites' behaviors and cross-interaction allow solving a global utility i.e. large scale CO problems.

In summary we argue that any large scale (eco) systems tends to move from the state with higher energy (higher cost) to the state with lower energy (lower cost), thus local minima of this functional are usually related to the stable stationary states (functional minimization).

Inspired by this metaphor, we argue that empowering future networks with autonomic and cognitive local capabilities will allow them to solve large scale constrained optimization problems. As an example, imagine an edge network

capable of self-organized learning, i.e., capable of learning from the environment and, through learning, capable of improving the performance. This without a Teacher, i.e., an Operator managing a network too complex. This means embedding into its nodes and devices autonomic, cognitive methods with a set of local rules, able to learn to compute input-output data mapping with desired actions or properties (local rules means rules capable of changing for example the "strength" of the interconnections of a node in the immediate neighborhood (moreover this would be in line with the Hebb's postulate of learning).

Maximize profits, minimize costs, minimize the loss are typical economics problems, which can be mathematically modelled as constrained optimization problems. It is argued that the same approach can be taken for designing and operating an highly flexible network architecture capable of self-adapting: i.e. solving network problems as constrained optimization.

A typical approach is looking for minimization (or maximization) of an objective function subject to constraints on the possible values of the independent variables. For example "Layering as Optimization Decomposition" (Chiang et al., 2006; Palomar & Chiang, 2006) integrates the various protocol layers into a single coherent theory, considering them as carrying out an asynchronous distributed computation over the network to implicitly solve a global Network Utility Maximization (NUM) problem. Since then, many research studies have been carried out on distributed network resource allocation using the language of NUM.

These efforts have found many applications in network resource allocation algorithms and Internet congestion control protocols, e.g., (Low, 2003; Kunniyur & Srikant, 2003, (La & Anantharam, 2002; Kelly, 1998). For example, the TCP/IP protocol can be seen as an example of an optimizer: its objective is to maximize the sum of source utilities (as functions of rates) with constraints on resources. In fact, each variant of a congestion control protocol can be seen as a distributed algorithm maximizing a particular utility function. The exact shape of the utility function can be reverse-engineered from the given protocol. Similarly, other recent results also show how to reverse engineer Border Gateway Protocols (BGPs) as a solution to the Stable Path Problem, and contention-based Medium Access Control (MAC) protocols as a game-theoretic selfish utility maximization.

Also cross-layer interactions can be characterized by viewing the process of network layering as the decomposition of a given NUM problem into many sub-problems. These sub-problems are then "combined together" by certain functions of the primal and dual variables (Palomar & Chiang, 2007).

We wish also defining a practical methodology, based on utility functions, for achieving both optimization and stability by means of a set of CO solvers, hereby called controllers. Practically, network self-organizing capabilities will be achieved through the exploitation of said controllers (CL) (Figure 5) spread across network layers.

The proposed methodology is based on a three-steps approach: 1) decompose networking and computing problems: this is required to develop and exploit the required set of controllers in charge of handling functionality (e.g. congestion control,

dynamic routing, scheduling, load balancing, resource optimization, etc.); 2) derive the controllers' utility functions: used to derive utility functions to be associated with the above controllers; each controller is seen as an optimizer whose objective is to maximize its utility, with the associated constraints; and 3) define and maximize an utility aggregated function: to derive the utility function to be associated with the network, which is an appropriate aggregation of the controllers' utility functions.

Revisiting the Concepts of Quality of Service

Cognition and autonomics can be used to improve the end-to-end performance objectives, for example in terms of resource management, Quality of Service (QoS), security, access control, etc. Normally, the effectiveness of said solutions depends on the adaptability of the underlying network elements and the capabilities of the cognitive and autonomic processes. In edge networks (both wireless and wired), however, ensuring QoS is a difficult problem because of its dynamic and unpredictable nature. The term soft QoS has been coined to express the idea of having QoS only during periods of combinatorial stability. Soft QoS differs from traditional QoS in that it only makes

Figure 5. Block diagram of a controller

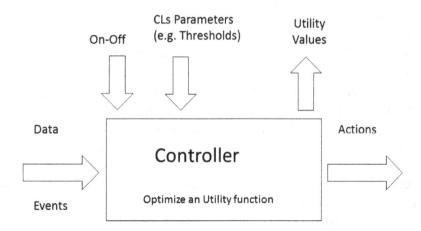

guarantees while the network dynamics are slower than the network update function. There several difficulties that researchers have to be solved to deal with end-to-end QoS problems in dynamic, complex environments.

We argue that concept of QoS has to be revisited in a network, as the edge one, characterized by different types of resources (storage, processing, sensing and communication related entities) and by a highly dynamic behavior of its elements.

One first reflection to consider is that each single constituent of the network is not (necessarily) stable, i.e., it can join and leave the network at any given instant. The topology of the network is variable because nodes aggregates in unpredictable ways. We can name this kind of edge networks ephemeral networks in order to give an idea of unpredictable behavior of each single constituent. In this contest a first notion of QoS can be defined in terms of a conservation principle: each constituent of an ephemeral network will put in place actions and strategies in order to get and maintain a minimum degree of connectivity. By degree of connectivity we mean a defined number of active connection between a specific nodes and its neighbors. Each node of an ephemeral network can be seen as a vertex v_i of a graph. The notation $\deg(v_i)$ denotes the number of links that connect v_i to its neighbors. Each single node in an ephemeral network will try to reach a minimal status characterized by the fact that $\deg(v_i) > 0$. In addition, the node will try to optimize its status by trying to reach a (optimal) status in which $\deg(v_i) = n$, where $n \in N$ and $n > 0$. The bigger is n the more the single node is connected and hence it will support a higher level of connectivity. In practical terms, each constituent node of an ephemeral network tries to reach be connected with n other nodes, the bigger is n and the more the node is connected. Hence each single node has several way to forward or receive data. One of the requirements (in terms of quality of service) for an ephemeral network is to be well connected, i.e., it should be highly probable to find a viable path

between any two possible nodes of the network. Wireless nodes will vary their power in order to reach a radius of connectivity that allows the communication with n other nodes. The higher the degree of nodes, the higher is the likelihood that the network will be fully connected. However, if n = n_t, where n_t is the total number of nodes of the ephemeral network, the network will be fully connected. This is a situation in which there is a direct connection, and hence an optimal path, between any two nodes. This is an optimal situation from a theoretical perspective, but in practice nodes should probably use their power in order to reach the maximum radius of connectivity, which can result in rapid battery exhaustion. One of the goal of a self-organizing ephemeral network is to reach an average degree of connectivity of nodes that guarantees a good connectedness of the network and does not overload each node. The number of n is the first parameter to determine in order to provide a minimal level of QoS. It should be noted that the concept of connectedness could be differently applied to the entire network. In those part of the network in which nodes are particularly dense the average connectedness value could sometimes exceed the goal number of n, while in other part of the network reaching the goal number n could be difficult and sometime even impossible (certain nodes will remain essentially leaf nodes).

Figure 6 represents the situation in which each node determines a radius r that allows connectivity with at least n = 3 nodes.

In ephemeral networks comprising different types of nodes, connectedness is only one of the properties that will influence the perceived Quality of Service. In fact, nodes can support connectivity, but also processing and storage. These capabilities can be used in order to compensate inadequacies in connectivity (and vice versa). For instance computation of functions is used in order to consume less bandwidth while forwarding relevant data to other nodes. A self-organizing ephemeral network will use its available capabilities in terms of connectivity, processing and

Figure 6. A network with deg(v_i) greater than three

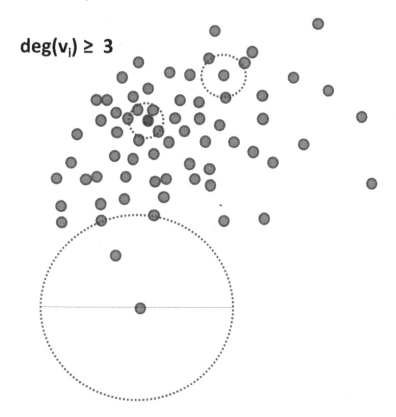

storage in order to achieve its goals. The goals of a self-organizing ephemeral network have to be stated in terms of non-functional requirements (e.g., make available to each node of the network an average of 1 Gb/s) and defining policies and simple algorithms that aims at reaching the goals.

There are two main settings in which an ephemeral network can operate: a) each node is essentially equal to all the others; there are some nodes that expose or offer more stable properties. These different settings can have an impact on how the ephemeral network reaches its goals. In the first situation each node should operate locally in order to support the global goal of the entire infrastructure: highly distributed policies for self-organization should occur essentially at each participating entity. This will guarantee that the network will cooperative work towards the (distributed) optimization of resources usage. In the second case, some nodes can take a coordinating

role and try to manage a sort of centralized view of the functioning of the infrastructure. These nodes can be thought as connected "poles" or kiosks in a smart environment. These entities will support a stable connectivity, they can provide for considerable processing and storage. Their goal could be to help the more dynamic nodes to reach the global goals of the ephemeral network by coordinating the allocation of resources. In other terms they act as "anchor nodes" and can implement optimization policies for the infrastructure (or a part of it). They are good candidate for being Brokers of dynamic resources. They could control the operation of these resources in order to provide the best possible arrangement of available resources in order to fulfil requirements of services and usage of the infrastructure.

Figure 7 shows the situation in which a node v_i needs some processing on data. It sends those data to the Anchor point A_1, that processes the

Figure 7. Example of scenario with nodes brokers of dynamic resources

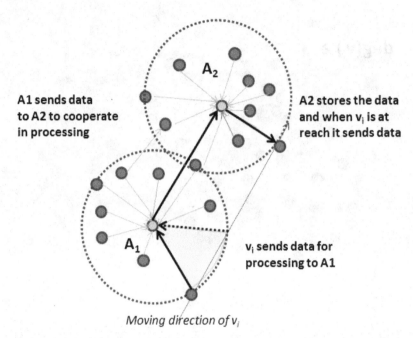

A1 sends data
to A2 to cooperate
in processing

A2 stores the data
and when v_i is at
reach it sends data

v_i sends data for
processing to A1

Moving direction of v_i

flow in cooperation with A_2 and then elaborated data are buffered in A_2. When v_i is at reach of A_2, processed data are returned to v_i.

It is important to stress out is that in edge networks made out of highly dynamic nodes, the concept of "density" could have a direct relationship with the possibility to provide a stable and performing infrastructure. When many nodes are close, the combination of processing, storage and connectivity achieved by the aggregation of constituents of the network could expose stable properties even if each individual is not stable at all. The determination of the values of $\deg(v_i) = n$ for which a change of state can be predicted (with huge impact on the quality of service) is still to be determined.

Further studies are needed in order to tackle these issues.

Optimization and Stability

Ensuring stability of a strategic asset like a Telco-ICT network is of paramount importance for most societies. In fact, instability in a network may have

pronounced primary effects jeopardizing the QoS and compromising the optimized use of resources.

The potential instability of an end-to-end path is a cross-layer issue: it may be linked to an undesired combination of diverse control and optimization mechanisms acting on either the underlying transport network or on the higher layers' components (e.g. flow admission control, TCP congestion control and dynamic routing).

The instability risks are already being experienced in today's networks (as well as in cloud computing infrastructures).

It has been widely demonstrated that even with the over-provisioning of resources, a network without an efficient flow admission control has instability regions that can lead to congestion collapse in certain configurations. Congestion control mechanisms represent another example of network stability measures. Currently available mechanisms (e.g. TCP Reno and Vegas) are large distributed control loops designed to ensure the stable congestion control of resources. However, these mechanisms are expected to be ill-suited, from a stability viewpoint, for future dynamic networks where transient devices and fluctuating capacity will potentially be much more present. Additional instability risks typical of any dynamically adaptive routing system, which can be (informally) defined as the quick change of network reachability and topology information, have a number of possible origins, including problems with connections, router failures, high levels of congestion, software configuration errors, transient physical and data link problems, and software bugs.

Earlier overviews of the state of the art concerning network stability issues offer other interesting examples. Starting from a simple model of a traditional network traffic dynamic system, (Ohira, Sawatari, 1998). showed that a phase transition point appears, separating the low-traffic phase (with no congestion) from the congestion phase as the packet creation rate increases. In (Sole, 2001), an enhanced model has exhibited nontrivial scaling properties close to the critical stability point, which reproduce some of the observed real Internet features. The possibility of phase transitions and meta-stability in various types of complex communication networks as well as the implication of these phenomena for network performance evaluation and control is discussed in (Marbukh, 2007). Specific cases include connection-oriented networks with dynamic routing, TCP/IP networks under random flow arrivals/departures, and multiservice wireless cellular networks. An investigation of the dynamics of traffic over scale-free networks (Wang, 2008) indicated the existence of the bi-stable state in traffic dynamics; specifically, that the capacity of the network has been quantified by the phase transition from a free flow state to a congestion state. Interestingly, (Ford, 2012) addresses the risk of instabilities in Cloud Computing infrastructures. That study points out some analogies between Cloud Computing infrastructures and complex systems and elaborates on the emergence of instabilities due to the unwanted coupling of several reactive mechanisms.

In summary we can argue that already in today's networks there are some potential risks of instabilities, but these risks are still limited and rather well-controlled.

If future networks architectures will be empowered with modular controllers pursuing network-wide multi objective optimizations, these risks of instabilities will dramatically increase, creating real threats for networks (which will become very complex, interconnected and dynamic, similar to natural ecosystems). These controllers have to be properly orchestrated to avoid unwanted couplings or interactions, potentially bringing non-linearity into the network behavior: in other words there is the

need to design and develop a methodology and practical approach for setting-up, configuring and tearing down sets with these multiple controllers in order to achieve both network optimization and stability (Manzalini, 2012). Figure 8 shows a methodology based on meta heuristics.

Use Case: Moving Dynamically Virtual Resources

This section presents a use case of a highly dynamic network in which it is possible for functionality and virtual resources to move across a physical infrastructure of combined IT resources (for virtual computing and storage) and network resources (virtual routers). This use case offers flexibility and programmability, but it poses several challenges, e.g. ensuring stability.

We assume that Virtual Machine (VM) and Virtual Router (VR) can be moved from one physical node to another (the physical node merely serves as the carrier substrate on which the actual virtual node operates).

A VR is a logical router (Schaffrath et al., 2009) that separates its functionality from the physical platform that hosts the entity, including mechanisms for management, configuration, monitoring and maintenance. Two VR solutions that allow logical routers to move among different physical platforms without causing network discontinuities and instabilities are proposed in (Wang, 2008) and (Agrawal, 2006).

Figure 8. Methodology for orchestrating multiple controllers in order to achieve both network optimization and stability

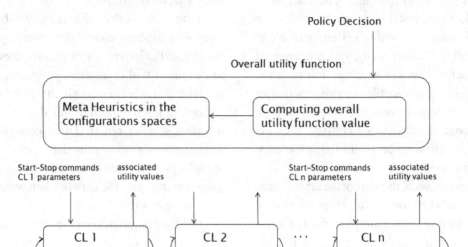

The dynamic provisioning of virtual resources (VMs and VRs) will allow load and traffic engineering to improve performance (e.g. limiting hotspots in IT resources) and to reduce power consumption in the routers' network. In other words, the size of the physical network can expand and contract according to load and traffic demand by idling or powering down nodes when they are not needed while having them ready to be activated to meet demand.

For example, in the case of hotspots in IT resources, operators can change the allocation or migration VMs to improve performance (e.g., the response time). At the same time, as the network traffic volume decreases, operators can move VRs to a smaller set of physical routers and shut down or 'hibernate' unneeded physical routers to save power. When the traffic starts to increase, physical routers can be brought up again and virtual routers can be migrated back accordingly.

It should be noted that although both control loops would be stable if operating alone, without a proper coordination, the combination of the two control loops may risk a positive feedback loop.

Analysis of this use case should be based on both forward and reverse engineering. In reverse engineering, the overall network utility function is implicitly determined by the two given control loops (moving VMs and VRs), and is to be discovered rather than designed. In forward engineering, the utility function must be properly selected (e.g. as a combination – sum or product -- of two sigmoid functions, one a function of response time, the other a function of the routers' energy consumption).

The utility function of the control-loop in charge of allocating or migrating VMs across multiple networks is based on optimizing a certain performance parameter (or set of parameters); for example, we may consider a function that indicates a decreasing utility as the response time increases (but any other functions could be considered depending on the required metrics). The control loop for moving VMs can be implemented with an algorithm.

The algorithm proceeds by considering the highest-loaded VM on the highest-loaded server and determines if it can be moved to the least-loaded physical server. The move is feasible only if that server has sufficient idle CPU to meet the desired resource allocation of the candidate VM.

If sufficient CPU is not available, then the algorithm examines the next least-loaded server and so on, until a match is found for the candidate VM. If no physical server can house the highest-loaded VM, then the algorithm moves on to the next-highest loaded VM and attempts to move it in a similar way. The process repeats until the utilization of all the resources on the physical server fall below their optimal thresholds.

The utility function of the control-loop in charge of migrating VRs to a smaller set of physical routers can be based on saving electrical power. The algorithm's objective function could be minimizing the overall CPU load for physical routers – depending on the traffic – in order to move the largest number of nodes into idle or sleeping states. The algorithm evaluates the heaviest physical routers and their nearest and lightest neighbor to exchange one or more virtual routers (Chabarek et al., 2008).

Regarding the energy savings, we utilized the data reported in [64]: the base router system (chassis, processor and switching fabric) consumes about 430W. It has 8 slots for line-cards and the average consumption of a line-card is about 70W. The overall power consumption is 990W when the router is operating at full load. We have assumed that the router consumes about 60% of its full load power consumption when it is idle (and from 10 to 20% when the node is in a sleeping state i.e., the router is switched off). For example, a line-card consumes 70W when working, 40W in an idle state. For simplicity, we assumed two states: full load and idle (i.e. hosting no VRs).

We now investigate how a critical situation can occur. Suppose during one minute a hot spot occurs in node 1. The VM control loop notices this and shifts some VM away from node 1 to node 2 in the next minute, while at the same time the VR control loop notices a traffic surge in node 1 and moves more VR to that node and reduces the number of VRs in node 2 (saving energy in node 2). While either of these actions alone would lead toward convergence, the two in combination cause overcompensation.

Therefore the two utility functions should not be maximized independently otherwise instabilities may occur. A global utility function should be addressed whose utility function is a combination of the above two functions. Optimization of the overall utility function means reaching a stable trade-off between response time and energy savings.

Figures 9 show an example of simulation results the migration of VM and VR, achieved through the two coordinated CL, allows reaching energy savings (about 23%) at the cost of an acceptable

Figure 9. Example of simulation results of the use case

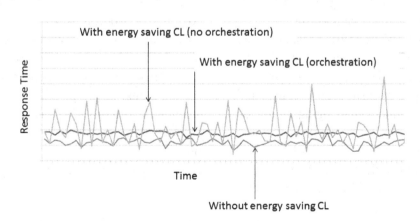

219

and controlled degradation of the response time of the IT servers. Importantly figure shows the occurrence of instabilities of the response time in case the two control loops are not orchestrated.

FUTURE RESEARCH DIRECTIONS

The analysis of the use case has just highlighted some of the potentialities enabled by a wide introduction of virtualization capabilities in IT and network nodes. Full exploitation of these potentialities will require fulfilling the challenging requirements about operating (in term of allocation, provisioning, migration, etc.) on ensembles VMs virtualizing network and IT resources: operations should be seamless, i.e., should have no (or very limited) impact on Users' QoE. Actually, VM migrations can be seen, at least, from two different perspectives. On one hand, there is the migration of VMs running an application (e.g. video streaming, interactive multi-media gaming): motivations for migrating a VM running an application could be intra- or inter-data center load balancing (e.g., avoiding performance degradations due to hot spots), or following Users' moving to other network attachment points (e.g. for QoE optimization). On the other hand, there is migration of VMs running a Virtual Router control plane (or any network function, fully developed in software): this might be even more challenging, especially when the migration is executed live (while the traffic is flowing in the network). Motivations could be traffic engineering (avoiding performance degradation due to congestion), other kind of network optimizations, energy savings, etc.

When virtualizing IT and network resources these two perspectives should be considered together, and, even more challenging, in a wide area context.

Normally the steps for moving VMs between two hosts in LAN are well established: 1) setting up the connectivity (e.g. layer-2 for intra-data center

operations) between the hosts; 2) transferring all disk state of the VM; 3) transferring the memory state of the VM to the target host as it continues running without interruption; 4) once the disk and memory states have been transferred, pausing the application for the final transition of memory and processor states to the target server. If all these steps are well understood in LAN environments, migrations over wide area connection poses new challenges. Constraints on bandwidth and latency of the networks connections will mainly impact steps 2 and 3. IP addressing will be an issue for step 4. These are the main open challenges.

In this direction, it will be important optimizing the performance parameters (e.g. total migration time and total downtime) of migrating a VM (running an applications characterized by a certain dirty page rate), with the network performance indicators (e.g. throughput, latency, etc). For example total migration time is roughly the number of dirty pages (depending on the VM workload) that should have been sent during the whole migration process divided by the available TCP bandwidth.

A complete analysis of these challenges is still missing and requires further RT&D activities.

Furthermore, Network Operators should be able to face the increasing complexity of management and control exacerbated by the needs of dynamic orchestration said virtual resources. This will require the integration of autonomic and cognitive capabilities within virtualization solutions. Future research directions in autonomic and cognitive networking should consider also how these technologies can provide solutions empowering software edge networks with self-organization capabilities. In particular, it appears interesting exploring the use of unsupervised machine learning techniques, such as Self-Organizing Maps (SOM), capable of mimicking how human perception functions and thus expected to be an adequate contribution to exploit network cognition.

CONCLUSION

Socio-economic drivers, technological advances and down-spiraling costs are steering the evolution of networks towards becoming a programmable environment of resources, interconnected dynamically by links, created and destroyed to serve multiple applications. Future networks will rely more and more on software, which will accelerate even more the pace of innovation (as it has been doing continuously in the computing and storage domains). This chapter has elaborated the vision of software networks at the edge as highly flexible and programmable environments, in which functionality is virtualized and run on a range of general purpose hardware: this allow dynamic migration, the instantiation of functionality in various locations in the network as required, without the need to exploit a new piece of equipment.

This evolution will transform the edge into a new business arena with multiple interacting sub-networks domains (operated by diverse private, public Players but even Users' Communities).

The reverse side of the coin is an increasing level of complexity: this creates the need to empower networks with autonomic and cognitive features (to ease and to limit human intervention), which in turn means increasing the capabilities of self-organization of the networks. It is argued that this can achieved by means of a set of interacting controllers capable of solving constrained optimization problems by optimizing aggregated utility functions. This chapter provided a brief overview of the state of the art of technologies enabling the proposed vision describes a use-case and concludes the next technical challenges to turn this vision in reality.

REFERENCES

AFI. (2012). *ETSI ISG autonomic network engineering for the self-managing future internet.* Retrieved December 10, 2012, from http://portal.etsi.org/afi

Agarwal, M., Bhat, V., Matossian, V., Putty, V., Schmidt, C., & Zhang, G. … Hariri, S. (2006). AutoMate: Enabling autonomic applications on the grid. In *Proceedings of the Autonomic Computing Workshop,* (pp. 48-57). IEEE.

Agrawal, M., Bailey, S., Greenberg, A., Pastor, J., Sebos, P., & Seshan, S. … Yates, J. (2006). *Towards a dynamic, manageable network edge.* Paper presented at ACM SIGCOMM Workshop on Internet Network Management. New York, NY.

Anderson, T., Peterson, L., Shenker, S., & Turner, J. (2005). Overcoming the internet impasse through virtualization. *IEEE Computer, 28*(4).

Biegel, G., & Cahill, V. (2004). A framework for developing mobile, context-aware applications. In *Proceedings of the International Conference on Pervasive Computing and Communications.* IEEE.

Bourse, D., Buljore, S., Delautre, A., Wiebke, T., Dillinger, M., & Brakensiek, J. … Alonistioti. (2003). The end-to-end reconfigurability (E2R) research. In *Proceedings of the SDR Forum Technical Conference.* Orlando, FL: SDR.

Bourse, D., & El-Khazen, K. (2005). End-to-end reconfigurability (E2R) research perspectives. *IEICE Transactions on Communications,* 4148 – 4157.

Bush, S. F., & Kulkarni, A. (2001). *Active networks and active network management: A proactive management framework.* New York: Kluwer Academic/Plenum Publishers.

Chabarek, J., Sommers, J., Barford, P., Estan, C., Tsiang, D., & Wright, S. (2008). Power awareness in network design and routing. [IEEE.]. *Proceedings - IEEE INFOCOM, 2008,* 457–465. doi:10.1109/INFOCOM.2008.93.

Chiang, M., Low, S. H., Calderbank, A. R., & Doyle, J. C. (2007). Layering as optimization decomposition: A mathematical theory of network architectures. *Proceedings of the IEEE, 95*(1), 255–312. doi:10.1109/JPROC.2006.887322.

Demestichas, P., Dimitrakopoloulos, G., Strassner, J., & Bourse, D. (2006). Introducing reconfigurability and cognitive network concepts in the wireless world. *IEEE Vehicular Technology Magazine*, *1*(1), 33–39.

Demestichas, P., Stavroulaki, V., Boscovic, D., Lee, A., & Strassner, J. (2006). m@ANGEL: Autonomic management platform for seamless cognitive connectivity to the mobile internet. *IEEE Communications Magazine*, *4*(6), 118–127. doi:10.1109/MCOM.2006.1668430.

Dong, S. (2004). *Methods for constrained optimization*. New York: Springer.

Dong, X., Hariri, S., Xue, L., Chen, H., Zhang, M., Pavuluri, S., & Rao, S. (2003). Autonomia: An autonomic computing environment. In *Proceedings of the IEEE International Conference on Performance, Computing, and Communications*. IEEE.

Fitzek, F., & Katz, M. (2006). *Cooperation in wireless networks: Principles and applications*. Berlin: Springer. doi:10.1007/1-4020-4711-8.

Fitzek, F., & Katz, M. (2007). *Cognitive wireless networks*. Berlin: Springer. doi:10.1007/978-1-4020-5979-7.

Ford, B. (2012). *Icebergs in the clouds: The other risks of cloud computing*. Retrieved December 10, 2012, from arXiv:1203.1979v1

Gelenbe, E., Xu, Z., & Seref, E. (1999). Cognitive packet networks. In *Proceedings of the 11th IEEE International Conference on Tools with Artificial Intelligence*, (pp. 47 – 54). IEEE.

Haykin, S. (2005). Cognitive radio: Brain-empowered wireless communications. *IEEE Journal on Selected Areas in Communications*, *23*, 201–220. doi:10.1109/JSAC.2004.839380.

Haykin, S. (2012). *Cognitive dynamic systems*. Cambridge, UK: Cambridge University Press.

Jennings, B., Van der Meer, S., Balasubramaniam, S., Botvich, D., Foghlu, M. O., Donnelly, W., & Strassner, J. (2007). Towards autonomic management of communications network. *IEEE Communications Magazine*, *45*(10), 112–121. doi:10.1109/MCOM.2007.4342833.

Kelly, F. P. (1997). Charging and rate control for elastic traffic. *European Transactions on Telecommunications*, *8*, 33–37. doi:10.1002/ett.4460080106.

Kelly, F. P., Maulloo, A., & Tan, D. (1998). Rate control in communication networks: Shadow prices, proportional fairness and stability. *The Journal of the Operational Research Society*, *49*, 237–252.

Kephart, J., & Chess, D. (2003). The vision of autonomic computing. *IEEE Computer*, *36*(1), 41–50. doi:10.1109/MC.2003.1160055.

Klein, C., Schmid, R., Leuxner, C., Sitou, W., & Spanfelner, B. (2008). A survey of context adaptation in autonomic computing. In *Proceedings of the International Conference on Autonomic and Autonomous Systems*. IEEE.

Kunniyur, S., & Srikant, R. (2003). End-to-end congestion control: Utility functions, random losses and ECN marks. *IEEE/ACM Transactions on Networking*, *10*(5), 689–702. doi:10.1109/TNET.2003.818183.

La, R. J., & Anantharam, V. (2002). Utility-based rate control in the Internet for elastic traffic. *IEEE/ACM Transactions on Networking*, *9*(2), 272–286. doi:10.1109/90.993307.

Lake, S. M. (2005). Cognitive networking with software programmable intelligent networks for wireless and wireline critical communications. In *Proceedings of the IEEE Military Communications Conference*, (pp. 1693 – 1699). IEEE.

Li, J., Powley, W., Martin, P., Wilson, K., & Craddock, C. (2009). A sensor-based approach to symptom recognition for autonomic systems. In *Proceedings of the International Conference on Autonomic and Autonomous Systems*. IEEE.

Liao, S., Wu, C., Yang, Q., Wang, B., & Jiang, M. (2011). A resource-efficient load balancing algorithm for network virtualization. *Chinese Journal of Electronics*, *20*(4).

Liu, H., & Parashar, M. (2004). Component-based programming model for autonomic applications. In *Proceedings of the International Conference on Autonomic Computing*, (pp. 10-17). IEEE.

Low, S. H. (2003). A duality model of TCP and queue management algorithms. *IEEE/ACM Transactions on Networking*, *11*(4), 525–536. doi:10.1109/TNET.2003.815297.

Manzalini, A. (2012). Mitigating systemic risks in future networks. In *Proceedings of the IEEE 17th International Workshop on Computer Aided Modeling and Design of Communication Links and Networks*. IEEE.

Manzalini, A., Zambonelli, F., Baresi, L., & Di Ferdinando, A. (2009). The CASCADAS framework for autonomic communications. In *Autonomic Communication*. Berlin: Springer-Verlag.

Marbukh, V. (2007). *Towards understanding of complex communication networks: Performance, phase transitions & control*. Sigmetrics Performance Evaluation Review.

McKeown, N. (2009). *Software-defined networking*. Paper presented at the 28th IEEE International Conference on Computer Communications. New York, NY.

Mitola, J. (2001). Cognitive radio for flexible mobile multimedia communications. *Mobile Networks and Applications*, *6*(5), 435–441. doi:10.1023/A:1011426600077.

NFV. (2012). *Network functions virtualisation white paper*. Retrieved December 10, 2012, http://portal.etsi.org/NFV/NFV_White_Paper.pdf

Ohira, T., & Sawatari, R. (1998). Phase transition in a computer network traffic model. *Physical Review E: Statistical Physics, Plasmas, Fluids, and Related Interdisciplinary Topics*, *58*, 193. doi:10.1103/PhysRevE.58.193.

Openstack. (2012). *Open source software for building private and public clouds*. Retrieved December 10, 2012, from http://www.openstack.org/

Palomar, D., & Chiang, M. (2007). *Alternative decompositions for distributed maximization of network utility: Framework and applications*. IEEE Transaction on Automatic Control.

Palomar, D. P., & Chiang, M. (2006). A tutorial on decomposition methods for network utility maximisation. *IEEE Journal on Selected Areas in Communications*, *24*(8), 1439–1451. doi:10.1109/JSAC.2006.879350.

Parashar, M., & Hariri, S. (2005). Autonomic computing: An overview. In *Unconventional Programming Paradigms*. Berlin: Springer-Verlag. doi:10.1007/11527800_20.

Raychaudhuri, D., Mandayam, N. B., Evans, J. B., Ewy, B. J., Seshan, S., & Steenkiste, P. (2006). CogNet: An architectural foundation for experimental cognitive radio networks within the future internet. In *Proceedings of ACM/IEEE MobiArch'06*, (pp. 11–16). ACM/IEEE.

Schaffrath, G., Werle, C., Papadimitriou, P., Feldmann, A., Bless, R., & Greenhalgh, A. ... Mathy, L. (2009). Network virtualization architecture: Proposal and initial prototype. In *Proceedings of the 1st ACM Workshop on Virtualized Infrastructure Systems and Architectures*. ACM.

Self-NET Project. (2007). *Self-management of cognitive future internet elements*. Retrieved December 10, 2012, from https://www.ict-selfnet.eu/

Sole, R. V. (2001). Information transfer and phase transitions in a model of internet traffic. *Physica, 289*(3-4), 595–605. doi:10.1016/S0378-4371(00)00536-7.

Srivastava, V., & Motani, M. (2005). Cross-layer design: A survey and the road ahead. *IEEE Communications Magazine, 43*(12), 112–119. doi:10.1109/MCOM.2005.1561928.

Sutton, P., Doyle, L. E., & Nolan, K. E. (2006). A reconfigurable platform for cognitive networks. In *Proceedings of the 1st International Conference on Cognitive Radio Oriented Wireless Networks and Communications*, (pp. 1 – 5). IEEE.

Thomas, R. W., Da Silva, L. A., & Mackenzie. (2005). Cognitive networks. In *Proceedings of IEEE DySPAN*, (pp. 352–60). IEEE.

Thomas, R. W., Friend, D. H., Da Silva, L. A., & Mackenzie, A. B. (2006). Cognitive networks: Adaptation and learning to achieve end-to-end performance objectives. *IEEE Communications Magazine, 44*(12), 51–57. doi:10.1109/MCOM.2006.273099.

Van der Meer, S., Davy, S., Davy, A., Carroll, S., Jennings, B., & Strassner, J. (2006). Autonomic networking: Prototype implementation of the policy continuum. In *Proceedings of the 1st Workshop on Broadband Convergence Networks*. IEEE.

Walsh, W. E., Tesauro, G., Kephart, J. O., & Das. (2004). Utility functions in autonomic systems. In *Proceedings of the International Conference on Autonomic Computing*, (pp. 70-77). IEEE.

Wang, B. H. (2008). Routing strategies in traffic network and phase transition in network traffic flow. *Pramana: Journal of Physics, 71*(2).

Wang, Y., Keller, E., Biskeborn, B., Van der Merwe, J., & Rexford, J. (2008). Virtual routers on the move: Live router migration as a network-management primitive. *SIGCOMM CCR, 38*(4), 231–242. doi:10.1145/1402946.1402985.

White, S. R., Hanson, J. E., Whalley, I., Chess, D. M., & Kephart, J. O. (2004). An architectural approach to autonomic computing. In *Proceedings of the International Conference on Autonomic Computing*. IEEE.

Winter, R., Schiller, J. H., Nikaein, N., & Bonnet, C. (2006). Crosstalk: Cross-layer decision support based on global knowledge. *IEEE Communications Magazine, 44*(1), 93–99. doi:10.1109/MCOM.2006.1580938.

Xu, J., Zhao, M., Fortes, J., Carpenter, R., & Yousif, M. (2007). On the use of fuzzy modeling in virtualized data center management. In *Proceedings of the 4th International Conference on Autonomic Computing*. IEEE.

ADDITIONAL READING

Anderson, J.A., & Rosenfeld. (Eds.). (1988). *Neurocomputing: Foundations of research*. Cambridge, UK: Cambridge.

Axelrod, R. (1977). *The complexity of cooperation: Agent-based models of competition and collaboration*. Princeton, NJ: Princeton Univ. Press.

CASCADAS. (2009). *ACE toolkit repository*. Retrieved December 10, 2012, from http://sourceforge.net/projects/acetoolkit/

Clark, D., Wroclawski, J., Sollins, K., & Braden, R. (2005). Tussle in cyberspace: Defining tomorrow's internet. *IEEE/ACM Transactions on Networking, 13*(3), 462–475. doi:10.1109/TNET.2005.850224.

Dobson, S., Denazis, S., Fernández, A., Gaiti, D., Gelenbe, E., & Massacci, F. et al. (2006). A survey of autonomic communications. *ACM Transactions on Autonomous and Adaptive Systems, 1*(2), 223–259. doi:10.1145/1186778.1186782.

Ferrari, L., Manzalini, A., Moiso, C., & Deussen, P. H. (2009). Highly distributed supervision for autonomic networks and services. In *Proceedings of the 5ᵗʰ Advanced International Conference on Telecommunications* (pp. 111-116). Washington, DC: IEEE Computer Society.

Friedman, R., Gavidia, D., Rodrigues, L., Viana, A. C., & Voulgaris, S. (2007). Gossiping on MANETs: The beauty and the beast. *SIGOPS Operative System Review, 41*(5), 67–74. doi:10.1145/1317379.1317390.

Hardin, G. (1968). The tragedy of the commons. *Science Magazine, 162*, 1243–1248. PMID:5699198.

Hoile, C., Wang, F., Bonsma, E., & Marrow, P. (2002). Core specification and experiments in DIET: A decentralised ecosystem-inspired mobile agent system. In *Proceedings of the 1ˢᵗ International Conference on Autonomous Agents and Multi-Agent Systems* (pp. 623-630). New York, NY: ACM.

Manzalini, A., Deussen, P. H., Nechifor, S., Mamei, M., Minerva, R., & Moiso, C. … Zambonelli, F. (2010). Self-optimized cognitive network of networks. *The Computer Journal*. doi: doi:10.1093/comjnl/bxq032.

Manzalini, A., Minerva, R., & Moiso, C. (2009). Exploiting P2P solutions in telecommunication service delivery platforms. In N. Antonopoulos, G. Exarchakos, M. Li, & A. Liotta (Eds.), Handbook of Research on P2P and Grid Systems for Service-Oriented Computing: Models, Methodologies, and Applications (pp. 937-955). Hershey, PA: IGI Global.

Matlin, M. W. (1998). *Cognition* (4th ed.). Orlando, FL: Harcourt Brace College Publishers.

Saffre, F., Tateson, R., Halloy, J., Shackleton, M., & Deneubourg, J. L. (2008). Aggregation dynamics in overlay networks and their implications for self-organized distributed applications. *The Computer Journal, 52*(4), 397–412. doi:10.1093/comjnl/bxn017.

Wang, Y. (2002). Keynote: On cognitive informatics. In *Proceedings of the 1st IEEE International Conference on Cognitive Informatics (ICCI'02)*. Calgary, Canada: IEEE CS Press.

Wang, Y. (2003a). Cognitive informatics: A new transdisciplinary research field. *Brain and Mind: A Transdisciplinary Journal of Neuroscience and Neurophilosophy, 4*(2), 115-127.

Wang, Y. (2003b). Keynote: Cognitive informatics models of software agent systems. In *Proceedings of the 1st International Conference on Agent-Based Technologies and Systems (ATS'03)*. Univ. of Calgary Press.

Wang, Y. (2009). On abstract intelligence: Toward a unified theory of natural, artificial, machinable, and computational intelligence. *International Journal of Software Science and Computational Intelligence, 1*(1), 1–18. doi:10.4018/jssci.2009010101.

KEY TERMS AND DEFINITIONS

Application Programmable Interface: A collection of specifications used to access a service, application, or program. Includes service calls, required parameters for each call, and the expected return values.

Ecosystem: A natural ecosystem is defined as a biological community of interacting organisms plus their physical environment. According to this metaphor, a business ecosystem is "the network of buyers, suppliers and makers of related products or services" plus the socio-economic environment, including the institutional and regulatory framework. Specifically, a service ecosystem is a shared environment, where several Players will share, use different types of resources and services up to the edge of the (wired and wireless) networks.

Edge Network: A network (wired and wireless) composed by a sheer number of cheap nodes and Users' devices (embedding communication, processing, and storage capabilities) at the edge of current networks, i.e., a few meters around the Users.

Network Functions Virtualization: It concerns the idea of developing network processing functions in software, running on standard hardware and that can be instantiated and moved in various locations in the network.

Network Operator: It is a traditional telecommunication operator owning both a network infrastructure (e.g., routers, switches, transport nodes) and a service delivery infrastructure (e.g., servers, data centers).

Quality of Service: It is a generic term referring to the level of quality of a certain service. QoS definition depends on the specific service quality parameters (e.g., jitter, delay, errors, interaction time, fault recovery time, service availability).

Self-Organization: It is a process where the organization of a system spontaneously emerges, without being controlled by the environment or an external supervising system.

Self-Organizing Map: It is a type of artificial neural network that is trained using unsupervised learning to produce a low-dimensional (typically two-dimensional), discretized representation of the input space of the training samples, called a map.

Software Defined Network: It is a network where the control and data planes are decoupled, network intelligence and state are logically centralized, and the underlying network infrastructure is abstracted from applications.

Virtual Machine: It is a software implementation of a machine (i.e. a computer) that executes programs like a physical machine.

Virtualization: It is the creation of a virtual version of an IT hardware platform, operating system (OS), storage device, or network resources.

Chapter 9
QoS Support in the Cognitive Radio Networks

Kiam Cheng How
Nanyang Technological University, Singapore

Maode Ma
Nanyang Technological University, Singapore

ABSTRACT

Wireless Mesh Networks (WMNs) are communications networks made up of radio nodes organized in a mesh topology. As a direct evolution from WMNs, the Cognitive Radio Networks (CRN) are similar to the WMNs in many ways. Correspondingly, CRNs are also expected to support delay sensitive and/or high bandwidth real-time streaming multimedia applications like live video streaming, VoIP (Voice-over-IP), video conferencing, online gaming, and so on. However, Quality-of-Service (QoS) provisioning in CRNs is very challenging due to various issues. In this chapter, issues that take place on different network layers, chiefly the physical, MAC (Medium Access Control), and network layer are examined. This chapter also studies and reviews existing proposals to tackle the challenging issue of QoS provisioning in CRNs. Based on these reviews, gaps are identified in existing proposals and some possible solutions are suggested. In the second part of the chapter, the authors look into how greater QoS provisioning capabilities are provided by two proposed routing protocols for CRNs utilizing a variety of techniques. A conclusion is provided at the last part of the chapter together with possible future research directions.

INTRODUCTION

The objective of this chapter is to examine existing medium access schemes and routing protocols that were proposed to meet the QoS requirements of broadband applications in CRNs. The motivation comes from the belief that even though it may not be possible to eliminate interference totally, performance improvement can be achieved by minimizing the effects of interference through the use of appropriate MAC layer, network layer or cross-layer protocols. We examine the different

DOI: 10.4018/978-1-4666-4189-1.ch009

Copyright © 2013, IGI Global. Copying or distributing in print or electronic forms without written permission of IGI Global is prohibited.

techniques that were utilized in existing schemes. These includes power control, rate control, multiple communication channels, cognitive radio and routing/cross-layer protocols that considers multiple network metrics like network topology, traffic level, noise level etc. By reviewing existing research literature, the chapter identifies inadequacy in terms of medium access control (MAC) and network layer solutions for QoS provisioning in CRNs. To address these gaps, the last part of the chapter look at two cognitive routing protocols that has the potential to tackle the challenging issue of QoS provisioning in CRNs through a cross-layer interaction across the three different networking layers, physical, MAC and network layer. These cognitive routing protocols are able to provide superior performance compared to existing protocols by considering a combination of different metrics like spectrum information, network topology, traffic pattern, interference and transmission properties like transmission power, modulation, rate etc.

BACKGROUND

The radio spectrum is a scarce and valuable resource. Due to the proliferation of diverse wireless communication systems, the unlicensed spectrum is becoming increasingly crowded.

Correspondingly, WMNs are also expected to have QoS support for delay sensitive and/or high bandwidth applications like live streaming multimedia, interactive video conferencing, online gaming, Internet TV and so on. In this chapter, QoS is defined as the ability to provide different priority to different applications, users, or data flows, or to guarantee a certain level of performance to a data flow. The performance of a data flow can be measured in terms of delay, throughput and packet loss. However, QoS provisioning in WMNs is very challenging due to various issues. These include physical layer issues such as fading or attenuation of a transmitted signal over the wireless medium which results in a loss of signal power at the receiver. Other factors include the dynamical changing of topology, capacity limitations, link variability and multi-hop communications. On the network layer, many existing dynamic routing protocols select paths based on only one criteria (shortest hops, delay etc), which do not take into account topology, interference or traffic pattern. This causes the traffic to flow through nodes that experience high interference and thus increases the occurrences of dropped packets and retransmissions.

Despite on-going research efforts, one key limitation to the performance of the WMNs is the interfering nature of wireless transmissions which degrades the network capacity. This is made worse, especially for the case of devices operating in the unlicensed spectrum where it is becoming increasingly crowded due to the proliferation of diverse wireless communication systems. The popularity of mobile wireless devices has also contributed to the increased utilisation of the unlicensed wireless spectrum. It is very commonplace nowadays to see people accessing popular Internet Websites or applications on the move. Popular examples of these applications include YouTube, Skype and Maple Story and so on.

The overcrowding of the unlicensed spectrum aggravates the interference issues which further reduces the performances of wireless devices. The interference is further exacerbated in CRNs where traffic takes multiple hops to reach the destination.

On the other hand, surveys (*FCC Spectrum Policy Task Force, FCC Report of the Spectrum Efficiency Working Group*, 2002) have shown that vast portions of the licensed spectrum remain underutilized across frequency, space and time. This development has presented new opportunities for improving the performance of WMNs as the underutilized spectrum can either be used to carry existing traffic, thus alleviating the interference problem on existing communication channels, or can be used to admit new traffic flows to increase network capacity.

Based on the software defined radio platform, Cognitive Radio (CR) (Mitola & Maguire, 1999) is a promising technology that can be used to sense and to access vacant channels dynamically. Particularly, CR based WMNs or Cognitive Radio Networks (CRNs) (Chowdhury & Akyildiz, Jan. 2008; Haykin, 2005) have gained much attention due to their capability to exploit frequency bands currently unoccupied for use. The set of frequency bands are also known as Spectrum Opportunity (SOP). The nodes in the CRNs communicate through dynamic channels and can be built upon physical or medium access techniques similar to those specified by existing standards such as IEEE 802.11, IEEE 802.15.4 and IEEE 802.16 (Sherman, Mody, Martinez, Rodriguez, & Reddy, 2008).

Notwithstanding the great potential, there are also pitfalls in the adoption of CR technology. In the following sections, we examined and reviewed existing proposals to tackle the challenging issue of QoS provisioning in CRNs. Based on these reviews, we identified gaps in existing proposals and suggest some possible solutions.

QOS SUPPORT AT PHYSICAL LAYER

CR was first proposed as a form of software radio. The idea is to configure the radio hardware through the use of software that allows the hardware to sense and to react to changes in the environment. According to the statistic of the Federal Communication Commission (FCC), temporal and geographical variations in the utilization of the assigned spectrum range from 15% to 85%. The limited available radio spectrum and the inefficiency in spectrum usage necessitate a new communication paradigm to exploit the existing spectrum dynamically. Thus, cognitive radio based wireless network (CRN) has been proposed to allow intelligent radios to provide unlicensed users with opportunistic access to the licensed bands without interfering with the existing users. In a CRN, a user can use spectrum sensing hardware

or software to sense idle spectrum, select the best channel and coordinate access to this channel with other users.

There are three CR modes (Goldsmith, Jafar, Maric, & Srinivasa, 2009), spectrum overlay, interweave and underlay. In spectrum overlay, the cognitive transmitter has prior knowledge of the primary users' codebooks and its messages. This can be obtained either through some publicized information or a periodical broadcast by the primary users. The information can then be exploited in a variety of ways to either cancel or mitigate the interference seen at both cognitive and primary users. The difficulty in this technique lies in the assumption that the primary users' message must be known at the cognitive transmitter when it begins its transmission as this may not be practical for an initial transmission.

In spectrum interweave, there exist temporary space-time frequency voids in the licensed band (spectrum hole) which can be exploited by the secondary users (SU) for its own communication. The SU must be able to monitor the radio spectrum periodically in order to detect spectrum holes that can be used for opportunistic transmission as these spectrum holes can change with time and geographic location. Because the SUs are basically transmitting on a license spectrum, the primary user (PU) may, at any time come back and take up the frequency bands currently available for secondary access. It simply implies that it is no longer valid to assume that the designated spectrum for secondary usage is fixed and always available. The lack of guaranteed resource availability is the primary reason for the difficulty in QoS provisioning in overlay CR systems.

The time-varying nature of the available resources in the spectrum interweave scenario can be mitigated through using spectrum underlay technique where simultaneous transmissions of primary and secondary systems are allowed. However, it means that the secondary transmitter must be very conservative in its output power so that the interferences introduced by the secondary system (SS) are below a certain threshold with regards to the primary system (PS). In this case, since the interference constraints in underlay systems are typically quite restrictive, SUs are limited to short range communications. While the underlay paradigm is most common in the license spectrum, it can also be used in unlicensed bands to provide different classes of service to different users (Goldsmith, et al., 2009). For both overlay and underlay CR systems, orthogonal frequency division multiplexing (OFDM) is particularly suitable as a potential transmission technology for overlay CR systems with its flexibility in filling spectral gaps within the PS (Weiss, Hillenbrand, Krohn, & Jondral, 2004).

To determine if a channel is occupied, direct sensing of the frequency band can be performed by using a matched filter or energy detector (Ghasemi & Sousa, Apr. 2008). However, due to fading or shadowing, sometimes it may not be possible to detect the primary transmitter. To solve the problem, cooperative detection has been proposed. Making use of sensing information from more nodes improves the accuracy of the transmitter detection. In (Ganesan, Li, Bing, & Li, Jan. 2008), the authors develop a fixed and a variable relay sensing scheme to leverage on the spatial diversity on the detection capabilities of CR networks. By using the cognitive users to sense the environment and then feeding the data to a central base station, the scheme is able to reduce the primary user detection time. This scheme is particularly suitable to be implemented in CRNs as it employs cognitive users distributed at various locations as relays to sense data and to improve detection capabilities.

The authors of (Hong, Sengupta, & Chandramouli, 23-27 May 2010) have also designed a cognitive radio prototype based on the IEEE 802.11 MAC air interface which can detect primary incumbents quickly with almost negligible sensing failure probability. In (Chowdhury & Akyildiz, Jan. 2008), the authors devised a scheme to allow nodes equipped with a single tuneable transceiver to monitor the primary channels while continuing operation in the secondary band. The monitoring is done by measuring the aggregated received power on a node and then isolating the leakage power for each transmitter. However it requires the mesh routers (MRs) to be aware of the location of other MRs which might not be feasible in the real-life implementation.

Once the vacant channels have been identified, new or existing traffic can be admitted to an available band according to the QoS requirements of the application. dynamic spectrum management (DSM) is performed to reconfigure operating parameters like transmission power, modulation or data rate to access the new frequency spectrum (Haykin, 2005). This help to reduce the node density per transmission channel and interference, thus improving the throughput and the delay. However, the time needed to access a new channel is non-trivial (Skalli, Ghosh, Das, Lenzini, & Conti, 2007) and thus requires judicious management.

QOS SUPPORT AT MAC LAYER

In the work (Wang, Wang, & Feng, 2011), the authors investigated the effects of the primary user reappearances on the QoS performance of spectrum management techniques. Due to the interruptions from the primary users, this causes multiple spectrum handoffs to take place for the secondary users which may have an adverse effect on the performance of secondary users. An analytical framework based on the pre-emptive resumption priority M/G/1 queuing theory that can incorporate various system parameters like spectrum sensing, spectrum decision, spectrum sharing, and spectrum mobility is developed. One of the important recommendations arising from the work suggests that an effective spectrum decision scheme should take into account of the interruptions from the primary users in addition to the traffic statistics of the primary and secondary users in order to evenly distribute the traffic loads of secondary users to candidate channels.

The authors of (Jia, Zhang, & Shen, 2008) have proposed a MAC protocol that utilizes multiple channels to improve the cognitive radio network throughput and overall spectrum utilization. The work takes into various constraints of CR used by SUs like sensing and transmission constraints, and PU constraints like maximum tolerable interference. The problem is formulated as an optimal stopping problem where both optimal solution and approximation rule are obtained. Simulation results show the good performance of SUs for various system configurations.

In the work done by (Salameh, Krunz, & Younis, 2009), the authors developed a distributed cognitive radio MAC (COMAC) protocol that enables unlicensed users to dynamically utilize the spectrum while limiting the interference on PUs. COMAC provides a statistical performance guarantee for PR users by limiting the fraction of the time during which the PUs' reception is negatively affected by CR transmissions. Based on the developed interference models, the authors derive a closed-form expression for the maximum allowable power for a CR transmission. Simulation results indicate that COMAC satisfies its target soft guarantees under different traffic loads and arbitrary user deployment scenarios. Results also show that exploiting the available channel information for the routing decisions can improve the end-to-end throughput of the CRN.

In (Timmers, Pollin, Dejonghe, Van der Perre, & Catthoor, 2010), the authors proposed a distributed multi-channel MAC (MMAC) protocol as enabler for CR networks. Different from existing work on MMAC protocols, which assumes that all nodes get equal access to the medium, the authors have developed a protocol with recognition of PUs in the network. The protocol is based on the timing structure from the PSM of IEEE 802.11 and is shown to improve performance by using spectral opportunities in licensed channels. It is shown to effectively protect the PUs from interference. For an active node, the scanning cost was shown to contribute only 5% to the total energy

cost. This cost is compensated by a reduction in overhearing cost to achieve a 40% decrease in global energy consumption.

(B. Wang & Zhao, 2010) studied the fair rate scheduling problem in an ad hoc cognitive wireless network with spectrum underlay. An optimal scheduling problem is formulated with an objective to achieve proportional fairness of the long-term average transmission rates among different links. As implementing the optimum scheduling is highly complex, two practical scheduling schemes are proposed. In the first scheme, transmission priorities of the links are determined by their potential contributions to an objective utility function, assuming there is no co-channel interference within the network. In the second scheme, transmission priorities are derived from both the objective function and interference to the primary network. The scheduling schemes can be implemented in a distributed manner in the ad hoc cognitive wireless network with limited assistance from the primary network. Results show that the proposed scheduling schemes can achieve high overall throughput and close-to-optimum fairness, and using exclusive regions can improve the system utility without compromising the fairness performance.

An optimal power loading algorithm for an OFDM-based CR system has been proposed in (Bansal, Hossain, & Bhargava, 2008). The loading scheme maximizes the downlink transmission capacity of the CR users while keeping the interference induced to the PUs below a specified threshold. A resource allocation framework has been presented for spectrum underlay in cognitive wireless networks (Le & Hossain, 2008). The authors consider both interference constraints for PUs and QoS constraints for SUs. Admission control algorithm were also designed for high network load conditions which are performed jointly with power control so that QoS requirements of all admitted SUs are satisfied while keeping the interference to PUs below the tolerable limit. The authors of (Bansal, Duval, & Gagnon, 16-19 May

2010) proposed a joint overlay and underlay power allocation scheme for OFDM-based CR system.

The authors of (Karipidis, Larsson, & Holmberg, 2009) have studied the NP-hard problem of scheduling and power control with QoS constraints and formulated the joint resource allocation problem as a mixed-integer programming (MIP) problem. In (Kang, Garg, Liang, & Zhang, 2010), the authors have considered a spectrum underlay network, where an OFDM-based CR system is allowed to share the subcarriers of an OFDMA-based PS. A new criterion referred to as rate loss constraint (RLC) in the form of an upper bound on the maximum rate loss of each primary user (PU) due to the CR transmission has been proposed to protect the PUs' transmission in the system.

Although the above mentioned research proposals are able to provide optimized solutions for resource allocation in CR systems, they have not taken into consideration of the effects of PU activities. One of the potential weaknesses of these schemes is that there is no consideration for the delay from the time that a channel is reclaimed or released by the PU until the time that the SU is aware of this. This delay could be due to channel sensing, adjustment of transmission parameters etc. required by the SU. As the availability of resources cannot be assumed in a dynamic environment which the CR systems operate, this means that the resource allocation performed by the above mentioned schemes could be based on already outdated information which is only valid in the past.

QOS SUPPORT AT NETWORK LAYER

In most routing protocols, the best route among nodes is considered to be the one with the best overall score. A score can be calculated in a number of ways, which includes contributions from individual nodes along the path. A combination of metrics can be used to derive the score, such as number of hops, delay, available capacity, etc. Most legacy wireless routing protocols such as AODV and DSR, etc. select paths based only on one criterion (shortest path, minimum delay etc.). The naive routing decisions based on a simple criterion cannot adequately capture the essence of the network dynamics and may perform poorly under certain conditions. For example, the shortest hop or the minimum delay route may route traffic through a node that is experiencing heavy noise and can result in a large number of packet losses or packet retransmissions.

Existing research work on CRNs has mainly focused on the physical layer and the issues of media access control (MAC) (Jia, et al., 2008; Salameh, et al., 2009). These approaches can provide optimal solutions in a single hop topology but are ineffective in multi-hop scenarios. For example, an optimized MAC protocol may provide the best joint-channel-power-rate assignment for a particular link. But such an assignment can be quite inefficient when considering the end-to-end path of a given flow possibly traversing several primary networks (PRNs). Thus, it is imperative to design appropriate cognitive multi-hop protocols capable of optimizing solutions over end-to-end paths (Khalife, Malouch, & Fdida, 2009).

There have been some research proposals to improve routing performance in WMNs by considering alternative routing criteria like interference (Wei & Zakhor, 2009), network topology (Feng, Hsu, & Lu, 2008) and traffic information (Wang, Liu, & Krishnaswamy, 2009), etc. They can generally provide much better performance compared to the legacy routing protocols.

As a direct evolution of the WMNs, the CRNs are similar to the WMNs in many ways. These similarities include physical layer constraints, layered protocol architecture, mesh network topology, support for multi-hop communications, and so on. Due to these similarities, many design principles applicable to WMN routing can also be applied to CRN routing. However, the issue of locating path is more complex in CRNs due to the inconsistency in frequency bands along with their respective parameters such as centre frequency and bandwidth. Additionally, in a CRN, the available channels at the source node may not be the same as the available channels at the destination node. Thus, a single path may have to be formed across multiple channels operating in different frequency bands and with different bandwidth. Furthermore, when a path is formed, any deviation in neighbourhood interference or primary user access will require the path to be recalculated and possibly dropped. In this instance, it would be necessary for a new route to be discovered and communication re-established. Due to these issues, routing protocols designed for CRNs tend to use on-demand routing schemes (Xiao & Hu, 2008).

In (Ma, Zheng, Ma, & Luo, 2008), the authors proposed an on-demand protocol for routing and channel assignment in multi-hop single transceiver CRN. The scheme quantifies the additional delay caused by channel switching and the corresponding reduction in back-off delay. Using this algorithm, a node can then determine whether to assign an existing channel to a flow, or if a new channel is needed. The simulation results show that the scheme is able to provide significant improvement in terms of network throughput compared to AODV in a network with high traffic load.

The authors of Delay motivated On-demand Routing Protocol (Cheng, Liu, Li, & Cheng, 2007) have proposed a joint interaction between on-demand routing and spectrum scheduling. The routing algorithm aims to minimize the sum of the switching delay, queuing delay and back-off delay for the considered route.

In (Pefkianakis, Wong, & Lu, 2008), the authors have proposed a spectrum-aware routing solution to opportunistically routes traffic across paths by considering the minimum aggregate throughput that can be supported by nodes along a path. A new routing metric, Path Spectrum Availability (PSA) is defined as the minimum aggregate throughput that can be supported by nodes along a path. However, this algorithm assumes that nodes

are able to communicate using several possibly disjoint channels at the same time. Furthermore, the routing algorithm works based on link state routing in which time is required to converge and to build a network topology map. As a result, this approach may not be suitable to the dynamic properties of the considered CRNs.

In the work performed by (Deng, Chen, He, & Tang, 2007), the authors proposed a routing scheme to identify paths that cause the least interference to the primary user. The path with the maximum interference margin among all possible paths is then selected that provides the best stability. In (Yang, Cheng, Liu, Yuan, & Cheng, 2008), the authors have proposed a framework of local coordination based routing and spectrum assignment algorithm. The algorithm is able to reduce multi-frequency switching delay at bottleneck nodes by redirecting flows to its neighbourhood. A capacity-based routing strategy for CRNs has been proposed in (Liu & Grace, 2008). A novel metric to measure the ability of a node to relay traffic has been used to determine the route. The scheme can improve performance by shifting the traffic to the edge of the network, away from the higher density regions. In (Ju & Evans, 2009), the authors have proposed a spectrum-aware routing scheme that uses the delay of the route request packet as the metric to assign the interface to a route, and throughput increment as the metric to select the path to route packets.

In (Talay & Altilar, 2009), the authors have designed a routing protocol that utilizes a link cost metric based on its spectrum usage history as opposed to its instantaneous state. Accordingly, a link's connectivity behavior is tracked and assigned a persistent cost metric that gets updated periodically to reflect its overall state. In this way, a route can be found between a source and destination even if there is no continuous end-to-end connectivity.

In (Liu & Grace, 2008), the authors proposed a capacity-based routing strategy for CRN. The scheme can improve performance by shifting traffic to the edge of the network, away from the higher density regions. However, the work did not consider issues like number of network interfaces needed, node synchronization issues and switching delay.

In (Filippini, Ekici, & Cesana, 2009), the proposed scheme aims to find the optimum path in CRNs using a novel metric that considers the maintenance cost of a route as channels or links that must be switched due to primary user activity. The authors have modelled the problem as an integer programming optimization model and have shown its polynomial time complexity in case of full knowledge of primary user activity. The authors in (Zhu, Akyildiz, & Kuo, 2008) have proposed a spectrum-tree based on-demand routing protocol. The routing metric combines the airtime cost of a link in conjunction with the available time of the spectrum.

QOS SUPPORT BY CROSS-LAYER APPROACH

One of the design principles for network protocols is that different protocol layers are required to be transparent from each other. This allows the protocol development and implementation to be scalable. However, this can lead to a less than optimum solution for as the lower layer solutions are only able to provide optimal solutions in a single hop topology but are ineffective in multi-hop scenarios. Thus a cross-layer approach has been proposed to allow the physical, MAC and network routing protocols to work collaboratively together for greater synergy.

One such example of a cross-layer approach was adopted by the work done by (Wu et al., 2006). The authors proposed a joint channel assignment and routing (JCAR) protocol in heterogeneous multi-radio multi-channel multi-hop wireless networks. A channel cost metric (CCM) was defined to capture the interference cost. JCAR then jointly coordinates the channel selection on each wireless interface and the route selection among interfaces

based on the CCM. The simulation results and experimental results through an experimental test bed demonstrated the efficacy and performance of the JCAR scheme.

In (Cheng, et al., 2007), the authors proposed a joint interaction between on-demand routing and spectrum scheduling. A delay-based metric was defined for evaluating the effectiveness of candidate routes. The path selection algorithm aims to minimize the sum of the switching delay, queuing delay and back-off delay for the considered route. Simulation results shows that the scheme can achieve a balance between assigning new frequency bands to allow simultaneous transmission and accommodating some nodes on one band to avoid expensive switching, thus achieves an overall optimal cumulative delay. However, the scheme requires that a common control channel be form between each node by using an additional dedicated wireless interface. This increases the cost, energy consumption and complexity of such a design. Furthermore, the common control channel can be overwhelmed by noise, thereby rendering it inoperable.

In (Zubow, Kurth, & Redlich, 2007), the authors devise a Multi-Channel Extremely Opportunistic Routing (MCExOR) for that makes use of multiple non overlapping RF channels in wireless multi-hop networks. The scheme improves the network performance by choosing the RF channel with the most promising candidate set for every transmission. However, the scheme requires nodes to discover neighbours through link probe packets. As MCExOR is a multi-channel protocol, link probes packets have to be broadcasted consecutively on different channels in a round robin manner. The combined switching delay can be non-trivial. To work around this, the authors assume a channel switching delay of 80μs which is several orders of magnitude lower than existing literature (Chandra & Bahl, 2004; Murray, Dixon, & Koziniec, 2007). However, even when a low channel switching delay is attainable, the total switching delay for multiple channels can be prohibitive, and therefore cannot be ignored.

The authors of (Su & Zhang, 2008) have proposed a cross-layer protocol which combines the spectrum sensing at physical layer with the packet scheduling at the MAC layer. The spectrum sensing strategies include both the random sensing and a negotiation-based sensing policy. For the random sensing policy, it is simpler to implement but it is not effective when the number of secondary users is smaller than the number of license users. The negotiation-based sensing policy is more effective but it incurs a higher overhead due to the message exchanges required. Once the vacant channels are identified, secondary users can then negotiate with one another to contend for the rights to transmit data packets over the vacant channels.

SOLUTIONS AND RECOMMENDATIONS

Many existing proposals for CRNs (Cheng, et al., 2007; Deng, et al., 2007; Ju & Evans, 2009; Liu & Grace, 2008; Ma, et al., 2008; Yang, et al., 2008) have assumed a static CRN that considers an available frequency band as a permanent resource indefinitely available during its activity. Clearly, such assumptions do not differ from those considered in multi-channel mesh networking. Other proposed solutions (Filippini, et al., 2009; Pefkianakis, et al., 2008; Talay & Altilar, 2009; Zhu, et al., 2008) have not considered the issue of QoS provisioning in CRNs.

In this section, we reviewed two routing protocols that addressed routing problem in CRNs by considering the dynamic property of the spectrum. The first protocol, the Opportunistic Service Differentiation Routing protocol (OSDRP) (How, Ma, & Qin, 2010, 2011) was proposed for the dynamic CRNs where the primary band can be exploited by a cognitive user while its intermittent availability can seriously affect the service offered for a CRN.

The second protocol, ROSA (Routing and Spectrum Allocation algorithm) was developed by (Ding, Melodia, Batalama, & Medley, 2009).

In this work, the authors proposed a cross-layer opportunistic spectrum access and dynamic routing algorithm for CRNs where local spectrum resources may change from time to time and hop-by-hop.

There are some similarities between the two schemes despite being very different in the approach taken to solve the QoS provisioning problem in CRNs. Both protocols make use of a common control channel that is used by all secondary users for spectrum access negotiation. This is done by equipping each node with a conventional wireless interface to form a common control channel among the nodes. Another similarity is that both protocols make use of transmit power control as a mean of QoS provisioning.

One of the key ideas of the OSDRP scheme is that the availability of SOP across the different PRNs which made up the CRN must be considered in the route selection to achieve an efficient end-to-end performance. To achieve this, OSDRP considers the availability of frequency band in addition to traditional metric like switching delay and queuing delay. It also combines the concept of Opportunistic Routing (OR) (Biswas & Morris, 2005) with Transmit Power Control (TPC) which can simplify the selection of candidate forwarding nodes (CFNs), improving the delivery ratios of CFNs and achieving service differentiation to traffic flows with different priorities.

In this work, the availability of the intermittent channel is modelled using the two-state semi-Markov model. The parameters used are the probability p of the primary user transmitting in the next time period and the mean duration of the channel as the exponential distribution with mean τ. The scheme also requires a power-control rate adaptive (M. Ma, Zheng, Zhang, Shao, & Fujise, 2006) scheme or a similar one to be implemented at the MAC layer. This allows the scheme to provide differentiated QoS through the use of adaptive modulation and coding technique. An overview of the OSDRP is shown in Figure 1.

Figure 1. OSDRP flow diagram

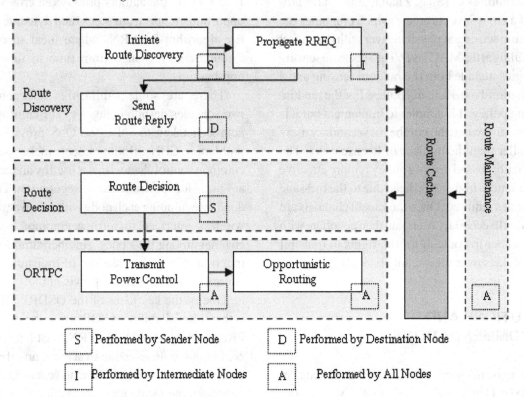

One of the distinguishing features of OSDRP is that it selects the minimum delay - maximum stability route to fulfil the required flow duration of the traffic flow. By monitoring and utilizing past channel histories to make predictions on future spectrum availability, the protocol selects a route that is most likely to be available for the entire duration of the transmission of the data. This helps to avoid costly route breakages and route re-discovery due to the re-appearance of the primary user.

Once a route has been selected, OR together with TPC is performed during the transmission to provide a differentiated service according to traffic priority. Different from existing OR techniques, OSDRP determines the next forwarding destination from the remaining hops along the selected route according to traffic priority. Due to the implementation of the power-control rate adaptive scheme at the MAC layer, higher priority packets will likely require a higher transmission power as compared to lower priority packets. Therefore, the high priority packet has a correspondingly higher chance of being received at a further away node as compared to the lower priority packets. OSDRP utilizes this fact to vary the range of the node selection. Thus, higher priority traffic will have a higher chance to skip intermediate nodes compared to lower priority traffic.

Using simulation experiments, the performance of OSDRP was compared with three other existing routing protocols, a modified version of DSR protocol (ccDSR) which uses traditional shortest-hop approach through the common control channel, the Delay motivated On-demand Routing Protocol (DORP) in (Cheng, et al., 2007) and the Spectrum Aware Mesh Routing Protocol (SAMER) in (Pefkianakis, et al., 2008).

Figure 2 shows the average number of hops for the different traffic priorities for values of p

Figure 2. Average number of hops vs. p

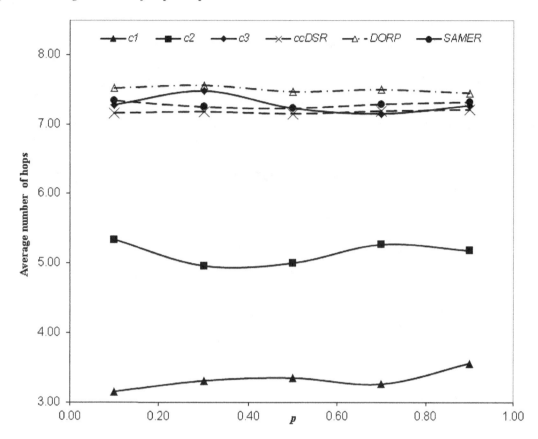

between 0.1 – 0.9. The average number of hops taken by the higher priority traffic is lower than those of other flows. The reason is because the higher transmission power coupled with larger OR candidate selection range for higher priority traffic enables it to skip more nodes along the route. The higher transmission power also makes it more likely for the opportunistic routing to succeed. The result also shows that the average number of hops is relatively constant under different values of p. It means that the "variability" of the SOP does not have any effect on the path length of the route taken by the traffic flows.

Figure 3 shows the average end-to-end delay for different traffic flows with values of p between 0.1 – 0.9. For the case of OSDRP, the higher priority traffic experiences less delay compared to the lower priority traffic. This is due to the less

number of intermediate nodes that the higher priority traffic has to go through in order to reach the destination. The result also shows that as the values of p increases, the end-to-end delay also increases. This is due to the increased likelihood of the primary user appearing that causes breakage in the end-to-end path. As a result, there is an increased channel switching and route rediscovery overhead. However, the delay for the higher priority traffic flows remains below 120ms which is acceptable for most multimedia broadband applications.

Figure 4 shows the total throughput for different schemes with values of p between 0.1 – 0.9. In the graph, we can see that OSDRP and SAMER provide the highest throughput. SAMER is able to perform better than OSDRP for p between 0.1 – 0.6 due to its ability to utilize multiple channels

Figure 3. Average end-to-end delay vs. p

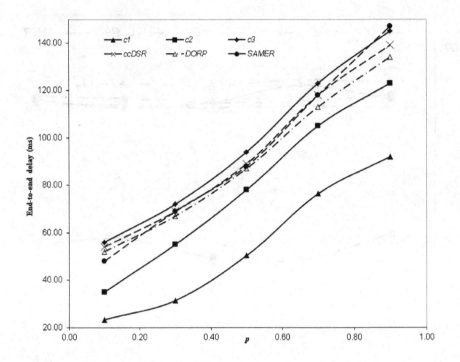

Figure 4. Total throughput vs. p

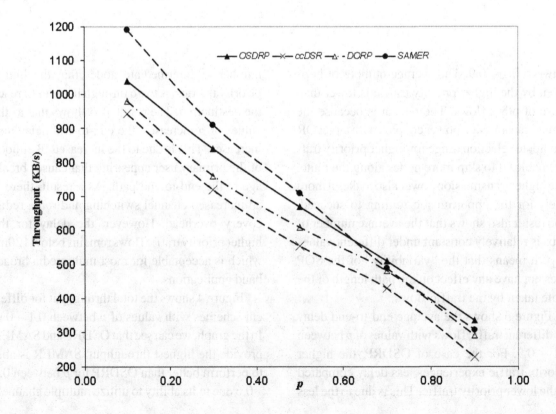

for concurrent transmissions. However, as p increases beyond 0.65, OSDRP starts to outperform SAMER as OSDRP is able to route traffic through nodes with greater spectrum stability.

To verify the effectiveness of the OSDRP notwithstanding the dynamic nature of the SOP, the authors designed a scenario where the route taken by OSDRP, DORP, ccDSR and SAMER all goes through the same primary network.

As τ decreases, the delays by DORP and ccDSR begin to increase due to the frequent changes in SOP in the primary network because both DORP and ccDSR are unable to react to the changes of SOP. Even though SAMER is designed primarily for CRNs, it also performs poorly because SAMER chooses its path via nodes with higher spectrum availability. For example, a node with N vacant channels will be favoured over another node with M vacant channels ($N>M$). However, it has not taken into full consideration of the statistical

behaviour of the spectrum usage. As a result, it is unable to react to the changes of τ. The delay experienced by OSDRP is quite constant despite the variation of τ, due to the selection of alternative routes through other primary networks when τ drops below certain level (see Figure 5).

Figure 6 shows the total throughput for different schemes when p is set to 0.5. As τ decreases, the throughputs by DORP, ccDSR and SAMER begin to decrease due to the frequent changes of SOP in the primary network. SAMER performs poorly when τ starts to drop below 30s, as it is unable to route traffic through nodes that can support the required traffic flow period of 30s. It further confirms that the duration of the availability of the communication channel needs to be taken into consideration when selecting a path. The throughput of OSDRP is quite constant despite the variation of τ, due to the selection of alterna-

Figure 5. Average end-to-end delay vs. τ for $p = 0.5$ (dynamic SOP scenario)

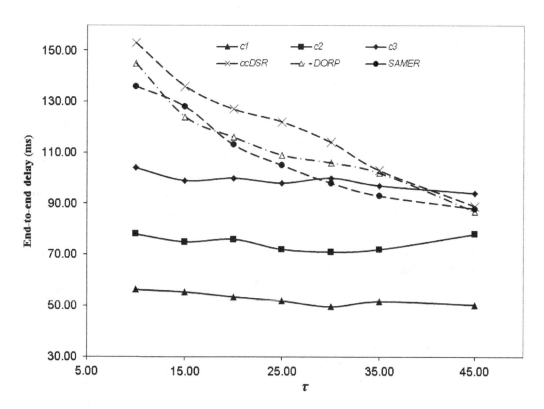

Figure 6. Total throughput vs. τ for p = 0.5 (dynamic SOP scenario)

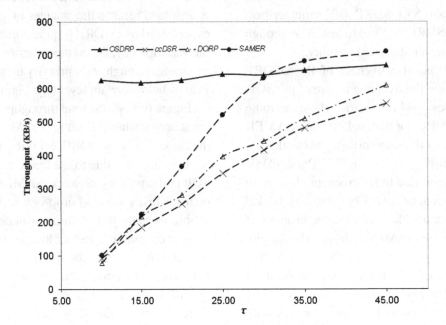

tive routes through other primary network when τ drops below a certain level.

From the above, it can be seen that the OSDRP scheme can provide a lower end-to-end delay and a higher throughput for the traffic flows at different levels of spectrum availability in various scenarios. The simulation results have also shown that the OSDRP can provide clear service differentiations for different traffic classes in various scenarios.

Similar to the OSDRP, ROSA also considers the existence of spectrum holes in the routing which is similar to the concept of SOP in the case of OS-DRP. At the same time, the routing in ROSA also considers the concept of spectrum utility which aims to maximize the capacity of the links. The spectrum utility function takes into consideration of processing gain, transmission loss, noise and power in order to provide BER (bit error rate) guarantees for both primary and secondary users. This is similar to the power allocation performed in the ROSA scheme where the algorithm tries to maximize the Shannon capacity of a link in a spectrum with a corresponding transmission power within the spectrum holes.

In order to sense the environmental parameters, ROSA makes use of a Collaborative Virtual Sensing (CVS) scheme. In this scheme, nodes share local sensing information with one another. These information are then combined with physical sensing information for better sensing results.

Once the sensing information has been obtained, ROSA opportunistically calculates the next hop. Depending upon queuing and spectrum dynamics, each packet may take a different path to the destination. The authors evaluated the performance of ROSA through the use of a discrete event simulator and the protocol was able to maximize the network throughput by performing joint routing, dynamic spectrum allocation, scheduling and transmit power control.

FUTURE RESEARCH DIRECTIONS

Currently, there has not been much work on the security aspect of cognitive radios. The implications of software-based radio implementation need to be rigorously investigated as it introduces an entirely new security loophole. One of the loopholes arises due to the fact that the behaviour of a CR is adapted according to its perceived environment from its own sensing observation or interaction with other CRs. One example of a CR specific attack can be launched easily against CR based networks by emulating the signals of primary users. Also known as the Primary User Emulation attack (Chen, Park, & Reed, 2008), this attack causes false alarm to the secondary network users and is a form of denial-of-service attack. There may also be various other types of security attacks made possible by this new security loophole. Researchers need to identify these attacks and proposed innovative solutions. One of the ideas that have been proposed utilizes the spectrum scanning and frequency agility associated with cognitive radios networks to allow secondary users to migrate away from frequency channels that are experiencing denial-of service attacks.

At the same time, additional research is required to develop a trusted security framework which can be easily implemented across different platforms and hardware architectures. There is a need to update existing schemes to support new authentication mechanisms that are needed in order to support the new trusted cognitive radio architecture.

Because CRNs are still in their infancy, there is a chance to make security part of the architecture of CRN from day one, instead of implementing security solutions as an afterthought. Doing this will require the effort and coordination of the research community.

CONCLUSION

The performance of CRNs and the issue of QoS provisioning can be tackled from the viewpoint of various network layers, physical, MAC and network layer. Physical layer factors like interference, fading, propagation losses are one of the reasons why the performance of wireless networks is not as good as their wired counterpart. In recent years,

the increased utilisation of the unlicensed wireless spectrum has also led to the aggravation of the interference issue in wireless networks. This has led to the development of opportunistic spectrum access through the use of Cognitive Radio.

Most routing protocols proposed for CRNs assume that all nodes operate in the same frequency spectrum, which is no longer valid in the CRN which utilizes multiple frequency bands. The issue of locating path is also more complex in CRNs due to the inconsistency in frequency bands along with their respective parameters such as centre frequency and bandwidth.

The review of the two Dynamic Cognitive Routing Protocols, OSDRP and ROSA has shown that a cross-layer approach that utilizes multi-metric routing with the consideration of spectrum availability information provided by the lower layers can improve performance over the traditional approach. At the same time, transmit power control and opportunistic routing techniques can also be integrated into the protocol design to provide differentiated service for different traffic priorities.

REFERENCES

Bansal, G., Duval, O., & Gagnon, F. (2010). *Joint overlay and underlay power allocation scheme for OFDM-based cognitive radio systems.* Paper presented at the IEEE 71st Vehicular Technology Conference (VTC 2010-Spring), 2010. New York, NY.

Bansal, G., Hossain, M. J., & Bhargava, V. K. (2008). Optimal and suboptimal power allocation schemes for OFDM-based cognitive radio systems. *IEEE Transactions on Wireless Communications*, *7*(11), 4710–4718. doi:10.1109/T-WC.2008.07091.

Biswas, S., & Morris, R. (2005). ExOR: Opportunistic multi-hop routing for wireless networks. *SIGCOMM Computer Communications Review*, *35*(4), 133–144. doi:10.1145/1090191.1080108.

Chandra, R., & Bahl, P. (2004). *MultiNet: Connecting to multiple IEEE 802.11 networks using a single wireless card*. Paper presented at the INFOCOM 2004. Twenty-third Annual Joint Conference of the IEEE Computer and Communications Societies. New York, NY.

Chen, R., Park, J.-M., & Reed, J. H. (2008). Defense against primary user emulation attacks in cognitive radio networks. *IEEE Journal on Selected Areas in Communications*, 26(1), 25–37. doi:10.1109/JSAC.2008.080104.

Cheng, G., Liu, W., Li, Y., & Cheng, W. (2007). *Joint on-demand routing and spectrum assignment in cognitive radio networks*. Paper presented at the IEEE ICC 2007. New York, NY.

Chowdhury, K. R., & Akyildiz, I. F. (2008). Cognitive wireless mesh networks with dynamic spectrum access. *IEEE Journal on Selected Areas in Communications*, 26(1), 168–181. doi:10.1109/JSAC.2008.080115.

Deng, S., Chen, J., He, H., & Tang, W. (2007). *Collaborative strategy for route and spectrum selection in cognitive radio networks*. Paper presented at the Future Generation Communication and Networking (FGCN 2007). New York, NY.

Ding, L., Melodia, T., Batalama, S., & Medley, M. J. (2009). *ROSA: Distributed joint routing and dynamic spectrum allocation in cognitive radio ad hoc networks*. Paper presented at the 12th ACM International Conference on Modeling, Analysis and Simulation of Wireless and Mobile Systems. New York, NY.

Feng, K.-T., Hsu, C.-H., & Lu, T.-E. (2008). Velocity-assisted predictive mobility and location-aware routing protocols for mobile ad hoc networks. *IEEE Transactions on Vehicular Technology*, 57(1), 448–464. doi:10.1109/TVT.2007.901897.

Filippini, I., Ekici, E., & Cesana, M. (2009). *Minimum maintenance cost routing in cognitive radio networks*. Paper presented at the IEEE MASS 2009. New York, NY.

Ganesan, G., Li, Y., Bing, B., & Li, S. (2008). Spatiotemporal sensing in cognitive radio networks. *IEEE Journal on Selected Areas in Communications*, 26(1), 5–12. doi:10.1109/JSAC.2008.080102.

Ghasemi, A., & Sousa, E. S. (2008). Spectrum sensing in cognitive radio networks: Requirements, challenges and design trade-offs. *IEEE Communications Magazine*, 46(4), 32–39. doi:10.1109/MCOM.2008.4481338.

Goldsmith, A., Jafar, S. A., Maric, I., & Srinivasa, S. (2009). Breaking spectrum gridlock with cognitive radios: An information theoretic perspective. *Proceedings of the IEEE*, 97(5), 894–914. doi:10.1109/JPROC.2009.2015717.

Haykin, S. (2005). Cognitive radio: Brain-empowered wireless communications. *IEEE Journal on Selected Areas in Communications*, 23(2), 201–220. doi:10.1109/JSAC.2004.839380.

Hong, K., Sengupta, S., & Chandramouli, R. (2010). *SpiderRadio: An incumbent sensing implementation for cognitive radio networking using IEEE 802.11 devices*. Paper presented at the IEEE International Conference on Communications (ICC), 2010. New York, NY.

How, K. C., Ma, M., & Qin, Y. (2010). *An opportunistic service differentiation routing protocol for cognitive radio networks*. Paper presented at the GLOBECOM 2010, IEEE Global Telecommunications Conference. New York, NY.

How, K. C., Ma, M., & Qin, Y. (2011). Routing and QoS provisioning in cognitive radio networks. *Computer Networks*, 55(1), 330–342. doi:10.1016/j.comnet.2010.09.008.

Jia, J., Zhang, Q., & Shen, X. (2008). HC-MAC: A hardware-constrained cognitive MAC for efficient spectrum management. *IEEE Journal on Selected Areas in Communications*, 26(1), 106–117. doi:10.1109/JSAC.2008.080110.

Ju, S., & Evans, J. B. (2009). *Spectrum-aware routing protocol for cognitive ad-hoc networks.* Paper presented at the IEEE Global Telecommunications Conference. New York, NY.

Kang, X., Garg, H., Liang, Y.-C., & Zhang, R. (2010). Optimal power allocation for OFDM-based cognitive radio with new primary transmission protection criteria. *IEEE Transactions on Wireless Communications, 9*(6), 2066–2075. doi:10.1109/TWC.2010.06.090912.

Karipidis, E., Larsson, E. G., & Holmberg, K. (2009). *Optimal scheduling and QoS power control for cognitive underlay networks.* Paper presented at the 3rd IEEE International Workshop on Computational Advances in Multi-Sensor Adaptive Processing (CAMSAP). New York, NY.

Khalife, H., Malouch, N., & Fdida, S. (2009). Multihop cognitive radio networks: To route or not to route. *IEEE Network, 23*(4), 20–25. doi:10.1109/MNET.2009.5191142.

Le, L. B., & Hossain, E. (2008). Resource allocation for spectrum underlay in cognitive radio networks. *IEEE Transactions on Wireless Communications, 7*(12), 5306–5315. doi:10.1109/TWC.2008.070890.

Liu, Y., & Grace, D. (2008). *Improving capacity for wireless ad hoc communications using cognitive routing.* Paper presented at the CrownCom 2008. New York, NY.

Ma, H., Zheng, L., Ma, X., & Luo, Y. (2008). *Spectrum aware routing for multi-hop cognitive radio networks with a single transceiver.* Paper presented at the 3rd International Conference on Cognitive Radio Oriented Wireless Networks and Communications. New York, NY.

Ma, M., Zheng, J., Zhang, Y., Shao, Z., & Fujise, M. (2006). *A power-controlled rate-adaptive MAC protocol to support differentiated service in wireless ad hoc networks.* Paper presented at the IEEE GLOBECOM 2006. New York, NY.

Mitola, J. III, & Maguire, G. Q. Jr. (1999). Cognitive radio: making software radios more personal. *IEEE Personal Communications, 6*(4), 13–18. doi:10.1109/98.788210.

Murray, D., Dixon, M., & Koziniec, T. (2007). *Scanning delays in 802.11 networks.* Paper presented at the 2007 International Conference on Next Generation Mobile Applications, Services and Technologies, 2007. NGMAST '07. New York, NY.

Pefkianakis, I., Wong, S. H. Y., & Lu, S. (2008). *SAMER: Spectrum aware mesh routing in cognitive radio networks.* Paper presented at the IEEE DySPAN 2008. New York, NY.

Salameh, H. A. B., Krunz, M. M., & Younis, O. (2009). MAC protocol for opportunistic cognitive radio networks with soft guarantees. *IEEE Transactions on Mobile Computing, 8*(10), 1339–1352. doi:10.1109/TMC.2009.19.

Sherman, M., Mody, A. N., Martinez, R., Rodriguez, C., & Reddy, R. (2008). IEEE standards supporting cognitive radio and networks, dynamic spectrum access, and coexistence. *IEEE Communications Magazine, 46*(7), 72–79. doi:10.1109/MCOM.2008.4557045.

Skalli, H., Ghosh, S., Das, S. K., Lenzini, L., & Conti, M. (2007). Channel assignment strategies for multiradio wireless mesh networks: Issues and solutions. *IEEE Communications Magazine, 45*(11), 86–95. doi:10.1109/MCOM.2007.4378326.

Su, H., & Zhang, X. (2008). Cross-layer based opportunistic MAC protocols for QoS provisionings over cognitive radio wireless networks. *IEEE Journal on Selected Areas in Communications, 26*(1), 118–129. doi:10.1109/JSAC.2008.080111.

Talay, A. C., & Altilar, D. T. (2009). *ROPCORN: Routing protocol for cognitive radio ad hoc networks.* Paper presented at the International Conference on Ultra Modern Telecommunications & Workshops. New York, NY.

Timmers, M., Pollin, S., Dejonghe, A., Van der Perre, L., & Catthoor, F. (2010). A distributed multichannel MAC protocol for multihop cognitive radio networks. *IEEE Transactions on Vehicular Technology, 59*(1), 446–459. doi:10.1109/TVT.2009.2029552.

Wang, B., & Zhao, D. (2010). Scheduling for long term proportional fairness in a cognitive wireless network with spectrum underlay. *IEEE Transactions on Wireless Communications, 9*(3), 1150–1158. doi:10.1109/TWC.2010.03.090802.

Wang, L.-C., Wang, C.-W., & Feng, K.-T. (2011). A queueing-theoretical framework for QoS-enhanced spectrum management in cognitive radio networks. *IEEE Wireless Communications, 18*(6), 18–26. doi:10.1109/MWC.2011.6108330.

Wang, W., Liu, X., & Krishnaswamy, D. (2009). Robust routing and scheduling in wireless mesh networks under dynamic traffic conditions. *IEEE Transactions on Mobile Computing, 8*(12), 1705–1717. doi:10.1109/TMC.2009.86.

Wei, W., & Zakhor, A. (2009). Interference aware multipath selection for video streaming in wireless ad hoc networks. *IEEE Transactions on Circuits and Systems for Video Technology, 19*(2), 165–178. doi:10.1109/TCSVT.2008.2009242.

Weiss, T., Hillenbrand, J., Krohn, A., & Jondral, F. K. (2004). *Mutual interference in OFDM-based spectrum pooling systems.* Paper presented at the IEEE 59th Vehicular Technology Conference, 2004. New York, NY.

Wu, H., Yang, F., Tan, K., Chen, J., Zhang, Q., & Zhang, Z. (2006). Distributed channel assignment and routing in multiradio multichannel multihop wireless networks. *IEEE Journal on Selected Areas in Communications, 24*(11), 1972–1983. doi:10.1109/JSAC.2006.881638.

Xiao, Y., & Hu, F. (2008). *Cognitive radio networks.* Boca Raton, FL: CRC Press. doi:10.1201/9781420064216.

Yang, Z., Cheng, G., Liu, W., Yuan, W., & Cheng, W. (2008). Local coordination based routing and spectrum assignment in multi-hop cognitive radio networks. *Mobile Networking Applications, 13*(1-2), 67–81. doi:10.1007/s11036-008-0025-9.

Zhu, G.-M., Akyildiz, I. F., & Kuo, G.-S. (2008). *STOD-RP: A spectrum-tree based on-demand routing protocol for multi-hop cognitive radio networks.* Paper presented at the IEEE Global Telecommunications Conference. New York, NY.

Zubow, A., Kurth, M., & Redlich, J. P. (2007). *An opportunistic cross-layer protocol for multichannel wireless networks.* Paper presented at the IEEE PIMRC 2007. New York, NY.

ADDITIONAL READING

Akyildiz, I., Lee, W.-Y., & Chowdhury, K. (2009a). Spectrum management in cognitive radio ad hoc networks. *IEEE Network, 23*(4), 6–12. doi:10.1109/MNET.2009.5191140.

Akyildiz, I. F., Lee, W.-Y., & Chowdhury, K. R. (2009b). CRAHNs: Cognitive radio ad hoc networks. *Ad Hoc Networks, 7*(5), 810–836. doi:10.1016/j.adhoc.2009.01.001.

Benveniste, M. (2008). *A distributed QoS MAC protocol for wireless mesh.* Paper presented at the Second International Conference on Sensor Technologies and Applications. New York, NY.

Cheng, H. T., & Zhuang, W. (2009). Novel packet-level resource allocation with effective QoS provisioning for wireless mesh networks. *IEEE Transactions on Wireless Communications, 8*(2), 694–700. doi:10.1109/TWC.2009.080739.

Cheng, X., Mohapatra, P., Lee, S.-J., & Banerjee, S. (2008). *MARIA: Interference-aware admission control and QoS routing in wireless mesh networks.* Paper presented at the IEEE International Conference on Communications. New York, NY.

Haykin, S., & Setoodeh, P. (2009). Robust transmit power control for cognitive radio. *Proceedings of the IEEE, 97*(5), 915–939. doi:10.1109/JPROC.2009.2015718.

Haykin, S., Thomson, D. J., & Reed, J. H. (2009). Spectrum sensing for cognitive radio. *Proceedings of the IEEE, 97*(5), 849–877. doi:10.1109/JPROC.2009.2015711.

How, K. C., Ma, M., & Qin, Y. (2012). A MAC-layer QoS provisioning protocol for cognitive radio networks. *Wireless Personal Communications, 65*(1), 203–222. doi:10.1007/s11277-011-0245-3.

Hu, H., Zhang, Y., & Chen, H.-H. (2008). An effective QoS differentiation scheme for wireless mesh networks. *IEEE Network, 22*(1), 66–73. doi:10.1109/MNET.2008.4435905.

Huang, J.-H., Wang, L.-C., & Chang, C.-J. (2008). QoS provisioning in a scalable wireless mesh network for intelligent transportation systems. *IEEE Transactions on Vehicular Technology, 57*(5), 3121–3135. doi:10.1109/TVT.2008.918701.

Lee, J., Liao, W., Chen, J.-M., & Lee, H.-H. (2009). A practical QoS solution to voice over IP in IEEE 802.11 WLANs. *IEEE Communications Magazine, 47*(4), 111–117. doi:10.1109/MCOM.2009.4907416.

Romdhani, L., & Bonnet, C. (2008). *Cross-layer QoS routing framework for wireless mesh networks*. Paper presented at the Fourth International Conference on Wireless and Mobile Communications. New York, NY.

Song, H., & Lin, X. (2008). *A group based MAC protocol for QoS provisioning in cognitive radio networks*. Paper presented at the 11th IEEE Singapore International Conference on Communication Systems. New York, NY.

Wang, L.-C., Chen, A., & Wei, D. S. L. (2007). *A cognitive MAC protocol for QoS provisioning in overlaying ad hoc networks*. Paper presented at the 4th IEEE Consumer Communications and Networking Conference. New York, NY.

Zhang, B., & Mouftah, H. T. (2005). QoS routing for wireless ad hoc networks: Problems, algorithms, and protocols. *IEEE Communications Magazine, 43*(10), 110–117. doi:10.1109/MCOM.2005.1522133.

Zhao, L., Wu, J. Y., Zhang, H., & Zhang, J. (2008). Integrated quality-of-service differentiation over IEEE 802.11 wireless LANs. *IET Communications, 2*(2), 329–335. doi:10.1049/iet-com:20070048.

KEY TERMS AND DEFINITIONS

Cognitive Radio: A cognitive radio is a transceiver which automatically detects available channels in wireless spectrum and accordingly changes its transmission or reception parameters.

Medium Access Control: In the seven-layer OSI model of computer networking, medium access control data communication protocol is a sub-layer of the data link layer.

Quality-of-Service: The quality of service refers to performance aspects of computer networks that allow the transport of traffic with special requirements like delay and throughput.

Routing Protocol: A routing protocol specifies how routers communicate with each other, disseminating information that enables them to select routes between any two nodes on a computer network.

Wireless Mesh Networks: A wireless mesh network is a communications network made up of radio nodes organized in a mesh topology.

Chapter 10
On the Performance of Transport Control Protocol in Cognitive Radio Networks

Yogesh Kondareddy
Cisco Systems, USA

Alireza Babaei
Virginia Tech, USA

Prathima Agrawal
Auburn University, USA

ABSTRACT

Transmission Control Protocol (TCP) is the most commonly used transport protocol on the Internet. All indications assure that it will be an integral part of the future Internetworks. In this chapter, the authors present how regular TCP, which was designed for wired networks, is not suitable for dynamic spectrum access networks. They develop an analytical model to estimate the TCP throughput of dynamic spectrum access networks. Dynamic spectrum access networks deal with opportunistic spectrum access leading to greater utilization of the spectrum. The extent of utilization depends on the primary user's traffic and also on the way the spectrum is accessed by the primary and secondary users. The proposed model considers primary and secondary user traffic in estimating the TCP throughput by modeling the spectrum access using continuous-time Markov chains, thus providing more insight on effect of dynamic spectrum access on TCP performance than the existing models.

1. INTRODUCTION

Radio spectrum allocation has traditionally been controlled rigorously by regulatory authorities through licensing processes. All countries have their own regulatory bodies, though regional regulators do exist. In the U.S., these spectrum-related regulations are done by the Federal Communications Commission (FCC). Spectrum has long been allocated in a first-come, first-served manner. Recent measurements indicate a substantial under-utilization of radio spectrum which is

DOI: 10.4018/978-1-4666-4189-1.ch010

Copyright © 2013, IGI Global. Copying or distributing in print or electronic forms without written permission of IGI Global is prohibited.

a consequence of static spectrum assignment. According to the FCC (FCC, 2003), temporal and geographical variations in the utilization of the assigned spectrum range from 15% to 85% (Akyildiz, Lee, Vuran & Mohanty, 2006). If radios could somehow use a portion of this unutilized spectrum without causing interference, then, there would be more room to operate and exploit. Such an idea relates to a broader concept of *Dynamic Spectrum Access* and is depicted in Figure 1 as was shown in (Akyildiz, Lee, Vuran & Mohanty, 2006). This figure shows a three-dimensional model of radio communication in which a device communicates in a finite band of frequency (called a channel in general) for a certain period of time and using a prescribed amount of power (regulated by FCC). Among such bands/channels of operation, those channels which are unused for a certain period of time are considered vacant and are referred to as *spectrum holes* or *spectrum opportunities*[1] (Zhao & Sadler, 2007).

The key technology which enables radio devices to shift their frequency of operation on demand to utilize the spectrum opportunities is called Software-defined Radio (Mitola & Maguire, 2001). A software-defined radio system is a radio communication system where components that are typically implemented in hardware (e.g. mixers, filters, amplifiers, modulators or de-

modulators, etc.) are instead implemented using software on embedded computing devices or on personal computers (Dillinger, Madani & Alonistioti, 2003). A more ambitious goal is to have a wireless device that is smart enough to analyze the radio environment and decide for itself the best spectral band and protocol at the lowest level of power consumption. Such a device has been called "Cognitive Radio". Cognitive radio represents a significant paradigm change in spectrum regulation and usage, from exclusive use by licensed users, also called primary users (PUs), to dynamic spectrum access by secondary users (SUs) and their coexistence with PUs. A network consisting of cognitive radios is called a Cognitive Radio Network (CRN). CRNs are opportunistic networks. The basic premise of these networks is that the owner of a licensed spectrum will not be using the spectrum always. Hence, this unused and licensed spectrum can be utilized on a non-interfering basis by other users who have a need for the same.

TCP is the most commonly used transport layer protocol used by most of the applications running on Internet. All indications assure that it will be an integral part of the future Internetworks. In a TCP connection, the transmitter uses an adaptive window based transmission strategy. The number of unacknowledged TCP segments cannot

Figure 1. Dynamic spectrum access concept

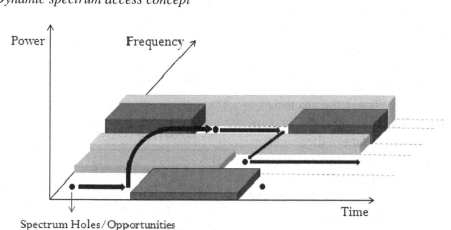

be more than the TCP *window size* (W_{max}) which can be adjusted by either the sender or the receiver based on the available buffers or the congestion. The transmitter, therefore, does not allow more than W_{max} unacknowledged packets outstanding at any given time. By adaptively changing the size of congestion window, TCP can control the flow of data based on the level of congestion in the network while the level of congestion is estimated through indicators like delay or packet loss.

TCP was designed and optimized primarily for wired networks. In wired media, the bit error rate is negligible and consequently it is safe to assume that, with a high probability, the packet loss is due to the congestion in the network. TCP reacts to the packet loss by shrinking its transmission (congestion) window size and initiating the congestion control and avoidance mechanisms. In a wireless environment, on the other hand, packets may get lost due to both congestion and corruption of the physical medium and as a result, many presumptions made by TCP may not apply. It is, therefore, a known fact that TCP is inherently inefficient in wireless environments and results in dramatic throughput degradation (Tian, Xu & Ansari, 2005).

TCP performance becomes even worse in cognitive radio networks for the following reasons:

- **Dynamic Topology:** A cognitive radio must relinquish its currently used channel once a primary user reclaims the channel back. If possible, the cognitive radio must choose another channel from the pool of available channels. Cognitive radios, therefore, dynamically change the channels on which they operate. As the channel of communication changes, some of the neighbors who were reachable on the previous channel might not be reachable on the current channel and vice versa. As a result the network topology changes with changes in frequency of operation resulting in route failures and packet loss.

- **Heterogeneity:** Different channels may support different transmission ranges, data rates and delay characteristics. Therefore, changes on the operating channels may also incur abrupt behavioral changes on TCP connections.

- **Spectrum-Handoff Delay:** In opportunistic spectrum access networks, a secondary user is forced to vacate the channels when the primary user of the respective channel becomes active. This is called *forced termination* (Zhu, Shen & Yum, 2007). The secondary user may then shift to another available channel and recover from that state. This is called *spectrum handoff*. Thus, the secondary users are serviced when the channels are free resulting in higher utilization of the spectrum. For each transition from one channel to another channel due to the PU's activity, there is a delay involved in the transition called *Spectrum-Handoff delay*.

All these factors decrease the predictability of the cause of transit-delay and subsequent packet loss on the network. The time latency during channel hand-off in cognitive networks might cause the TCP round trip timer to time out. TCP will wrongly recognize the delays and losses due to the above factors as network congestion and immediately take steps to reduce the congestion window size knowing not the cause of packet delay. This reduces the efficiency of the protocol in such environments.

2. BACKGROUND

There has been very few research focusing on the study and improvement of TCP in Dynamic spectrum access networks (See e.g., Kumar & Shin, 2012 and Luo, Yu, Ji & Lung, 2010). (Akyildiz,

Lee, Vuran & Mohanty, 2007) and (Kyasanur & Vaidya, 2005) discuss the transport layer design issues in such networks. Slingerland, Pawelczak, Prasad, Lo & Hekmat study the performance of different TCP flavors over dynamic spectrum access links using simulations. The proposed analytical model does not consider the effect of primary and secondary user's activity. It assumes the presence of a primary user and the effect of detection error is studied. In this chapter, we consider a more realistic scenario and modify the analytical model proposed in (Slingerland, Pawelczak, Prasad, Lo & Hekmat, 2005) to incorporate the effect of PU and SU traffic on the TCP performance. The PU and SU traffic are modeled using Markov chain and the blocking probability of the SUs is calculated. The obtained results will provide insight on the performance of TCP in a realistic dynamic spectrum access scenario.

Markov chains were used to model dynamic spectrum access networks in (Zhu, Shen & Yum, 2007; Tang, Chew, Ong & Haldar, 2006; Xing, Chandramouli, Mangold & Sai Shankar, 2006a; Xing, Chandramouli, Mangold & Sai Shankar, 2005b; Raspopovic, Thompson & Chandra, 2005). Some of these works do not capture the important details of dynamic spectrum access networks and some are too complex to be considered for just the throughput study in this chapter. Tang, Chew, Ong & Haldar propose a Markov model, but their model does not allow for the secondary users to reoccupy another free channel once it has been forced to vacate from a channel and considers the call to be completely dropped. The *spectrum hand-off* capability of the cognitive radio is thus not modeled in this work. Zhu, Shen & Yum try to reduce the forced termination of the secondary radios at the cost of increased blocking probability by reserving some of the channels for primary user access only. Both of these papers discuss on the optimal reservation of the channels for primary users to reduce the dropping probability and *forced termination* when in-fact these states

can be totally avoided with *spectrum hand-off* capability of a cognitive radio. Analysis in (Xing, Chandramouli, Mangold & Sai Shankar, 2006a; Xing, Chandramouli, Mangold & Sai Shankar, 2005b; Raspopovic, Thompson & Chandra, 2005; Capar, Martoyo, Weiss, Jondral, 2002), does not consider prioritized primary users. (Wang, Ji & Liu, 2007a; Wang, Ji & Liu, 2007b) propose Markov models to study secondary user contention and obtain fairness among them in a resource sharing environment. In this chapter the Markov model proposed in (Tang, Chew, Ong & Haldar, 2006) which is sufficiently accurate for this work, has been modified to accommodate the *spectrum hand-off* capability to capture the dynamic nature of the networks.

3. SYSTEM MODEL

The system consists of a Base Station (BS), a group of prioritized primary users and opportunistic secondary users as shown in Figure 2. There are a total of N channels in the system. The BS and the SUs scan their radio environment and maintain the information on the availability of channels with a certain confidence level (IEEE, 2007). The detection process is logically performed by a *Scanning Subsystem* of the Link Layer (SSLL) (Slingerland, Pawelczak, Prasad, Lo & Hekmat, 2005). The signal received by the SSLL from the PU is affected by noise only, i.e. fading and multi-path effects are not considered.

When a SU wants to start a communication it sends a request to the BS on a control channel which is dedicated for exchange of control information. After the BS acknowledges an end-to-end communication link is established at the transport layer. Once the communication link has been established, data segments flow to network layer and then to the data link layer.

At the link layer, the free channels are contended for on a frame-by-frame basis. Channels

Figure 2. Dynamic spectrum access with three SUs and two PUs

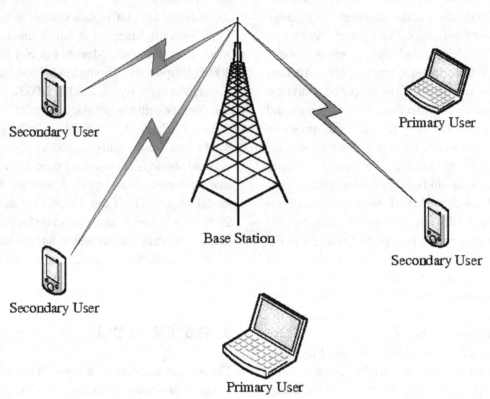

Secondary User

Primary User

Base Station

Secondary User

Secondary User

Primary User

are scanned periodically after fixed intervals (Pawelczak, Janssen & Prasad, 2006). This period of observing the channel is called *scanning phase* (SP). It is assumed that the SUs and the BS can scan the complete bandwidth one time in each SP. If a free channel was detected in the *scanning phase*, *the channel access phase* (CAP) follows during which the buffered frames are forwarded to the destination. TCP packets are secured by a Link Layer (LL) Stop and Wait ARQ mechanism (Cianca, Prasad, De Sanctis, De Luise, Antonini, Teotino & Ruggieri, 2005).

If there was no free channel (a blocked state) during the *scanning phase* the SSLL has to wait for the next SP to scan for a spectrum opportunity. The length of the *scanning phase*, T_i and *channel access phase*, T_o is not necessarily equal, but is the same for individual cycles. The *scanning phase* is not negligible when compared to *channel access phase* in dynamic spectrum access networks. The following derivations are assumed for the TCP steady state, i.e. a long lasting TCP connection with an infinite source of data. The scanning cycles are shown in Figure 3.

Figure 3. Scanning cycles used by the SSLL

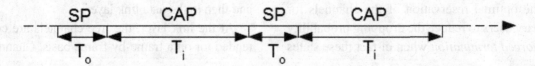

4. ANALYTICAL MODEL FOR TCP THROUGHPUT ESTIMATION

In this section, we will develop an analytical model to determine the TCP throughput of the SUs in the presence of PUs traffic and detection errors. If we do not take congestion related TCP packet loss into account, and assume a wireless link of infinite accessible capacity, the maximum throughput TCP can achieve depends only on the packet loss probability, segment size and RTT (Mathis, Semke, Mahdavi & Ott, 1997). The simple SQRT model for estimating maximum achievable TCP throughput or ('bandwidth') B is shown below. Though there are other TCP throughput analytical models (Padhye, Firoiu, Towsley & Kurose, 2000; Chen, Bu, Ammar & Towsley, 2006), we have chosen this formula since it is simple and sufficiently accurate model of TCP:

$$B = \frac{MSS}{RTT} \sqrt{\frac{3}{2p}}. \tag{1}$$

The parameters in the above equation are as follows:

- MSS is TCP segment size.
- p is the packet error probability. It can be computed as:

$$p = 1 - p_c^{N_F} \tag{2}$$

where p_c denotes the probability of correct frame reception at LL after at most $n_{\max}$ retransmissions. This can be written in a compact form as:

$$p_c = \left(1 - p_e\right) \sum_{i=0}^{n_{\max}} p_e^i = 1 - p_e^{n_{\max}+1} \tag{3}$$

where p_e denotes the LL frame error rate (FER). Here, we assume that the probability of LL frame error is uniformly distributed over all frames.

- RTT is the TCP packet round-trip time. RTT in the given network scenario can be formulated as (Slingerland, Pawelczak, Prasad, Lo & Hekmat, 2005):

$$RTT = 2T_{sr} + nT_p N_F + T_o + T_w \tag{4}$$

where

- T_{sr} denotes one-way packet delivery time (including transmission, propagation, packet queuing and processing delay).
- n is the average number of LL frame retransmissions. The average number of LL frame retransmissions is given as:

$$n = (1 - p_e) \sum_{i=1}^{n_{\max}-1} ip_e^i + n_{\max} p_e^{n_{\max}} \tag{5}$$

where $n_{\max}$ is the maximum number of retransmissions of one LL frame.

- N_F is the number of LL frames per TCP packet.
- T_p is the delay of the ARQ protocol, introduced by LL frame retransmissions.
- T_o is the channel observation time or the scanning time.
- T_w is the average delay that a packet incurs when either channel is not available or an improper decision is made by the scanner. In this chapter, we are concerned with the delay (T_w) caused due to the unavailability of the channels and detection errors which is derived below.

4.1. Estimation of Wait Time (T_w)

In each individual scan, either of the following events will increase the RTT by an inter-scanning interval of T_i :

1. A spectrum opportunity may be available or not based on the primary user's traffic. If there is no channel available then the user has to wait until the next scan interval (S) by waiting T_i seconds.
2. When a channel is available, a decision on the availability of the channel may result in an error, thus detecting that the channel is not available.

The average time a TCP packet must wait to gain access to the channel is given by T_w. We have

$$T_w = \lim_{n \to \infty} \sum_{k=1}^{n} \left[p_b + p_f(1 - p_b) \right]^k T_i$$
$$= \frac{T_i \left[p_b + p_f(1 - p_b) \right]}{1 - \left[p_b + p_f(1 - p_b) \right]} \qquad (6)$$

where,

$$p_f = \frac{\Gamma\left(WT_0, \dfrac{\nu}{2} \right)}{\Gamma(WT_0)} \qquad (7)$$

is the probability of false alarm, i.e. misinterpretation of a free channel as occupied and p_b is the blocking probability which means that that no channel is free. W is the bandwidth of the PU channel, ν is the threshold of the energy detector, and $\Gamma(., .)$ and $\Gamma(.)$ are upper incomplete gamma and gamma functions, respectively (Digham, Alouini & Simon, 2007; Pawelczak, Janssen & Prasad, 2006). The model proposed by Pawelczak, Janssen & Prasad assumes the absence of PUs. Our model considers PU traffic and takes

the effect of probability of detecting the PU on a DSA link, limiting the probability of introducing interference to the PU system by the DSA device.

4.2. Markov Model to Determine Blocking Probability

In this sub-section a Markov model to determine the blocking probability of SU frames is discussed. There are a total of N channels available for both secondary and primary users. Each channel is assumed to be of equal bandwidth. The PUs traffic in each channel is assumed to follow an ON/OFF pattern. A channel can be accessed by a SU if it is not being occupied by any PU. In this model it is assumed that both the PUs and SUs access the channels randomly. This is explained with the help of Figure 4. In this figure, there are a total of five channels of which two are occupied by PUs and one by an SU. When a new SU arrives, as shown in Figure 4a, it chooses a random free channel. A PU can choose any random channel and as shown in Figure 4b, if it chooses a secondary occupied channel, the SU jumps to a different free channel. If there is no other channel available, the SU's service is dropped as shown in Figure 4c. An SU cannot use a channel if it does not have an opportunity to do so as shown in Figure 4c.

There are four states in this model of which we are aiming to calculate the probability of the blocking state. The states are explained from the point of view of secondary users since the chapter focuses on the study of capacity of SUs.

- **Blocking State:** When all channels are occupied and no incoming traffic can be accommodated into the system, then the SU is said to be in Blocked state. On the occurrence of such an event, the SUs have to wait for the next *scanning phase* to scan for a spectrum opportunity.
- **Dropping State and Transition State:** When the primary user of a channel returns during the transmission of the SU's frame, the frame will be corrupted due to inter-

Figure 4. Random access in five channels

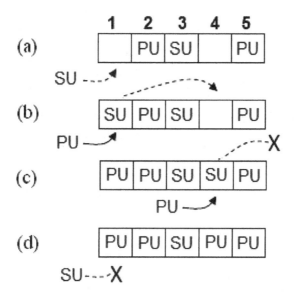

ruption. This is considered as collision by the link layer and a retransmission is attempted. Though the probability of occurrence of this event is very low due to the small frame transmission period, it is still considered in model for the sake of accuracy in calculating the blocking probability, p_b.

- **Non-Blocking State:** A secondary user is considered to be in this state if its frame has been transmitted successfully without being interrupted by a PU on that channel.

The Markov model for spectrum access with spectrum hand-off is explained in Figure 5. The PU's and SU's traffic are assumed to follow Poisson arrival processes with mean rates λ_p and λ_s respectively. They have a negative exponential service time distribution with mean rate $\dfrac{1}{\mu_p}$ and $\dfrac{1}{\mu_s}$ respectively. The numbers i, j, k represent the number of PUs, SUs and the type of state of the secondary user, respectively. Spectrum hand-off is accounted, for example, by letting the state

$(1, 1, 1)$ back to $(1, 2, 0)$ and not dropping it. If it were dropped then it has to be sent to $(1, 1, 0)$. $P(i, j, k)$ denotes the steady-state probability of state (i, j, k).

The balance equations as well as the equations for dropping and blocking probabilities are as follows (See Kondareddy & Agrawal, 2009 for more details in derivation of balance equations):

For $i = 0, \quad 0 \leq j \leq N-1, \quad k = 0,$

$$\begin{aligned}
\left[j\mu_s + i\mu_p + \lambda_s + \lambda_p \right] P(i, j, k) = \\
\delta\lambda_s P(i, j-1, k) + (j+1)\mu_s P(i, j+1, k) + \\
(i+1)\mu_p P(i+1, j, k)
\end{aligned} \tag{8}$$

where $\delta = 0$ for $j = 0$ and $\delta = 1$ for $j \neq 0$.

For $i \neq 0, \quad i + j \leq (N-1), \quad k = 0,$

$$\begin{aligned}
\left[j\mu_s + i\mu_p + \lambda_s + \lambda_p \right] P(i, j, k) = \\
\delta\lambda_s P(i, j-1, k) + (j+1)\mu_s P(i, j+1, k) + \\
\left(\frac{N-i-j}{N-i} \right) \lambda_p P(i-1, j, k) \\
+(i+1)\mu_p P(i+1, j, 0) + \delta P(i, j-1, k+1)
\end{aligned} \tag{9}$$

where $\delta = 0$ for $j = 0$ and $\delta = 1$ for $j \neq 0$.

For $k = i = 0$, $\quad j = N$,

$$\left[j\mu_s + \lambda_s + \lambda_p \right] P(i,j,k) = \\ \lambda_s P(i, j-1, k) + P(i, j, k+2) \tag{10}$$

For $i \neq 0 \neq N$, $\quad i + j = N$, $\quad k = 0$,

$$\left[\lambda_p + \lambda_s + i\mu_p + j\mu_s \right] P(i,j,k) = \\ \lambda_s P(i, j-1, k) + P(i, j, k+2) + \\ \left(\frac{N-i-j}{N-i} \right) \lambda_p P(i-1, j, k) + P(i, j-1, k+1) \\ + P(i, j, k+3) \lambda_s P(i, j-1, k) + \\ P(i, j, k+2) + \left(\frac{N-i-j}{N-i} \right) \lambda_p P(i-1, j, k) \\ + P(i, j-1, k+1) + P(i, j, k+3) \tag{11}$$

For $j = 0$, $\quad i = N$, $\quad k = 0$,

$$\left[j\mu_p + \lambda_s \right] P(i,j,k) = \\ P(i, j, k+3) + P(i, j, k+2) + \lambda_p P(i-1, j, k) \tag{12}$$

For $i + j = N$, $\quad k = 2$,

$$P(i,j,k) = \lambda_s P(i, j, k-2) \tag{13}$$

For $k = 1$, $\quad i + j \leq N$, $\quad 1 \leq i \leq N-1$,

$$P(i,j,k) = \lambda_p \left(\frac{j}{N-i} \right) P(i-1, j+1, k-1) \tag{14}$$

For $k = 1$, $\quad i + j = N$, $\quad i \neq 0$,

$$P(i,j,k) = \lambda_p P(i-1, j+1, k-3) \tag{15}$$

Equations (8)-(12) correspond to the non-blocking states. Equation (13) corresponds to the blocked states. Equation (14) corresponds to the

transition states and (15) to the dropping states. Note that we must have

$$\sum_{i=0}^{N} \sum_{j=0}^{N} \sum_{k=0}^{2} P(i,j,k) = 1$$

The dropping probability is given by the equation:

$$P_D = \sum_{i=1}^{N} \sum_{j=0, i+j=N}^{N} P(i, j, 2).$$

The blocking probability is by the equation:

$$P_B = \sum_{i=1}^{N} \sum_{j=0, i+j=N}^{N} P(i, j, 3).$$

Figure 6 shows the variation of blocking probability as a function of PU's arrival rate, λ_p. It can be observed that the dropping probability increases with increase in PU's arrival rate and with decrease in total number of channels, N. The value of blocking probability, p_b obtained using this Markov model will be used in the calculation of T_w in Equation (6). In the next section TCP throughput of SUs is studied using this analytical model.

5. RESULTS AND ANALYSIS

In this section the impact of primary and secondary user traffic as well as number of channels and scanning time on TCP throughput is studied using the proposed analytical model.

Figure 7 shows the variation of TCP throughput as a function of scanning time T_o. PU and SU traffic is maintained constant. *No scan* means that it is a perfect detection. It can be observed that throughput decreases with increase in the scan time. The impact of an incorrect detection

Figure 5. Markov model for dynamic spectrum access network with spectrum hand-off

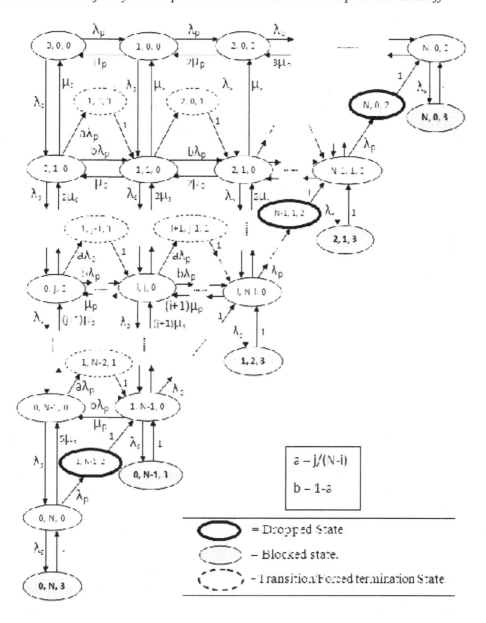

is not significant when T_o is large, since the length of the scanning phase is the dominating component for increasing the RTT. It can also be concluded that the throughput is always lower when compared to a *perfect scan* (*no scan*). These results are similar to (Slingerland, Pawelczak, Prasad, Lo, & Hekmat, 2005) because the PU and SU traffic rate is maintained at a constant rate for this graph. The actual advantage of the proposed model is that it allows studying the effect of the number of channels and PU, SU traffic as shown in the accompanying figures.

Figure 8 shows the variation of throughput as a function of total number of channels N. As the number of channels is increased there are more opportunities for a fixed PU and SU arrival rate. As a result the blocking probability p_b of the SU is reduced which in turn reduces the RTT, increasing the overall throughput.

Figure 6. Variation of SU blocking probability as PU's arrival rate is varied for different number of channels

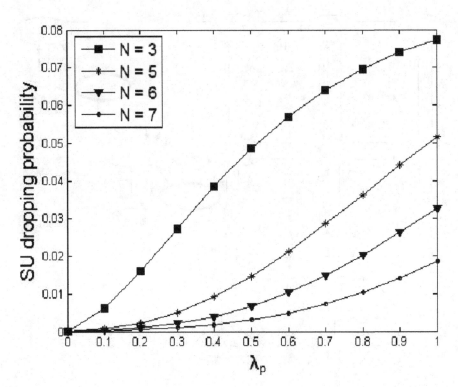

Figure 9 shows the variation of throughput as a function of primary user's traffic. It can be seen that as the PU's traffic is increased, the TCP throughput of the secondary user is reduced. This is due to the fact that with increase in PU traffic, smaller number of channels is available for SUs. As a result, the blocking probability, p_b increases which results in an increase in RTT and a decrease in overall TCP throughput. It can also be observed that as the number of channels, N, is increased, the throughput increases and the reasons are similar to the explanations of Figure 8.

Figure 10 shows the variation of TCP throughput as a function of SU traffic. The throughput decreases as the SU traffic increases because of the increased contention between the secondary users. The increased contention leads to increased blocking probability and RTT resulting in decreased throughput.

6. FUTURE RESEARCH DIRECTIONS

This chapter attempts to provide some analysis for the effect of dynamic spectrum access on the performance of TCP. The considered system model, however, was deliberately chosen to be simple to simplify the analysis and more focus was placed on gaining insight on the behavior of TCP in the presence of the dynamic topology, heterogeneity and spectrum handoff delay inherent in opportunistic access networks. For future research, the system model can be improved by considering factors like probability of misdetection, i.e. the misinterpretation of an occupied channel as free, in calculating the probability of packet error. The effect of exponential back-off in TCP can also be considered.

Figure 7. TCP throughput as a function of scanning time. $p_e = 10^{-7}$, $N_F = 2$, $MSS = 512$ *bytes*, $T_{sr} = T_p = 10\,ms$, $\lambda_s = \lambda_p = 0.5$, $N = 5$.

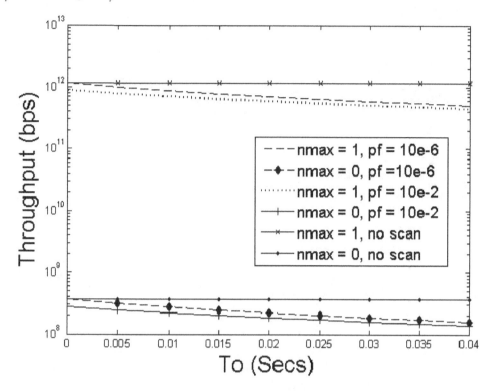

Figure 8. TCP throughput as a function of number of channels. $p_e = 10^{-7}$, $p_f = 10^{-6}$, $n_{max} = 1$, $N_F = 2$, $MSS = 512$ *bytes*, $T_{sr} = T_p = 10\,ms$, $\lambda_s = 0.5$.

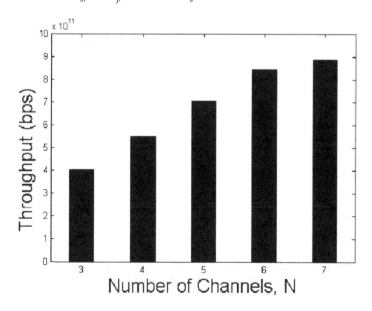

Figure 9. TCP throughput as a function of PU traffic rate, λ_p. $p_e = 10^{-7}$, $N_F = 2$, $MSS = 512$ *bytes,* $T_{sr} = T_p = 10\,ms$, $\lambda_s = 0.5$.

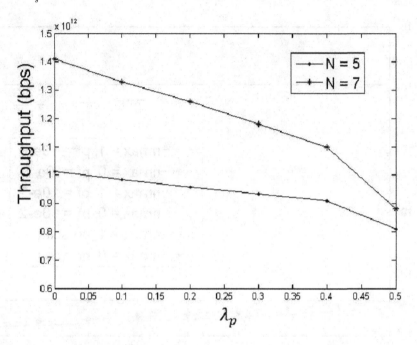

Figure 10. TCP throughput as a function of SU traffic rate, λ_s. $p_e = 10^{-7}$, $N_F = 2$, $MSS = 512$ *bytes,* $T_{sr} = T_p = 10\,ms$, $\lambda_p = 0.5$, $N = 7$.

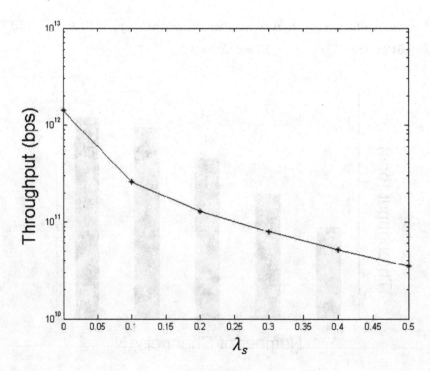

7. CONCLUSION

In this chapter, we discussed how regular TCP which was designed for wired networks is not suitable for dynamic spectrum access networks. We modified a simple yet sufficiently accurate TCP model to incorporate the delay caused by primary and secondary user's traffic and detection errors and analyze the throughput of Dynamic spectrum access networks by modeling the spectrum access using continuous-time Markov chains. Simulations were used to visualize the effect of primary and secondary user's traffic, number of channels and the length of the scan period on the performance of TCP throughput. The proposed analytical model proved to be efficient in capturing the dynamic nature of dynamic spectrum access networks unlike existing models.

REFERENCES

Akyildiz, I. F., Lee, W., Vuran, M. C., & Mohanty, S. (2006). NeXt generation/ dynamic spectrum access/cognitive radio wireless networks: A survey. *Computer Networks, 50*(13), 2127–2159. doi:10.1016/j.comnet.2006.05.001.

Capar, F., Martoyo, I., Weiss, T., & Jondral, F. (2002). Comparison of bandwidth utilization for controlled and uncontrolled channel assignment in a spectrum pooling system. In *Proceedings of the IEEE Vehicular Technology Conference*, (pp. 1069-1073). IEEE.

Chen, Z., Bu, T., Ammar, M., & Towsley, D. (2006). Comments on modeling TCP Reno performance: A simple model and its empirical validation. *IEEE/ACM Transactions on Networking, 14*(2), 451–453. doi:10.1109/TNET.2006.872541.

Cianca, E., Prasad, R., De Sanctis, M., De Luise, A., Antonini, M., Teotino, D., & Ruggieri, M. (2005). Integrated satellite-HAP systems. *IEEE Communications Magazine, 43*(12), supl.33-supl.39.

Digham, F., Alouini, M. S., & Simon, M. K. (2007). On the energy detection of unknown signals over fading channels. *IEEE Transactions on Communications, 55*(1), 21–24. doi:10.1109/TCOMM.2006.887483.

Dillinger, M., Madani, K., & Alonistioti, N. (2003). *Software defined radio: Architectures, systems and functions*. Chichester, UK: John Wiley & Sons.

FCC. (2003). ET docket no 03-222 notice of proposed rule making and order. Washington, DC: FCC.

IEEE. (2007). *Standard definitions and concepts for spectrum management and advanced radio technologies. Institute of Electrical and Electronics Engineers Standards Activities Department, P1900.1 Draft Standard (v0.28)*. IEEE.

Kondareddy, Y., & Agrawal, P. (2009). Effect of dynamic spectrum access on TCP performance. In *Proceedings of IEEE Globecom 2009*. IEEE.

Kumar, A., & Shin, K. G. (n.d.). DSASync: Managing end-to-end connections in dynamic spectrum access wireless LANs. *IEEE Transactions on Networking, 4*(20), 1068-1081.

Kyasanur, P., & Vaidya, N. H. (2005). Protocol design challenges for multi-hop dynamic spectrum access networks. In *Proceedings of IEEE DySPAN*, (pp. 645-648). IEEE.

Luo, C., Yu, F. R., Ji, H., & Lung, V. C. M. (n.d.). Cross-layer design for TCP Performance improvement in cognitive radio networks. *IEEE Transactions on Vehicular Technology, 59*(5), 2485-2495.

Mathis, M., Semke, J., Mahdavi, J., & Ott, T. (1997). The macroscopic behaviour of the TCP congestion avoidance algorithm. *ACM SIGCOMM Computer Communications Review, 27*(3), 67–82. doi:10.1145/263932.264023.

Mitola, J., & Maguire, G. Q. (1999). Cognitive radio: Making software radios more personal. *IEEE Personal Communications, 6*(4), 13–18. doi:10.1109/98.788210.

Padhye, J., Firoiu, V., Towsley, D. F., & Kurose, J. F. (2000). Modeling TCP Reno performance: A simple model and its empirical validation. *IEEE/ACM Transactions on Networking, 8*(2), 133–145. doi:10.1109/90.842137.

Pawelczak, P., Janssen, G. J. M., & Prasad, R. V. (2006). WLC10-4: Performance measures of dynamic spectrum access networks. In *Proceedings of IEEE Global Telecommunications Conference*, (pp. 1-6). IEEE.

Raspopovic, M., Thompson, C., & Chandra, K. (2005). Performance models for wireless spectrum shared by wideband and narrowband sources. [IEEE.]. *Proceedings of IEEE Milcom, 2005*, 1–6.

Slingerland, A. M. R., Pawelczak, P., Prasad, R. V., Lo, A., & Hekmat, R. (2007). Performance of transport control protocol over dynamic spectrum access links. [IEEE.]. *Proceedings of IEEE DySPAN, 2007*, 486–495.

Tang, P. K., Chew, Y. H., Ong, L. C., & Haldar, M. K. (2006). Performance of secondary radios in spectrum sharing with prioritized primary access. In *Proceedings of IEEE Milcom*. IEEE.

Tian, Y., Xu, K., & Ansari, N. (2005). *TCP in wireless environments: Problems and solutions*. IEEE Radio Communications.

Wang, B., Ji, Z., & Liu, K. J. R. (2007a). Primary-prioritized markov approach for dynamic spectrum access. [IEEE.]. *Proceedings of IEEE DySPAN, 2007*, 507–515.

Wang, B., Ji, Z., & Liu, K. J. R. (2007b). Self-learning repeated game framework for distributed primary-prioritized dynamic spectrum access. In *Proceedings of the IEEE Workshop on Networking Technologies for Software Define Radio Networks*, (pp. 1-8). IEEE.

Xing, Y., Chandramouli, R., Mangold, S., & Sai Shankar, N. (2005). Analysis and performance evaluation of a fair channel access protocol for open spectrum wireless networks. In *Proceedings of IEEE ICC 2005*, (pp. 1179-1183). IEEE.

Xing, Y., Chandramouli, R., Mangold, S., & Sai Shankar, N. (2006). Dynamic spectrum access in open spectrum wireless networks. *IEEE Journal on Selected Areas in Communications, 24*(3), 626–637. doi:10.1109/JSAC.2005.862415.

Zhao, Q., & Sadler, B. M. (2007, May). A survey of dynamic spectrum access: Signal processing, networking, and regulatory policy. *IEEE Signal Processing Magazine*.

Zhu, X., Shen, L., & Yum, T. P. (2007). Analysis of cognitive radio spectrum access with optimal channel reservation. *IEEE Communications Letters, 11*, 304–306. doi:10.1109/LCOM.2007.348282.

KEY TERMS AND DEFINITIONS

Cognitive Radio: A radio capable of learning from its environment and changing its operational parameters to maximize its throughput or minimize its interference to other radios.

Dynamic Spectrum Access: Spectrum access and coexistence of unlicensed cognitive radios with legacy licensed radios on a non-interfering basis.

Spectrum Handoff: Happens when a secondary unlicensed radio is forced to vacate a channel and switch to a different channel when a licensed radio requests it.

Throughput: The average rate of successful information transmission over a communication channel.

Transport Control Protocol: Is a protocol in data networks that provides a reliable and orderly stream of bytes from one application on a node to another application in a different node.

ENDNOTES

[1]   Note that the spectrum holes may be fractions of channels depending on the access method used in the network. For simplicity, we assume that spectrum holes are composed of one or a few whole channels as defined in the primary network.

Chapter 11
Dynamic Resource Configurations for the Convergence of Optical and Wireless Networks

Konstantinos Demestichas
Institute of Communication and Computer Systems (ICCS), Greece

Ioannis Loumiotis
Institute of Communication and Computer Systems (ICCS), Greece

Evgenia Adamopoulou
Institute of Communication and Computer Systems (ICCS), Greece

Theodora Stamatiadi
Institute of Communication and Computer Systems (ICCS), Greece

Efstathios Sykas
Institute of Communication and Computer Systems (ICCS), Greece

Nikolaos Papaoulakis
Institute of Communication and Computer Systems (ICCS), Greece

Ioanna Mesogiti
Cosmote Kinites Tilepikoinonies, Greece

ABSTRACT

In the current landscape of Mobile Communication Networks, evolved radio access technologies, such as Long Term Evolution (LTE), offer higher bitrates to mobile end users, providing support for a range of resource-demanding applications. In this context, one can imagine that the full potential of the communication infrastructures can be unleashed, in a cost-effective way, by enabling a smart convergence between the evolved access of the mobile world and the Passive Optical Networks (PONs) of the fixed world. In this context, this chapter introduces a novel management system called CONFES, Converged Network Infrastructure Enabling Resource Optimization and Flexible Service Provisioning, aiming at the proactive determination of PON clients' needs in bandwidth resources, and the efficient and reasonable allocation of resources to multiple clients according to such needs and the corresponding Service Level Agreements. Furthermore, the present chapter proposes, studies, and compares physical architecture solutions (both centralized and distributed) that can realize such advanced management systems.

DOI: 10.4018/978-1-4666-4189-1.ch011

Copyright © 2013, IGI Global. Copying or distributing in print or electronic forms without written permission of IGI Global is prohibited.

INTRODUCTION

In the current landscape of Mobile Communication Networks, evolved radio access technologies, such as Long Term Evolution (LTE) (Ekstrom, et al., 2006; Hadden, 2009), offer all the more higher bitrates to mobile end users, providing support for a range of resource-demanding applications, such as IPTV, media streaming, VoIP, social network applications and gaming (Zahariadis, Grüneberg, & Celetto, 2011; Amram, et al., 2011). In parallel to this evolution of the mobile world, we also witness the evolution of Passive Optical Networks (PONs) (Kramer & Pesavento, 2002; Byun, Nho, & Lim, 2003; Yang C., 2007) in the fixed access world. Optical networks are expanding, and their use, not just in the core and backbone parts of the communication infrastructure, but also towards the last-mile and the premises, is beginning to gain ground.

In this context, one can imagine that the full potential of the communication infrastructures can be unleashed, in a cost-effective way, by enabling a smart convergence between the evolved access of the mobile world and the PONs of the fixed world. To achieve this, the notion is clear: Utilize the optical network infrastructure not just as a backbone or solely for serving residential or business customers, but also as a backhaul for base stations of mobile network operators. Indeed, using a PON as a high-capacity medium shared among different mobile base stations (e.g., LTE eNodeBs) as well as other customers (business or residential) offers significant advantages:

- Enhanced support at the backhaul for the increasing capacities of the mobile radio access interfaces;
- Economies of scale, since more customers can be served through the same PON, making PON-related deployment investments more attractive.

At the same time, nonetheless, significant challenges arise: Although the PON is a medium of high capacity, its sharing (namely, at the OLT – Optical Line Terminal level (Amemiya, Imae, Fujii, Suzuyama, & Ohshima, 2005)) among multiple end-users with different and fluctuating needs implies that smart bandwidth management mechanisms should be in place, and associated Service Level Agreements (SLAs) should exist, making sure that the high –but restricted– capacity of the PON is continuously utilized in an efficient and fair manner. This becomes a necessity particularly for the case of mobile base stations acting as clients/customers of the PON. We will see that, in order to address this necessity, the introduction of cognitive technologies at the backhaul segment is in order. This comes as a natural complement to existing and future cognitive solutions that focus instead on the radio access part of wireless communications.

This chapter proposes a novel converged network infrastructure that considers a passive optical network (PON) (Lam, 2007) as the backhauling solution for multiple next generation telecommunications networks, as depicted in Figure 1. Contrary to the existing fixed capacity transmission network model, the proposed solution takes into account time varying bandwidth requirements and suggests an efficient learning-based mechanism for resource optimization and flexible service provisioning. Through an integrated management platform, suitable cognitive mechanisms are deployed towards the dynamic reconfiguration and automatic and proactive adaptation to network needs. The implementation of appropriate traffic management entities in both the wireless base station and the optical backhauling segment can guarantee high quality of service and end-to-end efficiency.

This novel management platform, called CON-FES – Converged Network Infrastructure Enabling Resource optimization and Flexible Service Provisioning is introduced and described in detail in

Figure 1. Envisioned converged network infrastructure

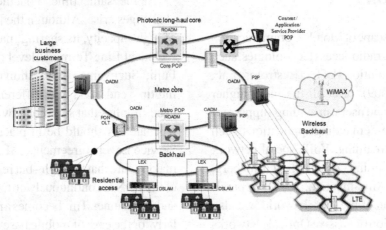

this chapter. CONFES is envisioned as an overlay network management system, particularly aiming at the proactive determination of PON clients' needs in bandwidth resources, and the efficient and reasonable allocation of resources to multiple clients according to such needs and the corresponding SLAs.

Hence, in a nutshell, CONFES is composed of two main cooperating entities:

- BS-ODORA, standing for Base Station-Optimal & Dynamic Optical Resource Allocation system, responsible for acting as a smart client at the Base Station (BS) side, predicting base station resource requirements (proactively) and announcing them to the CONFES Core.
- CONFES Core, constituting the management sub-system at the PON side, which gathers estimations and requests for resources by multiple base stations (BS-ODORA sub-systems) and potentially other clients (business or residential), and performs the resource allocation.

The proactive and intelligent nature of the functionality of BS-ODORA is of particular importance in this proposed management scheme, since it enables the PON to avoid making continu-

ous and unnecessary reconfigurations, and ensures that any resource reallocation is not arbitrary but based on actual and consolidated needs of the PON's clients.

In what follows, the chapter focuses in the proposed BS-ODORA system, whose functionality, to the authors' best knowledge, is innovative and not yet integrated in existing research management platforms or commercial network management products. In the following sections, the functionality of BS-ODORA is described and analyzed in detail. The corresponding modules as well as the interactions among them are detailed and explained. Moreover, physical architecture solutions (both centralized and distributed) that can realize such advanced management systems are proposed, studied and compared. Experimental results as well as future research directions are presented as well.

BACKGROUND

In the literature, there are a number of approaches that study the convergence of a fixed backhaul PON with a radio access technology. In (Shen, Tucker, & Chae, 2007), the authors propose four broadband access architectures that allow integration of EPON (Ethernet PON) and WiMAX technologies, and present the benefits from such integration. In (Yang, Ou, Guild, & Chen, 2009), the authors describe an architecture to achieve convergence of EPON and 802.16 networks, and propose a mechanism to map 802.16 differentiated traffics to the appropriate EPON queues and vice versa. Similarly, in (Ali, Ellinas, Erkan, Hadjiantonis, & Dorsinville, 2010) the author considers an NG-PON (Next Generation PON) and LTE network convergence. Furthermore, there are a number of Information and Communication Technology (ICT) projects studying the convergence of wireless and wired networks. Specifically, the ALPHA project (ICT-ALPHA project, 2008-2011) investigated the architectural and transmission solutions based on the manifold of optical fibres as well as wireless technology to support both wired and wireless services in a converged network infrastructure for all types of in-building networks. In the WOPROF project (WOPROF project, 2009-2011), the researchers studied the wavelength-division-multiplexing (WDM) optical phase modulated radio-over-fiber (RoF) system, as a solution to implement broadband seamless wireless-wireline access networks. A same research orientation is studied in the OFDM-PON project (OFDM-PON project, 2011-2013). However, in all the aforementioned approaches there is no consideration for proactiveness or cognition in backhaul resource allocation schemes, thus such schemes cannot function intelligently in scenarios of fluctuating traffic conditions and competitive traffic demand. Moreover,

current approaches only consider a single type of end users and usually a single type of radio access technology (either WiMAX or LTE), and do not provide for a generalized framework.

ABSTRACT RESOURCE MANAGEMENT FRAMEWORK

In order to accomplish the aforementioned converged approach, two key-elements are needed: (1) appropriate management modules both at the base station side, as well as at the optical elements side; (2) an appropriate protocol for transporting the base station backhaul resource requirements from the base station to the associated optical resource allocation module.

The first key-element is realized through the introduction and development of so-called Optimal and Dynamic Optical Resource Allocation (ODORA) management modules at the BS (Base Station), ONU (Optical Network Unit) and OLT (Optical Line Terminal) sides. The second key-element is realized through the introduction and implementation of the Optimal and Dynamic Optical Resource Allocation Protocol (ODORAP). The conceptual overview of this proposed management functionality is depicted in Figure 2.

In essence, the BS-ODORA management module is responsible for determining in real-time the backhaul resource requirements of the base station. This is feasible since the base station is aware of the traffic load that it handles on the

Figure 2. Conceptual overview of the proposed resource management framework

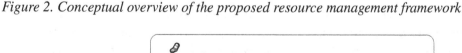

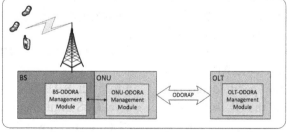

radio interface, thus the required backhaul resources can be inferred, by properly matching the radio traffic load degree into a level/amount of required backhaul resources. Parameters associated to the base station's traffic load include the number of active sessions, the number of standby users (EPS-only), traffic demand, user priorities, requested Quality of Service (QoS) levels, etc. The specifics of the implementation of this management module might differ for each type of RAN (Radio Access Network), e.g. between 2G/GPRS, UTRAN/HSPA and E-UTRAN, but, despite this fact, the BS-ODORA management module must in any case provide the same interface towards the ONU-ODORA management module, effectively hiding the implementation details. The proposed system also equips the BS-ODORA management module with traffic prediction functionality, by means of machine learning, based on historical traffic-load measurements and statistical data, which allows for efficient proactive resource allocation management.

As with all signalling functions, the goal of the proposed system is not to alter the main philosophy of the mobile network operations as specified by 3GPP, but rather to ensure 3GPP-compliant operation of the proposed converged network. This will eventually lead to faster development and reduced time-to-market. Session management, and Quality of Service (QoS) in particular, is an important operational aspect for 3GPP standards.

Moving forward, the ONU-ODORA management module is responsible for relaying the determined backhaul resources requirements to the OLT-ODORA management module, through the ODORAP protocol. The OLT-ODORA management module processes the requirements coming from multiple ONUs in order to produce an efficient resource allocation decision, which will affect the bandwidth that is made available to each of the served ONUs. The ODORAP protocol is designed so as to convey the specified data between the ONU-ODORA and the OLT-ODORA management modules.

Optimal and Dynamic Optical Resource Allocation Protocol: ODORAP

The optimal and dynamic optical resource allocation protocol is originally designed for the communication of ONU-ODORA and OLT-ODORA management modules. The resource requirements of each Base Station connected to the associated optical resource allocation module are gathered and transferred to the optical side. After the processing of the requirements, the optical side replies through the ODORA Protocol and allocates the available resources according to the agreed Service Level Agreements and Quality Indicators.

Mechanisms for controlling the periodicity in which resource requirements updates are received by the OLT are, also, developed. Both periodic and on-request retrieval and transmission of resource requirements are supported.

Technically, the design of ODORAP can rely on a standard high-level communication paradigm, such as Web Services using either SOAP (Simple Object Access Protocol) or REST (Representational State Transfer), or on an extension and evolution of the optional X2 Control plane interface (X2-C) encountered in Evolved Packet Systems (EPS) (3GPP Release 8). X2 is an optional interface between eNodeBs in an EPS system, primarily aiming at supporting mobility and user plane tunnelling features. According to 3GPP Release 8 Specifications, the X2-C interface proposes the "Load Indicator" procedure whose purpose is to allow an eNodeB to signal its load condition to neighbouring eNodeBs. The detailed use of the function is not further described in the standards, hence it constitutes an interesting topic of investigation for the present research activities.

QoS Provisioning

From an E-UMTS (Evolved UMTS) perspective, QoS implementation relies on the notion of "EPS bearer", which is an equivalent of the PDP

(Packet Data Protocol) context being used in 2G/ GPRS and 3G/UMTS standards. An EPS bearer corresponds to one Quality of Service policy applied within the EPC (Evolved Packet Core) and E-UTRAN, meaning that all the service data flows transported by the EPS bearer will be subject to the same packet scheduling algorithm, using the same priority, the same E-UTRAN RLC configuration, etc. This notion can also be regarded as the EPS equivalent to the UMTS Bearer Service of 3G/ UMTS networks. Additional mechanisms can also be present, such as enforcement of supplementary policies and use of the Differentiated Services (DiffServ) field. DiffServ re-uses an existing field that is present in the IP header (the IPv4 Type of Service field or IPv6 Traffic Class field), to define a new field known as DS (i.e., DiffServ), allowing packet classification and differentiated packet processing.

Generally, bearers can be classified into two categories, guaranteed bit rate (GBR) and non-guaranteed bit rate (non-GBR). Each bearer has an associated quality class indicator (QCI). The standardized QCIs for E-UMTS are depicted in Table 1 (Alcatel-Lucent, 2009).

In the context of the proposed converged network, such mechanisms must be further evolved to take into account the possibilities offered by the optical backhaul. As an interesting example, GPON Encapsulation Method (GEM) (Lam, 2007; Jiang & Senior, 2009) allows very efficient packaging of user traffic, with frame segmentation to allow for higher QoS for delay-sensitive traffic, such as voice and video communications. The joint utilization of methods such as these will enable enhanced QoS awareness and support within the proposed network.

The BS-ODORA management module, in order to guarantee high end-users' experience, plays an important role between the access network and the core network. Specifically, it calculates the QoS requirements of the BS proactively and transforms them into QoS demand requests for the PON. Furthermore, it is informed about malfunctions and unexpected network conditions in the backhaul network and employs mechanisms in the access network, in order to guarantee the QoS provided to the mobile operator's customers.

Table 1. Standardized QCIs for LTE

QCI	Resource Type	Priority	Packet Delay Budget (ms)	Packet Error Loss Rate	Example Services
1	GBR	2	100	10^{-2}	Conversational Voice
2	GBR	4	150	10^{-3}	Conversational Video (Live Streaming)
3	GBR	5	300	10^{-6}	Non-Conversational Video (Buffered Streaming)
4	GBR	3	50	10^{-3}	Real-time Gaming
5	Non-GBR	1	100	10^{-6}	IMS Signaling
6	Non-GBR	7	100	10^{-3}	Voice, Video (Live Streaming), Interactive Gaming
7	Non-GBR	6	300	10^{-6}	Video (Buffered Streaming)
8	Non-GBR	8	300	10^{-6}	TCP-based (for example WWW, e-mail), chat, FTP, p2p file sharing, progressive video and others
9	Non-GBR	9	300	10^{-6}	

FUNCTIONAL ARCHITECTURE

The functional architecture of BS-ODORA, i.e. the proposed CONFES management entity at the BS side is presented in Figure 3, by means of the ArchiMate modeling (Archimate Modeling Language, 2012). In the following sections, all of the involved functional entities as well as the interactions among them will be described in detail.

Message Exchange System

The Message Exchange System comprises the main entity through which the BS communicates with the CONFES Core. It is responsible for issuing requests and alerts from and towards the CONFES Core. Specifically, it is responsible for the following operations:

- Alert issuing in case the Intelligent Prediction System awaits the dissatisfaction of the short-term demand from the already allocated resources.

- Issuing of resource allocation request, as those are identified by the Intelligent Prediction System, for a mid-term period.
- Alert issuing to the CONFES Core in case a violation of the established SLA is detected.
- Issuing of SLA update requests in order to acquire and store an updated copy of the SLA.
- Reception of the updated SLAs and transfer to SLA Synchronization System.
- Reception of alerts from the CONFES Core and notification of the Fallback System, in order to tackle with unexpected conditions resulting in degradation of the offered quality of service.
- Reception of the updated allocated and requested resources, in order to maintain an updated record.

In detail, the Message Exchange System consists of the following sub-components:

Figure 3. BS-ODORA functional architecture

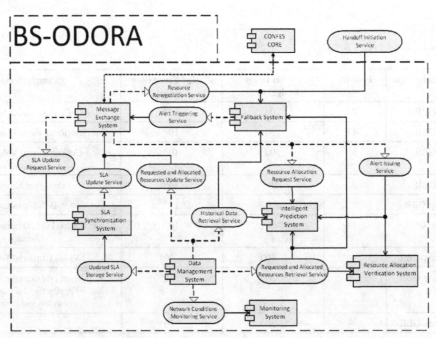

- **Alert Issuing Module:** The Alert Issuing Module receives messages of SLA violation (SLA alert messages) originating from the Resource Allocation Verification System and alerts messages originating from the Intelligent Prediction System, in case the short-term demand prediction cannot be satisfied by the resources already allocated to the BS. Consequently, this module forwards these alert messages to the CONFES Core.

- **Alert Reception Module:** The Alert Reception Module receives alert messages issued by the CONFES Core to the BS and notifies accordingly the Fallback System. This kind of messages refers to either the inability to offer the requested resources or potential malfunctions detected at the CONFES Core side.

- **Request Dispatching Module:** The Request Dispatching Module receives the resource allocation requests, based on the mid-term prediction of the Intelligent Prediction System as well as the resource negotiation messages from the Fallback System in case of not satisfying the initial demand. The role of this module is to forward these requests to the CONFES Core.

- **Communication Module for SLA Synchronization:** The purpose of the Communication Module for SLA Synchronization is to receive SLA update requests from the SLA Synchronization System and forward these requests to the CONFES Core. Moreover, this module is responsible for receiving the updated information (allocated/requested resources, SLA) and updating accordingly the Data Management and SLA Synchronization Systems.

Resource Allocation Verification System

The Resource Allocation Verification System is responsible for issuing alert messages when a violation of the agreed SLA is observed. For this reason, the Resource Allocation Verification System monitors in real-time the allocated, by the CONFES Core, resources. Then, it retrieves from the Data Management System the resources requested and received by the BS and detects any disagreement between the requested/allocated resources and the collected values.

In case of disagreement, a report is created and an SLA alert message is forwarded to the Message Exchange System. These messages include details on the percentage of the SLA violation, as the latter was recorded by the BS.

Monitoring System

The Monitoring System is responsible for fully monitoring current network conditions and recording them through the Data Management System. The Monitoring System records the number of served users, the number of active users, as well as the combination of user services and corresponding quality levels. These records, that are stored to the Database through the Data Management System, comprise the BS's historical data and are extremely important for the efficient performance of other systems, such as the Intelligent Prediction System.

SLA Synchronization System

The role of the SLA Synchronization System is to maintain an updated copy of the SLA at the BS side. For this reason, it issues update requests towards the CONFES Core, through the Data Exchange System and receives the updated version of SLAs. Consequently, it stores a copy of this version to the BS's Database through the Data Management System. The SLA Synchronization System performs two functions:

- **Update Decision:** The SLA Synchronization System takes periodically the decision to update the SLA. For this reason, it issues the appropriate request message to the Message Exchange System.
- **Update Execution:** Upon reception of the updated SLA, the Message Exchange System forwards the new version to the SLA Update Module, which maintains a copy of the SLA to the Database through the Data Management System.

Fallback System

The Fallback System comprises the main system for dealing with unexpected conditions that can potentially lead to degradation of the service quality offered by the BS. For this reason, it receives alert messages sent by the CONFES Core through the Message Exchange System and takes action for handling them.

In detail, the Fallback System consists of two sub-components:

- **The Resource Negotiation Module:** The Resource Negotiation Module receives alert messages from the CONFES Core and communicates with the Data Management System in order to retrieve (i) the current BS conditions (number of served users, number, services and quality classes of the active users), as these have been recorded by the Monitoring System and (ii) the resources requested by the BS at an earlier phase. It, then, decides to lower the requested resources. In this way, the BS is involved in a resource negotiation process and issues trough the Message Exchange System requests for new resources.

- **Handoff Triggering Module:** In case the resource renegotiation process does not result in an agreement, or the message alert refers to a failure/malfunction of the CONFES Core, the *Handoff Triggering Module* is responsible for deciding whether a handover should be initiated. Towards this end, it sends a proper message to the BS including the predicted number of users to be transferred to another cell, in order to avoid severe degradation of the offered quality of service.

Data Management System

The Data Management System is responsible for recording and accessing all data originating from or targeted for all the BS-ODORA components. Specifically, the interactions of the Data Management System with other modules included the following functions:

- Storage of the updated versions of the SLAs retrieved by the SLA Synchronization System;
- Storage of the current network conditions, as recorded by the Monitoring System;
- Storage of the requested and the allocated resources, as received by the Message Exchange System;
- Retrieval of all the necessary, for the prediction functionality, parameters from the Intelligent prediction System;
- Retrieval from the Resource Allocation Verification Module of all the parameters necessary to validate compliance with the agreed SLAs.
- Retrieval of all the parameters necessary for the resource renegotiation process from the Fallback System.

In detail, the Data Management System maintains a record of the current network status, which is stored in the BS's Database and consists of the historical data record, available to the other components through the historical data retrieval service. Moreover, the Data Management System maintains a record of the requested and allocated resources, which is accessible by the other systems through the requested and allocated resources retrieval service. Finally, the Data Management System maintains a copy of the SLA through the SLA synchronization service.

Intelligent Prediction System

The purpose of the Intelligent Prediction System is to predict the BS's needs, regarding the resources necessary to provide its mobile users with a certain quality of service level. The Intelligent prediction System retrieves the historical data from the Data Management System in order to use them for predicting, by means of machine learning methods, the necessary resources. After the prediction process is performed, the system issues, through

the Data Exchange System, a suitable request for resources allocation to the CONFES Core. Furthermore, the Intelligent Prediction System retrieves the updated requested and allocated resources, through the Data Management System, in order to verify that the predicted short-term demand is satisfied. In case the latter cannot be satisfied with the resources already allocated, the Intelligent Prediction System issues, through the Message Exchange System, appropriate message alerts to the CONFES Core, asking the short-term allocation of more resources in order to satisfy the predicted demand.

Specifically, the Intelligent Prediction System consists of five sub-components, which are further described subsequently (Figure 4):

- The Machine Learning Mid-term Prediction System
- The Machine Learning Short-term Prediction System

Figure 4. Intelligent prediction system: parameters and services

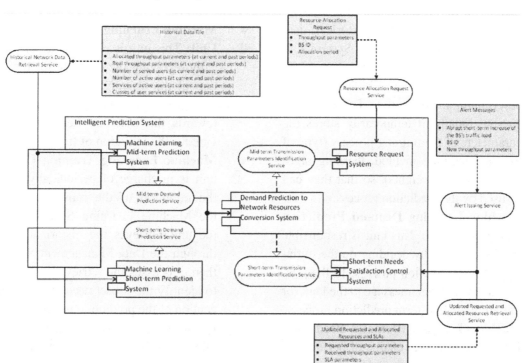

- The Demand Prediction to Network Resources Conversion System
- The Resource Request System
- The Short-term Needs Satisfaction Control System

Machine Learning Mid-Term Prediction System

The Machine Learning Mid-term Prediction System is responsible for predicting the mid-term needs of the BS by applying machine learning methods. In detail, it comprises the following components:

- **Machine Learning Training Scheduling Unit:** This unit is responsible for periodically deciding the initiation of the training process. It, then, issues a proper control message to the Machine Learning Training Scheduling Unit for the initiation of training.
- **Machine Learning Training Unit:** This unit is responsible for performing the training of the Machine Learning System. Initially, it retrieves the historical data from the Data Management System and selects the appropriate set of data required for prediction. Subsequently, it selects the best training method and performs the prediction. Finally, it temporarily stores the parameters of the training process (type of machine learning method, learning algorithm, learning weights), so that they can be used by the prediction process.
- **Machine Learning Demand Prediction Scheduling Unit:** This unit is responsible for the periodically deciding on the initiation of the prediction process. It, then, issues an appropriate message to the Unit for initiating the mid-term prediction process.
- **Machine Learning Demand Prediction Unit:** This unit is in charge of performing the mid-term prediction. Upon receiving

the foreseen control message for initiating the process, it decides on the time period upon the data of which the prediction will take place. It, then, utilizes the data formed by the training process in order to perform the prediction. The prediction result consists the demand, which is forwarded through a proper control message to the Demand Prediction to Network Resources Conversion System.

Machine Learning Short-Term Prediction System

The Machine Learning Short-term Prediction System is responsible for predicting the short-term resource needs of a BS, based on machine learning methods. Towards this direction, the system performs periodically the machine learning training process and reaches a prediction. In an optimal scenario, both the training and the prediction process are carried out at every monitored instance of the network conditions. In detail, the system is comprised of the following units:

- **Machine Learning Training Scheduling Unit:** This unit is responsible for periodically receiving the decision for the initiation of the training process. Upon reception, it issues a suitable control message towards the Machine Learning Training Unit for the initiation of training.
- **Machine Learning Training Unit:** This unit is in charge of periodically deciding the initiation of the training process of the Machine Learning System. Initially, the unit retrieves the historical data file through the Data Management System. It, then, processes the retrieved data in order to identify the subset necessary for the execution of the prediction process as well as the most suitable training method. Finally, after performing the prediction, the unit stores temporarily the data originating

from the training process (type of learning algorithm, learning weights, etc.)

- **Machine Learning Demand Prediction Scheduling Unit**: This unit is responsible for periodically deciding the initiation of the prediction process. It, then, issues a suitable control message to the Machine Learning Demand Prediction Unit for initiating the short-term prediction process.
- **Machine Learning Demand Prediction Unit:** The role of this unit is to perform the short-term demand prediction. After receiving a suitable control message, the Machine Learning Demand Prediction Unit selects the most suitable prediction method and utilizes the training data in order to perform the prediction. The prediction result consists the predicted demand, which is forwarded through an appropriate control message to the Demand Prediction to Network Resources Conversion System.

Demand Prediction to Network Resources Conversion System

The Demand Prediction to Network Resources Conversion System is in charge of retrieving the short-term and mid-term demand predictions from the corresponding Intelligent Prediction Systems, and converting them to appropriate network resources. The form of the parameters identified by this procedure must comply with the form of parameters included in the SLA (e.g. bandwidth segments, committed bandwidth, etc.). Subsequently, the parameters referring to mid-term predicted resources are forwarded to the Resources Request System while the ones preferring to short-term prediction are forwarded to the Short-term Needs Satisfaction Control System.

Resource Request System

The role of the Resource Request System is to retrieve the parameters relevant to the mid-term predicted resources and create the corresponding

request message for the allocation of the specific resources for the specified time period. This message is forwarded, through the Message Exchange System to the CONFES Core.

Short-Term Needs Satisfaction Control System

The main operation of the Short-term Needs Satisfaction Control System is to check whether the allocated resources are in accordance to the predicted short-term need of the BS. For this reason, the system retrieves the parameters relevant to the short-term predicted resources, as well as the allocated and requested resources through the Data Management System. It, then, verifies that the short-term predicted needs of the BS are satisfied by the allocated resources. In case the short-term demand exceeds the amount of allocated resources, a suitable alert message is sent to the CONFES Core including the new short-term resources that are necessary for the provision of the specified quality of service to the mobile users.

PHYSICAL IMPLEMENTATION SOLUTIONS

In the previous section, the functional architecture of the BS-ODORA module was presented. In brief, the BS-ODORA module:

- Observes the current network conditions using the Monitoring System.
- Orients its actions according to the above observation using the Fallback System in case of unexpected situations or the Intelligent Prediction System in order to calculate the required resources proactively.
- Plans the basic actions and evaluates the alternatives either at the Fallback System in case of unexpected situations or at the Intelligent Prediction System in case of the usual functionality of BS-ODORA module.

- Decides the needed actions according to the current state by using either the Intelligent Prediction System to calculate the long-term or short-term demand, or the Fallback System to recover from unexpected situations.
- Learns from the network conditions and past actions using Machine Learning techniques in the Intelligent Prediction System.
- Acts by sending requests or alarms to the Backhaul Network using the Message Exchange System.

As a result, the CONFES system is a cognitive technology (Haykin, 2005; Mitola & Maguire, 1999), that is agnostic to the Radio Access Technology (RAT) and can be implemented in any legacy or future access technology.

In the following, a thorough study and analysis of the physical implementation solutions (centralized or distributed) of BS-ODORA is given, indicating the advantages and the disadvantages of each one. Firstly, centralized architectural solutions are described, while subsequently possible distributed physical architectures are presented. A comparison between them is also provided in the CONCLUSION section.

CENTRALIZED PHYSICAL ARCHITECTURES

Generic Description

In the centralized approach for the physical architecture, quality indication parameters are collected by BS-ODORA either through the Network Management System (NMS) or through the central billing platform of the mobile operator.

The majority of the manufacturers/vendors propose solutions enabling a central system to supervise, using the same protocol, more than one access technologies, even heterogeneous ones, such as wired and mobile access networks, simultaneously. This is considered as an important advantage, since a centralized BS-ODORA entity will be able to extract network quality indication parameters without the need of analyzing different types of specialized messages for each technology. Figure 5 presents the collection of quality indication parameters from the NMS for each technology. It is worth noticing, however, that, even in infrastructures with a common manufacturer/vendor, there are separate NMSs for each access technology.

Every management system can communicate with the BS-ODORA using a standardized 3GPP (3GPP TS 32.615) XML structured document.

Figure 5. Statistical data collection through network management systems of different access technologies

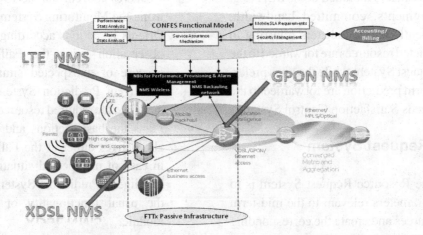

Specifically, such messages are already used for the existing and planned operational purposes of OAM (Operations And Management) systems and OSS (Operational Support System).

On the other hand, the centralized monitoring system of the NMS collects traffic information over a SNMPv3 protocol, in order to draw all the appropriate messages from the individual network entities or access points and calculate the quality indication parameters. The recording of quality indication parameters in a XML format file is not a real-time procedure but occurs in specific time intervals, for instance every 5 minutes. Furthermore, the kind and the multitude of quality indication parameters are usually limited to a certain number of standardized 3GPP parameters (3GPP TS 29.213). As a result, it is impossible to directly calculate specialized quality parameters for new services or for a combination of services. This can only be achieved indirectly, by processing a multitude of other measurements. The collection

of the XML files can be accomplished either by downloading the updated XML files from the NMS using ftp, or by using a JMS/XML protocol, as can be seen in Figure 6. In the following paragraphs, the advantages and disadvantages of the centralized architecture using a central NMS and a central billing platform are presented.

Advantages and Disadvantages of an NMS-Based Centralized Management Architecture

The advantages of a centralized architecture using an NMS mainly include:

- Direct access to quality indication parameters without the need of analyzing individual messages for each access technology.
- Low cost due to the use of software-based probes or XML files.

Figure 6. XML file collection

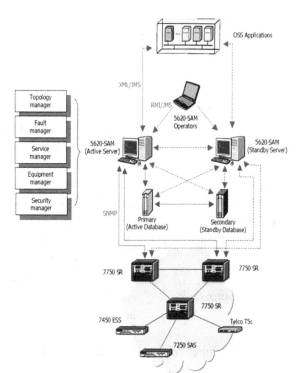

- No need for specialized software or hardware for the NMS-OMC interface.
- Use of a single protocol for the reception of quality indication parameters, regardless of the access technology.
- Compatibility with manufacturers that comply with the 3GPP XML format for statistical data.

While the following the most important disadvantages:

- Limitation in the kind and the number of quality indication parameters.
- Time limitation in the update process of the statistical data and the quality indication parameters.

Advantages and Disadvantages of a Billing Platform Based Centralized Architecture

The approach of having a centralized architecture that utilizes the mobile operator's central billing system presents both positive and negative aspects. Its advantages include:

- Functionality and compatibility regardless of the vendor.
- Flexibility in the supervision of heterogeneous networks that use the same billing method.
- Direct access to quality indication parameters without the need of analyzing individual messages for each access technology.
- Use of only one protocol for the reception of quality indication parameters regardless of the technology.

The main disadvantages of this approach include the following:

- Limitation in the kind and the number of the quality indication parameters.

- Time limitation in the update process of the statistical data and the quality indication parameters, as the billing reports are created at the end of the service period.
- Lack of detailed and low level information for important quality parameters, e.g. for IP data services.

DISTRIBUTED ARCHITECTURES

Use of Distributed Entities for Statistical Data Collection

A first step for migrating from a centralized architecture to a distributed one is to assign the task of statistics collection and extraction to dedicated distributed agents or probes, while retaining the more in-depth analysis of these statistics to a main entity (server). In this light, the communication process between a main BS-ODORA entity and several individual BS-ODORA sub-entities according to specific network interfaces is the basis for the distributed architecture. The sub-entities are connected, at physical layer, to the same interfaces where the access points are connected (base stations for wireless networks; xDSLAM or GPON (ITU-T G.984) for fixed networks). Each sub-entity consists of an embedded computer with at least two network Ethernet interfaces at bridge mode, so that it does not interfere with the network's information flaw. The software of the embedded computer is a special network analyzer, which supports the standardized connection protocol over Ethernet, in a way that, through the message analysis, data for the efficiency of the access point can be extracted.

This type of architecture exploits, in practice, the majority of backbone network Web infrastructures, which are based on Ethernet interfaces and IP networking, such as for LTE, WiMAX and WiFi networks, and offers a cost-effective modern solution. The interfaces must be able to support rates of 1 Gbps and the probe's processor must be able to parse data in real time through the protocol analyzer, and collect the necessary data through the messages at the application layer. The implementation of the protocol analyzer can be based upon the well-known TCPDUMP/ LIBPCAP library, which is used by Wireshark analyzers (TCPDUMP & LIBCAP library). Figure 7 depicts the points where network entities, as described above, can be connected to mobile networks. In any case, the network probes need to implement the standardized 3GPP protocols. The arrows highlight the exact interface where a CONFES probe can be inserted, for each technology under consideration.

Apart from the individual distributed subentities, a main BS-ODORA entity can be used for collecting the individual statistics from the distributed agents. Finally, in order for the above described structure to be fully functional, it is obvious that both parts have to support a statistics transfer protocol and an agent configuration protocol. This implies that each individual distributed sub-entity has to be automatically configurable. This can be achieved by using protocols like RT69. In this way, every agent can be automatically configured with settings specific for each technology and access point. Moreover, the abovementioned implementation can be used for traffic statistics exchange. Figure 8 depicts the distributed architecture of an LTE network. A

probe is introduced at an intermediate interface, with the aim to collect and extract individual quality indication data.

The advantages of using distributed entities for statistics collection include the following:

- Functionality and compatibility regardless of the equipment's vendor.
- Extraction of performance statistics at every level.
- Flexibility in the supervision of heterogeneous networks.
- Use of distributed BS-ODORA entities.
- Use of a simple central system for data analysis.
- Resource allocation for Monitoring, Feedback and Local Prediction.
- Real-time analysis of traffic data without time constraints from the management system.

While the disadvantages mainly focus on:

- Investment costs due to the need for hundreds of sub-entities in large-scale networks.
- Use of expensive equipment at interfaces of high capacity (10 Gbps).
- Possibility of time limitations in the extraction of data.

Figure 7. Connection points of distributed subunits-agents for mobile networks

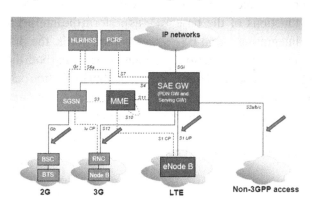

Figure 8. Use of CONFES probes at certain core network interfaces

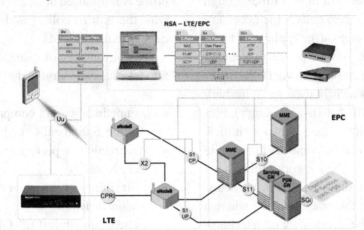

Use of Distributed Data Processing Entities

In the same context, the proposed system could be integrated through appropriate interfaces into GSM/GPRS/EDGE and UMTS/HSPA/HSPA+ networks. Specifically, the interfaces Abis and lub are defined as the backhaul network for GSM/GPRS/EDGE and UMTS/HSPA/HSPA+ networks, respectively, and could, in a future converged infrastructure, be served by a shared optical network.

At each base station, the required capacity that must be provided by the optical network varies in time according to the traffic served by the base station. The backhaul connection of a base station, at the edge of the optical network, can be served by a dedicated Optical Network Unit (ONU). On the other hand, the necessary resource prediction and resource negotiation functions of the base station can be realized by integrating into a BS-ODORA processing agent into each base station. At the same time, the collection of statistics and quality indication parameters can be performed by accessing the mobile operator's NMS. Figure 9 presents the corresponding architectural approach for the case of UMTS/HSPA/HSPA+ networks (lub interface).

Distributed Entities for Data Collection and Processing

In previous section, a distributed architectural approach was described, which collects statistics from the network through the use of distributed entities, and processes via a central main entity, while in the next section a solution of distributed entities which process data collected through the mobile operator's NMS was presented. Both of the above solutions are partly based on a centralized system, either for the data processing (first case) or for the statistics collection (second case). Evolving even further, towards a fully distributed architecture, all of the above functions must be performed by distributed entities. Therefore, a combined structure of the above solutions includes the use of distributed BS-ODORA entities, which will have to locally collect statistical data, as well as perform the intelligent processing of these data. In other words, the distributed entities are fully autonomous and both the collection and processing of quality indication parameters is done at the base station level, either directly, through the appropriate interfaces for base station data extraction, or indirectly by probes placed in the network.

Figure 9. Integration of CONFES solution in UMTS/HSPA networks

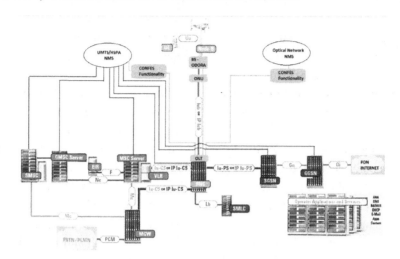

EXPERIMENTAL RESULTS

The role of CONFES as an overlay network management system is to proactively determine PON clients' needs in bandwidth resources, and to allocate these resources efficiently and reasonably to multiple clients according to their needs and their corresponding SLAs. The entity of BS-ODORA predicts base station resource requirements and announces them to the CONFES Core.

In this frame, an Artificial Neural Network (ANN) was implemented and employed inside the BS-ODORA management entity, which -after proper training- was able to satisfactorily predict the base station's backhaul resource requirements.

Artificial Neural Networks (Haykin, 1999), inspired by the human brain learning system, are among the most effective machine learning methods currently known. They use a training set consisting of input and output data in order to learn a target function. One major advantage of ANN is its robustness to errors in the training data. The basic unit element of Neural Networks is the neuron. A neuronal model consists of three basic elements:

A set of connecting links (synapses), each characterized by a weight w_{kj} which is the j input of the k neuron.

- An adder for summing the input signals.
- An activation function that limits the amplitude of the output of a neuron.

The input data is represented by a vector $X = [X_1; X_2; \ldots; X_n]$ and the model calculates a linear combination of these inputs and outputs. There is also an externally applied bias b_k that is used to increase or decrease the input of the activation function $\varphi(\bullet)$. The output u_k of the summation unit of neuron k is

$$U_k = \sum_{j=1}^{m} w_{kj} x_j \qquad (1)$$

and the output y_k of neuron k is

$$y_k = \varphi(u_k + b_k) \qquad (2)$$

There are plenty of different ANN types. For implementation and evaluation of the BS-ODORA prediction capability, a General Regression Neural Network (GRNN) was used, as compared to other ANNs, it was found to be give the best results for the problem at hand.

Figure 10 summarizes the mean absolute square error results that were extracted using three different Neural Networks, which were tested with the same type of input vector.

According to Figure 10, GRNN outperforms the other two network types and gives better results, regarding the mean absolute square error. Based on this analysis, the intelligent prediction system of BS-ODORA was finally implemented with a GRNN.

A General Regression Neural Network (Specht, 1991) is a one-pass neural network used for estimation of continuous variables. Its fast learning ability and the convergence to the optimal regression surface, as the samples become very large, consist among its main advantages. Furthermore, because the regression surface is instantly defined everywhere, GRNN is a perfect choice for situations with sparse data in a real-time environment, which renders GRNN ideal for load forecasting.

For the training process, a set of data collected by one of the largest mobile operators in Greece was used as input. The data were collected for a period of 4 months, every single hour, from a central base station in the center of Athens. The base station supports HSPA (High Speed Packet Access) connectivity. The neural network was trained to achieve a close to reality prediction of the bandwidth demand for the base station.

The collected data were processed to give the input vector that is presented in Box 1.

For the GRN network, a Gaussian function was used as kernel function, cross validation with one row left out of each model build was chosen as a validation method for the returned results, and sigma (σ) values for each single variable were taken into consideration. Sigma values control the influence degree that each variable has. One challenging issue is the right choice of the smoothing parameter σ. If σ is large, then the estimated density is smooth and in the limit case becomes a multivariate Gaussian. On the other hand, if σ is small, then the estimated density has non-Gaussian shapes, but at the risk that distant points may have a great effect on the estimate.

The implemented neural network was set up to choose different sigma value for each single variable, which gives the possibility to calculate one separate sigma value for each prediction variable and to differentiate the influence each variable has on its neighbors.

The results of the prediction process are given in Table 2.

Figure 10. Mean absolute square error for the general regression neural network (GRNN), the 3-layered perceptron neural network and the GMDH polynomial neural network

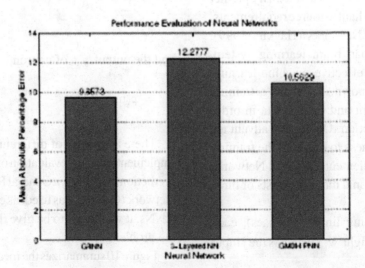

Box 1.

$$x = [month(1..12), date(1..31), day(1..7), time(in\ mins\ from\ 0\ to\ 1440), special\ event(0..1),$$
$$low\ bandwidth\ users(previous\ time\ period), mid\ bandwidth\ users(previous\ time\ period),$$
$$high\ bandwidth\ users(previous\ time\ period)]$$

As may be observed, the implemented learning mechanism is able to predict the backhaul resource requirements of the base station with a mean percentage error of 7,82%. This means that the resource requirements of the base station can proactively be requested (towards the PON) with satisfactory accuracy. Two parameter values can proactively be passed for optimal operation: a minimum and a maximum requested bandwidth, with the second one being approximately 7,82% greater than the first.

FUTURE RESEARCH DIRECTIONS

CONFES is a novel, future management platform that considers a passive optical network (PON) (Lescuyer & Lucidarme, 2008) as the backhauling solution for multiple next generation telecommunications networks. The proposed solution takes into account time varying bandwidth requirements and suggests an efficient learning-based mechanism for resource optimization and flexible service provisioning, as has already been described. The next steps include more validation and evaluation trials based on larger datasets. A demonstration network will be set up and installed at a pilot site. Apart from experiments with HSPA, the proposed system will also be tested on the emerging technology of LTE. More learning mechanisms, apart from those described in this chapter, can also be implemented and tested. The outcomes of such trials can help the improvement of the platform, so that the system may reach commercial operation.

CONCLUSION

This chapter introduced a novel overlay network management system for a converged wireless–optical infrastructure, aiming at the proactive determination of PON clients' needs in bandwidth resources, and the efficient and reasonable allocation of resources to multiple clients according to such needs and the corresponding SLA. To achieve this, a suitable functional architecture was identified and the role of its entity was described in detail. Special focus was given on the prediction entity, which is responsible for predicting the demand of a base station, by application of appropriate machine learning techniques, resulting in a cost-effective solution for the wireless network operator. First results show that prediction of the backhaul resource requirements of a base station can be achieved with an average percentage error of 7,82%, which makes the proposed solution feasible.

The physical architecture supporting this type of converged infrastructure is based on two main options. Firstly, at which network point will the collection of service quality indicators be performed; and secondly, where will the intelligent processing of this information, including the

Table 2. Experimental results

Error Type	Results
RMSE (Root Mean Squared Error)	2262,53kbps
MAE (Mean Absolute Error)	1773,81kbps
MAPE (Mean Absolute Percentage Error)	7,82

prediction process and the resource request issuing, be carried out. Therefore, as an overview of all possible choices, the collection of suitable quality parameters (such quality parameters are summarized per radio access technology type in Figure 11) can be performed by: (1) the BS directly, (2) the network provider's NMS, (3) the provider's billing system, and (4) distributed entities at certain network entities, equipped with protocol analyzers. The intelligent data processing can be performed by (1) the BS, (2) the network provider's NMS, (3) a server accessing the provider's NMS, (4) a server accessing the provider's billing system, (5) a server collecting data from the distributed, protocol analyzer enable probes, and (6) the distributed probes. Figure 12 summarizes the advantages and disadvantages of each of the discussed approaches.

ACKNOWLEDGMENT

This work has been performed under the Greek National project CONFES (2010 ΣΕ 01380022),

Figure 11. Statistical data and quality indication parameters that can be exploited by the BS-ODORA management system for backhaul resource prediction

Characteristics	Central Architecture	Distributed Architecture
Cost	low	high
Central System	Yes	Only at some cases
Distributed Units	No	Yes
Compatibility regardless the manufacturer	Yes (with xml)	Yes
Flexibility in the supervision of heterogeneous networks	Yes (when the same way of billing is used)	Yes
Need for specialized equipment	No	Yes (or at least when there is equipment with updated software)
Limitation of the number of exported quality indicators	Yes	No
Time limitation for renewal of quality indicators	Yes	No
Quality Indicators extraction	Directly download by using only one protocol, without the need to analyze the individual messages per technology.	Direct Calculation (statistic quality data extraction at any level)

Figure 12. Overview of architectural approaches

Quality Parameters	GSM	GSM/GPRS/EDGE	UMTS	HSPA/HSPA+	LTE	WiFi	WiMAX
Total number of users per access point	✓	✓	✓	✓	✓	✓	✓
Number of cells per BS	✓	✓	✓	✓	✓		
Total Bandwidth	✓	✓	✓	✓	✓	✓	✓
Average call duration	✓	✓	✓	✓	✓		
Bandwidth per type of service (voice, data)		✓	✓	✓	✓		
Bandwidth per user						✓	✓
Type of service (voice, data) and corresponding user percentage		✓	✓	✓	✓		
Data volume statistics per coding/modulation scheme		✓					
Signal level for every user and theoretic maximum speed per layer						✓	✓
Delay		✓	✓	✓	✓	✓	✓
Delay variance		✓	✓	✓	✓	✓	✓
Error rate		✓	✓	✓	✓	✓	✓

which has received research funding from the Operational Programme "Competitiveness & Entrepreneurship" of the National Strategic Reference Framework NSRF 2007-2013. This chapter reflects only the authors' views, and the Operational Programme is not liable for any use that may be made of the information contained therein.

REFERENCES

Alasti, M., Neekzad, B., Hui, J., & Vannithamby, R. (2010). Quality of service in WiMAX and LTE networks [Topics in Wireless Communications]. *IEEE Communications Magazine, 48*(5), 104–111. doi:10.1109/MCOM.2010.5458370.

Alcatel-Lucent. (2009). *The LTE Network Architecture.* White Paper.

Ali, M., Ellinas, G., Erkan, H., Hadjiantonis, A., & Dorsinville, R. (2010). On the Vision of Complete Fixed-Mobile Convergence. *Journal of Lightwave Technology.* doi:10.1109/JLT.2010.2050861.

Amemiya, M., Imae, M., Fujii, Y., Suzuyama, T., & Ohshima, S. (2005). Time and frequency transfer and dissemination methods using optical fiber network. *Frequency Control Symposium and Exposition* (pp. 914-918). Proceedings of the 2005 IEEE International.

Amram, N., Fu, B., Kunzmann, G., Melia, T., Munaretto, D., Randriamasy, S., et al. (2011). QoE-based Transport Optimization for Video Delivery over Next Generation Cellular Networks. *Proceedings of the IEEE Symposium on Computers and Communications*, (pp. 19-24).

Archimate Modeling Language. (2012). Retrieved December 2012, from http://www3.opengroup.org/subjectareas/enterprise/archimate

Butler, J., Lambea, J., Nolan, M., Theilmann, W., Torelli, F., Pistore, M. A., et al. (2011). SLAs empowering services in the future internet. Lecture Notes in Computer Science (including subseries Lecture Notes in Artificial Intelligence and Lecture Notes in Bioinformatics), 6656, 327-338.

Byun, H.-J., Nho, J.-M., & Lim, J.-T. (2003). Dynamic bandwidth allocation algorithm in Ethernet passive optical networks. *IEEE Electronics Letters, 39*(13), 1001–1002. doi:10.1049/el:20030635.

Chang, M., Abichar, Z., & Hsu, C. (2010). WiMAX or LTE: Who will Lead the Broadband Mobile Internet? *IT Professional, 12*(3), 26–32. doi:10.1109/MITP.2010.47.

Choi, S.-I., & Park, J. (2010). SLA-aware dynamic bandwidth allocation for QoS in EPONs. *Journal of Optical Communications and Networking, 2*(9), 773–781. doi:10.1364/JOCN.2.000773.

Chong, S., Li, S.-q., & Ghosh, J. (1995). Predictive dynamic bandwidth allocation for efficient transport of real-time VBR video over ATM. *IEEE Journal on Selected Areas in Communications, 13*(1), 12–13. doi:10.1109/49.363150.

Conti, J. (2010). LTE vs WiMax: the battle continues [COMMS WiMax vs LTE]. *Engineering & Technology, 5*(14), 63–65. doi:10.1049/et.2010.1417.

Cox, C. (2012). *An Introduction to LTE: LTE, LTE-Advanced, SAE and 4G Mobile Communications* (2nd ed.). Wiley. doi:10.1002/9781119942825.

Dahlman, E., Parkvall, S., & Skold, J. (2011). *4G: LTE/LTE-Advanced for Mobile Broadband* (1st ed.). Academic Press.

Ekstrom, H., Furuskar, A., Karlsson, J., Meyer, M., Parkvall, S., & Torsner, J. et al. (2006). Technical solutions for the 3G long-term evolution. *IEEE Communications Magazine, 44*(3), 38–45. doi:10.1109/MCOM.2006.1607864.

3GPP TS 29.213. (n.d.). Policy and charging control signalling flows and Quality of Service (QoS) parameter mapping.

3GPP TS 32.615. (n.d.). Telecommunication management; Configuration Management (CM); Bulk CM Integration Reference Point (IRP): eXtensible Markup Language (XML) file format definition.

Hadden, A. (2009). Mobile Broadband – Where the next generation leads us [industry perspectives]. *IEEE Wireless Communications, 16*(6), 6–9. doi:10.1109/MWC.2009.5361172.

Haykin, S. (1999). *Neural Networks, A Comprehensive Foundation* (2nd ed.). Prentice Hall.

Haykin, S. (2005). Cognitive Radio: Brain-Empowered Wireless Communications. *IEEE Journal on Selected Areas in Communications, 23*(2). doi:10.1109/JSAC.2004.839380.

Hood, D. (2012). *Gigabit-capable Passive Optical Networks* (1st ed.). Wiley. doi:10.1002/9781118156070.

ICT-ALPHA project. (2008-2011). Retrieved December 2012, from http://www.ict-alpha.eu/

ITU-T G.984. (n.d.). *Series recommendation* .

Jiang, J., & Senior, J. (2009). A new efficient dynamic MAC protocol for the delivery of multiple services over GPON. *Photonic Network Communications, 18*(2), 227–236. doi:10.1007/s11107-009-0186-x.

Kanonakis, K., Tomkos, I., Krimmel, H., Schaich, F., Lange, C., & Weis, E. et al. (2012). An OFDMA-based optical access network architecture exhibiting ultra-high capacity and wireline-wireless convergence. *IEEE Communications Magazine, 50*(8), 71–78. doi:10.1109/MCOM.2012.6257530.

Kantarci, B., & Mouftah, H. (2012). Ethernet passive optical network-long-term evolution deployment for a green access network. *IET Optoelectronics, 6*(4), 183–191. doi:10.1049/iet-opt.2010.0112.

Kramer, G., & Pesavento, G. (2002). Ethernet passive optical network (EPON): building a next-generation optical access network. *IEEE Communications Magazine, 40*(2), 66–73. doi:10.1109/35.983910.

Lam, C. (2007). *Passive Optical Networks, Principles and Practice*. Elsevier.

Lescuyer, P., & Lucidarme, T. (2008). *Evolved Packet System (EPS), The LTE and SAE Evolution of 3G UMTS*. Wiley. doi:10.1002/9780470723678.

Li, Q., Li, G., Lee, W., Lee, M.-i., Mazzarese, D., & Clerckx, B. et al. (2010). MIMO techniques in WiMAX and LTE: a feature overview. *IEEE Communications Magazine, 48*(5), 86–92. doi:10.1109/MCOM.2010.5458368.

Mitchell, T. (1997). *Machine Learning*. McGraw-Hill.

Mitola, J., & Maguire, G. (1999). Cognitive Radio: Making Software Radios More Personal. *IEEE Personal Communications*, 13-18.

Obele, B., Iftikhar, M., & Kang, M. (2011). On the QoS behavior of self-similar traffic in a converged ONU-BS under custom queueing. *Journal of Communications and Networks, 13*(3), 286–297.

OFDM-PON project. (2011-2013). Retrieved December 2012, from http://cordis.europa.eu/projects/rcn/96242_en.html

Ou, S., Yang, K., & Chen, H.-H. (2010). Integrated Dynamic Bandwidth Allocation in Converged Passive Optical Networks and IEEE 802.16 Networks. *IEEE Systems Journal, 4*(4), 467–476. doi:10.1109/JSYST.2010.2088750.

Oyman, O., Foerster, J., Tcha, Y.-j., & Lee, S.-C. (2010). Toward enhanced mobile video services over WiMAX and LTE [WiMAX/LTE Update]. *IEEE Communications Magazine, 48*(8), 68–76. doi:10.1109/MCOM.2010.5534589.

Ramaswami, R., Sivarajan, K., & Sasaki, G. (2009). *Optical Networks: A Practical Perspective* (3rd ed.). Morgan Kaufmann.

Ranaweera, C., Wong, E., Lim, C., & Nirmalathas, A. (2012). Next generation optical-wireless converged network architectures. *IEEE Network, 26*(2), 22–27. doi:10.1109/MNET.2012.6172271.

3. Release, G. P. P. 8. (n.d.). Retrieved April 12, 2012, from http://www.3gpp.org/Release-8

Sesia, S., Toufik, I., & Baker, M. (2011). LTE – The UMTS Long Term Evolution – From Theory to Practice (Second Edition including Release 10 for LTE-Advanced ed.). John Wiley & Sons.

Sheetal, A. (2012). *WDM-Passive Optical Networks*. LAP LAMBERT Academic Publishing.

Shen, G., Tucker, R., & Chae, C.-J. (2007). Fixed Mobile Convergence Architectures for Broadband Access: Integration of EPON and WiMAX. *IEEE Communications Magazine, 45*(8), 44–50. doi:10.1109/MCOM.2007.4290313.

Skene, J., Raimondi, F., & Emmerich, W. (2010). Service-level agreements for electronic services. *IEEE Transactions on Software Engineering, 36*(2), 288–304. doi:10.1109/TSE.2009.55.

Smith, E. (2012). The impact of network availabilty on meeting service level agreements. *Journal of the Institute of Telecommunications Professionals, 6*(1), 39–46.

Specht, D. (1991). A General Regression Neural Network. *IEEE Transactions on Neural Networks, 2*(6). doi:10.1109/72.97934 PMID:18282872.

Srikanth, S., Murugesa Pandian, P., & Fernando, X. (2012). Orthogonal frequency division multiple access in WiMAX and LTE: a comparison. *IEEE Communications Magazine, 50*(9), 153–161. doi:10.1109/MCOM.2012.6295726.

Tanaka, H. (2011). *Convergence of optical and wireless networks. OptoeElectronics and Communications Conference* (pp. 389–390). OECC.

TCPDUMP & LIBCAP library. (n.d.). Retrieved April 12, 2012, from http://www.tcpdump.org/

WOPROF project. (2009-2011). Retrieved December 2012, from http://cordis.europa.eu/projects/rcn/90604_en.html

Yang, C. (2007). CDMA Passive Optical Network Using Prime Code With Interference Elimination. *IEEE Photonics Technology Letters, 19*(7), 516–518. doi:10.1109/LPT.2007.893579.

Yang, K., Ou, S., Guild, K., & Chen, H.-H. (2009). Convergence of Ethernet PON and IEEE 802.16 Broadband Access Networks and its QoS-Aware Dynamic Bandwidth Allocation Scheme. *IEEE Journal on Selected Areas in Communications, 27*(2), 101–116. doi:10.1109/JSAC.2009.090202.

Zahariadis, T., Grüneberg, K., & Celetto, L. (2011). Seamless Content Delivery over Mobile 3G+/4G Networks. *Mobile Networks and Applications, 16*(3), 351–360. doi:10.1007/s11036-010-0259-1.

Zhang, i., & Ansari, N. (2011). On assuring end-to-end QoE in next generation networks: challenges and a possible solution. *IEEE Communications Magazine, 49* (7), 185-191.

Chapter 12
Architectures and Information Signaling Techniques for Cognitive Networks

Dzmitry Kliazovich
University of Luxembourg, Luxembourg

Nelson Fonseca
State University of Campinas, Brazil

Fabrizio Granelli
University of Trento, Italy

Pascal Bouvry
University of Luxembourg, Luxembourg

ABSTRACT

The introduction of self-awareness, self-management, and self-healing into networks leads to a novel paradigm known as cognitive networking. This chapter overviews recent developments of this concept, discussing possible cognitive node structure and candidate cognitive network architecture. It explains the functionality of cognitive algorithms and discusses opportunities for potential optimization. Furthermore, the concept of cognitive information services is introduced. Information signaling techniques are then classified, reviewed in details, and compared among them. Finally, the performance of cognitive communication protocols is presented for a choice of examples.

INTRODUCTION

The evolution of communication technologies has brought networking a step closer to a service provisioning on an "anytime, anywhere" basis, yet ensuring instantaneous secure communications. However, such an innovation is limited by the constraints imposed by the original design of the Internet which leads to the inefficient configuration and management of networks (Georgakopoulos, Tsagkaris, Karvounas, Vlacheas, & Demestichas, 2012).

Self-awareness, self-management, and self-healing have all been proposed for the optimization of network operation, reconfiguration, and

DOI: 10.4018/978-1-4666-4189-1.ch012

Copyright © 2013, IGI Global. Copying or distributing in print or electronic forms without written permission of IGI Global is prohibited.

management. The introduction of such "self-properties" contributes to an increase in network "intelligence", as well as creating a new paradigm, known as cognitive networking, which is expected to be part of the 4th generation wireless networks (4G) (Maravedis, 2006).

Cognition implies the awareness of the network of its own operational state, as well as its ability to automatically adjust operational parameters to accomplish specific tasks, such as the detection of environmental changes. Cognition depends on the support of network elements (routers, switches, base stations, etc.), to host active agents which can measure network status and configuration parameters in order to drive its reconfiguration when needed.

The ability to think, learn and benefit from past experience requires interaction between cognitive agents. Cognitive networks are usually composed of a set of cognitive engines, which can reside in a protocol layer, between different layers, or be distributed among various nodes (Kliazovich, Granelli, & Fonseca, 2009). Each cognitive agent operates locally but contributes to the achievement of global goals by interacting with other cognitive agents. Indeed, the efficiency of the operation of cognitive networks depends on the communication among these agents. Depending on the communication scope, which can be inter-layer, intra-layer, or network wide, different technologies can be used, each imposing specific constraints on the speed and delay of information exchange. Such constraints cannot be neglected and should be taken into account during the design of cognitive network architectures.

Cognitive networking encompasses multiple wireless technologies and is designed to deal with the complexities of network configuration, as well as the support of user applications. Cognitive networks can increase the profit of wireless service providers by reducing costs and developing new streams of revenue as a result of the provisioning of heterogeneous wireless access solutions (Zhang & Hanzo, 2010). The benefits for service providers deriving from the adoption of cognitive networks include the following: the possibility of relying on common hardware and software platforms while coping with the evolution of radio technologies, the development of new services, the minimization of infrastructure upgrades, accelerated innovation, and the maximization of return-on-investment (Clark at el., 2003).

Cognitive technologies allow network operators to continuously analyze network configuration and its performance. Moreover, reconfiguration can be triggered by application requirements, policies, or billing plans. Furthermore, cognitive networking offers extended sets of operations, allowing new ways of interaction between network operators and end-users (Demestichas, Dimitrakopoulos, & Strassner, 2006).

In the following sections, we discuss a reference network architecture which can be used to enable cognition properties, with an emphasis on aspects related to interoperability and incremental deployment. We also provide an extensive survey of various techniques which can be used for cognitive information exchange; this is the key to the design and successful deployment of such cognitive optimization techniques. Finally, the chapter presents cognitive communication protocols for the transport and the link layers.

BACKGROUND

Cognitive Node Architecture

Designing the architecture of a node in a cognitive network requires a careful balance between performance and interoperability. Indeed, interoperability represents a stringent constraint in network research.

Cognitive node is a generic network node, such as user terminal equipment, which carries complete or partial implementation of TCP/IP protocol stack and is capable of running a cognitive process for the purpose of reconfiguration of cognitive protocols stack parameters. Figure 1 shows the main functional blocks of a cognitive node. The design is oriented to support the requirements of interoperability with the TCP/IP protocol stack. In line with this, software modules are included in protocol layers, so that information internal to the layer can be obtained (observation) and parameter values tuned (action). Information monitored for different protocol layers is delivered to the cognitive engine implemented in a cognitive node. Quality of service requirements of running applications, such as a minimum bandwidth, delay bounds and packet loss rate are provided at the application layer. Information on round trip times and achievable sending rate is available at the transport layer. In case of a mismatch between these values and those required by the applications, the cognitive node can optimize transport layer parameters to achieve higher throughput or reduce delays. The cognitive node can, for example, force the application behavior to adapt itself to the current network conditions by selecting a lower bitrate codec. The network layer provides information on the network state, routing decisions, and the

selected Network Interface Card (NIC). The link layer signals changes in the link state (e.g., fading), reports bit and packet error rates, and enables higher layers to handle handover procedures. The physical layer can report transmission rate values and control the power emitted by transmitters.

The *cognitive engine* analyzes data and makes decisions. The goal is to properly configure communication protocols adequately on different layers and optimize protocol stack performance. To do this, the cognitive engine interacts with the running applications, controlling all protocol layers, and maintaining databases with observations of past performance, accumulated knowledge, and targeted goals. The cognitive adaptation algorithms are structured in steps, such as observation, data analysis, decision-making, and action. The cognitive engine periodically reconfigures protocol parameter values, monitors the obtained performance, and stores performance information in the database. Observations are used to derive knowledge which, after combined with the setup parameter values employed by the cognitive engine, can lead to optimal performance.

Figure 1. Cognitive node architecture

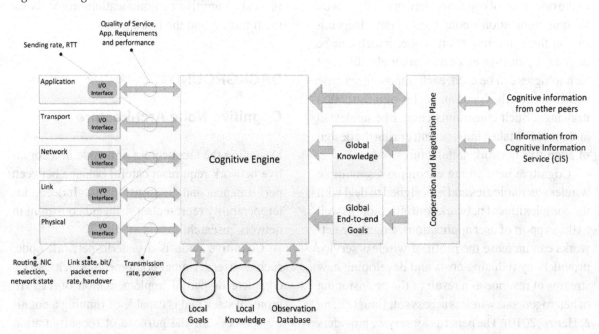

The decisions made by the cognitive engine at the node aim to optimize the protocol stack performance. They are driven by local goals for the specific nodes, specified and stored in the local database. Most goals are generated by the demands and QoS requirements of user applications. The cognitive engine also implements communication interfaces for information sharing. The decision-making process can take into account performance information available in the local knowledge base, as well that obtained from neighboring nodes.

The *cooperation and negotiation plane* attempts to perform network-wide cognitive optimization by allowing the exchange of cognitive information with other cognitive nodes in a distributed manner. Information harvesting can be either scheduled or undertaken by using instant requests or interrupts. Moreover, information can be either node-specific or data flow specific. In addition, the cognitive information can be exchanged using the Cognitive Information Service (CIS) which is a dedicated service in the network that receives and aggregates cognitive information from multiple nodes and provides information to other nodes upon request. The cooperation and negotiation plane allows nodes to obtain global knowledge, especially information on system-level goals. Nodes are required to cooperate in either a distributed or a centralized way to achieve global goals.

One of the main characteristics of the architecture of cognitive network is scalability. This is assured by the use of a combination of cognitive algorithms operating at the node level (centralized) and at the network level (distributed). Specifically, at the node level, the core cognitive techniques (such as data analysis, decision making, and learning) are concentrated on the cognitive planes of the nodes and centrally implemented. Moreover, observation and add-ons to the protocol layers are typically "non-intelligent". Distributing the cognitive process among the protocol layers (especially the learning and decision making functions) would require complex algorithms for synchronization and coordination between intra-layer cognitive processes. A simpler solution is the adoption of a centralized cognitive process.

Figure 2. Cognitive information service

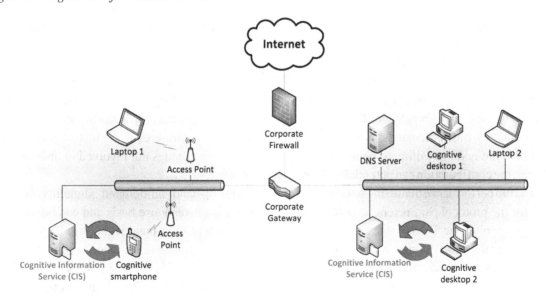

Cognitive Information Service

Cognition implies the actual or virtual existence of a database to enable the maintenance of the "history" of the network and support the decision-making process.

Figure 2 elaborates on such a concept by introducing the idea of the Cognitive Information Service (CIS) which is a network service that assists in the information exchange between cognitive nodes. It can receive, process, and aggregate cognitive information from any node in the network, as well as analyzing it and deriving system-level knowledge to guide future configuration decisions to be made by other nodes in the network.

The CIS, similar to the Domain Name Service (DNS), is implemented in a network segment with well-defined boundaries. The number of the nodes served and the size of the network segment should be limited by the design or implementation constraints to prevent CIS overload.

Both point-to-point and point-to-multipoint communications with the CIS server is possible. The latter is especially useful when the aggregation of cognitive information is sent to a large number of nodes. For this, either IP multicast at the network level or MAC broadcast at the link level can be used.

Whenever a new node joins the network, it can query the CIS for the optimal suggested configuration of its protocol stack parameters. However, the configuration offered by the CIS to a new node will not necessarily be optimal, as it will be computed without prior knowledge of the running applications, its traffic demands, and the peers with which the node is willing to communicate. However, the configuration can potentially offer a better startup performance than using fixed default values for the protocol parameters, as performed for the protocol of the TCP/IP stack.

The next presents a review and comparison between existing information signaling techniques that form the basis for implementation of different cognitive network techniques.

INFORMATION SIGNALING IN COGNITIVE NETWORKS

Many information signaling techniques are designed to overcome different limitations of the standard TCP/IP protocol reference model. Depending on the nature and requirements of information exchange information signaling solutions can be classified into in-band, on-demand, and broadcast signaling.

Signaling Methods

In-band signaling is the most effective signaling method from the point of view of overhead reduction. Cognitive information can be encapsulated into ongoing traffic flows, such as into optional packet header fields (Carrier Sense Multiple Access with Collision Detection, 1985), and delivered without waste of bandwidth resources.

Given its low overhead, in-band implementation of CIS is well suited for networks with wireless technologies used for networks access such as WiFi, WiMAX, and cellular (Zhang & Hanzo, 2010). One advantage of in-band signaling is that cognitive information can be associated with the portion of the application data with which it is delivered.

However, the main shortcoming of in-band signaling is that signaling is limited to the direction of the packet flow, making it unsuitable to cognitive schemes requiring instant communication between nodes not involved in ongoing data exchange.

Out-of-band on-demand signaling operates on a request-response basis and can be used as a complement to in-band signaling. It is designed for cases requiring instantaneous cognitive information delivery between network nodes. Since cognitive information is available at the requesting node only after some round-trip time delay has elapsed, on-demand signaling is well suited for the Wired/Wireless LAN scenario.

One of the core signaling protocols considered in on-demand signaling is the Internet Control Message Protocol (ICMP) (Postel, 1981). Generation of ICMP messages is not constrained by any specific protocol layer and can be performed on any layer of the protocol stack. However, signaling with ICMP messages involves operation with heavy protocol headers (IP and ICMP), checksum calculation, and other procedures which increase processing overhead.

Out-of-band broadcast signaling allows low-overhead point-to-multipoint cognitive information delivery from CIS server to the network nodes located in the same segment. Broadcasting is especially suited for wireless networks involving cellular organization.

In this approach, cognitive information is encapsulated into a beacon, which is periodically broadcasted by wireless gateways (access points or base stations), thus fitting scenarios where a

delay in the delivery of cognitive information can be tolerated so that the broadcasting can be performed at regular intervals.

According to their scope, signaling techniques can also be divided into two broad categories: node-level signaling and network-level signaling (see Table 1).

Node-Level Signaling

Node-level signaling techniques provide the means for information exchange between different layers of the TCP/IP stack initially designed to be standalone and separated.

Interlayer signaling pipe was one of the first approaches used for the implementation of cross-layer signaling (Wang & Abu-Rgheff, 2003) and to allow the propagation of signaling messages layer-to-layer along the packet data flow. Signaling information, included in an optional portion of packet headers, for example into an optional portion of IPv6 header (Deering & Hinden, 1998), follows the packet processing path within the pro-

Table 1. Comparison of signaling approaches

	Signaling Method	Scope	Type of Signaling	Signaling latency	Communication overhead	In-band / Out-of-band	Direction of signaling	Packet Association
Node-level Signaling	Interlayer signaling pipe	Node	Indication	Medium	High	In-band	Path dependent	Maintained
	Direct interlayer communication	Node	Request/ Response	Low	High	Out-of-band	Path independent	Not maintained
	Central cognitive plane	Node	Indication/ Request/ Response	Low	Medium	Out-of-band	Path independent	Not maintained
Network-level Signaling	ICMP messages	Network	Indication/ Request/ Response	High	High	Out-of-band	Path independent	Not maintained
	Packet headers	Network	Indication	High	Low	In-band	Path dependent	Maintained
	Explicit Notification	Network	Indication	High	Low	In-band	Path independent	Not maintained
	WCI	Network	Indication/ Request/ Response	High	High	Out-of-band	Path independent	Not maintained
	Cross-talk	Node/ Network	Indication/ Request/ Response	High	Low	In-band	Path dependent	Maintained

tocol stack, either in a top-down or in a bottom-up manner. One important property of this signaling method is that information can be associated with a specific packet, from the protocol stack either incoming or outgoing.

Generally, the signaling method using packet structures is preferable, due to a lower processing overhead as well as flexibility, and simplicity of access or modification of encapsulated information on any protocol layer.

Direct Interlayer Communication (DIC), proposed in (Wang at el., 2003), was designed to improve Interlayer signaling by introducing of "signaling shortcuts" performed out of band. DIC allows non-neighboring layers of the protocol stack to exchange messages, skipping processing on adjacent layers. Along with reduced processing overhead, DIC avoids insertion of signaling information into packet headers, which makes it suitable for bidirectional communication.

Despite the advantages of direct communication between protocol layers and standardized signaling, the ICMP-based approach involves significant overhead for protocol processing. Moreover, it is limited to request-response actions, while more complicated signaling should be adapted to handle asynchronous events. To this aim, a mechanism employing callback functions at the node level can be employed. Such mechanism allows a given protocol layer to register a specific procedure (callback function) with another protocol layer, with execution triggered by specific event at that layer.

The Central Cognitive Plane, which is implemented parallel to the protocol stack, is probably the most widely proposed interlayer signaling scheme. Each protocol layer is extended with a tiny interface that allows the exchange of information and configuration commands to be performed. These interfaces are interconnected with a cognitive engine using a common bus.

Implementation of this signaling method could be as simple as the access to a shared database by all layers (Chen, Shah & Nahrstedt, 2003),

while more advanced implementations needs to introduce interfaces to provide access to protocol layer parameters and functions (Raisinghani & Iyer, 2006).

Network-Level Signaling

Most of the existing cross-layer signaling proposals employ signaling between different protocol stack layers of a single node. However, cognitive processes have a network-wide scope and have end-to-end goals (Thomas, Friend, DaSilva & MacKenzie, 2006; Georgakopoulos, Tsagkaris, Karvounas, Vlacheas, & Demestichas, 2012). Consequently, cognitive networks require signaling approaches capable of effectively delivering signaling information between different nodes.

Packet headers can encapsulate signaling information and propagate it along the data flow making it available to network routers as well as to the end nodes. This method of signaling keeps overhead to the minimum and allows the association of signaling information with specific network packets. However, signaling information carried in the packet header implies a fixed direction of the signaling flow.

ICMP messages is usually the default signaling method, since signaling information carried by ICMP messages can be directed and processed at the destination in the same way ordinary IP data packets are processed. Moreover, ICMP messages are usually processed in the kernel, rather than in the user application domain.

Signaling using ICMP messages is desirable when instant communication is needed. However, these messages consume network bandwidth and have an impact on the delays experienced by other flows. They should be used only as a supplement to other signaling scheme to packet headers.

Explicit notification schemes, such as Explicit Congestion Notification (ECN) (Ramakrishnan, Floyd & Black, 2001), can be employed for network-level signaling. ECN signaling is performed in-band by letting network routers mark in-transit

TCP data packets with a congestion notification bit. At the receiver, this marking is feedback in TCP acknowledgement packets directed to the sender.

The main advantage of explicit notification schemes is the low overhead; the drawbacks include the limitation of signaling propagation to a specific path, the need to maintain of the signaling loop and the requirement for all network routers to support signaling and traffic generation functionalities.

The Wireless Channel Information (WCI) adopts a Central Cognitive Plane architecture to promote network-level signaling (Kim, 2001); this is accomplished by using a specifically dedicated network service that collects current wireless channel characteristics from both the link and the physical layers. Information is aggregated and sent to the mobile stations, allowing better adaptation to constantly changing channel conditions. In this method, communication is performed using standard TCP/IP protocols, such as SNMP and HTTP over TCP.

CrossTalk is a combination of node- and network-level signaling (Winter, Schiller, Nikaein & Bonnet, 2006). CrossTalk involves two cross-layer optimization planes: one responsible for the organization of cross-layer information exchange between protocol layers of a single node, and the other responsible for network-wide coordination. Most of the signaling is performed in-band, using packet headers, making it accessible not only to the end host but also to the network routers. Cross-layer information received from the network is aggregated and then employed jointly with information on global network conditions in the optimization of local protocol stack operation.

Comparison of Signaling Approaches

In this section, a comparison of the characteristics of the different signaling type, scope, latency, communication overhead, banding, signaling

direction and association with specific packet flows in the network.

There is no general scheme optimal for coping with both node- and network-wide signaling. Therefore, various signaling methods must be employed simultaneously in cognitive networks so that efficient functionality of cognitive algorithms can be ensured.

This comparison is summarized in Table 1. Further details can be found in (Kliazovich, Granelli & Fonseca, 2011).

Scope defines the boundaries of operation. Solutions limited to a single protocol stack tend to be flexible, since they can use internal protocol stack structures such as packet format and callback functions, thus avoiding the processing related to overhead.

Solutions operating at the node are suitable for signaling between reconfigurable elements of a cognitive network. Signaling can typically be implemented using direct interlayer communication methods and either interlayer signaling pipe or a central cognitive plane.

Type of signaling is related to the communication primitives supported by each signaling method. Approaches encapsulating signaling information into packet structures, such as, packet headers on the use of explicit notification, are limited to the use of these structures, while other approaches that transmit out-of-band support a wider range of communication, including request-response actions.

The choice of signaling depends on the actions required to be performed between cognitive agents. At the node level, a cognitive engine performing blind monitoring of the environment can be connected with a cognitive engine that employs methods based on packet structures, allowing for low-overhead communication. However, when a cognitive agent needs to setup certain parameters, request-response actions are unavoidable, which implies on heavy signaling overhead.

Signaling latency provides information on the delay associated with the delivery of signaling messages. This information is essential when signaling is to be performed across the network. The local delay resulting from signaling methods is usually several orders of magnitude less than that on the network-level. However, the interlayer signaling pipe method is slower than direct interlayer communication due to processing being carried out layer-by-layer. Moreover, the interlayer signaling pipe method can only suggest an asynchronous reaction to events, whereas direct communication allows instantaneous reactions.

Propagation delay also impacts on the efficiency of cognitive network implementation, as well as the on architecture design. It also influences information aggregation and the intervals for reporting adopted by cognitive engines involved in monitoring as well as impacting on the speed of cognitive engine, and of the reactions to changes in the network.

Communication overhead refers to the amount of network resources required for signaling. The encapsulation of signaling information into packets headers does not require additional network resources as long as reserved fields are used, leads to only a minor increase in processing when optional packet header fields are involved. The use of ICMP messages, however, requires additional overhead for delivery, which consumes network resources. The overhead for local signaling includes the number of operations (CPU cycles) required to deliver the message from one layer to another (his parameter does not include processing overhead of message encapsulation). The greatest communication overhead for local communications is associated with interlayer signaling pipe due to processing on several protocol layers prior to message delivery.

The least communication overhead is involved in signaling methods relying on existing data flow; other signaling methods, such as those using ICMP messages or WCI, require standalone transmission of signaling information encapsulated into low protocol headers, which consumes network band-width. Moreover, it is possible that the bandwidth consumed by signaling may nullify all the benefits to be obtained from cognitive optimization if the reporting interval of the cognitive engine is not chosen appropriately.

In-band/Out-of-band parameter indicates whether signaling information is transmitted in existing data traffic flow (in-band) or is transmitted separately (out-of-band). In-band signaling does not lead to any on significant overhead in term of network bandwidth and routing resources, although the primitives which can be utilized (packet headers, explicit notification and Crosstalk) are limited and delivery latency high. On the other hand, out-of-band signaling, since it is not constrained by signaling type, allows for faster information delivery, although this is achieved at the expense of greater network resource use.

Direction of signaling is related to the applicability of a signaling approach for a cross-layer optimization scheme. Out-of-band signaling schemes are path independent and can provide fast reactions to events, moreover, these reactions can take place simultaneously. Path dependent signaling, at the other hand, involves only asynchronous reaction. The speed and flexibility of path independent signaling is achieved at the expense of additional communication resources. Moreover, it does not allow packet association.

Packet association indicates whether signaling information can be associated with a specific packet transmitted through the network. Such a property is required by many optimization approaches. For example, at the network level, an ECN signal sent with a TCP data packet and echoed back with TCP acknowledgement by the receiver indirectly carries information related to the TCP flow for which ECN signal was sent. At the node level, information monitored on the physical layer (SNR or BER) must typically be associated with the packet for which it was measured.

In-band signaling techniques maintain indirect association between transferred signaling information transferred and the packet used to carry it. However, if out-of-band signaling is used such an association can be explicitly inserted. A good example is when the "Time Exceeded" ICMP message includes copies of the headers of the packet dropped.

Summarizing, we can observe that a large number of signaling methods exists that provide means for information exchange in cognitive network. Proper signaling methods should be selected at the design stage depending on the required scope and speed of signaling, signaling latency, and communication overhead. As a result, different cognitive networks may employ several information signaling techniques at the same time, especially those implementing cognitive process at the network level.

In the next section two examples of communication protocols implementing cognitive techniques at the transport and at the link layers are presented.

COGNITIVE COMMUNICATION PROTOCOLS

Cognitive Transmission Control Protocol

The Cognitive TCP (CogTCP) protocol (Kliazovich, Malheiros, Granelli, Madeira & Fonseca, 2010) continuously reconfigures its parameters, such as congestion window increase and decrease factors, to achieve optimal performance under constantly changing network conditions. These self-configuration capabilities are supported by a three step feedback loop: data analysis, decision making, and action.

A default value P_{def} is assigned to the parameter of interest for each a new flow. The cognitive engine periodically collects performance information on the current value of the parameter P. The average system performance obtained by using

the current value of P constantly being updated and stored in the local knowledge base. In the following equation T_a denotes system performance obtained with the current value of the parameter of interest (P). The average value of T_a is obtained using an exponentially weighted moving average (EWMA) as follows:

$$T_a = T_a * \left(w\right) + T_m * \left(1 - w\right),$$

where T_m is the current value of a system performance value obtained from using T_a, and w (the smoothing factor) is the weight assigned to the most recent performance measurement; i.e., the new value for average system performance is obtained as a sum of previously accumulated system performance and current performance measurement weighted by w.

During runtime, the values of P obtained considering a probability distribution which gives the deviation from the mean value. The smoothing factor s can be used to control the relevance of recent performance information, thus, providing a balance between stability and reactiveness to networks changes. The values of w close to zero increase the effect of the most recent performance measurements on average performance, thus enabling the algorithm to react quickly to changes while low values lead to more conservative behavior, resulting in more stable systems, since irrelevant transient changes do not affect the convergence to the optimal operational point.

During the decision making step, the cognitive mechanism continuously adjusts the mean of the distribution, in order to converge to the optimal value of P under current operational conditions. The mechanism can adjust the mean of the distribution by utilizing cognitive information and configuration policies from remote nodes or from a CIS service. Indeed, the decision making process is decentralized and can be performed by each node independently without communication with any other node or server.

Reconfiguration requires a generation of an update value for the controlled protocol parameter. In each time iteration, a new random value is generated according to a normal distribution, and assigned to the parameter P. The standard deviation (σ) of the normal distribution defines the aggressiveness of the mechanism. The lower the value of σ, the more conservative is the behavior of the algorithm on trying new values for P. Therefore, this parameter directly affects convergence and system stability.

In TCP, controlling the evolution of TCP window allows for the adjustment of network utilization, protocol fairness, and the level of network congestion. Higher values are desirable in high bandwidth-delay network with low or moderate congestion levels, but should otherwise be avoided. However, there is no effective way for a network node to determine, in advance, the available network bandwidth and the level of congestion along the end-to-end paths between the sender and the receiver (Croce, Mellia & Leonardi, 2010).

Figure 3 presents CogTCP performance results for a setup where the information sender and receiver are interconnected by links characterized with different error rates and round trip times. CogTCP is able to keep performance close to the optimal and outperforms configurations with

fixed values (represented in Figure 3 with bars 1-4) of the congestion window increase factor. These results demonstrate the benefits of dynamic adaptation in avoiding performance degradation under varying network conditions. A detailed benchmarking of the CogTCP solution is available in (Malheiros, Kliazovich, Granelli, Madeira, & Fonseca, forthcoming).

Cognitive Medium Access Control (MAC) Protocol

The Cognitive MAC (CogMAC) protocol (Kliazovich, Lima, Fonseca, Granelli & Madeira, 2009) is a technique for cognitive optimization of multiple link layer parameters, such as retry limit and contention window, in dynamic network environments. It does not rely on the explicit knowledge of network characteristics. CogMAC is implemented as a cognitive plane in parallel with the protocol stack but interfaces with all layers for the exchange of data and control information. CogMAC continuously infers dependencies between the achieved performance and protocol configuration parameters with this information, it builds and maintains a local knowledge base allowing it to trigger decisions using previous performance experience in a cognitive manner.

The data analysis, decision making, and action phases of the CogMAC protocol are similar to

Figure 3. CogTCP throughput performance

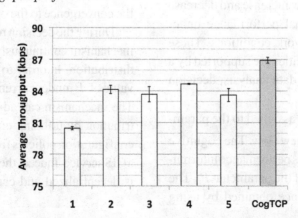

those of CogTCP, outlined in the previous section. The CogMAC performs dynamic runtime configuration of the following parameters: retry limit, contention window, and the RTS/CTS threshold when using the IEEE 802.11 link layer.

The retry limit parameter can limit the number of retransmission attempts made by a link layer before a data frame is dropped, with no notification being sent to upper layers. Low values of this parameter keep medium access delays bounded, but can only compensate for low channel error rates. High values, however, are appropriate for noisy channels although at the cost of increasing medium access delay.

The contention window parameter defines the size of the exponential backoff period and controls the rate of channel collisions. Large contention windows are recommended for dense networks where a large number of collisions can occur, while low congestion window values should be used in sparse networks to avoid unnecessary increases in medium access delay.

Finally, the RTS/CTS threshold parameter defines the minimum size of the data frame which transmission is accompanied by the RTC/CTS exchange. The optimal value depends on the number of cancelled nodes and the intensity of the traffic flow in the network.

The CogMAC approach aims to maximize the link layer throughput while ensuring bounds to the medium access delay experienced by individual nodes. Such a goal is easy to achieve when the exact number of mobile nodes is known, as well as their traffic demands and hidden nodes, and the error rates of the wireless channels. Figure 4 presents CogMAC throughput and delay performance. As the number of network nodes increases, the CogMAC shifts the points of operation to deliver optimal throughput while keeping the delay bounded. A detailed benchmarking of CogMAC solution is available in (Lima, Kliazovich, Granelli, Madeira, & Fonseca, 2013).

CONCLUSION AND FUTURE RESEARCH DIRECTIONS

This chapter presents an overview of the state-of-the-art in cognitive networking. Following the discussion on fundamental techniques of cognitive processes, reference architectures for cognitive node and cognitive network service are presented.

At the scope of a network node, the cognitive engine and the cooperation and negotiation plane, implemented in parallel to the protocol stack, control protocol configuration and performance in real

Figure 4. CogMAC a) delay and b) throughput performance

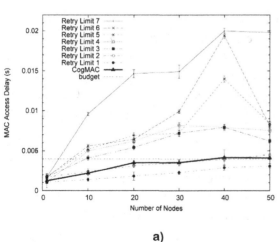

a)

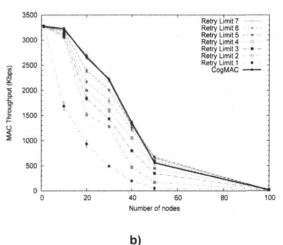

b)

time. At the scope of the network, the Cognitive Information Service (CIS) can be implemented to foster cognitive information exchange among the network nodes, thus enabling collaborative decision making. By the scope of operation CIS service is similar to DHCP service and can be implemented to serve network segments in both wired and wireless networks.

The chapter has reviewed several node and network level signaling techniques and provides a comparison of information signaling techniques considering their scope, type of signaling, signaling latency, communication overhead, method of signaling, direction of signaling, and available information association methods. Such a comparison contributes to the discussion of the applicability of various information signaling techniques in cognitive networks.

Finally, two examples of cognitive communication protocols are presented: the Cognitive TCP which works at the transport layer and the Cognitive MAC which operates at the link layer.

Cognitive functionalities are expected to become an essential component in the design of future communication systems, networks, and protocols simplifying management and enabling adaptability. The standardization activities will focus mostly on system architectures and information signaling techniques to ensure interoperability in cognitive systems.

REFERENCES

Chen, K., Shah, S. H., & Nahrstedt, K. (2003). Cross-layer design for data accessibility in mobile ad hoc networks. *Wireless Personal Communications, 21*, 49–75. doi:10.1023/A:1015509521662.

Clark, D. D., Partridge, C., Ramming, J. C., & Wroclawski, J. T. (2003). *A knowledge plane for the internet*. Paper presented at ACM SIGCOMM. Karlsruhe, Germany.

Croce, D., Mellia, M., & Leonardi, E. (2010). The quest for bandwidth estimation techniques for large-scale distributed systems. *SIGMETRICS Performance Evaluation Review, 37*(3), 20–25. doi:10.1145/1710115.1710120.

Deering, S., & Hinden, R. (1998). Internet protocol, version 6 (IPv6) specification. *RFC 2460*.

Demestichas, P., Dimitrakopoulos, G., & Strassner, J. (2006). Introducing reconfigurability and cognitive networks concepts in the wireless world. *IEEE Vehicular Technology Magazine, 1*(2), 32–39. doi:10.1109/MVT.2006.283572.

Georgakopoulos, A., Tsagkaris, K., Karvounas, D., Vlacheas, P., & Demestichas, P. (2012). Cognitive networks for future internet: Status and emerging challenges. *IEEE Vehicular Technology Magazine, 7*(3), 48–56. doi:10.1109/MVT.2012.2204548.

Kliazovich, D., Granelli, F., & Fonseca, N. L. S. (2009). Architectures and cross-layer design for cognitive networks. In *Handbook on Sensor Networks* (pp. 2-24). World Scientific Publishing Co, Inc.

Kliazovich, D., Granelli, F., & Fonseca, N. L. S. (2011). Survey on signaling techniques for cognitive networks. In *Proceedings of the IEEE International Workshop on Computer-Aided Modeling Analysis and Design of Communication Links and Networks (CAMAD)*. Kyoto, Japan: IEEE.

Kliazovich, D., Granelli, F., Fonseca, N. L. S., & Piesiewicz, R. (2009). *Cognitive information service: Basic principles and implementation of a cognitive inter-node protocol optimization scheme*. Paper presented at the IEEE Global Communications Conference (GLOBECOM). Honolulu, HI.

Kliazovich, D., Lima, J., Fonseca, N. L. S., Granelli, F., & Madeira, E. (2009). Cognitive link layer for wireless local area networks. In *Proceedings of the IEEE Latin-American Conference on Communications (LATINCOM)*. IEEE.

Kliazovich, D., Malheiros, N., Granelli, F., Madeira, E., & Fonseca, N. L. S. (2010). CogProt: A framework for cognitive configuration and optimization of communication protocols. In *Proceedings of the 2nd International Conference on Mobile Lightweight Wireless Systems (MOBILIGHT)*. Barcelona, Spain: MOBILIGHT.

Lima, J., Kliazovich, D., Granelli, F., Madeira, E., & Fonseca, N. L. S. (2013). *CogMAC - A cognitive link layer for wireless local area networks*. ACM/Springer Journal of Wireless Networks.

Malheiros, N., Kliazovich, D., Granelli, F., Madeira, E., & Fonseca, N. L. S. (2013). *A cognitive approach for self-configuration of communication protocols*. IEEE Transactions on Network and Service Management.

Malheirosa, N., Kliazovich, D., Granelli, F., Madeira, E., & Fonseca, N. L. S. (2013). A cognitive approach for self-configuration of communication protocols. *Computer Networks*.

Maravedis Market Research and Analysis. (2006). *Clash of the titans – WiMAX and 4G: The battle for convergence is joined*. Author.

Postel, J. (1981). *Internet control message protocol*. IETF. Kim, B.-J. (2001). A network service providing wireless channel information for adaptive mobile applications: I: Proposal. In *Proceedings of the IEEE International Conference on Communications (ICC)*, (pp. 1345 – 1351). IEEE.

Raisinghani, V. T., & Iyer, S. (2006). Cross layer feedback architecture for mobile device protocol stacks. *IEEE Communications Magazine, 44*(1), 85–92. doi:10.1109/MCOM.2006.1580937.

Ramakrishnan, K., Floyd, S., & Black, D. (2001). The addition of explicit congestion notification (ECN) to IP. *RFC 3168*.

Std, I. E. E. E. 802.3. (1985). Carrier sense multiple access with collision detection. IEEE.

Thomas, R. W., Friend, D. H., DaSilva, L. A., & MacKenzie, A. B. (2006). Cognitive networks: Adaptation and learning to achieve end-to-end performance objectives. *IEEE Communications Magazine, 44*(12), 51–57. doi:10.1109/MCOM.2006.273099.

Wang, Q., & Abu-Rgheff, M. A. (2003). Cross-layer signaling for next-generation wireless systems. In *Proceedings of the IEEE Wireless Communications and Networking (WCNC)*, (pp. 1084 – 1089). IEEE.

Winter, R., Schiller, J. H., Nikaein, N., & Bonnet, C. (2006). CrossTalk: Cross-layer decision support based on global knowledge. *IEEE Communications Magazine, 44*(1), 93–99. doi:10.1109/MCOM.2006.1580938.

Zhang, R., & Hanzo, L. (n.d.). Wireless cellular networks. *IEEE Vehicular Technology Magazine, 5*(4), 31-39.

ADDITIONAL READING

Liu, X., Hu, S., Xiao, Y., Liu, Y., Qu, G., & Kim, K. (2010). The multiple prioritized access mechanism of cognitive networks. In *Proceedings of IET 3rd International Conference on Mobile and Multimedia Networks (ICWMNN 2010)* (pp. 168-172). IET.

Lou, J., Luo, T., & Yue, G. (2010). Power allocation for cooperative cognitive networks. In *Proceedings of the 2010 3rd IEEE International Conference on Broadband Network and Multimedia Technology (IC-BNMT)* (pp. 412-416). IEEE.

Mihailovic, A., Nguengang, G., Borgel, J., & Alonistioti, N. (2009). Building knowledge lifecycle and situation awareness in self-managed cognitive future internet networks. In *Proceedings of the 2009 First International Conference on Emerging Network Intelligence* (pp. 3-8). IEEE.

Nolan, K. E., & Doyle, L. E. (2007). Teamwork and collaboration in cognitive wireless networks. *IEEE Wireless Communications, 14*(4), 22–27. doi:10.1109/MWC.2007.4300979.

Qi, J., Zhang, S., Sun, Y., & Tan, L. (2011). Research on available resource management model of cognitive networks based on intelligence agent. In *Proceedings of the 2011 IEEE 3rd International Conference on Communication Software and Networks (ICCSN)* (pp. 201-204). IEEE.

Qusay, M. (2007). *Cognitive networks: Towards self-aware networks.* New York: Wiley-Interscience.

Vu, M., Devroye, N., Sharif, M., & Tarokh, V. (2007). Scaling laws of cognitive networks. In *Proceedings of the 2nd International Conference on Cognitive Radio Oriented Wireless Networks and Communications* (pp. 2-8). IEEE.

Wang, Z.-D., Wang, H.-Q., Feng, G.-S., Li, B.-Y., & Chen, X.-M. (2010). Cognitive networks and its layered cognitive architecture. In *Proceedings of the 2010 Fifth International Conference on Internet Computing for Science and Engineering (ICICSE)* (pp. 145-148). ICICSE.

Wentao, H., & Xinbing, W. (2011). Throughput and delay scaling of general cognitive networks, *2011. Proceedings - IEEE INFOCOM,* 2210–2218.

Wentao, H., & Xinbing, W. (2012). Capacity scaling of general cognitive networks. *IEEE/ACM Transactions on Networking, 20*(5), 1501–1513. doi:10.1109/TNET.2011.2180400.

KEY TERMS AND DEFINITIONS

Cognitive Information Service: A network service assisting in cognitive information exchange between network nodes.

Cognitive Network: A communication network that makes use of cognitive processes to improve operation.

Cognitive Node: A network node running cognitive process.

Cognitive Process: A process, which involves active thinking and knowledge acquisition, and uses the acquired knowledge to trigger future decisions.

Cognitive Protocol: A protocol making use of cognitive process to optimize its operation.

Information Signaling: The process of information exchange between network nodes.

Chapter 13
Security in Cognitive Radio Networks

Krešimir Dabčević
University of Genova, Italy

Lucio Marcenaro
University of Genova, Italy

Carlo S. Regazzoni
University of Genova, Italy

ABSTRACT

While potentially solving the spectrum underutilization problem using methods such as dynamic and opportunistic spectrum access, Cognitive Radios (CRs) also bring a set of security issues and potential breaches that have to be addressed. These issues come from the two important capabilities implemented within CRs: their cognition ability and reconfigurability. This chapter focuses on identifying, presenting, and classifying the main potential security attacks and vulnerabilities, as well as proposing appropriate counter-measures and solutions for them. These are supplemented by simulation results and metrics, with the intention of estimating the efficiency of each of the observed attacks and its counter-measure. The presented simulations are performed in the proprietary C/C++ and Matlab/Simulink simulators. nSHIELD is a major ongoing European embedded systems security-related project, which is used to demonstrate the practicability of the potential implementation of the proposed countermeasures and solutions for the discussed security problems and issues.

INTRODUCTION

With the continuous market penetration of many spectrum-demanding radio-based services, such as video broadcasting, finding ways to increase the spectrum usage efficiency has become a ne- cessity. Cognitive Radio (CR) is a technological breakthrough that – by utilizing concepts such as Opportunistic Spectrum Access (OSA) and Dynamic Spectrum Access (DSA) – is expected to be an enabler for these improvements, making

DOI: 10.4018/978-1-4666-4189-1.ch013

Copyright © 2013, IGI Global. Copying or distributing in print or electronic forms without written permission of IGI Global is prohibited.

it a current "hot topic" within the radio-communication research community.

Cognitive radio can be described as an intelligent and dynamically reconfigurable radio that can adaptively regulate its internal parameters as a response to the changes in the surrounding environment. Namely, its parameters can be reconfigured in order to accommodate the current needs of either the network operator, spectrum lessor, or the end-user.

Although this doesn't necessarily need to be the case, Cognitive Radio (CR) is usually being defined as an upgraded and enhanced Software Defined Radio (SDR). Typically, full Cognitive Radios will have learning mechanisms based on some of the deployed machine learning techniques, and may potentially also be equipped with smart antennas, geolocation capabilities, biometrical identification, etc.

However, the newly-introduced cognitive capabilities are exactly what make Cognitive Radios susceptible to a whole new set of possible security issues and breaches. Furthermore, the threats characteristic to Software Defined Radios, as well as those characteristic to "traditional" wireless networks also need to be taken into account.

Cognitive Radio Network can be described as a network in which one or more users are Cognitive Radios. With the assumption of the potential attacker, as well as legitimate Secondary Users (SUs) always being CRs, the taxonomy of the threats within CRNs can be done with respect to the type of the Primary Users (PUs) considered, i.e.:

- PUs as "traditional" wireless systems,
- PUs as Software Defined Radios,
- PUs as Cognitive Radios.

It is worth noting that the proposed taxonomy is merely one of the possible approaches - the categorization can be done in several different ways. We have opted in for this particular approach because of its clarity and since it optimally fits

the CR security framework that we are proposing in the last subsection.

The following subsection defines the basic concepts and premises of cognitive radios, and gives an introductory classification and basic definitions of CR-related threats. Section 3 will deal with the security of traditional wireless systems, describing legacy methods for protecting wireless communications such as WEP, WPA and WPA2, as well as the general security issues in wireless cellular networks. Section 4 highlights the security issues related to Software Defined Radio systems, while Section 5 considers potential threats to Cognitive Radios. Results are shown for so-called Primary User Emulation Attacks and Smart Jamming Attacks.

BACKGROUND

One of the most important capacities of future Cognitive Radio systems is their capability to optimally adapt their operating parameters based on the observations and previous experience. There are several possible approaches towards realizing such cognitive capabilities, such as:

- Reinforcement learning,
- Learning based on neural networks,
- Game-theoretic approach.

Reinforcement learning refers to the machine learning method where radio learns through trial-and-error interactions in a scenario without perfect contextual information.

It is a kind of mathematical method used for the learning state in the cognition cycle, which will learn the information (recorded in the form of weighting factors) based on the external environment and previous states, which then influence the current activation. The weight is used to show the influence from the previous users or the factors based on circumstance, which will be updated on each activation (Hu, 2011).

Artificial Neural Networks (ANN) are mathematical models inspired by the structure and functioning of biological neural networks(Bishop, 1995). ANNs can change and adapt their structure based on data used during a learning phase and are able to discover and model complex relationships among acquired data. ANN can be trained by automatically selecting one model from the set of allowed models for the network and this is typically done by minimizing a cost criterion. There are numerous algorithms available for training neural network models; most of them can be viewed as a straightforward application of optimization theory and statistical estimation. Most of the algorithms used in training artificial neural networks employ some form of gradient descent. This is done by simply taking the derivative of the cost function with respect to the network parameters and then changing those parameters in a gradient-related direction. Evolutionary methods (Ilonen, Kamarainen, & Lampinen, 2003), simulated annealing (Kirkpatrick, Gelatt, & Vecchi, 1983), expectation-maximization, non-parametric methods and particle swarm optimization (Kennedy & Eberhart, 1995) are some commonly used methods for training neural networks.

Game theory is a mathematical study of strategic interaction processes between multiple independent decision makers. Since within Cognitive Radio Networks, users can be modeled as such decision makers, the game theory presents itself as a natural structure for analyzing users' behaviors and actions, as well as for modeling the suitable strategies in order to overcome the crucial interoperability issues between the cognitive users. Application of game theory to CRNs is multifold, ranging from ensuring a formalized approach for the dynamic spectrum sharing (DSS) related issues, through supplying different optimality criteria for the spectrum sharing, to deriving efficient distributed approaches for DSS by using the so-called non-cooperative game theory. Simpler game-theoretical solutions typically do not account for the learning capabilities of CRs,

however it is possible to model more advanced games, such as Bayesian games, for dealing with algorithms with learning capabilities.

Game theory can furthermore be viewed as an individual set of tools for analyzing the security-related issues, and has been studied e.g. in (Liu & Wang, 2011).

As stated, deployment of learning techniques represents one of the fundamental parts of the CR paradigm. By using one of the described approaches, CRs are able to observe and learn the status of the surrounding environment, which has an important application from the perspective of utilizing RF spectrum in a more efficient manner. The outcome of this learning process is used by the CR-enabled devices to improve the efficiency in accessing the available spectrum resources: CRs can, for example, learn different patterns of PUs' activities in order to be able to forecast the availability of the resource and to adapt dynamically to the sensed conditions. The knowledge about the spectrum usage can be built by each individual unlicensed user without interaction with other users. Alternatively, the unlicensed users can collaborate in order to not only exchange network information, but also to model and update the radio environments and typical activity patterns.

Deployment of these learning techniques, however, brings new potential weaknesses from the network security point of view. If a malicious user is aware of the learning capabilities of the CR devices in the network, it can adopt a specific activity pattern in order only to deceive the cognitive users, thus possibly dramatically decreasing the CRs' and the network's overall performance.

Whereas it is intuitive that each of the approaches for realization of the intelligent behavior within CRNs could suffer from their own potential vulnerabilities, these will not be considered separately. Instead, the main focus of the chapter will be on the vulnerabilities stemming out from the case where intelligent behavior within CRNs has been established, regardless of which approach was taken towards achieving it. The Objective Function Attack, described in the subsection "Other attacks and threats," is an example of the direct attack on CR's learning mechanism.

Security of traditional wireless systems is a well-studied topic, and a number of well-defined wireless security protocols are established and used nowadays. In cases where Primary Users within a CRN have only the properties and capabilities of the "traditional" (as opposed to Software Defined) digital transceivers, it is paramount to ensure the existence of such security measures and protocols.

Most widespread wireless security standards are Wired Equivalent Privacy (WEP), Wi-Fi Protected Access (WPA) and Wi-Fi Protected Access version 2 (WPA2), which are presented in the following section, as well as the common security issues of the wireless cellular networks.

Since Cognitive Radios are by and large defined as upgraded and enhanced Software Defined Radios, it is important to establish which security threats are relevant for SDR networks, as well as which counter-measures need to be deployed.

SECURITY OF "TRADITIONAL" WIRELESS SYSTEMS

As has been stated, there are several established and commonly used security standards for wireless networks used today. In this chapter, the general security issues in cellular networks, as well as the most widespread mechanisms for the WLAN security – WEP, WPA and WPA2 – will be reviewed.

Security Issues in Wireless Cellular Networks

The openness of communication characteristic to the wireless cellular networks brings a set of security issues that need to be addressed. Being

the standard that had the highest impact in the evolution of commercial wireless cellular networks, Global System for Mobile Communications (GSM) has throughout its existence been subjected to a particular attention from security standpoint.

GSM incorporates several built-in security features responsible for ensuring subscribers' safety and privacy, namely (European Telecommunications Standards Institute, 1996):

- Authentication of the registered subscribers only,
- Secure data transfer through the use of encryption,
- Subscriber identity protection,
- Mobile phones are inoperable without a SIM,
- Duplicate SIM are not allowed on the network,
- Securely stored Ki.

Most of the security mechanisms in GSM are based on crypto algorithms, which vary depending on the functionality they are designed to protect. The main such algorithms are A5 – a stream cipher used for encryption, A3 – an authentication algorithm, and A8 – the key agreement algorithm. Among the initial two A5 algorithms, A5/1 is the stronger one, and is used to achieve security and privacy of voice over the air interface. Originally kept secret, it became publicly known after being reverse-engineered, and has continued to serve as a good example for crypto-related security hazards. A5/2 is the version without any export limitations, which after also being reverse-engineered and cryptanalyzed, showed the need for a more powerful algorithm. Hence, in 2002, A5/3 was introduced using the block-cipher called KASUMI. Besides GSM, KASUMI is used as a crypto algorithm in GPRS and 3G networks as well.

Authors in (Barkan, Biham, & Keller, 2008) have analyzed several attacks against A5 cyphers, namely:

- **Class-Mark Attack:** The attacker changes the class-mark information that the phone sends to the network at the beginning of the conversation, such that the network thinks that the phone supports only A5/2. Although the network prefers to use A5/1, it must use either A5/2 (or A5/0 — no encryption), as it believes that the phone does not support A5/1. The attacker can then listen in to the conversation through the cryptanalysis of the weaker A5/2 cipher.
- **Recovering Crypto Key of Past or Future Conversations:** An attacker recovers the encryption key of an encrypted conversation that was recorded in the past.
- **Man in the Middle Attack:** The attacker uses a fake base-station in its communications with the mobile phone, and impersonates the mobile phone to the network, and forwards to the victim the authentication request that it got from the network. The victim sends the 32-bit Signed Response to the attacker, who holds on to it and, by performing a ciphertext attack finds the cypher key, and is able to authenticate himself on the network.

General Packet Radio Service (GPRS) is a protocol that enables the packet radio access for GSM users. From a security viewpoint, GPRS inherits many security problems from GSM, however the upgraded network architecture also brings several new ones.

Author in (Xenakis, 2008) has evaluated the security aspects of the GPRS architecture, identifying the following weaknesses:

- **Compromise of the Confidentiality of Subscriber Identity:** Whenever the serving network cannot associate the Temporary Mobile Subscriber Identity (TMSI) with the International Mobile Subscriber Identity (IMSI), the Service GPRS Support Node (SGSN) should request the MS to identify itself by means of IMSI on the radio path. This leaves the possibility of modeling the attacker pretending to be a new serving network, to which the user has to reveal his permanent identity.
- **One-Way Subscriber Authentication:** Does not assure that a mobile user is connected to an authentic serving network, thus enabling active attacks using a false BS identity. Furthermore, the A3 and A8 vulnerabilities are inherited from the GSM network, whereas re-using authentication triplets makes it possible to launch Man in the Middle Attack, or Replay Attack.
- **Encryption of Signalling and User Data is Optional:** Leading to attacker being able to mediate in the exchange of authentication messages between the legitimate user and the BS.
- **Unsupported Security Protection by the SS7 Technology:** This deficiency of the SS7 technology, which is used for signaling exchange in GPRS, increases the probability of an adversary to get access to the network or a legitimate operator to act maliciously as well as resulting in the unprotected exchange of signaling messages between the location registers.

Compared to its 2G and 2.5G predecessors, 3G has brought significantly better security features, mainly through the usage of the aforementioned KASUMI block cipher instead of the A5 stream cipher, and the Authentication and Key Agreement (AKA) protocol instead of CAVE-based authentication. Furthermore, 3G integrity algorithm with an Integrity Key (IK) introduces the feature of Data Integrity, whereas User to User Services Integrity Module (USIM) and USIM to Terminal Authentication provide the secure access to MS.

Long Term Evolution's (LTE) security is largely built upon the 3G one (usage of the AKA protocol in the first place), with several modifications, such as extended key hierarchy, introduction of longer keys, better backhaul protection and integrated interworking security for legacy and non-3GPP networks.

Wired Equivalent Privacy

Wired Equivalent Privacy (WEP) was "designed to provide the security of a wired LAN by encryption through use of the RC4 algorithm with two side of a data communication" (Lashkari, Danesh, & Samadi, 2009). It is an "optional encryption standard, implemented in the MAC layers, intended to provide user authentication, data privacy and data integrity in a manner that would make a wireless LAN equivalent to a wired LAN" (Borse & Shinde, 2005).

The RC4 algorithm – also known as a stream cipher – is a symmetric cipher in which every binary digit in a data stream is subjected separately to encrypting algorithm, by logically XOR-ing the key to the data. The key is shared between communicating nodes, clients and access points, and ensuring its secure exchange is needed.

One of the main vulnerabilities of the WEP protocol lies in the usage of the random Initialization Vector (IV), used in the encryption process. Namely, WEP's IV is only 24 bit long, allowing for a number of unique combinations that can be reached fairly easily in busy network conditions, bringing the need for the re-use of certain IVs. Hence, if RC4 for a certain IV is found, potential attacker can decrypt the packets with the same IV.

Furthermore, WEP does not define a key management protocol, leading to the need for manual change of the key for each wireless device by the network administrator. This presents a big security leak, since in case of a potential security breach all keys need to be changed, which – due to the lack of synchronization - is far from a trivial task.

The use of the RC4 also brings an issue of weak keys – the high correlation factor between the key and the output means that the attacker can somewhat easily filter out the "interesting

packets", substantially decreasing the number of combinations for possible keys that will allow him the access to the network.

There are two forms of authentication within 802.11 standards: Shared key and Open system. And while the latter one gives a more satisfactory performance in terms of security, the Shared key authentication – based on encryption of a challenge – brings a potential security breach in cases where attackers are able to monitor the encryption process.

Authors in (Borisov, Goldberg, & Wagner, 2001) define four basic types of attacks present in WEP-based wireless networks:

- **Passive Attack:** A passive eavesdropper can intercept all wireless traffic, until an IV collision occurs. Once the attacker obtains the XOR of the two plaintext messages, the resulting XOR can be used to infer data about the contents of the two messages. IP traffic is often very predictable and includes a lot of redundancy, which can be used to eliminate many possibilities for the contents of messages.
- **Active Attack to Inject Traffic:** If the attacker knows the exact plaintext for one encrypted message, he can use this knowledge to construct correct encrypted packets. The procedure involves constructing a new message, calculating the CRC-32, and performing bit flips on the original encrypted message to change the plaintext to the new message.
- **Active Attack from Both Ends:** The attacker makes a guess about the headers of a packet, which is usually easy to obtain or guess. The attacker can flip appropriate bits to transform the destination IP address to send the packet to a machine he controls, and transmit it using a rogue mobile station. Most wireless installations have Internet connectivity; the packet will

be successfully decrypted by the access point and forwarded unencrypted through appropriate gateways and routers to the attacker's machine, revealing the plaintext

- **Table-Based Attack:** The small space of possible initialization vectors allows an attacker to build a decryption table. Once he learns the plaintext for some packet, he can compute the RC4 key stream generated by the IV used, which can then be used to decrypt all other packets that use the same IV. Over time, the attacker can build up a table of IVs and corresponding key streams.

Wi-Fi Protected Access

Wi-Fi Protected Access (WPA) is an open standard aimed at solving problems present in WEP-based systems. Encryption is realized through the Temporal Key Integrity Protocol (TKIP), which provides per-packet key mixing function for reducing correlation between IVs from weak keys. Also, message integrity check, as well as the re-keying mechanism is added.

RC4 is also used within TKIP, with an addition of hashing, making for a significantly more robust mechanism.

Authors in (Lashkari, Danesh, & Samadi, 2009) break down the improvements that WPA brings over WEP as:

- A cryptographic message integrity code, or MIC, to defeat forgeries,
- A new IV sequencing discipline, to remove replay attacks from the attacker's arsenal,
- A per-packet key mixing function, to decorrelate the public IVs from weak keys,
- A re-keying mechanism, to provide fresh encryption and integrity keys, undoing the threat of attacks stemming from key reuse.

For home networks, a so-called WPA Pre-Shared Key (WPA-PSK) variation has been designed. It is a simplified algorithm, in which individual user must set a passphrase (key). Difference with WEP lies in automatic alteration of the key every *n* time intervals, making it more difficult for attackers to identify them.

However, WPA-PSK algorithm has proven to be more attack-prone. Several dictionary attacks were devised to somewhat efficiently exploit the Pairwise Master Key (PMK) – a feature obtained from the concatenation of the passphrase, Service Set Identifier (SSID), its length, and a number of bit strings used in a session.

Wi-Fi Protected Access Version 2

Wi-Fi Protected Access 2 (WPA2), also known as the 802.11i, is an amendment to the WPA standard, aiming at improving not only security and reliability, but also the ease of access of the WPA-based networks.

One of the most important novelties is the introduction of Counter Mode with Cipher Block Chaining Message Authentication Code Protocol (CCMP). It is based on Advanced Encryption Standard (AES) – an open-source algorithm that provides significant robustness improvements.

As is the case with WPA, the most exploitable vulnerability of WPA2 stems out from using the PSK key.

In WPA2, user authentication is separated from ensuring the privacy and integrity of the messages, and, like WPA, it operates in two modes:

- **WPA-Personal (or Pre-Shared Key (PSK)):** Performed between the client and the access point, and typical for home networks,
- **WPA-Enterprise (or Extensible Authentication Protocol (EAP)):** Typical for business networks. Authentication server named RADIUS is used for authorization decisions - it provides the Master Session Key to the client and the access point.

Up to date, WPA2 is considered the most reliable Wi-Fi security protocol, however few vulnerabilities are still present.

Authors in (Dengg, Friedl, Hörtler, Jäger, Lehner, & Macskási, n.d.) recognize the following attacks on WPA2-secured systems:

- **PSK Brute Force Dictionary Attack:** Based on attacking the PSK, recognized as WPA2's biggest weakness. To perform an attack on the passphrase the attacker must eavesdrop the network during the 4way handshake in phase 4 for the PTK, where he receives all but the passphrase, and then perform the attack.

- **Security Level Rollback Attack:** Based on WPA2's feature of defining a TSN (Transient Security Network). The attacker sends wrong Beacon or Probe requests to establish a Pre-RSNA connection, even if both would support a more secure RSNA connection like WPA2. As PreRSNA does not support a cipher suite, they won't be able to detect the fraud and accept the insecure connection. The attacker is now able to get the default keys by exploiting WEP's weaknesses.

- **Reflection Attack:** Present in ad-hoc networks, where a device is not allowed to play both the supplicant and authenticator roles at the same time. The original device starts the handshake as authenticator, the attacker starts another 4way handshake using the same parameters but the device as supplicant. Once the device starts to send messages as supplicant, the attacker can use these messages as a valid message for the initial 4wayhandshake of the attacker's target.

In addition to those, (AirTightNetworks, 2012) recognize the so-called "Hole196" vulnerability, which exposes WPA2-secured network to insider attacks. The attack is enabled by the usage of the group temporal key (GTK), shared among all authorized clients in a WPA2 network. The data traffic encrypted using the GTK should be transceived between an access point and a legitimate user, however a malicious inside user can potentially eavesdrop and decrypt data from other authorized users as well as scan their Wi-Fi devices for vulnerabilities, install malware and possibly compromise those devices.

Wi-Fi Alliance continuously works on improving the WPA and WPA2 standards, offering different EAP types, allowing for greater interoperability and higher security. Nevertheless, certain security issues still exist, and improvements still need to be made.

In future Cognitive Radio Networks, it is feasible to expect the presence of non-CR and non-SDR wireless terminals, i.e. the systems that are commonly deployed today. But also, the wireless nature of SDRs and CRs points to the fact that such systems will also be prone to inheriting the threats present to the aforementioned, "traditional" systems. Hence, ensuring maximum security and privacy of such systems will be paramount, and addressing the known security issues in the current state-of-the-art security standard – WEP2 – can be considered a good starting point.

SECURITY OF SOFTWARE DEFINED RADIOS

There is no unanimous definition of what requirements a radio must satisfy in order to be considered software defined. One of the most recognizable, and in the same time very intuitive ones is Wireless Innovation Forum's one, which recognizes SDR as "a radio in which some or all of the physical layer functions are software defined" (Wireless Innovation Forum). These functions usually include – but are not limited to – frequency, modulation technique, cryptography, used bandwidth, coding technique, etc. However, the level of reconfigurability/reprogrammabillity needed for the radio to be labeled as an SDR isn't strictly defined.

Hence, depending on this level of software reconfigurability, different authors establish a division between, for example, Software Capable, Software Programmable, and Software Defined Radios.

For the sake of the simplicity, all of these will from now on be marked as Software Defined Radios, as from the security point of view, they mostly share common threats and problems.

For the future purposes, it is useful to categorize the types of software present in Software Defined Radios, as per Wireless Innovation Forum's guidelines, since this categorization is widely accepted in the scientific environment, and is commonly referred to.

Following that, it is possible to classify the software in SDRs as:

- **Radio Operating Environment (ROE):** Consists of the core framework, the operating system, device drivers, middleware, installer and any other software fundamental to the operation of the radio platform,
- **Radio Applications (RA):** Software which controls the behavior of the RF function of the radio. This includes any software defining the air interface and the modulation and communication protocols, as well as software used to manage or control the radio in a network environment,
- **Service Provider Applications (SPA):** Software used to support network and other service provider support for the user of the radio. It includes voice telephone calls, data delivery, paging, instant messaging service, video pictures, emergency assistance, and geolocation,
- **User Applications (UA):** Application software not falling into any of the above categories.

General SDR-Related Security Threats

One of the potential hazards in SDRs lies in the possibility of tampering the hardware of SDRs. Since these hazards apply to all wireless systems and are not unique to the new features that SDRs bring, the focus will be on the other types of threats – the ones stemming out from the software reconfigurability. Main threats to the reconfigurability come from faulty and buggy software, so the deployed schemes need to protect the system from download and usage of the improper software.

In general, security-enabling mechanisms for SDRs can be divided into hardware-based and software-based ones, each with their own advantages and disadvantages.

Hardware-based mechanisms include hardware modules for monitoring the SDR's reconfigurable parameters. However, unlike the SDRs they are securing, these mechanisms themselves are typically not easily reconfigurable, and updating the security parameters or policies may be problematic and expensive.

Software-based mechanisms rely on deploying the tamper-resistance techniques, providing safe and secure authentication, communication security and integrity, as well as safe algorithms for download, updating and distribution of the software. The potential vulnerability of such schemes is the openness to malicious modification.

In (Li, Raghunathan, & Jha, 2009), authors present a security architecture based on separation of the application environment and the radio operation environment, so that the compromise of one doesn't affect the other. Furthermore, SDR reconfiguration parameters produced by the application environment are checked against security policies before they take effect in the radio environment. So, in cases where application environment is tampered with and becomes malicious, it cannot infect the radio environment and thus the RF characteristics can be ensured to be in compliance with the desired policies.

For software classification, the authors have used Wireless Innovation Forum's guidelines, as was described before, where on top of the ROE, RA, and SPA they are defining the User Application Environment (UAE) as the environment (OS) where UA are executed.

Authors define a new separate layer called *secure radio middleware* (SRM) – a layer implemented below UAE, which includes the most security-critical components, namely RA and ROE. SRM is composed of:

- **Bypass:** In charge of non-critical operations,
- **Memory Management Unit:** Controls the behavior of the OS,
- **Virtualized Hardware:** Where all the radio applications are performed,
- **Security Policy Monitor:** Tries to decide a normal value or range for the radio parameters and compare them to the ones the OS passes to Virtualized Hardware, leading to initialization of the appropriate recovery mechanisms in cases of violation.

As the authors themselves note, their implementation has several constraints. Since a desktop PC has been used as a testbed, the implementation doesn't reflect the performance in the potential real-life scenarios, where platforms will typically be far more resource-constrained. Furthermore, their architecture doesn't incorporate mechanisms for encryption/decryption, information integrity, access control and secure radio software download, which are issues that need to be addressed separately.

Authors in (Brawerman, Blough, & Bing, 2004) propose the lightweight version of a Secure Socket Layer (SSL) protocol. SSL provides bulk encryption, end point authentication and data integrity protection. For encryption, symmetric key algorithms are used, whereas for authentication, client and server can mutually authenticate each other.

LSSL redesigns the SSL protocol in order to decrease the computational complexity of the performed operations and perform most of the cryptography at the server side, thus making it suitable for power-constrained devices, such as SDR terminals.

The authors have defined several possible attacks, and the corresponding defense feature employed within the protocol, namely:

- **Access Control:** Countered by the authentication mechanism.
- **Masquerade Attack:** Attacker emulates the manufacturer server or a client, which protocol counters using mutual authentication.
- **Confidentiality:** Secrecy of information is ensured by establishing secure connections.
- **Replay:** Attacker re-transmits messages after a certain time period. Protocol tackles this by using timestamps.
- **R-CFG Validation:** Installation of the non-approved R-CFG, resolved by digitally signing every R-CFG by the regulatory agency.
- **R-CFG Integrity:** Possibility of modifying R-CFG after it has been approved, countered by using one-way hash functions.

Potential Threats to Common SDR Architectures

Currently, there are two predominant open-source architectures for SDRs: GNU Radio – particularly appealing to academic environment due to the relative simplicity of use and compatibility with the low-cost off-the-shelf SDR platforms such as USRP, and Software Communications Architecture (SCA) – architecture adopted by the Wireless Innovation Forum.

GNU Radio is an open-source software toolkit that, coupled with hardware equipment such as USRP, allows for a complete platform for building Software Defined Radios (although GNU

Radio can also be used as a stand-alone software package).

Most of GNU Radio's applications are written in Python, whereas C++ is used for implementing signal processing blocks. Python commands are used to control all of the USRP's software defined parameters, such as transmit power, gain, frequency, antenna selection, etc.

GNU Radio is built on two main structural entities – signal processing blocks and flow graphs. Blocks are structured to have a certain number of input and output ports, consisting of small signal-processing components. When the blocks are appropriately connected, a flow graph is made.

Authors in (Hill, Suvda, & Campbell, 2005) have analyzed threats related to GNU Radio-based SDR systems. They refer to the GNU Radio Software Applications – written in C++ – as to the Radio Applications (RA), and to the Python functions as to the Radio Operating Environment (ROE).

As such, they identify the following shortcomings related to the ROE of GNU Radio:

- At the moment, there is no embedded functionality for verification, i.e. securing the SDR device from being reconfigured by the malicious code.
- Presence of the risks related to the execution of models in the graph – since a single address space is shared among all the software modules, there is a possibility for the malicious user to alter the data in the whole address space. To counter this, they propose restricting each module to only be able to access its dedicated address space.
- Possibility of a buffer overflow, coming out from the use of the shared buffer. Mechanisms for restricting the amount of data possibly written to the buffer are needed.

They also define three possible attacks, depending on the parameter targeted:

- **Modulation Attack:** Improper change of the modulation format,
- **Frequency Attack:** Jamming attacks where an impostor is transmitting on the frequencies that it's not allowed to,
- **Output Power Attack:** Where an attacker can continuously transmit at high power, forcing other users to increase their power level, which leads to increased battery drain.

Authors go on to suggest that GNU Radio ROE has to provide mechanisms for evaluating and enforcing policies for specifying the operating constraints of the SDRs, defined by the network administrators and regulators.

Software Communications was originally defined by the US government with the purpose of securing waveform portability and improving software reuse. Built originally for US military's Joint Tactical Radio System (JTRS) program, it has been accepted as a communication standard in military services of many other countries, but also by commercial organizations such as Wireless Innovation Forum. It is an always-evolving standard - with first version dating from 2000 – that provides standardized set of methods for installing, managing and de-installing new waveforms, therefore maintaining interoperability of various SDR systems.

The Software Communications Architecture (SCA) is an open architecture framework that instructs the designers as to how the elements of hardware and software should operate in harmony within the JTRS. It governs the structure and operation of the JTRS, enabling programmable radios to load waveforms, run applications, and be networked into an integrated system. Design engineers use the Software Communications SCA definition document just as an architect or planner uses a local building code to design and build homes.

Security is a very important aspect of radios featuring SCA. The architecture provides the foundation to solve issues like programmable cryptographic capability, certificate management, user identification and authentication, key management, and multiple independent levels of classification. Manufacturers and users are embracing the approach, albeit much more slowly than preferred. For example, the Security Supplement to the JTRS SCA requires that SDR devices "shall only accept cryptographic algorithms/algorithm packages signed by National Security Agency (NSA)," that "NSA shall digitally sign all Security Policy XML files," and that "the operating system invocation method shall be a NSA digitally signed script". However, SDR middleware and tools vendors supporting JTRS customers do not yet support digital signature features within their products, although they express openness to including such features in future releases. Similarly, user and manufacturer representatives in the SDR Forum's Public Safety SIG are trying to identify alternatives to digital signatures before committing to such an approach, largely due to perceptions about public key infrastructure (PKI) technology complexity.

SECURITY OF COGNITIVE RADIOS

As described before, cognitive radios can be considered as intelligent devices that are able to learn from the experience and dynamically adapt to the features of the environment. Major research efforts have been devoted towards the study and development of learning and reasoning techniques without considering security related issues in detail. Typically, security is tackled by means of adding authentication on encryption mechanism to the data communication within the network, but this is not always sufficient due to the improved capabilities of the cognitive paradigm. In particular, as artificial intelligence engines represent the core of cognitive devices, potential threats that are able to feed CRs with false sensory inputs – thus

purposely affecting its trained knowledge and subsequently its behavior – should be considered.

Table 1 summarizes the attacks and the proposed defense mechanisms addressed in this section, also describing their basic characteristics.

Primary User Emulation Attacks

Two types of users can be differentiated in CRNs: Primary Users (PUs) and Secondary Users (SUs). The main premise of the opportunistic spectrum access lies in the SUs' ability to access the channels normally assigned to PUs when they are free of occupancy. In order to decide whether the channel is momentarily free, or is in use by the PU or the other SU, the cognitive radio needs to perform spectrum sensing (alternatively, two other methods – geolocation/database and beacons are proposed in the literature, and were addressed in the subsection "Alternative spectrum occupancy decision methods and the related security threats"). Several spectrum sensing approaches, such as energy detection, cyclostationary feature detection, second-order statistics detection, filterbank-based detection, etc., have been proposed up to date, each with its advantages and disadvantages in terms of ease of implementation, decoding complexity and sensing accuracy in various channel conditions. In case that the CR decides that the specific channel is momentarily not in use by the PU, it competes with other potentially present SUs in order to acquire the rights to access the channel. Furthermore, once that it has been assigned the rights to use the channel, the CR will still need to periodically perform spectrum sensing and, should it sense the presence of a PU, vacate the channel immediately.

Primary User Emulation Attack (PUEA) is a type of attack where a secondary user falsely advertises itself as a primary user, either to acquire exclusive right to the spectrum occupancy, or to cause Denial of Service (DoS) within the network. Depending on the spectrum sensing technique that

Table 1. Summary of the threats to cognitive radios and the proposed solutions

Attack type	Contribution	Attacker's special characteristics	Proposed defense scheme
PUEA – emulating characteristics of a primary user to acquire exclusive spectrum rights	Chen, Park, & Reed, 2008	Altering its transmit power, modulation mode and frequency; injecting false data to the localization system	3-step mechanism: verification of signal characteristics, RSS measurement, localization of the signal
	Chen, Cooklev, Chen, & Pomalaza-Raez, 2009	Applying the estimation techniques to enhance its performance	Assumes that emulating the channel features is not feasible for the attacker. Invariants of communication channels are used as means of differentiating between the PUE attackers from legitimate PUs
	Liu, Ning, & Dai, 2010	-	Novel physical layer authentication mechanism, which incorporates cryptographic and wireless link signatures
	Dabcevic, Marcenaro & Regazzoni, 2012 (our proposed scheme)	Ability to emulate any of the PU's transmission characteristics	Location integrity checking as means of deciding on the credibility of a user
Byzantine – providing wrong data to other nodes in collaborative spectrum sensing	Wang, Li, Sun, & Han, 2009	Two operating modes: causing False Alarm attack, or causing False Alarm & Miss-detection	Each user is attributed a suspicious level, turned into a trust value, but also a consistency value
	Min, Shin, & Hu, 2009	Two types of attacks: false-positive and false-negative. The attackers are assumed to able to estimate the channel occupancy with 100% precision	Double-defense mechanism: the correlations between the reported RSS values using correlation filters are observed and the suspicious nodes are outlined; usage of the weight-combining data fusion rule
	Noon & Li, 2010	Hit-and-run attacker - able to estimate its current suspicious level and adapt its attacking scheme	Novel reputation algorithm - the user is permanently excommunicated once his reputation value is below a threshold
SJA – sending spurious RF data, disrupting the normal communication	Dabcevic, Marcenaro & Regazzoni, 2012 (our proposed scheme)	The attacker tries to emulate the "good" radio node	Frequency switching algorithm
OFA – disrupting CR's learning mechanism	Qingqi, Hongning, & Kefeng, 2011	-	Set of general guidelines, e.g. Multi-Objective Programming module verifies all of the reconfigured parameters in each iteration
Lion attack – multi-layer attack with the goal of causing DoS at the transport layer	Hernandez-Serrano, Leon, & Soriano, 2010	-	Set of general guidelines for reducing the efficiency of the attack
Attacks on CCC	Zhu & Zhou, 2008 /	two types of attacks: DoS attack in multi-hop networks, and the greedy MAC layer behavior	-
	Safdar & O'Neill, 2009	-	Authentication of communicating CR nodes as the key security feature
Spectrum trading security issues	Zhu, Suo, & Gao, 2010	Attacker decreases the QoS while declaring that it remains the same	Once it observes illegal behavior, PU decreases the amount of spectrum shared with SU, thus reducing its overall utility
802.22-specific	Bian & Park, 2008	Identification of the possible attacks: DoS; Replay; Jamming in QPs; PUEA; Threats to WMBs; Attacks on Self-Coexistence mechanism	Security sublayer deals with some of the vulnerabilities, mainly through: Privacy Key Management v2; message authentication codes; Advanced Encryption Standard

the legitimate SUs use, the adversary emulates certain characteristics of a PU – i.e. in CRNs where SUs use energy detectors, the PUE attacker will try to create signals of similar power, whereas in networks with feature-based detectors the attacker will emulate the corresponding feature of the PU. To counter the PUE attacks, the appropriate defense scheme able to distinguish between real and mimicking PUs needs to be implemented within the network.

One of the aggravating factors in devising such a scheme is Federal Communication Commission's instruction that "no modification to the incumbent signal should be required to accommodate opportunistic use of the spectrum by SUs."

PUEAs have arguably been given the most attention in the literature out of all the threats specific to CRNs. The PUEA-defense contributions can be divided into those where the locations of the PUs are supposed to be known a-priori, such as in cases when PUs are for example TV towers or base stations, and those where the PUs' locations cannot be assumed to be known beforehand.

Authors in (Chen, Park, & Reed, 2008) propose a location-based method, applicable to the network where PUs are TV towers, with high transmission power and high transmission range.

The authors model a CR attacker capable of altering its transmit power, modulation mode and frequency. Two types of attacks are possible: in the first one, the attacker alters the RSS measurements by changing the transmit power, whereas in the second one, the attackers inject false data to the localization system.

To counter such attackers, they propose a scheme that „estimates a location of the signal source and, if it deviates from the known location of the TV towers and the signal characteristics resemble those of primary user signals, then it is likely that the signal source is launching a PUE attack", assuming that „it would be infeasible for an attacker to mimic both the primary user signal's transmission location and energy level since the transmission power of the attacker's CR is several orders of magnitude smaller than that of a typical TV tower". The scheme consists of three steps: verification of signal characteristics, RSS measurement, and localization of the signal source.

Simulation results show the effectiveness of the scheme, designed for the networks in which PUs have fixed locations and high transmit powers. In cases of mobile PUs with relatively small power (directly leading to higher RSS fluctuations), alternative approaches need to be used.

In (Chen, Cooklev, Chen, & Pomalaza-Raez, 2009), authors propose another location-based method for dealing with advanced PUE attackers. The modeled attacker is capable of applying the estimation techniques to enhance its performance, i.e. it „can employ a maximum likelihood estimator to infer the transmit power of the primary user and a channel parameter, and use the inferred parameters and a mean-field approach to generate primary user emulation". It is assumed that the attacker has the location information of all the entities in the network. The authors also assume the use of energy detectors as spectrum sensing mechanisms, meaning that the attacker needs to try and transmit signals whose energy will be as similar as possible to the one transmitted by the legitimate PU, from the viewpoint of the targeted SUs. To do this, attacker estimates the PU's transmit power and the channel parameter, and then, taking into account its distance to the targeted SU and PU's distance to the SU, launches a PUE attack.

The designed defense mechanism lies on the presumption that the attacker cannot successfully emulate the channel features. Invariants of communication channels are used as means of differentiating between the PUE attackers from legitimate PUs.

The simulation results show that, while such attacker can successfully defeat a „naive" detection method, the proposed mechanism successfully distinguishes between mimicking and real PUs with high accuracy.

Authors in (Liu, Ning, & Dai, 2010) have modeled a non-location-based mechanism, which uses a helper node placed proximate to the PU in order to counter PUEAs. The helper node „serves as a "bridge" to enable a secondary user to verify the cryptographic signature carried by the helper node's signals, and then obtain the helper node's authentic link signatures to verify the primary user's signals". The authors propose a novel physical layer authentication mechanism, which incorporates cryptographic and wireless link signatures. It is assumed that all SUs have reliable ways to obtain the correct public key of each helper node, and that the helper node cannot be compromised by an attacker.

Proposed Scheme and Simulator for Countering PUEA

We are presenting a naive location-based method for identifying PUE attackers, with the assumption of the a-priori knowledge of the locations of all of the users. The method is based on the credibility calculation for all of the SUs, and the final decision of whether the SU is the actual PU or the PUE attacker is done by comparing its credibility to the predefined threshold for the given SNR level.

The following assumptions were made:

- Each user has the a-priori information of other users' locations,
- The attackers are capable of emulating one or more of the PU's features, including the ability to transmit at the same power as the PU,
- Prior to encountering PUE attacker, the CR is ensured to have established communication with the legitimate PU, in order to derive the appropriate threshold value for user classification for a given channel.

The algorithm decides on the credibility of the user in a following way:

- Based on the coordinates on the playground, the distance between the SU (CR) and the legitimate PU is calculated.
- The RSS values of the legitimate PU transmitting a signal at constant power are calculated for different SNR values. The expected distance between the SU and legitimate PU can be calculated from the RSS value.
- The credibility of each user is calculated as the ratio of the real distance (derived from coordinates) and approximated distance (derived from RSS values). This value is used as a „ground truth", and the threshold value for future user classification is derived from this credibility.
- The RSS values of subsequent users are calculated depending on their distance and transmit power, and their credibility is derived using the previous method. The credibility is then compared to the threshold, where it is decided whether a user is a legitimate PU or a PUE attacker.

It should be noted that the algorithm performs better as more samples from legitimate PUs can be obtained for calculation of the threshold.

In the simulations, AWGN free-space channel with corresponding path loss values has been used in channel modeling. The transmit powers of the legitimate PU and the emulating SU are equal.

For calculating the threshold, we have performed Monte Carlo simulations with 1000 iterations, where position on the playground was randomized in every iteration. The threshold is calculated as:

$$\gamma = 0.995 * total\_trust.$$

The credibility of each subsequent user is then compared to the threshold and, if its value is higher than the threshold, the user is regarded as a legitimate PU.

Security in Cognitive Radio Networks

Figure 1 shows the distribution of the average calculated credibility over 1000 iterations, versus SNR, whereas probabilities of the correct detection of the legitimate PU, and the successful detection of the attacker are given in Figure 2.

Because of the noise power causing high RSS fluctuations in low-SNR environments, the credibility of legitimate PUs is relatively low in such harsh channel conditions.

The algorithm fares substantially better in higher-SNR environments. For SNR=15dB, the algorithm is able to correctly identify legitimate PUs with a 98% accuracy, and malicious users with 92% accuracy, whereas for SNR=25 dB, legitimate PUs are correctly categorized with a 100%, and malicious users with 98% accuracy.

Different results can be obtained for different threshold constraints.

Alongside the aforementioned poor channel conditions, the main vulnerabilities of the algorithm arise when the attacker is close to the real PU. In those cases, either a more complex RSS-based scheme, such as the one previously mentioned proposed by (Chen, Park, & Reed, 2008), or an alternative, non-RSS-based scheme need to be used for the successful detection of PUEAs.

Byzantine Attacks

Once the sensing part is finished, the CR needs to decide how to use the acquired data in order to correctly estimate the channel occupancy state. While it is possible for each entity to make this decision solely based on their own spectrum sensing outputs, more precise results can be achieved if the users can exchange the information among themselves. This is the idea behind collaborative spectrum sensing, where SUs either send the results of the spectrum sensing to each other, or to a centralized entity which then decides on the channel occupancy and feeds this decision back to the SUs. This way, the correct detection probability of a channel occupancy, potentially impaired due to the problems such as a „hidden node", equipment malfunction, or poor channel conditions, can be improved significantly.

However, collaborative spectrum sensing also has its drawbacks – besides the increase of computational complexity (in cases where each

Figure 1. Distribution of the average calculated credibility over 1000 iterations vs. SNR

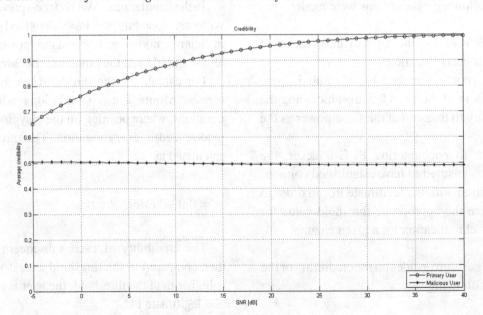

Figure 2. Probabilities of the correct detection of the legitimate PU and the successful detection of the attacker

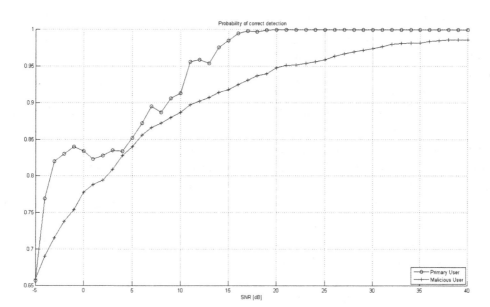

node has to make the decision for itself based on the data acquired from multiple users) or the need for use of the additional data fusion entity (in cases of centralized collaborative sensing), certain security issues arise as well.

Byzantine attackers send false spectrum sensing information to the other users or the centralized entity, thus increasing the probability of the wrong decision of the spectrum occupancy. Furthermore, a malfunctioning node may unintentionally also cause faulty reports. In both cases, the ability to correctly estimate the channel availability – arguably the most important feature of CRs – can be degraded severely.

Hence, with regards to the type of the misbehaving CR node, the users can be classified as:

- **Greedy:** With the intention of acquiring exclusive privileges to the free channels by constantly sending the information of a channel being occupied,
- **Malicious:** With the intention of causing harmful interference between the other

users, or reducing the spectrum usage efficiency,

- **Temporarily Malfunctioning:** Who unknowingly send incorrect information regarding the spectrum occupancy.

Coming up with a reliable method for countering the byzantine failures imposes itself as a critical task in order for the collaborative sensing to be able to be safely and successfully implemented.

Various strategies for addressing byzantine issues have been proposed in the literature, different from each other mainly with respect to the data fusion algorithm, reputation algorithm and the attackers' special features considered.

Authors in (Wang, Li, Sun, & Han, 2009) propose a relatively simple defense scheme for singling out the malicious user by computing the suspicious level, trust values and consistency values. The authors consider a single malicious attacker, and show how the algorithm, which eliminates the observations from the node marked as malicious, performs depending on the collaborative sensing scheme used. The attacker can operate in two modes: causing False Alarm attack, where it reports a higher sensed power whenever the power is below its set threshold, or causing False Alarm & Miss-detection, where it reports higher sensed power when it's below the threshold, or lower sensed power when it is above it.

Each user is attributed a suspicious level, which is then turned into a trust value. Since the trust value itself is not reliable in cases when there are either not enough observations, or there is no malicious user present, each user is also assigned a consistency value. By eliminating the reports from the users with consistently low trust values, and then using the OR rule for the remaining nodes, the scheme shows satisfying improvements compared to simpler, more straightforward schemes, for both attacking strategies. The main limitation of the scheme is the fact that only one malicious user is considered at any time.

In (Min, Shin, & Hu, 2009), authors propose a double-defense mechanism for the centralized collaborative sensing, which they refer to as the „Attack-tolerant Distributed Sensing Protocol" (ADSP). Two types of attacks are taken into account: false-positive, classifying a non-primary user as a primary thus increasing the probability of a misdetection, and false-negative, causing failure to detect a primary signal and increasing the probability of the false alarm. The attackers are assumed to be able to correctly estimate whether the PU is using the channel or not at all times, regardless of the decision the centralized entity makes, therefore being able to switch between their attacking modes.

The proposed defense framework „consists of three building blocks:

- Sensing manager that manages sensor clusters and directs the sensors to report their readings at the end of each scheduled sensing period,
- Attack detector that detects and discards (or penalizes) the abnormal sensing reports

based on the pre-established shadowing correlation profile,

- Data-fusion center that determines the presence or absence of a primary signal based on the filtered sensing results".

The mechanism is implemented in a way that the clustered sensors send their RSS values and location information to the data fusion center, which is being done in two phases. First, the correlations between the reported RSS values using correlation filters are observed, and the nodes whose reports appear inconsistent with the others are deemed suspicious, so their reports are not taken into account for making the decision on the channel occupancy. The other line of defense – implemented because of the inaccuracy of the first one when the attackers produce low-strength attacks – is a weight-combining data fusion rule, where weights to sensors are allocated based on their Conditional Probability Density Function (CPDF). This way, the misbehaving sensors are likely to be given low weight factors, meaning that their reports to the data fusion center will be less likely to affect the final decision.

The simulation results shows the proposed algorithm to be able to minimize the probability of a false-alarm by up to 99.2% (for the first type of attack), and to achieve the probability of correct detection of up to 97.4% (for the second type of attack), showing significantly better performances than the other algorithms considered.

In (Noon & Li, 2010), authors present a specific type of an advanced attacking strategy, called Hit-and-run, and the corresponding defense mechanism. The attacking strategy is based on the assumption that the attacker is able to estimate its current suspicious level assigned by the data fusion center, and act appropriately. Namely, when it feels that it's suspicious level is high, and there is a potential for it to be expelled from the network, it stops sending false observations, and starts acting honestly. Once that it calculates that it's safe again, it re-starts its malicious behavior, and from there continues to use this Hit-and-run strategy. It is assumed that the attacker is aware of the other nodes' reports to the DFC, and can model its report based on this information.

The conventional reputation-based schemes are unable to deal with this kind of attacker, so the authors have proposed a new point-system. The system permanently bans the user from the network once it has accumulated enough negative reputation points, where each negative point is assigned to the user whenever its suspicion level surpasses a pre-defined threshold. By applying the Wald's equality, the algorithm can approximate the expected time for the attacker to reach the threshold, and also the time for the attacker to decrease its suspicion level. By combining these approximations, the time needed for detecting the attacker can be estimated.

For the set number of 10 secondary users in the network, the authors show how the algorithm fares when faced with up to three attackers. As the number of attackers increases, the algorithm needs more iterations for successful detection, however still successfully manages to excommunicate the malicious users.

Smart Jamming Attacks

RF jamming attacks refer to the illicit transmissions of RF signals with the intention of disrupting the normal communication on the targeted channels. RF jamming is a known problem in modern wireless networks, and not an easy one to counter with the traditional „hardware-based" equipment. Since RF spectrum is an extremely valuable asset, whose lessor in most countries is a state itself, RF jamming is typically seen as a property theft, with fines and repercussions for the identified intentional jammers being substantial.

There are many different types of jammers depending on their allocation, ranging from disrupting the signal receipt at the target receivers, to more sophisticated ones, such as deceiving the targets into accepting false information. Software

Defined Radios and Cognitive radios bring the prospect for improving both the jamming capabilities of the malicious user, but also developing advanced protection- and counter-mechanisms.

Proposed Scheme for Countering Smart Jamming Attacks and the Simulator

We define a *smart jammer* as a particular type of an attacker that is able to scan the entire spectrum and selectively jam specific channels, thus causing anomalous spectrum usage and actually interfering with dynamic spectrum access techniques (Morerio, Dabcevic, Marcenaro, & Regazzoni, 2012).

The considered *smart jammer* consists of three major components:

- A spectrum sensor, which senses and locates target's physical channel,
- A spectrum analyzer, which analyzes the sensed spectrum data and, combining it with the prior knowledge of the target channel, consequently devises an action,
- A radio transmitter, which is dedicated to radiating jamming signals.

In our scenario, we are considering a case with an arbitrary number of legitimate mobile Cognitive Nodes (CNs), and one Malicious Node (MN) equipped with a mobile jamming device – the *smart jammer*. This network is controlled by a centralized Data Fusion Entity (DFE) with a fixed location, which collects the following data from each of the SUs in each timeframe:

- Their position (coordinates *x*, *y*) on the playground,
- Their Received Signal Strength (RSS) value,
- Their transmit frequency.

The *smart jammer* is designed with the following characteristics and capabilities:

- Ability to jam one frequency at the time, but able to alter the jamming frequency every *n* timeframes,
- Altering its transmit power – specifically, it refrains from transmitting when it approaches the legitimate node, in order to make the DFE think that it is being jammed by the legitimate node,
- Trying to emulate a legitimate node, sending its true coordinates to the DFE.

The DFE continuously calculates the distance between all pairs of users, as well as their RSS value. Whenever the RSS value for a certain user drops below a pre-defined threshold, it assumes that the user has found himself in the jammer-influenced area, initiates the frequency switching algorithm for the given user, and assigns a negative reputation point to the user suspected of jamming. Upon collecting a certain number of negative reputation points, the user is deemed a jammer, all the legitimate nodes are notified of its presence, and its observations to the DFE are disregarded in the future.

The jammer strategically tries to confuse the DFE into thinking that the other nodes are in fact jammers. By ceasing to transmit whenever it gets close to another node, it causes the decrease in the reputation value for the said legitimate node.

A simulator was realized, where the DFE is implemented as a set of C/C++ interacting modules running on an IGEPv2 - a compact ARM-based industrial processor board. The DFE is able to sense signal strength of detected mobile entities and - by comparing the RSS values - has the ability to detect jammers within the monitored environment. Implemented prototype is able to deal with fixed and mobile jammers - after a jammer is detected, the cooperative mobile entity automatically modifies its operating frequency, as per DFE's instructions. It is assumed that the frequency switching initialization protocol between the DFE and the cooperative nodes is being done over a dedicated channel, which cannot be jammed.

The scenario consists of a number of entities (agents) carrying a mobile device which is able to transmit and receive data at 3 different frequencies (namely 800, 900, and 1800 and MHz) to a centralized control center. The agents move intelligently (in a sense that they are able to alter their trajectories in order to avoid the obstacles) throughout the jamming-polluted environment. The considered playground is a virtual depiction of a standard urban environment, 40m x 40m large, and the agents are simulated at moving at a constant speed of 5 km/h. The jammers can be either fixed or mobile, and their emitted signal strength follows the Rayleigh distribution with fixed parameters. Fixed jammers' positions and characteristics are stored in an XML file, which is loaded in the setup stage together with the map of the ground. An example of a scenario with 2 moving agents (Agent1 and Agent2) originally transmitting at the frequency of 1800 MHz, and three fixed jammers (J0 - J3) jamming at 800 MHz, 800 MHz and 1800 MHz respectively, with their respective radii of sensing and influence is depicted in Figure 3.

The agents periodically send a single radio data to the control center, where the running cognitive node receives and processes it.

Radio data sent by an agent contains the following information:

- **Position of the Agent (x, y) on the Mapped Ground:** This is generated by the trajectories simulator. It simulates a GPS sensor on the mobile device. If video monitoring of the ground area is available, positioning data coming from the tracker can potentially be fused with the GPS data in order to obtain a better position estimation.
- **Frequency of the Transmission:** Initial transmission frequency can be chosen at the beginning of the simulation, whereas information of the updated frequencies are sent in every timeframe.
- **Power of the Transmitted Signal:** Fixed.

Figure 3. Scenario with two agents and three fixed jammers

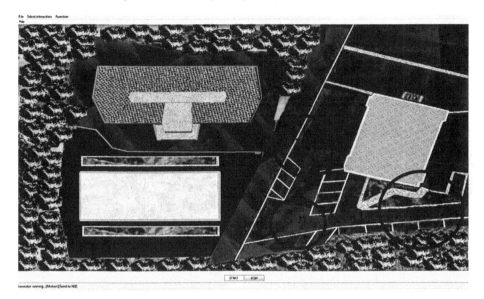

- **Possibly Detected Jammers' Estimated Power:** Each jammer has a typical radius (coded in the XML configuration file) of influence, inside which the agent can estimate its power (knowing that the signal strength follows the Rayleigh distribution).
- **IDs of the Possible Neighboring Agents** (within a fixed sensing radius).

We can also look at a slightly different scenario by introducing a moving jammer: now, an additional agent (Agent3), carrying a jamming device, has been added to the scene. Besides disturbing communication at its operating frequency within its jamming radius, it also transmits spurious data to the DFE regarding its position. A scenario with 2 moving agents transmitting at the frequency of 1800 MHz and one Jammer transmitting at the same frequency, with their respective radii of sensing and influence is depicted in Figure 4.

Frequency switching process for one of the agents (Agent1) as a function of time, and depending on the jamming power of the nearby jammers is given in Figure 5.

The same process for both agents (Agent1 and Agent2) for the modified (mobile-jammer) scenario is given in Figure 6. As can be seen, in this case the frequency switching only occurs once for each of the agents: since mobile jammer doesn't have the capability of jamming multiple frequencies, there is no reason for agents 1 and 2 to deviate from their newly-set frequencies once they start transmitting at a frequency not influenced by the malicious agent.

The radio data reception represents, from the node point of view, the "sensing" stage of the cognitive cycle. The agents' mobile terminals are equipped with sensors which monitor the environment, sending a radio survey (radio sensors) and positioning (GPS sensor) information to the cognitive node.

The cognitive node - acting as a data fusion center - then analyzes all the information received from each agent. For each agent, the signal-to-noise and distortion ratio (SINAD) of the received data packet is computed. Also, agents' relative positions are compared, and by the means of the voting algorithm, rankings are assigned to each

Figure 4. Scenario with mobile jammer (intruder)

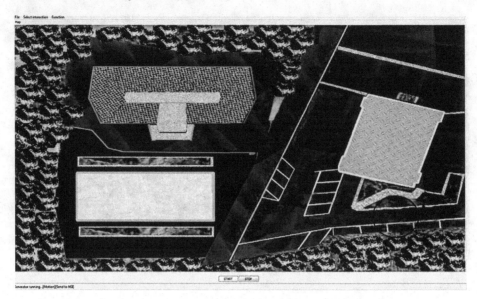

agent's ID. Then, intruder's position and ID are worked out.

In the decision stage, the SINAD datum is compared to an acceptable (fixed to 10 dB) threshold. If the communication with an agent under the jamming influence proves to be below the acceptable threshold, a suitable strategy is chosen in order to schedule a change in the transmit frequency.

The "action" stage leads to the change in the state of the system. As was previously explained, this module implements the active interaction of the system towards the surrounding environment or towards itself: the action of changing frequency

Figure 5. Frequency switching depending on the jammer power (two agents and three fixed jammers)

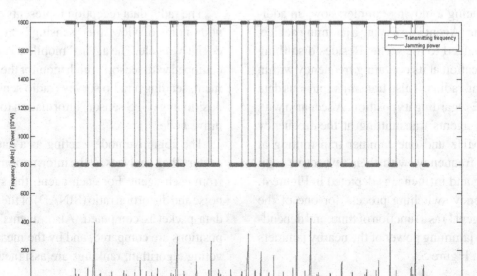

Figure 6. Frequency switching depending on the jammer power (mobile jammer)

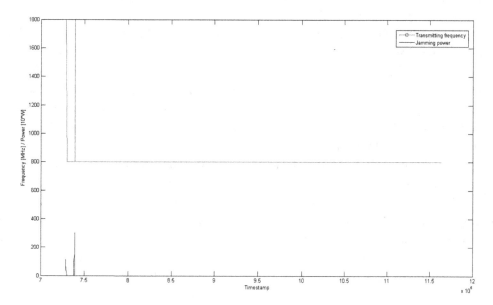

is selected based on the strategy ST chosen during the previous step.

Hence, detection of the intruder does not trigger a decision and a subsequent action in the cognitive cycle. Instead, the information relative to the malevolent agent is transmitted to the third party agent, which in real-life application could, for example, display data on the mobile devices, thus leaving the decision step under human control. Alternatively, a learning-based-on-experience strategy could be deployed within the DFE in the future perspective.

Alternative Spectrum Occupancy Decision Methods and the Related Security Threats

Besides spectrum sensing, two other methods have been proposed by the NPRM – Notice of the Proposed Rule Making – Unlicensed Operation in the TV Broadcast Bands (Check, Scott, Mace, Brenner, & Nicoll, 2004) as alternative ways of acquiring spectrum occupancy information: geo-location/database and beacon signals.

Overcoming some of the drawbacks of the spectrum sensing approaches (which vary depending on the sensing technique used) – such as possibly long sensing periods, unknown/incomplete waveform information, or bad channel conditions – geolocation/database approach has recently sparked interest in the CR research community. This approach requires the SU to have a perfect awareness of its location, and to be able to access the database containing the list of the currently available frequencies at a given location. One particular feature makes usage of the geolocation/database approach especially appealing from the regulatory point of view: the possibility of easier management of the frequencies or frequency bands that the lessor wishes to declare as "available" or "busy" at any given time.

Naturally, this approach brings its own set of security issues and concerns, primarily:

- **Continuous Database Accessibility:** Ensuring that the database is always „up-and-running", and updated with the list of (un)available frequencies is a necessity.

- **Database Management and Updating:** Since databases need to be regularly updated, there is a need for a reliable mechanism for the processes of updating and downloading the updated content to the cognitive device.

- **Database Tampering:** While originally the communication between the database and the SU is intended to be one-way (SU downloading the content from the database), ensuring that malicious content cannot be uploaded by the SU by deploying anti-tampering methods is paramount.

- **Database Emulation:** Similarly to PUEA, if the SU retrieves information from a source pretending to be a spectrum lessor in a given geographical area, it can make wrong estimations of the spectrum occupancy of a given frequency band – i.e. it may try accessing a channel currently marked as "busy" by the spectrum lessor (malicious attack), or may refrain itself from accessing a channel that is in fact marked as "available" (selfish attack).

- **Providing False Geolocation Information:** Whereas many CRs are expected to have direct geolocation capabilities due to the embedded navigation systems, such as GPS (Global Positioning System) or GLONASS (Globalnaya Navigatsionnaya Sputnikovaya Sistema), there might be instances where this is not the case, or where the navigation system is malfunctioning. In this case, CRs may have the capability of finding out their coordinates by triangulation with other cooperative or non-cooperative devices, which opens up the possibility of providing false data, thus causing the targeted device to perform the triangulation erroneously.

Beacon signals method refers to the usage of beacons as means of providing the prospective SUs information of the available frequencies in their proximity. SUs tune to a dedicated channel in order to extract the information of the spectrum availability from the beacons, and then decide upon the optimal way to proceed. In the case of the absence of the beacon, the SUs should refrain themselves from using the spectrum opportunistically.

The main issues from a security and privacy standpoint that impose themselves are as follows:

- **Beacon Emulation:** Emulation attacks are a common security issue in CRNs, regardless of the approach taken towards realizing the spectrum occupancy. That being said, Beacon signals seem particularly prone to such attacks, since they represent a single point of failure. The attacker may intercept the beacon, alter its parameters and/or predict the behavior of the cognitive users.

- **Security of the Common Control Channel:** With the assumption that the beacons are being transmitted over a dedicated channel, it is necessary to address the related security problems. CCC-related security issues and the proposed defense mechanisms are discussed in the subsection "Other attacks and threats."

- **Beacon Misinterpretation:** One of the challenges lies in preventing the beacon to be received outside of the designated geographical area, thus causing the incorrect interpretation of the contained information, e.g. a SU receiving a beacon from the neighbouring cell, and mistakenly concluding that the channel X is free for accessing opportunistically. Furthermore, in case of multiple beacons co-existing in the same location at the same time, there is a problem of deciding upon which is the one carrying the correct information for a given geographical spot.

Whereas beacon designs have been proposed in the literature, such as (Lei & Chin, 2008), architecture dealing with the aforementioned security problems is still an open issue.

Threats to Reputation Systems

In Cognitive Radios, usage of the reputation systems has a particular purposefulness in the networks where some sort of collaboration between the users exists such as in the context of collaborative spectrum sensing. Whereas threats to the reputation systems were somewhat covered in the subsection "Byzantine attacks," it is useful to provide a more detailed coverage of the potential attacks and issues.

Authors in (Sun & Liu, 2012) have given a detailed comparison of the attacks on feedback-based reputation systems, recognizing:

- **Whitewashing and Traitor Attacks:** Whitewashing attacker is able to discard its current ID, and re-enter the system (network) with a new ID. Traitor attacker is able to restore his reputation score by behaving non-maliciously for a certain time period (see "Hit-and-run attacker" under "Byzantine attacks"). The authors propose increasing the cost/complexity for acquiring a new user ID, as well as low initial reputation for new users as a defense strategy against whitewashing. Against traitor attacks, the adaptive forgetting scheme with the fading factor is proposed.
- **Attacking Object Quality Reputation Through Dishonest Feedback:** Refers to providing false feedback information in order to lead the reputation system towards the erroneous decision. The authors recognize three different approaches towards tackling dishonest feedback attacks:
  - **Increasing the Cost of Dishonest Feedback:** Users are needed to have certain credentials to be able to provide feedback.
  - **Detection of Dishonest Feedback:** Deployment of a defense scheme that detects dishonest feedback based on the majority rule, i.e. the feedback that significantly differs from the majority's opinion is disregarded
  - **Mitigating the Effects of Dishonest Feedback:** Feedback of users with lower feedback reputation will have less impact on the overall score. There are several proposed methods for calculating the feedback reputation of a user, such as computing a weight of a user's feedback in the feedback aggregation algorithm as the inverse of the variance in all of his or her feedback.
- **Self-Promotion Attacks:** Attackers can provide honest feedback for the objects they are not interested in – for example, in case of collaborative spectrum sensing, for frequency bands that they are not interested in opportunistically accessing. For countering self-promoting attacks, the defense schemes used against whitewashing and traitor attacks can be applied.
- **Complicated Collusion Attacks:** In order to enhance the efficiency of attacks and reduce the probability of being detected, attackers may collude. The authors differentiate two types of complex collaboration attacks:
  - **Oscillation Attack (Srivatsa, Xiong, & Liu, 2005):** Malicious users are divided into different groups, each group performing different role at a given time – i.e. while one group focuses on providing dishonest feedback, the other may focus on improving its reputation by providing honest feedback to the non-targeted objects. The focuses of these groups may switch dynamically.
  - **RepTrap Attack (Yang, Feng, Sun, & Dai, 2008):** Malicious users fo-

cus on breaking the "majority rule" of an object by making the majority of feedback for the given object dishonest.

For countering the complicated collusion attacks, two different defense schemes were proposed: a scheme using temporal analysis, which explores the information in the time domain (e.g. changing trend of rating values), and a user correlation analysis, which aims at finding the patterns between the malicious users.

Other Attacks and Threats

Several other attacks that are directly related to the cognitive functionalities of CRs have been devised, and studied in the literature.

Objective Function Attacks (OFA) are aimed at disrupting the most complex of the CR's functionalities – its learning mechanism. Learning mechanism will typically be on top of triggering the reconfiguration process of most of the reconfigurable radio parameters, such as frequency, modulation type, power and coding rate, in order to improve the overall performance – e.g. increase of the data-rate, decrease of the energy consumption, or enabling or disabling certain security protocols and functions. The malicious users can try and tamper with some of these parameters, in order to prevent the CR from the adapting in an optimal way.

To counter OFAs, (Qingqi, Hongning, & Kefeng, 2011) propose a simple method called Multi-Objective Programming module, which verifies all of the reconfigured parameters. The model is based on Particle Swamp Optimization (PSO) – a computational method for solving optimization problems in which software agents move through the problem space, trying to improve the candidate solution. Upon reconfiguration, the algorithm is supposedly able to detect the attackers, and reset the parameters to previous state.

Lion attack is a cross-layer attack characteristic for CRNs, where the malicious node targets the physical layer, in order to cause DoS at the transport layer. The attacker performs either a PUEA, or a jamming attack, thus forcing the SU currently using the channel to perform frequency handoff. Because of the high latencies of data flow within the TCP protocol, the situation where the transport layer is unaware of the temporary disconnection due to the handoff can occur. The transport layer keeps streaming data, which is then not transmitted, but queued at the lower layers, leading to certain TCP segments being delayed, or even permanently lost, and the throughput suffering substantially.

Authors in (Hernandez-Serrano, Leon, & Soriano, 2010) evaluate the impacts of Lion attack on TCP performance, validating its efficiency through simulations. The authors provide general guidelines for reducing the efficiency of Lion attacks, namely freezing the TCP connection parameters during the frequency handoffs, and deploying the CRN-adapted intrusion detection systems.

Common Control Channel (CCC) is expected to be present in most Cognitive Radio Networks, both centralized (enabling communication between base station and SU) and distributed (for the communication between SUs), and as such imposes itself as one of the potential points of attack. The attacker can, for example, forge the MAC frames in multi-hop networks, where there is no mechanism for the MAC frames authentication, thus causing DoS.

In (Zhu & Zhou, 2008), the authors analyze two types of attacks on the CCC: the aforementioned DoS attack in multi-hop networks, and the greedy MAC layer behavior, where a "CR device is being reconfigured to exploit implicit fairness mechanisms in lower-layer wireless network protocols for the advantage of that CR device's performance", or where "the greedy nodes refuse to transmit data to legitimate nodes so as to obtain better channel allocation for themselves."

Authors in (Safdar & O'Neill, 2009) propose a framework for a secure Common Control Channel in multi-hop CRNs, suggesting that "channel announcements, selection and reservation takes place in the common control channel, whereas data exchange in the selected data channel between two cognitive radio nodes occurs in the data channel part of the MAC super frame," and pointing out to authentication of communicating cognitive radio nodes as the key feature of the framework.

Spectrum trading refers to assigning the RF spectrum through administrative means, allowing a spectrum license holder to directly control the process of spectrum lease or a sell to a non-licensed user. As such, it is one of the most interesting capacities of Cognitive Radios from the license holders' point of view. Whereas security of spectrum trading by itself has mainly regulatory, as opposed to technical, significance, thus differing from the mechanisms considered throughout the rest of the chapter, it is useful to point out towards such mechanisms as well.

Authors in (Zhu, Suo, & Gao, 2010) have addressed the security aspects of the spectrum trading by using a game-theoretical approach, formulating the process as a reversed Stackelberg game. The authors assume cooperation between a PU and a SU, where:

The primary base station (BS) communicates with the primary users, and trades unused frequency spectrum with the secondary network. Then, the secondary BS could act as a relay for the primary network, where a contract is required between the primary network and the secondary network to ensure a QoS level in the relay work. The secondary network can gain some utility from the relay work. Moreover, unused frequency spectrum in secondary network could also be leased to secondary users (Zhu, Suo, & Gao, 2010).

Applying a game theoretical concept to a wanted model and searching for its Nash equilibrium(s) requires defining a finite set of actions that each of the players can take, as well as each player's utility functions. The authors define five factors that compose PUs' utility function: satisfaction of its transmission, profit from selling spectrum, gain, and payment from the SUs' relay work, and performance loss due to the shared spectrum with SUs. SUs' utility is comprised by: gain from its data transmission, profit and cost from acting as relay, and the payment for the purchased spectrum. The observed security issue refers to the scenario where SU tries to cheat the primary PU by decreasing the QoS while declaring that the QoS remains the same. The proposed scheme tackles this by continuously supervising SU's performance parameter and, in case that illegal behavior occurs, the PU punishes the SU by decreasing the shared spectrum with SU, thus reducing its overall utility.

802.22 Standard for CRNs and the Related Security Threats

The IEEE 802.22 is a Cognitive Radio standard for Wireless Regional Area Networks, WRANs developed by the IEEE 802 LAN/MAN standards committee, specifying the methods for opportunistic usage of the white spaces in the 54 - 862 MHz TV bands.

Following the general paradigms of the Opportunistic Spectrum Access, the 802.22 standard prescribes the set of rules for the OSA, whilst ensuring that the normal operation of the TV services remains undisrupted by the interference. The standard considers two approaches for achieving the knowledge of the spectrum occupancy: spectrum sensing and geolocation/database. Centralized network architecture is defined, where in the case of the spectrum sensing method being used as means for determining the occupancy, secondary base stations are in charge of directly coordinating the cognitive users to achieve spectrum sensing synchronously. The sensing outputs are then forwarded to the centralized entity (data fusion center), which makes a decision on the spectrum occupancy.

Several security threats directly related to 802.22 standard can be identified. Whereas the standard defines the existence of the security sublayer, able to tackle several common security issues, it does not contain any specific technique for protecting spectrum sensing or geolocation information, or the data coming from the database. Examples of potential 802.11-related security threats are (Bian & Park, 2008):

- **Denial of Service (DoS):** Attackers create messages for disturbing spectrum sensing and allocation processes. This type of threat is managed by the 802.22 security sublayer through PKMv2 (Privacy Key Management v2) and message authentication codes.
- **Replay Attacks:** The attacker captures and replays the local sensing reports sent by wireless terminals to their base station. This may cause the base station to make incorrect spectrum sensing decision. IEEE 802.22 uses AES (Advanced Encryption Standard) for dealing with this type of attack.
- **Spurious Transmissions in QPs:** The attacker transmits spurious data (jamming) in quiet periods (QPs). By transmitting spurious messages in QPs, an adversary can interfere with the various coexistence-related control mechanisms carried out during QPs.
- **Incumbent Signal Emulation:** In PUEAs, a malicious CR transmits signals whose characteristics emulate those of incumbent signals. This type of attack is also known as "incumbent ghosting."

- **Security Threats Against WMBs:** The IEEE 802.11 standard proposes two solutions for detecting the presence of Part 74 devices (i.e., low-power wireless devices, such as wireless microphones, which are licensed to operate in the TV broadcast bands). If Part 74 signals are detected, a wireless terminal sends a wireless microphone beam (WMB) to collocated base stations in its vicinity. The 802.22 standard specifies that each wireless terminal needs to possess pre-programmed security keys that enable the use of an authentication mechanism to prevent the forgery and modification of WMBs. The security sublayer protects WMBs from replay attacks in the same manner as it protects intra-cell management messages.
- **Security Vulnerabilities in Coexistence Mechanism:** One of the most significant security oversights in IEEE 802.22 is the lack of protection provided to inter-cell beacons. All inter-cell control messages are vulnerable to unauthorized modification, forgery, or replay.

Being one of the main novelties that the standard defines, the last point warrants somewhat more in-depth explanation. Self-coexistence is a cooperation mechanism performed between the overlapping WRANs with the intention of improving performance and minimalizing interference. In cases where the base station wishes to perform a spectrum handoff to a channel whose Signal-to-Interference Ratio is lower than acceptable, the On-Demand Spectrum Contention (ODSC) protocol is used. The protocol includes transmitting the intercell beacons between base stations with the goal of sharing spectrum occupancy information. However, attackers may disrupt the synchronization and the exclusive spectrum sharing process by sending false, modified, or replayed beacons. This is known as the Beacon Falsification (BF) attack.

TOWARDS THE COMPLETE SECURITY FRAMEWORK FOR THE COGNITIVE RADIO NETWORKS

So far, the common threats present in Cognitive Radio Networks, and the suggested countermeasures to them, have been addressed separately. Constructing the complete security framework able to encompass the most suitable security solutions for each of the potential threats is the ultimate task for ensuring the safe and secure operations within the future Cognitive Radio Networks.

nSHIELD(ARTEMIS Joint Undertaking, 2012) is an ongoing European project, whose goal is ensuring the Security, Privacy, and Dependability (SPD) in the context of Embedded Systems. The nSHIELD project is, at the same time, a complement and significant technological breakthrough of pSHIELD, a pilot project funded in ARTEMIS Call 2009, as the first investigation towards the realization of the SHIELD Architectural Framework for SPD. The roadmap, already started in the pilot project, will bring to address SPD in the context of Embedded Systems as a "built in" rather than as "add-on" functionalities, proposing and perceiving with this strategy the first step toward SPD certification for future ESs.

One of the main novelties that the nSHIELD structural framework brings is the introduction of a different reference model. In addition to three horizontal layers: node, network and middleware, it will also contain one vertical layer – the so-called "Overlay." It is exactly overlay that is an enabler for the desired composability of the system, as this is where a set of security agents will be placed, which will then be properly selected depending on the considered scenario. Each security agent is in charge of monitoring the proper selection of the security measurements and parameters on one of the mentioned vertical layer. The measurements observed by each agent are transformed into metadata, and distributed to the other agents. The aggregated metadata allows for the forming the dynamic context, used for deciding which of

the actions and algorithms need to be performed and activated at one of the three vertical layers, in order to achieve the desired SPD level.

One of the key features of the concerned radio-based Embedded Systems is the introduction of the so-called "Smart Transmission Layer," able to receive and transmit a variety of different radio waveforms based on the software used. This sublayer – implemented within the network layer of the system – is to rely on the Software Defined Radio platform which – once equipped with the possibilities of maintaining scenario awareness, detecting possible threats and adapting to the new situations by itself – will evolve towards the Cognitive Radio. Hence, one of the central points of interest of the project is developing the aforementioned complete, secure framework for CRs and CRNs.

Even though the development is still in its early phase, the general ideas have been established.

Namely, through a feasible set of hardware-based and software-based security measures, the following is to be achieved within the framework:

- Secure authentication mechanisms,
- Confidentiality,
- Data integrity,
- Accessibility,
- Multimodal strategies for the isolation of adversary nodes,
- Ability to differentiate between adversaries and unintentionally misbehaving SUs.

The security mechanisms deployed in the current wireless networks are usually constructed as a two-fold line of defense, the first one being proactive mechanisms, and the second reactive ones. The proactive mechanisms common to such wireless networks can serve as the foundation for the considered security framework for CRNs. Namely, these include the sets of cryptographic primitives such as *Public Key Cryptography* and *Hash functions* for ensuring the confidentiality and authentication within the network.

The more challenging task is finding a way for combining the proposed reactive mechanisms.

Advanced Intrusion Detection Systems (IDSs) impose themselves as a means for resolving this task. IDSs have the task of recognizing the unauthorized access or attack attempts, and triggering the appropriate security mechanism.

Furthermore, it is necessary to ensure that the proposed architecture can accommodate embedded systems with different capabilities. The future intrusion detection system shall, once the security risk or malfunction has been detected, evaluate the ES's capabilities, as well as the required SPD level imposed by the Overlay, and deploy the appropriate security mechanism. Several state-of-the-art security mechanisms for each of the security threats shall be available for the system at all times, with the possibility of the Internet-based scheme updating. A simplified model is presented in Figure 7.

For example, in cases where the observed ES has only basic SDR capabilities, one of the software tampering protection mechanisms implemented within the Framework should be deployed, depending on the currently demanded SPD level. The SPD level can continuously change during the scenario, depending on the internal states of the system (e.g. battery level), and the external parameters from the environment (e.g. harsh channel conditions, or approaching an area where certain problematic behaviors have been experienced in the past, such as presence of a jammer). Alternatively, in case that the observed ES is the state-of-the-art CR device, security mechanisms for each of the identified threats at a given time need to be triggered, also depending on the required SPD level.

The current activities regarding the development of the Security-aware framework are focused on devising the algorithms for successfully countering different Smart Jamming strategies. The future work will focus on developing the appropriate algorithms for other SDR-related and CR-related threats studied throughout this chapter, and integrating them within the described constructed framework, ultimately leading to the complete, adaptable security system for the embedded SDR and CR devices.

Figure 7. Basic scheme of the security-aware framework

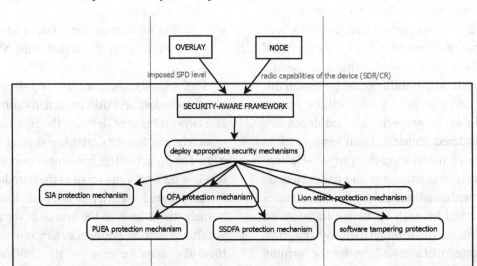

CONCLUSION

Cognitive Radio, and the most important features associated with it – Opportunistic Spectrum Access and Dynamic Spectrum Access – undoubtedly make for exciting, innovative and above all beneficial research topics. However, the advanced features linked with CRs bring new sets of security breaches and issues, addressing which is paramount in constructing efficient Cognitive Radio Networks.

This chapter has given a breakdown of the main standards, security problems, and corresponding solutions for "traditional" wireless networks, Software Defined Radio networks, and Cognitive Radio Networks, respectively (where each subsequent network inherits the issues found in the previous ones).

Most of the considered security issues stem out from the deployment of one of the spectrum occupancy decision methods, usually one of the methods of spectrum sensing, and the self-reconfigurability of the radios. As such, the main threats to such mechanisms are identified as Primary User Emulation Attacks, Byzantine Attacks, and Smart Jamming Attacks. Depending on type of the learning mechanism deployed, a great security hazard is present in the form of the Objective Function Attack, targeting CR's learning mechanism, which is still a somewhat understudied topic in the community.

Although there is a number of works in the research community where these security issues have been studied separately, there is only a limited number of works that propose schemes for unification and integration of the security mechanisms into a security framework. Building such a framework is one of the tasks of the ongoing nSHIELD project, the basic foundations for constructing which were presented in the chapter.

As the device capabilities and the prospective ideas behind the Cognitive Radio technology continue to evolve, so do the existing threats and attacks, with some new ones arising on-the-go.

Because of the numerous possibilities of variations, keeping up with them from a security perspective is often not an easy task, with challenges on multiple fields still unresolved.

REFERENCES

AirTightNetworks. (2012). *WPA2 Hole196 Vulnerability*. Retrieved July 2012, from AirTight-Networks: http://www.airtightnetworks.com/WPA2-Hole196/

ARTEMIS Joint Undertaking. (2012). *New Shield Project. Towards the Architectural Framework for Security, Privacy and Dependability (SPD)*. Retrieved 2012, from New Shield Project. Towards the Architectural Framework for Security, Privacy and Dependability (SPD): http://www.newshield.eu/

Barkan, E., Biham, E., & Keller, N. (2008, Volume 21 Issue 3). Instant Ciphertext-Only Cryptanalysis of GSM Encrypted Communication. *Journal of Cryptology*, 392-429.

Bian, K., & Park, J.-M. (2008). Security vulnerabilities in IEEE 802.22. *Proceedings of the 4th Annual International Conference on Wireless Internet (WICON '08)* (p. 9). Brussels, Belgium: Institute for Computer Sciences, Social-Informatics and Telecommunications Engineering.

Bishop, C. (1995). *Neural Networks for Pattern Recognition*. Oxford, UK: Oxford University Press.

Borisov, N., Goldberg, I., & Wagner, D. (2001). *Security of the WEP algorithm*. Retrieved July 15, 2012, from University of California, Berkeley: http://www.isaac.cs.berkeley.edu/isaac/wep-faq.html

Borse, M., & Shinde, H. (2005). Wireless Security & Privacy. *Proceedings on the Personal Wireless Communications, 2005 (PWC 2005), 2005 IEEE International Conference on* (pp. 424-428). Prague: Springer.

Brawerman, A., Blough, D., & Bing, B. (2004). Securing the Download of Radio Configuration Files for Software Defined Radio Devices. *Mobiwac '04: Proceedings of the Second International Workshop on Mobility Management & Wireless Access Protocols* (pp. 98-105). Philadelphia: Association for Computing Machinery (ACM).

Check, W. A., Scott, A., Mace, S. L., Brenner, D. L., & Nicoll, D. L. (2004, November 30). Notice of the Proposed Rule Making - Unlicensed Operation in the TV Broadcast Bands. Washington, D.C., Washington, United States of America.

Chen, R., Park, J.-M., & Reed, J. H. (2008, January). Defense against Primary User Emulation Attacks in Cognitive Radio Networks. *IEEE Journal on Selected Areas in Communications, 26*, 25–37. doi:10.1109/JSAC.2008.080104.

Chen, Z., Cooklev, T., Chen, C., & Pomalaza-Raez, C. (2009). Modeling Primary User Emulation Attacks and Defenses in Cognitive Radio Networks. *Performance Computing and Communications Conference (IPCCC), 2009 IEEE 28th International*, (pp. 208-215). Fort Wayne.

Dengg, J., Friedl, W., Hörtler, P., Jäger, M., Lehner, M., & Macskási, C. (n.d.). *WLAN Security & Encryption*. Retrieved July 2012, from Tuxworld: http://tuxworld.homelinux.org/papers/Wlan_Security_paper.pdf

European Telecommunications Standards Institute. (1996, November). Recommendation GSM 02.09, "Security Aspects". Sophia Antipolis, Valbonne, France.

Hernandez-Serrano, J., Leon, O., & Soriano, M. (2010). Modeling the Lion Attack in Cognitive Radio Networks. *EURASIP Journal on Wireless Communications and Networking* .

Hill, R. L., Suvda, M., & Campbell, R. (2005). Threat Analysis of GNU Software Radio. *Proceedings of the World Wireless Congress*.

Hu, N. (2011). *Investigations of radio behaviours and security threats in cognitive radio networks*. Hoboken, NJ.

Ilonen, J., Kamarainen, J.-K., & Lampinen, J. (2003). Differential Evolution Training Algorithm for Feed-Forward Neural Networks. *Neural Processing Letters, 17*(1), 93–105. doi:10.1023/A:1022995128597.

Kaigui, B., & Jung-Min, P. (2008). Security Vulnerabilities in IEEE 802.22. *Proceedings of the 4th Annual International Conference on Wireless Internet - WICON '08* (p. article no. 9). Brussels: ICST (Institute for Computer Sciences, Social-Informatics and Telecommunications Engineering).

Kennedy, J., & Eberhart, R. (1995). Particle Swarm Optimization. *Proceedings of IEEE International Conference on Neural Networks*, (pp. 1942-1948).

Kirkpatrick, S., Gelatt, C. D., & Vecchi, M. P. (1983). Optimization by Simulated Annealing. *Science, 220*(4598), 671–680. doi:10.1126/science.220.4598.671 PMID:17813860.

Lashkari, A. H., Danesh, M. M., & Samadi, B. (2009). A Survey on Wireless Security protocols (WEP, WPA and WPA2/802.11i). *Computer Science and Information Technology, 2009. ICCSIT 2009. 2nd IEEE International Conference on*, (pp. 48-52). Kuala Lumpur.

Lei, Z., & Chin, F. (2008, June). A Reliable and Power Efficient Beacon Structure for Cognitive Radio Systems. *Broadcasting. IEEE Transactions on, 54*, 182–187.

Li, C., Raghunathan, A., & Jha, N. K. (2009). An Architecture for Secure Software Defined Radio. Design, Automatione and Test in Europe 2009 - DATE, (pp. 448-453). Dresden.

Liu, R. K., & Wang, B. (2011). *Cognitive Radio Networking And Security: A Game-Theoretic View*. Cambridge, New York: Cambridge University Press.

Liu, Y., Ning, P., & Dai, H. (2010). Authenticating Primary Users' Signals in Cognitive Radio Networks via Integrated Cryptographic and Wireless Link Signatures. *2010 IEEE Symposium on Security and Privacy*, (pp. 286-301).

Mathur, C. N., & Subbalakshmi, K. (2007). Security Issues in Cognitive Radior Networks. In Mahmoud, Q. H. (Ed.), *Cognitive Networks: Towards Self-Aware Networks* (pp. 271–292). West Sussex: John Wiley & Sons, LTD. doi:10.1002/9780470515143.ch11

Min, A. W., Shin, K. G., & Hu, X. (2009). Attack-Tolerant Distributed Sensing for Dynamic Spectrum Access Networks. *Network Protocols, 2009. ICNP 2009. 17th IEEE International Conference on*, (pp. 294-303). Ann Arbor.

Morerio, P., Dabcevic, K., Marcenaro, L., & Regazzoni, C. S. (2012). Distributed cognitive radio architecture with automatic frequency switching. *2012 Complexity in Engineering (COMPENG 2012) Proceedings*. Aachen.

Noon, E., & Li, H. (2010). Defending Against Hit-and-run Attackers in Collaborative Spectrum Sensing of Cognitive Radio Networks: A Point System. *Vehicular Technology Conference (VTC 2010-Spring), 2010 IEEE 71st*, (pp. 1-5). Knoxville, TN.

Qingqi, P., Hongning, L., & Kefeng, F. (2011). Defense Against Objective Function Attacks in Cognitive Radio Networks. *Chinese Journal of Electronics*, 138-142.

Safdar, G., & O'Neill, M. (2009). Common Control Channel Security Framework for Cognitive Radio Networks. *Proceedings on Vehicular Technology Conference, 2009. VTC Spring 2009. IEEE 69th*, (pp. 1-5). Barcelona.

Srivatsa, M., Xiong, L., & Liu, L. (2005). TrustGuard: countering vulnerabilities in reputation management for decentralized overlay networks. *Proceedings of the 14th international conference on World Wide Web* (pp. 422-431). Chiba: ACM New York.

Sun, Y. L., & Liu, Y. (2012, March). Security of Online Reputation Systems: The evolution of attacks and defenses. *Signal Processing Magazine, IEEE*, pp. 87-97.

Wang, W., Li, H., Sun, Y. L., & Han, Z. (2009). *Attack-Proof Collaborative Spectrum Sensing in Cognitive Radio Networks* (pp. 130–134). doi:10.1109/CISS.2009.5054704

Wireless Innovation Forum. (n.d.). *Wireless Innovation Forum*. Retrieved August 2012, from SDR Forum: http://www.wirelessinnovation.org/

Xenakis, C. (2008). Security Measures and Weaknesses of the GPRS Security Architecture. *International Journal of Network Security*, 158-169.

Yang, Y., Feng, Q., Sun, Y. L., & Dai, Y. (2008). RepTrap: A Novel Attack on Feedback-based Reputation Systems. *Proceedings of the 4th international conference on Security and privacy in communication networks - SecureComm '08* (p. Article No. 8). Istanbul: ACM New York.

Zhu, L., & Zhou, H. (2008). Two types of attacks against Cognitive Radio Network MAC Protocols. *Proceedings on the 2008 International Conference on Computer Science and Software Engineering*, (pp. 1110-1113). Washington DC: IEEE Computer Society.

Zhu, Y., Suo, D., & Gao, Z. (2010). Secure Cooperative Spectrum Trading in Cognitive Radio Networks: A Reversed Stackelberg Approach. *Proceedings on 2010 International Conference, MEDIACOM 2010*, (pp. 202-205). Hong Kong.

ADDITIONAL READING

Baldini, G., Sturman, T., Biswas, A. R., Leschhorn, R., Godor, G., & Street, M. (2012). Security aspects in software defined radio and cognitive radio networks: A survey and a way ahead. *IEEE Communications Surveys & Tutorials, 14*(2), 355–379. doi:10.1109/SURV.2011.032511.00097.

Brawerman, A., Blough, D., & Bing, B. (2004). Securing the download of radio configuration files for software defined radio devices. In *Proceedings of the Second International Workshop on Mobility Management & Wireless Access Protocols* (pp. 98-105). Philadelphia, PA: IEEE.

Brawerman, A., & Copeland, J. A. (2005). An anti-cloning framework for software defined radio mobile devices. [Seoul, South Korea: IEEE.]. *Proceedings of Communications, 2005*, 3434–3438.

Burbank, J. L. (2008). Security in cognitive radio networks: The required evolution in approaches to wireless network security. In *Proceedings of the Cognitive Radio Oriented Wireless Networks and Communications, 2008.* Singapore: CrownCom.

Dawoud, D. S. (2004). A proposal for secure software download in SDR. [Africon.]. *Proceedings of AFRICON, 2004*, 77–82.

Debar, H. (2007). Intrusion detection in cognitive networks. In Mahmoud, Q. H. (Ed.), *Cognitive Networks: Towards Self-aware Networks* (pp. 293–314). West Sussex, UK: John Wiley & Sons Ltd. doi:10.1002/9780470515143.ch12.

El-Hajj, W., Safa, H., & Guizani, M. (2011). Survey of security issues in cognitive radio networks. *Journal of Internet Technology*, 1-18.

Fragkiadakis, A. G., Tragos, E. Z., & Askoxylakis, I. G. (2012). A survey on security threats and detection techniques in cognitive radio networks. *IEEE Communications Surveys & Tutorials*, 1-18.

Hu, N. (2011). *Investigations of radio behavio and security threats in cognitive radio networks*. Hoboken, NJ: Pearson.

Jin, Z., Anand, S., & Subbalakshmi, K. P. (2009). Detecting primary user emulation attacks in dynamic spectrum access networks. In *Proceedings of IEEE ICC 2009* (pp. 1-5). Dresden, Germany: IEEE.

Kaligineedi, P., Khabbazian, M., & Bhargava, V. K. (2008). Secure cooperative sensing techniques for cognitive radio systems. In *Proceedings of ICC 2008* (pp. 3406-3410). IEEE.

León, O., Hernández-Serrano, J., & Soriano, M. (2010). Securing cognitive radio networks. *International Journal of Communication Systems*, 633–652.

León, O., Román, R., & Hernández-Serrano, J. (2011). Towards a cooperative intrusion detection system for cognitive radio networks. In *Proceedings of the Workshop on Wireless Cooperative Network Security - WCNS'11*. Springer.

Li, X., Chen, J., & Ng, F. (2008). Secure transmission power of cognitive radios for dynamic spectrum access applications. [Princeton, NJ: IEEE.]. *Proceedings of the Information Sciences and Systems, 2008*, 213–218.

Liu, R. K., & Wang, B. (2011). *03 cognitive radio networking and security - A game-theoretic view*. New York: Cambridge University Press.

Mathur, C. N., & Subbalakshmi, K. P. (2007). Security issues in cognitive radio networks. In Mahmoud, Q. H. (Ed.), *Cognitive Networks: Towards Self-Aware Networks* (pp. 271–292). West Sussex, UK: John Wiley & Sons Ltd. doi:10.1002/9780470515143.ch11.

Michael, L. B., Mihaljevic, M. J., Haruyama, S., & Kohno, R. (2002, July). A framework for secure download for software-defined radio. *IEEE Communications Magazine*, 88–96. doi:10.1109/MCOM.2002.1018012.

Newman, T. R., & Clancy, C. T. (2009). Security threats to cognitive radio signal classifiers. In *Proceedings of the Virginia Tech Wireless Personal Communications Symposium*. Blacksburg, VA: IEEE.

Prasad, S., & Thuente, D. J. (2011). Jamming attacks in 802.11g – A cognitive radio based approach. In *Proceedings of the Military Communications Conference - MILCOM 2011* (pp. 1219-1224). Baltimore, MD: MILCOM.

Rawat, A. S., Anand, P., Chen, H., & Varshney, P. K. (2010). Countering byzantine attacks in cognitive radio networks. In *Proceedings of the Acoustics Speech and Signal Processing (ICASSP)*, (pp. 3098-3101). Dallas, TX: IEEE.

Safdar, G. A., & O'Neill, M. (2009). Common control channel security framework for cognitive radio networks. In *Proceedings of the Vehicular Technology Conference, 2009*. IEEE.

Uchikawa, H., Umebayashi, K., & Kohno, R. (2002). Secure download system based on software defined radio composed of FPGAs. In Proceedings of Personal, Indoor and Mobile Radio Communications, 2002 (pp. 437-441). IEEE.

Wang, W. L. S. Y., Li, H., & Han, Z. (2010). Cross-layer attack and defense in cognitive radio networks. [Miami, FL: IEEE.]. *Proceedings of Globecom, 2010*, 1–6.

Wyglinski, A. M., Nekovee, M., & Hou, T. Y. (2010). *Cognitive radio communications and networks: Principles and practice*. London: Elsevier.

Xiao, S., Park, J.-M. J., & Ye, Y. (2009). Tamper resistance for software defined radio software. In *Proceedings of the 2009 33rd Annual IEEE International Computer Software and Applications Conference*, (vol. 1, pp. 383-391). Seattle, WA: IEEE.

Zhang, X., & Li, C. (2009). The security in cognitive radio networks: A survey. In *Proceedings of the 2009 International Conference on Wireless Communications and Mobile Computing: Connecting the World Wirelessly* (pp. 309-313). Lepizig, Germany: IEEE.

KEY TERMS AND DEFINITIONS

Byzantine Attack: Cognitive Radio-specific attack unique to collaborative spectrum sensing, where attacker provides false spectrum sensing information to the collaborating nodes.

IEEE 802.22 WRAN: A Cognitive Radio standard for Wireless Regional Area Networks which specifies the methods for opportunistic usage of the white spaces in the 54 - 862 MHz TV bands.

Jamming Attack: Attack common to all wireless networks, where attacker intentionally sends spurious data on one or more channels in order to disrupt services of legitimate nodes.

Lion Attack: Cognitive Radio-specific attack where the malicious node performs a series of PUEAs or Jamming Attacks at the physical layer, in order to cause DoS at the transport layer.

Primary User Emulation Attack: Cognitive Radio-specific attack where attacker emulates some characteristics of Primary Users.

Software Communications Architecture (SCA): An open software architecture for SDR systems, also used by the current state-of-the-SDR system – Joint Tactical Radio System (JTRS).

Spectrum Sensing: Method of acquiring knowledge of spectrum occupancy by scanning the channels of interest for the presence of Primary Users.

Chapter 14
Cognitive Techniques for the Development of Services in Broadband Networks:
The Case of Vocabulary Learning Management Systems

Yiouli Kritikou
University of Piraeus, Greece

Maria Paradia
Pedagogical Institute, Greece

Panagiotis Demestichas
University of Piraeus, Greece

ABSTRACT

Information and Communication Systems have tremendously evolved in the past years. This has resulted to the respective increase of the use of communication systems, devices, and applications. To follow this evolution, the applications now focus not only on the delivery of each application, but also on adaptability, so as to meet users' needs. This is aimed to be achieved by adapting to these needs in the most efficient and seamless way, thus offering an advanced experience to the user. To this end, this chapter focuses on an application of cognitive networks, presenting the mechanism by which self-adaptation can be added. More specifically, this chapter discusses e-learning management systems and showcases the methodology by which such a system may be adapted to users' preferences and achieve effective learning. This is achieved by using vocabulary teaching as a specific instance of e-learning. Scenarios and the respective results of this methodology are also presented.

DOI: 10.4018/978-1-4666-4189-1.ch014

Copyright © 2013, IGI Global. Copying or distributing in print or electronic forms without written permission of IGI Global is prohibited.

INTRODUCTION

As Information and Communication Technologies have tremendously evolved in the last years, people are more and more accustomed to using their portable devices for not only communicating with their acquaintances, friends and colleagues through voice and data, but also to be able to exploit the potentials of such a device. More specifically, it is part of peoples routine to take advantage of their time "on-the-go" to check and respond to e-mails, make bank checks and transfers or read a book; all these through their portable device (mobile phone, or tablet).

Further to this, as mentioned by Cisco, by 2016, one-quarter of mobile users will have more than one mobile-connected device, and 9 percent will have three or more mobile-connected devices (Cisco, 2012). Moreover, in the same study, it is mentioned that by 2016 smart phones and tablets will equal the amount of laptops/ netbooks. This practically means that portable devices will be very commonly used.

It is therefore imperative in the context of this new era to provide the users the potential of not only to access plain material through their device, but also enhance this experience with further features for an advanced user experience and effective exploitation of the time and effort invested.

On the other hand, Information and Communication Technologies have obliterated physical distance and natural borders. The communication between people of different countries and culture is now performed on a daily basis for most of the modern professions, but also for personal life. Consequently, people need to be acquainted and be able to communicate using more than one language, their mother language, in order to facilitate their interactions. Therefore, taking also into consideration the abovementioned increase of usage of mobile devices and the need to expand the knowledge horizons, the e-learning systems have significantly gained ground in the recent years. More specifically, as also discussed in the forthcoming section, the e-learning systems are used more and more to enhance peoples' knowledge remotely.

This work discusses on the approaches followed by the researchers throughout the years, with respect to personalized e-learning systems, focusing on the current trends of vocabulary learning systems. Furthermore, the architecture of such a system is presented, providing also details on the functionality of the different components of the system. Finally, scenarios of the system's operation and their respective results are concluding this chapter. Future research directions, as well as the conclusion of this research are given in the end of this work.

BACKGROUND

General Approach

During the last two decades, several research attempts have led to the design and development of various electronic environments that aim at facilitating learning, through specialized forms of teaching, namely e-learning environments. Such systems have been many times discussed and presented, for instance by Alomyan (2004), Brusilovsky (2001), Dagger et al. (2003), Dolog et al. (2004), Hsu et al. (2008), Juvina and Oostendorp (2004), Ong and Hawryszkiewycz (2003). In Alomyan (2004) the focus is placed on the individual differences in the context of Web-based learning, as well as the personalisation approach that may be followed. Proposed architectures and methodologies for achieving personalisation are described in Brusilovsky (2001), Dagger et al. (2003), Dolog et al. (2004), Hsu et al. (2008), Juvina and Oostendorp (2004), Ong and Hawryszkiewycz (2003). These approaches are mainly based on the structure of the system, while Dolog et al. (2004), Hsu et al. (2008), and Ong & Hawryszkiewycz (2003) use mechanisms to detect the personal preferences of each student.

Moreover, recent research findings have paved the way towards new models and new learning theories that are associated with multimedia, in conjunction with the consideration of various factors in learning, with the goal of achieving a deeper understanding of the way multimedia influence teaching and learning (Samaras et al., 2006). On the other hand, Zhang and Fang (2010) support that the direct interaction between tutors and students during self regulated learning through the e-learning instructional platform can be realized with specific design modules, so as to enhance the teaching and learning effect. Therefore, the inclusion of multimedia in the context of the e-learning procedure is highly encouraged, instead of using them separately (Zhang and Fang, 2010).

In the context of the research done by Tan & Pearce (2012) it is confirmed that the use of multimedia, and more specifically of video, in education can be an effective way of engaging students and supporting their understanding. The results show that the use of open educational resources is not viewed by students as a poor alternative and that, as long as properly facilitated and integrated into the lesson, the perceptions of students of this material do not diminish the perceived effectiveness of this method.

Taking this a step further, in (Meekyeong et al., 2012) the Multimedia Presentation Authoring System (MPAS) is introduced. This system produces multimedia e-learning contents for mobile environment, making it possible to create multimedia presentations that integrate diverse media types including images, video, sound, and texts for mobile devices. In a similar manner, mobile agents are used in the system presented in (Meguro et al., 2010), for developing a distributed asynchronous Web based training system for mobile devices.

Naturally, commercial software systems have been developed in order to assist students learn a new language. One of these systems is Rosetta Stone Software (Rosetta Stone, 2012), which offers quite a variety of languages. Similar to

Rosetta Stone is "Tell me More" software (Tell Me More, 2012), which has a number of languages available as well and also provides the option of choosing Professional or Individual contexts to learn the language. There are of course systems that specialize in a single language, such as Ouino French (Ouino French, 2012), which specializes in French language. Finally, there are also types of software that assist students with grammar or vocabulary and do not emphasise in interactions or personalisation, such the White Smoke system (White Smoke, 2012).

Conclusively, the e-learning systems have drastically evolved in the last decade, exploiting the potentials given by the advances of technology. To this end, the e-learning systems use multimedia in the context of the lessons, so as to enhance their learning experience and make learning more effective.

The next section presents how the e-learning systems have been further developed, so as to be able to adapt to students' personal preferences.

Personalisation of E-Learning Systems

In the light of the above, several approaches have been centered on the personalisation of e-learning systems as well, so as to increase the efficiency of their interactions with the student and consequently achieve better results in the learning process. This is achieved by using monitoring and evaluation methods during the learning procedure. For instance, a student modeling server may be used (Brusilovsky et al., 2005), taking explicitly or implicitly input by the student through the Detection Mechanism (Garzotto & Cristea, 2004) or an adaptation filter, which removes the implied unnecessary information for the user (Zakaria et al., 2003). Another method is used in (Juvina & Oostendorp, 2004), where it is supported that Web navigation can be modeled by studying individual differences and behavioural metrics, using Latent

Semantic Analysis (LSA) (LSA Website, 2012). The DEPTHS system (Jeremić et al., 2009) is a system using design patterns, incorporating semantic annotation service and context-aware learning services, so as to facilitate and enrich students learning experience and performance. The GRAPPLE system (Oneto et al., 2009) serves as a platform for Learning Management Systems to be integrated and, despite the fact that it integrates personalisation and adaptation features, it does not emphasize on the detailed and direct interactions with students, but only infers their preferences, by detecting their behaviour when using the system. Moodle (Moodle Website, 2012), on the other hand, is an Open Source Course Management System, which encourages collaboration between students, it is rather flexible regarding the organization of the courses, yet personalisation and adaptation are still at a very basic level. Furthermore, personalisation in vocabulary learning management systems has also been researched. More specifically, in (Gamper & Knapp, 2002) psycholinguistic methods are applied along with adaptive hypermedia, yet the system does not take direct feedback from the students. This means that the system can only make "assumptions" on the student's preferences, which can thus be verified by applying the adapted content. The VocaTest system (Kazi, 2005) is based on indirect student feedback as well, which takes into consideration the student's scores in test, in order to assume the preferences. In more recent researches as (Jung & Graf, 2008) and (Yoshimoto, 2008), a more modern approach is followed; in this particular system the strategy of creating Games is used, in order to help the student absorb the new vocabulary introduced. Yet, in these cases as well, the policy of the systems is based on assumptions and not on applied mathematics/ algorithms. Finally, in (Deng, 2011) the way learning styles and theories are being used within a personalized adaptable e-learning adaptive system is discussed. This paper aims to establish conditions for creating versatile online courses adjusted to individual

student's needs, which enable students to choose their own learning path.

Finally, in another study (Chen, 2009) self-regulated learning assisted mechanisms are presented in the personalized e-learning systems. These mechanisms can save students' self-regulated learning abilities, by using the proposed self-regulated learning assessment mechanism. This mechanism provides immediate feedback as a response from students and a heteronomy mechanism is being used on the tutor's side as a reminder.

Detection and Personalisation Mechanisms

This subsection goes through the detection and personalisation mechanisms that have been used within research throughout the years. These mechanisms are used separately in the learning management systems investigated.

Item Response Theory

Item Response Theory (IRT) considers both the course material difficulty and the student ability to provide individual learning paths for students. The item characteristic function, which was proposed by Rasch, uses a single difficulty parameter and is used to model the course materials (Chen, 2005).

Having considered the importance of the tests, the paper (Baylari & Montazer, 2009) proposes a personalized multiagent e-learning system based on item response theory (IRT) and artificial neural network (ANN) which presents adaptive tests (based on IRT) and personalized recommendations (based on ANN). These agents add adaptivity and interactivity to the learning environment and act as a human instructor which guides the students in a friendly and personalized teaching environment. In this study, a framework for constructing adaptive tests is proposed that is used as a post-test in the system. This system has the capability of estimating the students' ability based on explicit responses on these tests and presents to the student a personalized and adaptive test based on that ability. Also the system can discover student's problems via their responses on review tests by using an ANN approach and then recommends appropriate learning materials to the student (Baylari & Montazer, 2009).

Similarly, several researches have been conducted; the work performed by (Chen & Duh, 2008) presents a modeling process to determine the difficulty parameters of courseware and construct the content of courseware for the personalized recommendation services using fuzzy-based Item Response Theory. An approach for designing a personalised learning system by analysing the ability of the student based on Item Response Theory is discussed in (Yarandi et al., 2011), while in (Jeong & Hong, 2011) the Item Response Theory is used for supporting the item selection for students in Computerized Adaptive Testing, with the aim to use existing data to streamline and individualize the measurement process.

Conclusively, the Item Response Theory focuses each time on one part of the learning procedure; either the course construction or on identifying the student preferences and needs.

Bayesian Concepts

The detection mechanism using the Bayesian concepts can serve as a tool to detect the personal preferences of each student. More specifically, the system takes into consideration personal student preferences and historic activity, both directly and indirectly. This is achieved through acquiring knowledge from previous interactions with the student and mapping personal preferences to the specific learning style, for enhancing the student's learning experience and maximizing its effectiveness. This gradual transformation of past interactions to knowledge and experience endows the system with cognitive capabilities (Thomas et al., 2006). The advantage of the resulting system

lies in the increase of the probability of successfully adapting to the student's learning preferences and consequently facilitating the learning process. The simplest components were taken into account, comprising the system's architecture (Paradia et al., 2012). In some researches performed, the learning functionality is influenced by Bayesian networks. More specifically, for the technical approach and application of analyses such as in García et al. (2007), Jeon and Su (2011), Nguyen and Pham (2011), Santos et al. (1999), Sbattella and Tedesco (2004), Tedesco et al. (2006), the concepts of the Bayesian Networks have been used, as they constitute robust techniques for modeling and solving stochastic problems, and therefore, are main technologies for the development of cognitive systems. The Bayesian principles were taken into consideration in such cases and then adapted to the e-learning platform requirements. More specifically, in (Garcia, 2007) Bayesian Networks are used for the detection of learning styles. In (Jeon & Su, 2011) and (Sbattella & Tedesco, 2004) user models are managed through the use of Bayesian Networks. In (Jeon & Su, 2011) the system through Bayesian Networks adapts according to user profile and performance data using information not only of the particular students, but also from previous ones, while in (Sbattella & Tedesco, 2004) the system takes also into consideration learning attitudes, efficiency of learning strategies, and attitude to cooperation and communication. Both in (Nguyen & Pham, 2011) and (Santos et al., 1999) Bayesian Networks are used to manage user models and adapt according to the identified changes. Finally, in (Tedesco et al, 2006) a partial user model is created for the user model management across different systems.

The aforementioned approaches have differences, when it comes to the part of the system the Bayesian Networks are used for. Yet, in all cases, the most probable behaviour and requirements of the student is calculated, based on the stored experience.

Ontologies and Semantic Web

Another way to develop personalized learning content is by using ontologies. An ontology is the clue in integrating data/ knowledge base objects with distributed objects systems in diverse integrative collaborative applications (Elisabeta & Răzvan, 2010). Moreover, due to their powerful knowledge representation formalism and associated inference mechanisms, ontology-based systems are emerging as a natural choice for the next generation of Knowledge Management Systems (KMSs) operating in organizational and interorganizational, as well as community contexts (Razmerita et al., 2003).

To this end, in the paper (Gaeta, 2009) methodologies and techniques for supporting a community of experts in modeling educational domains (e.g. mathematics domain, English literature domain, etc.) are described. This takes place through the management of convenient educational ontologies namely e-Learning ontologies and exploiting them, in order to define and execute personalised e-Learning experiences within blended learning activities. Further to this, as Semantic Web technologies have not yet been applied widely to deliver learning objects, the paper (Raju & Ahmed, 2011) introduces the idea of enabling technologies for developing next-generation learning object repository for construction. This work also demonstrates how the ontologies and Semantic Web technologies can be used to develop and deliver intelligent, sharable and dynamic learning objects. The paper also outlines the development of repository using the ontology-driven Semantic Web approach and discusses the construction education ontology and semantic databases. This concept is further enhanced by investigating ontologies and metadata for three types of resources, namely domain, user, and observation (Henze et al., 2004).

Another approach is followed in (Navigli & Velardi, 2004); in this work, the tool OntoLearn is used to first extract a domain terminology from available documents in certain Web sites. Then, complex domain terms are semantically interpreted and arranged in a hierarchical fashion. Finally, a general-purpose ontology, namely WordNet, is trimmed and enriched with the detected domain concepts. The major novel aspect of this approach is semantic interpretation, that is, the association of a complex concept with a complex term.

Furthermore, Draganidis et al (2006) have developed an ontology based application for competency management and learning paths. Razmerita et al. (2003) present a generic ontology-based user modeling architecture, namely OntobUM, applied in the context of a Knowledge Management System (KMS). On the other hand, user models, often addressed as user profiles, have been included in KMSs mainly as simple ways of capturing the user preferences and/or competencies. This view is extended by including other characteristics of the users relevant in the KM context. The proposed user modeling system relies on user ontology, using Semantic Web technologies, based on the IMS LIP specifications (Instructional Management Systems - Learner Information Package) and it is integrated in an ontology-based KMS called Ontologging. Finally, Machine Learning and Natural Language Processing are used by Brewster et al., (2002) for developing a user-centred methodology for ontology construction. In this approach, the student selects a corpus of texts and sketches a preliminary ontology (or selects an existing one) for a domain with a preliminary vocabulary associated to the elements in the ontology (lexicalisations). Examples of sentences involving such lexicalization in the corpus are automatically retrieved by the system.

Therefore, it can be concluded that ontologies are used for modeling the structure of a learning system, as well as the user model, either indirectly or directly. To this end, ontologies can be considered a useful tool for modeling a learning system.

Emphasizing on Vocabulary

An e-learning system can focus on many different aspects and many different disciplines; history, mathematics, physics, technologies, language. The list is ongoing and can be enhanced and focused, depending on the developers' inspiration, as well as the students' needs for learning and specialized content.

In this context, many research activities have focused on e-learning vocabulary systems. The integration of technology in a regular, physical classroom is being discussed in (Constantinescu, 2007); this work focuses on the way that technology can be embraced in the regular classroom, integrating multimedia in the learning procedure. In another approach for physical classrooms, Bekleven and Yilmaz (Bekleyen & Yilmaz, 2011) use a certain software, namely JING™ in classes to teach new vocabulary in an enjoyable and innovative way, and more specifically the use of a vocabulary test, in order to measure the students' knowledge of the target vocabulary, before and after a teaching period. In addition, an interview is conducted to acquire the students' opinion about their learning experience. Finally, in (Dalton & Grisham, 2011) Ten (10) eVoc strategies are highlighted that hold promise for improving vocabulary learning in intermediate grades and that employ digital tools and resources that are readily available and feasible to implement in today's schools. Yet, in this study it is suggested that the use of digital tools has to be supported by the tutor in the context of a physical classroom.

Studying the virtual environments, in the approach of (Chen & Hsu, 2008), the aim is to provide an effective and flexible learning environment for learning of English language. This study adopts the advantages of mobile learning to present a personalized intelligent mobile learning system, which can appropriately recommend English news articles to students, based on the evaluation of students' reading abilities. This system also relies on the ability of students' to automatically discover and retrieve the unknown vocabulary from reading, by the proposed fuzzy Item Response Theory (FIRT). The fuzzy Item Response Theory can conduct personalized curriculum sequencing, for supporting effective English reading learning for individual learners. On the other hand, a system using the Fuzzy Theory and the Memory Cycle Theory assists a student to memorize vocabularies easily is introduced in (Wang et al., 2008). More specifically, in this system, it is possible to find the content that best suits a student by using fuzzy inferences and personal memory cycles. After reading an article, a quiz is provided for the student to improve his/her memory of the vocabulary in the article.

The paper (Huang et al., 2012) develops a ubiquitous English vocabulary learning (UEVL) system to assist students in experiencing a systematic vocabulary learning process, in which ubiquitous technology is used to develop the system. In this system, video clips are being used as the material for doing so. User preferences, system requirements, and content characteristics are taken into consideration in this study. From another point of view, the study (Wang, 2011) proposes an Adaptive Learning in Teaching English as a Second Language for e-learning system that considers various student characteristics (learning performance) using a data mining technique, which is an artificial neural network (ANN), as the core of the e-learning system. Three different levels of teaching content are set for adaptive learning in this e-learning system; vocabulary, grammar, and reading. Finally, an adaptive mobile learning model for learning new languages based on ability of student is presented in (Jahankhani et al., 2011). This system uses an ontology-based knowledge modelling technique to classify language learning materials and to describe user profile, so as to provide adaptive learning environment.

In this section an analysis of the e-learning systems throughout the years has been made, presenting also the respective mechanisms developed for enhancing personalisation. In this chapter Bayesian Concepts are used for developing a mechanism for storing information on the past activity of each student and taking into account current activity. Of course, in case the system detects unexpected behaviour on the part of the student, then it adapts accordingly, in order to alleviate the unexpected phenomenon and normalize the respective behaviour and learning experience, as shown in the end of this chapter.

MAIN FOCUS OF THE CHAPTER

Issues, Controversies, Problems

Taking into account the theoretical basis and the research done as presented in Section 2, it is essential to consider the development of a novel teaching methodology, which will have to incorporate the essentials of e-learning, along with the potential to adapt to student's specific needs, making learning more effective and indirect for the student. An e-learning system needs to be able to proactively adapt to the user's profile, provide the appropriate material, be able to evaluate the performance and guide the student appropriately, towards improving the performance (Huang, et al., 2012; Wang & Liao, 2011). This could increase the quality of the electronically delivered knowledge, contributing, in turn, in time and effort saving. In this sense, it is essential to form a structure, a specific architecture, in order to serve as a basis for the development of an e-learning platform in general, engaging cognitive capabilities for adapting to student's personalized requirements and specific needs. To this end, this section presents the architecture of such a platform, engaging all the characteristics derived from the various researches conducted so far.

The main concept behind creating this specific architecture is simplicity, in order to achieve adaptability. More specifically, the architecture is as simple as possible, so as to be able to be used not only for this specific application of e-learning presented in this work, that is vocabulary learning,

but also for other e-learning applications in general, which embrace cognitive characteristics. To this end, the components, as well as the functionality of each of these components are described in detail in the following sections. The specific characteristics for a vocabulary learning system are also presented hereinafter.

Solutions and Recommendations

Architecture and System Components

The architecture of such a system has to be based on simplicity, in order to be adaptive to the requirements of each of the focus areas chosen, as also mentioned previously. Therefore, the components that the system is comprised of have to be organised properly so as to store distinct information from each other, but also be able to interact with each other at any time to provide the requested information. In this way, the best learning experience is offered to the student, based on knowledge collected from each component of the system, even if the student requirements change in an unexpected way.

More specifically, the proposed architecture is comprised by the following components:

- User Profile;
- Content Provider;
- System Interface; and
- User Monitoring/ Detection Mechanism.

Figure 1 presents the components of the system and gives an overview of the information exchanged between them. The functionality and role of each component is described hereinafter (see Figure 2).

User Profile

Each student has certain, unique characteristics that are associated with his personal information. These characteristics include information on the student as a person (name, age, etc.), knowledge

Figure 1. Overview of the e-learning mechanisms used throughout the years for the e-learning systems

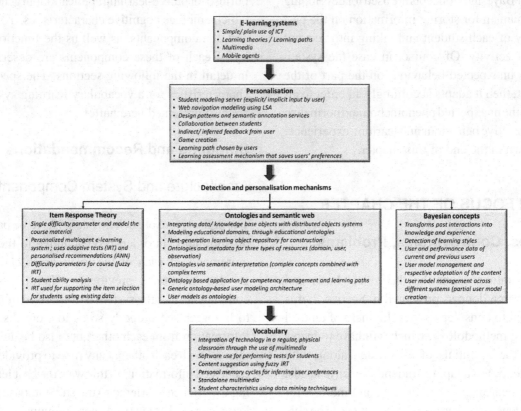

Figure 2. The architecture of a web-based learning management system

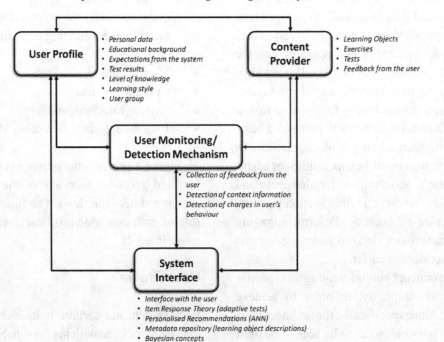

background and level, as well as the expectations from the specific learning experience. These are the data collected and stored in the User Profile component and are continuously updated, based on the progress within the system.

As concluded from the literature, the personal information of the student is collected directly by him, as he enters the system for the first time. In this initial phase, the student completes a form depicting all the personal information with respect to his name, age, gender, etc. Then, the student gives information on his educational background, the focus of his interests and finally provides information on the anticipated outcome of his experience within the system. Alternatively, this can be done through an interview or a questionnaire, depending on the system's structure.

Of course, the derived information may change, as the student progresses using the system and further enhances his knowledge and experience in the specific field. This happens because the student is giving feedback to the system through tests performed, after a specific block of information is processed. This basically depicts his progress in the field and marks respectively a new level of knowledge conquered. In other words, this procedure can "upgrade" a student from "Novice" to "Intermediate" and finally to "Expert" in terms of level of knowledge.

Additionally to the above-mentioned information, learning styles are also widely used for grouping students in the context of an e-learning system, depending on the way they prefer to have the content delivered to them or the learning procedure is mostly efficient. Thereof, learning styles categorization is used, along with the level of knowledge, so as to have the specific style of learning experience fully adapted to their preferences, needs and expectations from their learning experience.

In summary, the User Profile component has to infer the following information:

- Students' preferences concerning the content of each course; and
- Students' preferences regarding the structure of the interface/ platform.

Furthermore, it has to store the following information:

- The users' profiles, i.e. personal information about each student;
- Information about each student group, i.e. which members it consists of, what are its main characteristics (e.g., group of novice or expert students);
- Log files about each student's behaviour during his navigation through the system;
- The answers each student provided to each of the set of questions, tests and interviews when entering the system for the first time;
- The scores in the exercises and evaluation tests, when completing a course, as well as the feedback provided by the administrator of the course, for each student (Wang & Liao, 2011).

Content Provider

The Content Provider component stores information about the learning material that will be delivered to the students. The Content Provider stores the learning courses, or learning blocks in different forms. Depending on the information required by the component "User Monitoring/ Detection Mechanism", the Content Provider component in turn sends the appropriate information to the component "System Interface". The information stored in the Content Provider is based on the technique used by the Content Provider itself, in cooperation with the System Interface, as will be analysed in the following section.

Conclusively, when the component receives a request for a specific type of learning block, it provides the appropriate information to the System

Interface component, utilizing the instructions sent by the User Profile, about each student/ student group's preferences.

System Interface

The System Interface is in essence the component that collects information from all the other components of the system, makes the appropriate synthesis and then delivers the requested content to the student. This information can make use of the Item Response Theory (adaptive tests), personalised recommendations (ANN), metadata repository (learning object descriptions), Bayesian concepts or ontologies and semantic Web, as also analysed in section "Detection and personalisation mechanisms". This depends on the system structure and methodology that has been chosen to be followed. The different approaches were presented in the section "Detection and personalisation mechanisms" and it is in the designer's decision to select the best methodology, or combination of them, in order to better depict the requested information and meet the student's personalized needs and expectation from his/ her learning experience.

User Monitoring/Detection Mechanism

Finally, the User Monitoring/Detection Mechanism component has the role of acquiring the necessary context information for delivering the structure content to the student, in the best form for achieving the most efficient learning experience. More specifically, the component monitors each student's behaviour during the navigation in the e-learning system (moving from one course to another), detecting the student's interest on certain subjects, or weaknesses in understanding in some others (Huang et al., 2012; Wang & Liao, 2011). Moreover, this component collects information on the student's environment (i.e. the network he is logged in to, the type of device he is using,

etc.) and the feedback sent from the student as he navigates within the system, either implicitly (monitoring his behaviour) or explicitly (through taking tests).

The data collected in the User Monitoring/ Detection Mechanism component are transferred to the User Profile, Content Provider and System Interface components, in order to serve as input for the adaptation of the final structure of the content. To this end, this component detects user preferences, the level of the student's knowledge, information on the context of the student (type of network, device used, etc), as well as information on potential changes in student's behaviour.

User Interaction with the System

As previously mentioned, the design, development and appropriate exploitation of an electronic teaching system is essential, in the sense of developing an interactive and efficient Web based (vocabulary) teaching system. This teaching model, having the necessary structure and information (through the initial questionnaire and the evaluation process of student's behaviour, as will be analyzed in the sequel), groups the student in an appropriate set, based on the learning style, offering guidance within the learning material through certain activities and strategies, which completely adapt to it.

The answers of the student in the respective set of questions in the beginning of his learning experience will help the system in forming the student's initial profile, adding him in a group of students, having the same learning style and the same level of knowledge. The questionnaires that are dealing with the initial learning style detection will be formed based on learning style's categorization that is closer to the school routine and teaching reality (Felder, & Henriques, 1995; Jahankhani et al., 2011, Kritikou et al., 2008; Paradia et al., 2012). After the initial categorization of the student, the student officially enters the course. In this context, the learning material is accessed, studying the course, referring to the respective further studying incentives, solving the exercises and generally following the suggested learning itinerary by the system. In case the student chooses not to take the questionnaire, the system classifies the student in the novice group and the procedure continues by monitoring the student's behaviour throughout the navigation in the system (see Figure 3).

The originally formed learning material starts at this point to adapt to the student's special preferences and learning pace. This means that the learning material included in the system is scaled in levels of difficulty and at the same time is structured in a way so as to provide to each level the strategies that realize different learning styles. Moreover, the student's activity is evaluated so as to detect potential weaknesses and problems encountered, and record the respective performance and behaviour. The aim is the adaptation of the learning material, consequently leading to the overall improvement of the student's performance.

At the same time, the system monitors the learning pace, the amount of the material and the specific needs of the students, in the context of the certain learning style, making the process personalized. Such an environment is considered to serve as incentive for the student, to make a bigger effort during the learning process, as the student feels more confident in the learning environment.

Finally, the system evaluates the student's progress, by providing the student with a test to assess the amount of information perceived, offering paradigms and presenting information instances that need the student's feedback. The test corresponds to a course completed by the student, containing questions formed so as to not overload the student and in order to be able to be answered using simple and short responses. This means that even students with very basic skills in technology are able to answer such questions easily, with the minimum interaction possible.

Conclusively, the proposed teaching system (which can focus on vocabulary teaching) has the following characteristics, which are extremely difficult and time consuming to be incorporated in the traditional teaching process. These charac-

Figure 3. The student navigation procedure and the system's respective actions

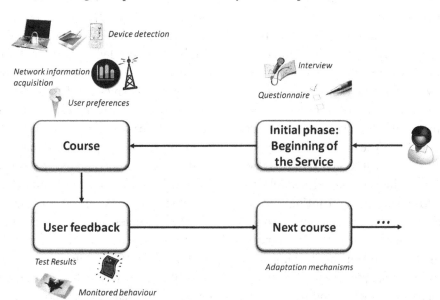

teristics further enhance the learning experience from the student's side and complete the process of effective and efficient learning.

- Personalisation;
- Adaptability;
- Interactivity;
- Variety in the levels of difficulty the way of presenting the learning material (Huang et al., 2012; Wang & Liao, 2011).

User Profile Parameters Classification

As mentioned above, user preferences might be changing over time, along with progressively studying the offered courses, enhancing knowledge and viewing versatile aspects of a subject. This means that the system should revise certain aspects of the offered learning procedure, in order to better meet the student's evolved needs. Each of these aspects is influenced by one or more factors that reflect the student's behaviour within the system, namely the user profile parameters. This means that the student's behaviour can be monitored through parameters concerning the navigation in the system and certain points of student's behaviour and, by being kept in log files, this information can be updated accordingly.

User profile parameters can be classified following this approach presented in (Ahmad et al., 2004; Juvina & Oostendorp, 2004), so as to facilitate their evaluation. Therefore, it is assumed that a student's e-learning profile consists of two types of parameters: the "input parameters" and the "output parameters". The input parameters are countable parameters, that a certain value may be attributed to them, while the output parameters are more abstractly counted and are influenced by the input parameters. The output parameters map the student and learning procedure preferences and based on them, the student and learning procedure preferences are adapted. In the following sections, two output parameters and three input parameters are presented and analyzed in details.

More complex models may incorporate a higher number of parameters, yet the nature of the analysis remains the same.

Input Parameters

As mentioned previously and will be analysed thoroughly in the subsequent paragraphs, the output parameters are difficult to measure. This happens as in most cases, even the student is not in position to realistically estimate the educational level, the level of familiarity on a subject, the learning style or the expected outcomes of taking a specific course. Therefore, setting a number of input (evaluation) parameters is necessary, in order to aid the system to evaluate the preferences of the student (output parameters), as progressing with the study of the provided material. Those parameters include the Course Duration, the Test Duration, and the Performance.

More precisely, Course Duration refers to the time that a user spends for completing a didactic unit/course. This time is measured and then compared by the system to a set of (pre-estimated) threshold values, which depend on the particular course. The result is the classification of the student in one of the following four classes: low, medium, high, or very high. The value of Course Duration subsequently affects the determination of the output parameters' values. The Test Duration parameter is similar in nature, but it is related to the time that a student spends to complete a test.

What is also measured and taken into account in the process of user preferences prediction is the Performance parameter. By keeping the student's test scores, the system can estimate how well the student has comprehended the concepts of the course. This parameter is assumed to have four possible values: 'A', 'B', 'C', or 'D'.

The dependencies between input and output parameters are depicted in Figure 4.

Therefore, the system groups certain parameter values, so as to evaluate the student's preferences on the learning experience, as shown in Table 1. In case the system has inferred after the

Figure 4. Dependencies between input and output parameters

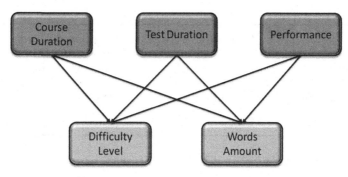

initial short questionnaire that the student is Novice, it presents the corresponding information and adapts itself accordingly, using the information by Table 2.

Thereafter, the student takes the course and the system monitors the student's navigation within the course and the respective behaviour/reactions. This is done by measuring the evaluation parameters, as discussed previously. Comparing the values of these parameters with the data of Table 2, the system can conclude whether the parameters' group will have to be changed or not. This is also combined with the feedback that the student has provided the system with. For instance, in case the student provides the system with low evaluation, despite the high scores and good performance, the system concludes that it needs to rearrange the content to fit the appropriate learning style of the student.

The next subsection describes the knowledge acquisition and adaptation methodology.

Output Parameters

The output parameters are practically the parameters that affect the student's performance, but cannot be easily measured. Yet, as it is essential for the system to be aware of their value, they are composed by other measurable parameters (input parameters, discussed in the previous section) and they can thus be inferred through them. The exact procedure is presented in detail in section 5.

The output parameters include Difficulty Level and Number of Words. By keeping these parameters updated, the system is able to provide the student with the appropriate content, in the most suitable way. The values of these parameters are modified according to the student's behaviour in each didactic unit.

Difficulty Level is influenced by the level of the student's knowledge on the subject, being a novice, intermediate or expert. As the student takes more and more courses, the level of knowledge

Table 1. Input parameters and user groups

	Course Duration	Test Duration	Performance
Novice	High	High	D
Intermediate	Medium	Medium	B/ C
Expert	Low	Low	A

Table 2. Output parameters and user groups

	Difficulty Level	Number of Words
Expert	High/Medium	High/Medium
Intermediate	Medium	Medium
Novice	Low	Low

changes, from novice to intermediate, or from intermediate to expert, and consequently asks for more complex content, with more detailed information on the subject and more advanced resources to explore. Difficulty Level may be attributed to one of the following three values: low, medium, or high.

Number of Words refers to the amount of information the student wishes to explore in the course to study. Low, medium, or high are the values that Number of Words can be set to. For instance, Low corresponds to a small amount of words defined and presented in each course, so as to be easily absorbed by the novice student. Medium and high are formed respectively, by including for instance fifteen (15) and twenty-five (25) words in the course.

System Implementation

Methodology for Knowledge Acquisition and Adaptation to User Preferences

The process of developing knowledge regarding personal preferences of the student comprises two phases. The initial phase is the collection of information on the student. For the initial phase, the approach proposed in this section is to monitor the student's behaviour, collect feedback from him and calculate rankings of Number of Words and Difficulty Level combinations. The next phase is the approximation of future student preferences based on the gathered feedback, using Bayesian

statistics principles, in order to improve the behaviour of the e-learning platform towards the student.

Concepts from Bayesian statistics are applied in order to estimate the probability of the Difficulty Level and Number of Words for a specific content provided. This can be done through updating instantaneous estimations, by taking into account existing information on the user (Kritikou et al., 2008; Stavroulaki et al., 2009).

The first step of the application of this methodology is to create the Conditional Probability Table (CPT) for each Output Parameter (Table 3). Practically, the CPT Table serves as an input for the instantaneous estimated probabilities of utility volume, which is the second step of this methodology. As the student is being delivered with a specific content, the instantaneous estimations are changing, depicted by and depending on the monitored behaviour of the user within the system. This means that the instantaneous probability estimations are changing in time and act as input to the estimation of the adapted probability.

The third step of this procedure is the calculation of adapted probabilities. The calculation of these probabilities is based on the following formula (Kritikou et al., 2008):

$$p_{adapted,n} = w_{hist} \cdot p_{adapted,n-1} + w_{instant} \cdot (1 - |p_{adapted,n-1} - p_{instant,n}|) \cdot p_{instant,n} \quad (1)$$

where:

- $|x|$: represents the absolute value of x;
- n: denotes the current instant;

Table 3. CPT for "difficulty level" output parameter

Parent Node(s)			LevelDifficulty			
CourseDuration	TestDuration	Performance	High	Medium	Low	bar charts
High	High	A	0,1	0,35	0,55	
		B	0,25	0,35	0,4	
		C	0,05	0,35	0,6	
	Medium	A	0,3	0,35	0,35	
		B	0,2	0,45	0,35	
		C	0,15	0,3	0,55	
	Low	A	0,5	0,3	0,2	
		B	0,35	0,35	0,3	
		C	0,1	0,3	0,6	
Medium	High	A	0,1	0,35	0,55	
		B	0,15	0,6	0,25	
		C	0,05	0,4	0,55	
	Medium	A	0,25	0,45	0,3	
		B	0,25	0,55	0,2	
		C	0,1	0,5	0,4	
	Low	A	0,55	0,35	0,1	
		B	0,15	0,45	0,4	
		C	0,1	0,25	0,65	
Low	High	A	0,15	0,55	0,3	
		B	0,25	0,3	0,45	
		C	0,15	0,35	0,5	
	Medium	A	0,6	0,3	0,1	
		B	0,2	0,45	0,35	
		C	0,25	0,45	0,3	
	Low	A	0,5	0,3	0,2	
		B	0,3	0,45	0,25	
		C	0,2	0,25	0,55	

- $p_{adapted,n}$: represents the adapted probability estimation at moment n;
- $p_{adapted,n-1}$: represents the adapted probability's previous value;
- $p_{instant,n}$: stands for the current instantaneous estimation;
- w_{hist} and $w_{instant}$: reflect the weights attributed to the historical estimation and the current instantaneous estimation, respectively. Their value is in the interval (0, 1) and the formula $w_{hist} + w_{instant} = 1$ is always true.

Indicative Results

This section aims at evaluating the proposed system through indicative results. Two scenarios are used for the evaluation. The first scenario presents a regular case, while the second scenario aims at showing how the system responds to an unexpected monitored behaviour and the third scenario describes the role of weights in the overall process.

Plain Scenario

The simplest case to test the functionality and results of a system is to use the data of the first time the student enters and uses the system, without any change in his behaviour and requirements, or network and device configuration. In this sense, a student enters the system as a Novice, which means that the student has no particular vocabulary knowledge of this language. The student uses a laptop in his home and the network is provided through wired access, hence there is no change in the device and network.

The system stores information on the activities of the student as he navigates through the system; the time to complete a course, the time for taking the respective test and the feedback the student gives to the system after his learning experience. This way the system creates an "experience" for handling the particular student on his preferences, needs, and level of knowledge. Of course, as the student becomes more efficient on the vocabulary of the foreign language and he learns by using the system, the latter updates the respective information and provides advanced content, in order to assist the student increase his knowledge and efficiency in the new perceived content. This also means that the student's status is being changed from Novice to Intermediate and from Intermediate to Expert, in order to depict student's increased knowledge and provide him with the appropriate content. Figure 5 presents the instantaneous estimations for the parameter "Difficulty Level". Historical and instantaneous estimations are taken equally into consideration. As can be observed, the behaviour of the student is rather unstable, which can cause confusion to the system. This means that the system may not have a clear view on the level of difficulty that best suits the student's knowledge and preferences. When applying the Bayesian Networks technique, the system can estimate the preferences of the student in a smoother manner and thus provide him with a more stable content, as depicted in Figure 6.

User Behaviour Change

In the second scenario, the student continues to use the platform and learns the respective blocks of content delivered to him, responds to the respective tests, while the system detects and stores the appropriate information in its components. The student is now in the Intermediate level of knowledge in the field of vocabulary of the foreign language he has chosen to learn.

In one of the tests, the student has unexpectedly low performance. While a certain difficulty level was expected to have been reached so far by the student at this point of the course, the student has an extremely low percentage of correct responses.

In this case the system acts in a twofold way; first, it adapts the interface design, in the case the interface is too complicated and inflexible and distracts the student. Then, through the component Content Provider a simpler block of courses is chosen, so as to avoid discouraging the student and also double check that his potentials have indeed reached the level Intermediate.

This piece of information (student behaviour and system's adaptation) is stored in the User Profile component, so as to serve as an input for future reference in potentially similar situations.

The results of this unexpected behaviour are depicted in the following scenario. More specifically, in Figure 7 the instantaneous estimations of this behaviour are depicted. After applying the Bayesian Networks technique, the results of Figure 8 are produced. In other words, the adapted estimations provide the system with a more balanced view of the student's preferences, taking both historical and instantaneous estimations into consideration equally. Therefore, as can be observed in Figure 8, the system, through the adapted estimations can offer to the user Medium Difficulty Level, something rather hard to infer by the instantaneous estimations (Figure 7).

Figure 5. Instantaneous estimations for the parameter "difficulty level"

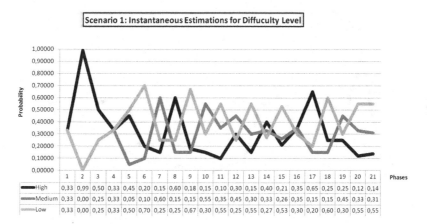

FUTURE RESEARCH DIRECTIONS

As the next step of this work, the implementation of this system will be done, in order to verify its efficiency and effectiveness, when used by students. This procedure will take place in a real world environment, with actual students from different levels of technology acquaintance, different ages and various fields of knowledge and educational level. In this way, the usability of the system can be tested in a more complete and multifaceted manner, aiming at revealing potential flaws and empowering the advantages of the system.

Finally, using the conclusions and test results, a vocabulary platform will be established, able to provide to students an easy, adapted to their own preferences and needs, and effective system for learning the vocabulary of a foreign language.

CONCLUSION

This work presented an application of cognitive networks, presenting the mechanism by which self adaptation can be added. More specifically, the evolution of e-learning management systems were presented, showcasing the methodology by

Figure 6. Adapted estimations for the parameter "difficulty level"

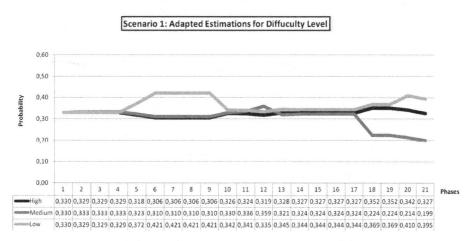

Figure 7. Instantaneous estimations for the scenario "user behaviour change"

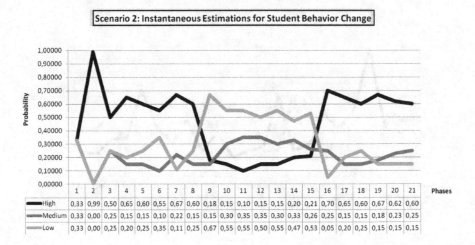

	1	2	3	4	5	6	7	8	9	10	11	12	13	14	15	16	17	18	19	20	21
High	0,33	0,99	0,50	0,65	0,60	0,55	0,67	0,60	0,18	0,15	0,10	0,15	0,15	0,20	0,21	0,70	0,65	0,60	0,67	0,62	0,60
Medium	0,33	0,00	0,25	0,15	0,15	0,10	0,22	0,15	0,15	0,30	0,35	0,35	0,30	0,33	0,26	0,25	0,15	0,15	0,18	0,23	0,25
Low	0,33	0,00	0,25	0,20	0,25	0,35	0,11	0,25	0,67	0,55	0,55	0,50	0,55	0,47	0,53	0,05	0,20	0,25	0,15	0,15	0,15

which such a system may be adapted to users' preferences and achieve effective learning. Vocabulary teaching was used as a specific instance of e-learning. Scenarios and the respective results of this methodology were also presented.

Conclusively, it can be derived that many different approaches have been evolved in order to embrace offer and enhanced learning experience to the student, by adapting to his personal characteristics and preferences. In this sense, Bayesian

Networks application may offer a more balanced content, considering both historical, as well as instantaneous data.

ACKNOWLEDGMENT

This work has been performed in the framework of the ACROPOLIS (Advanced Coexistence technologies for Radio Optimisation in Licenced and

Figure 8. Adapted estimations for the scenario "user behaviour change"

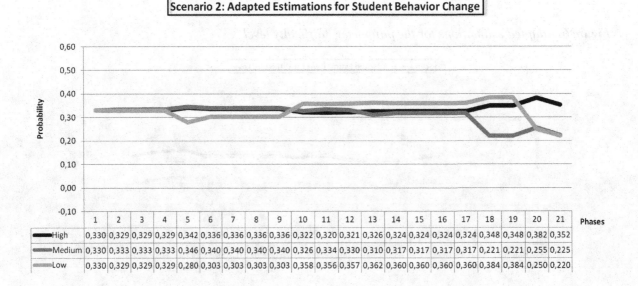

	1	2	3	4	5	6	7	8	9	10	11	12	13	14	15	16	17	18	19	20	21
High	0,330	0,329	0,329	0,329	0,342	0,336	0,336	0,336	0,336	0,322	0,320	0,321	0,326	0,324	0,324	0,324	0,324	0,348	0,348	0,382	0,352
Medium	0,330	0,333	0,333	0,333	0,346	0,340	0,340	0,340	0,340	0,326	0,334	0,330	0,310	0,317	0,317	0,317	0,317	0,221	0,221	0,255	0,225
Low	0,330	0,329	0,329	0,329	0,280	0,303	0,303	0,303	0,303	0,358	0,356	0,357	0,362	0,360	0,360	0,360	0,360	0,384	0,384	0,250	0,220

Unlicensed Spectrum – Network of Excellence) project (http://www.ict-acropolis.eu). Moreover, evolved versions of this work support training activities in the context of this project as well. This paper reflects only the authors' views and the Community is not liable for any use that may be made of the information contained therein.

REFERENCES

Ahmad, A. R., Basir, O., & Hassanein, K. (2004). *Adaptive user interfaces for intelligent e-learning: Issues and trends.* Paper presented at the Fourth International Conference on Electronic Business. Beijing, China.

Alomyan, H. (2004). Individual differences: Implications for web-based learning design. *International Education Journal, 4*(4), 188–196.

Baylari, A., & Montazer, G. A. (2009). Design a personalized e-learning system based on item response theory and artificial neural network approach. *Journal of Expert Systems with Applications, 36,* 8013–8021. doi:10.1016/j.eswa.2008.10.080.

Bekleyen, N., & Yilmaz, A. (2011). *The impact of computer-assisted language learning on vocabulary teaching: jing™ and instant messaging.* Paper presented at the 5th International Computer & Instructional Technologies Symposium. Elazig, Turkey.

Brewster, C., Ciravegna, F., & Wilk, Y. (2002). *User-centred ontology learning for knowledge management.* Paper presented at 6th International Conference on Applications of Natural Language to Information Systems-Revised Papers. Stockholm, Sweden.

Brusilovsky, P. (2001). Adaptive hypermedia. In Kobsa, A. (Ed.), *User modeling and user-adapted interaction* (pp. 87–110). Dordrecht, The Netherlands: Kluwer Academic Publishers.

Brusilovsky, P., Sosnovsky, S. A., & Shcherbinina, O. (2005). User modeling in a distributed e-learning architecture. In Ardissono, L., Brna, P., & Mitrovic, A. (Eds.), *User Modeling 2005, Lecture Notes in Artificial Intelligence* (pp. 387–391). Berlin: Springer-Verlag. doi:10.1007/11527886_50.

Chen, C.-M. (2009). Personalized e-learning system with self-regulated learning assisted mechanisms for promoting learning performance. *Journal of Expert Systems with Applications, 36,* 8816–8829. doi:10.1016/j.eswa.2008.11.026.

Chen, C.-M., & Duh, L.-J. (2008). Personalized web-based tutoring system based on fuzzy item response theory. *Journal of Expert Systems with Applications, 34,* 2298–2315. doi:10.1016/j.eswa.2007.03.010.

Chen, C.-M., & Hsu, S.-H. (2008). Personalized intelligent mobile learning system for supporting effective English learning. *Journal of Educational Technology & Society, 11*(3), 153–180.

Chen, C.-M., Lee, H.-M., & Chen, Y. H. (2005). Personalized e-learning system using item response theory. *Journal of Computers & Education, 44,* 237–255. doi:10.1016/j.compedu.2004.01.006.

Cisco. (2012, February 14). *Cisco visual networking index: Global mobile data traffic forecast update, 2011–2016.* Retrieved December 10, 2012, from http://www.cisco.com/en/US/solutions/collateral/ns341/ns525/ns537/ns705/ns827/white_paper_c11-520862.pdf

Constantinescu, A. I. (2007). Using technology to assist in vocabulary acquisition and reading comprehension. *The Internet TESL Journal, 8*(2).

Dagger, D., Conlan, O., & Wade, V. (2003). Towards anytime, anywhere learning: The role and realization of dynamic terminal personalization in adaptive eLearning. In D. Lassner & C. McNaught (Eds.), *Proceedings of World Conference on Educational Multimedia, Hypermedia and Telecommunications* (pp. 32-35). Chesapeake, VA: IEEE.

Dalton, B., & Grisham, D. L. (2011). eVoc strategies: 10 ways to use technology to build vocabulary. *The Reading Teacher Journal, 64*(5), 306–317. doi:10.1598/RT.64.5.1.

Deng, S. (2011). *Using learning styles to implementing personalized e-learning system.* Paper presented at the International Conference on Management and Service Science (MASS). Wuhan, China.

Dolog, P., Henze, N., Nejdl, W., & Sintek, M. (2004). *Personalization in distributed e-learning environments.* Paper presented at the Thirteenth international World Wide Web conference. New York, NY.

Draganidis, F., Chamopoulou, P., & Mentzas, G. (2006). *An ontology based tool for competency management and learning paths.* Paper presented at 6th International Conference on Knowledge Management, Special track on Integrating Working and Learning. Graz, Austria.

Elisabeta, T.-E., & Răzvan, C.-A. (2010). *Ontology for an e-learning model.* Paper presented at the 5th International Conference on Virtual Learning. Targu-Mures, Romania.

Felder, R. M., & Henriques, E. R. (1995). Learning and teaching styles in foreign and second language education. *Foreign Language Annals Journal, 28*(1), 21–31. doi:10.1111/j.1944-9720.1995.tb00767.x.

Gaeta, M., Orciuoli, F., & Ritrovato, P. (2009). Advanced ontology management system for personalised e-learning. *Journal of Knowledge-Based Systems, 22,* 292–301. doi:10.1016/j.knosys.2009.01.006.

Gamper, J., & Knapp, J. (2002). *A web-based language learning system.* Paper presented at the Nineteenth International Conference on Machine Learning. Sydney, Australia.

García, P., Amandi, A., Schiaffino, S., & Campo, M. (2007). Evaluating Bayesian networks' precision for detecting students' learning styles. *Journal of Computers and Education, 49*(3), 794–808. doi:10.1016/j.compedu.2005.11.017.

Garzotto, F., & Cristea, A. (2004). *ADAPT major design dimensions for educational adaptive hypermedia.* Paper presented at the World Conference on Educational Multimedia, Hypermedia and Telecommunications. Chesapeake, VA.

Henze, N., Dolog, P., & Nejdl, W. (2004). Reasoning and ontologies for personalized e-learning in the semantic web. *Journal of Educational Technology & Society, 7*(4), 82–97.

Hsu, M. H. (2008). A personalized English learning recommender system for ESL students. *Expert Systems with Applications Journal, 34*(1), 683–688. doi:10.1016/j.eswa.2006.10.004.

Huang, Y. M., Huang, Y. M., Huang, S. H., & Lin, Y. T. (2012). A ubiquitous English vocabulary learning system: Evidence of active/passive attitudes vs. usefulness/ease-of-use. *Computers & Education Journal, 58,* 273–282. doi:10.1016/j.compedu.2011.08.008.

Jahankhani, H., Yarandi, M., & Tawil, A. R. (2011). *An adaptive mobile learning system for learning a new language based on learner's abilities.* Paper presented at the Advances in Computing and Technology Conference. London, UK.

Jeon, S. S., & Su, S. Y. W. (2011). Deriving prior distributions for Bayesian models used to achieve adaptive e-learning. *Journal of Knowledge Management & E-Learning: An International Journal, 3*(2), 251–270.

Jeong, H., & Hong, B. (2011). An application of SCORM based CAT for e-learning. In Park, J. J., Yang, L. T., & Lee, C. (Eds.), *FutureTech 2011* (pp. 230–236). Berlin: Springer. doi:10.1007/978-3-642-22333-4_29.

Jeremić, Z., Jovanović, J., & Hatala, M. (2009). Project-based collaborative learning environment with context-aware educational services. *Journal of Learning in the Synergy of Multiple Disciplines, 5794,* 441–446. doi:10.1007/978-3-642-04636-0_42.

Jung, J., & Graf, S. (2008). *An approach for personalized Web-based vocabulary learning through word association games.* Paper presented at the International Symposium on Applications and the Internet. Turku, Finland.

Juvina, I., & Oostendorp, H. V. (2004). Individual differences and behavioral metrics involved in modeling Web navigation. In Stary, C., & Stephanidis, C. (Eds.), *User-Centered Interaction Paradigms for Universal Access in the Information Society* (pp. 258–269). Berlin: Springer. doi:10.1007/978-3-540-30111-0_7.

Kazi, S. A. (2005). *VocaTest: An intelligent tutoring system for vocabulary learning using the mLearning approach.* Paper presented at Re-designing Pedagogy: Research, Policy, Practice Conference. Singapore.

Kritikou, Y., Demestichas, P., Adamopoulou, E., Demestichas, K., Theologou, M., & Paradia, M. (2008). User profile modeling in the context of web-based learning management systems. *Journal of Network and Computer Applications, 31,* 603–627. doi:10.1016/j.jnca.2007.11.006.

Latent Semantic Analysis (LSA). (2012). Retrieved December 10, 2012, from http://lsa.colorado.edu/

Meekyeong, K., Hong, C., Kwon, D., & Hong, S. (2012). Multimedia presentation authoring system for e-learning contents in mobile environment. *Journal of Applied Mathematics & Information Sciences, 6*(2), 705–711.

Meguro, K., Yamamoto, D., Motomura, S., Sasama, T., Kawamura, T., & Sugahara, K. (2010). *Journal of World Academy of Science, Engineering and Technology, 66.*

Moodle. (2012). Retrieved December 10, 2012, from http://moodle.org

Navigli, R., & Velardi, P. (2004). Learning domain ontologies from document warehouses and dedicated web sites. *Journal of Computational Linguistics archive, 30*(2), 151-179.

Nguyen, V. A., & Pham, V. C. (2011). Bayesian network to manage learner model in context-aware adaptive system in mobile learning. In Chang, M. et al. (Eds.), *Edutainment 2011* (pp. 63–70). Berlin: Springer. doi:10.1007/978-3-642-23456-9_13.

Oneto, L., Herder, E., Abel, F., & Smits, D. (2009). *Making today's learning management systems adaptive.* Paper presented at Learning in the Synergy of Multiple Disciplines Conference. Berlin, Germany.

Ong, S. S., & Hawryszkiewycz, I. (2003). *Towards personalised and collaborative learning management systems.* Paper presented at the Third IEEE International Conference on Advanced Learning Technologies. Athens, Greece.

Ouino French. (2012). Retrieved December 10, 2012, from http://www.ouinofrench.com/

Paradia, M., Kritikou, Y., Stavroulaki, V., Demestichas, P., Dimitrakopoulos, G., & Glavas, S. et al. (2012). Introducing cognition in web-based, learning management systems for vocabulary teaching. *Journal of Network and Communication Technologies, 1*(1), 51–66.

Raju, P., & Ahmed, V. (2011). Enabling technologies for developing next-generation learning object repository for construction. *Journal of Automation in Construction, 22,* 247–257. doi:10.1016/j.autcon.2011.07.008.

Razmerita, L., Angehrn, A., & Maedche, A. (2003). *Ontology-based user modeling for knowledge management systems.* Paper presented at 9th International Conference on User Modeling. Johnstown, PA.

Rosetta Stone. (2012). Retrieved December 10, 2012, from http://www.rosettastone.eu

Samaras, H., Giouvanakis, T., Bousiou, D., & Tarabanis, K. (2006). Towards a new generation of multimedia learning research. *AACE Journal, 14*(1), 3–30.

Santos, E., Brown, S., Lejter, M., Ngai, G., Banks, S., & Stytz, M. (1999). *Dynamic user model construction with Bayesian networks for intelligent information queries*. Paper presented at the Twelfth International Florida Artificial Intelligence Research Society Conference. Orlando, FL.

Sbattella, L., & Tedesco, R. (2004). *Profiling and tutoring users in virtual campus*. Paper presented at the Fifth International Conference on Information Technology Based Higher Education and Training. Istanbul, Turkey.

Stavroulaki, V., Kritikou, Y., & Darra, E. (2009). *Acquiring and learning user information in the context of cognitive device management*. Paper presented at Joint Workshop on Cognitive Wireless Networks and Systems - Cognitive Radio Networking, held in conjunction with IEEE International Conference on Communications. Dresden, Germany.

Tan, E., & Pearce, N. (2012). *Open education videos in the classroom: exploring the opportunities and barriers to the use of YouTube in teaching introductory sociology*. Research in Learning Technology. doi:10.3402/rlt.v19s1/7783.

Tedesco, R., Dolog, P., Nejdl, W., & Allert, H. (2006). *Distributed Bayesian networks for user modeling*. Paper presented at World Conference on E-Learning in Corporate, Government, Healthcare, and Higher Education. Chesapeake, VA.

Tell Me More. (2012). Retrieved December 10, 2012, from http://www.tellmemore.com

Thomas, R., Friend, D., DaSilva, L., & McKenzie, A. (2006). Cognitive drivers: Adaptation and learning to achieve end-to-end performance objectives. *IEEE Communications Magazine, 44*(12), 51–57. doi:10.1109/MCOM.2006.273099.

Wang, T., Chiu, T. K., Huang, L. J., Fu, R. X., & Hsieh, T. C. (2009). An English vocabulary learning system based on fuzzy theory and memory cycle. In Spaniol, M. et al. (Eds.), *Advances in Web Based Learning – ICWL 2009* (pp. 420–423). Berlin: Springer. doi:10.1007/978-3-642-03426-8_50.

Wang, Y. H., & Liao, H. C. (2011). Data mining for adaptive learning in a TESL-based e-learning system. *Journal of Expert Systems with Applications, 38*, 6480–6485. doi:10.1016/j.eswa.2010.11.098.

White Smoke. (2012). Retrieved December 10, 2012, from http://www.whitesmoke.com

Yarandi, M., Jahankhani, H., Dastbaz, M., & Tawil, A. R. (2011). *Personalised mobile learning system based on item response theory*. Paper presented at the 6th Annual Conference in Advances in Computing and Technology. London, UK.

Yoshimoto, B., McGraw, I., & Seneff, S. (2009). *Rainbow rummy: A web-based game for vocabulary acquisition using computer-directed speech*. Paper presented at International Workshop on Speech and Language Technology in Education. Warwickshire, UK.

Zakaria, M. R., Moore, A., Stewart, C. D., & Brailsford, T. J. (2003). *'Pluggable' user models for adaptive hypermedia in education*. Paper presented at the Fourteenth ACM Conference on Hypertext and Hypermedia. Nottingham, UK.

Zhang, C., & Wang, F. (2010). *E-learning instructional platforms based on network and multimedia technology*. Paper presented at the Second International Workshop on Education Technology and Computer Science (ETCS). Wuhan, China.

ADDITIONAL READING

Bantouna, A., Stavroulaki, V., Kritikou, Y., Tsagkaris, K., Demestichas, P., & Moessner, K. (2012). An overview of learning mechanisms for cognitive systems. *EURASIP Journal on Wireless Communications and Networking*, 22. doi:10.1186/1687-1499-2012-22.

Brusilovsky, P. (2001). Adaptive hypermedia. In Kobsa, A. (Ed.), *User modeling and user-adapted interaction* (pp. 87–110). Dordrecht, The Netherlands: Kluwer Academic Publishers.

Chamot, A. U. (2005). Language learning strategy instruction: Current issues and research. *Annual Review of Applied Linguistics Journal*, *25*, 112–130.

Claypool, M., Le, P., Wased, M., & Brown, D. (2001). *Implicit interest indicators*. Paper presented at ACM Intelligent User Interfaces Conference (IUI). Santa Fe, New Mexico.

Cohen, A. D. (2003). The learner's side of foreign language learning: Where do styles, strategies and tasks meet? *International Review of Applied Linguistics in Language Teaching Journal*, *41*(4), 279–291.

Conati, C., & Zhao, X. (2004). *Building and evaluating an intelligent pedagogical agent to improve the effectiveness of an educational game*. Paper presented at ACM Intelligent User Interfaces Conference. Madeira, Spain.

Demestichas, P. (2010). Introducing cognitive systems in the wireless B3G world: Motivations and basic engineering challenges. *Telematics and Informatics Journal*, *27*, 256–268. doi:10.1016/j.tele.2009.08.002.

Demestichas, P., Katidiotis, A., Tsagkaris, K., Adamopoulou, E., & Demestichas, K. (2009). Enhancing channel estimation in cognitive radio systems by means of Bayesian networks. *Wireless Personal Communications Journal*, *49*(1), 87–105. doi:10.1007/s11277-008-9559-1.

Dunn, R., & Dunn, K. (1978). *Teaching students through their individual learning styles: A practical approach*. Reston, VA: Reston Publishing Company.

Heckmann, D., Schwartz, T., Brandherm, B., Schmitz, M., & Wilamowitz-Moellendor, M. V. (2005). *The general user model ontology*. Paper presented at the Tenth International Conference on User Modeling. Edinburgh, UK.

Kalaydjiev, O., & Angelova, G. (2002). *Adaptive hypermedia in elearning*. Paper presented at Next Generation Network Workshop. Heidelberg, Germany.

Koutsorodi, A., Adamopoulou, E., Demestichas, K., & Theologou, M. (2006). Terminal management and intelligent access selection in heterogeneous environments. *Mobile Networks and Applications Journal*, *11*(6), 861–871. doi:10.1007/s11036-006-0054-1.

Koutsorodi, A., Adamopoulou, E., Demestichas, K., & Theologou, M. (2007). Service configuration and user profiling in 4G terminals. *Journal of Wireless Personal Communications*, *43*(4), 1303–1321. doi:10.1007/s11277-007-9303-2.

Mariani, L. (1996). Investigating learning styles. *Perspectives, a Journal of TESOL*, *11*(2).

Paradia, M., Mitsis, N., Solomonidou, C., & Raptis, A. (2004). Design and development of an online educational platform for bilingual students of advanced level written Greek. *Journal of Applied Linguistics*, *20*, 45–61.

Paradia, M., Mitsis, N., Solomonidou, C., & Raptis, A. (2005). The impact of applying supportive teaching by means of an online educational platform, aimed at helping Greek bilingual pupils with writing. *Journal of Applied Linguistics*, *21*, 55–71.

Sprenger, M. (2003). *Differentiation through learning styles and memory*. Thousand Oaks, CA: Sage.

Stavroulaki, V., Bantouna, A., Kritikou, Y., De-mestichas, P., Tsagkaris, K., & Blasco, P. et al. (2012). Learning and Knowledge Management toolbox for Cognitive Radio Network applications. *IEEE Vehicular Technology Magazine*, *7*(2), 91–99. doi:10.1109/MVT.2012.2190196.

Stavroulaki, V., Koutsouris, N., Tsagkaris, K., & Demestichas, P. (2010). *Virtualisation platform for the introduction of cognitive systems in the future internet*. Paper presented at Future Networks and Mobile Summit 2010. Florence, Italy.

Stavroulaki, V., Kritikou, Y., & Demestichas, P. (2009). *Acquiring and learning user information in the context of cognitive device management*. Paper presented at IEEE International Conference on Communications 2009 (ICC 2009). Dresden, Germany.

Tsagkaris, K., Katidiotis, A., & Demestichas, P. (2010). Performance evaluation of artificial neural networks based learning schemes for cognitive radio systems. *Computers and Electrical Engineering Journal*, *36*(3), 518–535. doi:10.1016/j.compeleceng.2009.12.005.

KEY TERMS AND DEFINITIONS

Adaptivity: The process of customising something, in order to meet certain needs or expectations.

Cognition: Acquiring knowledge by exploiting past experience.

Detection Mechanisms: The application of methodology for explicitly or implicitly learning something.

Learning Management System: The system or software that offers learning content.

Personalisation: The procedure of making adaptations for meeting the person's specific and unique needs.

System Components: The set of factors comprising a system and realising its proper functonality. Each of the factors is irreplaceable.

Vocabulary: The set of words with a certain meaning that comprise a language.

Compilation of References

3GPP TS 29.213. (n.d.). Policy and charging control signalling flows and Quality of Service (QoS) parameter mapping.

3GPP TS 32.615. (n.d.). Telecommunication management; Configuration Management (CM); Bulk CM Integration Reference Point (IRP): eXtensible Markup Language (XML) file format definition.

3GPP. (2008). *TR 36.913, Requirements for further advancements for E-UTRA (LTE-Advanced)*. Technical Report.

3GPP. (2011). *Technical specification group radio access network, evolved universal terrestrial radio access network (E-UTRAN), self-configuring and self-optimizing network (SON) use cases and solutions, TR 36.902, V9.3.1, release 9.*

3GPP Release 8. (n.d.). Retrieved April 12, 2012, from http://www.3gpp.org/Release-8

Abu-Dayya, A. A., & Beaulieu, N. C. (1992). Outage probabilities of diversity cellular systems with cochannel interference in Nakagami fading. *IEEE Transactions on Vehicular Technology, 41*(4), 343–355. doi:10.1109/25.182583.

Acharya, P. A. K., Singh, S., & Zheng, H. (2006). Reliable open spectrum communications through proactive spectrum access. In *Proceedings of TAPAS*. TAPAS.

AFI. (2012). *ETSI ISG autonomic network engineering for the self-managing future internet*. Retrieved December 10, 2012, from http://portal.etsi.org/afi

Agarwal, M., Bhat, V., Matossian, V., Putty, V., Schmidt, C., & Zhang, G. … Hariri, S. (2006). AutoMate: Enabling autonomic applications on the grid. In *Proceedings of the Autonomic Computing Workshop*, (pp. 48-57). IEEE.

Agrawal, M., Bailey, S., Greenberg, A., Pastor, J., Sebos, P., & Seshan, S. … Yates, J. (2006). *Towards a dynamic, manageable network edge*. Paper presented at ACM SIGCOMM Workshop on Internet Network Management. New York, NY.

Ahmad, A. R., Basir, O., & Hassanein, K. (2004). *Adaptive user interfaces for intelligent e-learning: Issues and trends*. Paper presented at the Fourth International Conference on Electronic Business. Beijing, China.

AirTightNetworks. (2012). *WPA2 Hole196 Vulnerability*. Retrieved July 2012, from AirTightNetworks: http://www. airtightnetworks.com/WPA2-Hole196/

Akin, S., & Gursoy, M. C. (2010). Effective capacity analysis of cognitive radio channels for quality of service provisioning. *IEEE Transactions on Wireless Communications, 9*(11), 3354–3364. doi:10.1109/TWC.2010.092410.090751.

Akin, S., & Gursoy, M. C. (2011). Performance analysis of cognitive radio systems under QoS constraints and channel uncertainty. *IEEE Transactions on Wireless Communications, 10*(9), 2883–2895. doi:10.1109/TWC.2011.062911.100743.

Akyildiz, I. F., Lee, W., Vuran, M. C., & Mohanty, S. (2006). NeXt generation/ dynamic spectrum access/ cognitive radio wireless networks: A survey. *Computer Networks, 50*(13), 2127–2159. doi:10.1016/j.comnet.2006.05.001.

Akyildiz, I. F., Lee, W.-Y., Vuran, M. C., & Mohanty, S. (2008, April). A Survey on Spectrum Management in Cognitive Radio Networks. *IEEE Communications Magazine*, 40–48. doi:10.1109/MCOM.2008.4481339.

Akyildiz, I. F., Su, W., Sankarasubramaniam, Y., & Cayirci, E. (2002). Wireless sensor networks: A survey. *Computer Networks*, *38*(4), 393–422. doi:10.1016/S1389-1286(01)00302-4.

Alamouti, S. M. (1998). A simple transmit diversity technique for wireless communications. *IEEE Journal on Selected Areas in Communications*, *16*(8), 1451–1458. doi:10.1109/49.730453.

Alasti, M., Neekzad, B., Hui, J., & Vannithamby, R. (2010). Quality of service in WiMAX and LTE networks[Topics in Wireless Communications]. *IEEE Communications Magazine*, *48*(5), 104–111. doi:10.1109/MCOM.2010.5458370.

Alavi, S. M. M., Walsh, M., & Hayes, M. (2009). Robust distributed active power control technique for IEEE 802.15.4 wireless sensor networks — A quantitative feedback theory approach. *Journal in Control Engineering Practice*, *17*(7), 805–814. doi:10.1016/j.conengprac.2009.02.001.

Alcatel-Lucent. (2009). *The LTE Network Architecture*. White Paper.

Alexandrescu, A. (2001). *Modern C++ Design*. Addison Wesley.

Ali, M., Ellinas, G., Erkan, H., Hadjiantonis, A., & Dorsinville, R. (2010). On the Vision of Complete Fixed-Mobile Convergence. *Journal of Lightwave Technology*. doi:10.1109/JLT.2010.2050861.

Al-Mogren, A. (2008). Energy adaptive approach in a multi-channel dissemination-based network. In Proceedings of New Technologies, Mobility and Security, NTMS '08, (pp. 1 –6). NTMS.

Alomyan, H. (2004). Individual differences: Implications for web-based learning design. *International Education Journal*, *4*(4), 188–196.

Alouini, M.-S., & Goldsmith, A. J. (2000). Adaptive modulation over Nakagami fading channels. *Wireless Personal Communications*, *13*, 119–143. doi:10.1023/A:1008979107539.

Amemiya, M., Imae, M., Fujii, Y., Suzuyama, T., & Ohshima, S. (2005). Time and frequency transfer and dissemination methods using optical fiber network. *Frequency Control Symposium and Exposition* (pp. 914-918). Proceedings of the 2005 IEEE International.

Amram, N., Fu, B., Kunzmann, G., Melia, T., Munaretto, D., Randriamasy, S., et al. (2011). QoE-based Transport Optimization for Video Delivery over Next Generation Cellular Networks. *Proceedings of the IEEE Symposium on Computers and Communications*, (pp. 19-24).

Analysis of Mason. (2012). Retrieved February 12, 2012 from http://www.analysysmason.com/consulting/services/strategy-consulting/spectrummanagement/Digital-dividend/Our-digital-dividend-experience/Digital-dividend-study-forDutch-Ministry-of-Economic-Affairs/

Anantharamu, L., Chlebus, B., Kowalski, D., & Rokicki, M. (2010). Deterministic broadcast on multiple access channels. In *Proceedings IEEE INFOCOM*. IEEE.

Andersen, P. (2012). *Application delivery networking in the cloud*. Retrieved October 13, 2012, from http://cloud-times.org/2012/08/27/application-delivery-networking-in-the-cloud/

Anderson, T., Peterson, L., Shenker, S., & Turner, J. (2005). Overcoming the internet impasse through virtualization. *IEEE Computer*, *28*(4).

Anggraeni, P., Mahmood, N., Berthod, J., Chausson-niere, N., My, L., & Yomo, H. (2008). Dynamic channel selection for cognitive radios with heterogenous primary bands. *Wireless Personal Communications*, *45*, 369–384. doi:10.1007/s11277-008-9464-7.

Anghel, P. A., & Kaveh, M. (2004). Exact symbol error probability of a cooperative network in a Rayleigh-fading environment. *IEEE Transactions on Wireless Communications*, *3*(5), 1416–1421. doi:10.1109/TWC.2004.833431.

Anker, P. (2010a). Cognitive radio, the market and the regulator. In *Proceedings of the IEEE Symposium on New Frontiers in Dynamic Spectrum Access Networks*. IEEE.

Anker, P. (2010b). Does cognitive radio need policy innovation? *Competition and Regulation in Network Industries*, *11*(1), 2–26.

Archimate Modeling Language. (2012). Retrieved December 2012, from http://www3.opengroup.org/subjectareas/enterprise/archimate

Arslan, H., & Yarkan, S. (2007). Cross-Layer Adaptation and Optimization for Cognitive Radio. I H. Arslan, Cognitive Radio, Software Defined Radio, and Adaptive Wireless Systems (s. 421-452). Springer.

Arslan, M. Y., Yoon, J., Sundaresan, K., Krishnamurthy, S. V., & Banerjee, S. (2011). FERMI: A FEmtocell Resource Management System for Interference Mitigation in OFDMA Networks. *International Conference on Mobile Computing and Networking (Mobicom)*, (s. 25-36).

ARTEMIS Joint Undertaking. (2012). *New Shield Project. Towards the Architectural Framework for Security, Privacy and Dependability (SPD)*. Retrieved 2012, from New Shield Project. Towards the Architectural Framework for Security, Privacy and Dependability (SPD): http://www.newshield.eu/

ASGARD. (2012). Retrieved from ASGARD: Cognitive Radio Experimentation Platform: http://asgard.lab.es.aau.dk

Asterjadhi, A., Kumar, R., La Porta, T., & Zorzi, M. (2011). Broadcasting in multi channel wireless networks in the presence of adversaries. In *Proceedings of the 8th Annual IEEE Communications Society Conference on Sensor, Mesh and Ad Hoc Communications and Networks (SECON)*, (pp. 377 –385). IEEE.

Atia, G., Sahai, A., et al. (2008). spectrum enforcement and liability assignment in cognitive radio systems. In *Proceedings of the 3rd IEEE Symposium on New Frontiers in Dynamic Spectrum Access Networks*. IEEE.

Australian Communication and Media Authority (ACMA). (2007). *The economics of spectrum management: A review*. ACMA.

Bajaj, J., Wooseong, K., Oh, S. Y., & Gerla, M. (2011). Cognitive Radio Implementation in ISM Bands with Microsoft SORA., (s. 531-535).

Baldo, N., & Zorzi, M. (2008, April). Fuzzy Logic for Cross-Layer Optimization in Cognitive Radio networks. *IEEE Communications Magazine*, 64–71. doi:10.1109/MCOM.2008.4481342.

Baldwin, R., & Cave, M. (1999). *Understanding regulation: Theory, strategy, and practice*. Oxford, UK: Oxford University Press.

Bansal, G., Duval, O., & Gagnon, F. (2010). *Joint overlay and underlay power allocation scheme for OFDM-based cognitive radio systems*. Paper presented at the IEEE 71st Vehicular Technology Conference (VTC 2010-Spring), 2010. New York, NY.

Bansal, G., Hossain, M. J., & Bhargava, V. K. (2008). Optimal and suboptimal power allocation schemes for OFDM-based cognitive radio systems. *IEEE Transactions on Wireless Communications*, 7(11), 4710–4718. doi:10.1109/T-WC.2008.07091.

Bao, X., & Li, J. (2007). Efficient message relaying for wireless user cooperation: Decode-amplify-forward (DAF) and hybrid DAF and coded-cooperation. *IEEE Transactions on Wireless Communications*, 6(11), 3975–3984. doi:10.1109/TWC.2007.06117.

Barkan, E., Biham, E., & Keller, N. (2008, Volume 21 Issue 3). Instant Ciphertext-Only Cryptanalysis of GSM Encrypted Communication. *Journal of Cryptology*, 392-429.

Barr, N. (2004). *Economics of the welfare state. New York*. USA: Oxford University Press.

Baylari, A., & Montazer, G. A. (2009). Design a personalized e-learning system based on item response theory and artificial neural network approach. *Journal of Expert Systems with Applications*, 36, 8013–8021. doi:10.1016/j.eswa.2008.10.080.

Beck, K. (2002). *Test Driven Development: By Example*. Addison-Wesley Professional.

Beek, J. V. D., & Riihijarvi, J. (2011). UHF white space in Europe – A quantitative study into the potential of the 470–790MHz band. In *Proceedings of the IEEE International Symposium on Dynamic Spectrum Access Networks (DySPAN)*. Aachen, Germany: IEEE.

Bekleyen, N., & Yilmaz, A. (2011). *The impact of computer-assisted language learning on vocabulary teaching: jing™ and instant messaging*. Paper presented at the 5th International Computer & Instructional Technologies Symposium. Elazig, Turkey.

Bennis, M., & Niyato, D. (2010). A q-learning based approach to interference avoidance in self-organized femtocell networks. In *Proceedings of GLOBECOM Workshops (GC Wkshps)* (pp. 706-710). doi: 10.1109/GLOCOMW.2010.5700414

Bian, K., & Park, J.-M. (2008). Security vulnerabilities in IEEE 802.22. *Proceedings of the 4th Annual International Conference on Wireless Internet (WICON '08)* (p. 9). Brussels, Belgium: Institute for Computer Sciences, Social-Informatics and Telecommunications Engineering.

Biegel, G., & Cahill, V. (2004). A framework for developing mobile, context-aware applications. In *Proceedings of the International Conference on Pervasive Computing and Communications*. IEEE.

Bin Sediq, A., & Yanikomeroglu, H. (2009). Performance analysis of soft-bit maximal ratio combining in cooperative relay networks. *IEEE Transactions on Wireless Communications, 8*(10), 4934–4939. doi:10.1109/TWC.2009.081187.

Bishop, C. (1995). *Neural Networks for Pattern Recognition*. Oxford, UK: Oxford University Press.

Biswas, S., & Morris, R. (2005). ExOR: Opportunistic multi-hop routing for wireless networks. *SIGCOMM Computer Communications Review, 35*(4), 133–144. doi:10.1145/1090191.1080108.

Bletsas, A., Khisti, A., Reed, D. P., & Lippman, A. (2006). A simple cooperative diversity method based on network path selection. *IEEE Journal on Selected Areas in Communications, 24*(3), 659–672. doi:10.1109/JSAC.2005.862417.

Bloem, M., Alpcan, T., & Başar, T. (2007). A stackelberg game for power control and channel allocation in cognitive radio networks. In *Proceedings of the 2nd International Conference on Performance Evaluation Methodologies and Tools*. ICST. ISBN: 978-963-9799-00-4

Borisov, N., Goldberg, I., & Wagner, D. (2001). *Security of the WEP algorithm*. Retrieved July 15, 2012, from University of California, Berkeley: http://www.isaac.cs.berkeley.edu/isaac/wep-faq.html

Borse, M., & Shinde, H. (2005). Wireless Security & Privacy. *Proceedings on the Personal Wireless Communications, 2005 (PWC 2005), 2005 IEEE International Conference on* (pp. 424-428). Prague: Springer.

Bourdena, A., Pallis, E., Kormentzas, G., & Mastorakis, G. (2012). A centralised broker-based CR network architecture for TVWS exploitation under the RTSSM policy. In *Proceedings of the 2nd IEEE Workshop on Convergence among Heterogeneous Wireless Systems in Future Internet (CONWIRE 2012)*. IEEE.

Bourdena, A., Pallis, E., Kormentzas, G., Skianis, C., & Mastorakis, G. (2011). Real-time TVWS trading based on a centralised CR network architecture. In *Proceedings of the IEEE Globecom2011*. IEEE.

Bourdena, A., Pallis, E., Kormentzas, G., & Mastorakis, G. (2013). A prototype cognitive radio architecture for TVWS exploitation under the real time secondary spectrum market policy. *Physical Communication*.

Bourse, D., & El-Khazen, K. (2005). End-to-end reconfigurability (E2R) research perspectives. *IEICE Transactions on Communications*, 4148 – 4157.

Bourse, D., Agusti, R., et al. (2007). *The E2R II flexible spectrum management (FSM) framework and cognitive pilot channel (CPC) concept – Technical and business analysis and recommendations*. E2R II White Paper.

Bourse, D., Buljore, S., Delautre, A., Wiebke, T., Dillinger, M., & Brakensiek, J. ... Alonistioti. (2003). The end-to-end reconfigurability (E2R) research. In *Proceedings of the SDR Forum Technical Conference*. Orlando, FL: SDR.

Boyer, J., Falconer, D. D., & Yanikomeroglu, H. (2004). Multihop diversity in wireless relaying channels. *IEEE Transactions on Communications, 52*(10), 1820–1830. doi:10.1109/TCOMM.2004.836447.

Bradford, G. J., & Laneman, J. (2009). An experimental framework for the evaluation of cooperative diversity. *43rd Annual Conference on Information Sciences and Systems*, (s. 641-645).

Brawerman, A., Blough, D., & Bing, B. (2004). Securing the Download of Radio Configuration Files for Software Defined Radio Devices. *Mobiwac '04: Proceedings of the Second International Workshop on Mobility Management & Wireless Access Protocols* (pp. 98-105). Philadelphia: Association for Computing Machinery (ACM).

Brewster, C., Ciravegna, F., & Wilk, Y. (2002). *User-centred ontology learning for knowledge management*. Paper presented at 6th International Conference on Applications of Natural Language to Information Systems-Revised Papers. Stockholm, Sweden.

Brusilovsky, P. (2001). Adaptive hypermedia. In Kobsa, A. (Ed.), *User modeling and user-adapted interaction* (pp. 87–110). Dordrecht, The Netherlands: Kluwer Academic Publishers.

Brusilovsky, P., Sosnovsky, S. A., & Shcherbinina, O. (2005). User modeling in a distributed e-learning architecture. In Ardissono, L., Brna, P., & Mitrovic, A. (Eds.), *User Modeling 2005, Lecture Notes in Artificial Intelligence* (pp. 387–391). Berlin: Springer-Verlag. doi:10.1007/11527886_50.

Buddhikot, M., & Ryan, K. (2005). Spectrum management in coordinated dynamic spectrum access based cellular networks. In *Proceedings of the First IEEE International Symposium on New Frontiers in Dynamic Spectrum Access Networks, DySPAN'05*, (pp. 299 –307). IEEE.

Burkard, R. E., & Rendl, F. (1991). Lexicographic bottleneck problems. *Operations Research Letters, 10*(5), 303–308. doi:10.1016/0167-6377(91)90018-K.

Bush, S. F., & Kulkarni, A. (2001). *Active networks and active network management: A proactive management framework*. New York: Kluwer Academic/Plenum Publishers.

Butler, J., Lambea, J., Nolan, M., Theilmann, W., Torelli, F., Pistore, M. A., et al. (2011). SLAs empowering services in the future internet. Lecture Notes in Computer Science (including subseries Lecture Notes in Artificial Intelligence and Lecture Notes in Bioinformatics), 6656, 327-338.

Byun, H.-J., Nho, J.-M., & Lim, J.-T. (2003). Dynamic bandwidth allocation algorithm in Ethernet passive optical networks. *IEEE Electronics Letters, 39*(13), 1001–1002. doi:10.1049/el:20030635.

Cabric, D., Mishra, S. M., & Brodersen, R. W. (2004). Implementation issues in spectrum sensing for cognitive radios. In *Proceedings of Asilomar Conference on Signals, Systems and Computers*. Asilomar.

Cao, L., & Zheng, H. (2005). Distributed spectrum allocation via local bargaining. In *Proceedings of the IEEE Sensor and Ad Hoc Communications and Networks (SECON '05)*, (pp. 475–486). IEEE.

Capar, F., Martoyo, I., Weiss, T., & Jondral, F. (2002). Comparison of bandwidth utilization for controlled and uncontrolled channel assignment in a spectrum pooling system. In *Proceedings of the IEEE Vehicular Technology Conference*, (pp. 1069-1073). IEEE.

Capozzi, F., Piro, G., Grieco, L., Boggia, G., & Camarda, P. (2013). *Downlink packet scheduling in LTE cellular networks: Key design issues and a survey*. IEEE Communications Surveys & Tutorials.

Cattoni, A. F., Sørensen, T. B., & Mogensen, P. E. (2012). Architecture Design Approaches and Issues in Cross Layer Systems. I H. F. Rashvand, & Y. S. Kavian, Using Cross-Layer Techniques for Communication Systems (s. 29-52). IGI Global.

Cave, M. (2002). *Review of radio resource management*. Retrieved May 24, 2012, from http://icttoolkit.infodev. org/en/Document.2245.pdf

Chabarek, J., Sommers, J., Barford, P., Estan, C., Tsiang, D., & Wright, S. (2008). Power awareness in network design and routing.[IEEE.]. *Proceedings - IEEE INFOCOM, 2008*, 457–465. doi:10.1109/INFOCOM.2008.93.

Chandra, R., & Bahl, P. (2004). *MultiNet: Connecting to multiple IEEE 802.11 networks using a single wireless card*. Paper presented at the INFOCOM 2004. Twenty-third Annual Joint Conference of the IEEE Computer and Communications Societies. New York, NY.

Chandrasekhar, V., Andrews, J., & Gatherer, A. (2008). Femtocell Networks: a survey. *IEEE Communications Magazine, 46*(9), 59–67. doi:10.1109/MCOM.2008.4623708.

Chang, C. S. (1994). Stability, queue length, and delay of deterministic and stochastic queuing networks. *IEEE Transactions on Automatic Control, 39*(5), 913–931. doi:10.1109/9.284868.

Chang, C. S. (2000). *Performance guarantees in communication networks*. Berlin, Germany: Springer-Verlag. doi:10.1007/978-1-4471-0459-9.

Chang, C., Wawrzynek, J., & Brodersen, R. W. (2005). BEE2: a high-end reconfigurable computing system. *IEEE Design & Test of Computers, 22*(2), 114–125. doi:10.1109/MDT.2005.30.

Chang, M., Abichar, Z., & Hsu, C. (2010). WiMAX or LTE: Who will Lead the Broadband Mobile Internet? *IT Professional, 12*(3), 26–32. doi:10.1109/MITP.2010.47.

Charilas, D. E., & Panagopoulos, A. D. (2010). A survey on game theory applications in wireless networks. *Computer Networks, 54*(18), 3421–3430. doi:10.1016/j. comnet.2010.06.020.

Chatzikokolakis, K., Arapoglou, R., Merentitis, A., & Alonistioti, N. (2012). Fair power control in cooperative systems based on evolutionary techniques. In *Proceedings of the International Conference on Mobile Ubiquitous Computing, Systems, Services and Technologies, UBI-COMM 2012*. ACM.

Check, W. A., Scott, A., Mace, S. L., Brenner, D. L., & Nicoll, D. L. (2004, November 30). Notice of the Proposed Rule Making - Unlicensed Operation in the TV Broadcast Bands. Washington, D.C., Washington, United States of America.

Chen, D., Zhang, Q., & Jia, W. (2008). Aggregation aware spectrum assignment in cognitive ad-hoc networks. In *Proceedings of the Third International Conference on Cognitive Radio Oriented Wireless Networks and Communications (CrownCom 2008)*, (pp. 1-6). CrownCom.

Chen, Z., Cooklev, T., Chen, C., & Pomalaza-Raez, C. (2009). Modeling Primary User Emulation Attacks and Defenses in Cognitive Radio Networks. *Performance Computing and Communications Conference (IPCCC), 2009 IEEE 28th International*, (pp. 208-215). Fort Wayne.

Chen, C.-M. (2009). Personalized e-learning system with self-regulated learning assisted mechanisms for promoting learning performance. *Journal of Expert Systems with Applications*, *36*, 8816–8829. doi:10.1016/j.eswa.2008.11.026.

Chen, C.-M., & Duh, L.-J. (2008). Personalized web-based tutoring system based on fuzzy item response theory. *Journal of Expert Systems with Applications*, *34*, 2298–2315. doi:10.1016/j.eswa.2007.03.010.

Chen, C.-M., & Hsu, S.-H. (2008). Personalized intelligent mobile learning system for supporting effective English learning. *Journal of Educational Technology & Society*, *11*(3), 153–180.

Chen, C.-M., Lee, H.-M., & Chen, Y. H. (2005). Personalized e-learning system using item response theory. *Journal of Computers & Education*, *44*, 237–255. doi:10.1016/j.compedu.2004.01.006.

Chen, D., & Laneman, J. N. (2006). Modulation and demodulation for cooperative diversity in wireless systems. *IEEE Transactions on Wireless Communications*, *5*(7), 1785–1794. doi:10.1109/TWC.2006.1673090.

Cheng, G., Liu, W., Li, Y., & Cheng, W. (2007). *Joint on-demand routing and spectrum assignment in cognitive radio networks*. Paper presented at the IEEE ICC 2007. New York, NY.

Chen, I. R., Yilmaz, O., & Yen, I. L. (2006). Admission control algorithms for revenue optimization with QoS guarantees in mobile wireless networks. *Springer Wireless Personal Communications*, *38*(3), 357–376. doi:10.1007/s11277-006-9037-6.

Chen, K., Shah, S. H., & Nahrstedt, K. (2003). Cross-layer design for data accessibility in mobile ad hoc networks. *Wireless Personal Communications*, *21*, 49–75. doi:10.1023/A:1015509521662.

Chen, R., Park, J.-M., & Reed, J. H. (2008). Defense against primary user emulation attacks in cognitive radio networks. *IEEE Journal on Selected Areas in Communications*, *26*(1), 25–37. doi:10.1109/JSAC.2008.080104.

Chen, Y. X., & Tellambura, C. (2005). Performance analysis of three-branch selection combining over arbitrarily correlated Rayleigh fading channels. *IEEE Transactions on Wireless Communications*, *4*(3), 861–865. doi:10.1109/TWC.2005.847109.

Chen, Z., Bu, T., Ammar, M., & Towsley, D. (2006). Comments on modeling TCP Reno performance: A simple model and its empirical validation. *IEEE/ACM Transactions on Networking*, *14*(2), 451–453. doi:10.1109/TNET.2006.872541.

Chiang, M., Low, S. H., Calderbank, A. R., & Doyle, J. C. (2007). Layering as optimization decomposition: A mathematical theory of network architectures. *Proceedings of the IEEE*, *95*(1), 255–312. doi:10.1109/JPROC.2006.887322.

Chiani, M., Win, M. Z., Zanella, A., Mallik, R. K., & Winters, J. H. (2003). Bounds and approximations for optimum combining of signals in the presence of multiple cochannel interferers and thermal noise. *IEEE Transactions on Communications*, *51*(2), 296–307. doi:10.1109/TCOMM.2003.809265.

Choi, W., Hong, J.-P., Kim, D. I., & Kim, B.-H. (2009). An error detection aided GSC/MRC switching scheme in AF based cooperative communications. In *Proceedings of the IEEE 69th Vehicular Technology Conference (VTC Spring 2009)*, (pp. 1-5). IEEE.

Choi, S.-I., & Park, J. (2010). SLA-aware dynamic bandwidth allocation for QoS in EPONs. *Journal of Optical Communications and Networking, 2*(9), 773–781. doi:10.1364/JOCN.2.000773.

Chong, S., Li, S.-q., & Ghosh, J. (1995). Predictive dynamic bandwidth allocation for efficient transport of real-time VBR video over ATM. *IEEE Journal on Selected Areas in Communications, 13*(1), 12–13. doi:10.1109/49.363150.

Chou, C. T., & Shin, K. G. (2004). Analysis of adaptive bandwidth allocation in wireless networks with multilevel degradable quality of service. *IEEE Transactions on Mobile Computing, 3*(1), 5–17. doi:10.1109/TMC.2004.1261813.

Chowdhury, K. R., & Akyildiz, I. F. (2008). Cognitive wireless mesh networks with dynamic spectrum access. *IEEE Journal on Selected Areas in Communications, 26*(1), 168–181. doi:10.1109/JSAC.2008.080115.

Chowdhury, K. R., & Melodia, T. (2010). Platforms and testbeds for experimental evaluation of cognitive ad hoc networks. *IEEE Communications Magazine, 48*(9), 96–104. doi:10.1109/MCOM.2010.5560593.

Chu, S.-I. (2012). Performance of amplify-and-forward cooperative diversity networks with generalized selection combining over Nakagami-m fading channels. *IEEE Communications Letters, 16*(5), 634–637. doi:10.1109/LCOMM.2012.031212.112443.

Cianca, E., Prasad, R., De Sanctis, M., De Luise, A., Antonini, M., Teotino, D., & Ruggieri, M. (2005). Integrated satellite-HAP systems. *IEEE Communications Magazine, 43*(12), supl.33-supl.39.

Cisco. (2012, February 14). *Cisco visual networking index: Global mobile data traffic forecast update, 2011–2016.* Retrieved December 10, 2012, from http://www.cisco.com/en/US/solutions/collateral/ns341/ns525/ns537/ns705/ns827/white_paper_c11-520862.pdf

Clancy, T. C., & Walker, B. D. (2006). Predictive dynamic spectrum access. In *Proceedings of SDR Forum Technical Conference.* Orlando, FL: SDR.

Clark, D. D., Partridge, C., Ramming, J. C., & Wroclawski, J. T. (2003). *A knowledge plane for the internet.* Paper presented at ACM SIGCOMM. Karlsruhe, Germany.

Cognitive Radio Tutorial. (2012). Retrieved June 11, 2012, from http://www.radio-electronics.com/info/rf-technology-design/cognitive-radio-cr/technology-tutorial.php

Constantinescu, A. I. (2007). Using technology to assist in vocabulary acquisition and reading comprehension. *The Internet TESL Journal, 8*(2).

Conti, J. (2010). LTE vs WiMax: the battle continues[COMMS WiMax vs LTE]. *Engineering & Technology, 5*(14), 63–65. doi:10.1049/et.2010.1417.

Cordeiro, C., Challapali, K., Birru, D., & Shanka, S. N. (2006). IEEE 802.22: An introduction to the first wireless standard based on cognitive radios. *The Journal of Communication, 1*(1), 38–47.

Cover, T. M., & Gamal, A. A. E. (1979). Capacity theorems for the relay channel. *IEEE Transactions on Information Theory, 25*(5), 572–584. doi:10.1109/TIT.1979.1056084.

Cox, C. (2012). *An Introduction to LTE: LTE, LTE-Advanced, SAE and 4G Mobile Communications* (2nd ed.). Wiley. doi:10.1002/9781119942825.

Croce, D., Mellia, M., & Leonardi, E. (2010). The quest for bandwidth estimation techniques for large-scale distributed systems. *SIGMETRICS Performance Evaluation Review, 37*(3), 20–25. doi:10.1145/1710115.1710120.

da Costa, D. B., & Aissa, S. (2009). Performance of cooperative diversity networks: Analysis of amplify-and-forward relaying under equal-gain and maximal-ratio combining. In *Proceedings of the IEEE International Conference on Communications, (ICC 2009)*, (pp. 1-5). Dresden, Germany: IEEE.

Dagger, D., Conlan, O., & Wade, V. (2003). Towards anytime, anywhere learning: The role and realization of dynamic terminal personalization in adaptive eLearning. In D. Lassner & C. McNaught (Eds.), *Proceedings of World Conference on Educational Multimedia, Hypermedia and Telecommunications* (pp. 32-35). Chesapeake, VA: IEEE.

Dahlman, E., Parkvall, S., & Skold, J. (2011). *4G: LTE/LTE-Advanced for Mobile Broadband* (1st ed.). Academic Press.

Dalton, B., & Grisham, D. L. (2011). eVoc strategies: 10 ways to use technology to build vocabulary. *The Reading Teacher Journal, 64*(5), 306–317. doi:10.1598/RT.64.5.1.

DaSilva, L. A., MacKenzie, A. B., da Silva, C. R., & Thomas, R. W. (2008). Requirements of an Open Platform for Cognitive Networks Experiments. *3rd Symposium on New Frontiers in Dynamic Spectrum Access Networks. DySPAN 2008* (s. 1-8). IEEE.

Deering, S., & Hinden, R. (1998). Internet protocol, version 6 (IPv6) specification. *RFC 2460*.

Demestichas, P., Dimitrakopoulos, G., & Strassner, J. (2006). Introducing reconfigurability and cognitive networks concepts in the wireless world. *IEEE Vehicular Technology Magazine*, *1*(2), 32–39. doi:10.1109/MVT.2006.283572.

Demestichas, P., Stavroulaki, V., Boscovic, D., Lee, A., & Strassner, J. (2006). m@ANGEL: Autonomic management platform for seamless cognitive connectivity to the mobile internet. *IEEE Communications Magazine*, *4*(6), 118–127. doi:10.1109/MCOM.2006.1668430.

Deng, S. (2011). *Using learning styles to implementing personalized e-learning system*. Paper presented at the International Conference on Management and Service Science (MASS). Wuhan, China.

Deng, S., Chen, J., He, H., & Tang, W. (2007). *Collaborative strategy for route and spectrum selection in cognitive radio networks*. Paper presented at the Future Generation Communication and Networking (FGCN 2007). New York, NY.

Digham, F., Alouini, M. S., & Simon, M. K. (2007). On the energy detection of unknown signals over fading channels. *IEEE Transactions on Communications*, *55*(1), 21–24. doi:10.1109/TCOMM.2006.887483.

Dillinger, M., Madani, K., & Alonistioti, N. (2003). *Software defined radio: Architectures, systems and functions*. Chichester, UK: John Wiley & Sons.

Ding, L., Melodia, T., Batalama, S., & Medley, M. J. (2009). *ROSA: Distributed joint routing and dynamic spectrum allocation in cognitive radio ad hoc networks*. Paper presented at the 12th ACM International Conference on Modeling, Analysis and Simulation of Wireless and Mobile Systems. New York, NY.

Dirani, M., & Altman, Z. (2010). A cooperative reinforcement learning approach for inter-cell interference coordination in OFDMA cellular networks. In *Proceedings of the 8th International Symposium on Modeling and Optimization in Mobile, Ad Hoc and Wireless Networks (WiOpt)*, (pp. 170-176). WiOpt.

Dolog, P., Henze, N., Nejdl, W., & Sintek, M. (2004). *Personalization in distributed e-learning environments*. Paper presented at the Thirteenth international World Wide Web conference. New York, NY.

Dong, X., Hariri, S., Xue, L., Chen, H., Zhang, M., Pavuluri, S., & Rao, S. (2003). Autonomia: An autonomic computing environment. In *Proceedings of the IEEE International Conference on Performance, Computing, and Communications*. IEEE.

Dong, S. (2004). *Methods for constrained optimization*. New York: Springer.

Draganidis, F., Chamopoulou, P., & Mentzas, G. (2006). *An ontology based tool for competency management and learning paths*. Paper presented at 6th International Conference on Knowledge Management, Special track on Integrating Working and Learning. Graz, Austria.

Du, Q., & Zhang, X. (2009). *QoS-driven power-allocation game over fading multiple-access channels*. Paper presented at IEEE Global Telecommunications Conference (GLOBECOM). New York, NY.

EC. (1999). Directive 1999/5/EC of the European parliament and of the council of 9 March 1999 on radio equipment and telecommunications terminal equipment and the mutual recognition of their conformity. *Official Journal, L 091*, 0010 - 0028.

EC. (2002a). *Decision no 676/2002/EC of the European parliament and of the council of 7 March 2002 on a regulatory framework for radio spectrum policy in the European community (radio spectrum decision)*. Brussels, Belgium: EC.

EC. (2002b). Directive 2002/20/EC of the European parliament and of the council of 7 March 2002 on the authorisation of electronic communications networks and services (authorisation directive). *Official Journal, L 108*, 0021 - 0032.

EC. (2002c). Directive 2002/21/EC of the European parliament and of the council of 7 March 2002 on a common regulatory framework for electronic communications networks and services (framework directive). *Official Journal. L 108*, 0033 - 0050.

EC. (2009). Directive 2009/140/EC of the European parliament and of the council of 25 November 2009 amending directives 2002/21/EC on a common regulatory framework for electronic communications networks and services, 2002/19/EC on access to, and interconnection of, electronic communications networks and associated facilities, and 2002/20/EC on the authorisation of electronic communications networks and services. *Official Journal, L 337*, 0037 - 0069.

ECC. (2008). *CEPT report 24: A preliminary assessment of the feasibility of fitting new/future applications/services into non-harmonised spectrum of the digital dividend (namely the so-called white spaces between allotments)*. Electronic Communications Committee (ECC) within the European Conference of Postal and Telecommunications Administrations (CEPT).

ECC. (2011). ECC report 159 technical and operational requirements for the possible operation of cognitive radio systems in the 'white spaces' of the frequency: *Vol. 470-790. MHz.* Cardiff: ECC.

Ekstrom, H., Furuskar, A., Karlsson, J., Meyer, M., Parkvall, S., & Torsner, J. et al. (2006). Technical solutions for the 3G long-term evolution. *IEEE Communications Magazine, 44*(3), 38–45. doi:10.1109/MCOM.2006.1607864.

ElBatt, T. A., Krishnamurthy, S. V., Connors, D., & Dao, S. (2000). Power management for throughput enhancement in wireless ad-hoc networks. In *Proceedings of the IEEE Communications, 2000,* (pp. 1506-1513). IEEE. doi: 10.1109/ICC.2000.853748

Elisabeta, T.-E., & Răzvan, C.-A. (2010). *Ontology for an e-learning model.* Paper presented at the 5th International Conference on Virtual Learning. Targu-Mures, Romania.

Elkourdi, T., & Simeone, O. (2011). Femtocell as a relay: An outage analysis. *IEEE Transactions on Wireless Communications, 10*(12), 4204–4213. doi:10.1109/TWC.2011.100611.102046.

Elwalid, A. I., & Mitra, D. (1993). Effective bandwidth of general Markovian traffic sources and admission control of high speed networks. *IEEE/ACM Transactions on Networking, 1*(3), 329–343. doi:10.1109/90.234855.

Erman, A. T., & Havinga, P. (2010). Data dissemination of emergency messages in mobile multi-sink wireless sensor networks. In *Proceedings of the 9th IFIP Annual Mediterranean Ad Hoc Networking Workshop (Med-Hoc-Net),* (pp. 1 –8). IFIP.

Esmailpour, A., & Nasser, N. (2011). Dynamic QoS-based bandwidth allocation framework for broadband wireless networks. *IEEE Transactions on Vehicular Technology, 60*(6), 2690–2700. doi:10.1109/TVT.2011.2158674.

ETSI. (2009). *ETSI TR 102 683 V1.1.1: Reconfigurable radio systems (RRS), cognitive pilot channel (CPC).* ETSI.

Ettus Research. (2012). Retrieved from Ettus Research: http://www.ettus.com

EU. (2012). Decision no 243/2012/EU of the European parliament and of the council of 14 March 2012 establishing a multiannual radio spectrum policy programme. *Official Journal, L. 81*, 7-17.

EU. (n.d.). *Press release on maximising radio spectrum efficiency by sharing it.* Retrieved on October 15, 2012 from http://europa.eu/rapid/press-release_MEMO-12-636_en.htm

European Telecommunications Standards Institute. (1996, November). Recommendation GSM 02.09, "Security Aspects". Sophia Antipolis, Valbonne, France.

Falowo, O. E., & Chan, H. A. (2008). Joint call admission control algorithms: Requirements, approaches and design considerations. *Elsevier Computer Communications, 31*(6), 1200–1217. doi:10.1016/j.comcom.2007.10.044.

Fang, Y. (2003). Thinning algorithms for call admission control in wireless networks. *IEEE Transactions on Computers, 52*(5), 685–687. doi:10.1109/TC.2003.1197135.

Fang, Y., & Zhang, Y. (2002). Call admission control schemes and performance analysis in wireless mobile networks. *IEEE Transactions on Vehicular Technology, 51*(2), 371–382. doi:10.1109/25.994812.

Fattah, H., & Leung, C. (2002). An overview of scheduling algorithms in wireless multimedia networks. *IEEE Wireless Communications*, *9*(5), 76–83. doi:10.1109/MWC.2002.1043857.

Faulhaber, G. R. (2005). *The question of spectrum: Technology, management, and regime change*. AEI-Brookings Joint Center for Regulatory Studies.

Faulhaber, G. R., & Farber, D. J. (2003). Spectrum management: Property rights, markets and the commons. In Craven, F., & Wildeman, S. (Eds.), *Rethinking Rights and Regulations: Institutional Response to New Communications Technologies*. MIT Press.

FCC 10-174. (2010). *Second memorandum opinion and order*. Retrieved July 27, 2012 from http://www.ic.gc.ca/eic/site/smt-gst.nsf/vwapj/SMSE-012-11-adaptrum-annexj.pdf/$FILE/SMSE-012-11-adaptrum-annexj.pdf

FCC Spectrum Policy Task Force. (2002). *Report of the spectrum efficiency working group*. Retrieved July 15, 2012 from http://www.fcc.gov/sptf/reports.html

FCC. (2003). ET docket no 03-222 notice of proposed rule making and order. Washington, DC: FCC.

FCC. (2004). FCC 04-113 notice of proposed rulemaking: In the matter of unlicensed operation in the TV broadcast bands (ET docket no. 04-186) and additional spectrum for unlicensed devices below 900 MHz and in the 3 GHz band (ET docket no. 02-380). Washington, DC: Federal Communications Commission.

FCC. (2006). FCC 06-156 first report and order and further notice of proposed rule making in the matter of unlicensed operation in the TV broadcast bands (ET docket No. 04-186) and additional spectrum for unlicensed devices below 900 MHz and in the 3 GHz band (ET docket No. 02-380). Washington, DC: Federal Communications Commission.

FCC. (2008). *FCC 08-260 second report and order and memorandum opinion and order in the matter of unlicensed operation in the TV broadcast bands*. Washington, DC: Federal Communications Commission.

FCC. (2010). FCC 10-174 second memorandum opinion and order in the matter of unlicensed operation in the TV broadcast bands (ET docket No. 04-186) and additional spectrum for unlicensed devices below 900 MHz and in the 3 GHz band (ET docket No. 02-380). Washington, DC: Federal Communications Commission.

FCC. (2012). FCC12-36 third memorandum opinion and order in the matter of unlicensed operation in the TV broadcast bands (ET docket No. 04-186) and additional spectrum for unlicensed devices below 900 MHz and in the 3 GHz band (ET docket No. 02-380). Washington, DC: Federal Communications Commission.

Federal Communications Commission. (2012). Retrieved from http://www.fcc.gov/

Felder, R. M., & Henriques, E. R. (1995). Learning and teaching styles in foreign and second language education. *Foreign Language Annals Journal*, *28*(1), 21–31. doi:10.1111/j.1944-9720.1995.tb00767.x.

Feng, Q. Xue, Guangxi, S., & Yanchun, L. (2009). Smart channel switching in cognitive radio networks. In *Proceedings of CISP, 2009*. CISP.

Feng, W. Liang, & Zhu. (2010). A greedy strategy of data dissemination over multi-channel in mobile computing environments. In *Proceedings of the 3rd International Conference on Advanced Computer Theory and Engineering (ICACTE)*, (vol. 5, pp. V5–322 –V5–326). ICACTE.

Feng, K.-T., Hsu, C.-H., & Lu, T.-E. (2008). Velocity-assisted predictive mobility and location-aware routing protocols for mobile ad hoc networks. *IEEE Transactions on Vehicular Technology*, *57*(1), 448–464. doi:10.1109/TVT.2007.901897.

Feng-Seng, C., Kwang-Cheng, C., & Fettweis, G. (2012). Green resource allocation to minimize receiving energy in OFDMA cellular systems. *IEEE Communications Letters*, *16*(3), 372–374. doi:10.1109/LCOMM.2012.010512.2339.

Fernández-Prades, C., Arribas, J., Closas, P., Avilés, C., & Esteve, L. (2011). GNSS-SDR: an open source tool for researchers and developers. *ION GNSS Conference*. Portland.

Filippini, I., Ekici, E., & Cesana, M. (2009). *Minimum maintenance cost routing in cognitive radio networks.* Paper presented at the IEEE MASS 2009. New York, NY.

Fitzek, F., & Katz, M. (2006). *Cooperation in wireless networks: Principles and applications.* Berlin: Springer. doi:10.1007/1-4020-4711-8.

Fitzek, F., & Katz, M. (2007). *Cognitive wireless networks.* Berlin: Springer. doi:10.1007/978-1-4020-5979-7.

Fodor, G., Koutsimanis, C., Racz, A., Reider, N., Simonsson, A., & Muller, W. (2009). Intercell interference coordination in OFDMA networks and in the 3GPP long term evolution system. *The Journal of Communication, 4*(7), 445–453.

Ford, B. (2012). *Icebergs in the clouds: The other risks of cloud computing.* Retrieved December 10, 2012, from arXiv:1203.1979v1

Forge, S., Horvitz, R., et al. (2012). *Perspectives on the value of shared spectrum access.* Princes Risborough: SCF Associates Ltd. IDA. (2012). *Commercial trial for white space applications.* Retrieved from http://www.ida.gov.sg/Policies%20and%20Regulation/20100730141139.aspx

Fourati, S., Hamouda, S., & Tabbane, S. (2011). Rmc-mac: A reactive multi-channel mac protocol for opportunistic spectrum access. In *Proceedings of the 4th IFIP International Conference on New Technologies, Mobility and Security (NTMS),* (pp. 1 –5). IFIP.

FP7 EU COGEU. (2010). *COGnitive radio systems for efficient sharing of TV white spaces in EUropean context.* Retrieved June 10, 2012, from http://www.ict-cogeu.eu/index.htm

FP7 EU FEDERICA. (2008). *Federated e-infrastructure dedicated to European researchers innovating in computing network architectures.* Retrieved June 10, 2012, from www.fp7-federica.eu

FP7 EU GEYSERS. (2010). *Generalized architecture for dynamic infrastructure services.* Retrieved June 10, 2012, from www.geysers.eu/

FP7 EU NOVI. (2010). *Networking innovation over virtualized infrastructures.* Retrieved June 10, 2012, from www.fp7-novi.eu

FP7 EU QoSMOS. (2010). *Quality of service and mobility driven cognitive radio systems.* Retrieved June 10, 2012, from http://www.ict-qosmos.eu/home.html

FP7 EU SACRA. (2010). *Spectrum and energy efficiency through multi-band cognivite radio.* Retrieved June 10, 2012, from http://www.ict-sacra.eu/

FP7 EU SENDORA. (2008). *Sensor network for dynamic and cognitive radio access.* Retrieved June 10, 2012, from http://www.sendora.eu/

FP7 EU UniverSelf. (2010). Retrieved June 10, 2012, from http://www.univerself-project.eu/

FP7-ICT-248303 QUASAR Project. (n.d.). Retrieved from http://www.quasarspectrum.eu/

FP7-ICT-248454 QoSMOS Project. (n.d.). Retrieved from http://www.ict-qosmos.eu/

FP7-ICT-248560 COGEU Deliverable 3.1. (2010). *Use-cases analysis and TVWS systems requirements.* Retrieved December 2012 from http://www.ict-cogeu.eu/deliverables.html

FP7-ICT-248560 COGEU Project. (2012). *Cognitive radio systems for efficient sharing of TV white spaces in European context.* Retrieved from http://www.ict-cogeu.eu

FP7-ICT-249060 SACRA Project. (n.d.). Retrieved from http://www.ict-sacra.eu/

Fragouli, C., Le Boudec, J. Y., & Widmer, J. (2006). Network coding: An instant primer. *ACM Computer Communication Review, 36*(1), 63–68. doi:10.1145/1111322.1111337.

Frisanco, T., Tafertshofer, P., Lurin, P., & Ang, R. (2008). Infrastructure sharing and shared operations for mobile network operators: From a deployment and operations view. In *Proceedings of Network Operations and Management Symposium (NOMS 2008),* (pp. 129-136). NOMS. doi: 10.1109/NOMS.2008.4575126

Gaeta, M., Orciuoli, F., & Ritrovato, P. (2009). Advanced ontology management system for personalised e-learning. *Journal of Knowledge-Based Systems, 22,* 292–301. doi:10.1016/j.knosys.2009.01.006.

Gamper, J., & Knapp, J. (2002). *A web-based language learning system.* Paper presented at the Nineteenth International Conference on Machine Learning. Sydney, Australia.

Ganesan, G., & Li, Y. G. (2005). Cooperative spectrum sensing in cognitive radio networks. In *Proceedings of IEEE DySPAN.* DySPAN.

Ganesan, G., Li, Y., Bing, B., & Li, S. (2008). Spatiotemporal sensing in cognitive radio networks. *IEEE Journal on Selected Areas in Communications, 26*(1), 5–12. doi:10.1109/JSAC.2008.080102.

Garcia, L. G., Costa, G. W., Cattoni, A. F., Pedersen, K. I., & Mogensens, P. E. (2010). Self-Organizing Coalitions for Conflict Evaluation and Resolution in Femtocells. *Global Telecommunications Conference (GLOBECOM)* (pp. 1-6). IEEE.

Garcia, L. G. U., Pedersen, K. I., & Mogensen, P. E. (2009). Autonomous component carrier selection: Interference management in local area environments for LTE-advanced. *IEEE Communications Magazine, 47*(9), 110–116. doi:10.1109/MCOM.2009.5277463.

García, P., Amandi, A., Schiaffino, S., & Campo, M. (2007). Evaluating Bayesian networks' precision for detecting students' learning styles. *Journal of Computers and Education, 49*(3), 794–808. doi:10.1016/j.compedu.2005.11.017.

Garzotto, F., & Cristea, A. (2004). *ADAPT major design dimensions for educational adaptive hypermedia.* Paper presented at the World Conference on Educational Multimedia, Hypermedia and Telecommunications. Chesapeake, VA.

Gelenbe, E., Xu, Z., & Seref, E. (1999). Cognitive packet networks. In *Proceedings of the 11th IEEE International Conference on Tools with Artificial Intelligence,* (pp. 47 – 54). IEEE.

Georgakopoulos, A., Karvounas, D., Stavroulaki, V., Tsagkaris, K., Tosic, M., Boskovic, D., & Demestichas, P. (2012). Scheme for expanding the capacity of wireless access infrastructures through the exploitation of opportunistic networks. *Mobile Networks and Applications, 17*(4), 463–478. doi:10.1007/s11036-012-0379-x.

Georgakopoulos, A., Tsagkaris, K., Karvounas, D., Vlacheas, P., & Demestichas, P. (2012). Cognitive networks for future internet: Status and emerging challenges. *IEEE Vehicular Technology Magazine, 7*(3), 48–56. doi:10.1109/MVT.2012.2204548.

Ghasemi, A., & Sousa, E. S. (2005). Collaborative spectrum sensing for opportunistic access in fading environments. In *Proceedings of IEEE DySPAN.* DySPAN.

Ghasemi, A., & Sousa, E. S. (2008). Spectrum sensing in cognitive radio networks: Requirements, challenges and design trade-offs. *IEEE Communications Magazine, 46*(4), 32–39. doi:10.1109/MCOM.2008.4481338.

Gigaom. (2012). *Article on spectrum sharing among operators.* Retrieved October 13, 2012 from http://gigaom.com/europe/europe-wants-operators-to-share-their-spectrum/

GNU Radio. (2012). Retrieved from GNU Radio: http://www.gnuradio.org

Goldsmith, A. J. (2005). *Wireless communications.* Cambridge, UK: Cambridge University Press. doi:10.1017/CBO9780511841224.

Goldsmith, A. J., & Varaiya, P. (1997). Capacity of fading channels with channel side information. *IEEE Transactions on Information Theory, 43*(6), 1986–1992. doi:10.1109/18.641562.

Goldsmith, A., Jafar, S. A., Maric, I., & Srinivasa, S. (2009). Breaking spectrum gridlock with cognitive radios: An information theoretic perspective. *Proceedings of the IEEE, 97*(5), 894–914. doi:10.1109/JPROC.2009.2015717.

Gonzalez, C., Dietrich, C. B., Sayed, S., Volos, H. I., Gaeddert, J. D., & Robert, P. M. et al. (2009). Open-source SCA-based core framework and rapid development tools enable software-defined radio education and research. *IEEE Communications Magazine, 47*(10), 48–55. doi:10.1109/MCOM.2009.5273808.

Grauballe, A., Jensen, M. G., Paramanathan, A., Fitzek, F. H. P., & Madsen, T. K. (2009). Implementation and performance analysis of cooperative medium access control protocol for CSMA/CA based technologies. In *Proceedings of the European Wireless Conference (EW 2009),* (pp. 107-112). EW.

Guo, X., & Xia, X.-G. (2008). A distributed space-time coding in asynchronous wireless relay networks. *IEEE Transactions on Wireless Communications*, 7(5), 1812–1816. doi:10.1109/TWC.2008.070042.

Haas, Z., Halpern, J., & Li, L. (2002). Gossip-based ad hoc routing. In *Proceedings of the Twenty-First Annual Joint Conference of the IEEE Computer and Communications Societies INFOCOM*, (vol. 3, pp. 1707 – 1716). IEEE.

Hadden, A. (2009). Mobile Broadband – Where the next generation leads us[industry perspectives]. *IEEE Wireless Communications*, 16(6), 6–9. doi:10.1109/MWC.2009.5361172.

Hanly, S., & Tse, D. N. C. (1998). Multiaccess fading channels–Part I: Polymatroid structure, optimal resource allocation and throughput capacities. *IEEE Transactions on Information Theory*, 44(7), 2796–2815. doi:10.1109/18.737513.

Haykin, S. (1999). *Neural Networks, A Comprehensive Foundation* (2nd ed.). Prentice Hall.

Haykin, S. (2005). Cognitive radio: Brain-empowered wireless communications. *IEEE Journal on Selected Areas in Communications*, 23(2), 201–220. doi:10.1109/JSAC.2004.839380.

Haykin, S. (2012). *Cognitive dynamic systems*. Cambridge, UK: Cambridge University Press.

Heissenbuttel, M., Braun, T., Walchli, M., & Bernoulli, T. (2006). Optimized stateless broadcasting in wireless multi-hop networks. In *Proceedings of the 25th IEEE International Conference on Computer Communications INFOCOM*. IEEE.

Hentilä, L., Kyösti, P., Käske, M., Narandzic, M., & Alatossava, M. (2012, July 16). *MATLAB Implementation of the WINNER Phase II Channel Model*. Retrieved from WINNER+: http://projects.celtic-initiative.org/winner+/phase_2_model.html

Henze, N., Dolog, P., & Nejdl, W. (2004). Reasoning and ontologies for personalized e-learning in the semantic web. *Journal of Educational Technology & Society*, 7(4), 82–97.

Hernandez-Serrano, J., Leon, O., & Soriano, M. (2010). Modeling the Lion Attack in Cognitive Radio Networks. *EURASIP Journal on Wireless Communications and Networking*.

Hill, R. L., Suvda, M., & Campbell, R. (2005). Threat Analysis of GNU Software Radio. *Proceedings of the World Wireless Congress*.

Hoang, D. T., Niyato, D., & Wang, P. (2012). Optimal admission control policy for mobile cloud computing hotspot with cloudlet. In *Proceedings of the IEEE Wireless Communications and Networking Conference (WCNC)*. Paris, France: IEEE.

Holland, G., Vaidya, N., & Bahl, P. (2001). A rate-adaptive MAC protocol for multihop wireless networks. In *Proceedings of the ACM Mobicom Conference*, (pp. 236-251). Rome, Italy: ACM Press.

Hong, K., Sengupta, S., & Chandramouli, R. (2010). *SpiderRadio: An incumbent sensing implementation for cognitive radio networking using IEEE 802.11 devices*. Paper presented at the IEEE International Conference on Communications (ICC), 2010. New York, NY.

Hood, D. (2012). *Gigabit-capable Passive Optical Networks* (1st ed.). Wiley. doi:10.1002/9781118156070.

Hossain, E., Niyato, D., & Han, Z. (2009). *Dynamic spectrum access and management in cognitive radio networks*. Cambridge, UK: Cambridge University Press. doi:10.1017/CBO9780511609909.

Host-Madsen, A. (2004). Capacity bounds for cooperative diversity. *IEEE Transactions on Information Theory*, 52(4), 1522–1544. doi:10.1109/TIT.2006.871576.

Hou, F., & Huang, J. (2010). Dynamic channel selection in cognitive radio network with channel heterogeneity. In *Proceedings of IEEE Globecom*. IEEE.

How, K. C., Ma, M., & Qin, Y. (2010). *An opportunistic service differentiation routing protocol for cognitive radio networks*. Paper presented at the GLOBECOM 2010, IEEE Global Telecommunications Conference. New York, NY.

How, K. C., Ma, M., & Qin, Y. (2011). Routing and QoS provisioning in cognitive radio networks. *Computer Networks*, 55(1), 330–342. doi:10.1016/j.comnet.2010.09.008.

Hoyhtya, M., Pollin, S., & Mammela, A. (2008). Performance improvement with predictive channel selection for cognitive radios. In *Proceedings of the First International Workshop on Cognitive Radio and Advanced Spectrum Management, CogART 2008*. CogART.

Hoyhtya, M., Pollin, S., & Mammela, A. (2010). Classification-based predictive channel selection for cognitive radios. In *Proceedings of IEEE ICC*. IEEE.

Hsu, A. C.-C., Wei, D. S.-L., & Kua, C.-C. J. (2007). A cognitive mac protocol using statistical channel allocation for wireless ad-hoc networks. In *Proceedings of WCNC*. WCNC.

Hsu, M. H. (2008). A personalized English learning recommender system for ESL students. *Expert Systems with Applications Journal, 34*(1), 683–688. doi:10.1016/j.eswa.2006.10.004.

Huang, J., Berry, R. A., & Honig, M. L. (2005). Spectrum sharing with distributed interference compensation. In *Proceedings of the 1st IEEE International Symposium on New Frontiers in Dynamic Spectrum Access Networks 2005 (DySPAN '05)*, (pp. 88-93). IEEE. doi: 10.1109/DYSPAN.2005.1542621

Huang, J., Berry, R. A., & Honig, M. L. (2006). Distributed interference compensation for wireless networks. *IEEE Journal on Selected Areas in Communications, 24*(5), 88–93.

Huang, Y. M., Huang, Y. M., Huang, S. H., & Lin, Y. T. (2012). A ubiquitous English vocabulary learning system: Evidence of active/passive attitudes vs. usefulness/ease-of-use. *Computers & Education Journal, 58*, 273–282. doi:10.1016/j.compedu.2011.08.008.

Hu, N. (2011). *Investigations of radio behaviours and security threats in cognitive radio networks*. Hoboken, NJ.

Hunter, T. E., & Nosratinia, A. (2006). Diversity through coded cooperation. *IEEE Transactions on Wireless Communications, 5*(2), 283–289. doi:10.1109/TWC.2006.1611050.

Hu, Q., & Tang, Z. (2011). ATPM: An energy efficient MAC protocol with adaptive transmit power scheme for wireless sensor networks. *Journal of Multimedia, 6*(2), 122–128. doi:10.4304/jmm.6.2.122-128.

Hu, W., Willkomm, D., Abusubaih, M., Gross, J., Vlantis, G., Gerla, M., & Wolisz, A. (2007). Cognitive radios for dynamic spectrum access - Dynamic frequency hopping communities for efficient IEEE 802.22 operation. *IEEE Communications Magazine, 45*(5), 80–87. doi:10.1109/MCOM.2007.358853.

ICT-ALPHA project. (2008-2011). Retrieved December 2012, from http://www.ict-alpha.eu/

IEEE P1900.4/D1.5. (2008). *Draft standard for architectural building blocks enabling network-device distributed decision making for optimized radio resource usage in heterogeneous wireless access networks*. IEEE.

IEEE Standard 802.21. (2009). *IEEE standard for local and metropolitan area networks-part 21: Media independent handover services*. IEEE.

IEEE. (2007). *Standard definitions and concepts for spectrum management and advanced radio technologies. Institute of Electrical and Electronics Engineers Standards Activities Department, P1900.1 Draft Standard (v0.28)*. IEEE.

Ikki, S. S., & Ahmed, M. H. (2009a). Performance analysis of generalized selection combining for amplify-and-forward cooperative-diversity networks. In *Proceedings of the IEEE International Conference on Communications (ICC '09)*, (pp. 1-6). Dresden, Germany: IEEE.

Ikki, S., & Ahmed, M. H. (2007). Performance analysis of cooperative diversity using equal gain combining (EGC) technique over Rayleigh fading channels. In *Proceedings of the IEEE International Conference on Communications (ICC 2007)*, (pp. 5336-5341). Glasgow, UK: IEEE.

Ikki, S. S., & Ahmed, M. H. (2009b). Performance of cooperative diversity using equal gain combining (EGC) over Nakagami-m fading channels. *IEEE Transactions on Wireless Communications, 8*(2), 557–562. doi:10.1109/TWC.2009.070966.

Ilonen, J., Kamarainen, J.-K., & Lampinen, J. (2003). Differential Evolution Training Algorithm for Feed-Forward Neural Networks. *Neural Processing Letters, 17*(1), 93–105. doi:10.1023/A:1022995128597.

Industry Canada. (2012). *Consultation on policy and technical framework for the use of non-broadcasting applications in the television broadcasting bands below 698 MHz*. Industry Canada. ITU-R. (2009). *Report ITU-R SM.2152 definitions of software defined radio (SDR) and cognitive radio system (CRS)*. Geneva: ITU.

Insights, T. (2012). *Report on current and future prospects for MIMO – A bird's eye view*. Retrieved September 10, 2012, from http://trends-in-telecoms.blogspot.gr/2012/07/current-and-future-prospects-for-mimo.html

Intanagonwiwat, C., Govindan, R., Estrin, D., Heidemann, J., & Silva, F. (2003). Directed diffusion for wireless sensor networking. *IEEE/ACM Transactions on Networking*, *11*(1), 2–16. doi:10.1109/TNET.2002.808417.

Issariyakul, T., & Krishnamurthy, V. (2009). Amplify-and-forward cooperative diversity wireless networks: Model, analysis, and monotonicity properties. *IEEE/ACM Transactions on Networking*, *17*(1), 225–238. doi:10.1109/TNET.2008.925090.

ITU. (2004). *Radio spectrum management for a converging world*. Paper presented at the Workshop on Radio Spectrum Management for a Converging World. Geneva, Switzerland.

ITU. (2008). Radio regulations: *Vol. 1. Articles*. Geneva: International Telecomunication Union.

ITU-T G.984. (n.d.). *Series recommendation*.

Jahankhani, H., Yarandi, M., & Tawil, A. R. (2011). *An adaptive mobile learning system for learning a new language based on learner's abilities*. Paper presented at the Advances in Computing and Technology Conference. London, UK.

Jennings, B., Van der Meer, S., Balasubramaniam, S., Botvich, D., Foghlu, M. O., Donnelly, W., & Strassner, J. (2007). Towards autonomic management of communications network. *IEEE Communications Magazine*, *45*(10), 112–121. doi:10.1109/MCOM.2007.4342833.

Jeong, H., & Hong, B. (2011). An application of SCORM based CAT for e-learning. In Park, J. J., Yang, L. T., & Lee, C. (Eds.), *FutureTech 2011* (pp. 230–236). Berlin: Springer. doi:10.1007/978-3-642-22333-4_29.

Jeon, S. S., & Su, S. Y. W. (2011). Deriving prior distributions for Bayesian models used to achieve adaptive e-learning. *Journal of Knowledge Management & E-Learning: An International Journal*, *3*(2), 251–270.

Jeremić, Z., Jovanović, J., & Hatala, M. (2009). Project-based collaborative learning environment with context-aware educational services. *Journal of Learning in the Synergy of Multiple Disciplines*, *5794*, 441–446. doi:10.1007/978-3-642-04636-0_42.

Jia, J., Zhang, Q., & Shen, X. (2008). HC-MAC: A hardware-constrained cognitive MAC for efficient spectrum management. *IEEE Journal on Selected Areas in Communications*, *26*(1), 106–117. doi:10.1109/JSAC.2008.080110.

Jiang, J., & Senior, J. (2009). A new efficient dynamic MAC protocol for the delivery of multiple services over GPON. *Photonic Network Communications*, *18*(2), 227–236. doi:10.1007/s11107-009-0186-x.

Jin, S., Yue, W., & Sun, Q. (2012). Performance analysis of the sleep/wakeup protocol in a wireless sensor network. [ICIC]. *International Journal of Innovative Computing, Information, & Control*, *8*(5), 3833–3844.

Ju, S., & Evans, J. B. (2009). *Spectrum-aware routing protocol for cognitive ad-hoc networks*. Paper presented at the IEEE Global Telecommunications Conference. New York, NY.

Ju, M., & Kim, I.-M. (2009). ML performance analysis of the decode-and-forward protocol in cooperative diversity networks. *IEEE Transactions on Wireless Communications*, *8*(7), 3855–3867. doi:10.1109/TWC.2009.081470.

Jung, J., & Graf, S. (2008). *An approach for personalized Web-based vocabulary learning through word association games*. Paper presented at the International Symposium on Applications and the Internet. Turku, Finland.

Juvina, I., & Oostendorp, H. V. (2004). Individual differences and behavioral metrics involved in modeling Web navigation. In Stary, C., & Stephanidis, C. (Eds.), *User-Centered Interaction Paradigms for Universal Access in the Information Society* (pp. 258–269). Berlin: Springer. doi:10.1007/978-3-540-30111-0_7.

Kaigui, B., & Jung-Min, ". P. (2008). Security Vulnerabilities in IEEE 802.22. *Proceedings of the 4th Annual International Conference on Wireless Internet - WICON '08* (p. article no. 9). Brussels: ICST (Institute for Computer Sciences, Social-Informatics and Telecommunications Engineering).

Kaltenberger, F., Ghaffar, R., Knopp, R., Anouar, H., & Bonnet, C. (2010, April). Design and implementation of a single-frequency mesh network using OpenAirInterface. *EURASIP Journal on Wireless Communications and Networking*. doi:10.1155/2010/719523.

Kam, A. C., Minn, T., & Siu, K. Y. (2001). Supporting rate guarantee and fair access for bursty data traffic in W-CDMA. *IEEE Journal on Selected Areas in Communications*, *19*(11), 2121–2130. doi:10.1109/49.963799.

Kamerman, A., & Monteban, L. (1997). WLAN-II: A high-performance wireless LAN for the unlicensed band. *Bell Labs Technical Journal*, *2*(3), 118–133. doi:10.1002/bltj.2069.

Kang, X., Garg, H., Liang, Y.-C., & Zhang, R. (2010). Optimal power allocation for OFDM-based cognitive radio with new primary transmission protection criteria. *IEEE Transactions on Wireless Communications*, *9*(6), 2066–2075. doi:10.1109/TWC.2010.06.090912.

Kanonakis, K., Tomkos, I., Krimmel, H., Schaich, F., Lange, C., & Weis, E. et al. (2012). An OFDMA-based optical access network architecture exhibiting ultra-high capacity and wireline-wireless convergence. *IEEE Communications Magazine*, *50*(8), 71–78. doi:10.1109/MCOM.2012.6257530.

Kantarci, B., & Mouftah, H. (2012). Ethernet passive optical network-long-term evolution deployment for a green access network. *IET Optoelectronics*, *6*(4), 183–191. doi:10.1049/iet-opt.2010.0112.

Karagiannidis, G. K. (2003). Performance analysis of SIR-based dual selection diversity over correlated Nakagami-m fading channels. *IEEE Transactions on Vehicular Technology*, *52*(5), 1207–1216. doi:10.1109/TVT.2003.816612.

Karagiannidis, G. K., Zogas, D. A., & Kotsopoulos, S. A. (2003). Performance analysis of triple selection diversity over exponentially correlated Nakagami-m fading channels. *IEEE Transactions on Communications*, *51*(8), 1245–1248. doi:10.1109/TCOMM.2003.815070.

Karipidis, E., Larsson, E. G., & Holmberg, K. (2009). *Optimal scheduling and QoS power control for cognitive underlay networks*. Paper presented at the 3rd IEEE International Workshop on Computational Advances in Multi-Sensor Adaptive Processing (CAMSAP). New York, NY.

Karvounas, D., Georgakopoulos, A., Stavroulaki, V., Koutsouris, N., Tsagkaris, K., & Demestichas, P. (2012). Resource allocation to femtocells for coordinated capacity expansion of wireless access infrastructures. *EURASIP Journal on Wireless Communications and Networking*, (1): 310. doi:10.1186/1687-1499-2012-310.

Katti, S., Rahul, H., Hu, W., Katabi, D., Medard, M., & Crowcroft, J. (2008). XORs in the air: Practical wireless network coding. *IEEE/ACM Transactions on Networking*, *16*(3), 497–510. doi:10.1109/TNET.2008.923722.

Kaya, O., & Ulukus, S. (2007). Power control for fading cooperative multiple access channels. *IEEE Transactions on Wireless Communications*, *6*(8), 2915–2923. doi:10.1109/TWC.2007.05858.

Kazi, S. A. (2005). *VocaTest: An intelligent tutoring system for vocabulary learning using the mLearning approach*. Paper presented at Redesigning Pedagogy: Research, Policy, Practice Conference. Singapore.

Kelly, F. P. (1997). Charging and rate control for elastic traffic. *European Transactions on Telecommunications*, *8*, 33–37. doi:10.1002/ett.4460080106.

Kelly, F. P., Maulloo, A., & Tan, D. (1998). Rate control in communication networks: Shadow prices, proportional fairness and stability. *The Journal of the Operational Research Society*, *49*, 237–252.

Kennedy, J., & Eberhart, R. (1995). Particle Swarm Optimization. *Proceedings of IEEE International Conference on Neural Networks*, (pp. 1942-1948).

Kephart, J., & Chess, D. (2003). The vision of autonomic computing. *IEEE Computer*, *36*(1), 41–50. doi:10.1109/MC.2003.1160055.

Kesidis, G., Walrand, J., & Chang, C. S. (1993). Effective bandwidths for multiclass Markov fluids and other ATM sources. *IEEE/ACM Transactions on Networking*, *1*(4), 424–428. doi:10.1109/90.251894.

Khalife, H., Ahuja, S., Malouch, N., & Krunz, M. (2008). Probabilistic path selection in opportunistic cognitive radio networks. In *Proceedings of the IEEE Globecom Conference*. IEEE.

Khalife, H., Malouch, N., & Fdida, S. (2009). Multihop cognitive radio networks: To route or not to route. *IEEE Network*, *23*(4), 20–25. doi:10.1109/MNET.2009.5191142.

Khattab, A., Camp, J., Hunter, C., Murphy, P., Sabharwarl, A., & Knightly, E. (2008). WARP - A Flexible Platform for Clean-Slate Wireless Medium Access Protocol Design. *ACM SIGMOBILE Mobile Computing and Communications Review*, *12*(1), 56–58. doi:10.1145/1374512.1374532.

Kirkpatrick, S., Gelatt, C. D., & Vecchi, M. P. (1983). Optimization by Simulated Annealing. *Science, 220*(4598), 671–680. doi:10.1126/science.220.4598.671 PMID:17813860.

Kiskani, M. K., Khalaj, B. H., & Vakilinia, S. (2010). Delay QoS provisioning in cognitive radio systems using adaptive modulation. In *Proceedings of the 6th ACM Workshop on QoS and Security for Wireless and Mobile Networks (Q2SWinet)*. ACM.

Klein, C., Schmid, R., Leuxner, C., Sitou, W., & Spanfelner, B. (2008). A survey of context adaptation in autonomic computing. In *Proceedings of the International Conference on Autonomic and Autonomous Systems*. IEEE.

Kliazovich, D., Granelli, F., & Fonseca, N. L. S. (2011). Survey on signaling techniques for cognitive networks. In *Proceedings of the IEEE International Workshop on Computer-Aided Modeling Analysis and Design of Communication Links and Networks (CAMAD)*. Kyoto, Japan: IEEE.

Kliazovich, D., Granelli, F., Fonseca, N. L. S., & Piesiewicz, R. (2009). *Cognitive information service: Basic principles and implementation of a cognitive inter-node protocol optimization scheme*. Paper presented at the IEEE Global Communications Conference (GLOBECOM). Honolulu, HI.

Kliazovich, D., Lima, J., Fonseca, N. L. S., Granelli, F., & Madeira, E. (2009). Cognitive link layer for wireless local area networks. In *Proceedings of the IEEE Latin-American Conference on Communications (LATINCOM)*. IEEE.

Kliazovich, D., Malheiros, N., Granelli, F., Madeira, E., & Fonseca, N. L. S. (2010). CogProt: A framework for cognitive configuration and optimization of communication protocols. In *Proceedings of the 2nd International Conference on Mobile Lightweight Wireless Systems (MOBILIGHT)*. Barcelona, Spain: MOBILIGHT.

Kondareddy, Y. R., & Agrawal, P. (2008). Selective broadcasting in multi-hop cognitive radio networks. In *Proceedings of the IEEE Sarnoff Symposium*. IEEE.

Kondareddy, Y., & Agrawal, P. (2009). Effect of dynamic spectrum access on TCP performance. In *Proceedings of IEEE Globecom 2009*. IEEE.

Kong, P. Y., & the, K. H. (2004). Performance of proactive earliest due date packet scheduling in wireless networks. *IEEE Transactions on Vehicular Technology, 53*(4), 1224–1234. doi:10.1109/TVT.2004.830942.

Korakis, T., Knox, M., Erkip, E., & Panwar, S. (2009). Cooperative Network Implementation Using Open-Source Platforms. *IEEE Communications Magazine, 47*(2), 134–141. doi:10.1109/MCOM.2009.4785391.

Kowalik, K., Bykowski, M., Keegan, B., & Davis, M. (2008). An evaluation of a conservative transmit power control mechanism on an indoor 802.11 wireless mesh testbed. In *Proceedings of the International Conference on Wireless Information Networks and Systems (WINSYS'08)*, (pp. 5-14). ISBN: 978-989-8111-61-6

Kramer, G., Gastpar, M., & Gupta, P. (2005). Cooperative strategies and capacity theorems for relay networks. *IEEE Transactions on Information Theory, 51*(9), 3037–3063. doi:10.1109/TIT.2005.853304.

Kramer, G., & Pesavento, G. (2002). Ethernet passive optical network (EPON): building a next-generation optical access network. *IEEE Communications Magazine, 40*(2), 66–73. doi:10.1109/35.983910.

Kritikou, Y., Demestichas, P., Adamopoulou, E., Demestichas, K., Theologou, M., & Paradia, M. (2008). User profile modeling in the context of web-based learning management systems. *Journal of Network and Computer Applications, 31*, 603–627. doi:10.1016/j.jnca.2007.11.006.

Kulkarni, R., & Zekavat, S. A. (2006). Traffic-aware inter-vendor dynamic spectrum allocation: Performance in multi-vendor environments. In *Proceedings of the 2006 International Conference on Wireless Communications and Mobile Computing*. ACM Press.

Kumar, A., & Shin, K. G. (n.d.). DSASync: Managing end-to-end connections in dynamic spectrum access wireless LANs. *IEEE Transactions on Networking, 4*(20), 1068-1081.

Kunniyur, S., & Srikant, R. (2003). End-to-end congestion control: Utility functions, random losses and ECN marks. *IEEE/ACM Transactions on Networking, 10*(5), 689–702. doi:10.1109/TNET.2003.818183.

Kyasanur, P., & Vaidya, N. H. (2005). Protocol design challenges for multi-hop dynamic spectrum access networks. In *Proceedings of IEEE DySPAN*, (pp. 645-648). IEEE.

Lai, L., & El Gamal, H. (2008). The water-filling game in fading multiple-access channels. *IEEE Transactions on Information Theory, 54*(5), 2110–2122. doi:10.1109/TIT.2008.920340.

Lake, S. M. (2005). Cognitive networking with software programmable intelligent networks for wireless and wireline critical communications. In *Proceedings of the IEEE Military Communications Conference*, (pp. 1693 – 1699). IEEE.

Lam, C. (2007). *Passive Optical Networks, Principles and Practice*. Elsevier.

Laneman, J. N., Wornell, G. W., & Tse, D. N. C. (2001). An efficient protocol for realizing cooperative diversity in wireless networks. In *Proceedings of the IEEE International Symposium on Information Theory (ISIT 2001)*, (p. 294). Washington, DC: IEEE.

Laneman, J. N., Tse, D. N. C., & Wornell, G. W. (2004). Cooperative diversity in wireless networks: Efficient protocols and outage behavior. *IEEE Transactions on Information Theory, 50*(12), 3062–3080. doi:10.1109/TIT.2004.838089.

Laneman, J. N., & Wornell, G. W. (2003). Distributed space-time-coded protocols for exploiting cooperative diversity in wireless networks. *IEEE Transactions on Information Theory, 49*(10), 2415–2425. doi:10.1109/TIT.2003.817829.

La, R. J., & Anantharam, V. (2002). Utility-based rate control in the Internet for elastic traffic. *IEEE/ACM Transactions on Networking, 9*(2), 272–286. doi:10.1109/90.993307.

Lashkari, A. H., Danesh, M. M., & Samadi, B. (2009). A Survey on Wireless Security protocols (WEP,WPA and WPA2/802.11i). *Computer Science and Information Technology, 2009. ICCSIT 2009. 2nd IEEE International Conference on*, (pp. 48-52). Kuala Lumpur.

Latent Semantic Analysis (LSA). (2012). Retrieved December 10, 2012, from http://lsa.colorado.edu/

Leaves, P., Moessner, K., Tafazolli, R., Grandblaise, D., Bourse, D., Tonjes, R., & Breveglieri, M. (2004). Dynamic spectrum allocation in composite reconfigurable wireless networks. *IEEE Communications Magazine, 42*(5), 72–81. doi:10.1109/MCOM.2004.1299346.

Lee, J.-F., Wang, C.-S., & Chuang, M.-C. (2010). Fast and reliable emergency message dissemination mechanism in vehicular ad hoc networks. In *Proceedings of the IEEE Wireless Communications and Networking Conference (WCNC)*. IEEE.

Lehr, W., & Jesuale, N. (2008). Spectrum pooling for next generation public safety radio systems. In *Proceedings of the 3rd IEEE Symposium on New Frontiers in Dynamic Spectrum Access Networks, 2008*. IEEE.

Lei, X., Fuja, T., Kliewer, J., & Costello, D. (2007). A network coding approach to cooperative diversity. *IEEE Transactions on Information Theory, 53*(10), 3714–3722. doi:10.1109/TIT.2007.904990.

Lei, Z., & Chin, F. (2008, June). A Reliable and Power Efficient Beacon Structure for Cognitive Radio Systems. *Broadcasting. IEEE Transactions on, 54*, 182–187.

Le, L. B., & Hossain, E. (2008). Resource allocation for spectrum underlay in cognitive radio networks. *IEEE Transactions on Wireless Communications, 7*(12), 5306–5315. doi:10.1109/T-WC.2008.070890.

Lemstra, W., & Anker, P. et al. (2011). Cognitive radio: Enabling technology in need of coordination. *Competition and Regulation in Network Industries, 12*(3), 210–235.

Lescuyer, P., & Lucidarme, T. (2008). *Evolved Packet System (EPS), The LTE and SAE Evolution of 3G UMTS*. Wiley. doi:10.1002/9780470723678.

Li, C., Raghunathan, A., & Jha, N. K. (2009). An Architecture for Secure Software Defined Radio. Design, Automatione and Test in Europe 2009 - DATE, (pp. 448-453). Dresden.

Li, J., Chen, D., Wang, Y., & Wu, J. (2013). Performance evaluation of cloud-RAN system with carrier frequency offset. In *Proceedings of the IEEE Global Communications Conference, Exhibition & Industry Forum*. IEEE.

Li, J., Powley, W., Martin, P., Wilson, K., & Craddock, C. (2009). A sensor-based approach to symptom recognition for autonomic systems. In *Proceedings of the International Conference on Autonomic and Autonomous Systems*. IEEE.

Liang, O., Sekercioglu, Y. A., & Mani, N. (2006). A survey of multipoint relay based broadcast schemes in wireless ad hoc networks. *IEEE Communications Surveys Tutorials*, 8(4), 30–46. doi:10.1109/COMST.2006.283820.

Liao, S., Wu, C., Yang, Q., Wang, B., & Jiang, M. (2011). A resource-efficient load balancing algorithm for network virtualization. *Chinese Journal of Electronics*, 20(4).

Li, B., Li, L., Li, B., Sivalingam, K. M., & Cao, X.-R. (2004). Call admission control for voice/data integrated cellular networks: performance analysis and comparative study. *IEEE Journal on Selected Areas in Communications*, 22(4), 706–718. doi:10.1109/JSAC.2004.825987.

Lien, S. Y., Tseng, C. C., Chen, K. C., & Su, C. W. (2010). Cognitive radio resource management for QoS guarantees in autonomous femtocell networks. In *Proceedings of the IEEE International Conference on Communications (ICC)*, (pp. 1-6). IEEE. doi: 10.1109/ICC.2010.5502784

Li, L., & Goldsmith, A. J. (2001). Capacity and optimal resource allocation for fading broadcast channels: Ergodic capacity. *IEEE Transactions on Information Theory*, 47(3), 1083–1102. doi:10.1109/18.915665.

Lima, J., Kliazovich, D., Granelli, F., Madeira, E., & Fonseca, N. L. S. (2013). *CogMAC - A cognitive link layer for wireless local area networks*. ACM/Springer Journal of Wireless Networks.

Lin, Z., Erkip, E., & Ghosh, M. (2005). Adaptive modulation for coded cooperative systems. In *Proceedings of the International Workshop on Signal Processing Advances for Wireless Communications (SPAWC 2005)*. New York: SPAWC.

Li, Q., Li, G., Lee, W., Lee, M.-i., Mazzarese, D., & Clerckx, B. et al. (2010). MIMO techniques in WiMAX and LTE: a feature overview. *IEEE Communications Magazine*, 48(5), 86–92. doi:10.1109/MCOM.2010.5458368.

Liu, H., & Parashar, M. (2004). Component-based programming model for autonomic applications. In *Proceedings of the International Conference on Autonomic Computing*, (pp. 10-17). IEEE.

Liu, Y., & Grace, D. (2008). *Improving capacity for wireless ad hoc communications using cognitive routing*. Paper presented at the CrownCom 2008. New York, NY.

Liu, Y., Ning, P., & Dai, H. (2010). Authenticating Primary Users' Signals in Cognitive Radio Networks via Integrated Cryptographic and Wireless Link Signatures. *2010 IEEE Symposium on Security and Privacy*, (pp. 286-301).

Liu, P., Tao, Z., Narayanan, S., Korakis, T., & Panwar, S. S. (2007). CoopMAC: A cooperative MAC for wireless LANs. *IEEE Journal on Selected Areas in Communications*, 25(2), 340–354. doi:10.1109/JSAC.2007.070210.

Liu, R. K., & Wang, B. (2011). *Cognitive Radio Networking And Security: A Game-Theoretic View*. Cambridge, New York: Cambridge University Press.

Liu, X. (2006). Sensing-based opportunistic channel access. *Mobile Networks and Applications*, 11, 577–591. doi:10.1007/s11036-006-7323-x.

Lopez-Perez, D., Guvenc, I., De La Roche, G., Kountouris, M., Quek, T. Q. S., & Zhang, J. (2011). Enhanced intercell interference coordination challenges in heterogeneous networks. *IEEE Wireless Communications Magazine*, 18(3), 22–30. doi:10.1109/MWC.2011.5876497.

Low, S. H. (2003). A duality model of TCP and queue management algorithms. *IEEE/ACM Transactions on Networking*, 11(4), 525–536. doi:10.1109/TNET.2003.815297.

Luo, C., Yu, F. R., Ji, H., & Lung, V. C. M. (n.d.). Cross-layer design for TCP Performance improvement in cognitive radio networks. *IEEE Transactions on Vehicular Technology*, 59(5), 2485-2495.

Lyrtech, R. D. Incorporated. (2012). *Small form factor SDR development platforms*. Retrieved July 2012, from Lyrtech RD: http://lyrtechrd.com/en/products/view/+small-form-factor-sdr-development-platforms

Ma, H., Zheng, L., Ma, X., & Luo, Y. (2008). *Spectrum aware routing for multi-hop cognitive radio networks with a single transceiver*. Paper presented at the 3rd International Conference on Cognitive Radio Oriented Wireless Networks and Communications. New York, NY.

Ma, L., Han, X., & Shen, C. C. (2005). Dynamic open spectrum sharing MAC protocol for wireless ad hoc networks. In *Proceedings of the 1st IEEE International Symposium on New Frontiers in Dynamic Spectrum Access Networks 2005 (DySPAN '05)*, (pp. 203-213). IEEE.

Ma, M., Zheng, J., Zhang, Y., Shao, Z., & Fujise, M. (2006). *A power-controlled rate-adaptive MAC protocol to support differentiated service in wireless ad hoc networks.* Paper presented at the IEEE GLOBECOM 2006. New York, NY.

Ma, R.-T., Hsu, Y.-P., & Feng, K.-T. (2009). A pomdp-based spectrum handoff protocol for partially observable cognitive radio networks. In *Proceedings of WCNC.* WCNC.

Magdalinos, P., Kousaridas, A., Spapis, P., Katsikas, G., & Alonistioti, N. (2011). Enhancing a fuzzy logic inference engine through machine learning for a self-managed network. *ACM Springer Mobile Networks and Applications, 16*(4), 475–489. doi:10.1007/s11036-011-0327-1.

Makris, P., & Skianis, C. (2008). Multi-scenario based call admission control for coexisting heterogeneous wireless technologies. In *Proceedings of IEEE GLOBECOM.* New Orleans, LA: IEEE.

Makris, P., Skoutas, D. N., & Skianis, C. (2012). On networking and computing environments' integration: A novel mobile cloud resources provisioning approach. In *Proceedings of the IEEE International Conference on Telecommunications and Multimedia (TEMU).* IEEE.

Makris, P., Skoutas, D. N., & Skianis, C. (2013). *A survey on context-aware mobile and wireless networking: On networking and computing environments integration.* IEEE Communications Surveys & Tutorials. doi:10.1109/SURV.2012.040912.00180.

Malheirosa, N., Kliazovich, D., Granelli, F., Madeira, E., & Fonseca, N. L. S. (2013). A cognitive approach for self-configuration of communication protocols. *Computer Networks.*

Manzalini, A. (2012). Mitigating systemic risks in future networks. In *Proceedings of the IEEE 17th International Workshop on Computer Aided Modeling and Design of Communication Links and Networks.* IEEE.

Manzalini, A., Zambonelli, F., Baresi, L., & Di Ferdinando, A. (2009). The CASCADAS framework for autonomic communications. In *Autonomic Communication.* Berlin: Springer-Verlag.

Mao, L., Xu, S., Fu, T., & Huang, Q. (2012). *Game theory based power allocation algorithm in high-speed mobile environment.* Paper presented at Vehicular Technology Conference Fall (VTC 2012-Fall). Québec City, Canada.

Maravedis Market Research and Analysis. (2006). *Clash of the titans – WiMAX and 4G: The battle for convergence is joined.* Author.

Marbukh, V. (2007). *Towards understanding of complex communication networks: Performance, phase transitions & control.* Sigmetrics Performance Evaluation Review.

Mathis, M., Semke, J., Mahdavi, J., & Ott, T. (1997). The macroscopic behaviour of the TCP congestion avoidance algorithm. *ACM SIGCOMM Computer Communications Review, 27*(3), 67–82. doi:10.1145/263932.264023.

Mathur, C. N., & Subbalakshmi, K. (2007). Security Issues in Cognitive Radior Networks. In Mahmoud, Q. H. (Ed.), *Cognitive Networks: Towards Self-Aware Networks* (pp. 271–292). West Sussex: John Wiley & Sons, LTD. doi:10.1002/9780470515143.ch11.

Ma, Y., Zhang, H., Yuan, D., & Chen, H. H. (2009). Adaptive power allocation with quality-of-service guarantee in cognitive radio networks. *Computer Communications, 32*(18), 1975–1982. doi:10.1016/j.comcom.2009.06.012.

McHenry, M. A., McCloskey, D., & Lane-Roberts, G. (2004). *New York City spectrum occupancy measurements.* Shared Spectrum Company.

McKeown, N. (2009). *Software-defined networking.* Paper presented at the 28th IEEE International Conference on Computer Communications. New York, NY.

Meddour, D. E., Rasheed, T., & Gourhant, Y. (2011). On the role of infrastructure sharing for mobile network operators in emerging markets. *International Journal of Computer and Telecommunications Networking, 55*(7), 1576–1591.

Meekyeong, K., Hong, C., Kwon, D., & Hong, S. (2012). Multimedia presentation authoring system for e-learning contents in mobile environment. *Journal of Applied Mathematics & Information Sciences, 6*(2), 705–711.

Meguro, K., Yamamoto, D., Motomura, S., Sasama, T., Kawamura, T., & Sugahara, K. (2010). *Journal of World Academy of Science, Engineering and Technology, 66.*

Merentitis, A., & Triantafyllopoulou, D. (2010). Transmission power regulation in cooperative cognitive radio systems under uncertainties. In *Proceedings of the IEEE International Symposium on Wireless Pervasive Computing (ISWPC)*, (pp. 134-139). IEEE. doi: 10.1109/ISWPC.2010.5483742

Merentitis, A., Kaloxylos, A., Stamatelatos, M., & Alonistioti, N. (2010). Optimal periodic radio sensing and low energy reasoning for cognitive devices. In *Proceedings of the 15th IEEE Mediterranean Electrotechnical Conference (MELECON 2010)*, (pp. 470-475). IEEE. doi: 10.1109/MELCON.2010.5476231

Merentitis, A., Patouni, E., Alonistioti, N., & Doubrava, M. (2008). To reconfigure or not to reconfigure: Cognitive mechanisms for mobile devices decision making. In *Proceedings of the Vehicular Technology Conference (VTC 2008)*, (pp. 1-5). IEEE. doi: 10.1109/VETECF.2008.267

Meshkova, E., Ansari, J., Denkovski, D., Riihijärvi, J., Nasreddine, J., Pavlovski, M., et al. (2011). Experimental Spectrum Sensor Testbed for Constructing Indoor Radio Environmental Maps. *International Symposium on Dynamic Spectrum Access Networks (DySPAN)*. IEEE.

Mhatre, V. P., Papagiannaki, K., & Baccelli, F. (2007). Interference mitigation through power control in high density 802.11 WLANs. In *Proceedings of INFOCOM 2007 26th IEEE International Conference on Computer Communications* (pp. 535-543). IEEE. doi: 10.1109/INFCOM.2007.69

Michalopoulos, D. S., & Karagiannidis, G. K. (2008). PHY-layer fairness in amplify and forward cooperative diversity systems. *IEEE Transactions on Wireless Communications*, 7(3), 1073–1082. doi:10.1109/TWC.2008.060825.

Mihovska, A., Meucci, F., Prasad, N. R., Velez, F. J., & Cabral, O. (2009). Multi-operator resource sharing scenario in the context of IMT-advanced systems. In *Proceedings of the Second International Workshop on Cognitive Radio and Advanced Spectrum Management (CogART 2009)*, (pp. 12-16). CogART. doi: 10.1109/COGART.2009.5167225

Min, A. W., Shin, K. G., & Hu, X. (2009). Attack-Tolerant Distributed Sensing for Dynamic Spectrum Access Networks. *Network Protocols, 2009. ICNP 2009. 17th IEEE International Conference on*, (pp. 294-303). Ann Arbor.

Mishra, A. S. S., & Brodersen, R. (2006). Cooperative sensing among cognitive radios. In *Proceedings of IEEE ICC*. IEEE.

Mitchell, T. (1997). *Machine Learning*. McGraw-Hill.

Mitola, J., III, & Maguire, G. Q. (1999). Cognitive radio: Making software defined radio more personal. In *Proceedings of the IEEE International Conference of Personal Communications*. IEEE.

Mitola, J., III. (2000). *Cognitive radio: An integrated agent architecture for software defined radio*. (PhD Dissertation). Royal Institute of Technology, Stockholm, Sweden.

Mitola, J. (2001). Cognitive radio for flexible mobile multimedia communications. *Mobile Networks and Applications*, 6(5), 435–441. doi:10.1023/A:1011426600077.

Moodle. (2012). Retrieved December 10, 2012, from http://moodle.org

Morerio, P., Dabcevic, K., Marcenaro, L., & Regazzoni, C. S. (2012). Distributed cognitive radio architecture with automatic frequency switching. *2012 Complexity in Engineering (COMPENG 2012) Proceedings*. Aachen.

Murray, D., Dixon, M., & Koziniec, T. (2007). *Scanning delays in 802.11 networks*. Paper presented at the 2007 International Conference on Next Generation Mobile Applications, Services and Technologies, 2007. NGMAST '07. New York, NY.

Musavian, L., & Aissa, S. (2009). Fundamental capacity limits of cognitive radio in fading environments with imperfect channel information. *IEEE Transactions on Communications*, 57(11), 3472–3480. doi:10.1109/TCOMM.2009.11.070410.

Musavian, L., & Aissa, S. (2010). Effective capacity of delay-constrained cognitive radio in Nakagami fading channels. *IEEE Transactions on Wireless Communications*, 9(3), 1054–1062. doi:10.1109/TWC.2010.03.081253.

Musavian, L., Aissa, S., & Lambotharan, S. (2011). Adaptive modulation in spectrum-sharing channels under delay quality-of-service constraints. *IEEE Transactions on Vehicular Technology*, 60(3), 901–911. doi:10.1109/TVT.2010.2097282.

Nash, J. F. (1950). Equilibrium points in n-person games. *Proceedings of the National Academy of Sciences of the United States of America, 36*(1), 48–49. doi:10.1073/pnas.36.1.48 PMID:16588946.

Navigli, R., & Velardi, P. (2004). Learning domain ontologies from document warehouses and dedicated web sites. *Journal of Computational Linguistics archive, 30*(2), 151-179.

Nekovee, M. (2012). *QUASAR deliverable D 1.4: Final report on regulatory feasibility assessment*. Retrieved from http://www.quasarspectrum.eu/

Nekovee, M. (2006). Dynamic spectrum access - Concepts and future architectures. *BT Technology Journal, 24*(2), 111–116. doi:10.1007/s10550-006-0047-4.

Nekovee, M., Irnich, T., & Karlsson, J. (2012). Worldwide trends in regulation of secondary access to white spaces using cognitive radio. *IEEE Wireless Communications, 19*(4), 32–40. doi:10.1109/MWC.2012.6272421.

Newman, T. R., Hasan, S. M., DePoy, D., Bose, T., & Reed, J. H. (2010). Designing and Deploying a Building-Wide Cognitive Radio Network Testbed. *IEEE Communications Magazine, 48*(9), 106–112. doi:10.1109/MCOM.2010.5560594.

NFV. (2012). *Network functions virtualisation white paper*. Retrieved December 10, 2012, http://portal.etsi.org/NFV/NFV_White_Paper.pdf

Nguyen, G. D., & Kompella, S. (2010). Channel sharing in cognitive radio networks. In *Proceedings of MILCOM*. MILCOM.

Nguyen, V. A., & Pham, V. C. (2011). Bayesian network to manage learner model in context-aware adaptive system in mobile learning. In Chang, M. et al. (Eds.), *Edutainment 2011* (pp. 63–70). Berlin: Springer. doi:10.1007/978-3-642-23456-9_13.

Ni, S.-Y., Tsend, Y.-C., Chen, Y.-S., & Sheu, J.-P. (1999). The broadcast storm problem in a mobile ad hoc network. In *Proceedings of the 5th Annual ACM/IEEE International Conference on Mobile Computing and Networking (MOBICOM '99)*. ACM/IEEE.

Niyato, D., & Hossain, E. (2007). A game-theoretic approach to competitive spectrum sharing in cognitive radio networks. In *Proceedings of the Wireless Communications and Networking Conference, WCNC 2007*. Hong Kong: WCNC.

Niyato, D., & Hossain, E. (2008). Spectrum trading in cognitive radio networks: A market-equilibrium-based approach. *Wireless Communications, 15*(6).

Niyato, D., & Hossain, E. (2005). Call admission control for QoS provisioning in 4G wireless networks: Issues and approaches. *IEEE Network Magazine, 19*(5), 5–11. doi:10.1109/MNET.2005.1509946.

Niyato, D., & Hossain, E. (2008). Competitive spectrum sharing in cognitive radio networks: A dynamic game approach. *IEEE Transactions on Wireless Communications, 7*(7), 2651–2660. doi:10.1109/TWC.2008.070073.

Niyato, D., & Hossain, E. (2009). Cognitive radio for next-generation wireless networks: An approach to opportunistic channel selection in IEEE 802.11-based wireless mesh. *IEEE Wireless Communications, 16*(1), 46–54. doi:10.1109/MWC.2009.4804368.

Nolan, K. E., Sutton, P. D., Doyle, L. E., Rondeau, T. W., Le, B., & Bostian, C. W. (2007). Dynamic Spectrum Access and Coexistence Experiences Involving Two Independently Developed Cognitive Radio Testbeds. *2nd IEEE International Symposium on New Frontiers in Dynamic Spectrum Access Networks*, (s. 270-275).

Nolte, K., Kaloxylos, A., Tsagkaris, K., Rosowski, T., Stamatelatos, M., & Galani, A. et al. (2010). The E3 architecture: Enabling future cellular networks with cognitive and self-x capabilities. *International Journal of Network Management*.

Noon, E., & Li, H. (2010). Defending Against Hit-and-run Attackers in Collaborative Spectrum Sensing of Cognitive Radio Networks: A Point System. *Vehicular Technology Conference (VTC 2010-Spring), 2010 IEEE 71st*, (pp. 1-5). Knoxville, TN.

Obele, B., Iftikhar, M., & Kang, M. (2011). On the QoS behavior of self-similar traffic in a converged ONU-BS under custom queueing. *Journal of Communications and Networks, 13*(3), 286–297.

Ofcom Consultation on White Space Device Requirements. (2012). Retrieved November 23, 2012 from http://stakeholders.ofcom.org.uk/consultations/whitespaces/?utm_source=updates&utm_medium=email&utm_campaign=whitespaces

Ofcom. (2007). *Digital dividend review - A statement on our approach to awarding the digital dividend*. OFCOM.

OFCOM. (2008). *Digital dividend review: Geographic interleaved awards 470 - 550 MHz and 630 - 790 MHz consultation on detailed award design*. OFCOM.

Ofcom. (2009). *Digital dividend: Cognitive access - Statement on licence-exempting cognitive devices using interleaved spectrum*. OFCOM.

Ofcom. (2011). *Implementing geolocation - Summary of consultation responses and next steps*. OFCOM.

OFDM-PON project. (2011-2013). Retrieved December 2012, from http://cordis.europa.eu/projects/rcn/96242_en.html

Ogbonmwan, S. E., & Li, W. (2006). Multi-threshold bandwidth reservation scheme of an integrated voice/data wireless network. *Elsevier Journal on Computer Communications*, 29(9), 1504–1515. doi:10.1016/j.comcom.2005.09.007.

Ohira, T., & Sawatari, R. (1998). Phase transition in a computer network traffic model. *Physical Review E: Statistical Physics, Plasmas, Fluids, and Related Interdisciplinary Topics*, 58, 193. doi:10.1103/PhysRevE.58.193.

Olafsson, S., & Glover, B. et al. (2007). Future management of spectrum. *BT Technology Journal*, 25(2), 52–63. doi:10.1007/s10550-007-0028-2.

Oneto, L., Herder, E., Abel, F., & Smits, D. (2009). *Making today's learning management systems adaptive*. Paper presented at Learning in the Synergy of Multiple Disciplines Conference. Berlin, Germany.

Ong, S. S., & Hawryszkiewycz, I. (2003). *Towards personalised and collaborative learning management systems*. Paper presented at the Third IEEE International Conference on Advanced Learning Technologies. Athens, Greece.

Openstack. (2012). *Open source software for building private and public clouds*. Retrieved December 10, 2012, from http://www.openstack.org/

Osborne, M. J., & Rubinstein, A. (1994). *A course in game theory*. Cambridge, MA: MIT.

Ouino French. (2012). Retrieved December 10, 2012, from http://www.ouinofrench.com/

Ou, S., Yang, K., & Chen, H.-H. (2010). Integrated Dynamic Bandwidth Allocation in Converged Passive Optical Networks and IEEE 802.16 Networks. *IEEE Systems Journal*, 4(4), 467–476. doi:10.1109/JSYST.2010.2088750.

Oyman, O., Foerster, J., Tcha, Y.-j., & Lee, S.-C. (2010). Toward enhanced mobile video services over WiMAX and LTE[WiMAX/LTE Update]. *IEEE Communications Magazine*, 48(8), 68–76. doi:10.1109/MCOM.2010.5534589.

Paavola, J., & Ekman, R. (2011). *WISE – White space test environment for broadcast frequencies*. Retrieved from http://wise.turkuamk.fi

Padhye, J., Firoiu, V., Towsley, D. F., & Kurose, J. F. (2000). Modeling TCP Reno performance: A simple model and its empirical validation. *IEEE/ACM Transactions on Networking*, 8(2), 133–145. doi:10.1109/90.842137.

Palomar, D. P., & Chiang, M. (2006). A tutorial on decomposition methods for network utility maximisation. *IEEE Journal on Selected Areas in Communications*, 24(8), 1439–1451. doi:10.1109/JSAC.2006.879350.

Palomar, D., & Chiang, M. (2007). *Alternative decompositions for distributed maximization of network utility: Framework and applications*. IEEE Transaction on Automatic Control.

Panwar, S. S., Towsley, D., & Wolf, J. K. (1988). Optimal scheduling policies for a class of queues with customer deadlines to the beginning of service. *Journal of the ACM*, 35(4), 832–844. doi:10.1145/48014.48019.

Paradia, M., Kritikou, Y., Stavroulaki, V., Demestichas, P., Dimitrakopoulos, G., & Glavas, S. et al. (2012). Introducing cognition in web-based, learning management systems for vocabulary teaching. *Journal of Network and Communication Technologies*, 1(1), 51–66.

Parashar, M., & Hariri, S. (2005). Autonomic computing: An overview. In *Unconventional Programming Paradigms*. Berlin: Springer-Verlag. doi:10.1007/11527800_20.

Parekh, A. K., & Gallager, R. G. (1993). A generalized processor sharing approach to flow control in integrated services networks: The single-node case. *IEEE/ACM Transactions on Networking, 1*(3), 344–357. doi:10.1109/90.234856.

Pateromichelakis, E., Shariat, M., Quddus, A., & Tafazolli, R. (2013). *On the evolution of multi-cell scheduling in 3GPP*. IEEE Communications Surveys & Tutorials.

Pauli, V., & Seidel, E. (2011). *Inter-cell interference coordination for LTE-A*. Retrieved May 28, 2012 from http://www.nomor.de/uploads/1d/19/1d196a493af55 11cc92466089924cc5c/2011-09-WhitePaper-LTE-A-HetNet-ICIC.pdf

Pavloska, V., Denkovski, D., Atanasovksi, V., & Gavrikovska, L. (2010). A policy reasoning architecture for cognitive radio networks. In *Proceedings of the 8th International Conference in Communications (COMM)*, (pp. 531-534). ACM. doi: 10.1109/ICCOMM.2010.5509059

Pawelczak, P., Hoeksema, F., Prasad, R. V., & Hekmat, R. (2010). Dynamic Spectrum Access:An Emergency Network Case Study. IEEE DySPAN (s. 601-606). Singapore: IEEE Press.

Pawelczak, P., Janssen, G. J. M., & Prasad, R. V. (2006). WLC10-4: Performance measures of dynamic spectrum access networks. In *Proceedings of IEEE Global Telecommunications Conference*, (pp. 1-6). IEEE.

Pawelczak, P., Prasad, R. V., et al. (2005). Cognitive radio emergency networks–Requirements and design. In *Proceedings of the First IEEE International Symposium on New Frontiers in Dynamic Spectrum Access Networks*. IEEE.

Pawelczak, P., Nolan, K., & Doyle, L., Ser Wah Oh, & Cabric, D. (2011). Cognitive Radio: Ten years of experimentation and development. *IEEE Communications Magazine, 49*(3), 90–100. doi:10.1109/MCOM.2011.5723805.

Pefkianakis, I., Wong, S. H. Y., & Lu, S. (2008). *SAMER: Spectrum aware mesh routing in cognitive radio networks*. Paper presented at the IEEE DySPAN 2008. New York, NY.

Peng, C., Zheng, H., & Zhao, B. Y. (2006). Utilization and fairness in spectrum assignment for opportunistic spectrum access. *Journal in Mobile Network Applications, 11*(4), 555–576. doi:10.1007/s11036-006-7322-y.

Pereirasamy, M., Luo, J., Dillinger, M., & Hartmann, C. (2005). Dynamic inter-operator spectrum sharing for umts fdd with displaced cellular networks. In *Proceedings of the IEEE Wireless Communications and Networking Conference*, (vol. 3, pp. 1720 – 1725). IEEE.

Petrova, M., & Mahonen, P. (2007). Cognitive Resource Manager. I F. H. Fitzek, & M. D. Katz (Red.), Cognitive Wireless Networks (s. 397-422). Springer.

Pham, T. T., Nguyen, H. H., & Tuan, H. D. (2012). Relay assignment for max-min capacity in cooperative wireless networks. *IEEE Transactions on Vehicular Technology, 61*(5), 2387–2394. doi:10.1109/TVT.2012.2192508.

Piro, G., Grieco, L. A., Boggia, G., Fortuna, R., & Camarda, P. (2011). Two-level downlink scheduling for real-time multimedia services in LTE networks. *IEEE Transactions on Multimedia, 13*(5), 1052–1065. doi:10.1109/TMM.2011.2152381.

Polson, J. (2004). Cognitive Radio Applications in Software Defined Radio. *Software Defined Radio Technical Conference*. Phoenix.

Postel, J. (1981). *Internet control message protocol*. IETF.

Qiao, D., Gursoy, M. C., & Velipasalar, S. (2010). A noncooperative power control game in multi-access fading channels with quality of service (QoS) constraints. *Physical Communication, 3*(2), 97–104. doi:10.1016/j.phycom.2010.03.003.

QinetiQ, Ltd. (2006). *A study of the provision of aggregation of frequency to provide wider bandwidth services*. Final report for Office of Communications (Ofcom). Ofcom.

Qingqi, P., Hongning, L., & Kefeng, F. (2011). Defense Against Objective Function Attacks in Cognitive Radio Networks. *Chinese Journal of Electronics*, 138-142.

Rahul, H., Kushman, N., Katabi, D., Sodini, C., & Edalat, F. (2008). Learning to share: Narrowband-friendly wideband wireless networks. *ACM SIGCOMM, 38*(4), 147–158. doi:10.1145/1402946.1402976.

Raisinghani, V. T., & Iyer, S. (2006). Cross layer feedback architecture for mobile device protocol stacks. *IEEE Communications Magazine, 44*(1), 85–92. doi:10.1109/MCOM.2006.1580937.

Raju, P., & Ahmed, V. (2011). Enabling technologies for developing next-generation learning object repository for construction. *Journal of Automation in Construction, 22,* 247–257. doi:10.1016/j.autcon.2011.07.008.

Ramachandran, K., Kokku, R., Zhang, H., & Gruteser, M. (2010). Symphony: Synchronous two-phase rate and power control in 802.11 WLANs. *IEEE/ACM Transactions on Networking, 18*(4), 1289–1302. doi:10.1109/TNET.2010.2040036.

Ramakrishnan, K., Floyd, S., & Black, D. (2001). The addition of explicit congestion notification (ECN) to IP. *RFC 3168.*

Ramaswami, R., Sivarajan, K., & Sasaki, G. (2009). *Optical Networks: A Practical Perspective* (3rd ed.). Morgan Kaufmann.

Ranaweera, C., Wong, E., Lim, C., & Nirmalathas, A. (2012). Next generation optical-wireless converged network architectures. *IEEE Network, 26*(2), 22–27. doi:10.1109/MNET.2012.6172271.

Rao, V. S., Prasad, R. V., Yadati, C., & Niemegeers, I. (2010). Distributed heuristics for allocating spectrum in cr ad hoc networks. In *Proceedings of IEEE Globecom.* IEEE.

Raspopovic, M., Thompson, C., & Chandra, K. (2005). Performance models for wireless spectrum shared by wideband and narrowband sources.[IEEE.]. *Proceedings of IEEE Milcom, 2005,* 1–6.

Ratasuk, R., Tolli, D., & Ghosh, A. (2010). Carrier aggregation in LTE-advanced. In *Proceedings of the Seventy-First IEEE Vehicular Technology Conference (VTC 2010 Spring),* (pp. 1-5). IEEE.

Raychaudhuri, D., Mandayam, N. B., Evans, J. B., Ewy, B. J., Seshan, S., & Steenkiste, P. (2006). CogNet: An architectural foundation for experimental cognitive radio networks within the future internet. In *Proceedings of ACM/IEEE MobiArch'06,* (pp. 11–16). ACM/IEEE.

Razavi, R., Klein, S., & Claussen, H. (2010). A fuzzy reinforcement learning approach for self-optimization of coverage in LTE networks. *Bell Labs Technical Journal, 15*(3), 153–175. doi:10.1002/bltj.20463.

Razmerita, L., Angehrn, A., & Maedche, A. (2003). *Ontology-based user modeling for knowledge management systems.* Paper presented at 9th International Conference on User Modeling. Johnstown, PA.

Reddy, Y. B., & Bullmaster, C. (2008). Cross-Layer Design in Wireless Cognitive Networks. *International Conference on Parallel and Distributed Computing, Applications and technologies* (s. 462-467). IEEE Computer Society.

Rehmani, M. H., Viana, A. C., Khalife, H., & Fdida, S. (2011). Improving data dissemination in multi-hop cognitive radio ad-hoc networks. In *Proceedings of the 3rd International ICST Conference on Ad Hoc Networks (ADHOCNETS 2011).* Paris, France: ADHOCNETS.

Ren, S., & Letaief, K. B. (2009). Maximizing the effective capacity for wireless cooperative relay networks with QoS guarantees. *IEEE Transactions on Communications, 57*(7), 2148–2159. doi:10.1109/TCOMM.2009.07.070585.

Rezaei, Z., & Mobininejad, S. (2012). Energy saving in wireless sensor networks. *International Journal of Computer Science & Engineering Survey, 3*(1), 20–27. doi:10.5121/ijcses.2012.3103.

Rezki, Z., & Alouini, M. (2012). Ergodic capacity of cognitive radio under imperfect channel-state information. *IEEE Transactions on Vehicular Technology, 61*(5), 2108–2119. doi:10.1109/TVT.2012.2195042.

Robinson, D. L., Shukla, A. K., Burns, J., & Atefi, A. (2005). Resource trading for spectrum aggregation and management. In *Proceedings of the First IEEE International Symposium on New Frontiers in Dynamic Spectrum Access Networks (DySPAN'05),* (pp. 666-671). IEEE.

Rosetta Stone. (2012). Retrieved December 10, 2012, from http://www.rosettastone.eu

Rostamzadeh, K., & Gopalakrishnan, S. (2011). Analysis of emergency message dissemination in vehicular networks. In *Proceedings of the IEEE Wireless Communications and Networking Conference (WCNC),* (pp. 575 –580). IEEE.

RSPG. (2010). *RSPG10-306 radio spectrum policy group report on cognitive technologies*. Brussels: RSPG.

RSPG. (2011a). *RSPG10-348 final RSPG opinion on cognitive technologies*. Brussels: RSPG.

RSPG. (2011b). *RSPG11-392 report on collective use of spectrum (CUS) and other spectrum sharing approaches*. Brussels: RSPG.

Safdar, G., & O'Neill, M. (2009). Common Control Channel Security Framework for Cognitive Radio Networks. *Proceedings on Vehicular Technology Conference, 2009. VTC Spring 2009. IEEE 69th*, (pp. 1-5). Barcelona.

Sahai, N. H. A., & Tandra, R. (2004). Some fundamental limits on cognitive radios. In *Proceedings of the 42 Allerton Conference on Communication, Control and Computing*. Allerton.

Sahai, R. T. A., & Hoven, N. (2006). Opportunistic spectrum use for sensor networks: The need for local cooperation. In *Proceedings of IPSN*. IPSN.

Salameh, H. A. B., Krunz, M. M., & Younis, O. (2009). MAC protocol for opportunistic cognitive radio networks with soft guarantees. *IEEE Transactions on Mobile Computing*, *8*(10), 1339–1352. doi:10.1109/TMC.2009.19.

Salami, G., Attar, A., Holland, R. T., Oliver, & Aghvami, H. (2011). A comparison between the centralized and distributed approaches for spectrum management. *IEEE Communications Surveys and Tutorials*, *13*(2), 274–290.

Salem, M., Adinoyi, A., Rahman, M., Yanikomeroglu, H., Falconer, D., & Young-Doo, K. et al. (2010). An overview of radio resource management in relay-enhanced OFDMA-based networks. *IEEE Communications Surveys & Tutorials*, *12*(3), 422–438. doi:10.1109/SURV.2010.032210.00071.

Samaras, H., Giouvanakis, T., Bousiou, D., & Tarabanis, K. (2006). Towards a new generation of multimedia learning research. *AACE Journal*, *14*(1), 3–30.

Santos, E., Brown, S., Lejter, M., Ngai, G., Banks, S., & Stytz, M. (1999). *Dynamic user model construction with Bayesian networks for intelligent information queries*. Paper presented at the Twelfth International Florida Artificial Intelligence Research Society Conference. Orlando, FL.

Sato, H. (1976). *Information transmission through a channel with relay*. Tech Report B76-7. Honolulu, HI: University of Hawaii.

Sbattella, L., & Tedesco, R. (2004). *Profiling and tutoring users in virtual campus*. Paper presented at the Fifth International Conference on Information Technology Based Higher Education and Training. Istanbul, Turkey.

Schaffrath, G., Werle, C., Papadimitriou, P., Feldmann, A., Bless, R., & Greenhalgh, A. ... Mathy, L. (2009). Network virtualization architecture: Proposal and initial prototype. In *Proceedings of the 1st ACM Workshop on Virtualized Infrastructure Systems and Architectures*. ACM.

Scutari, G., & Barbarossa, S. (2005). Distributed space-time coding for regenerative relay networks. *IEEE Transactions on Wireless Communications*, *4*(5), 2387–2399. doi:10.1109/TWC.2005.853883.

Self-NET Project. (2007). *Self-management of cognitive future internet elements*. Retrieved December 10, 2012, from https://www.ict-selfnet.eu/

Sen, A. (1993). Markets and freedom: Achievements and limitations of the market mechanism in promoting individual freedoms. *Oxford Economic Papers*, *45*(4), 519–541.

Sendonaris, A., Erkip, E., & Aazhang, B. (1998). Increasing uplink capacity via user cooperation diversity. In *Proceedings 1998 IEEE International Symposium on Information Theory*. IEEE.

Sendonaris, A., Erkip, E., & Aazhang, B. (2003). User cooperation diversity: Part II: Implementation aspects and performance analysis. *IEEE Transactions on Communications*, *51*(11), 1939–1948. doi:10.1109/TCOMM.2003.819238.

Sengupta, S., Hong, K., Chandramouli, R., & Subbalakshmi, K. P. (2011). SpiderRadio: A Cognitive Radio Network with Commodity Hardware and Open Source Software. *IEEE Communications Magazine*, *49*(3), 101–109. doi:10.1109/MCOM.2011.5723806.

Sesia, S., Toufik, I., & Baker, M. (2011). LTE – The UMTS Long Term Evolution – From Theory to Practice (Second Edition including Release 10 for LTE-Advanced ed.). John Wiley & Sons.

Shah, A., & Haimovich, A. M. (2000). Performance analysis of maximal ratio combining and comparison with optimum combining for mobile radio communications with cochannel interference. *IEEE Transactions on Vehicular Technology*, *49*(4), 1454–1463. doi:10.1109/25.875282.

Shakkottai, S., & Srikant, R. (2002). Scheduling real-time traffic with deadlines over a wireless channel. *Springer Wireless Networks*, *8*(1), 13–26. doi:10.1023/A:1012763307361.

Shannon, C. E. (1948). A mathematical theory of communication. *The Bell System Technical Journal*, *27*, 379–423.

Shannon, P. C. E. (1949). Communication in the presence of noise. *Proceedings of the Institute of Radio Engineers*, *37*, 10–21.

Sheetal, A. (2012). *WDM-Passive Optical Networks*. LAP LAMBERT Academic Publishing.

Shen, G., Tucker, R., & Chae, C.-J. (2007). Fixed Mobile Convergence Architectures for Broadband Access: Integration of EPON and WiMAX. *IEEE Communications Magazine*, *45*(8), 44–50. doi:10.1109/MCOM.2007.4290313.

Sherman, M., Mody, A. N., Martinez, R., Rodriguez, C., & Reddy, R. (2008). IEEE standards supporting cognitive radio and networks, dynamic spectrum access, and coexistence. *IEEE Communications Magazine*, *46*(7), 72–79. doi:10.1109/MCOM.2008.4557045.

Shiang, H. P., & Schaar, M. V. D. (2008). Delay-sensitive resource management in multi-hop cognitive radio networks. In *Proceedings of IEEE DySpan*. IEEE.

Shin, H., & Song, J. B. (2008). MRC analysis of cooperative diversity with fixed-gain relays in Nakagami-m fading channels. *IEEE Transactions on Wireless Communications*, *7*(6), 2069–2074. doi:10.1109/TWC.2008.070812.

Simoens, S., Muñoz Medina, O., Vidal, J., & del Coso, A. (2010). Compress-and-forward cooperative MIMO relaying with full channel state information. *IEEE Transactions on Signal Processing*, *58*(2), 781–791. doi:10.1109/TSP.2009.2030622.

Simon, R., Huang, L., Farrugia, E., & Setia, S. (2005). Using multiple communication channels for efficient data dissemination in wireless sensor networks. In *Proceedings of the IEEE International Conference on Mobile Adhoc and Sensor Systems Conference*. IEEE.

Simon, M. K., & Alouini, M.-S. (1999). A unified performance analysis of digital communication with dual selective combining diversity over correlated Rayleigh and Nakagami-m fading channels. *IEEE Transactions on Communications*, *47*(1), 33–44. doi:10.1109/26.747811.

Simon, M. K., & Alouini, M.-S. (2005). *Digital communications over fading channels* (2nd ed.). New York: Wiley-IEEE Press.

Skalli, H., Ghosh, S., Das, S. K., Lenzini, L., & Conti, M. (2007). Channel assignment strategies for multiradio wireless mesh networks: Issues and solutions. *IEEE Communications Magazine*, *45*(11), 86–95. doi:10.1109/MCOM.2007.4378326.

Skene, J., Raimondi, F., & Emmerich, W. (2010). Service-level agreements for electronic services. *IEEE Transactions on Software Engineering*, *36*(2), 288–304. doi:10.1109/TSE.2009.55.

Skiena, S. S. (2008). *The algorithm design manual* (2nd ed.). Berlin: Springer. doi:10.1007/978-1-84800-070-4.

Skordoulis, D., Ni, Q., Chen, H.-H., Stephens, A. P., Liu, C., & Jamalipour, A. (2008). IEEE 802.11n MAC frame aggregation mechanisms for next-generation high-throughput WLANs. *IEEE Transactions on Wireless Communications*, *15*(1), 40–47. doi:10.1109/MWC.2008.4454703.

Skoutas, D. N., & Rouskas, A. N. (2010). Scheduling with QoS provisioning in mobile broadband wireless systems. In *Proceedings of the European Wireless Conference (EW)*, (pp. 422-428). EW.

Skoutas, D. N., Makris, P., & Skianis, C. (2013). *Optimized admission control scheme for coexisting femtocell, wireless and wireline networks*. Springer Telecommunication Systems Journal.

Skoutas, D. N., & Rouskas, A. N. (2009). A scheduling algorithm with dynamic priority assignment for WCDMA systems. *IEEE Transactions on Mobile Computing*, *8*(1), 126–138. doi:10.1109/TMC.2008.106.

Slingerland, A. M. R., Pawelczak, P., Prasad, R. V., Lo, A., & Hekmat, R. (2007). Performance of transport control protocol over dynamic spectrum access links.[IEEE.]. *Proceedings of IEEE DySPAN, 2007*, 486–495.

Smith, E. (2012). The impact of network availabilty on meeting service level agreements. *Journal of the Institute of Telecommunications Professionals*, 6(1), 39–46.

Sokolowski, C., Petrova, M., de Baynast, A., & Mähönen, P. (2008). Cognitive Radio Testbed: Exploiting Limited Feedback in Tomorrow's Wireless Communication Networks. *IEEE International Conference on Communications Workshops*, (s. 493-498).

Sole, R. V. (2001). Information transfer and phase transitions in a model of internet traffic. *Physica*, 289(3-4), 595–605. doi:10.1016/S0378-4371(00)00536-7.

Song, Y., & Xie, J. (2010). Common hopping based proactive spectrum handoff in cognitive radio ad hoc networks. In *Proceedings of GlobeCom*. IEEE. doi:10.1109/GLOCOM.2010.5683840.

Spapis, P., Katsikas, G., Stamatelatos, M., Chatzikokolakis, K., Arapoglou, R., & Alonistioti, N. (2011). Learning enhanced environment perception for cooperative power control. In *Proceedings of the International Conference on Mobile Ubiquitous Computing, Systems, Services and Technologies, UBICOMM 2011*. UBICOMM. ISBN: 978-1-61208-171-7

Specht, D. (1991). A General Regression Neural Network. *IEEE Transactions on Neural Networks*, 2(6). doi:10.1109/72.97934 PMID:18282872.

Srikanth, S., Murugesa Pandian, P., & Fernando, X. (2012). Orthogonal frequency division multiple access in WiMAX and LTE: a comparison. *IEEE Communications Magazine*, 50(9), 153–161. doi:10.1109/MCOM.2012.6295726.

Srivastava, V., & Motani, M. (2005). Cross-layer design: A survey and the road ahead. *IEEE Communications Magazine*, 43(12), 112–119. doi:10.1109/MCOM.2005.1561928.

Srivatsa, M., Xiong, L., & Liu, L. (2005). TrustGuard: countering vulnerabilities in reputation management for decentralized overlay networks. *Proceedings of the 14th international conference on World Wide Web* (pp. 422-431). Chiba: ACM New York.

Starobinski, D., & Xiao, W. (2010). Asymptotically optimal data dissemination in multichannel wireless sensor networks: Single radios suffice. *IEEE/ACM Transactions on Networking*, 18(3), 695–707. doi:10.1109/TNET.2009.2032230.

Stavroulaki, V., Kritikou, Y., & Darra, E. (2009). *Acquiring and learning user information in the context of cognitive device management*. Paper presented at Joint Workshop on Cognitive Wireless Networks and Systems - Cognitive Radio Networking, held in conjunction with IEEE International Conference on Communications. Dresden, Germany.

Stavroulaki, V., Tsagkaris, K., Logothetis, M., Georgakopoulos, A., Demestichas, P., Gebert, J., & Filo, M. (2011). Opportunistic networks: An approach for exploiting cognitive radio networking technologies in the future Internet. *IEEE Vehicular Technology Magazine*, 6(3), 52–59. doi:10.1109/MVT.2011.941892.

Std, I. E. E. E. 802.3. (1985). Carrier sense multiple access with collision detection. IEEE.

Strinati, E., Yang, S., & Belfiore, J.-C. (2007). Adaptive modulation and coding for hybrid cooperative networks. In *Proceedings of the IEEE International Conference on Communications (ICC '07)*, (pp. 4191 – 4195). Glasgow, UK: IEEE.

Su, H., & Zhang, X. (2008). Cross-layer based opportunistic MAC protocols for QoS provisionings over cognitive radio wireless networks. *IEEE Journal on Selected Areas in Communications*, 26(1), 118–129. doi:10.1109/JSAC.2008.080111.

Sun, L., & Wang, W. (2011). On distribution and limits of information dissemination latency and speed in mobile cognitive radio networks. In *Proceedings IEEE INFOCOM*. IEEE.

Sun, Q., Zeng, X., Chen, N., Ke, Z., & Rasool, R. (2008). A non-cooperative power control algorithm for wireless ad hoc and sensor networks. In *Proceedings of the Second International Conference on Genetic and Evolutionary Computing (WGEC '08)*, (pp. 181-184). WGEC. doi: 10.1109/WGEC.2008.95

Sun, Y. L., & Liu, Y. (2012, March). Security of Online Reputation Systems: The evolution of attacks and defenses. *Signal Processing Magazine, IEEE*, pp. 87-97.

Sutton, P., Doyle, L. E., & Nolan, K. E. (2006). A reconfigurable platform for cognitive networks. In *Proceedings of the 1st International Conference on Cognitive Radio Oriented Wireless Networks and Communications*, (pp. 1 – 5). IEEE.

Sutton, P. D., Nolan, K. E., & Doyle, L. E. (2008). Cyclostationary Signatures in Practical Cognitive Radio Applications. *IEEE Journal on Selected Areas in Communications, 26*(1), 13–24. doi:10.1109/JSAC.2008.080103.

Sutton, P., Lotze, J., Lahlou, H., Fahmy, S., Nolan, K. E., & Rondeau, T. W. et al. (2010, September). Iris: An Architecture for Cognitive Radio Networking Testbeds. *IEEE Communications Magazine*, 114–122. doi:10.1109/MCOM.2010.5560595.

Suzhi, B., & Zhang, Y. J. A. (2012). Outage-optimal TDMA based scheduling in relay-assisted MIMO cellular networks. *IEEE Transactions on Wireless Communications, 11*(4), 1488–1499. doi:10.1109/TWC.2012.021512.111150.

Tairan, W., Cano, A., & Giannakis, G. B. (2005). Efficient demodulation in cooperative schemes using decode-and-forward relays. In *Proceedings of the Conference Record of the Thirty-Ninth Asilomar Conference on Signals, Systems and Computers,* (pp. 1051- 1055). Asilomar.

Tairan, W., Giannakis, G. B., & Renqiu, W. (2008). Smart regenerative relays for link-adaptive cooperative communications. *IEEE Transactions on Communications, 56*(11), 1950–1960. doi:10.1109/TCOMM.2008.060688.

Talay, A. C., & Altilar, D. T. (2009). *ROPCORN: Routing protocol for cognitive radio ad hoc networks.* Paper presented at the International Conference on Ultra Modern Telecommunications & Workshops. New York, NY.

Tan, K., Wan, Z., Zhu, H., & Andrian, J. (2007). CODE: Cooperative medium access for multirate wireless ad hoc network. In *Proceedings of the 4th Annual IEEE Communications Society Conference on Sensor, Mesh and Ad Hoc Communications and Networks (SECON '07)*, (pp. 1-10). IEEE.

Tanaka, H. (2011). *Convergence of optical and wireless networks. OptoeElectronics and Communications Conference* (pp. 389–390). OECC.

Tan, E., & Pearce, N. (2012). *Open education videos in the classroom: exploring the opportunities and barriers to the use of YouTube in teaching introductory sociology.* Research in Learning Technology. doi:10.3402/rlt.v19s1/7783.

Tang, L., Sun, Y., Gurewitz, O., & Johnson, D. (2011). PW-MAC: An energy-efficient predictive-wakeup MAC protocol for wireless sensor networks. In *Proceedings of the IEEE Infocom* (pp. 1305-1313). IEEE. doi: 10.1109/INFCOM.2011.5934913

Tang, P. K., Chew, Y. H., Ong, L. C., & Haldar, M. K. (2006). Performance of secondary radios in spectrum sharing with prioritized primary access. In *Proceedings of IEEE Milcom*. IEEE.

Tang, J., & Zhang, X. (2007a). Quality-of-service driven power and rate adaptation over wireless links. *IEEE Transactions on Wireless Communications, 6*(8), 3058–3068. doi:10.1109/TWC.2007.051075.

Tang, J., & Zhang, X. (2007b). Quality-of-service driven power and rate adaptation for multichannel communications over wireless links. *IEEE Transactions on Wireless Communications, 6*(12), 4349–4360. doi:10.1109/TWC.2007.06031.

Tang, J., & Zhang, X. (2007c). Cross-layer modeling for quality of service guarantees over wireless links. *IEEE Transactions on Wireless Communications, 6*(12), 4504–4512. doi:10.1109/TWC.2007.06087.

Tang, J., & Zhang, X. (2008). Cross-layer-model based adaptive resource allocation for statistical QoS guarantees in mobile wireless networks. *IEEE Transactions on Wireless Communications, 7*(6), 2318–2328. doi:10.1109/TWC.2008.060293.

Tan, K., Zhang, J., Fang, J., Liu, H., Ye, Y., & Wang, S. et al. (2009). *Sora: High Performance Software Radio using General Purpose Multi-core Processors.* Boston: USENIX NSDI.

Tarokh, V., Seshadri, N., & Calderbank, A. R. (1998). Space-time codes for high data rate wireless communication: Performance criterion and code construction. *IEEE Transactions on Information Theory, 44*(2), 744–764. doi:10.1109/18.661517.

TCPDUMP & LIBCAP library. (n.d.). Retrieved April 12, 2012, from http://www.tcpdump.org/

Tedesco, R., Dolog, P., Nejdl, W., & Allert, H. (2006). *Distributed Bayesian networks for user modeling.* Paper presented at World Conference on E-Learning in Corporate, Government, Healthcare, and Higher Education. Chesapeake, VA.

Telatar, E. (1999). Capacity of multi-antenna Gaussian channels. *European Transactions on Telecommunications, 10*(6), 585–595. doi:10.1002/ett.4460100604.

Tell Me More. (2012). Retrieved December 10, 2012, from http://www.tellmemore.com

Tellambura, C., Annamalai, A., & Bhargava, V. K. (2003). Closed-form and infinite series solutions for the MGF of a dual-diversity selection combiner output in bivariate Nakagami fading. *IEEE Transactions on Communications, 51*(4), 539–542. doi:10.1109/TCOMM.2003.810870.

The, K. H., Kong, P. Y., & Jiang, S. (2003). Proactive earliest due date scheduling in wireless packet networks. In *Proceedings of the International Conference on Communication Technology,* (pp. 816–820). ACM.

Thomas, R. W., Da Silva, L. A., & Mackenzie. (2005). Cognitive networks. In *Proceedings of IEEE DySPAN,* (pp. 352–60). IEEE.

Thomas, R. W., Friend, D. H., Da Silva, L. A., & Mackenzie, A. B. (2006). Cognitive networks: Adaptation and learning to achieve end-to-end performance objecives. *IEEE Communications Magazine, 44*(12), 51–57. doi:10.1109/MCOM.2006.273099.

Thomas, R., Friend, D., DaSilva, L., & McKenzie, A. (2006). Cognitive drivers: Adaptation and learning to achieve end-to-end performance objectives. *IEEE Communications Magazine, 44*(12), 51–57. doi:10.1109/MCOM.2006.273099.

Tian, Y., Xu, K., & Ansari, N. (2005). *TCP in wireless environments: Problems and solutions.* IEEE Radio Communications.

Timmers, M., Pollin, S., Dejonghe, A., Van der Perre, L., & Catthoor, F. (2010). A distributed multichannel MAC protocol for multihop cognitive radio networks. *IEEE Transactions on Vehicular Technology, 59*(1), 446–459. doi:10.1109/TVT.2009.2029552.

Tkachenko, A., Cabric, D., & Brodersen, R. W. (2007). Cyclostationary Feature Detector Experiments using Reconfigurable BEE2. *International Conference on Dynamic Spectrum Access Networks.*

Tseng, Y.-C., Ni, S.-Y., & Shih, E.-Y. (2001). Adaptive approaches to relieving broadcast storms in a wireless multihop mobile ad hoc network. In *Proceedings of the 21st International Conference on Distributed Computing Systems.* IEEE.

Van der Meer, S., Davy, S., Davy, A., Carroll, S., Jennings, B., & Strassner, J. (2006). Autonomic networking: Prototype implementation of the policy continuum. In *Proceedings of the 1st Workshop on Broadband Convergence Networks.* IEEE.

Van Der Meulen, E. C. (1971). Three-terminal communication channels. *Advances in Applied Probability, 3,* 120–154. doi:10.2307/1426331.

Vartiainen, J., Hoyhtya, M., Lehtomaki, J., & Braysy, T. (2010). Priority channel selection based on detection history database. In *Proceedings of CROWNCOM.* CROWNCOM.

Vassaki, S., Poulakis, M., & Panagopoulos, A. D., & Constantinou, P. (2011). *Optimal power allocation under QoS constraints in cognitive radio systems.* Paper presented at the IEEE 8th International Symposium on Wireless Communication Systems (ISWCS '11). Aachen, Germany.

Vassaki, S., Panagopoulos, A. D., & Constantinou, P. (2012). Effective capacity and optimal power allocation for mobile satellite systems and services. *IEEE Communications Letters, 16*(1), 60–63. doi:10.1109/LCOMM.2011.110711.111881.

Vecchio, M., Viana, A. C., Ziviani, A., & Friedman, R. (2010). Deep: Density-based proactive data dissemination protocol for wireless sensor networks with uncontrolled sink mobility. *Computer Communications, 33*(8), 929–939. doi:10.1016/j.comcom.2010.01.003.

Viana, A. C., Herault, T., Largilliers, T., Peyronnet, S., & Zaidi, F. (2010). Supple: A flexible probabilistic data dissemination protocol for wireless sensor networks. In *Proceedings of the 13th ACM International Conference on Modeling, Analysis, and Simulation of Wireless and Mobile Systems.* ACM Press.

Walsh, W. E., Tesauro, G., Kephart, J. O., & Das. (2004). Utility functions in autonomic systems. In *Proceedings of the International Conference on Autonomic Computing*, (pp. 70-77). IEEE.

Wang, B. H. (2008). Routing strategies in traffic network and phase transition in network traffic flow. *Pramana: Journal of Physics, 71*(2).

Wang, B., Ji, Z., & Liu, K. J. R. (2007b). Self-learning repeated game framework for distributed primary-prioritized dynamic spectrum access. In *Proceedings of the IEEE Workshop on Networking Technologies for Software Define Radio Networks*, (pp. 1-8). IEEE.

Wang, C.-W., Wang, L.-C., & Adachi, F. (2010). Modeling and analysis for reactive-decision spectrum handoff in cognitive radio networks. In *Proceedings of the IEEE Global Telecommunications Conference (GLOBECOM 2010)*. IEEE.

Wang, H., Ren, J., & Li, T. (2010). Resource allocation with load balancing for cogntive radio networks. In *Proceedings of IEEE GlobeCom*. IEEE.

Wang, L.-C., & Wang, C.-W. (2008). Spectrum handoff for cognitive radio networks: Reactive-sensing or proactive-sensins? In *Proceedings of the IEEE International Performance, Computing and Communications Conference (IPCCC 2008)*. IEEE.

Wang, Q., & Abu-Rgheff, M. A. (2003). Cross-layer signaling for next-generation wireless systems. In *Proceedings of the IEEE Wireless Communications and Networking (WCNC)*, (pp. 1084 – 1089). IEEE.

Wang, B., Ji, Z., & Liu, K. J. R. (2007a). Primary-prioritized markov approach for dynamic spectrum access. [IEEE.]. *Proceedings of IEEE DySPAN, 2007*, 507–515.

Wang, B., & Liu, K. J. R. (2011). Advances in cognitive radio networks: A survey. *IEEE Journal of Selected Topics in Signal Processing, 5*(1), 5–23. doi:10.1109/JSTSP.2010.2093210.

Wang, B., Wu, Y., & Liu, K., J., R. (2010). Game theory for cognitive radio networks: An overview. *Computer Networks, 54*(14), 2537–2561. doi:10.1016/j.comnet.2010.04.004.

Wang, B., & Zhao, D. (2010). Scheduling for long term proportional fairness in a cognitive wireless network with spectrum underlay. *IEEE Transactions on Wireless Communications, 9*(3), 1150–1158. doi:10.1109/TWC.2010.03.090802.

Wang, F., Krunz, M., & Cui, S. (2008). Price-based spectrum management in cognitive radio networks. *IEEE Journal of Selected Topics in Signal Processing, 2*(1), 74–87. doi:10.1109/JSTSP.2007.914877.

Wang, H.-M., Yin, Q., & Xia, X.-G. (2010). Fast Kalman equalization for time-frequency asynchronous cooperative relay networks with distributed space-time codes. *IEEE Transactions on Vehicular Technology, 59*(9), 4651–4658. doi:10.1109/TVT.2010.2076352.

Wang, L.-C., Wang, C.-W., & Adachi, F. (2011). Load-balancing spectrum decision for cognitive radio networks. *IEEE Journal on Selected Areas in Communications, 29*(4), 757–769. doi:10.1109/JSAC.2011.110408.

Wang, L.-C., Wang, C.-W., & Feng, K.-T. (2011). A queueing-theoretical framework for QoS-enhanced spectrum management in cognitive radio networks. *IEEE Wireless Communications, 18*(6), 18–26. doi:10.1109/MWC.2011.6108330.

Wang, T., Chiu, T. K., Huang, L. J., Fu, R. X., & Hsieh, T. C. (2009). An English vocabulary learning system based on fuzzy theory and memory cycle. In Spaniol, M. et al. (Eds.), *Advances in Web Based Learning – ICWL 2009* (pp. 420–423). Berlin: Springer. doi:10.1007/978-3-642-03426-8_50.

Wang, W., & Huang, A. (2010). Spectrum aggregation: Overview and challenges. *Network Protocols and Algorithms, 2*(1), 184–196. doi:10.5296/npa.v2i1.329.

Wang, W., Li, H., Sun, Y. L., & Han, Z. (2009). *Attack-Proof Collaborative Spectrum Sensing in Cognitive Radio Networks* (pp. 130–134). doi:10.1109/CISS.2009.5054704.

Wang, W., Liu, X., & Krishnaswamy, D. (2009). Robust routing and scheduling in wireless mesh networks under dynamic traffic conditions. *IEEE Transactions on Mobile Computing, 8*(12), 1705–1717. doi:10.1109/TMC.2009.86.

Wang, X. G., Min, G., Mellor, J. E., Al-Begain, K., & Guan, L. (2005). An adaptive QoS framework for integrated cellular and WLAN networks. *Elsevier Journal on Computer Networks*, *47*(2), 167–183. doi:10.1016/j.comnet.2004.07.003.

Wang, X., Vasilakos, A. V., Chen, M., Liu, Y., & Kwon, T. T. (2012). A survey of green mobile networks: Opportunities and challenges. *Springer Mobile Networks and Applications*, *17*(1), 4–20. doi:10.1007/s11036-011-0316-4.

Wang, Y. H., & Liao, H. C. (2011). Data mining for adaptive learning in a TESL-based e-learning system. *Journal of Expert Systems with Applications*, *38*, 6480–6485. doi:10.1016/j.eswa.2010.11.098.

Wang, Y., Keller, E., Biskeborn, B., Van der Merwe, J., & Rexford, J. (2008). Virtual routers on the move: Live router migration as a network-management primitive. *SIGCOMM CCR*, *38*(4), 231–242. doi:10.1145/1402946.1402985.

Wan-Jen, H., Hong, Y.-W. P., & Kuo, C.-C. J. (2008). Lifetime maximization for amplify-and-forward cooperative networks. *IEEE Transactions on Wireless Communications*, *7*(5), 1800–1805. doi:10.1109/TWC.2008.061075.

Wannstrom, J. (2012). *LTE-advanced*. Retrieved May 10, 2012, from http://www.3gpp.org/IMG/pdf/lte_advanced_v2.pdf

Webb, W. (2012). On using white space spectrum. *IEEE Communications Magazine*, *50*(8), 145–151. doi:10.1109/MCOM.2012.6257541.

Weiss, T., Hillenbrand, J., Krohn, A., & Jondral, F. K. (2004). *Mutual interference in OFDM-based spectrum pooling systems*. Paper presented at the IEEE 59th Vehicular Technology Conference, 2004. New York, NY.

Wei, W., & Zakhor, A. (2009). Interference aware multipath selection for video streaming in wireless ad hoc networks. *IEEE Transactions on Circuits and Systems for Video Technology*, *19*(2), 165–178. doi:10.1109/TCSVT.2008.2009242.

Wei, Y., Song, M., & Song, J. (2008). An AODV-improved routing based on power control in WiFi mesh networks. In *Proceedings of Electrical and Computer Engineering, 2008* (pp. 001349–001352). CCECE.

White Smoke. (2012). Retrieved December 10, 2012, from http://www.whitesmoke.com

White, S. R., Hanson, J. E., Whalley, I., Chess, D. M., & Kephart, J. O. (2004). An architectural approach to autonomic computing. In *Proceedings of the International Conference on Autonomic Computing*. IEEE.

Wieselthier, J., Nguyen, G., & Ephremides, A. (2000). On the construction of energy-efficient broadcast and multicast trees in wireless networks. In *Proceedings of the Nineteenth Annual Joint Conference of the IEEE Computer and Communications Societies INFOCOM*, (vol. 2, pp. 585–594). IEEE.

Winter, R., Schiller, J. H., Nikaein, N., & Bonnet, C. (2006). CrossTalk: Cross-layer decision support based on global knowledge. *IEEE Communications Magazine*, *44*(1), 93–99. doi:10.1109/MCOM.2006.1580938.

Winters, J. H. (1984). Optimum combining in digital mobile radio with cochannel interference. *IEEE Journal on Selected Areas in Communications*, *2*(4), 528–539. doi:10.1109/JSAC.1984.1146095.

Winters, J. H., & Salz, J. (1998). Upper bounds on the bit-error rate of optimum combining in wireless systems. *IEEE Transactions on Communications*, *46*(12), 1619–1624. doi:10.1109/26.737400.

Wireless Innovation Forum. (n.d.). *Wireless Innovation Forum*. Retrieved August 2012, from SDR Forum: http://www.wirelessinnovation.org/

WOPROF project. (2009-2011). Retrieved December 2012, from http://cordis.europa.eu/projects/rcn/90604_en.html

Wu, D., & Negi, R. (2003). Effective capacity: a wireless link model for support of quality of service. *IEEE Transactions on Wireless Communications*, *2*(4), 630–643.

Wu, H., Yang, F., Tan, K., Chen, J., Zhang, Q., & Zhang, Z. (2006). Distributed channel assignment and routing in multiradio multichannel multihop wireless networks. *IEEE Journal on Selected Areas in Communications*, *24*(11), 1972–1983. doi:10.1109/JSAC.2006.881638.

Wu, S. H., Chao, H. L., Ko, C. H., Mo, S. R., Jiang, C. T., & Li, T. L. et al. (2012). A cloud model and concept prototype for cognitive radio networks. *IEEE Wireless Communications*, *19*(4), 49–58. doi:10.1109/MWC.2012.6272423.

Wyglinski, A. M., Nekovee, M., & Hou, T. (2010). *Cognitive Radio Communications and Networks: Principles and Practice*. Academic Press.

Wyglinski, A. M., Nekovee, M., & Hou, Y. T. (2009). *Cognitive radio communications and networks: Principles and practice*. London: Elsevier.

Wyner, A. D., & Ziv, J. (1976). The rate-distortion function for source coding with side information at the receiver. *IEEE Transactions on Information Theory, 22*(1), 1–11. doi:10.1109/TIT.1976.1055508.

Xenakis, C. (2008). Security Measures and Weaknesses of the GPRS Security Architecture. *International Journal of Network Security*, 158-169.

Xiao, Q., Li, Y., Zhao, M., Zhou, S., & Wang, J. (2009). Opportunistic channel selection approach under collision probability constraint in cognitive radio systems. *Computer Communications, 32*(18), 1914–1922. doi:10.1016/j.comcom.2009.06.015.

Xiao, Y., & Hu, F. (2008). *Cognitive radio networks*. Boca Raton, FL: CRC Press. doi:10.1201/9781420064216.

Xie, X., & Guo, W. (2011). *Fundamental effective capacity limits of cognitive radio in fading environments with imperfect channel information*. Paper presented at International Conference on Computational Problem-Solving (ICCP '11). Aachen, Germany.

Xing, Y., Chandramouli, R., Mangold, S., & Sai Shankar, N. (2005). Analysis and performance evaluation of a fair channel access protocol for open spectrum wireless networks. In *Proceedings of IEEE ICC 2005*, (pp. 1179-1183). IEEE.

Xing, Y., Chandramouli, R., Mangold, S., & Sai Shankar, N. (2006). Dynamic spectrum access in open spectrum wireless networks. *IEEE Journal on Selected Areas in Communications, 24*(3), 626–637. doi:10.1109/JSAC.2005.862415.

Xu, J., Zhao, M., Fortes, J., Carpenter, R., & Yousif, M. (2007). On the use of fuzzy modeling in virtualized data center management. In *Proceedings of the 4th International Conference on Autonomic Computing*. IEEE.

Ya-Feng, W., Yin-long, X., Guo-Liang, C., & Kun, W. (2004). On the construction of virtual multicast backbone for wireless ad hoc networks. In *Proceedings of the IEEE International Conference on Mobile Ad-hoc and Sensor Systems*, (pp. 294 – 303). IEEE.

Yang, L., Cao, L., Zheng, H., & Belding, E. (2008). Traffic-aware dynamic spectrum access. In *Proceedings of the Fourth International Wireless Internet Conference (WICON 2008)*. WICON.

Yang, Y., Feng, Q., Sun, Y. L., & Dai, Y. (2008). RepTrap: A Novel Attack on Feedback-based Reputation Systems. *Proceedings of the 4th international conference on Security and privacy in communication networks - SecureComm '08* (p. Article No. 8). Istanbul: ACM New York.

Yang, C. (2007). CDMA Passive Optical Network Using Prime Code With Interference Elimination. *IEEE Photonics Technology Letters, 19*(7), 516–518. doi:10.1109/LPT.2007.893579.

Yang, C. G., Li, J. D., & Tian, Z. (2010). Optimal power control for cognitive radio networks under coupled interference constraints: A cooperative game-theoretic perspective. *IEEE Transactions on Vehicular Technology, 59*(4), 1696–1706. doi:10.1109/TVT.2009.2039502.

Yang, H.-C., & Alouini, M.-S. (2003). Performance analysis of multibranch switched diversity systems. *IEEE Transactions on Communications, 51*(5), 782–794. doi:10.1109/TCOMM.2003.811408.

Yang, K., Ou, S., Guild, K., & Chen, H.-H. (2009). Convergence of Ethernet PON and IEEE 802.16 Broadband Access Networks and its QoS-Aware Dynamic Bandwidth Allocation Scheme. *IEEE Journal on Selected Areas in Communications, 27*(2), 101–116. doi:10.1109/JSAC.2009.090202.

Yang, L., Cao, L., & Zheng, H. (2008). Proactive channel access in dynamic spectrum networks. *Elsevier Physical Communications Journal, 1*, 103–111. doi:10.1016/j.phycom.2008.05.001.

Yang, Z., Cheng, G., Liu, W., Yuan, W., & Cheng, W. (2008). Local coordination based routing and spectrum assignment in multi-hop cognitive radio networks. *Mobile Networking Applications, 13*(1-2), 67–81. doi:10.1007/s11036-008-0025-9.

Yan, Z., Rong, Y., Nekovee, M., Yi, L., Shengli, X., & Gjessing, S. (2012). Cognitive machine-to-machine communications: visions and potentials for the smart grid. *IEEE Network, 26*(3), 6–13. doi:10.1109/MNET.2012.6201210.

Yao, J., Mark, J. W., Wong, T. C., Chew, Y. H., Lye, K. M., & Chua, K.-C. (2004). Virtual partitioning resource allocation for multiclass traffic in cellular systems with QoS constraints. *IEEE Transactions on Vehicular Technology, 53*(3), 847–864. doi:10.1109/TVT.2004.825746.

Yarandi, M., Jahankhani, H., Dastbaz, M., & Tawil, A. R. (2011). *Personalised mobile learning system based on item response theory.* Paper presented at the 6th Annual Conference in Advances in Computing and Technology. London, UK.

Ye, W., Heidemann, J., & Estrin, D. (2002). An energy-efficient MAC protocol for wireless sensor networks. In *Proceedings of the IEEE Infocom,* (pp. 1567-1576). IEEE. doi: 10.1109/INFCOM.2002.1019408

Yick, J., Mukherjee, B., & Ghosal, D. (2008). Wireless sensor network survey. *The International Journal of Computer and Telecommunications Networking, 52*(12), 2292–2330.

Yilmaz, O., Chen, I. R., Kulczycki, G., & Frakes, W. B. (2010). Performance analysis of spillover-partitioning call admission control in mobile wireless networks. *Springer Wireless Personal Communications, 53*(1), 111–131. doi:10.1007/s11277-009-9673-8.

Yindi, J., & Hassibi, B. (2006). Distributed space-time coding in wireless relay networks. *IEEE Transactions on Wireless Communications, 5*(12), 3524–3536. doi:10.1109/TWC.2006.256975.

Yi, S., Blostein, S. D., & Julian, C. (2003). Exact outage probability for equal gain combining with cochannel interference in Rayleigh fading. *IEEE Transactions on Wireless Communications, 2*(5), 865–870. doi:10.1109/TWC.2003.816796.

Yi, Z., & Kim, I.-M. (2008). Diversity order analysis of the decode-and-forward cooperative networks with relay selection. *IEEE Transactions on Wireless Communications, 7*(5), 1792–1799. doi:10.1109/TWC.2008.061041.

Yoon, S.-U., & Ekici, E. (2010). Voluntary spectrum handoff: A novel approach to spectrum management in CRNS. *Proceedings of, ICC,* ICC.

Yoshimoto, B., McGraw, I., & Seneff, S. (2009). *Rainbow rummy: A web-based game for vocabulary acquisition using computer-directed speech.* Paper presented at International Workshop on Speech and Language Technology in Education. Warwickshire, UK.

Young-Chai, K., Alouini, M.-S., & Simon, M. K. (2000). Analysis and optimization of switched diversity systems. *IEEE Transactions on Vehicular Technology, 49*(5), 1813–1831. doi:10.1109/25.892586.

Younis, O., Kant, L., Chang, K., & Young, K. (2009). Cognitive manet design for mission-critical networks. *IEEE Communications Magazine,* 64–71. doi:10.1109/MCOM.2009.5273810.

Yu, C. H., Doppler, K., Ribeiro, C. B., & Tirkkonen, O. (2011). Resource sharing optimization for device-to-device communication underlaying cellular networks. *IEEE Transactions on Wireless Communications, 10*(8), 2752–2763. doi:10.1109/TWC.2011.060811.102120.

Yue, W., Sun, Q., & Jin, S. (2010). Performance analysis of sensor nodes in a WSN with sleep/wakeup protocol. In *Proceedings of the Ninth International Symposium on Operations Research and Its Applications (ISORA'10),* (pp. 370–377). ISORA.

Zahariadis, T., Grüneberg, K., & Celetto, L. (2011). Seamless Content Delivery over Mobile 3G+/4G Networks. *Mobile Networks and Applications, 16*(3), 351–360. doi:10.1007/s11036-010-0259-1.

Zakaria, M. R., Moore, A., Stewart, C. D., & Brailsford, T. J. (2003). *'Pluggable' user models for adaptive hypermedia in education.* Paper presented at the Fourteenth ACM Conference on Hypertext and Hypermedia. Nottingham, UK.

Zhang, C., & Wang, F. (2010). *E-learning instructional platforms based on network and multimedia technology.* Paper presented at the Second International Workshop on Education Technology and Computer Science (ETCS). Wuhan, China.

Zhang, i., & Ansari, N. (2011). On assuring end-to-end QoE in next generation networks: challenges and a possible solution. *IEEE Communications Magazine, 49* (7), 185-191.

Zhang, R., & Hanzo, L. (n.d.). Wireless cellular networks. *IEEE Vehicular Technology Magazine, 5*(4), 31-39.

Zhang, Q. T., & Lu, H. G. (2002). A general analytical approach to multi-branch selection combining over various spatially correlated fading channels. *IEEE Transactions on Communications*, 50(7), 1066–1073. doi:10.1109/TCOMM.2002.800804.

Zhang, X., Tang, J., Chen, H. H., Ci, S., & Guizani, M. (2006). Cross-layer-based modeling for quality of service guarantees in mobile wireless networks. *IEEE Communications Magazine*, 44(1), 100–106. doi:10.1109/MCOM.2006.1580939.

Zhang, Z. (1988). Partial converse for a relay channel. *IEEE Transactions on Information Theory*, 34(5), 1106–1110. doi:10.1109/18.21243.

Zhao, J., Zheng, H., & Yang, G. H. (2005). Distributed coordination in dynamic spectrum allocation networks. In *Proceedings of the First IEEE International Symposium on New Frontiers in Dynamic Spectrum Access Networks (DySPAN)*, (pp. 259–268). IEEE.

Zhao, Y., Mao, S., Neel, J. O., & Reed, J. H. (April 2009). Performance Evaluation of Cognitive Radios: Metrics, Utility Functions, and Methodology. *Proceedings of the IEEE*, 642-659.

Zhao, Q., Geirhofer, S., Tong, L., & Sadler, B. M. (2008). Opportunistic spectrum access via periodic channel sensing. *IEEE Transactions on Signal Processing*, 56(2), 785–796. doi:10.1109/TSP.2007.907867.

Zhao, Q., & Sadler, B. M. (2007). A survey of dynamic spectrum access. *IEEE Signal Processing Magazine*, 24(3), 79–89. doi:10.1109/MSP.2007.361604.

Zhao, Q., Tong, L., Swami, A., & Chen, Y. (2007). Decentralized cognitive mac for opportunistic spectrum access in ad hoc networks: A pomdp framewrok. *IEEE Journal on Selected Areas in Communications*, 25(3), 589–600. doi:10.1109/JSAC.2007.070409.

Zhao, Y., Adve, R., & Lim, T. J. (2007). Improving amplify-and-forward relay networks: Optimal power allocation versus selection. *IEEE Transactions on Wireless Communications*, 6(8), 3114–3123.

Zheng, K., Hu, F., Wang, W., Xiang, W., & Dohler, M. (2012). Radio resource allocation in LTE-advanced cellular networks with M2M communications. *IEEE Communications Magazine*, 50(7), 184–192. doi:10.1109/MCOM.2012.6231296.

Zhu, G.-M., Akyildiz, I. F., & Kuo, G.-S. (2008). *STOD-RP: A spectrum-tree based on-demand routing protocol for multi-hop cognitive radio networks.* Paper presented at the IEEE Global Telecommunications Conference. New York, NY.

Zhu, J., & Li, S. (2006). Channel allocation mechanisms for cognitive radio networks via repeated multi-bid auction. In *Proceedings of ICWMMN 2006*. ICWMMN.

Zhu, L., & Zhou, H. (2008). Two types of attacks against Cognitive Radio Network MAC Protocols. *Proceedings on the 2008 International Conference on Computer Science and Software Engineering*, (pp. 1110-1113). Washington DC: IEEE Computer Society.

Zhu, Y., Suo, D., & Gao, Z. (2010). Secure Cooperative Spectrum Trading in Cognitive Radio Networks: A Reversed Stackelberg Approach. *Proceedings on 2010 International Conference, MEDIACOM 2010*, (pp. 202-205). Hong Kong.

Zhu, H., & Cao, G. (2006). rDCF: A relay-enabled medium access control protocol for wireless ad hoc networks. *IEEE Transactions on Mobile Computing*, 5(9), 1201–1214. doi:10.1109/TMC.2006.137.

Zhu, P., Li, J., & Wang, X. (2007). A new channel parameter for cognitive radio. In *Proceedings of CrownCom, 2007*. CrownCom. doi:10.1109/CROWNCOM.2007.4549845.

Zhu, X., Shen, L., & Yum, T. P. (2007). Analysis of cognitive radio spectrum access with optimal channel reservation. *IEEE Communications Letters*, 11, 304–306. doi:10.1109/LCOM.2007.348282.

Zimmermann, E., Herhold, P., & Fettweis, G. (2003). On the performance of cooperative diversity protocols in practical wireless systems. In *Proceedings of the IEEE 58th Vehicular Technology Conference (VTC 2003-Fall)*, (pp. 2212- 2216). Orlando, FL: IEEE.

Zlatanov, N., Hadzi-Velkov, Z., Karagiannidis, G. K., & Schober, R. (2011). Cooperative diversity with mobile nodes: Capacity outage rate and duration. *IEEE Transactions on Information Theory*, 57(10), 6555–6568. doi:10.1109/TIT.2011.2165794.

Zogas, D. A., Karagiannidis, G. K., & Kotsopoulos, S. A. (2005). Equal gain combining over Nakagami-*n* (Rice) and Nakagami-*q* (Hoyt) generalzied fading channels. *IEEE Transactions on Wireless Communications*, 4(2), 374–379. doi:10.1109/TWC.2004.842953.

Zubow, A., Kurth, M., & Redlich, J. P. (2007). *An opportunistic cross-layer protocol for multi-channel wireless networks*. Paper presented at the IEEE PIMRC 2007. New York, NY.

Zyba, G., Voelker, G., Ioannidis, S., & Diot, C. (2011). Dissemination in opportunistic mobile ad-hoc networks: The power of the crowd. In *Proceedings IEEE INFOCOM* (pp. 1179–1187). IEEE. doi:10.1109/INFCOM.2011.5934896.

About the Contributors

Thomas Lagkas received the BSc degree (with honors) in Computer Science from the Department of Informatics, Aristotle University, Thessaloniki, Greece. He received the PhD degree on "Wireless Communication Networks" from the same department, in 2006. During his PhD studies, he was awarded the PhD candidates' scholarship by the Research Committee of the Aristotle University. He is a Lecturer at the Computer Science Department, International Faculty of the University of Sheffield, CITY College. He has been an adjunct Lecturer at the Department of Informatics and Telecommunications Engineering, University of Western Macedonia, Greece, since 2007. He was also a Laboratory Associate at the Technological Educational Institute of Thessaloniki, since 2004, and a Scientific Associate, since 2008. Dr. Lagkas has been awarded the postdoctoral research fellowship by the State Scholarships Foundation of Greece. His interests are in the areas of wireless communication networks, medium access control, QoS provision, mobile multimedia communications, power saving, fairness ensure, resource allocation in wireless sensor networks, bandwidth distribution in cooperative wireless networks, scheduling in wireless broadband networks, and health/environmental monitoring networks with relevant publications at a number of widely recognized international scientific journals and conferences.

Panagiotis G. Sarigiannidis received the B.Sc. and Ph.D. degrees in computer science from the Aristotle University of Thessaloniki, Thessaloniki, Greece, in 2001 and 2007, respectively. He is currently a Lecturer with the University of Western Macedonia, Kozani, Greece. His research interests include medium access protocols in optical networks, dynamic bandwidth allocation schemes in passive optical networks, scheduling policies in IEEE 802.16 wireless networks, wireless push systems design and optimization, quality of service provisioning in optical and wireless networks, traffic estimation and prediction via numerical analysis, and design of burst allocation for optical burst switching networks. He has published over 40 papers in international journals, conferences, and book chapters.

Malamati Louta is Assistant Professor at the Department of Informatics and Telecommunications Engineering, University of Western Macedonia, Greece. She holds M.Eng. (1997) and Ph.D. (2000) degrees in Electrical and Computer Engineering from the National Technical University of Athens (N.T.U.A) and M.B.A. degree from the N.T.U.A., the National & Kapodistrian University of Athens and the University of Piraeus. From 1999 to 2005, she was a member of the staff of Public Power Corporation, working as a senior engineer, as a member of the team that developed the telecommunications section of PPC S.A. and as Information System Security Sub-Sector Manager. From 2005 to 2008, Dr. Louta was Assistant Professor at the Department of Business Administration, Technological Educational Institute of Western Macedonia, Greece, and additionally was Adjunct Assistant Professor at the Department of Informatics and Telecommunications Engineering, University of Western Macedonia, Greece. From 2008 to 2010, she was Lecturer at the Department of Informatics and Telematics of Harokopio University of Athens. Her research interests include the design and performance evaluation of communication networks, autonomic / cognitive networking, ad-hoc wireless networking, telecommunications service and software engineering, algorithms and complexity theory. She is the author of over 65 peer-reviewed publications in these areas. Dr Louta has been actively involved in a number of research and development projects of the E.U.. She serves as a member of the editorial board of three international journals, as a technical program committee member and as a reviewer in a number of international conferences and journals. She is a member of the IEEE, the ACM, and the Technical Chamber of Greece, and served as a member of the committee of National, European Programs and Innovation at the Department of Western Macedonia of the Technical Chamber of Greece. Additional information may be found at http://users.uowm.gr/louta.

Periklis Chatzimisios serves as an Assistant Professor with the Computing Systems, Security, and Networks (CSSN) Research Lab of the Department of Informatics at the Alexander TEI of Thessaloniki, Greece. He currently participates in several European and National research projects acting in research and management positions. Since 2010, Dr. Chatzimisios serves as a Member of the Standards Development Board for the IEEE Communication Society (ComSoc). He is very active in several IEEE activities such as handling Dissemination activities and International relations for the VTS & AESS Joint Greece, serving as Chapter Associate Editor for the Newsletter of the IEEE Greece Section as well as Counselor of the IEEE Student Branch of the Alexander TEI of Thessaloniki. He is also acting as Departmental Erasmus Coordinator and as a member of the Institutional Erasmus Committee, having established many agreements of Alexander TEI of Thessaloniki with high-quality European Universities, Research Centers, and Telecommunication Operators. Dr. Chatzimisios serves as Organizing/TPC member and co-Chair for several conferences and he holds editorial board positions for many IEEE and non-IEEE journals. He has been an Organizer/Invited Speaker for many dissemination events, talks, and seminars. He is the author of 8 books and more than 60 peer-reviewed papers and book chapters in the areas of multimedia communications (mainly Quality of Service and Quality of Experience), wireless communications (mainly in IEEE 802.11 and 802.16 protocols) and security. His published research work has received more than 500 citations by other researchers.

* * *

Evgenia Adamopoulou received her Diploma as well as her Ph.D. degree in Mobile Communications (2009) from the School of Electrical and Computer Engineering of the National Technical University of Athens. Since 2005, she has been working as a researcher at the same institution, in the Computer Networks Laboratory of the Institute of Communication and Computer Systems. Her primary research interests include mobile and computer networks, cognitive and software-defined radio, computer and smartphone application development, mobile services, ICT applied in transport, and machine learning techniques. Currently, she serves as Task Leader and Dissemination Manager in the FP7 projects EcoGem and EMERALD. She has been actively involved in several European and national research project in the aforementioned fields. She has participated in the Technical Program Committees in international conferences and served as a reviewer for top ranked scientific journals. She has authored over 50 publications in the aforementioned fields.

Nancy Alonistioti has a B.Sc. degree and a PhD degree in Informatics and Telecommunications (Dept. of Informatics and Telecommunications, University of Athens). She has working experience as senior researcher and project manager in the Dept. of Informatics and Telecommunications at University of Athens. She has participated in several national and European projects, (MOBIVAS, ANWIRE, E2R, E3, SELFNET, UNIVERSELF etc.) and has experience as Project and Technical manager of the IST-MOBIVAS, IST-ANWIRE, ICT-SELFNET projects, which had a focus on reconfigurable mobile systems, cognitive mobile networks and FI. She has served as PMT member and WP Leader of the FP6 IST- E2R project. She is co-editor and author in *Software Defined Radio, Architectures, Systems and Functions*, published by John Wiley in May 2003. She has served as lecturer in University of Piraeus and she has recently joined the faculty of Dept. Informatics and Telecommunications of Univ. of Athens. She is TPC member in many conferences in the area of mobile communications and mobile applications for systems and networks beyond 3G. She has over 55 publications in the area of mobile communications, reconfigurable, cognitive, and autonomic systems and networks and Future Internet.

Peter Anker is a Senior Research Fellow at the section Economics of Infrastructure of the Delft University of Technology. Peter is performing PhD research on spectrum management, including the role of new technologies, such as cognitive radio. In 1988 Peter graduated in Electrical Engineering at the Delft University of Technology. He has been working in the field of telecommunications ever since. At the moment, he is working as a senior policy advisor on frequency management at the ministry of Economic Affairs. He is actively involved in policy to further liberalize spectrum usage at both the European and national level. As such, he is co-founder of the Dutch CRplatform.nl.

Roi Arapoglou received her B.Sc and M.Sc in Advanced Informational Systems, from the Department of Informatics and Telecommunications NKUA, in 2009 and 2011, respectively. She has been working as a research associate for the SCAN group since February 2011. She has been involved in several EU FP7 ICT projects and she is currently pursuing her PhD at the Department of Informatics and Telecommunications NKUA, under the guidance of Lecturer Nancy Alonistioti. Her main research interests include energy efficient techniques for future autonomous communication networks.

Alireza Babaei is currently a research scientist in Wireless@VT at Virginia Tech. He has served as a guest editor for *IEEE Wireless Communications* Magazine special issue in "Dynamic Spectrum Management" and a symposium TPC chair for the IEEE ICNC 2013. He has been TPC member and technical reviewer for numerous IEEE conferences and journal publications. He received a Ph.D. degree in Electrical and Computer Engineering from George Mason University in 2009 where he also received an outstanding graduate student award. His areas of active research include modeling and performance evaluation of wireless networks, information and communications theory, and cognitive radio communications and networks. He is a member of IEEE.

Gilberto Berardinelli received his Ph.D. degree in wireless communication from Aalborg University, Denmark, in 2010. In 2006, he worked with the Radio Frequency Engineering Department in Vodafone NV, Padova, where he studied issues related to the coverage of HSDPA services, and also radio propagation in urban and suburban environments. He is currently a postdoctoral researcher in the Radio Access Technology Section at Aalborg University. His research interests are mostly focused on physical layer design for 4G and Beyond 4G systems, thus including multiple access schemes, multi-antenna systems, and iterative turbo receivers. He collaborates with Nokia-Siemens Networks in the development of solutions for future wireless systems.

Athina Bourdena received her B.Sc. from the Department of Applied Informatics and Multimedia of Technological Educational Institute of Crete in 2007 and her M.Sc. in Digital Communications and Networks from the Department of Digital Systems of the University of Piraeus in 2009. She is working towards her Ph.D. within the field radio resource management in cognitive radio networks, at the University of the Aegean, Department of Information & Communication Systems Engineering. She has actively participated in several EU funded research projects of FP7. She has more than 20 publications at various international conferences proceedings, workshops, scientific journals and book chapters. She has acted as a reviewer for several scientific journals and member of conferences technical program committees. Her research interests include cognitive radio networks, radio resource management, networking traffic analysis, end-to-end QoS, dynamic bandwidth management, and next generation networks.

Pascal Bouvry received the Ph.D. degree in computer science from the University of Grenoble, Grenoble, France, in 1994. He is currently a Professor with the Faculty of Sciences, Technology and Communication, University of Luxembourg, Luxembourg City, Luxembourg, and is heading the Computer Science and Communication Research Unit (http://csc.uni.lu). He specializes in parallel and evolutionary computing. His current research interests include the application of nature-inspired computing for solving reliability, security, and energy-efficiency problems in clouds, grids, and ad hoc networks.

Andrea F. Cattoni received his Master Degree in Telecommunications Engineering and his PhD in Information and Communication Sciences and Technologies from the University of Genova, Genova, Italy, in 2004 and 2008, respectively. Since 2008, he has been chief scientist in a joint research lab between the University of Genova and Selex Communications. From November 2008, he works as Post Doc researcher first and Associate Professor then at Aalborg University. Andrea is also Research Consultant at Nokia Siemens Network, Aalborg, Denmark. Andrea F. Cattoni is author of more than 30 scientific publications. He is Danish Substitue Member in the Management Committee and Working Group Leader in the COST Action IC0902. He serves as Technical Program Committee Member and as a reviewer in several International Conferences and Journals. His current research topics include Cognitive Radio, Radio Resource Management, Local Area access methods, Beyond 4G systems.

Konstantinos Chatzikokolakis received his BSc from the Department of Informatics and Telecommunications of the National Kapodistrian University of Athens in 2008. He received his MSc in "Computer System Technologies" at the same department on 2012. He is currently a PhD candidate at the same department. Since October 2010, he serves as a researcher in the SCAN group of Lecturer Nancy Alonistioti, in the Department of Informatics and Telecommunications of the National and Kapodistrian University of Athens (UoA), in the context of several EU-funded ICT Projects and he has served as PMT member and WP Leader of the FP7 SACRA project. His research interests include Dynamic Resource Allocation, Cognitive Radio Networks, Future Networks, Network Management, and Evolutionary Algorithms. Parts of his work have already been published in conferences and journals.

Philip Constantinou received the Diploma degree in physics from the National University of Athens (NTUA), Athens, Greece, in 1971, the M.S. degree in applied science from the University of Ottawa, Ottawa, ON, Canada in 1976, and the Dr. Eng. (Ph.D.) degree in electronics from the University of Carleton, Ottawa, in 1983. From 1980 to 1984, he was a Spectrum Engineer and the Head of the Equipment Approval Section, Department of Communications, Ottawa. From 1984 to 1989, he was a Senior Research Scientist on Digital Mobile Communications with the National Center for Scientific Research Demokritos, Athens, Greece. In 1989, he became a Faculty Member with the Department of Electrical and Computer Engineering, NTUA, where he became a Full Professor in 1996 and is currently the Director of the Mobile Radio Communications Laboratory. His research interests include mobile radio communications, mobile satellite and digital communications, radio channel modeling, radio coverage measurements, and interference problems.

Noël Crespi holds Masters' degrees from the Universities of Orsay and Canterbury, a Diplome d'ingénieur from Telecom ParisTech and a Ph.D and Habilitation from Paris VI University. From 1993-95 he worked at CLIP, Bouygues Telecom, and in 1995 joined France Telecom R&D where he was involved in Intelligent Network paradigms for value added services. For Orange (France Telecom's Internet, mobile and television division) he led the Mobicarte prepaid service project to define, architect and deploy an infrastructure that hosted more than 10 million mobile subscribers. He has played a key role in standardisation as a delegate in a number of committees and as the editor for CAMEL, the Intelligent Network standard for mobile networks; he was appointed as the coordinator for France Telecom's standardisation activities for the core network and then for all GSM/UMTS standards at ETSI's plenary committee. In 1999, he joined Nortel Networks as Telephony Programme manager for France and Middle East-Africa. He was responsible for the evolution of the switching area, and led key programmes for the evolution of Nortel products. He has also worked for ETSI as an independent contractor. He joined Institut Mines-Telecom in 2002 and is currently professor and MSc Programme Director, leading the Service Architecture Laboratory. He coordinates the standardisation activities for Institut Telecom at ETSI, 3GPP and ITU-T. He is also a Visiting Professor at the Asian Institute of Technology as well as Adjunct Professor at KAIST (Korea), and is on the 4-person Scientific Advisory Board of FTW (Austria). His current research interests are in Service Architectures, Communication Services, P2P Social Networks, and the Internet of Things/Services. He is the author/co-author of than 160 research papers and 140 contributions in standardization.

Krešimir Dabčević obtained his titles of Bachelor of Science in Electrical Engineering and Information Technology, and Master of Science in Information and Communication Technology from the Faculty of Electrical Engineering and Computing, University of Zagreb, Croatia, in 2009 and 2011, respectively. Since 2012, he is a PhD student in Space Science and Engineering with the focus on Cognitive Radio Technologies at the University of Genova, Italy. His research interests include security aspects of Cognitive Radio technology, and application of Game Theory to Cognitive Radio.

Konstantinos Demestichas received his Diploma, as well as his Ph.D. degree in Mobile Communications (2009), from the School of Electrical and Computer Engineering of the National Technical University of Athens. Since 2005, he has been working as a researcher at the same institution, in the Computer Networks Laboratory of the Institute of Communication and Computer Systems. His primary research interests include B3G wireless networks, cognitive radio, computer and telecommunication software engineering, intelligent transport and smart mobility services, and machine learning techniques. He has been actively involved in several European and national research project in the aforementioned fields. Currently, he serves as Group Leader in the FP7 project EcoGem and as Technical Manager in the FP7 project EMERALD. He has participated in the Technical Program Committees of international conferences and served as a reviewer for top ranked scientific journals. He has authored over 50 publications in the aforementioned fields.

Panagiotis Demestichas is Professor at the University of Piraeus, Department of Digital Systems since April 2012, where he also drives the development of the laboratory of Telecommunication Networks and integrated Services (TNS). He is also the head of the department since September 2011. Furthermore, Prof. Demestichas has 20 years of experience in international and national R&D projects and has served as a Project Coordinator (FP7/ ICT OneFIT) and a Technical Manager (FP7/ ICT E3). He is the chairman of WG6 titled "Cognitive Systems and Networks for a Wireless Future Internet", of the Wireless World Research Forum. Prof. Demestichas has many publications in international journals and refereed conferences. He is a member of the IEEE, ACM and of the Technical Chamber of Greece. His research interests include the design and performance evaluation of high-speed, wireless and wired, broadband networks, software engineering, network management, algorithms and complexity theory, and queuing theory.

Yasir Faheem received Ph.D. degree in Networks and Information Technology from Université Paris Nord, France in 2012. Prior to that, he obtained MS Research degree with specialization in Networks and Distributed Systems from Université Nice Sophia Antipolis, France in 2008, and BS (Computer Science) degree from NUCES-FAST, Pakistan in 2006. Currently, he is an Assistant Professor in the department of Computer Science at COMSATS Institute of Information Technology, Islamabad, Pakistan. His current research interests include wireless sensor networks, mobile ad-hoc networks and cognitive radio networks.

Nelson Luis Saldanha da Fonseca received his Ph.D degree in Computer Engineering from The University of Southern California in 1994. He is a Full Professor at Institute of Computing of The University of Campinas, Campinas, Brazil. He has published 300+ papers and supervised 50+ graduate students. As Visiting Professor, he lectured at the University of Trento, the University of Pisa and the University of Basque Country. He is the recipient of the 2012 IEEE Communications Society (ComSoc) Joseph LoCicero Award for Exemplary Service to Publications and the 2011 ComSoc Latin America Service award. He received the Medal of the Chancelor of the University of Pisa (2007). He is also the recipient of the Elsevier Computer Network Journal Editor of Year 2001 award. He is past EiC of the *IEEE Communications Surveys and Tutorials*, past EiC of *ComSoc Electronic Newsletter*, and past Editor of the *Global Communications Newsletter*. He is Senior Editor for the *IEEE Communications Surveys and Tutorials* and Senior Editor for the *IEEE Communications Magazine*, a member of the editorial board of *Computer Networks, Peer-to-Peer Networking and Applications, Journal of Internet Services and Applications*, and *International Journal of Communication Systems*. He served in the editorial board of *IEEE Transactions on Multimedia*.He founded the IEEE Latin America Conference on Communications (LATINCOM) and the Latin America Conference on Cloud Computing and Communications

(LATINCLOUD). He was technical chair of over 10 IEEE conferences. Nelson is an active volunteer of the IEEE Communications Society. Currently, he is ComSoc Vice Chair Member Relations. He served as Member-at-Large in ComSoc Board of Governors, Director of Latin America Region and Director of on-line Services.

Fabrizio Granelli is IEEE ComSoc Distinguished Lecturer for 2012-13, and Associate Professor at the Dept. of Information Engineering and Computer Science (DISI) of the University of Trento (Italy). From 2008, he is deputy head of the academic council in Information Engineering. He received the "Laurea" (M.Sc.) degree in Electronic Engineering and the Ph.D. in Telecommunications Engineering from the University of Genoa, Italy, in 1997 and 2001, respectively. In August 2004 and August 2010, he was visiting professor at the State University of Campinas (Brasil). He is author or co-author of more than 130 papers with topics related to networking, with focus on performance modeling, wireless communications and networks, cognitive radios and networks, green networking and smart grid communications. Dr. Granelli was guest-editor of *ACM Journal on Mobile Networks and Applications, ACM Transactions on Modeling and Computer Simulation*, and *Hindawi Journal of Computer Systems, Networks, and Communications*. He is Founder and General Vice-Chair of the First International Conference on Wireless Internet (WICON'05) and General Chair of the 11th and 15th IEEE Workshop on Computer-Aided Modeling, Analysis, and Design of Communication Links and Networks (CAMAD'06 and IEEE CAMAD'10). He is TPC Co-Chair of IEEE GLOBECOM Symposium on "Communications QoS, Reliability and Performance Modeling" in the years 2007, 2008, 2009, and 2012. He was officer (Secretary 2005-2006, Vice-Chair 2007-2008, Chair 2009-2010) of the IEEE ComSoc Technical Committee on Communication Systems Integration and Modeling (CSIM), and Associate Editor of *IEEE Communications Letters* (2007-2011).

Kiam Cheng How received the BE degree in Computer Engineering in 1999 and the MSc degree in Communication Software and Networks in 2004 from the Nanyang Technological University. He is currently working towards the PhD degree at the Nanyang Technological University. His research interests include wireless networking, optical networking, network security, and so forth.

Alexandros Kaloxylos received the B.Sc. degree in Computer Science from the University of Crete, Greece, in 1993, the M.Phil. degree in Computing and Electrical Engineering from the Heriot-Watt University, Scotland, in 1994, and the Ph.D. degree in Informatics and Telecommunications from the University of Athens in 1999. From 1990 to 1993, he was a staff member of the Computer Centre of the University of Crete, and a researcher in the Foundation of Research and Technology Hellas (FORTH). From 1994 to 1995, he was a research associate at the University of Wales. From 1995 until today, he is a researcher at the Communications Network Laboratory of the University of Athens. In 2002, he joined the faculty of the University of Peloponnese, where he is presently an Assistant Professor in the Department of Telecommunications Science and Technology. He has participated in numerous projects realized in the context of EU programs as well as National Initiatives. He has currently published over 80 papers in international journals and conferences. He is a senior member of IEEE and a member of the editorial board of the *IEEE Communication's Society Survey and Tutorials Electronic Journal*.

George T. Karetsos was born in Karditsa, Greece. He received the diploma in electrical engineering in 1992 and the Ph.D. in telecommunication systems in 1996, both from the National Technical University of Athens (NTUA), Greece. He is currently an associate professor in the Information Technology and Telecommunications department of the Technology Education Institute of Larissa, Greece, and a senior research associate at the Technological Research Center of Thessaly, Greece. He has participated in the Technical Program Committees of more than fifty international conferences and workshops. He has also acted as reviewer in various journals related to computer communications and wireless networking. His research interests are in the areas of active networking, cognitive radios, heterogeneous wireless networking, performance evaluation, and resource management for fixed and wireless networks. He is a member of the IEEE and of the Technical Chamber of Greece.

George Katsikas has received his B.Sc. degree from the Department of Informatics and Telecommunications of the National and Kapodistrian University of Athens (NKUA) in June 2010, and he is currently pursuing his M.Sc. studies in Communication Systems and Networks in the same department. He pursued the 1st year of his M.Sc. studies with honours. He serves as a research fellow in the Self-Evolving Cognitive and Autonomic Networking (SCAN) Group of NKUA and has already participated in EU-funded ICT Projects. Parts of his work have been published in several conferences. His main research interests are Cloud computing and networking, network management, machine learning, B3G communication systems, and Software Engineering. Since February 2011, he is also a laboratory assistant in Department of Informatics and Telecommunications, for the courses "Communication Networks" and "'Software Development for Telecommunications."

Dzmitry Kliazovich is a Research Fellow at the Faculty of Science, Technology, and Communication of the University of Luxembourg. He holds an award-winning Ph.D. in Information and Telecommunication Technologies from the University of Trento, Italy. Prior to joining the University of Luxembourg, he was an ERCIM Research Fellow at the VTT Technical Research Centre of Finland and a Scientific Advisor for Wireless Communications at the Create-Net Research Centre, Italy. In 2005, he was a Visiting Researcher at the Computer Science Department of the University of California at Los Angeles (UCLA). A year later he joined Nokia Siemens Networks with the responsibility of starting up a research direction focusing on 3G Long-Term Evolution (LTE). Dr. Kliazovich is a holder of several scientific awards including fellowship grants provided by the European Research Consortium for Informatics and Mathematics (ERCIM), the IEEE Communication Society, Italian Ministry of Education, and the University of Trento. His work on energy-efficient scheduling in cloud computing environments received Best Paper Award at the IEEE/ACM International Conference on Green Computing and Communications (GreenCom) in 2010. Dr. Kliazovich is the author of more than 70 research papers, Editorial Board Member of the *IEEE Communications Surveys and Tutorials*, Features Editor of the *ICaST Magazine*, and contributing member of the *IEEE ComSoc Technical Committee on Communication Systems Integration and Modeling* (CSIM). His main research activities are in the field of energy efficient communications, cloud computing, and next-generation networking.

Yogesh Kondareddy earned the PhD degree in Electrical Engineering from Auburn University in 2010. Since that time he has been working in Cisco Systems Inc. His research areas include Cognitive

Networks, Vehicular Networks and Software Defined Networks. He has several published papers in conference and journals in the above topics including a patent in modeling vehicular networks.

George Kormentzas received the Diploma in Electrical and Computer Engineering and the Ph.D. in Computer Science both from the National Technical University of Athens (NTUA), Greece, in 1995 and 2000, respectively. He is currently working as an Assistant Professor in the Information & Communication Systems Engineering department at the University of the Aegean. His research interests are in the fields of traffic analysis, network control, resource management, and quality of service in broadband networks. He has published extensively in the fields above, in international scientific journals, edited books, and conference proceedings. He is a member of pronounced professional societies, an active reviewer, and guest editor for several journals and conferences and EU-evaluator for Marie Curie Actions.

Yiouli Kritikou received her diploma in 2003 and her Ph.D. degree in 2009 from the Department of Digital Systems in University of Piraeus. Since September 2003, she is research engineer at the University of Piraeus, Laboratory of Telecommunication Networks and Services. As of January 2011, Dr. Kritikou conducts a post-doc research in Advanced Services in the context of the Future Internet. She has participated to number of national and international projects. Currently she is working in the FP7/ICT UniverSelf Integrated Project (09.2010-08.2013) and the FP7/ICT ACROPOLIS (Advanced Coexistence technologies for Radio Optimization in Licensed and unlicensed Spectrum) Network of Excellence (10.2010-09.2013). Her research interests are in the design, specification, and development of services for wireless networks, concentrating on user profile, ubiquitous service delivery, and technoeconomic aspects of services delivery.

Ioannis Loumiotis was born in Athens, Greece, in October 1986. He received his Diploma (2009) from the School of Electrical and Computer Engineering of the National Technical University of Athens. He is currently working towards a PhD degree at the same institution. He is a member of the Mobile and Personal Communications Laboratory, and from December 2010 he is participating in the Greek national ICT project "CONFES." His primary research interests include next generation wireless networks (4G), computer networks, and machine learning. He is a member of the Technical Chamber of Greece.

Maode Ma received the BE degree in Computer Engineering from Tsinghua University in 1982, the ME degree in Computer Engineering from Tianjin University in 1991, and the PhD degree in Computer Science from Hong Kong University of Science and Technology in 1999. He is an associate professor in the School of Electrical and Electronic Engineering, Nanyang Technological University, Singapore. He has extensive research interests including wireless networking, optical networking, grid computing, bioinformatics, and so forth. He has been a member of the technical program committee for more than 70 international conferences. He has been a technical track chair, tutorial chair, publication chair, and session chair for more than 40 international conferences. He has published more than 120 international academic research papers on wireless networks and optical networks. He currently serves as an associate editor for IEEE Communications Letters, an editor for IEEE Communications Surveys and Tutorials. He is a member of the IEEE.

Prodromos Makris was born in Samos Island, Greece, in 1985. He holds a five-year Diploma in Information and Communication Systems Engineering (2007) and a MSc (honors) in Communication and Computer Networking Technologies (2009) both from the University of the Aegean, Greece. He is currently pursuing his PhD and works as an ICT engineer for the Computer and Communications Systems Laboratory in the department of Information and Communication Systems Engineering. During the last years, he has been actively participating in several national and EC-funded projects (e.g. FP6-IST-UNITE, FP7-ICT-HURRICANE, FP7-ICT-PASSIVE, FP7-ICT-COGEU, COSMOTE PEDION 24, etc.). His research interests include QoS provisioning in 4G heterogeneous network technologies, context-aware mobile and wireless networking and mobile cloud computing issues. He is an IEEE member and also a member of Technical Chamber of Greece.

Antonio Manzalini received the M. Sc. Degree in Electronic Engineering from the Politecnico of Turin. In 1990 he joined CSELT, which became Telecom Italia Lab. He started with activities on technologies and architectures of future optical transport networks. He has been awarded 5 patents on network and systems. He was author of a book on Network Synchronization, his RTD results have been published in several papers, and he served the TCP of several internal Conferences. He has been active in ITU-T as Chairman. He has been actively involved in several EURESCOM and European Project. Since 2003, he has been a member of the Scientific Committee of Centre Tecnologic de Telecomunicacions de Catalunya. In 2008, he was awarded with the International Certification of Project Manager by PMI. He is now joining the Future Centre of the Strategy Dept. of Telecom Italia. His current research interests are mainly in the area of cognitive and autonomic networks, software defined networks and virtualization, primarily for design and management of future networks.

Lucio Marcenaro graduated in Electronic Engineering at the University of Genova, Italy, in 1999, and received the PhD in Computer Science and Electronic Engineering from the same University in 2003. From 2003 to 2010, he was a CEO and a development manager at TechnoAware srl. From March 2011, he became assistant professor in Telecommunications at the Department of Biophysical and Electronic Engineering (now Department of Electrical, Electronic, Telecommunications Engineering, and Naval Architecture) at Faculty of Engineering, University of Genova, Italy.

George Mastorakis received his B.Eng. in Electronic Engineering from UMIST in 2000, his M.Sc. in Telecommunications from UCL in 2001, and his Ph.D. in Telecommunications from University of the Aegean in 2008. He currently serves as an Assistant Professor at Technological Educational Institute of Crete and as a research associate at Centre for Technological Research of Crete. He has actively participated in a large number of EC and national funded research projects. He has more than 60 publications at various international conferences proceedings, workshops, scientific journals, and book chapters. He is an editor of *Journal of Networks*, a reviewer with several scientific journals and a member of conferences technical program committees. His research interests include cognitive radio networks, radio resource management, interactive television broadcasting, networking traffic analysis, end-to-end QoS, mobile networks, and dynamic bandwidth management.

Ioanna Mesogiti received her Diploma in electrical and computer engineering from the National Technical University of Athens (NTUA) in 2002. She holds an M.B.A. degree from Athens University of

Economics and Business (AUEB) and NTUA since 2003. During 2001–2002, she worked as a research associate in NCSR Demokritos participating in EU funded research projects, while from 2003 through 2005 she was employed as a software engineer in Siemens S.A. in the Fixed Networks Department. In 2005, she joined COSMOTE initially in the New Technologies Sub-Department and, since 2009, in the Research & Development Section as Senior Engineer, specializing in access network technologies and participating in projects such as the specification, design, and integration of novel access technologies in COSMOTE's network. Her fields of expertise include wireless network technologies (broadband and broadcast) and telecommunications protocols design, testing, and implementation.

Roberto Minerva, manager, Head of Innovative Architectures within the Future Center of Telecom Italia. He held many responsibilities within Telecom Italia Lab: Network Intelligence, Wireless Architecture, and Business Services Area Manager. Roberto has a Master Degree in Computer Science. Since 1987 he has been involved in the development of Service Architectures for Telecom (TINA, OSA/Parlay and SIP), in activities related to IMS, and in the definition of services for the Business market (context-awareness, ambient intelligence and automotive). He is author of several articles and paper presented in international conferences and journals.

Preben Elgaard Mogensen received his M.Sc. E.E. and Ph.D. degrees in 1988 and 1996 from Aalborg University, Denmark. He is currently Professor at Aalborg University leading the Ratio Access Technology Section. Preben Mogensen is also part time associated with Nokia Siemens Networks. His current research work is related to heterogenous networks deployment, cognitive radio, and beyond 4G.

Evangelos Pallis is an Associate Professor in the Department of Applied Informatics and Multimedia at Technological Educational Institute of Crete. He received his B.Sc. in Electronic Engineering from the Technological Educational Institute of Crete in 1994, his M.Sc. and his Ph.D. in Telecommunications from University of East London in 1997 and 2002, respectively. His research interests are in the fields of wireless networks, mobile communication systems, interactive television systems, QoS/QoE techniques and network management technologies. He has participated in a large number of national and European funded R&D projects and has acted as Technical/Scientific coordinator of IST-2002-FP6-507312 "ATHENA" project. He has more than 80 publications in international referred journals, conference papers, and book-chapters in the above scientific areas. He is the general chairman of the international conference on Telecommunications and Multimedia (TEMU), member of IET/IEE and active contributor to the IETF interconnection of content distribution networks (CDNi).

Athanasios D. Panagopoulos received the Diploma degree in electrical and computer engineering and the Dr. Eng. degree from the National Technical University of Athens (NTUA), Athens, Greece, in 1997 and 2002, respectively. From January 2005 to May 2008, he was the Head of the Wireless and Satellite Communications Department, Hellenic Authority of Information Security and Communication Privacy, Athens. From May 2008 to October 2012, he has been a Lecturer with the School of Electrical and Computer Engineering, NTUA and now he is an Assistant Professor. He has published more than 240 publications in international journals, book chapters, and conference proceedings. His research interests include mobile computing technologies, radio communication systems design, and wireless and satellite communications networks. Dr. Panagopoulos has been the Vice-Chair of the Hellenic IEEE

Communication Chapter since 2010. He also serves as an Associate Editor for the *IEEE Communication Letters* and the *IEEE Transactions on Antennas and Propagation*.

Nikolaos Papaoulakis received the degree and Ph.D of Electrical and Computer Engineer from the Electrical Engineering and Computer Science School of the National Technical University of Athens, in the area of Radio Resource Management for Wireless Networks. He currently works in the field of mobile and fixed networking in both National and European projects, as a senior research associate of the Telecommunications Laboratory of the Institute of Communication and Computer Systems. He has participated in several EU projects, and has served as technical manager in the FP7 project My-e-Director (2012). His research interests are in the areas of heterogeneous mobile Internetworking, radio resource management - radio planning - network optimisation in wireless networks. Also, he has significant research experience on Wireless Sensor networking and routing protocols. He has published a large number of journals, book chapters, conferences and standardization contributions, and has participated in organizing committees of international conferences.

Maria Paradia is a philologist as well as a School Consultant in the secondary education sector. Dr. Paradia has served as Deputy in the Office of the Pedagogical Institute under the subject of 'The teaching of the Greek language with the use of ICTs'. Her academic interests focus on applied linguistics, teaching methodology and educational technology areas which she covers in her doctoral dissertation, her research activities and her published articles in academic journals and conference proceedings. Moreover, Dr. Paradia has participated to a number of national and international projects related to teaching Greek language using Information and Communication Technologies.

Petar Popovski received the Dipl.Ing. in electrical engineering and Magister Ing. in communication engineering from Sts. Cyril and Methodius University, Skopje, Macedonia, in 1997 and 2000, respectively and Ph. D. from Aalborg University, Denmark, in 2004. He is currently a Professor at Aalborg University, where he held faculty positions since 2004. From 2008 to 2009 he held part-time position as a wireless architect at Oticon A/S. He has more than 140 publications in journals, conference proceedings, and books and has more than 25 patents and patent applications. He has received the Young Elite Researcher award and the SAPERE AUDE career grant from the Danish Council for Independent Research. He has received six best paper awards, including three from IEEE. Dr. Popovski serves on the editorial board of several journals, including *IEEE Communications Letters* (Senior Editor), *IEEE JSAC Cognitive Radio Series*, *IEEE Transactions on Communications,* and *IEEE Transactions on Wireless Communications*. His research interests are in the broad area of wireless communication and networking, information theory and protocol design.

Marios I. Poulakis received the Diploma degree in electrical and computer engineering from the National Technical University of Athens (NTUA), Athens, and the M.Sc. degree in economics and administration of telecommunication networks from the National and Kapodistrian University of Athens, Athens, in 2006 and 2008, respectively. He is currently working toward the Ph.D. degree at NTUA. Since October 2007, he has been an Associate Researcher with the Mobile Radio Communications Laboratory, School of Electrical and Computer Engineering, NTUA, participating in various industry and research-oriented projects, including electromagnetic field and QoS measurements in GSM and

UMTS networks and technical reports on electromagnetic emissions of antenna stations. His research interests include wireless and satellite communications with emphasis on radio resource management, optimization theory, cross layer design and cognitive radios. Mr. Poulakis has been a Member of the Technical Chamber of Greece since 2007.

Carlo Regazzoni received the "laurea" degree in Electronic Engineering and the Ph.D. in Telecommunications and Signal Processing from the University of Genova, Italy, in 1987 and 1992, respectively. He is Full Professor since 2006. Since 1990, he is responsible of the video & Signal Processing for telecommunications Group (ISIP40) area of the Signal Processing & Telecommunications Group (SP&T) at DITEN (formerly DIBE). He is the coordinator of the Erasmus Mundus Joint Doctorate on Interactive and Cognitive Environments (EMJD-ICE).

Mubashir Husain Rehmani has done Post Doctorate from PASNET, Université Paris Est, France in 2012. He has done PhD under the supervision of Dr. Aline Carneiro Viana and Prof. Serge Fdida from Université Pierre et Marie Curie, Paris, France in 2011. He did M.S. in Networks and Telecommunications from L2S, Laboratory of Signals and Systems, Supelec and University of Paris Sud-11 in 2008. He obtained B.E. (Bachelors of Engineering) Degree in Computer Systems Engineering from Mehran University of Engineering and Technology, Pakistan, in 2004. His current research interests include wireless self-organizing networks such as cognitive radio ad-hoc networks, wireless sensor networks, mobile ad-hoc networks.

Charalabos Skianis is director of Computer and Communications Systems Lab at the Department of Information and Communication Systems at the University of the Aegean in Samos, Greece. His current research activities take upon Novel Internet Architectures and Services, Cloud Computing & Networking, Energy & Context aware Next Generation Networks and Services, Management of Mobile and Wireless Networks, E2E QoS for heterogeneous networks and performance modeling and evaluation. He acts within Technical Program and Organizing Committees for numerous conferences and workshops and as a Guest Editor for scientific journals. He is at the editorial board of journals, member of pronounced professional societies (senior member of IEEE), an active reviewer for scientific journals, and an active member of several Technical Committees within the IEEE ComSoc, and member of IEEE BTS; IEEE TVT and IEEE CS. His research attracts both National and International funding and has coordinated several such initiatives.

Dimitrios N. Skoutas holds a PhD degree in Communication Networks and a Dipl.-Eng (5 years degree) in Electrical and Computer Engineering with major in Telecommunications. His current research activities include context aware Next Generation Networks and Quality of Service provisioning in heterogeneous networks environment. He has also been keenly working on the area of Resource Management and Quality of Service Provisioning in Mobile and Wireless Broadband Networks where he has proposed several algorithmic and architectural optimizations. He has several publications in the above fields in international scientific journals and conference proceedings, which received more than 60 citations by other scholars. Dr Skoutas has also been involved in various European and National funded R&D projects (e.g. FP7-ICT-PASSIVE, FP6-IST-UNITE, ESF-NR ARCHIMEDES I). He acts within Technical Program and Organizing Committees for conferences and he is an active reviewer for several scientific journals and conferences. He is a member of pronounced professional societies (IEEE Communications Society, Greek Computer Society, and Technical Chamber of Greece).

Troels B. Sørensen graduated in 1990 (M.Sc. EE) from Aalborg University and received the PhD degree from the same university in 2002. From 1991 to 1997 he worked with a Danish telecom operator, developing type approval test methods for the DECT cordless system; in the course of this work he participated in ETSI standardisation. In 1997 he joined the Center for PersonKommunikation (CPK) at Aalborg University where initially his involvement was in propagation modelling for cellular communication systems. Later, his work focused on system related issues, including cellular system modelling, radio resource management, and specifically distributed antenna systems as the topic of his PhD. Recent activities have included physical layer research for the long-term evolution of the Evolved Universal Terrestrial Radio Access, scalable network deployment studies, and related experimental activities. Troels B. Sørensen is an associate professor in the Radio Access Technology (RATE) section at Aalborg University, Department of Electronic Systems, where his primary involvement is in the supervision of Master and PhD students. He is a member of IEEE and The Society of Danish Engineers.

Panagiotis Spapis received the diploma in Electrical and Computer Engineering from the University of Patras, Greece, 2008. Since September 2008 serves as research fellow in the Self-evolving Cognitive & Autonomic Networking (SCAN) Laboratory of the National and Kapodistrian University of Athens (NKUA) and have participated in several research project. His main research interests are in the area of learning and decision making techniques in cognitive networks; parts of his work have already been published in several conferences and journals (his work has been selected/awarded as a very interesting work in UBICOMM 2011 and received invitation for extended article journal version).

Makis Stamatelatos is a researcher in the SCAN group of Lecturer Nancy Alonistioti, in the Department of Informatics and Telecommunications of the National and Kapodistrian University of Athens (NKUA). He holds a M.Sc. in Communication Systems and Networks from NKUA and a B.Sc. degree in Informatics and Telecommunications from the same department. He has been working as a research associate for the SCAN group since 2004 and has participated in a number of European research projects. His research interests focus on information modeling for network management, knowledge management, and business modeling for future networks. He has acted as Designated Representative of NKUA in the IEEE P1900.4 WG and SCC41 TC and has contributed to the standard development. He has also contributed to OMA and OMG; he is currently following ETSI TC RRS.

Theodora Stamatiadi received her Diploma (2003), as well as her master degree at Techno-economical Systems-MBA (2006), from the School of Electrical and Computer Engineering of the National Technical University of Athens. In 2008, she received her master degree at Environmental & Sanitary Engineering from the School of Environmental Engineering of the Technical University of Crete. From 2002 to 2010, she worked at Siemens S.A. in Greece, starting by doing her internship and leaving the company as Software Project Manager for Telephone Switches for MME companies. During her job at Siemens, she worked in different departments of the company, acquiring extensive experience about the processes and operation of a multinational company. From 2007 to 2009, she worked as a research associate at European and National Projects. Since October 2010, she is a researcher at the Institute of

Communication and Computer Systems. Her primary research interests include mobile and computer networks.

Eftathios Sykas is a Professor in the School of Electrical Engineering of the National Technical University of Athens. Since 1988, before 2nd generation mobile networks became commonplace, he started working in 3rd generation personal and mobile communications projects. He is now involved in pervasive and ubiquitous communications. He has participated in several RACE, ACTS, and IST projects, being a work-package and/or project leader. He has served as Director of the Computer Science Division (1997-2000), as a member of the board of Governors of the Institute of Communication and Computer Systems (1999-2002), and as a member of the Greek Parliament Committee for the Security of Communications Networks (1995-2003). He is a reviewer for several international journals, and a member of IEEE, ACM, IEEE Standard 802 Committee, and the Technical Chamber of Greece.

Fernando M. L. Tavares received his Electrical Engineer and M.Sc. degrees from University of Brasília, Brazil, in 2005 and 2009, respectively. He worked at Nokia Institute of Technology (INdT) as a researcher for four years. He is currently working toward a Ph.D. degree at Aalborg University, Denmark, in close cooperation with Nokia Siemens Networks (NSN). His current research interests are mostly related to interference suppression concepts for beyond 4G networks.

Oscar Tonelli received his Master Degree in Telecommunication Engineering from the University of Trento, Italy, in 2010, with a joint Master Thesis at Aalborg University, Denmark. He joined Aalborg University in 2009, where he is now currently working toward a Ph.D. degree, in close cooperation with Nokia Siemens Networks. His current research topics include Cognitive Radio, Radio Resource Management algorithms for IMT-A, and the realization of Software Defined Radio-based, network testbeds.

Shah Muhammad Emad Uddin has graduated from Politecnico di Torino, Italy specializing in Wireless Systems and Related Technologies in September 2012. He also holds a Master's degree in I.T. Management from Mälardalen University, Sweden and BS Computer Science from University of Karachi, Pakistan. He recently made a stage in Telecom Italia concerning future software networks at the edge. His main research interests include Self Organizing Networks, VANETs, and Future Networks.

Stavroula Vassaki received the Diploma degree in electrical and computer engineering from the National Technical University of Athens (NTUA) in 2006 and the M.Sc. degree in economics and administration of telecommunication networks from the National and Kapodistrian University of Athens in 2008. Since November 2006, she has been an Associate Researcher with the Mobile Radio Communications Laboratory, School of Electrical and Computer Engineering, NTUA. She is currently working toward her Ph.D. degree at NTUA. Her research interests include wireless and satellite communications with emphasis on radio resource management, game theory, optimization theory and cognitive radio networks. She has been a Member of the Technical Chamber of Greece since 2007.

Index